Latin American Cultural Studies:
A Reader

Featuring twenty-five key essays from the *Journal of Latin American Cultural Studies (Traves/sia)*, this book surveys the most influential themes and concepts, as well as scouring some of the polemics and controversies, which have marked the field over the last quarter of a century since the *Journal*'s foundation in 1992.

Emerging at a moment of crisis of revolutionary narratives, and at the onset of neoliberal economics and emergent narcopolitics, the cultural studies impetus in Latin America was part of an attempted intellectual reconstruction of the (centre-) left in terms of civil society, and the articulation of social movements and agencies, thinking beyond the verticalist constructions from previous decades.

This collection maps these developments from the now classical discussions of the 'cultural turn' to more recent responses to the challenges of biopolitics, affect theory, posthegemony and ecocriticism. It also addresses novel political constellations including resurgent national-popular or eco-nativist and indigenous agencies. Framed by a critical introduction from the editors, this volume is both a celebration of influential essays published over twenty five years of the *Journal* and a representative overview of the field in its multiple ramifications, entrenchments and exchanges.

Jens Andermann, Benjamin Bollig, Lorraine Leu, Daniel Mosquera, Rory O'Bryen and **David M. J. Wood** are editors of the *Journal of Latin American Cultural Studies*.

Latin American Cultural Studies: A Reader

Edited by
Jens Andermann, Benjamin Bollig,
Lorraine Leu, Daniel Mosquera,
Rory O'Bryen and David M.J. Wood

LONDON AND NEW YORK

First published 2018
by Routledge
2 Park Square, Milton Park, Abingdon, Oxon, OX14 4RN, UK

and by Routledge
711 Third Avenue, New York, NY 10017, USA

Routledge is an imprint of the Taylor & Francis Group, an informa business

© 2018 Taylor & Francis

All rights reserved. No part of this book may be reprinted or reproduced or utilised in any form or by any electronic, mechanical, or other means, now known or hereafter invented, including photocopying and recording, or in any information storage or retrieval system, without permission in writing from the publishers.

Trademark notice: Product or corporate names may be trademarks or registered trademarks, and are used only for identification and explanation without intent to infringe.

British Library Cataloguing in Publication Data
A catalogue record for this book is available from the British Library

ISBN13: 978-0-415-78652-2

Typeset in Times New Roman
by RefineCatch Limited, Bungay, Suffolk

Publisher's Note
The publisher accepts responsibility for any inconsistencies that may have arisen during the conversion of this book from journal articles to book chapters, namely the possible inclusion of journal terminology.

Disclaimer
Every effort has been made to contact copyright holders for their permission to reprint material in this book. The publishers would be grateful to hear from any copyright holder who is not here acknowledged and will undertake to rectify any errors or omissions in future editions of this book.

Contents

Citation Information   ix
Notes on Contributors   xiii
Introduction   1

Temporalities

1. War and Cultural Studies: Reflections on Recent Work in Peru and Argentina   18
   William Rowe

2. The Reconfigurations of Post-dictatorship Critical Thought   27
   Nelly Richard

3. For Whom the Eye Cries: Memory, Monumentality, and the Ontologies of Violence in Peru   37
   Paulo Drinot

4. The Last Sacred Image of the Latin American Revolution   55
   Mariano Mestman

Territories

5. Hemispheric Domains: 1898 and the Origins of Latin Americanism   77
   Julio Ramos

6. Patagonia as Borderland: Nature, Culture, and the Idea of the State   92
   Gabriela Nouzeilles

7. The Return of Coatlicue: Mexican Nationalism and the Aztec Past   106
   Jean Franco

8. A Short Andean History of Photography: *Yawar Fiesta*   120
   John Kraniauskas

9. Cuba: A Curated Culture   140
   Guillermina De Ferrari

CONTENTS

Aesthetics

10. Argentina's Secret Poetry Boom — 162
    Nestor Perlongher

11. Tin Tan: The Pachuco — 166
    Carlos Monsiváis

12. (Queer) Boleros of a Tropical Night — 176
    José Quiroga

13. Heavy Metal Music in Postdictatorial Brazil: Sepultura and the Coding of Nationality in Sound — 185
    Idelber Avelar

Affects

14. Sabina's Oranges: The Colours of Cultural Politics in Rio de Janeiro, 1889–1930 — 203
    Tiago de Melo Gomes and Micol Seigel

15. Mob Outrages: Reflections on the Media Construction of the Masses in Venezuela (April 2000–January 2003) — 227
    Luis Duno Gottberg

16. The City Cross-dressed: Sexual Rights and Roll-backs in De la Rúa's Buenos Aires — 248
    Ana Gabriela Álvarez

17. Conspicuous Consumption and the Performance of Identity in Contemporary Mexico: Daniela Rossell's *Ricas y Famosas* — 265
    Elaine Luck

Cityscapes

18. From Urb of Clay to the Hypodermic City. Improper Cities in Modern Latin America — 282
    Marzena Grzegorczyk

19. Obverse Colonization: São Paulo, Global Urbanization and the Poetics of the Latin American City — 297
    Justin A. Read

20. Favelas and the Aesthetics of Realism: Representations in Film and Literature — 317
    Beatriz Jaguaribe

21. *Amores Perros*: Exotic Violence and Neoliberal Fear — 333
    Ignacio M. Sánchez-Prado

Medialities

22. Post/Colonial Toponymy: Writing Forward 'in Reverse' — 352
    Quetzil Castañeda

CONTENTS

23. Material Culture, Slavery, and Governability in Colonial Cuba: The Humorous Lessons of the Cigarette *Marquillas*   368
    Agnes Lugo-Ortiz

24. Indigenous Media and the End of the Lettered City   393
    Freya Schiwy

25. Subjective Displacements and 'Reserves of Life'   411
    Ivana Bentes

    Index   427

Citation Information

The chapters in this book were originally published in the *Journal of Latin American Cultural Studies*. When citing this material, please use the original page numbering for each article, as follows:

Chapter 1
War and Cultural Studies: Reflections on Recent Work in Peru and Argentina
William Rowe
Journal of Latin American Cultural Studies, volume 1, issue 1 (1992) pp. 18–37

Chapter 2
The Reconfigurations of Post-dictatorship Critical Thought
Nelly Richard
Journal of Latin American Cultural Studies, volume 9, issue 3 (2000) pp. 273–282

Chapter 3
For Whom the Eye Cries: Memory, Monumentality, and the Ontologies of Violence in Peru
Paulo Drinot
Journal of Latin American Cultural Studies, volume 18, issue 1 (March 2009) pp. 15–32

Chapter 4
The Last Sacred Image of the Latin American Revolution
Mariano Mestman
Journal of Latin American Cultural Studies, volume 19, issue 1 (March 2010) pp. 23–44

Chapter 5
Hemispheric Domains: 1898 and the Origins of Latin Americanism
Julio Ramos
Journal of Latin American Cultural Studies, volume 10, issue 3 (2001) pp. 237–251

Chapter 6
Patagonia as Borderland: Nature, Culture, and the Idea of the State
Gabriela Nouzeilles
Journal of Latin American Cultural Studies, volume 8, issue 1 (1999) pp. 35–48

CITATION INFORMATION

Chapter 7
The Return of Coatlicue: Mexican Nationalism and the Aztec Past
Jean Franco
Journal of Latin American Cultural Studies, volume 13, issue 2 (August 2004)
pp. 205–218

Chapter 8
A Short Andean History of Photography: Yawar Fiesta
John Kraniauskas
Journal of Latin American Cultural Studies, volume 21, issue 3 (September 2012)
pp. 359–378

Chapter 9
Cuba: A Curated Culture
Guillermina De Ferrari
Journal of Latin American Cultural Studies, volume 16, issue 2 (August 2007)
pp. 219–240

Chapter 10
Argentina's Secret Poetry Boom
Nestor Perlongher
Journal of Latin American Cultural Studies, volume 1, issue 2 (1992) pp. 178–184

Chapter 11
Tin Tan: The Pachuco
Carlos Monsiváis
Journal of Latin American Cultural Studies, volume 3, issues 1–2 (1994)
pp. 179–198

Chapter 12
(Queer) Boleros of a Tropical Night
José Quiroga
Journal of Latin American Cultural Studies, volume 3, issues 1–2 (1994)
pp. 199–214

Chapter 13
Heavy Metal Music in Postdictatorial Brazil: Sepultura and the Coding of Nationality in Sound
Idelber Avelar
Journal of Latin American Cultural Studies, volume 12, issue 3 (2003)
pp. 329–346

Chapter 14
Sabina's Oranges: The Colours of Cultural Politics in Rio de Janeiro, 1889–1930
Tiago de Melo Gomes and Micol Seigel
Journal of Latin American Cultural Studies, volume 11, issue 1 (2002) pp. 5–28

CITATION INFORMATION

Chapter 15
Mob Outrages: Reflections on the Media Construction of the Masses in Venezuela (April 2000–January 2003)
Luis Duno Gottberg
Journal of Latin American Cultural Studies, volume 13, issue 1 (March 2004) pp. 115–135

Chapter 16
The City Cross-dressed: Sexual Rights and Roll-backs in De la Rúa's Buenos Aires
Ana Gabriela Álvarez
Journal of Latin American Cultural Studies, volume 9, issue 2 (2000) pp. 137–153

Chapter 17
Conspicuous Consumption and the Performance of Identity in Contemporary Mexico: Daniela Rossell's Ricas y Famosas
Elaine Luck
Journal of Latin American Cultural Studies, volume 19, issue 3 (December 2010) pp. 299–315

Chapter 18
From Urb of Clay to the Hypodermic City. Improper Cities in Modern Latin America
Marzena Grzegorczyk
Journal of Latin American Cultural Studies, volume 7, issue 1 (1998) pp. 55–74

Chapter 19
Obverse Colonization: São Paulo, Global Urbanization and the Poetics of the Latin American City
Justin A. Read
Journal of Latin American Cultural Studies, volume 15, issue 3 (December 2006) pp. 281–300

Chapter 20
Favelas and the Aesthetics of Realism: Representations in Film and Literature
Beatriz Jaguaribe
Journal of Latin American Cultural Studies, volume 13, issue 3 (December 2004) pp. 327–342

Chapter 21
Amores Perros: *Exotic Violence and Neoliberal Fear*
Ignacio M. Sánchez-Prado
Journal of Latin American Cultural Studies, volume 15, issue 1 (March 2006) pp. 39–57

Chapter 22
Post/Colonial Toponymy: Writing Forward 'in Reverse'
Quetzil Castañeda
Journal of Latin American Cultural Studies, volume 11, issue 2 (2002) pp. 119–134

CITATION INFORMATION

Chapter 23
Material Culture, Slavery, and Governability in Colonial Cuba: The Humorous Lessons of the Cigarette Marquillas
Agnes Lugo-Ortiz
Journal of Latin American Cultural Studies, volume 21, issue 1 (March 2012) pp. 61–85

Chapter 24
Indigenous Media and the End of the Lettered City
Freya Schiwy
Journal of Latin American Cultural Studies, volume 17, issue 1 (March 2008) pp. 23–40

Chapter 25
Subjective Displacements and 'Reserves of Life'
Ivana Bentes
Journal of Latin American Cultural Studies, volume 20, issue 1 (March 2011) pp. 5–19

For any permission-related enquiries please visit:
http://www.tandfonline.com/page/help/permissions

Notes on Contributors

Ana Gabriela Alvarez is Visiting Assistant Professor in the Departments of Social and Cultural Analysis and of Spanish and Portuguese at New York University, USA. She holds a degree in anthropology from the University of Buenos Aires and a Ph.D. from Birkbeck College, University of London. For twenty years, she has undertaken fieldwork among travesti and trans communities in Buenos Aires, Argentina, on which she has published in academic journals and newspapers in Argentina, the UK, Germany and the US. She currently conducts research among migrant trans sex workers from Latin America and the European market of prostitution.

Idelber Avelar is Professor of Spanish and Portuguese at Tulane University, USA. His latest books are *Figuras de la violencia: Ensayos sobre política, narrativa y música popular* (2016), *Transculturación en suspenso: Los orígenes de los cánones narrativos colombianos* (2015) and *Crônicas do Estado de Exceção* (2014). He is also the author of *The Untimely Present: Postdictatorial Latin American Fiction and the Task of Mourning* (1999), winner of the MLA Kovacs award and translated into Spanish and Portuguese. He has published numerous articles in scholarly journals in Europe and the Americas. His article on music in Machado de Assis won the Brazilian Foreign Ministry international essay contest.

Quetzil Castañeda is a Lecturer in the Center for Latin American and Caribbean Studies and Research Associate in the Department of Anthropology at Indiana University, USA. He is the founding director of the Open School of Ethnography and Anthropology – an independent, non-degree school that offers field study abroad, writing workshops, research methods, conferences, and consulting services. He has over 20 years of experience conducting research in México on identity politics, heritage, tourism, anthropology of art, ethics, visual ethnography, applied anthropology, language revitalization, and representation. His publications include an award winning ethnographic film, *Incidents of Travel in Chichén Itzá* (DER 1997), which explores Maya New Age spiritualism and 2012 prophecies. He has published books including *In the Museum of Maya Culture* (1996); *Estrategias Identitarias* (2004); and *Ethnographic Archaeologies* (2008). His areas of expertise include Mayan language and culture, México, Guatemala, heritage, tourism, museum studies, ethnography of archaeology, ethnographic fieldwork/methods, New Age spiritualism, and 2012 the End of the World.

Guillermina De Ferrari (Ph.D. Columbia University) is Professor of Caribbean Literature and Visual Culture at the University of Wisconsin-Madison, USA. She is the author of *Vulnerable States: Bodies of Memory in Contemporary Caribbean Fiction* (2007) and

NOTES ON CONTRIBUTORS

Community and Culture in Post-Soviet Cuba (2014). She curated the exhibition *Apertura: Photography in Cuba Today* (Chazen Museum of Art, March-June 2015). She is currently the Director of the Center for Visual Cultures at University of Wisconsin-Madison.

Paulo Drinot is a Senior Lecturer in Latin American history at the Institute of the Americas, University College London, UK, and coeditor of the Journal of Latin American Studies. He is the author of *The Allure of Labor: Workers, Race, and the Making of the Peruvian State* (2011), published in Spanish translation as *La seducción de la clase obrera: Trabajadores, raza y la formación del Estado peruano* (2016); editor of *Che's Travels: The Making of a Revolutionary in 1950s Latin America* (2010), and *Peru in Theory* (2014); and coeditor of *Más allá de la dominación y la resistencia: Estudios de historia peruana, siglos XVI–XX* (with Leo Garofalo, 2005), and *The Great Depression in Latin America* (with Alan Knight, 2014), also published in Spanish as *La Gran Depresión en América Latina* (2014). He has two books forthcoming, a co-edited collection titled *Comics and Memory in Latin America* (2016) and a co-edited volume on the government of Velasco Alvarado (1968–1975) (forthcoming).

Luis Duno-Gottberg is Associate Professor in the Department of Spanish, Portuguese and Latin American Studies at Rice University, USA. His research and teaching interests focus on nineteenth, twentieth and twenty-first-century Caribbean Culture, with an emphasis on race and ethnicity, politics, violence and visual culture. He is the author of *Albert Camus. Naturaleza: Patria y Exilio* (1994), *Solventar las diferencias: La ideología del mestizaje en Cuba* (2003) and *La humanidad como mercancía. La esclavitud moderna en América* (2014). His current book project, *Dangerous People: Hegemony, Representation and Culture in Contemporary Venezuela*, explores the relationship between popular mobilization, radical politics and culture in Venezuela.

Jean Franco is Professor Emerita at Columbia University, USA, and a pioneering figure not just of Latin American literary and cultural studies in the English-speaking world but also of research in Latin American women's writing and of intersections between coloniality, gender and cultural forms more widely. Her work was recognized through the 1996 PEN award for the lifetime contribution to disseminating Latin American literature in English. Among her many books are *The Modern Culture of Latin America* (1967), *Spanish American Literature Since Independence* (1969), *César Vallejo: The Dialectics of Poetry and Violence* (1976), *Plotting Women: Gender and Representation in Mexico* (1989), *Critical Passions* (1999), *The Decline and Fall of the Lettered City: Latin America and the Cold War* (2002) and *Cruel Modernity* (2013).

Tiago de Melo Gomes was Professor of Contemporary History at the Rural Federal University of Pernambuco, Brazil, where he worked on popular theatre, mass culture, race and national identity. His many publications included articles in *Sophie – Periódico Acadêmico de História*; *Revista de História*; *História. Questões e Debates*; *Afro-Asia*; *Estudos Afro-Asiáticos*; and *Revista Brasileira de História*. He is the author of *Um Espelho no Palso: identidades sociais e massificacao cultural no teatro de revista dos anos 1920* (2004). He was extraordinarily generous with his mentorship, advising dozens of students in his years at UFRPE. He was working on a social history the role of tradition and Brazilian regionalism in 1920s culture in Recife when he fell ill and died suddenly in February 2016.

Marzena Grzegorczyk obtained her Ph.D. in in Spanish and Comparative Literature from Stanford University and served as Assistant Professor of Spanish at Emory University,

USA, where she taught critical theory, literature and film, before moving to a career in film production. She has published work on Latin American literature and urban culture in Spanish, English and Polish, most notably her book *Private Topographies: Space, Subjectivity and Political Change in Modern Latin America* (2005). As an independent filmmaker, she has directed the short film *Faithful* (2002) and the documentary *Desertopia* (2000).

Beatriz Jaguaribe is a Professor in the School of Communications of the Federal University of Rio de Janeiro, Brazil. Her awards include a Guggenheim Fellowship (2004), the Andrés Bello Chair at the King Juan Carlos of Spain Center at NYU (2012), and the CNPq scholarship for research projects. She has authored *Fins de século* (1998), *Mapa do Maravilhoso do Rio de Janeiro* (2001), *Choque do Real* (2007), and *Rio de Janeiro: Urban life through the Eyes of the City* (2014), among other books. Her research explores how literature, photography, architecture, and cinema reveal subjectivities and collective imaginaries in modernist and contemporary urban and national scenarios in Brazil and also in Hispanic America. Her current research project is centered on discussing the dilemmas of nation building in Brazil in the first decades of the Twentieth Century by contrasting the positivist cartographical and photographic endeavors of the Rondon Commission in Mato Grosso in the first decades of the Twentieth Century with the avant-garde re-invention of the Indian in the 1920s.

John Kraniauskas is Professor of Latin American Studies at Birkbeck College, University of London, UK. He was a founding editor of the *Journal of Latin American Cultural Studies* and has published widely on the relation between cultural forms (in particular, literature and film) and socio-political formations in the Americas, including essays on Rodolfo Walsh, Manuel Puig, Osvaldo Lamborghini, Roberto Bolaño, and on the work of Antonio Negri and Ernesto Laclau. He is the author of *Políticas literarias: política y acumulación en la cultura latinoamericana* (2012) and of *Capitalism and its Discontents. Power and Accumulation in Latin American Culture* (2017).

Elaine Luck completed her Ph.D. in Latin American Cultural Studies at the University of Manchester, UK, working on manifestations of contemporary Mexican visual culture in the context of economic shifts and its impact on the reproduction of cultural narratives. In particular, she focuses on museums, exhibitions and photography. Her work has appeared in the *Journal of Latin American Cultural Studies* and the Modern Humanities Research Association's *Working Papers* series.

Agnes Lugo-Ortiz is Associate Professor of Latin American and Caribbean Literatures at the University of Chicago, USA. She is the author of *Identidades imaginadas: Biografía y nacionalidad en el horizonte de la guerra (Cuba, 1860-1898)* (1999); and co-editor of *Herencia: The Anthology of US Hispanic Writing* (2001), *En otra voz: Antología de la Literatura Hispana de los Estados Unidos* (2002), and *Recovering the US Hispanic Literary Hertiage, volume V* (2006). She is currently working on a book-length project on the visual culture of slavery in colonial Cuba (specifically from 1727 to 1886—the dates that frame the emergence and final collapse of the large slaveholding plantations system on the island), underlining its transamerican and transatlantic connections. Akin to this endeavor, she has recently completed an edited volume, in collaboration with Angela Rosenthal, entitled *Slave Portraiture in the Atlantic World* (2013).

Mariano Mestman is a Researcher at CONICET and the Gino Germani Institute of the Faculty of Social Sciences, University of Buenos Aires, Argentina, where he directs the

NOTES ON CONTRIBUTORS

Masters in Communication and Culture. He is the author of *Del Di Tella a Tucumán Arde. Vanguardia artística y política en el 68 argentino* (2000, with A. Longoni) and *Estados Generales del Tercer Cine. Los Documentos de Montreal* (2014). He is also the editor of *Masas, pueblo y multitud en cine y televisión* (2013, with M. Varela) and *Las rupturas del 68 en el cine de América Latina* (2016). His studies on the history of Latin American cinema and the Third World were published in collective books such as *Il Nuovo Cinema, Ieri e Oggi* (2001), *Cine documental en América Latina* (2003), The Cinema of Latin America (2003), Global Neorealism: The Transnational History of a Film Style, 1930–1970 (2011), The Grierson Effect: Tracing Documentary's International Movement (2014), Political Documentary Cinema in Latin America (2014).

Gabriela Nouzeilles is Emory L. Ford Professor of Spanish at Princeton University, USA. She was co-founder and executive editor of the interdisciplinary journal *Nepantla: Views from South*. Her book *Ficciones somáticas* (2000) studies the interplay of medical, literary, and visual narratives of disease in late nineteenth-century Argentine culture. She is the editor of *La naturaleza en disputa. Retóricas del cuerpo y el paisaje* (2002) and co-editor of *The Argentina Reader* (2004) and the *The Itinerant Languages of Photography* (2013). Her most recent book, *Of Other Places: Patagonia and the Production of Nature* (forthcoming), studies the modern production of natural spaces, and traces the textual and visual inventions of Patagonia as an alternative geography outside modernity. Her current work addresses the relationship between photography and other media in the work of Latin American writers and artists such as Guillermo Cabrera Infante, Julio Cortázar, Salvador Elizondo, Diamela Eltit, and Frida Kahlo.

Nestor Perlongher was one of the most important Argentine poets of the second half of the twentieth century as well as an essayist, anthropologist, and gay rights activist. Born in Avellaneda in 1949 he studied sociology in Buenos Aires and then later in Campinas (Brazil) and Paris. In the 1960s and 70s he belonged to anarchist and Trotskyite political formations, before founding some of the earliest gay rights groups in Argentina, including the FLH or Homosexual Liberation Front. His Master's thesis, entitled *O negócio do michê* (published in Spanish as *La prostitución masculina*) was a pioneering analysis of male prostitution in São Paulo that drew on contemporary urban anthropology and the work of Gilles Deleuze and Félix Guattari. As a poet, he published six volumes, of which *Alambres* (Wires, 1987) stands out as a collection marking an epoch in Argentine poetry, not least with its inclusion of one of the most striking poems about the dictatorship of the 1970s, "Cadáveres" (Corpses). He also broke ground as a theorist and anthologist of the continental literary movement known as the *neobarroco*, or in his coinage the *neobarroso*, in which the Caribbean baroque turns muddy in the waters of the River Plate. Perlongher died in São Paulo in 1992. Much of his work has been collected or republished posthumously: *Poemas completos* (poems, 1997); *Prosa plebeya* (essays, 1997); and *Correspondencia* (letters, 2016).

José Quiroga is Professor of Comparative Literature at Emory University, USA. His research interests are contemporary Latin American and Latino literatures and cultures, gender and queer studies, contemporary Cuba and the Caribbean, and Latin American poetry. His published books include *Mapa Callejero* (2010), *Law of Desire: A Queer Film Classic* (2009), *Cuban Palimpsests* (2005) and *Sexualidades en Disputa* (with Daniel Balderston, 2005). In addition, he has also published *Tropics of Desire: Interventions from Queer Latino America* (2001) and *Understanding Octavio Paz* (2000). He has been an invited keynote speaker at numerous U.S. and foreign universities, and is presently completing both an edited collection for Duke University Press titled The Havana Reader, and a book on dissident practices in Cuba and Argentina, for which he has been awarded a Guggenheim Fellowship for the year 2010–2011.

Julio Ramos is Professor Emeritus at the University of California, Berkeley, USA. His recent publications include *Sujeto al limite: ensayos de cultura literaria y visual*, as well as articles on experimental film and music. He co-directed and co-produced the documentary *Retornar a La Habana con Guillen Landrian* and is currently completing a *Detroit's Rivera: The Labors of Public Art*.

Justin A. Read is Associate Professor of Romance Languages and Literatures at the University at Buffalo, USA. His current research focuses on the modernization and urbanization of Latin America over the long 20th century, with particular emphasis on Argentina and Brazil. Specifically, his interests lie in 'poetic ecology', or the emergence of citizenship and national sovereignty as elements of the built environment. He is currently completing the manuscript of his second book, *Buenos Aires and the Birth of the Non-Subject*. He has published on poetics, politics, space, and critical theory in such venues as *Cuadernos de Literatura*, *Modernism/Modernity*, *Revista de Estudios Hispánicos*, *Journal of Architecture*, *CR: New Centennial Review*, *Yearbook of Futurist Studies*, and of course the *Journal of Latin American Cultural Studies*.

Nelly Richard is among the most influential Latin American art critics of the twentieth and twenty-first century. Born in Caen, France, she arrived in Chile after completing her studies at the Sorbonne in 1970, the year Salvador Allende won the presidential elections, and went on to become the visual arts coordinator at the National Museum of Fine Arts in Santiago. She resigned from her post after Pinochet's military coup and became a critical spokesperson for the artistic and literary underground known as the 'Escena Avanzada', not least through the ground-breaking essay *Margins and Institutions* she contributed for a show of Chilean art under dictatorship exhibited in Australia in 1986. Besides directing the *Revista de Crítica Cultural*, Chile's most important platform for critical theory, for over a decade, Richard is the author of many books, of which *Cultural Residues* (2004), *Masculine/Feminine: Practices of Difference* (2004) and *The Insubordination of Signs* (2004) have been translated into English.

William Rowe is Emeritus Professor of Poetics at Birkbeck College, University of London, UK. He is a Fellow of the British Academy, holds an Honorary Doctorate at the Catholic University of Peru and is an Honorary Professor of the University of San Marcos, Lima.

Ignacio M. Sánchez-Prado is Professor of Spanish and Latin American Studies at Washington University in Saint Louis, USA. His research focuses on the relationship between aesthetics, ideology and cultural institutions in Mexico, with a particular focus on literature and cinema. He is the author of *El canon y sus formas. La reinvención de Harold Bloom y sus lecturas hispanoamericanas* (2002); *Naciones intelectuales. Las fundaciones de la modernidad literaria mexicana (1917–1959)* (2009); *Intermitencias americanistas. Ensayos académico y literarios (2004–2009)* (2012), which won the LASA Mexico 2010 Humanities Book Award; and *Screening Neoliiberalism: Transforming Mexican Cinema 1988–2012* (2014). He has edited and co-edited nine scholarly collections, the most recent of which are *Democracia, Otredad y Melancolía. Roger Bartra ante la crítica* (with Mabel Moraña. 2015) and the forthcoming *A History of Mexican Literature* (with Anna Nogar and José Ramón Ruisánchez, 2016).

NOTES ON CONTRIBUTORS

Freya Schiwy is Associate Professor of Media and Cultural Studies at the University of California, Riverside, USA. She is author of *Indianizing Film: Decolonization, the Andes, and the Question of Technology* (2009) and co-editor of *Adjusting the Lens. Community and Collaborative Video in Mexico* (forthcoming); *Digital Media, Cultural Production, and Speculative Capitalism* (2011), and *(In)disciplinar las ciencias sociales* (2002). Currently, she is completing a monograph titled *The Open Invitation. Video Activism, Mexico, and the Politics of Affect*.

Micol Seigel is Associate Professor of American Studies and History at Indiana University, Bloomington, USA, where she teaches and studies policing, prisons, and race in the Americas. Her current manuscript on the transnational circulation of policing policy and practice during the Cold War, *Violence Work: State Power and the Limits of* Police, is under advanced review. Her previous work has appeared in *Social Text, Transition, Social Justice,* the *Journal of American History, Hispanic American Historical Review*, and elsewhere; and her book *Uneven Encounters: Making Race and Nation in Brazil and the United States* (2009) received a finalist mention for the Lora Romero first book prize of the American Studies Association. Her research has been supported by FLAS, Fulbright, the ACLS, the Rockefeller Foundation, the Cornell Society for the Humanities, and the United States Studies Centre at the University of Sydney. She is a long-time member of Critical Resistance, a founding and active member of Decarcerate Monroe County, and an Inside-Out Prison Exchange Program instructor.

Introduction

It is probably no accident that '*emergencia*' – alluding both to a process of emergence and a state of emergency – has such critical potential in Spanish and Portuguese, especially in this post-Rio Olympics present, in which Latin America seems once again to be heading towards a ruffle of catastrophic changes engulfing most of the region. Twenty-five years after the foundation of the *Journal of Latin American Cultural Studies*, we are witnessing a historical moment that, more than just the commodities-crisis-induced implosion of the Latin American 'pink tide's' neo-Keynesian state projects, has also seen the rise of militantly reactionary mass movements centred on the urban middle classes, a new politics of resentment relentlessly drummed up through increasingly belligerent audiovisual and digital media. The political history of the Latin American cultural studies project had been closely interrelated with the 'democratic transitions' that took place across the region during the final decades of the twentieth century and their critique, be that as a result of the demise of military dictatorships, as in Brazil and the Southern Cone, or as the outcome of peace accords and post-civil war settlements, as in large parts of Central America and Peru. The peace accords signed in Havana between the FARC *guerrilla* and the Colombian government and plebiscite as well as, in a wider sense, the recent US–Cuban *rapprochement* itself, are a kind of belated final chapter to this 'post-dictatorial' moment in Latin American politics and culture. This moment follows on the brutal counterinsurgency wars waged in the aftermath of the Cuban revolution and cutting short a range of experiences of socio-economic 'modernization' that were predicated on the notion of 'development' and extended in its political expressions from Arbenz's presidency in Guatemala to Perón and Frondizi in Argentina or Kubitschek and Goulart in Brazil. Even though it also drew on previous, vernacular strands of cultural analysis and critique, Latin American cultural studies largely framed its questions, categories and approaches in terms of the actors and shifting constellations emerging within the regionally diversified playing field of the Latin American post-dictatorships of the 1980s and 1990s. A shared focus in these early years, allowing for the configuration of something like a 'field' of conversation across national and linguistic boundaries, included responses from the vantage point of theory and aesthetics to contemporary interventions heralding new kinds of governmentality under neoliberal prerogatives.

Yet the analysis of the cultural and mass-medial underpinnings of this new order also attempted to move away from the ideological critiques which, in the 1960s and 1970s, had dominated approaches to 'popular' and 'mass culture', during a period of intense intellectual involvement in decolonizing struggles of 'national liberation', that culminated in, among others, Ariel Dorfman's and Armand Mattelart's (1972) influential critique of Disney or in Roberto Schwarz's (1970) acerbic balance of Brazilian cultural production before and after the military coup of 1964. Rather, the emphasis now lay with the attempt to map and reconstruct democratic-popular agencies from within the mediatic apparatuses of subject formation put into place during or after the dictatorships: Ernesto Laclau's and Chantal Mouffe's neo-Gramscian *Hegemony and Socialist Strategy* (1985) and the communication theory work of Eliseo Verón, Jesús Martín-Barbero or Roger Bartra, among others, provided early reference points for this quest for understanding how the behavioural codes and sentimental economies set in motion through 'new-media' circuits were actually being put into everyday intimate as well as communal practice, not just as modes of 'alienated' consciousness but also – at least in equal measure – as everyday forms of symbolization and political appropriation and inscription. How, then – the emergent network of researchers from the social sciences and the humanities assembled around the concept of 'cultural studies' asked – could these everyday experiences of 'culture' (in the 'wide', anthropological sense put forward by Raymond Williams) actually be articulated to forge novel and emancipatory demands in the struggle for citizenship and justice?

At the same time, as highlighted by Jean Franco, responding to the 'cultural studies questionnaire' that the *Journal of Latin American Cultural Studies* began circulating among leading figures of the field in the early 1990s, 'there is a difference between the politics of culture and the politics of politics. Cultural studies can and should theorize change, but cannot replace public sphere politics' (Franco 1993: 156). Others also called for caution when entrusting notions of agency and identity with ultimate legitimizing functions – in George Yúdice's words: 'Why should group culture function as the ultimate warrant of legitimacy? If culture is a construct, then how can it be a warrant of legitimacy?' (Yúdice 1997: 220). In synthesis, then, the questions this emerging, transdisciplinary network of Latin American cultural studies was raising were very much the ones expressed in William Rowe's opening essay to this collection, originally published in the first number of the *Journal* – both in relation to the politics playing out within the field of culture itself and to the political conditions of possibility of a given cultural field and its transfigurations: 'What I would like to suggest is that the study of culture needs to ask the question: what are the conditions of existence of a given cultural field? And in what ways is the cultural field in which we find ourselves currently changing?' (Rowe 1992: 20).

These questions remain of an uncanny actuality today, as the – however timid and contradictory – national-popular processes that appeared to have taken root in Latin America over the last two decades are collapsing one by one, due to internal fractures as well as the sustained and concerted efforts of large mediatic and judiciary corporations: a novel combination, perhaps, of the colonial matrix Ángel Rama theorized in his posthumously published *The Lettered City* (1984). Neo-autonomist and Schmittian currents in cultural and political theory have been quick to seize on this 'posthegemonic' moment in Latin American politics, but their often timely and acute critiques of the nation-state and institution-centred framework of cultural and political models of analysis have mostly turned a blind eye to the hegemonic *re-articulations* recently converging around themes of consumption, religion and the racist/sexist re-assertion of patriarchal identity, mobilized as a moral crusade against 'corruption', the new shorthand phrase through which any attempt at redistribution, social justice and the enhancement of citizenship is now instantly put under suspicion. Biopolitical conceptions of governmentality and affect have at least started addressing these new configurations, yet on the whole Latin American cultural studies – a field which, to quote Abril Trigo's (2004: 3–4) useful definition, proclaimed to analyse 'the symbolic production and living experiences of social reality in Latin America [. . .] as intricately connected to social, political and material relations' – has failed rather calamitously in addressing, let alone foreseeing, the current leap to the right across most of its supposed constituency. Indeed, over almost two decades, Latin American cultural studies has grown more and more out of touch with its core business of, to quote Trigo again, the intimate exchange between culture and 'what is experienced at the social and political spheres' (Trigo 2004: 4), mainly because its own critical vocabularies have become increasingly distant from the passionate languages of the political forged in Latin America since the millennium. Or, more seriously even, the languages of the field of Latin American cultural studies, which had emerged over the 1980s and 1990s within contexts of 'new social movements' and identity politics, have shown little resistance against their active co-optation by a bogus right-wing 'Republicanism' or by a vapid, PR-treated neoliberal idiom of tolerance, participation, and sustainability, which now sits comfortably alongside anemic and self-referential stances of campus leftism.

Of course, many of the dead ends of Latin American cultural criticism and theory had already been highlighted from as early as the mid-1990s by the likes of Nelly Richard (1996), Román de la Campa (1999), and Alberto Moreiras (2001), and quite a substantial number of pages from the *Journal*'s twenty-five-year history, including dossiers and special issues, were dedicated to these diagnoses and their implications. Rather than retelling that story, then, as an ongoing success story, perhaps today we need to revisit the family history of our field in the mindset of Walter Benjamin's theses on history, using to our own advantage the present moment of danger, as the lightning flash that illuminates those shards and leftovers that might still be wielded against an enemy we barely know – because, as weapons, they at least begin to define the organs and functions of the body against which they might come in handy. This is, indeed, the wager of this 'anthology' celebrating the *Journal*'s twenty-fifth anniversary: to assume both the failure *and* the ongoing potential of the Latin American cultural studies project, to sift through its archives once more in search for eccentric, off-mainstream propositions, the productivity of which we are only fully grasping today when their pregnancy with future meanings is unfolding.

Founded initially under the name of *Traves/sia*, the *Journal*'s stated aim had been to open up a space of translation and cross-fertilization between several fields still – to use Raymond Williams's terms – in a state of 'formation', including the various ways in which the concept of 'culture' was then reconfiguring disciplinary constellations in UK and US academia, as well as giving rise, in Latin America, to novel conversations between literary and anthropological traditions with social and communication studies work on audiovisual media, all in the context of a post-1989 rethinking of leftist politics and strategy. Yet in its double spelling, referenced by a shadowed second 's', *Traves/sia* also upheld its allegiance to an aesthetic radicalism many of these new 'culturalisms' were now viewing with suspicion, and one that the journal subsequently re-asserted through collaborations from the likes of Néstor Perlongher, Margo Glantz, Raúl Zurita, and João Gilberto Noll. '*Travesia*', in Spanish, had also been a key concept of the poetic-artistic experiment of *Amereida* by the collective of Valparaíso-based architects, writers and artists who would go on to found the 'Ciudad Abierta' in 1972: a lyrical as well as performative reclaiming of historico-geographical space, which the Portuguese '*Travessia*' puts into an intricate and somewhat enigmatic relation with João Guimarães Rosa's epic monologue *Grande Sertão: Veredas*, of which it is the last word and final sentence; not least because both the Spanish and Portuguese terms are also intimately connected, in their historical semantics, with travel and discovery and, thus, with the coloniality of knowledge.

In a similar balancing act as, say, the Chilean *Revista de Crítica Cultural* in its close relationship with the aesthetic legacies of the '*escena avanzada*' of the Pinochet years, the *Journal* sought to reconcile a radical poetics with a hermeneutics of culture, to paraphrase the title of a book by William Rowe (2014 [1996]), one of the *Journal*'s founding editors, and thus also to translate not just to and from different geopolitical and linguistic locations of 'cultural theory' but also between these and a neo- or post-avantgardist aesthetic production which, as the Brazilian art critic Mário Pedrosa had already foreseen in 1966, was now in itself 'no longer purely artistic but rather cultural' in its scope and materialities (Pedrosa 1966: 207). As in all translations, a considerable amount of noise was unleashed in this attempt to mediate between critical idioms that often seemed to be pulling in opposing directions. When rereading today the first volumes of *Traves/sia*, one finds 'cultural studies questionnaires' sitting right next to essayistic and experimental-narrative work and article-length contributions that are often 'switching between [...] Latin American cultural criticism and critical US Latin Americanism,' as John Kraniauskas (2005: 3) put it in an earlier balance of the *Journal*'s trajectory more than ten years ago, adding: 'Herein lies our (the Journal's) drama.'

In attempting to provide a discursive space for exchanges between various critical departures from Frankfurt School or Althusserian modes of ideology critique (Birmingham School-inspired cultural studies with the new media and mediations theories then emerging out of Latin America's social theory engine, FLACSO, and somewhat later subalternist and postcolonial strands of thought entering the field from US academia) while at the same time also holding on to the 'exceptionality' of the aesthetic, the *Journal* remained – for better or worse – in a position of eccentricity towards some of the field's major waves or critical fashions. Rather, from very early on its pages also played host to incisive critiques by the likes of Ricardo Kaliman (1998), Ana del Sarto (2000), and Gabriela Nouzeilles (2001), among others, which hinted at the intellectual and political cost of Cultural Studies' divorce from (mainly) Marxist-inspired earlier strands of radical reflection and critique. From Mariátegui to Retamar, this vernacular Latin American tradition of cultural analysis had taken culture as an ideological battlefield in which the critic intervened, as Arturo Jauretche put it in his book-length X-ray of Argentina's petty bourgeoisie, 'colocándome "a la paleta" en el método' [taking methodology as it comes] (1966: 9), that is: by actively embracing the 'amateurism' of 'an impassioned actor and observer' rather claiming the detached vantage point of the social scientist. Ironically, critiques such as those by Kaliman, Del Sarto, and Nouzeilles appeared at a time when the journal, and the 'field' to which it was now catering, were themselves experiencing a process of rapid institutionalization, as manifest in the move from the initial, more artisanal mode of production and distribution to academic publisher Carfax (subsequently Taylor & Francis). This shift coincided with the promotion of the previous subtitle to the name under which the journal has been circulating ever since, further cutting off its moorings in region-specific genealogies of aesthetic and critical radicalism.

The mutable collective of intellectuals editing the journal – with backgrounds in Anglo-American but also Latin American and European academia – were plainly aware of the pitfalls involved in this balancing act and attempted to make explicit the difficult fit of its intellectual constituency with the professional protocols of the Anglo-American knowledge economy. The *Journal*'s 'politics of translation' received in those years a renewed emphasis. New sections such as 'From the Archive' made available for the first time to English-language audiences the work of classics such as Ángel Rama, Antonio Cornejo Polar, and the South American forays of the Collège de Sociologie, among others, while the *Journal* also documented and translated controversies within Latin America itself such as the debate around Oscar del Barco's *No matarás* open letter in 2006–7. 'Dispatches', a new rubric rolled in since 2010 for short, essayistic chronicles 'from the field' on events and processes during or just after their unfolding, has sought to rekindle something of the spirit of active intellectual witnessing invoked by Jauretche; thus far, contributions have covered the deaths of Néstor Kirchner and Hugo Chávez, counter-terrorist discourse under

Alan García's second presidency and force-feeding of Mapuche prisoners in Chile, the pre-World Cup *protestos* in Brazil, and the Mexican student movement against electoral fraud, further to special dossiers on the election of Latin America's first pope and the rise of *macrismo* in Argentina.

However, the 'user data' provided at regular intervals by the *Journal*'s commercial publishers reveal a not too surprising preference among its readership for a more consolidated set of topics – indicative, if anything, of the meanings and role of cultural studies for the classroom of today. For some time now, the *Journal*'s 'top-selling' article has been a piece on the importance of Dominican and Central American wrestling culture in Junot Díaz's *Brief and Wondrous Life of Oscar Wao* (Garland Mahler 2010) – a novel written in English. In all likelihood, 'Latin Americanist' input is being sought here as 'cultural background' from outside the field itself, whereas other topics popular with readers – contemporary Mexican, Brazilian and Argentine cinema, particularly films set on the urban margins, the work of Roberto Bolaño, or the literary and filmic manifestations of post-dictatorial memory in the Southern Cone – are at least indicative of the current contents of undergraduate syllabi in Spanish and Portuguese programmes in the US and UK. By comparison, the *Journal*'s own attempts to push different agendas and to reconnect with off-campus politics as they have unfolded across Latin America have enjoyed a far more limited success, especially where they have not been made available through Open Access. Indeed, the commodification of critical work and its circulation through professional platforms plugged into a largely privatized knowledge economy are likely to actively obstruct today the gathering of heterodox audiences such as the journal was seeking to bring to the same table at the moment of its inception. This is particularly true for Latin America itself where, for linguistic reasons but also for the vastly uneven access to commercial library packages, the *Journal* circulates far less than in the Anglosphere.

On one level, these technicalities shed light on the extent to which the very condition of possibility of critical production also as a public good is predicated on techno-economic logistics that are indifferent (rather than actively hostile) to particular modes of thought, and which, on another level, complicate the possibility of maintaining the kinds of two- or three-way conversations which had once provided the ethical and political *raison d'être* of the field of Latin American cultural studies. Indeed, we must reflect on the ways in which political economies of knowledge foreclose today particular modes of critical labour predicated on figures and gestures of aesthetic and intellectual autonomy or negativity – a process that Willy Thayer, in a book written more than fifteen years ago and specifically referring to the Chilean context, pointedly associated with the political, economic, and administrative concept of 'transition' (Thayer et al. 2000). Today, on a global scale for which Chile, in hindsight, was in so many ways an early laboratory, the question facing scholars and intellectuals working in the realm of Cultural Studies is very much about how, from within our professional practices inescapably enmeshed in systems of self-reification and the neoliberalization of thinking, we can recover some of the hermeneutics of compassion, confrontation, and enmity, which had propelled previous waves of cultural critique in Latin America as well as elsewhere.

The present Reader, celebrating twenty-five years of the *Journal of Latin American Cultural Studies*, is also a first attempt to re-chart the map of the field with a view to these new challenges. Rather than once more to document key moments and polemics from the past – a task that previous anthologies such as those by Del Sarto, Ríos, and Trigo (2004) and more recently Szurmuk and McKee Irwin (2012) have already fulfilled remarkably well – we have asked for the ongoing or renewed validity of the questions and issues raised in the *Journal*'s pages. Readers might be surprised at first sight by the absence of key names in the field whose work the *Journal* has accompanied and published over the years (Jesús Martín-Barbero, Josefina Ludmer, Néstor García Canclini, or Silviano Santiago may come to mind) and the presence of others whose work, while in conversation with it, has not necessarily been identified with Latin American cultural studies but rather with art history, anthropology or even literary writing. No judgment of quality or critical value is intended here, merely the suggestion that, twenty-five years onward from the *Journal*'s foundation, the question of what cultural studies needs to be and of what might be specifically Latin American about them, is perhaps not as settled as some of its resident curators and gravediggers might think. Rather than a museum of Latin American cultural studies, this collection wants to offer something like an open archive and therefore an invitation to read anew. Its six thematic areas provide cross-sections, each in its own fashion, through concerns and controversies that have run through the *Journal*'s pages, yet which also acquire a new urgency in the light of present critical and political challenges.

'Temporalities', the opening section, includes essays that deal first and foremost with the historical reconfigurations of cultural memory, particularly in relation to the epochal shift ushered in by successive military blows to the progressive social and political experiments of the 1960s: the capture and assassination of Ernesto 'Che' Guevara in Bolivia in 1967; Pinochet's 1973 military coup and subsequent restructuring of Chilean society along the lines dictated by Chicago-school neoliberal economics; the *Proceso de Reorganización Nacional* that began with the 1976 coup in Argentina; as well as the drawn out struggles between the Sendero Luminoso guerrilla and the Peruvian state in the 1980s and 1990s. Yet beyond underscoring Latin America's both privileged and eccentric relation to the global rise of memory, and of 'memory studies' as cultural and political phenomena in recent decades, they also open up the fraught struggle between competing cultural, historical, and political teleologies that diverse forms and genres of memory-work encode. Indeed, in charting these competing teleologies they illuminate the simultaneous non-simultaneity of lived worlds that make up the discontinuous, heterotropic texture of the neoliberal present in Latin America.

William Rowe's 'War and Cultural Studies: Reflections on Recent Work in Peru and Argentina' (1992) underscores the need, not only to map out violence's destructive social and political effects (the traumatic erasures of memory, the 'emptying out' of the social fabric, and the short-circuiting and rewiring of whole ways of living and perceiving), but also to discard – as so much romantic nostalgia – any hope that culture might still constitute a stable foundation from which to counteract such destructive 'unworldings'. Reconstruction of the broken universes left in the wake of such processes thus involves thinking beyond the disciplinary frameworks that continue to constrain the study of 'culture' today, even – or perhaps especially – now that cultural studies finds itself comfortably accommodated by corporate university programmes. Indeed, only work that remains critically attuned to the historically precarious territorialization of culture by national-popular registers, can shed light on the processes whereby popular forms counter the deterriorializations of capital. Essays by Viñas, Ludmer, and Sarlo in Argentina (which blast open the illusory aesthetic-political sutures binding literature to the construction of the national) as well as writings by Rodrigo Montoya, Alberto Flores Galindo and José María Arguedas in Peru (who re-anchor literature in its anthropological 'other scene') are cited as exemplary guides in this ongoing task.

If Rowe's essay warns of the dangers of assuming any continuity of popular cultural formations, Nelly Richard's 'The Reconfigurations of Post-dictatorship Critical Thought' (2000) – eloquently rendered in English by John Kraniauskas – offers insights into the inherent instability and non self-identity of the post-dictatorial, neoliberal present. Dwelling on the emblematic insistence on the figures of trauma, mourning and melancholy in post-dictatorship thinking, Richard insists that it is from a critical vindication of the *remainder* that culture might imagine alternative futures to those imposed by the *golpe* and its homogenizing 'aftershock' pragmatics. Thus, she insists that sustained attention to the traces of loss that fissure the discourse of a certain post-political realism – attention, that is, to the semantic, affective, and political reverberations of what is 'spectral' and 'untimely' – allow for a critical defamiliarization of the neoliberal present as a precariously assembled montage of 'reality effects'. The figures of spectrality and untimeliness, powerfully constelled in works such as Idelber Avelar's *The Untimely Present* (1999), continue to guide efforts to re-emplot the post-dictatorial present by interdisciplinary researchers who are reaching beyond literature to test the less familiar interstices between film, photography, architecture, and land art.

Complementing Richard's anxiety that those same residual alterities – deployed in some neo- and post-avant-garde scenarios to fracture neoliberal consensus – nonetheless risk incorporation by the laws of supply and demand that fuel late capitalism's 'cultural turn', Paulo Drinot's (2009) account of the polemic surrounding 'The Eye That Cries' (a monument to the victims of political violence, created in Lima in 2005) alerts us to the ways in which 'post-conflict' memory-work may, by contrast, also fix and entrench irreconcilable 'ontologies' of the present. The monument – a constellation of some 30,000 plus stones, each of which was inscribed with the name of a victim of political violence – refused to enshrine a 'top-down' *Fujimorista* narrative about the triumphant demise of the Sendero Luminoso and, with this, of the age of armed struggle. Rather, it sought to provide a space of democratic redress in which to correct the social invisibility of those sectors of Peruvian society – principally Andean *campesinos* – whose historic inhabitation of the precarious intersections between social, sexual, and racial exclusion, made their deaths at the hands of both state and counter-state forces 'unremarkable'. Yet disagreement over whether to include within the monument's fabric the names of some 41 *Senderistas* massacred in 1992 by state forces brought these competing aims to a head. To include such names seemed – to some at least – to vitiate both collectivist *and* individualist understandings of violence, victimhood, and responsibility. To suppress the inclusion of these 'terrorists' – the aim of certain particularly colourful vandals – would, for others, lead to the reintroduction, under the terms of 'post-conflict' peace and reconciliation, of biopolitical distinctions between legitimate and illegitimate forms of violence, and, crucially, between deaths worthy and not worthy of being mourned.

Drinot's illumination of the difficulty involved in stabilizing the meanings of past, present and future in 'post-conflict' Peru, offers proleptic insights for what will no doubt be a fraught and drawn out process of social and political reconstruction in Colombia following the peace talks held in La Habana with Latin America's oldest *guerrilla* insurgency in 2015 and 2016 and a subsequent referendum. Will 'peace' continue to represent the pursuit of 'war by other means'? Mariano Mestman's closing essay in the section, 'The Last Sacred Image of the Latin American Revolution' (2010), adds new layers to these questions in its final unpacking of the competing iconographies that shape the narrativization of post-1960s Latin American history, its ruptures and continuities, its moments of epic heroism and collective disappointment. His forays into the 'afterlives' of two photographs of 'Che' Guevara – Alberto Korda's 1960 image of the heroic *guerrilla* fighter whose fixed stare beholds an epic future, and Freddy Alborta's shot of the recently expired corpse of the hero-turned-fallen- Christ in Vallegrande, Bolivia – certainly expose the labour performed by the image in particular in the making of epochs. They also demonstrate how, beyond their evidentiary or testimonial claims, such images condense multiple emplotments of past, present, and future, especially in their tensile balancing of scientific, military, religious, and aesthetic registers. The political 'reality-effect' of the Bolivian army's displaying of the corpse may thus have breathed new life into radical forms of political subjectivation, and precisely at the moment when the image of the living *guerrillero* became an insignia for the culture industry's imposition of a very different set of values. Such an image, moreover – that of the corpse that lives on – might also, in this sense, stand as a symbol for the vital potentialities and multiple futures still lying dormant in a present epoch that continues to labour under the sign of defeat.

'Territories', the concept that constitutes the second section's unifying thread, underscores the spatial underpinnings of many questions raised in the first section. Its connotations encompass the demarcations that European imperial projects used to map colonial aspirations and possessions and the impact their imposition had on colonial life, to the various manifestations of political and cultural sovereignty that have informed Latin American republican configurations from the nineteenth century to the globalized, transnational and, in concretely geopolitical ways, tenuous present. These articles have in common an interest in revisiting spatial intersections where national symbolic economies inform the political, revealing, as it were, schemes of 'worlding' – to use a Heideggerian concept deployed by Julio Ramos – whose tactical and ideological contours have given form to Latin American ideas and realities in profound ways. Rather than frame the articles as oracular in scope, we would like to emphasize their critical sagacity in detecting instances of experimentation where certain discourses and national compositions blended into cyclical structures, following John Kraniauskas' reference to Arguedas's penchant in *Yawar Fiesta* for 'experiment[ing] with cultural and political possibility'.

If Ramos's 'Hemispheric Domains: 1898 and the Origins of Latin Americanism' (2001) revisits two significant moments in Latin American territorial reconfiguration, namely the secession of Panama and creation of the Panama Canal, and the 1898 Spanish American War, in order to map out a biopolitics of capital and regional reordering, casting a critical light especially on the economic and cultural implosions within which Antonio Cornejo Polar's 1997 interpellation of US-based Latin Americanism plays an important role, Gabriela Nouzeilles's 'Patagonia as Borderland: Nature, Culture, and the Idea of the State' (1999) reexamines the symbolic construction of Patagonia as the product of a multifarious imperial imagination and its reinvention at the hands of the state, emphasizing new spatial-iconic coordinates of hegemony that give birth to fetishisms pregnant with problematic values of cultural cohesion as well as economic and political authority. That we read these articles today (2016), at a time when both Argentina and Puerto Rico find themselves subject to dislocating and rapacious transnational financial opportunism, reveals illuminating and distressing resonances.

By looking at the long-term use of colonial symbols and geo-cultural formations, their fluid, accrued value, but also at their paradoxical appropriation, Jean Franco's 'The Return of Coatlicue: Mexican Nationalism and the Aztec Past' (2004) and John Kraniauskas's 'A Short Andean History of Photography: *Yawar Fiesta*' (2012), develop nuanced readings of regional foundations where human relations and artifacts compose haunting legacies of cultural fetishizing and commodification, dislocation and fragmentation, and where dominant structures are reproduced into conflicting, periodic regimes of meaning. Ending with a poignant analogy between Coatlicue, human trafficking, and dismembering, Franco's article appears today, to echo her own deliberation, 'eerily relevant'; as eerily relevant as Kraniauskas's analyses of *Yawar fiesta*, when read in the context of waves of dispossession and resurgence in Andean regions, and where radical structures of capitalization and alteration of social relations display visible neocolonial lineages. Taking us into a more contemporary realm, Guillermina De Ferrari, in the final contribution to this section, highlights the unstable and paradoxical status of national cultures as transnational commodities mined for local colour and authenticity on global art and literary markets. Zooming in on Cuba during the 'Special Period', her analysis productively cross-fertilizes literary and art-historical ways of approaching 'the contemporary', both to draw out the singularity of Cuban aesthetic production during that time and to suggest wider-ranging implications for Latin American art and culture as a whole. Indeed, it is very much its mode of circulation (in particular its legibility inside Cuba as well as abroad) that determines the kind of ambiguous, double-coded expression shared by so many artistic and literary works of the time. The management, distribution, and contextualization of meaning, which by that time (the 1990s) was starting to become universally known as 'curatorship', is characterized by De Ferrari as a 'technique of power' that allows the negotiation of 'local' as well as 'global' valences of *cubanidad* and, thus, also shapes ways of thinking about the country's peculiar, idiosyncratic insertion into global-capitalist circuits since then.

'Aesthetics', the third section, brings together four essays on cultural production, circulation, and reception, focused on Argentina, Mexico, Brazil and, broadly speaking, the Caribbean region. The Argentine Néstor Perlongher (1949–1992) was known for his work both in poetry and urban anthropology, as a writer and anthologist closely associated with the *neobarroco*, and as a pioneering researcher of male prostitution in São Paulo, where he lived in the 1980s and 1990s. His essay on Argentina's 'secret poetry boom' (1992) was accompanied in the *Journal* by a translation of his era-defining poem 'Cadáveres' (Corpses), and remains unpublished in Spanish. As a poet, sociologist, and founding member of gay rights groups (including the Homosexual Liberation Front, or FLH, in Argentina), Perlongher was uniquely well-placed to observe cultural shifts in the late- and post-dictatorship period. He examined a series of phenomena linked to a 'flowering of bards' in late 1980s and early 1990s Buenos Aires: the catalogue of Último Reino, a longstanding publisher of neoromantic and later neobaroque poetry; the relative commercial success of *Diario de Poesía*, a bimonthly newspaper dedicated to poetry, sold in bookshops and *kioscos*; and the growing popularity of literary workshops. These all gave him cause for cautious optimism. His analysis links such developments to political circumstances: the destruction of networks of militancy by the 1976–83 dictatorship, and with it the need to find alternative forms and spaces of expression, including a highly coded, even mannerist style of writing. The latter fed into the so-called *neobarroco* poetry, whose practitioners include Tamara Kamenszain and Arturo Carrera, as well as Perlongher himself, and several Uruguayan writers, including Eduardo Espina. Opposition came in the shape of a move towards 'objectivist' styles, championed by the *Diario de Poesía*. Whatever his own aesthetic preferences, Perlongher pronounced the controversy enriching.

Perlongher's observations on the artisanal and scantly funded publications of the 1980s foreshadow later work such as Andrea Giunta's 2009 book on 'post-crisis' art or Cecilia Palmeiro's 2011 study of the 'trash aesthetic' of Argentine art spaces Eloísa Cartonera and Belleza y Felicidad. Within this collection, Perlongher's work should be read alongside William Rowe's analysis of cultural and theoretical production from Peru and Argentina during this period, and Ana Gabriela Álvarez's work on *travesti* activism in Buenos Aires. Justin Read's essay on São Paulo also chimes with Perlongher's work as an anthropologist, especially his thesis – later published in book form – *O negocio do michê* (The Business of Masculine Prostitution). Perlongher's interest in poetry as a genuinely popular form of cultural production also links up with Freya Schiwy's piece on indigenous media.

Carlos Monsiváis (1938–2010) was perhaps Mexico's best-known and most respected contemporary cultural commentator. He was also a movie critic and his piece 'Tin Tan: The Pachuco' (1994) demonstrates his encyclopaedic knowledge of Mexican cinema. Just like Perlongher's text, it demonstrates the *Journal*'s commitment to the translation of emerging writing for an Anglophone public. Tin Tan was the screen name of Germán Valdés, a Mexican entertainer who made dozens of popular but low-grade musical films from 1944 onwards. These popularized the *pachuco* style of dress, in a distinctive oversized 'zoot suit', and of language, predating celebratory appraisals of Spanglish by several decades. The *pachuco* was studied, famously, by Octavio Paz in *The Labyrinth of Solitude* (1950), in a melancholy and rather disapproving vein. Tin Tan, whose career partly coincided with the Golden Age of Mexican cinema, was commercially exploited, but never wholly accepted. Monsiváis sketches the standard repertoire of the Mexican comic character, embodied in Cantinflas, who has come to monopolize 'the emblematization of the people.' In contrast, the *pachuco* figure as embodied by Tin Tan became a symbol of cultural resistance and popular modernity, employing a linguistic collage that was at once offensive to the guardians of good taste and ever more popular with audiences. His vitality on screen, for Monsiváis, lifted mediocre and even bad films; Tin Tan mastered parody and the 'hatred of boredom', against more obviously commercial – and conservative – films. Monsiváis examines the interactions between popular culture and the culture industry, not merely for purposes of denunciation, but with a view to uncovering the conflicted spaces that emerge in such an encounter. Of particular importance is the role of the audience, and the fan (which the author clearly was) of Tin Tan's pictures. The essay demonstrates Monsiváis at his most virtuoso and compelling as a cultural critic. It is also an early example of the importance of film for the *Journal*'s contributors – see, for example, the essay included in this anthology by Ignacio Sánchez Prado on *Amores perros*.

José Quiroga, in 'Queer Boleros of a Tropical Night' (1994), writes on the resurgent interest in the 1990s in sentimental *boleros* of the 1940s and 1950s, in particular in cultural works by or depicting gay men. Manuel Puig, and especially the popular film version of *Kiss of the Spider Woman*, would be perhaps the best-known example. The *bolero* re-emerged as a seductive voice from the past, drawing readers and spectators into what Quiroga calls 'a meta-Caribbean space.' From his perspective as an expert in both Latino studies and queer theory, Quiroga reads this as something other than camp or nostalgia, not simply a tired post-modern gesture of longing for times past, expressed in tacky and sentimental songs. Context is important, not least the effects of NAFTA and the end of the Cold War on regional realpolitik and its cultural echoes. Quiroga hones in on the role of performance in both the original *boleros* – Agustín Lara's compositions especially – and the 'undecideability' occasioned by their re-use in ostensibly queer settings. This re-use transcends borders and binaries. Quiroga's essay obviously has points of contact with Perlongher's research, including the latter's writings on transvestism and on the work of Puig himself. It also connects to Elaine Luck's essay on upper-class identity performance; as well as the border-crossing analysis of William Rowe's contribution.

Idelber Avelar's contribution, 'Heavy metal music in postdictatorial Brazil' (2003), originally presented at the *Journal*'s annual conference in London that same year, was accompanied by a heavily amplified broadcast of the music of Sepultura, the Brazilian thrash/death metal band on which his article throws a spotlight. Avelar situates Brazilian heavy metal in both its political context – the tail end of the dictatorship and the first (unelected) civilian government since the 1960s – and the ongoing 'national cultural battle' over authenticity in Brazilian music. Heavy metal, as performed by Sepultura and their peers, fell victim to multiple exclusions: as nihilistic; as technically impoverished; as foreign; and as politically alien to the broadly progressive values of the absorbent genre of MPB, or Brazilian Popular Music. Avelar, via a reading of Nietzsche, defends Sepultura against the charge of nihilism, highlighting the celebration of the power of life in metal, not least through the ubiquitous power chord. In a musical genre characterised by its fans' (and performers') selective exclusions, Sepultura have pulled off twin feats: to remain almost universally recognised as an authentic death/thrash metal group; and to have changed constantly over the decades of their existence. Avelar notes the growing incorporation of Afro-Brazilian rhythms into their soundscapes, alongside other elements from outside the staples of death metal, such as distortion, noise, speed, and syncopation. For young people in Brazil, heavy metal represents a metaphor for the absence of the nation and also an antidote to social exclusion. Sepultura manage to reject the false universality of MPB while also resisting the neo-colonial logic of 'world music'. Like Quiroga, Avelar engages in close analysis of music, but also of its reception. His piece links to a strong tradition of music writing in the *Journal*: the same issue included a piece on taste in Brazilian music by João Freire Filho and Micael Herschmann; one might also cite articles by David Treece, Jack A. Draper III, and most recently Lara Putnam.

Spinoza's famous observation that 'no one has yet determined what a body can do' (1959: 87) has become something of a founding statement for the 'affective turn' in the humanities and social sciences, and might also serve as a common point of reference for the essays collected in the section that follows, on 'Affects'. Interest in what we might call the circulation of social energy and in the affective capacities of bodies both human and nonhuman, has been widespread across many strands of Latin American(ist) cultural theory, as several of the contributions to this Reader across all of the sections demonstrate. Carlos Monsiváis's and Jean Franco's writings, for example, have, from very early on, highlighted the affective, meaning-defying dimensions of cultural experience, which were also a focal point of anthropological, literary, and art-historical research, from Alberto Flores Galindo's studies on indigenous insurgencies in the Andes to Doris Sommer's work on *testimonio* or Nelly Richard's writings on post-dictatorial aesthetics of memory and mourning. The essays collected here choose a more restricted, yet also more systematic, approach to the problem of affect as 'a new configuration of bodies, technology, and matter' (Ticineto Clough 2007: 2). They depart from a similar, Foucauldian framework concerned with the biopolitical production of normatized and 'deviant' bodies, in which the latter (which encompass not only gendered, racialized bodies, but also, in a more generic, unspecified fashion, the collective body of the mass or 'mob') fulfil a dual role as both the foundation and the abyss of the classificatory, taxonomic organization of populations on behalf of the apparatuses of state, science, and capitalism. As a constitutive excess, a body that is (in)defined by its very resistance to definition or classification, the deviant body thus becomes a kind of representational energy reserve, a source of fundamental anxiety that is there to be mobilized for the discursive production of moral panic. As a surface onto which fears of contamination, violence, and self-loss can be projected, this deviant body whose 'dangerousness is never quite graspable', as Ana Gabriela Álvarez puts it in her discussion of the special powers awarded to the police by the modern Argentine state, thus also becomes a source of legitimacy for a specifically modern kind of power, which feeds on that which exceeds it – in Álvarez's words: 'Power which tries to grasp desire and desire which is nourished on escaping from power.'

Yet the essays in this section also attempt to push this Foucauldian framework to its limits by asking about the 'affective capacities' unleashed by these bodies; their powers of counter-acting upon, or through, the very apparatuses that produce and reproduce them.

These counter- or retro-actions should not be confounded with 'agency' or with an emergent political subjectivity assuming its own representation, although – evidence perhaps of the belated reception of Deleuzian, queer, neo-phenomenological, or bio-informatic theories of affect in the field of Latin American studies – the texts occasionally struggle to move beyond terminologies drawn from the sociology of cultural identities or from a Laclauian conception of hegemony. Nevertheless, the main focus of attention shifts in all four pieces from the (critique of) representations of social subjects to the much more intricate and hard-to-grasp dimension of the mutual affectations between bodies and representations, and between bodies and other bodies, 'the ebbs and swells of intensities that pass between "bodies" (bodies defined not by an outer skin-envelope or other surface boundary but by their potential to reciprocate or co-participate in the passages of affect)' (Gregg and Seigworth 2010: 2).

In the opening article, 'Sabina's oranges' (2002), the late Tiago de Melo Gomes and Micol Seigel weave a richly textured cultural history of urban race relations in Rio de Janeiro during the turn from the nineteenth to the twentieth century, a period of intense political change and 'urban reformism' grounded in real estate speculation and social segregation. Through the subsequent iterations of 'Sabina' – a black, female street vendor who became an icon of Republicanism when medical students took to the streets on her behalf protesting a police prohibition on selling food in public places – Melo Gomes and Seigel construct a critical archaeology of 'cordiality', the paternalistic framework of interracial/interclass loyalties on which the myth of Brazilian 'racial democracy' has been predicated. In their minutious analysis, which draws out the intersectional aspects of Sabina's production as 'poor, old, female, black, ex-slave', Melo Gomes and Seigel argue that, from the very first public display of 'affection' towards this 'other' on the part of elite subjects – the male, white students – the very system of differences and hierarchies in which Sabina's alterity and subordination are grounded, is also simultaneously re-affirmed and reified. The excess and abjection of her multiply 'othered' body, in fact, become the measure of the elite subjects' charitable 'affection' towards her – yet, in being thus banished from the realm of normatized bodies, Sabina's dangerously polyvalent body also causes the students' and other subsequent 'appropriations' of her figure to 'get out of hand', unleashing its excess of signification.

The subsequent essays by Luis Duno Gottberg (2004), Ana Gabriela Álvarez (2000), and Elaine Luck (2010) all situate the questions raised by Melo Gomes and Seigel about the discursive production of 'deviance' and its affective 'counter-actings' in the context of the neoliberal city and its associated mediascapes. Thus, they also suggest a kind of post-disciplinary, or post-developmental, return to some of the tropes that first emerged in the context of nineteenth-century mass psychology and urban 'hygienism' – a resonance nicely flagged up by Álvarez in her opening quotation from José María Ramos Mejía's turn-of-the-century psychopathology of the popular multitude. Duno Gottberg's contribution traces through the audiovisual and discursive mass-media coverage of the 2002 coup against Hugo Chávez in Venezuela 'how the media produce the crowd' as well as – by justifying the latter's violent 'containment' as a necessary re-establishment of order from anomie – the naturalness of the norms that the crowd infringes. Tracing these tropings back to the foundational romances of modern Venezuelan literature (which, the author argues, are also those of the modern nation-state's political-institutional make-up, both being similarly founded on 'the erasure of the Black subject'), Duno sketches out a powerful critique of mediation theories focused on the agency and empowerment of consuming publics. Rather than to think about audiovisual media as a democratic space of negotiated meanings, he suggests, we need to rethink the relation between 'mediatic mediation' and 'social mediation', especially in relation to the mass-medial forging of 'counter-insurgent imaginaries'.

Like Duno Gottberg, Álvarez performs in her contribution a multi-layered close reading of a key political moment, here the constitutional debates in the city of Buenos Aires from which the short-lived 'Alianza' national government, formed under the mayor-turned-president De la Rúa, subsequently emerged. Here, debates about civil liberties against arbitrary police detention soon zeroed in – thanks once more to a concerted media effort – on the issue of street prostitution, and especially on the figure of the *travesti* (transvestite) sex worker, against whom 'neighborhood values' had to be defended at any price. In her/his defiance of the heteronormative matrix, the *travesti* becomes not just a shorthand for all the kinds of 'deviance' that require 'extraordinary' police intervention (and which, Álvarez argues, cannot be named in their own right in order not to reveal the various kinds of social and class repression performed 'in their name'). The *travesti* also serves as a projection surface for all kinds of fantasies, particularly of release from the very containment of desire that 'ordinary citizens' demand be imposed on others, and that they impose on themselves. Just like Duno Gottberg, then, Álvarez analyses the discursive stimulation of resentment as a dominant political affect, inquiring – in a series of close-readings of political-mediatic scenes – into the ways in which political discourse, its actors and audiences, are all 'affected' by that which this discourse mobilizes as the 'unspeakable' underwriting its enunciation.

This logic of excess, which constantly returns to yet also hollows out, previous, 'high-modern' figurations of race, gender, and class, as Elaine Luck suggests in her analysis of Daniela Rossell's photographic portraits of Mexican upper-class women, is closely related to the neoliberal re-articulation of these values through consumer culture. Against the homogenizing drive of modern nationalism, she suggests, neoliberalism has multiplied and fractured identity tokens as a way of diversifying and expanding supply and demand, thus also levelling the relation between an external, object world vis-à-vis the body as the urn or shrine of the self. Following Susan Stewart's work on bourgeois material culture, Luck reads Rossell's photographs as engaging with a world in which 'the body occupies one more position within a seriality and diversity of objects', which are thus invested with bodily valences and affects to the same extent as the body is being objectified and commodified. Taken together, and in drawing on propositions from visual studies, performance theory, media studies, and feminist/queer theory, the four pieces signal an emerging interest, to quote Luck once more, in 'objects' relations to the body and space, and the body's insertion into the material environment as another object, one that is constructed externally through images.'

The articles in the section 'Cityscapes' all survey the impact of imperialism and neoliberalism's chokehold on the continent at a moment when the 'pink tide' promised to address their effects. In addition to issues of governance and citizenship in urban environments, the pieces share a concern with the commodification of Latin America's cities – of its peoples, its poverty, and its violence. They all contemplate the role of geographical stories in the production and contestation of urban spaces and imaginaries. Writing on Brazil, Cuba, Argentina, and Mexico, the authors explore lived space – the city as the stage for intersecting, conflicting subjectivities. The central consideration that criss-crosses the four pieces is the drama of modernity – its dreams and realities – that plays out in Latin America's cities.

Marzena Grzegorczyk's reflections on the latter (1998) invoke Ángel Rama's notion of reading the imprints that the city's symbolic order leaves on the material one. However, she focuses instead on what happens when the symbolic urban lawmaker crosses paths with material reality and is unable to mould it. These *desencuentros* give rise to 'improper cities': zones of conflict where urban bodies and the urban unconscious undo the European ordering impulse. Grzegorczyk examines the dynamics of this disturbing of Western mentality through what appears to be a disparate trio of texts: Euclides da Cunha's *Os Sertões* (1902), Cabrera Infante's *La Habana para un infante difunto* (1941), and the paintings of Guillermo Kuitca. What emerge from her corporeally focused readings are the racialized and gendered logics of both the symbolic and material cities. In *Os Sertões* the rebels' unplanned city is 'monstrous' because of their miscegenation, with racial purity fundamental to national progress. Cabrera Infante's narrator disturbs the city's order and re-maps it with his prodigious sexual appetite that persists in introducing sexualized female bodies into the narrative. Kuitca's abstracted maps of Buenos Aires that evoke bodies only as traces and as abjection imagine what an excess of order does to bodily differences.

Grzegorczyk's 'improper cities' are thoroughly modern, in as much as modernity in the Americas, which has its structural foundations in the political economy of slavery, continues to shape racial and gendered forms of subjugation today. Her starting point is Rama's lettered city, but her counter reading of the production of city spaces gestures towards Aníbal Quijano's fundamental point about modernity in Latin America: that racial hierarchy was its ordering principle (see for example 2000). Unfortunately, although Latin American Cultural Studies as a field has focused considerable attention on urban issues since the publication of this article, the importance of race for the production of space remains woefully understudied. Countless geographical stories of dislocation, migration, and segregation stem from that enduring way of ordering society based on upholding white supremacy. However, many otherwise acute and astute commentators have preferred to understand Latin America's urbanization primarily through the prism of class relations. Justin Read's (2006) notion of 'obverse colonization' in the context of globalization focuses on this 'fault-line' between rich and poor in São Paulo. He contemplates the way that Latin America's less enviable qualities, such as great wealth disparities and ghettoization, are now 'transfecting' nominally rich nations of the West, obliging a rethink of First, Third, and even Fourth Worlds as national, geographic places. Instead, they are interspersed and coexist often within a single neighbourhood in São Paulo, London, or New York. A key contribution of Read's article is his casting of cultural critique as a productive tool to understand urban, global networks at a moment when social scientists were struggling to measure the extensive and intermeshed nature of such networks and flows. Read seeks to demonstrate that cultural critique can map a mega-city like São Paulo in which real and virtual landscapes overlap. He uses Google satellite maps to demonstrate the amorphous non-location that is São Paulo, as well as a poem by Concretist Haroldo de Campos that 'translates' the Third World city into the First. However, the provocative spirit of his concept of 'obverse colonialism' also demands that we look beyond high-tech satellite images and the lyricism of the *letrados*, to focus on less privileged ethnic and racialized or gendered geopolitical subjects and spatialities (as he does in his brief consideration of *forró* music by Northeastern migrants).

Beatriz Jaguaribe's article (2004) also ponders the issue identified by Read that globalization has created cities that have become increasingly difficult for geographers to map. The overlap of 'real', imagined, and virtual cityscapes that the media present and invent for us forms the focus of her piece. The urban environment that lies at the centre of her analysis is the favela. Jaguaribe begins by reflecting on Brazil's inconsistent, vexed relationship with a space that it has seen simultaneously as a locus of national identity and a site of barbarity that obstructs the project of modernity. Although Jaguaribe does not reflect in any sustained way on race, the piece can help us to think about how this profoundly racialized/ethnicized space (the majority of Brazil's favela dwellers are black and Northeasterners represent a significant part of its population) has become de-coupled from the country's modern, integrationist narratives. At the time this article was written the favelas were experiencing a moment of extremely high visibility in cultural representation and public discourse that imagined them as a powerful threat to the so-called formal city. Jaguaribe identifies the predominant mode of representation as a new realism, or an 'aesthetics of realism'. If realist codes have always been fundamental to articulating the contradictions of Brazilian modernity, the article seeks to explore what forms realism takes when those modernizing narratives unravel in the face of globalization and modernity's discontents. What emerges, the author contends, is a battle over the nature of 'the real' that admits subjectivity and the imagination, demonstrates a consciousness of mediation, or comes packaged for a market. In the years following the millennium, the national and international market's appetite for favela representations hinged on portrayals of violence. In the fierce polemic generated by the film *Cidade de Deus* (2002) Jaguaribe sees how this new aesthetics of realism can become part of the culture of the spectacle and simultaneously politicize representation.

Ignacio Sánchez-Prado does not share Jaguaribe's guarded optimism about the political possibilities of hit films depicting urban violence in Latin America. In his contribution (2006), a lucid and blistering critique of *Amores Perros* (2000), he examines the commodification of a Latin American imaginary for the consumption of the West and for the beneficiaries of neoliberalism at home in Mexico. His analysis reveals a conservative morality that underpins the film and stymies any reflection on violence as an outcome of socio-economic inequalities. Although critics have read the film as a reflection on an uncertain political moment in which the paternalistic state unravels, the author observes a complete absence of political institutions in the narrative in which a violence born of moral decline, rather than corruption, social injustice, or neoliberalism, produces the spaces of the city. For Sánchez-Prado, for all its slick cosmopolitanism as it portrays the spaces through which Mexico City's rich and poor transit, modernity is a mask in this film behind which lurk the country's profound inequalities. Ultimately, he argues, the city of *Amores Perros* is an unreal non-place invented as part of the branding of Latin America in a cinematic world market, and he leaves us in no doubt as to what is at stake in such representations: these naturalizations of social conflict are complicit with neoliberalism. A key takeaway from Sánchez-Prado's intervention must be his admonition to cultural studies scholars who increasingly use violence as the framework to understand Latin American society and culture as a whole. He warns that they must guard against de-politicization and the re-articulation of neo-colonialism in their own work.

The final section, entitled 'Medialities', brings together a group of articles that explore the linguistic, cultural, aesthetic, and technological dynamics of mediation and interstitiality, building on the journal's foundational interest in translation as a mode of thinking in-between fields, as laid out in the introductory section above. In the first issue of *Travesia*, as the *Journal* was then still called, media and communications scholar Jesús Martín-Barbero called for a politicized understanding of culture *as* mediation, problematizing old informational modes of analysis that 'identifie[d] communication with the process of transmission of signifieds that are already given' (1992: 59), which in turn were associated with what he called an instrumentalist conception of democracy that limited the Left to 'a substantialist conception of social subjects' (1992: 58). Martín-Barbero, drawing on earlier work in media and cultural studies by authors such as Manuel Martín Serrano and Raymond Williams, placed a new emphasis on the reception and social uses of culture as a way not just of understanding but also of energizing then-emerging forms of democracy in Latin America. The legacy of Martín-Barbero's work is felt strongly throughout this reader, both developed and critiqued in contributions as diverse as those by Luis Duno Gottberg, Ignacio Sánchez-Prado, Julio Ramos, Beatriz Jaguaribe, and William Rowe, to name just a few. The four articles gathered in this final section are variously located at the crossroads of cultural formations and political discourse, laying bare different processes of mediation, or of encoding and decoding, to use Stuart Hall's terminology, that together work to find politically productive forms of critique.

Quetzil Castañeda's 'Post/Colonial Toponymy: Writing Forward "in Reverse"' (2002) tackles the related problems of translation and coloniality, sifting through the accumulation of mistranslations (from an array of possible Mayan source terms), misinterpretations, and misreadings that are lodged in successive debates over the Spanish colonisers' mythologized action of naming the Yucatán peninsula, which the author sees as overwritten by a process of Derridean dissemination. While Castañeda articulates a powerful critique of the colonial discursivity inherent in this toponymic event, he is equally forceful in identifying postcolonial criticism's own failure to overcome the temporalities and teleologies of European modernity and racism. Where Castañeda addresses the textual configurations of coloniality, Agnes Lugo-Ortiz, in her article 'Material Culture, Slavery, and Governability in Colonial Cuba: The Humorous Lessons of the Cigarette *Marquillas*' (2012), reads everyday objects – the lithographed paper *marquillas* that served to wrap bundles of cigarettes in late nineteenth-century Cuba – as sites of discursive power that acted as conduits for the racism of white elites on the defensive. Rather than opening themselves up to the potential polysemy of their visual subjects – for instance, the cultural references to the African diaspora that might be encompassed by the Afro-Cuban characters' dress – the *marquillas* close down the possibility of such readings by converting their 'black' subjects into vehicles of crude, racist humour, converting them into atemporal markers of Western superiority. The artefacts analysed by Lugo-Ortiz thus disenfranchise the Cubans of colour who populate them by casting them beyond the social mobility promised by the temporality of modernity, seeking to discipline them by nipping in the bud Afro-Cubans' emerging self-conceptions as subjects of revolutionary agency.

The pair of articles that close this section, by contrast, open up the possibilities of agencial political subjectivity on the part of subaltern actors who have taken it upon themselves to seize control of the processes of media production and transmission. In 'Indigenous Media and the End of the Lettered City' (2008), Freya Schiwy situates indigenous video production (focusing mainly on the work of the Bolivian organizations CEFREC [Centro de Formación y Realización Cinematográfica] and CAIB [Coordinadora Audiovisual Indígena Originaria de Bolivia]) in productive dialogue with other forms and vehicles of knowledge transmission in Latin America, both hegemonic and subaltern: oral memory, weaving, topography, and the written word. Schiwy finds that by both activating preconquest cultural signifiers and influencing their social uses and modes of reception, indigenous media producers partake of a highly politicized process of 'decolonising the soul', a term borrowed from Frantz Fanon via Silvia Rivera Cusicanqui. But rather than celebrating a putative substitution of 'lettered' culture by a newly decolonised orality, Schiwy – echoing Quetzil Castañeda's critique of postcolonial discourse – holds that the commonly held binary that pits orality against literacy is itself a construct of colonial temporality. Indeed, her article shares with Ivana Bentes' 'Subjective Displacements and "Reserves of Life"' (2011) the conviction that the cultural dynamics of mass-mediated late modernity render unsustainable the concept of the lettered city and its hierarchized dichotomy between orality and literacy, which for Schiwy entails an implicit teleology of social and intellectual progress. Bentes, though, does hold out for a mode of social mobility embodied in productions by community television and video projects in Brazilian favelas, which, the author argues, have been capable of 'transmuting' the urban precariat's life experiences into radically new audiovisual languages. These spaces of radical aesthetic autonomy thus become vehicles through which the erstwhile protagonists of so many sensationalized representations of urban decay and gang warfare attain meaningful political subjecthood; by constituting themselves as processes of spatial and temporal disruption into the social life of the community, following Rancière, they show themselves to embody alternative sensibilities, to be 'reserves of life' rather than of human detritus. In Bentes' reading, then, these new audiovisual subjects become able to fully assume the terms of their own mediation.

References

Avelar, Idelber. 1999. *The Untimely Present: Post-dictatorial Latin American Fiction and the Task of Mourning.* Durham, NC: Duke University Press.

De la Campa, Román. 1999. *Latin Americanism.* Minneapolis: University of Minnesota Press.

Del Sarto, Ana. 2000. 'Cultural Critique in Latin America or Latin American Cultural Studies?' *Journal of Latin American Cultural Studies* 9, 3: 235–247.

Dorfman, Ariel and Mattelart, Armand. 1972. *Para leer al Pato Donald. Comunicación de masa y colonialismo.* México, D. F.: Siglo XXI.

Franco, Jean. 1993. 'Cultural Studies Questionnaire,' *Journal of Latin American Cultural Studies* 2, 1: 154–158.

Garland Mahler, Anne. 2010. 'The Writer as Superhero: Fighting the Colonial Curse in Junot Diaz's *The Brief and Wondrous Life of Oscar Wao*,' *Journal of Latin American Cultural Studies* 19, 2: 119–140.

Giunta, Andrea. 2009. *Poscrisis. Arte argentino después de 2001.* Buenos Aires: Siglo Veintiuno.

Gregg, Melissa and Seigworth, Gregory J. 2010. 'An Inventory of Shimmers,' in *The Affect Theory Reader.* Durham, NC: Duke University Press.

Jauretche, Arturo. 1966. *El medio pelo en la sociedad argentina. Apuntes para una sociología nacional.* Buenos Aires: Peña Lillo.

Kaliman, Ricardo. 1998. 'What is "Interesting" in Latin American Cultural Studies,' *Journal of Latin American Cultural Studies* 7, 2: 261–272.

Kraniauskas, John. 2005. 'The Cultural Turn? On the *Journal of Latin American Cultural Studies* (1992–2004),' *Revista de Estudios Hispánicos* 39, 3: 561–569.

Martín-Barbero, Jesús. 1992. 'Notes on the Communicative Fabric of Democracy,' *Journal of Latin American Cultural Studies* 1, 1: pp. 48–68.

Moreiras, Alberto. 2001. *The Exhaustion of Difference: The Politics of Latin American Cultural Studies.* Durham, NC: Duke University Press.

Nouzeilles, Gabriela. 2001. 'Apocalyptic Visions: National Tales and Cultural Analysis in a Global Argentina,' *Journal of Latin American Cultural Studies* 10, 3: 291–301.

Palmeiro, Cecilia. 2011. *Desbunde y felicidad. De la Cartonera a Perlongher.* Buenos Aires: Título.

Pedrosa, Mário. 1966. 'Arte ambiental, arte pós-moderna, Hélio Oiticica,' *Correio da Manhã*, 26 June 1966; republished in *Dos murais de Portinari aos espaços de Brasília*. São Paulo, Perspectiva, 1981: 205–209.

Quijano, Aníbal. 2000. 'Coloniality of Power, Eurocentrism, and Latin America,' *Nepantla: Views from South* 1, 3: 533–580.

Rama, Ángel. 1984. *La ciudad letrada.* Hanover, NJ: Ediciones del Norte.

Richard, Nelly. 1996. 'The Cultural Periphery and Postmodern Decentering of Borders,' in *Rethinking Borders*, ed. Jonathan Welchman. Minneapolis: University of Minnesota Press: 71–84.

Rowe, William. 2014 [1996]. *Hacia una poética radical. Ensayos de hermenéutica cultural.* México, D. F.: Fondo de Cultura Económica.

Schwarz, Roberto. 1970. 'Cultura e politica no Brasil: 1964-1969,' in *Pai de família e outros ensaios.* São Paulo: Paz e Terra, 1978 (orig. published in *Les Temps Modernes*, Paris).

Spinoza, Baruch. 1959. *Ethics; On the Correction of Understanding.* London: Everyman's Library.

Szurmuk, Mónica and McKee Irwin, Robert (eds.) 2012. *Dictionary of Latin American Cultural Studies.* Gainesville: University of Florida Press.

Thayer, Willy, Guadelupe Santa Cruz, Federico Galende and Pablo Oyarzún. 2000. 'Conversation on Willy Thayer's *The Unmodern Crisis of the Modern University*,' *Nepantla: Views From South* 1, 1: 229–254.

Ticineto Clough, Patricia. 2007. 'Introduction,' in *The Affective Turn: Theorizing the Social.* Durham, NC: Duke University Press.

Trigo, Abril. 2004. 'General Introduction,' in *The Latin American Cultural Studies Reader*, ed. Ana del Sarto, Alicia Ríos and Abril Trigo. Durham, NC, Duke University Press: 1–14.

Yúdice, George. 1997. 'Cultural Studies Questionnaire,' *Journal of Latin American Cultural Studies* 6, 2: 217–222.

War and Cultural Studies: Reflections on Recent Work in Peru and Argentina

WILLIAM ROWE

Memory and the Cultural World

At a recent festival of Quechua theatre in Peru, one of the plays took as its theme the widespread disappearance of people in the Emergency Zones, where the state is engaged in what is known as a dirty war with the forces of the Communist Part of Peru, better known as Sendero Luminoso. Disappearances have occurred over the past two decades in a large number of Latin American countries. How does one investigate their cultural effect? For a start, they imply a network of threats, silences and other invasions of violence into the web of symbolic production. In the play I refer to, the stage is divided into three simultaneous spaces: one of them shows a young man being taken away by the army; in the second, his family are weeping for the absent son; in the third, the dead man himself appears and recounts his experience. Obviously, the multiplication of spaces comes out of the need to recompose a divided reality, where memory, communication and knowledge have been broken into fragments.[1] What is most moving is perhaps the presence of the dead man on the stage; the dead, in this circumstance, are memory — and without the accumulations of memory there is no culture. Specifically, where there is no social memory there can be no ethics. Historically the state has presented itself as guarantor of order and meaning, offering itself, as Pedro Morandé shows, as a coherent body in the face of the chaos of discontinuity (Morandé 1987, 95–96). And yet if the state cannot exist without its representation of continuities, these are selective, since we find states engaged in the deliberate creation of social amnesia.

These conclusions are obvious, perhaps. But if the debate about cultural studies does not confront the question of memory and violence — military, social and symbolic — then it will become increasingly nostalgic and irrelevant. A study of social amnesia in the shantytowns of Córdoba, Argentina, during the last military government shows that memory does not survive without a social space where it can be articulated. The inhabitants remembered perfectly well the times before 1976, but the period of military government was a kind of blank space. The reduction of the capacity for memory even affected their personal lives. The researchers reached the conclusion that the main cause was the suppression of the usual contexts of communication: 'the forms of continuity most affected were those connected with people's ways of relating to each other, that is with symbolic processes, rather than with modes of economic reproduction. . .people did not get together any more, not even to play cards or to talk about football on a street corner. . .in the schools, the students were not allowed to have meetings or singing sessions during break, on pain of military intevention.' Predominantly, though, the amnesia effect owed less to direct state intervention than to self-surveillance: '"it was a society which patrolled itself"' (Mata et. al. 1988, 241–242).

The two examples given draw attention to a conflict between state and culture, not at the level of cultural policy [*las políticas culturales*] but at the more fundamental one of the cultural world and its bases. The term cultural world is the one used by Merleau-Ponty to refer to the way in which the composition of perceptions into a perceived world depends upon and contributes to a shared cultural world (Merleau-Ponty 1989, 23–25, 346–365). In the civil war in Peru, both material and cultural bases of Andean life are under threat of destruction, and in response the indigenous peasantry are inventing ways of reconstituting their universe. More precisely, in the Quechua play, it is a question of reinventing a space in which to reflect upon experience — without that the cultural field becomes simply a network of obediences. Under the Argentine military government, the suppression of social memory appears to have been carried out with considerable success. Quite probably, opposite examples could be found in each country — the aim is not to classify the historical processes. What I would like to suggest is that the study of culture needs to ask the question: what are the conditions of existence of a given cultural field? And in what ways is the cultural field in which we find ourselves currently changing? Clearly these are questions that can never fully be answered, especially the second one; but I believe they are vital for defining the bases for cultural studies.

The destruction of symbolic processes is not the exclusive property of states of open war. In an analysis of the first year of Carlos Menem's government, Beatriz Sarlo has noted that this government imposes 'the idea that politics consists merely in the taking of decisions and not in the construction of the alternatives within whose limits one chooses'; this diminution of the political sphere 'ends up in a government that operates as if it was always having to confront states of emergency. That is exactly what happened with the sending of Argentine troops to the Gulf.' The neutral, de-ideologising [*desideologizante*] appearance of the decisions hides something else, the imposition of a new rationalisation: '*The neutral mask of decisions* expresses both that the politics of rationalisation is the only possible one and that it is not the product of any ideology.' In the final analysis neutral would be that which is not marked by evaluative codes, in other words an apparently non-cultural sphere; the italics are in Sarlo's original, reflecting the violence implicit in the obliteration of cultural signs, in 'the concealment of evaluative aspects'.

'The danger of this type of intervention', writes Sarlo as she develops her argument, 'is the emptying of the symbolic [*vaciamiento simbólico*]; once the narrative and myths of historical peronism had been deconstructed, they were only replaced by the bourgeois novel of market rationalisation, very poor material for replacing the political identity which Menemism proposes to dissolve' (Sarlo 1990, 7–8). That thinning of the texture of politics in which Menem and Fujimori (other names could be added, such as Collor) have taken the lead, carries with it an undeclared violence: not only against the economic situation of the millions of inhabitants who are not functional for end-of-century capitalism, but also against those signs of identity which are not functional either. This violence is as legal as the other one of open war, and external war and the use of the methods of war within the nation have become closely interconnected. The connections had already appeared in the National Security State, but new dimensions have accreted in the past two decades. When Mario Vargas Llosa, whose presidential programme has been adopted in broad measure by Fujimori, resorts to external and internal war in *The Real Life of Alejandro Mayta*, he does not do so in order to condemn war ethically but to reduce cultural differences to a simplified political polarity. The whole sphere of cultural signs is affected by the debilitation of symbols of difference, and this is done not merely with the aim of demonstrating the unviability of socialist ideology, something he had already attempted in *The War of the End of the World*, but in order to create an ethical and political vacuum, fillable only with neo-liberal rationalisation. *The Storyteller* finishes off the job. Political emptiness and emptyness of the symbolic become the same thing. The parody of indigenism and anthropology destroys the possibility of any linguistic or cultural plurality as constitutive of the nation. In fact the emptying goes further: the possibility of there being a repertory of symbols which could be called national disappears and there remains a scenario capable of being written only in neo-liberal language. The question therefore arises, what are the alternatives to market rationalisation and the weakening of the symbolic? A provocative solution is given by Morandé: if market rationality is not neutral and value free, but actually as sacrificial a form of communality as the traditional Christian notions of the social, which have had a longer history in Latin America, then why not return to the Christian idea? (Morandé 1987, chapters 5,6,10,11).

Some brief points need making here regarding the debate about the effects of the mass media. Until recently, and most often on the basis of the Chilean experience of the Pinochet government, it was said that the mass media, given their imperialist orientation, were bound to debilitate national cultures. Lately, however, there has been increasing recognition that this attitude rested upon the supposed passivity of the audience and ideological omnipotence of the media. It is therefore becoming accepted that criticism should not be directed at the presumed messages in isolation from the larger cultural field, and that it needs to consider the media as forms of cultural mediation — mediation of popular memory, for example. When codes of reception are taken into account, the telenovela can then be investigated as an encounter between popular memory and the mass imaginary (Martín-Barbero 1987). The question, once again, is that of the continuities and discontinuities of the symbolic. If television converts distances into simultaneities and floods local spaces with global images, it is also capable of reformulating local cultural materials. Of themselves, therefore, the media do not provide an answer to the problem.

The emptying of the symbolic field on the one hand, and the reinvention of continuities (whether by subaltern or hegemonic groups) on the other, can be understood within a larger historical context. Crucial among the changes that affect the current horizon is the fact that '"the notion of an authentic culture in terms of an autonomous and internally coherent universe is no longer viable" either in the Third World or the First, "except perhaps as a useful fiction or revealing distorsion."'

The statement is made by Néstor García Canclini in *Culturas híbridas: estrategias para entrar y salir de la modernidad* (García Canclini, 1990a). Among the effects of cultural hybridism is the fact that 'at the end of the century, access to multicultural perspectives is not confined to writers, artists and exiled politicians, but is available to people from all social strata.' A vast migratory process is occurring and it includes cultural materials as well as human beings; you don't have to be a rural Mexican migrant to the USA in order to experience the flows which cross frontiers: it's enough to stay at home and turn on the television. Hybridization cuts across any polar opposition between continuity and destruction; in this context change as a process requiring chronological interpretation is less important than lateral movements, and these are not unifiable and require multiple perspectives.

Deterritorialization/Reterritorialization

The word culture itself is affected by these destabilisations. Its traditional referent, bound up with the formation of nation-states, is becoming irrelevant: 'Why go on thinking culture in an etymological sense, as the "cultivation" of a territory, when national frontiers become porous, when the disarticulation of both urban and peasant forms casts doubt on whether the key to cultural systems can be found in the relationship between populations and particular types of territory which would generate particular behaviours?' (García Canclini 1990b, 9) García Canclini points to two processes which can help to understand this situation: decollection [*descolección*] and deterritorialization: 'There was a time when the identities of groups were formed through two movements: the occupation of a territory and the constitution of collections — of objects, of monuments, of rituals — in terms of which the signs distinguishing a group were affirmed and celebrated. To have an identity was, above all, to have a country, a city or a neighbourhood, an entity within which everything shared by those who inhabited that place became identical or interchangeable. Those who did not share the territory and therefore did not have the same objects and symbols, the same rituals and customs, were the others, the different ones. What is left of that paradigm in the epoch of the decentralization and planetary expansion of big companies, of the transnationalization of communications and of multidirectional migrations?'

To respond to deterritorialization without nostalgia can be difficult, but the difficulty must be faced. Otherwise, if one fails to grasp the movements of deterritorialization and is drawn into defence of a past which is being destroyed, this is no answer to neo-liberal market pragmatism, increasingly dominant in Latin America. And it becomes difficult to explain cultural continuities except one-sidedly, in terms of crass inertia and repetition. Take for example the successful promotion of the Gulf War as a Just War, a phenomenon which epitomizes the continuities celebrated by the dominant Western states. It is not enough to say that the ideology of Just War goes back to the Crusades and to point to its continuities as a theme of Western superiority. It is also necessary to ask what possibilities of redistribution of regional power made necessary its most recent resuscitation, and what were the communicative forms of this resuscitation. The shifting grounds and forms of inscription need to be analysed, not just the context.

As soon as deterritorialization occurs, pressures for restabilization, for reterritorialization also occur. That is why it is difficult to think within the terms of García Canclini's proposition. The pressures for reterritorialization are immediate and simultaneous and often more perceptible than the movement of deterritorialization. Continuities and traditions that occur on the back of deterritorialization are not therefore returns to or of the past, however much they may seem that. 'The force and obstinacy of a deterritorialization can only be evaluated through the types of reterritorialization that represent it; the one is the reverse side of the other' (Deleuze and Guattari 1983, 316).

If we consider the actions of Sendero Luminoso in these terms, there are ways in which the attempt to destroy existing political forces and institutions, although carried out in the name of social revolution, could be argued to constitute a form of reterritorialization. This raises a further issue: what deterritorialization does the latter coincide with? The most obvious face of its actions is the use of violence. If in some ways this seems merely indiscriminate and excessive, it does on the other hand have an exemplifying and codifying function. That is, the cruelty with which victims who are members of the local population are treated has two sides. There appears to be an attempt to eradicate all cultural signs, leaving mere emptiness and silence. Considered as a tactic, this links with the decision not only to eliminate the presence of the state in the 'liberated zones' but also that of all popular organisations apart from Sendero — to liquidate the officials, the habits and the signs of all other organisations. This seems to have been the aim when the leaders of the mining unions in the central highlands, a key force in the labour movement, were murdered. The other side is the attempt to emplace itself as the sole popular organisation: a new authoritarian territorialization, through which Sendero takes on the characteristics of a state. This is accompanied by a lack of interest in Quechua culture: Sendero's political programme is concerned only with class, not with cultural differences of an ethnic type.

If the current political violence in the Andean region is accelerating change, the question arises how far is it change towards authoritarianism and dogmatism. The mixture of rapid change with rigid containment can be traced in the ways authoritarian violence has been legitimated. In the first place, Sendero substituted an already existing social violence, connected with the structures of gamonalismo, in other words with the power relations of precapitalist commercial capital. Peasants were able to consider this violence as 'normal', while it could also appear to be 'the foundation of a new order' (Manrique 1989, 165). But if at first the victims were those peasants who had become part of *gamonalista* structures, 'the category "enemies of the revolution or of the party" would later become terrifyingly all-inclusive, referring to anyone who stood in the way of Sendero's aims, or who simply refused to collaborate.' The logic shows considerable symmetry with the rules for a Just War that were used to draw up the notorious Requirement of the sixteenth century, a document to be read out by Spanish forces to the Indians, requiring the latter to show allegiance to the crown and threatening them with war should they fail to do so. But if an antimodernizing violence resting upon a pre-political violence is the most visible feature of this war, it nevertheless obscures a massive deterritorialization of Andean culture arising out of the increasing migration of populations and of cultural features. This is the 'time of convulsion' explored in José María Arguedas's later novels and investigated by the historian Alberto Flores Galindo (Arguedas 1960, 10; Flores Galindo 1986, 321–372).

Cultural Criticism in Argentina and Peru

What is the situation of the academic disciplines in an epoch of migrations and hybridism? Clearly, they should not be impervious to the transformations their traditional objects are undergoing. One area of difficulty is that the bland aggregation of disciplines, which characterises much of what is currently called Cultural Studies, is insufficient; disciplinary frontiers tend to get reestablished, behind a façade of apparent synthesis. And equally debilitating is the narrow range of materials which are actually studied and taught; often, materials which cannot be called popular are excluded. One of Andrés Bello's great insights, in his struggle to assemble a Latin American theory of knowledge, was that if the work of analysis is done thoroughly, it then becomes possible to enter a place where all truths touch each other. The task is to discover the intersections of the different practices of knowledge in order to be able to break down and recompose whole cultural fields.

Cultural criticism, a phrase little heard some five years ago, is becoming a new intellectual fashion. But its current acceptance entails the risk that it can be taken to be a mere updating of previously existing practices, extended to new objects of study. Literary criticism begins to include popular cultures, sociology learns to appreciate cultural texts, historians interpret artistic texts. All of this is happening, and it is valuable that it should be. But to leave it at that is to run the risk of missing out what is most vital: the new importance of cultural analysis does not arise simply from changed relationships between disciplines in the intellectual field, but from changes which are shaking the bases of sociability, politics and of symbolic activity in general. It is becoming increasingly accepted that there is a need to rethink the past, present and future of Latin American societies from the viewpoint of the cultural field.

Let us consider, in this light, the characteristics of two traditions of cultural criticism that have arisen independently in Argentina and Peru but have some interesting similarities. David Viñas's book, *Indios, ejército y frontera*, probes those continuities which can be traced between 1879, the year when the oligarchic republic was consolidated with Buenos Aires as its centre, and the period of military government initiated in the latter part of the 1970s. This book documents the genocidal treatment of the Indians in the military campaign to push them south of the Río Negro, known as the 'Conquest of the Desert', and asks what happens when the key historical continuity lies in what has disappeared, in what is not said by public discourses but nevertheless permeates the systems of state power, regardless of different governments. Viñas traces the shift between a fixed and porous frontier based on military forts to a mobile but impermeable frontier resting upon the new speed of the 'holy trinity' of the Remington repeater rifle, the telegraph and railways; and a further shift to internal and internalised frontiers also based in the final analysis on the army ('dieu caché' of Argentine history) and their connection with the socio-economic and discursive homogenisations imposed as a result of 1879. In the process of this oligarchic and ethnocidal modernity, culture becomes, as Viñas puts it, 'ontological', the force of the newly imposed national culture seeming natural and immanent, just at the moment of massive deterritorialisations. 'And the violence exercised against the Indians and their lands turned back and impregnated with all its irrationality the foundations of the oligarchic republic' (Viñas 1982, 105).

Viñas does not locate the continuities implied in this type of statement within a Freudian unconscious nor within ideology. But he does not entirely resolve the problem of where to situate them. He attempts to facilitate transition between material history and the production of meaning by using a vocabulary of relative densifications and rigidifications, made up of terms like 'calcification' and 'colloidal' (Viñas 1982, 12).

Josefina Ludmer, in *El género gauchesco: un tratado sobre la patria*, is concerned with similar problems, which she extends to include the legitimacy of criticism itself. Her text refuses the specialised language of literary criticism and allows itself to be permeated both by common speech and by the language of state power. It parodies the state's use of legal discourse, especially in its dense overcoding and multiple semantic superimpositions, and exposes ironically the complicity of literary criticism insofar as its procedures rest upon the same enunciative statutes.

Ludmer formulates a strategy for an interrogation of enunciation (more precisely, of the enunciative field) within specific limits, those of the gauchesque genre. She analyses the foundational genre of Argentine national literature as a double embedding of literature in the organisation of war and civil code, and vice versa. In this sense she traces a superimposition of law in the sense of literary code and of law as code within the legal system; the whole process allows the penetration of the state in literary production and reception and sets up a connective stabilisation of epic potential (Ludmer 1988, 236). The major dilemma, given all this, is where can criticism speak/write from? What are the alternatives, if it is not going to embed itself within the rigidifications it analyses? Ludmer's approach to the problem is ironical, rather than offering a positive alternative.

There are two stories by Borges that belong to the margins of the gauchesque genre and can help reveal its limits and those of Ludmer's study as well. In 'El otro duelo', body and code become disconnected: the race between two beheaded men, the crass inertia of bodies turned into corpses which still uphold the rules of the game, unpeals the code from its material supports. The bodies die, the code lives on, grotesquely. In 'Funes el memorioso', infinite, undifferentiated recall prevents memory and the story not only places the gauchesque at a limit where it collapses — Funes is called a 'compadrito' but his mentality entirely resists identity — it also challenges all stabilizations, continuities, incorporations and overcodings which make the production of a state possible. A massive decodification (deterritorialization) pushes readers not only outside the genre but outside any genre and in some ways outside culture itself, placing on the agenda the necessity for a Renegotiation of cultural fixities in order to escape the other stasis, that of extreme decodification, that of Funes's immobilised body.

Beatriz Sarlo, in her book, *Una modernidad periférica, Buenos Aires 1920 y 1930*, seeks to avoid fixities of genre and discourse and defines the culture of Buenos Aires between 1920 and 1930 as a mixture, not in the sense of a passive aggregate of elements, inherited from the past or received from outside, but as forms and discourses which become refunctionalized (Sarlo, 1988). The result is not single focus but a multiplicity of readings which modify each other mutually. Paradigms and ideological frames such as national versus cosmopolitan literature are excluded; this type of schematics is replaced by a densification of the literary and cultural field, achieved not through the consolidation of law but through an extraordinary richness of writings and readings. Sarlo allows texts and not theoretical procedures to define both the field and the methods of criticism. The ideal model of her approach, if one can speak in such terms, would be not so much the multiple location of the critical voice as allowing it to vary and move according to the heterogeneity of the field under study, making use of a fertile tension between monograph multiple writings. What is demonstrated is the possibility of a plural modern culture, resistant to the homogenizations sought by current power systems; and a possible resolution to the incarceration of criticism within the institutions and languages of imposed continuity.

The examples mentioned, to which other names could be added, are distinguished among other things by a multidisciplinary openness. In Peru, the need to break down discursive frontiers has had a different dynamic, while also being a response to the current historical conjuncture, in particular the experience of violence. 'Sendero Luminoso covers the whole national territory, the intellectuals do not', in the words of the Peruvian anthropologist Rodrigo Montoya (Montoya 1990). For Montoya, there is an urgent need to achieve an integral vision of Peru, beyond existing fragmentations. Among the resources available for this task are: 1) the tradition of mestizo writing, whose key figures are the Inca Garcilaso, Felipe Guaman Poma and José María Arguedas; 2) anthropology as the study of marginalised cultures from inside their own autonomy; 3) economics, history and sociology for their capacity to discuss society globally. But there is no question here of constructing a hierarchical totality: 'there are two ways of seeing totality. One, if you retain the metaphor of a building and therefore of the vertical structure of society; the other is to do with thinking totality in horizontal terms, where economic, cultural and political phenomena would occur in the same plane, at the same time and not superimposed like ecological floors within a vertical structure' (Montoya 1989).

For Alberto Flores Galindo, the young Peruvian historian who died recently, it has only been possible 'to think and imagine Peru as a totality' since the middle of the twentieth century (Flores 1986, 322). The historical changes which have made this possible are new mercantile flows, the extension of the road network, urbanisation and migrations. Another factor needs adding to those mentioned by Flores. Though its relationship with modernity is more ambiguous, the political violence of the past decade is implicit in all of his argument. Its context is the failure of the Creole State, whose framework has proved incapable of containing current social forces or of offering political structures which do not oppress the ethnic populations. Montoya invited a group of primary schoolteachers to report on how they perceive their identity. One of them asks, 'Am I Peruvian?...We really do not know why this land is called Peru...I personally am a Quechua, I live as a Quechua but my heart is not big for this territory which is called Peru because this Peru is the property of those who control economic power' (Montoya and López 1987, 39). From what place can the Creole State be confronted critically, given that its ethnocentric (and ethnocidal) bases have penetrated the majority of cultural criticism in Peru? In the struggle to create alternative enunciative spaces Andean culture has been a key resource. Here is another testimony from Montoya's book: 'I am thinking that Peru is no longer ours. The head of Peru is in Lima; its mouth forgot its language and doesn't speak it any more because it learned another "more perfect" one. Its eyes don't know any more how to look at the other parts of its body. Is it that Peru has been cut into pieces? Will it look, hear and speak again when the head returns to the body?' (Montoya and López 1987, 80) The idea of the broken and scattered body articulates an Andean mythical substrate, the cycle of Inkarrí, a utopian figuration of the Inka. Here once again the capacity of the Andean social imagination to recompose a fragmented reality and give meaning to experiences is evident. A particular difficulty is to grasp this necessary totalisation alongside the cultural hybridizations taking place.

A further problem is whether it might not be impossible to imagine, within the terms of Western political reason, a new culturally plural state, not dependent upon an ethnically oppressive modernity. One line of thinking passes through a reconsideration of magic, taking its direction from the popular re-use of magical images and practices in new social contexts. These latter include intersections between the experience of generalised violence (economic as well as political) and the inadequacy of public languages, of the dominant social imagination, and of traditional political formulae. In this scenario, Andean magical beliefs have appeared in resemantized forms in the cities. This is the case, for example, of the *pishtaku* (sometimes pronounced pistaco), a figure originating in colonial times. The *pishtaku* beheads human beings in order to extract grease from them. In previous periods the grease was said to be used for casting bells and manufacturing candles; in the nineteenth century, for locomotives; in the nineteen sixties, for the NASA space programme. But in 1987 *pishtakus* appeared in Huamanga, a city flooded by migrants escaping from the violence of the armed forces or Sendero. They wore yellow raincoats and carried machine guns, machetes and an identity card provided by the President of the Republic.[2] The grease extracted by them was sent away for the manufacture of medicines and beauty products, and the profit obtained would be used for paying the foreign debt. But, as Isbell has pointed out, for peasants in some parts of Ayacucho, the *pishtaku* (known there as *ñakak*) is believed to carry off fat in order to 'feed the Sendero army on the flesh of peasants' (Isbell, 1991). The *pishtaku* is an obviously vampiric figure whose magic is far from being a merely archaic and folkloric nostalgia; on the contrary, it can be used for diagnosing capitalist modernity.[3] Moreover, the symbolic effectiveness of the *pishtaku* cannot be interpreted from the viewpoint of the social and economic rationality subscribed to by the dominant groups, the educational system and even the majority of intellectuals. It implies a society of colonial social relationships, an ethnic rather than a class logic and a magical not an instrumental rationality.

When *pishtakus* began to appear in Lima in 1988, metamorphosed into a group of gringo doctors with assistants wearing white coats who went through the shanty-towns kidnapping children and removing their eyes for transplants, a debate arose as to whether the eye-stealers (*saca-ojos*) could be interpreted as a regression to ethnic as opposed to class identities. According to this viewpoint, the transition from ethnic to class identities, a precondition for the creation of a genuinely national society, had been interrupted by Sendero, and was causing the social fabric to collapse and bringing about a return to local and ethnic identities. The opposing argument maintained that if the renunciation of ethnic identities was necessary for modernity, then this was an ethnocidal modernity. If such widespread magical perceptions are responses to an emptying of the symbolic field, do they also imply a return to premodern identities, do they indicate a possible resource for an alternative sociability, or are they simply projections of an anxiety which can find no other outlet? The answer is not yet known; but it is also clear that the question can only be pursued from a new attitude to the cultural field.

Notes

1. Billie Jean Isbell has documented the way in which Senderista and state violence have produced a situation in which 'there is no consensus on dates, no agreed-upon shared histories across communities. No construction of political explanations...As one man put it: "We can't even protect the rights of our dead or our disappeared. We have no control over anything."' (Isbell 1991).
2. I owe these data to Nelson Manrique.
3. See, for example, *Pistaco Perú*, an unpublished play by Julio Ortega.

References

Arguedas, J.M., 1960 'Discusión de la narración peruana', *La Gaceta de Lima*, July-August
Deleuze, G. and Guattari, F., 1983 *Anti-Oedipus*, Minneapolis
Flores Galindo, A., 1986 *Buscando un Inca, identidad y utopía en los Andes*, La Habana
García Canclini, N., 1990a *Culturas híbridas: estrategias para entrar y salir de la modernidad*, Mexico
García Canclini, N., 1990b 'Escenas sin territorio: estética de las migraciones e identidades en transición', *Revista de Crítica Cultural*, 1, 1
Isbell, B.-J., 1991 'Texts and Contexts of Terror in Peru', paper presented at the Symposium on Textuality in Amerindian Cultures, London, Centre for Latin American Cultural Studies.
Ludmer, J., 1988 *El género gauchesco: un tratado sobre la patria*, Buenos Aires
Manrique, N., 1989 'La década de la violencia', *Márgenes*, III, 5–6, 137–180
Martín-Barbero, J., 1987 *De los medios a las mediaciones*, Barcelona
Mata, M.C. et. al., 1988 'Memoria y acción popular', in N. García Canclini, ed., *Cultura transnacional y culturas populares*, Lima, Instituto Para América Latina
Merleau-Ponty, M., 1989 *The Phenomenology of Perception*, London
Montoya, R., 1989 'El socialismo mágico es posible', *Nariz del diablo* (Quito), 14
Montoya, R., 1990 'Politics and violence in Peru', lecture at the Institute of Latin American Studies, London
Montoya, R., and López, L.E., eds., 1987 *¿Quiénes somos? El tema de la identidad en el altiplano*, Lima and Puno
Morandé, P., 1987 *Cultura y modernización en América Latina*, Madrid
Sarlo, B., 1988 *Una modernidad periférica:* Buenos Aires 1920 y 1930, Buenos Aires
Sarlo, B., 1990 'Menem, cinismo y exceso', *Revista de Crítica Cultural*, 2,3, p. 7. Originally published in *Punto de Vista*, 39 (December 1990).
Viñas, D., 1982 *Indios, ejército y frontera*, Mexico

The Reconfigurations of Post-dictatorship Critical Thought

NELLY RICHARD

The military coup did not only materially destroy the continuity of the social and political order that sustained the democratic tradition of Chile. In so far as it unleashed a series of breaks and ruptures within the whole system of categories which had, until 1973, made possible a determinate understanding of the social based on shared rules of intelligibility, it was also experienced—symbolically—as what the philosopher Patricio Marchant has called a 'coup against representation'. The military coup constituted an event—in the strong sense of an irruption and disruption—that disturbed not only the linear development of historical continuity but also the rationale of history itself: its logical causality and its forms of self-comprehension. Such a disturbance of a whole system of understanding which, before the coup, had organized how the social was named and thought, was lived, according to Marchant, as a 'loss of the word'.[1] The traumatic suspension of speech caused by the shredding of identity and representation brought about by the brusque clash of the *familiar* (the symbolic, institutional and communicative normality of the social order; its habitual modes of signification and participation) with the calamitous *unknown* (the destruction of homicidal violence).

The figures of trauma, mourning and melancholy became the emblematic figures of a certain form of critical thought of post-dictatorship. They connote the sense of abandonment and lack of recognition that affects the subject of historical break when they no longer possess names and concepts that are sufficiently trustworthy to verbalize their experience: the catastrophic radicality of their devastated experience. Trauma, mourning and melancholy (the coup as trauma, mourning as the loss of the object and melancholy as the unresolved suspension of mourning[2]) are figures that, taken from the Freudian repertory, lent their affective tone to the expression of post-dictatorship—an expression marked by the problematic character of a tension between *loss of knowledge* (of confidence in knowledge as a secure foundation) and *knowledge of loss* (the critical vindication of waste, of the *remainder*, as the condition of a thought of an 'afterwards' now irreconcilable with previous models of finitude and the totalization of truth). This theoretical tension, moreover, is inscribed into a present divided (at its extremes), on the one hand, by fixed memorization of the past (nostalgic contemplation of a memory petrified in time; that is, monumental) and, on the other, by the complete dissolving of the traces of that historical past subjected to the electronic erasure of the communicative flows of contemporary media acting in syntactic complicity with capitalist globalization.

Trauma, mourning and melancholy traced a state of melancholization of though of/in post-dictatorship which found a key source of its philosophical-aesthetic productivity in Benjaminian allegory: historical devastation, the ruining of meaning, but also the work on the ruins of a disfigured totality that transformed its traces into the redemptive promise of a broken historicity that continued to vibrate in the folds of its falling. According to Idelber Avelar, 'the epochal importance of allegory in post-dictatorship' is that it is ' the trope of the impossible'; that it 'responds to a fundamental impossibility, the irrecuperable breaking of representation' (Avelar, 1997, p. 302).[3]

It is this *break in signification* (which Avelar emblematizes in the figure of allegory), that—in post-dictatorship—subjects thought, categories and languages to a broken, wounded, incomplete, disintegrated, convulsed condition. These were all different responses to the break in signification that were formulated by key sectors of the artistic, cultural and political fields in Chile. Some languages of post-dictatorship (for example, those of the social sciences) disavowed, hid or disguised the signs of the vulnerability of thought so as to reconstruct—as if nothing had happened—*efficient discourses*: discourses able to re-order the disorder of the social thanks to the technical character of its quantitative and statistical instruments which processed the fact of violence but without permitting itself to be disturbed by any breakage or unfixing of meaning. Other narratives desperately tried to re-integrate the disintegrated (the broken emblems of the national-historical and popular) into new organic wholes synthesizing grand world-views—such was the case of the ideological narratives of the militant left. Meanwhile, a critical poetics made use of fragmentation and breakage, of the post-symbolic remainder, to exhibit vulnerablity, wounds, in solidarity with the historical ruining of vocabularies fallen into social and political disintegration—but also to restyle the fragments by way of the techniques of montage and cutting.

We know the effects that unprocessed mourning has on the subject: psychic blockages, libidinal withdrawal, the paralysing of the will and desire when confronted by the loss of something that cannot be reconstituted (the body, truth, ideology, representation). Unprocessed mourning tends to generate depressive-melancholic symptoms that immobilize the subject into sad and self-absorbed contemplation of loss, without the energy necessary to creatively escape from the 'meaningless' drama. According to Julia Kristeva, the depressive-melancholic effect comes not only from the sadness of the irrecuperability of loss, but also from the destructive alteration of *significant relations* that blocks the ability to represent and communicate, that is, to generate symbolic equivalences to transform the symptom of loss into recreative words and images (Kristeva, 1987, pp. 13–78). In Kristeva's view, coming out of mourning implies putting certain mechanisms of *substitution* into action (thanks to which what is lost is replaced by the representation of loss) as well as mechanisms of *transposition* that displace experience into registers of figuration and expression where experience is redrawn through metaphoric artifice.[4] Kristeva's reading trusts in artistic and literary creation as the privileged register for an expressive reconfiguration of the traumatic value of limit experiences. This trust is based on having confidence in the *networks of semantic polyvalency* that metaphor generates around what is suppressed[5] as the imaginary surrounds absence with an expressive multiplicity of connotations of meaning that displace lack into a surplus of images.

If we translate this reading into the scene of social memory, it suggests the importance of confiding in critical aesthetics, so that the most shivering zones of memory find force, value and intensity in a labour *on forms at the point of signification*—which is where art works.[6]

The forms of memorization that have predominated within the Transition are divided between memory as *monument* (ritualistic celebration of a memory heroically frozen into historical symbol: the reification of the past into a commemorative block without fissure) or memory as *document* (objectification of truth through the descriptive neutrality of commentary and its institutional rhetorics of information; the mono-referential simplicity of the fact exhausted in the denotative and informational). Art and literature work, thankfully, against this dual citational usage of memory as practised within the Transition, and it is thanks to their polysignifying and irruptive labour on forms (images, stories and narratives) that the aesthetic gesture is able to intensify memory as a battle of symbolizations. It is thanks to such irruptions that art and culture have become the registers most attuned to the exploration of the disaggregated, the split, the residual, the convulsed (of all that vibrates as fragment, detail and broken singularity after the death of the organic symbol).

But let us return to critical thought and the challenges of its reconfiguration in post-dictatorship, when it is not only a matter of sharing mourning with those in grief but also of committing the subject of historical mourning to the labour of *resignification*: how does one account for what upset our forms of life and knowledge in a language that accuses 'the coup' ('el golpe')—and recognizes the *accident* of loss—without renouncing the task of *conceptually reformulating* the meanings of the experience? How does one articulate a *reflexive distance* that stands back from the simple testimonial realism of the affectively lived, such that the hierarchy inherent in the concept does not at the same time erase the subjective texture of what is lived and suffered? How to re-emplot significant articulations and operative connections so that critical thought may reactivate itself as such, but without letting the promise of a recovery of thought merely accommodate loss? How, in sum, to express the *loss of sense*, but without renouncing to critically reconjugate the *sense of loss*?

The experiential and categorial disaster brought about by the coup rocked subjectivities and consciousnesses to such a degree that a thought or speech sensitive to it could not but be sensitive also to the cuts and wounds of the precarious. This explains its suspicion of scientific rationality—whose research frameworks and professional lexicon are exhibited without ruptures or breaks, unharmed.[7] For this reason too, the critical value of the expressive tremors that permeate those languages unhappy with the domain of knowledge that is associated with technical competence and academic formalism. Hence the need for what has been socially broken to enter into figurative equivalence with the traces of discontinuity that mark certain critical poetics as they explore the breaches and fissures of representation. But, how are we to conjugate signalling such breaches and fissures within the tormented plot of enunciation with the refusal to renounce a critical activity able to take *conceptual leaps* and *subjective mutations* that *transform* the suffering images of past defeat into something else?

A line of thought that has been unravelling in Chilean post-dictatorship philosophy underlines the need 'to not lose loss',[8] that is, to not erase the weight and gravity of the traces that are left as the *remains* of decomposition: to not betray the trembling fragility of such traces by resorting to the machines of critical reason (and their politics of meaning) that forever threaten with the exercise of argumentative control and rule of that which, according to this line of thought, should remain vibrating as *catastrophic torsion*. The philosophical-deconstructive turn of such thought of/in post-dictatorship that seeks to keep and maintain the catastrophe of meaning thus radicalizes its distrust of the instrumentality of explanatory knowledge, of administrative knowledge that translates the historical fact of loss into a simple reconstructive, and thus normalizing, language. Such suspicion and distrust shown by philosophy contribute, no doubt, to reinforce the metacritical value of the thought of/in post-dictatorship, acting as its *necessary* condition. But, in my view at least, they do not constitute a *sufficient* condition if the challenge is to recover the word after 'the loss of the word', saving this word from the shipwreck of the unsayable, and drifting within the pure discourse of the unnamable, but on the contrary, 'finding new forms of critical incidence in the present' (Moreiras, 1999).

To simply track the signs of melancholy as the allegorical figuration of mourning in the social and historical imaginary of post-dictatorship, or the monotonous insistence on the *irrecoverability of signification* as pure undoing as against the 'doing' of the market, might end up indulging the final vocabulary of a complete and definitive 'loss of capacity to critically transform the real'.[9] To recover this lost ability implies, as suggested by Alberto Moreiras, 'bringing mourning for the past to a close, or beginning to consider it as a symptomatic, relative inscription, and so subsumable into a larger field' towards which to shift the marks of 'a wound that is still open in the experiential orders of the socio-political' and which, although always 'spectrally present', must effectuate a 'separation' from the previous scene so as not to become nostalgically identified with a time before the coup lived as simple muteness (Moreiras, 1999).

It seems to me that this irrepressible tension between what has been *destroyed in representation*, on the one hand, and the need to recreate new forms of *critical incidence* that contain the image of this destruction without remaining contemplatively adhered to it, condenses one of the most arduous tasks of the intellectual field of post-dictatorship—at least, for those of us who believe that it is not enough to rigorously examine the negative conditions of thought, but that it is also necessary to design new modes of intervention that do not aspire to leaving the present *as given*. This supposes practices of the production and insertion of meaning into the polemical contexts of the present which are able to occasion a clash of statements, institutional friction.

To reflect upon the conditions for the critical intervention of theoretical practice in present-day debates presents us with the problem of *limits* in two senses: the *internal limits* of the academic field, inasmuch as the limitations imposed by disciplinary frontiers that separate specialisms might be guilty of restricting the displacement of objects that our reading energies must mobilize with regard to social and cultural processes of renewed complexity; and the *external limit*, in so far as referring to critical intervention in the *living* present supposes travelling the gap between the discursive universe of the academy and the extra-academic territories of action—two zones that are ruled by specific and unequal laws of competence, validity and social efficacy.

If we look to the question of the internal limit that concerns the distribution of disciplines, we should revise the actual processes of *decentring* and *transversality* with which practices such as cultural studies or cultural critique pretend to challenge the criteria of autonomy and purity—of non-interference—associated with traditional criticism, by revitalizing other archives of knowledge with non-canonical readings of extended social and cultural practices. I leave aside here any evaluation of such decentrings and transversalities, as well as any answer to whether these have produced emancipatory results with regard to previous hierarchies and classifications; or whether their extreme particularism and segmenting of differences, their unlimited juxtaposition of objects and indiscriminately valid knowledges in the theoretical-academic supermarket of marginalities and subalternities—today reclassified by cultural studies—are only producing obscene promiscuity and suspicious relativisms of value (see Galende, 1996; Sarlo, 1997; Grüner, 1998; Thayer, 1999).

But even if we decide to rescue the pluralizing effect of the decanonizations actually in progress, it might be that the contamination and dissemination of texts proposed by cultural critique reveals itself only to be capable of producing 'changes in the relationship between the disciplines in the intellectual field' on the same map of academic culture, without affecting in the least the relations 'between sociality, politics and culture' (Rowe).

I thus leave aside this first limit, well known to cultural critique, between *disciplines* and *transdisciplinarity*, and the risk of its becoming the latest academic novelty of a reading machine—whose only virtue would be that it is more hybrid than others. I am rather interested in examining the frontier between academic interiority and exteriority, between *academic culture* (the professional universe of discursive thinking) and *intellectual practice* (criticism's networks of social intervention and public debate[10]), because this is the site perhaps over which there is the least consensus in our discussion about intellectual activity and post-dictatorship.[11] The difficulties in thinking about such a site or location which presupposes heterogeneous tensions between the 'inside' and 'outside' of academic culture, has to do with present-day risks (a relation with the present) and with the conflict between *actuality* and the *language of criticism* (see Thayer, 1997); between cultural market and critical resistance to the standardization of signs and values; between *cultural assimilation* and *critical irrecoverability*.

We have many reasons with which to convince ourselves that the present is nothing more than the factual reign of the *given*; a clumsy plot made up of media redundancies based on a trivial mix of common sense and opinion simplistically reduced to a descriptive brand-name that is exhausted in the immediacy of the conjuncture. How do we thus dare to create a critique of an actuality that is able to separate itself from the simplifications of this banal state? How may we establish a 'distance' from the advertising of an actuality that passes itself off as the present, confusing it with the official realism of a 'today' trivially framed by the mass media?

But, at the same time, and this is what interests me: why abandon the present to its fate without according it the benefit of suggesting that all that is formulated in its name does not speak in the same language of common places articulated as simple, unreflective actuality? Why cast aside the possibility that in the gaps of official vocabularies certain other voices are producing alternative, discordant meanings; and if this is the case, how do we not take on a certain responsibility for them, *take their side* in the struggle over meaning which sets them constantly against hegemonic definition?

Reality is also the zone in which the 'actual'—in Foucault's sense—signals the potential 'becoming-other' of the present: a 'becoming-other' that is played out in each dissonant relation of codes, each time the contestatory emergence of difference (a difference that is never assured or concluded—not difference as a 'product', rather difference in action, in *process*) must dispute terrain with capitalist mercantile orderings that look to make reality equivalent to the forms and signs of a neo-liberal suture. The present is not stamped with a uniform grammar of signs that are integrated into the Whole that is the market without rupture or disruptions of its self-representation. The present is composed in a stratification of statements which, because they are arranged according to always unstable relations of force, present less solid and coordinated zones in which to *test* ('ensayar') difference. And these 'testing' zones, in which what is in formation (ways of being, seeing and reading) does not yet coincide with a complete or definitive meaning, are key sites in which cultural critique can fine tune its arms so as to attempt to modify the ideological configuration of the present.

To introduce itself into the folds of non-coincidence that divide signifieds from signifiers so as to foreground the *montage*-like quality of actuality; to reveal the discursive pacts mobilized by cultural ideologies to naturalize meaning, remain the tasks of criticism, allowing it to exercise a 'vigilant counter-interpretation' on what Derrida calls the 'artifactuality of the real' (Derrida, 1998, p. 15). These folds of non-coincidence also allow criticism to distinguish the present from actuality, inserting the paradoxes of the inactual and its residues (any scrap that makes the operational smoothness and transparency of 'today' opaque) between them so as to make this present strange to itself, 'untimely': out of step, in times and ways, with the conventions of the majorities that formulate the passive agreement of signs.[12]

On the other hand, if 'conflict is the moral state of difference' (as Barthes once said) it falls to intellectual criticism to recover for the dominant systems of values and legitimization the conflicting points of view which the conformist pluralism of the market of diversity insists in erasing so that it does not block our view of the de-diffentiation of differences. Re-introducing conflicting points of view into dominant systems of valorization so that hegemonic definitions find themselves shaken by the confrontation of values, powers and meanings is also one of cultural criticism's tasks which should, therefore, occupy cracks in official systematizations that upset its sets (and subsets) of statements. To ignore the present or actuality because they are merely the products of official translation and reduction would be equivalent to renouncing 'the struggle for meaning, and considering culture as a *battlefield*' (Grüner, 1998, p. 23), in which, daily, the emergent and the residual must struggle for their lives against the blocs of dominant formalization. If intellectual criticism abstains from participating in these struggles under the (aristocratic) pretext that the present is too promiscuous, from where will the *clashes of accentuation* be made that will shatter the arranged false consensus with which actuality pretends to maintain its signs in order?

Fragments and totality; abstract equivalence and singularity of difference; homogeneity of the system's general law—neoliberalism, globalization—and local heterogeneity of its concrete agency; capitalist saturation and points of breakage in the diagram through which to put it, interstitially, into contradiction: these are the tensions that demand of post-dictatorship critical thought that it face the dilemma of daring (or not) to put into circulation social theories and interpretations, critical fictions, that look to break open the dominant reality—effect of standardized culture, without knowing—for sure—whether its *pulsion of otherness* will (or will not) open up a path in the midst of the uniform and the conformity that politically, academically, and through the media, domesticates it. On the one hand, by risking intervention in the public realm of culture we run the risk that the critical voice is subsumed by actuality and becomes mere leftovers, without having its 'difference' from the dominant trivializing communicative regime noticed (see Thayer, 1997). On the other, ignoring the public realm when faced with contemporary abuses (and withdrawing into the passive autocritical exercise of negation, or renouncing public intervention due to excessive epistemological vigilance) produces a complicit silence that transforms academic refuge into a comfortable zone of non-intervention from which to avoid all risk of social engagement with the heterogeneity and resistance of the actual forces of disorder.

It is true that the landscape of Transition has been marked by the loss of history and politics as the objects of a previous struggle for meaning that has now waned, and it is also true that this loss has been accompanied by the slippage of subjects and objects into a world in which *consensus* and the *market* have mapped out a horizon that now lacks all intensive vibration. Nevertheless, as in every formation of statements, the present reality of the Transition (consensual homogeneity, market seriality) shows fissures and disjunctures which expose the grammar of order to unforeseeable zones of agitation and turbulence from where criticism can rescue whatever refuses assimilation into the functional languages of institutional culture and politics. (It would be enough to mention the Pinochet 'case' to illustrate how, at a time in which all appeared to be harmonized ['concertado'] and foreseen by the systems of control set in place by the Transition, an incident-accident succeeds in disorganizing the prefixed modes of naming and arranging, freeing—onto the surface of actuality—discordant flows of expressivity that make for a revolt of meaning not easily integrated into official codes.)

It is also true, a number of end-of-the-century theses warn us, that 'alterity, like the rest, has fallen prey to the laws of the market, supply and demand'; that 'the discourse of differences' only fabricates simulacra of alterity as a circulating part of a system of 'regulated exchange' (Baudrillard, 1991, p. 138). According to this thesis, nothing (neither excess nor remainder) can succeed in de-regulating the systematicity of the system because the capitalist machine has become expert in incorporating dissonances and transgressions of the production of multiplicity and heterogeneity with which the market logic of diversification reactivates itself. But no law of appropriation exists whose rule is so hermetic—in its ability to *totally* reunify capitalist fragmentation—that all times and subjectivities can be inexorably captured by the seriality of the market-place (see Williams, 1979, p. 252). The struggle between the tendencies of processes of *seriality-repetition* and *alterity-transformation* is never decided before the event, amongst other reasons because the play of difference—before being subordinated by a regime of general, translatory equivalence—vibrates as an *acting* potentiality, as singular opening and adventure. It is precisely the critical vibration of these *zones of uncertainty* around the *risks* of difference that challenges the model of 'imaginary subjectivity' characteristic of capitalism 'which poses a Totality without fissures, differences, closed in the form of a multiple universal system of abstract equivalences' (Grüner, 1998, p. 50). Moreover, no construction of knowledge, unless it considers itself to be infallible, could certify that there do not exist—within both the present and actuality—lines of flight and dissidence that break away from the absolute predictability of the system.

All of this is just to say that to transform the present and actuality into a zone of critical labour does not imply surrendering to its simple pragmatics, but rather to read—out of and against its time—what runs through the present as ambivalence, disagreement or resistance. Without this reading of the present for what speaks or labours against its grain, we would not know how to intervene in the debate on the inconclusive formulation of the new, saving what is still in the process of invention (works, texts, critical fictions) from states of normative consolidation looking to *fix* their value. Maintaining this oscillating value that is also in suspense, and making it contradictory in the undoing and redoing of meaning, are ways of working with texts and culture that contradicts the conceptual and mercantile reifications of 'circulating'-form and 'exchange'-form.

To re-emplot post-dictatorship along new lines of critical thought, we must *activate* determinate forces of alterity and alteration. If not, what is criticism for? To mobilize these forces supposes detecting *how* and *when* grand or small insurrections of meaning are formulated: social rebellion, but also poetics of writing, twists in genre (and gender), institutional fractures. Without conforming to the rules of understanding that fix the dominant reality effect (its practical realism, its common sense), but struggling on the inside of discursive conjunctures, is how intellectual criticism travels the folds of disobedience that striate the real so as, from *incompleteness* and the *uncertainty* of difference, to oppose the anti-Utopian closure of the real imposed by end-of-the-century neoliberalism as well as the vocabularies of impotence.

Translated by John Kraniauskas

Notes

1. In their prologue to *Escritura y temblor*, Pablo Oyarzún and Willy Thayer locate the writing of Marchant in relation to the consciousness of the 'loss of the word' as theorized by him as a 'tremor zone' of experiential disaster and a catastrophe of names (see Marchant, 2000, p. 5).
2. According to Idelber Avelar: 'By oscillating between the positions of object and subject of mourning, postdictatorial literature finds itself permanently on the brink of melancholy. In its strict Freudian sense, the distinction between mourning and melancholy lies in the place of loss, located either outside of the subject, exercising a profound impact on him but being in the end understandable as a loss suffered by someone for something or someone else (mourning), or everywhere, to the point of including the grieving subject in loss itself, such that the separation between subject and object of loss disappears (melancholy) … . Thus melancholy emerges as a specific kind of mourning, of that which has closed its circle including the mourning subject as object of loss. In this sense, melancholy is nothing less than a privileged symptom of a blockage in the resolution of the work of mourning' (Avelar, 1997, p. 302).
3. Avelar's interpretation of allegory opposes this figure to metaphor, in so far as metaphor does no more than assimilate any remainder into the substituting chains of a present unified by the homogeneous translation codes of the market.

4. According to Kristeva (1987, pp. 53–54): 'to trans-pose, in the Greek *métaphorein*: transport–from the start language is a translation, but in a register heterogeneous to the register in which affective loss… operates'. Metaphoric translation 'takes signs from their signifying neutrality', breaks with 'asymbolics: the loss of sense', multiplying networks of translation and figurative conversion around loss.
5. Here 'metaphor' is not to be understood in opposition to 'allegory' and conceived to be a procedure (comparatively) devalued in its critical potential as in Avelar's interpretation (see Avelar, 1997, p. 22).
6. Déotte points to the importance of the artist's role 'of putting into words and images, of proportioning representations'. They should 'take sides with what remains, with the annihilated, disappeared, with the vanquished' (Déotte, 1998, p. 150). In turn Rella foregrounds the 'modalities of thought, other forms of entering into a cognitive relation with the real: that of art, poetry and narrative' for creating new forms of sense and new dispositions of the subject (Rella, 1992, p. 215).
7. According to Marchant: 'One day, suddenly ('de golpe'), so many of us lost the word, totally lost the word. Others in contrast–strength or weakness–lost that loss: they could carry on talking, writing, and, if change in content, nevertheless, no change in the rhythm of their speech, their writing' (Marchant, forthcoming).
8. Trujillo, rereading Marchant, writes: 'Suddenly ('de golpe') thought and loss appeared together. And apparently, neither the loss of thought can be thought nor the thought of loss lost. The thought of loss has lost loss. Insofar as it is the thought of loss that drags all into disappearance, there is enormous difficulty for a thought to begin to think…. Errant metonymy: the thought of loss is the loss that can no longer be lost' (Trujillo, 1999, n.p.).
9. 'Melancholy is the loss of the ability to critically transform the real', says Federico Galende in a reflection on how a crisis of recomposition of the tradition of the left 'results from the impossibility of mourning, of a coup ('golpe') that, through trauma, shifted the mirrors in which a field might recompose itself …' (Galende, 1998, p. 47).
10. With regard to this distinction between academic labour and intellectual practice, Said speaks about 'choosing the risks and uncertain results of the public sphere–a conference, a book or article, that circulate without blocks–rather than the complicit space controlled by experts and profesionals' (Said, 1996, p. 94).
11. When I say 'our' I am referring especially to a space of reflection and collective discussion that united us for three years in the Seminar of Cultural Critique of Arcis University organized within the framework of the Rockefeller Foundation project on Postdictatorship and Democratic Transition 1997–1999. Many of my reflections here are the product of the singular experience of that Seminar that gathered together students and professors of philosophy, sociology, art and literature–whom I thank for the quality and stimulus of their contributions.
12. Horacio González leaves open the possibility for cultural criticism of rescuing the present from itself owing to the 'heterogeneity of the actual', writing that 'the present always contains cultural identities, but *diffuse presences*; ethical imperatives, but *valorative instability*; thematic hegemony, but *argumentative dispersion*; visibility of the new, but *persistence of archaisms*' (quoted in Podlubne, 1998, p. 77).

References

Idelber Avelar, 'Alegoría y postdictadura: notas sobre la memoria del mercado', *Revista de Crítica Cultural*, No. 14 (June 1997).

Jean Baudrillard, *La transparencia del mal* (Barcelona: Editorial Anagrama, 1991).

Jean Louis Déotte, *Catástrofe y olvido: las ruinas, Europa, el museo* (Santiago: Editorial Cuarto Propio, 1998).

Jacques Derrida, *Ecografías de la televisión* (Buenos Aires: Eudeba, 1998).

Federico Galende, 'Un desmemoriado espíritu de época', *Revista de Crítica Cultural*, No. 13 (November 1996).

Federico Galende, 'La izquierda entre el duelo, la melancolía y el trauma', *Revista de Crítica Cultural*, No. 17 (November 1998).

Eduardo Grüner, 'El retorno de la teoría crítica de la cultura', in *Fredric Jameson, Slavoj Zizek: Estudios culturales, reflexiones sobre el multiculturalismo* (Buenos Aires: Paidos, 1998).

Julia Kristeva, *Soleil noir: dépression et mélancolie* (Paris: Gallimard, 1987).

Patricio Marchant, *Escritura y temblor* (Santiago: Editorial Cuarto Propio, 2000).
Patricio Marchant, *Sobre árboles y madres* (forthcoming).
Alberto Moreiras, 'La exterioridad de la no liberación: subalternismo y práctica teórica', unpublished manuscript.
Judith Podlubne, 'Beatriz Sarlo/Horacio González: perspectivas de la crítica cultural', in *Las operaciones de la crítica*, ed. by Alberto Giordano and María Cecilia Vásquez (Rosario: Beatriz Viterbo Editora).
Franco Rella, *El silencio y las palabras: el pensamiento en tiempo de crisis* (Barcelona: Paidos, 1992).
William Rowe, 'La crítica cultural: problemas y perspectivas', *Nuevo Texto Crítico*, Nos 14/15 (1997).
Edward Said, *Representaciones del intelectual* (Barcelona: Paidos, 1996).
Beatriz Sarlo, 'Los estudios culturales y la crítica literaria en la encrucijada valorativa', *Revista de Crítica Cultural*, No. 15 (November 1997).
Willy Thayer, 'Como se llega a ser lo que se es', *Revista de Crítica Cultural*, No. 15 (November 1997).
Willy Thayer, 'Tercer espacio e ilimitación capitalista', *Revista de Crítica Cultural*, No. 18 (June 1999).
Iván Trujillo, 'Pensar la pérdida', unpublished manuscript.
Raymond Williams, *Politics and Letters: Interviews with New Left Review* (London: New Left Books, 1979).

Paulo Drinot

FOR WHOM THE EYE CRIES: MEMORY, MONUMENTALITY, AND THE ONTOLOGIES OF VIOLENCE IN PERU

This paper explores the polemic that erupted in early 2007 in Peru over the monument called The Eye that Cries (El ojo que llora). *This monument, which commemorates the victims of Peru's recent political violence, has become key to Peru's ongoing 'battles for memory' or 'memory struggles', struggles that pit opposing memories of the decade and a half of violence in the 1980s and 1990s. I argue that this polemic offers a privileged perspective from which to consider the ways in which two opposing interpretations of Peru's recent violent past have emerged in the last few years.*

On the night of 23 November 2007, under the cover of darkness, a group of people entered a small gated section of Lima's Campo de Marte (Martian Field).[1] One of the few green areas in a city of some eight million people, the Campo de Marte is also the scene of military parades on 28 July, Peru's national day. The intruders were carrying buckets full of paint and sledgehammers. They had beaten and then tied up a municipal policeman guarding the area. They approached a central section of the gated area and proceeded to attack and throw the paint over a large rock jutting out of the ground. The following day, the attack's symbolic content was plain for all to see. The paint used in the attack, a bright orange, is the colour associated with former president Alberto Fujimori and his ten-year rule of the country (1990–2000).[2] Only two days earlier the Chilean authorities had extradited Fujimori to Peru, where he is now standing trial for a range of charges, including corruption and human rights abuses. The rock that the attackers defaced is the central piece in a larger monument to the victims of Peru's recent violent past.[3] This monument, called *The Eye that Cries* (*El ojo que llora*), has become key to Peru's ongoing 'battles for memory' or 'memory struggles', struggles that pit opposing memories of the decade and a half of violence in the 1980s and 1990s.

The report of the Truth and Reconciliation Commission (Comisión de la Verdad y Reconciliación – CVR) published in 2003 laid bare the trauma of Peru's internal war. The violence, the report revealed, had left a far greater number of victims, some 70,000, than had until then been assumed.[4] Although the report established that the responsibility and culpability for the violence lay ultimately with Shining Path, it also blamed the forces of order for the various abuses that they committed. More importantly, the report framed its analysis of the direct causes of violence in a broader socio-historical analysis which underlined the ways in which the violence reflected and reproduced entrenched and intersecting class, ethnic and gender inequalities that separate the included few from the excluded many in Peru. As Salomon Lerner, the president of the CVR, noted in his speech of 28 August 2003, the report reveals that Peru is 'a country where exclusion is so absolute that tens of thousands of citizens can disappear without anyone in integrated society, in the society of the non-excluded, noticing a thing'.[5] The report was met with intense hostility by various sectors of Peruvian society and its recommendations have for the most part been ignored.[6] *The Eye that Cries* monument, as we will see, was inspired by the report of the CVR, and is part of a broader attempt by human rights organizations and civil society in Peru to keep open the debate on the broader reasons for Peru's descent into violence; a debate that the report sought to initiate and that many, including the present administration of President Alan García, seek to silence. In February 2009 it emerged that the Garcia government had rejected a two million dollar donation from the German government to build and maintain a Museum of Memory that would have housed the Yuyanapaq photographic exhibition on the years of violence.

The attack on the monument was expressive of a desire to silence, indeed destroy, debate. But it was also expressive of the fact that Fujimori and his associates, now standing trial for historical misdeeds, could not erase history. As Slajov Zizek has recently noted: 'The Chinese Cultural Revolution serves as a lesson [. . .]: destroying old monuments proved not to be a true negation of the past. Rather it was an impotent *passage à l'acte*, an acting out which bears witness to the failure to get rid of the past' (2008: 176). Indeed, the attack was a telling colophon to the polemic surrounding *The Eye that Cries* that erupted in early 2007 and which I discuss below.[7] This polemic offers a privileged perspective from which to consider the ways in which two opposing interpretations of Peru's recent violent past have emerged in the last few years. These interpretations are not necessarily identifiable with specific viewpoints or ideological stances (although there may be some coincidences). They do not correspond necessarily to a right-wing and a left-wing position. They do correspond to underlying ideas, assumptions perhaps, that shape particular analyses. I have no intention of providing a detailed study of these analyses. But I think it is useful to consider these underlying ideas; ideas that are often not fully articulated by those who draw upon them in their analyses. I argue, in the final section of this paper, that these ideas produce different conclusions about the causes of the violence that Peru experienced, about the responsibilities and culpabilities of the violent and non-violent actors, and about the ways in which Peruvian society should confront its recent violent past in a post-violent context. However, before briefly retracing the steps of the polemic that surrounded the sculpture, I will consider in a first section the ways in which the sculpture's function, the memorialization of violence, inserts it into broader global processes of memorialization.

Memorializing the violence in Peru

On 3 January 2007, Peruvians woke to the news that a monument to terrorism existed in the country. The headline of the newspaper *Expreso* left no room for doubt: 'There is a monument to terrorists!'[8] A brief article informed the newspaper's readers, in a language that has sadly become rather common in some of the printed press in Peru, that the monument had been built 'by the dreadful Truth Commission created by the champagne socialists (*izquierda caviar*) who rose to power in the shadow of Valentín

Paniagua and Alejandro Toledo'.[9] According to the article, the monument consisted of a 'sculpture surrounded by circles made up of little stones which have been inscribed with the names of terrorists mixed in with the names of innocent victims'. The article further indicated that Luis Enrique Ocrospoma, the mayor of Jesus María, the district where the monument is located, had declared that the neighbours of the district 'are outraged by this situation' and that it was necessary to 'safeguard the interests of the neighbours, and this implies their right to life. We are against all acts of violence, and for this reason we reject tributes to terrorist delinquents who committed execrable crimes'.

What was odd about this headline is that the monument in question was none other than *The Eye that Cries*, created by Lika Mutal, a Dutch sculptor residing in Peru. The monument had been inaugurated more than a year earlier, on 28 August 2005. According to the webpage of APRODEH, a human rights organization, the *Yuyanapaq* photographic exhibition organized by the Truth and Reconciliation Commission had inspired Mutal to design a sculpture that 'in addition to being a tribute to the victims, will be an efficient instrument to make the population gain greater awareness of what happened in Peru during the years of internal armed conflict and to promote reflection and invite the memory and construction of a more just, democratic and solidary Peru'.[10] The sculpture, which consists of a large rock from which water spurts surrounded by small pebbles inscribed with the names of some 30,000 victims of the violence, had been conceived as 'a space whose purpose was to pay tribute to and preserve the memory of all the victims and to bring to light Peru's recent history'. The sculpture is the centrepiece of a larger project, called *La alameda de la memoria* (*The Boulevard of Memory*), which was to incorporate 'additional spaces whose function will be to provide information on the internal war [. . .] and to present the "Quipus of memory" elaborated in 2005 as part of the effort to raise consciousness and as a symbolic reparation to victims of political violence'.[11] The webpage adds that the sculptural project 'brings together the efforts of a range of civil society institutions and the Municipality of Jesus María, which agreed to bring the proposal to fruition in the Campo de Marte'.

The Eye that Cries monument presents a departure in terms of Lima's monumental and sculptural landscape. The expansion in public sculpture which occurred in mid nineteenth-century Lima, as documented by Natalia Majluf, produced monuments that were 'like disciplinary lighthouses, an attempt to create and shape a collective memory and to create a national spatiality' (1994). This project failed, Majluf concludes, because the elite vision it sought to project was overtaken by the 'irruption of the popular'. The elites' projected cultural hegemony failed to become dominant and the monuments today stand as 'exclusive and exclusionary spaces'. It would be unfair to accuse Mutal of having created a 'disciplinary lighthouse' (for one thing hers is a wounded piece of art, an art of suffering, not of domination), but she evidently shares with her predecessors the belief in the sculpture's capacity 'to create and shape a collective memory and to create a national spatiality'. But I would suggest that the monument does more interesting work than its sculptor herself recognizes since it invites both a collective memory and an individuated memory as part of, but not subsumed within, the collective. The pebbles inscribed with the names of the victims of the violence both help remember (in a cognitive sense) those who died but also help re-member (in an embodied sense) those whose bodies were dis-membered by the violence. The monument serves not simply to remember the past but more importantly to inscribe literally into the most basic stuff of Peruvian territoriality (its pebbles) the names of those who were erased from it by the violence. In fact, by virtue of the marginality of the vast majority of those who died to official Peruvian nationhood, the inscription of their names in the pebbles should be seen not as a recording of their death but as their coming into being as actually existing, if dead, Peruvians.

In short, the function of *The Eye that Cries* is the memorialization of the violence that Peru experienced as a tribute to its victims. As suggested by the name of monumental complex in which the sculpture is located, *The Boulevard of Memory*, the civil society organizations that backed the construction of the monument sought to privilege memory as the concept through which to confront collectively the past and, concretely, the political violence that the country experienced in the 1980s and 1990s. In this way, the sculptor and promoters of *The Eye that Cries* inserted it into a broader phenomenon: the rise of the 'culture of memory', the 'industry of memory' or even the 'empire of memory' in Peru, which, in turn, inserts Peru into a far broader process.[12] In order to get a sense of the memory phenomenon in Peru it suffices to note the number of recent local publications that have the word 'memory' in the title.[13] This raises the question: where does this interest in memory come from? Why is memory favoured over other concepts related to the past (such as history)? What consequences does the focus on memory (some would say the obsession for memory) have?

It may be worth briefly examining the rise of memory as a cultural and political phenomenon in the last few decades.[14] According to Andreas Huyssen, the source of the memory phenomenon is to be found in the decolonization processes and in the social movements of the 1960s, as well in the rise of the 'Other', but even more so in the debate surrounding the Holocaust that occurred in the 1980s in the light of various media events (such as the TV series *Holocaust*) and the anniversaries of a series of key events in the rise of the Third Reich. In the 1990s, the genocides in Rwanda, Bosnia and Kosovo contributed to extending the memory discourse on the Holocaust beyond its original point of reference. In Europe and in the United States, Huyssen argues, memory has developed unusual commercial dimensions, in evidence in the rise of the nostalgia industry, the interest in the construction of museums, and what Huyssen calls 'self-musealization', that is, the popular obsession for video cameras, life memories and confessional literature (a phenomenon increasingly subject to technological transformation as witnessed by the rise of personal blogs and cyberspaces such as Myspace and Facebook) (2000: 22–25).

Alongside the commercialization of memory, we are witnessing the increasing political use of memory, 'ranging from a mobilization of mythic pasts to support aggressively chauvinist or fundamentalist politics (e.g., post-communist Serbia and Hindu populism in India) to fledgling attempts, in Argentina and Chile, to create public spheres of "real" memory that will counter the politics of forgetting pursued by postdictatorship regimes either through "reconciliation" and official amnesties or through repressive silencing'. But as Huyssen points out, 'the fault line between mythic past and real past is not always that easy to draw – one of the conundrums of any politics of memory anywhere. The real can be mythologized just as the mythic may engender strong reality effects. In sum, memory has become a cultural obsession of monumental proportions across the globe' (2000: 26). Pierre Nora may be right to argue that the memory discourse is an attempt to confront the anxiety produced by a threatening globalization by anchoring lived experience in the local, the intimate, and the community-based.[15] But, insists Huyssen, 'securing the past is no less risky an enterprise than securing the future. Memory, after all, can be no substitute for justice, and justice itself will inevitably be entangled in the unreliability of memory' (2000: 37).

One of the most salient aspects of the memory phenomenon has been the new interest in what we could call monumentality, that is the cultural and political use of public monuments.[16] The memorialization of the Holocaust in particular, but also of the slave trade, of the two World Wars, of decolonization in Africa and Asia, and most recently of the attack on New York's Twin Towers, among other historical traumas, has generated a series of debates on monumentality and memory that cannot be properly addressed here.[17] However, it is important to recognize that these debates on (historical) monumentality, commemoration, collective remembrance and 'sites of memory' represent a broader frame of reference within which the polemic surrounding *The Eye that Cries* can be understood.[18] Although that polemic reflected in some ways local – Peruvian – prerogatives, the ways in which Peruvians confront the past, as well as remembering and forgetting, echo global processes and have a global resonance.

The focus on memory in the Peruvian context is intimately, although not exclusively, linked to the work of the Truth and Reconciliation Commission. As Carlos Iván Degregori, one of the former commissioners (and one of Peru's foremost anthropologists), notes in a recently published article, the 'genealogy' of the CVR points to an attempt, beginning in the mid 1990s, on the one hand, to counteract the forgetting of the violence that Peru had experienced, a forgetting that was being imposed by the Fujimori government (a forgetting, moreover, that appeared consecrated by the amnesty law of 1995) and, on the other, the official *fujimorista* narrative, that presented itself, as the official *pinochetista* narrative in Chile had done, as a 'memory of salvation'. According to Degregori, despite the attempts, from within the corridors of power, to impose both forgetting and a 'memory of salvation', 'there existed always [...] narratives that questioned that official history. The most visible were those produced by human rights organisations or the opposition press. But there were also the silenced memories, reduced to the local or family context, out of fear or and because of a lack of channels of expression in the public sphere' (2004: 76).

In this interpretation, the 'official history' of the violence is expressed as a product of a dialectic between two memories in struggle with one another: one, from above, produced by *fujimorismo*, and the other, from below, produced by the human rights organizations, democratic civil society organizations and the Truth and Reconciliation Commission, which formulates it most clearly. The armed conflict is replaced by another conflict over how to comprehend the past. 'To remember' and to make audible the 'silenced memories' thus becomes the fundamental challenge that the CVR sets itself and more importantly, proposes to Peruvian society. As Degregori makes clear: 'to move from a vague passive sympathy to an active memory, not only showing solidarity with the victims, but also capable of formulating new meanings of the past and a new political proposal for the future, is the difficult challenge of the years to come' (2004: 85). It is no surprise then that the activities organized by the CVR, as well as their publications, reprise and celebrate this idea: hence the organization of the photographic exhibition *Yuyanapaq – Para recordar (In order to remember)*; hence the title of the book that compiles Salomon Lerner's speeches: *La rebelión de la memoria (The Rebellion of Memory)*; hence the projected construction of the *Boulevard of Memory*.

It is easy to understand the use (indeed, perhaps, the abuse) of the memory discourse by the CVR and by post-CVR projects/initiatives. Memory, unlike history, and particularly 'official history', appears to be (although it seldom is) something more immediate, authentic, even more democratic. The idea, as Degregori notes, is to forge an 'active' collective memory, that is to say a memory that is politically and culturally usable. Degregori understands well that, as Joanna Bourke has pointed out, 'the collective does not possess a memory, only barren sites upon which individuals inscribe shared narratives, infused with power relations' (2004: 474). Collective memory, in other words, is as constructed or imagined as history: memory 'is not "something" that exists in some ethereal sphere, beyond culture' (Bourke, 2004: 484). To the 'memory as salvation' (*memoria salvadora*) constructed by Fujimori and peddled by his cronies is opposed a 'democratic' or perhaps 'inclusionary' memory, which posits a different reading of the past and a new vision of the future. And, as I discuss below, this is precisely the memory that *The Eye that Cries* seeks to promote. As Lika Mutal explains (to repeat), the monument was designed so that 'in addition to being a tribute to the victims, it will [become] an efficient instrument to make the population gain greater awareness of what happened in Peru during the years of internal armed conflict and to promote reflection and invite the memory of and construction of a more just, democratic and solidary Peru'.[19]

However, although it is easy to share the desire to forge a collective memory, or, better still, a historical consciousness, that can help create a 'more just, democratic and solidary Peru', it is important to reflect upon the limits of memory projects.[20] Wolf Kansteiner is not wrong when he argues that those peoples who have lived through traumatic war experiences 'only have a chance to shape the national memory if they command the means to express their visions, and if their vision meets with compatible social or political objectives and inclinations among other important social groups, for instance, political elites or parties' (2002: 187–188). It is therefore in the political sphere and not merely in the symbolic or monumental sphere that the struggles for memory must be conducted. Again, as Huyssen argues, 'memory, after all, can be no substitute for justice' (2000: 37). It is most likely the lack of any real political power that forces those who share the ideas reflected in the report of the Peruvian Truth and Reconciliation Commission to act primarily in the sphere of representation. But it is important to recognize that as long as the ideas about the past and about the national project included in the CVR report and in *The Eye that Cries* are not expressed and represented in a concrete political project it is unlikely that this inclusive memory will become the national memory. This is precisely what the polemic over *The Eye that Cries* demonstrates.

The polemic

If the *The Eye that Cries* monument already existed in August 2005 and if the Municipality of the district had collaborated in its creation, how do we then explain the headline in *Expreso* (to recall: 'There is a monument to terrorists!')? The immediate explanation resides in the ruling of 25 November 2006 of the Inter-American Court of Human Rights (CIDH), the highest judicial instance in the region, on the massacre that occurred in the Castro Castro penitentiary in 1992, when 41 inmates were executed extra-judicially by police officers and soldiers sent in to quell a riot.[21] The ruling, which runs to 200 pages, concludes that the Peruvian state violated the right to life of 41 persons, and establishes that the state has to provide indemnities to the relatives of the dead and that 'the State must carry out, within a one-year period, a public act of acknowledgment of its responsibility in relation to the violations declared in this Judgment and as an apology to the victims and for the satisfaction of their next of kin, in a public ceremony with the presence of high State authorities and of the victims and their next of kin, and it must transmit said act through the media, including the transmission on radio and television'.[22] At the same time, the CIDH established that 'the State must guarantee that, within a one-year period, all the persons declared as deceased victims in the present Judgment are represented in the monument called "The Eye that Cries", for which it must coordinate, with the next of kin of the mentioned victims the realization of an act in which they may include an inscription with the name of the victim as corresponds pursuant to the monument's characteristics'.[23]

The CIDH's ruling caused consternation among the political class and public opinion in Peru. President Alan García declared that 'it is indignant that a tribunal has reached a conclusion that harms a country that was the victim of the insanity and diabolic destruction of a sect that sought to destroy our Fatherland'.[24] According to García, Peru would not accept the ruling since it made no sense for the victims to indemnify their victimizers: 'if the court wants to punish those responsible, then it should go ahead and do it, but the people have been wronged and they cannot be forced to pay, with their taxes, hundreds of millions [of dollars] to those who destroyed the country'. Regarding the symbolic act that the CIDH ordered the Peruvian state to perform, the President, perhaps a little confused by the reference to Mutal's sculpture in the ruling, suggested in a tone that mixed sarcasm and bravura, 'I have to assume that the Court will have to come here in order to build it, because it will not find a single Peruvian willing to place a brick in favour of the assassins of Peru'.[25]

The ruling unleashed a polemic that illustrated, and reflected, how different sectors of Peruvian society made sense of, and sought to represent, the recent violent past. The differentiated reactions to the ruling and, as we will see, to the *Eye that Cries*, arguably, are expressions of the differentiated interpretations that exist in Peru of the causes of, and nature of, the violence. As such, the polemics over the ruling of the CIDH, and over *The Eye that Cries*, illustrated and reflected the polarization of Peruvian society over the recent violent past, and, in particular, over the interpretation of the recent violent past that the CVR had put forward in its report. For those opposed to the CVR, the polemics were further evidence, and channels for demonstrating, that in the final analysis the CVR was, in the best case, misguided or, in the worst, philo-terrorist. For those who supported the CVR, the polemics were further evidence of, and channels for demonstrating, the incapacity of conservative sectors in Peruvian society to understand the need to end the country's culture of impunity for human rights violators and to uphold the rule of law.

Many viewed the ruling of the CIDH as a serious error and some as a pro-Shining Path act. The Peruvian representative to the OAS, Antero Flores Aráoz, commented that 'we know that many of them were terrorists, which means that to accept or decree that they be honoured and indemnified is, frankly, an excess'.[26] According to Cardinal Juan Luis Cipriani, the ruling demonstrated that the CIDH espoused 'a clear ideology in favour of terrorism'.[27] The director of *Correo*, a right-wing daily, used the ruling as an opportunity to engage in his favourite activity (to accuse the 'caviar' left of all the ills of the country) and published an editorial titled 'The Eye that Cries is Hidrogo's' where he berated journalists and left-wing intellectuals for their silence regarding 'the policeman called Hidrogo [...], the martyr, who during the prison uprising had his eyes gouged out by the *senderistas* [Shining Path militants] and who suffered a thousand other barbarities before he was rescued and before he died thanks, no doubt, to divine pity'.[28]

These views were countered by others, who defended the ruling, arguing that it was the duty of the State to always act within the law, which implied recognizing past errors, the jurisdiction of the CIDH on this matter, and the need to comply with its rulings. A communiqué published in various newspapers and signed by Mario Vargas Llosa (Peru's foremost novelist and a former presidential candidate) and Gustavo Gutiérrez (a Dominican priest and one of the intellectual fathers of Liberation Theology) among others suggested that 'just as it is necessary to carry out fair trials that result in severe sentences for criminals, it is equally necessary to recognize one's errors and crimes, to sanction those responsible and to make reparations as mandated by law. To not do so would be to renounce the very rule of law that the terrorists sought to destroy. This does not imply an equivalence between the victims of Shining Path with the terrorist victimizers. It implies demanding of the State an ethical and legal behaviour that is consonant with democracy'.[29]

Others, though they recognized that the ruling had to be observed, disagreed with its essence. Martin Tanaka, a political scientist and former director of the prestigious Institute of Peruvian Studies, declared that 'the ruling contains elements that are highly objectionable' and ironically commented on the idea that Peru should 'apologize to the members of the Central Committee of Shining Path'. Regarding the suggestion in the 'concurring opinion' of Judge Antônio Augusto Cançado Trindade, one of the five judges of the CIDH, that 'many of the victims bombed in the brutal armed attack of the Castro Castro Prison resemble Joans of Arc of the end of the [twentieth] century ... [like] the historical character, they had their ideas to free the social environment, for which they were imprisoned, some submitted to a trial without means of defence, and some were not even given this opportunity'[30], Tanaka retorted: 'although the crimes of the forces of order are reproachable, this does not turn the murdered *senderistas* into saints'.[31] Finally, Tanaka objected to the recommendation of the CIDH regarding Lika Mutal's sculpture and argued that 'with regard to this, I subscribe entirely to the statement issued by the promoters of this project: "It is inadmissible that The Eye that Cries be used for acts that aim to forget [as was indicated by the Truth and reconciliation Commission] that the internal war that began in 1980 was caused by the criminal decision of Shining Path to destroy the State and society in Peru"'.

It is interesting to note that this last opinion was shared by the sculptor of the monument. Asked by Doris Bayly of *El Comercio* newspaper whether she would include the names of the 41 assassinated *senderistas* in the monument, Lika Mutal answered: 'I would not. They were criminals, murdered outside the rule of law, but criminal nonetheless. If some form of reparation needs to be paid, perhaps it could be focused on putting right what they damaged'.[32] Similarly, Salomón Lerner, the former dean of the Catholic University and former President of the Truth and Reconciliation Commission, indicated that the monument did not include the names of terrorists: 'any person who has taken the trouble to visit *The Eye that Cries* will have been able to confirm that the names are those of the victims of the violence that devastated Peru. There are the names of months-old children who have died, of old women, and also of members of the forces of order who sacrificed their lives. Not of terrorists'.[33] As this shows, the polemic over the CIDH ruling brought to the fore a key question that divided how Peruvians understood the recent violent past: who were the victims and who were the victimizers of Peru's recent violent past? Or, to be more precise, under what circumstances could victimizers be considered victims?

The polemic over the ruling of the CIDH dovetailed with the polemic over *The Eye that Cries* when, on 11 January, *Correo* announced on its front page: 'Terrorists in the Eye that Cries – Unbelievable! The 41 *senderistas* from Castro Castro have already been honoured!'[34] During a visit to the monument, two of the newspaper's reporters had found 'the inscription of Carlos Aguilar Garay and Roberto River Espinoza, whose names appear on two separate stones (several rocks [sic] have been wiped out by the sun) next to the inscription of the year they died: 1992. They died in Castro Castro'. This discovery, according to the newspaper, established that the 'obviously unjustified' homage/tribute ordered by the CIDH 'has already been performed by those who built the monument' and that these people 'will have to answer to the nation for an action as unjustified as it is absurd'. Meanwhile, the mayor of Jesus María declared that he would forthwith remove the names of the *senderistas* from the monument '[to preserve] national dignity and out of respect for the [district's] neighbours'.

Many agreed that the *senderistas* should not be included among the victims of the violence memorialized in the *Eye that Cries*. Lika Mutal herself declared that she had had no knowledge of the presence of their names. She declared: '*The Eye that Cries* was created as a space to awaken the consciousness of all Peruvians. I have only now realised that the lists of the Truth and Reconciliation Commission and the Human Rights Ombudsman contained the total register of victims. They gave me the lists to use as I saw fit. We included all the names in what amounted to a mystical action' ['casi como una actitud mística incluimos todos los nombres'].[35] In other words, according to Mutal, the inclusion of the names of the *senderistas* had been a mistake. At the very least, it was a consequence not of a conscious decision to include the names of the *senderistas*, but rather of the fact that they had been considered victims of the political violence by the CVR and the Ombudsman's Office. But as I have already pointed out, Mutal believed that their names should not figure in the monument, because she considered them to be criminals. In a sense, Mutal agreed with Aldo Mariátegui when the journalist berated her: 'No, *señora* Mutal. Don't come to me with poems about reconciliation and articles by Mario Vargas Llosa (geniuses also can slip up), there are dead people and then there are dead people. One thing is the victim and another thing is the victimizer. Take those assassins out of there'.[36] However, not everyone agreed. Carlos Tapia, a former member of the Truth and Reconciliation Commission, declared around that time that he believed that the *senderistas'* names should be included in the monument because he considered them to be victims of the internal violence.[37]

The discovery of the presence of the names of murdered *senderistas* in the monument sharpened the controversy. The mayor of Jesus María declared that he would put a halt to the projected phases of the monument and that 200,000 soles destined for the construction of the *Quipu of memory* would be used for children's playgrounds.[38] He also suggested that the offending stones should be removed. This provoked a series of public reactions, including that of Francisco Soberón, the director of APRODEH, a human rights organization, who declared: 'we believe that no discriminations should occur because all the names that appear [in the stones] are of victims of terrorism or of extrajudicial killings'; and that of the artist Victor Delfín, who suggested that the mayor's proposal was an act of 'ignorance'.[39] Around that time, marches and pickets in favour and against the monument were organized.

'Is there a way of solving this impasse?' asked Mario Vargas Llosa in an article published in the Spanish daily *El País* and reproduced in *El Comercio*. 'Yes', he answered, 'Turn the stones with the names upside down, concealing them temporarily from public light, until time heals the wounds, appeases the tempers and establishes the consensus that will allow us all to accept that the horror that Peru lived as a consequence of the attempt of Shining Path – to repeat a Maoist revolution in the Peruvian Andes – and the terrible abuses and wickedness that the forces of order committed during the struggle against terror, stained us all, by commission or omission, and that only with this acceptance can we start to build a democracy worthy of the name, where disgraces such as those that soiled our eighties and nineties are inconceivable'.[40] Vargas Llosa's proposal was met with approval in the media. *El Comercio* declared that 'Vargas Llosa's proposal to turn around some of the stones while tempers calm down is sensible'.[41]

Reading the polemic

As I suggested in the previous section, the polemic regarding *The Eye that Cries* monument was framed by a broader debate that resulted from the ruling of the CIDH. It also coincided with a debate regarding a proposal put forward by the government to establish the death penalty for child rapists and for terrorists. At the time, many observers concluded that the debates over the CIDH ruling and the death penalty proposal were, in effect, political manoeuvres. Some suggested that what the government wanted was to avoid paying the reparations indicated by the CIDH to the victims of violence caused by agents of the state. Others argued that what was sought was to favour the fugitive former president Alberto Fujimori, and more broadly a supposed alliance between Apristas and Fujimoristas, by forcing the country into a situation where it would have to leave the jurisdiction of the CIDH (which was convenient for Alan Garcia, Fujimori and all those who sought to re-establish a Mafioso order in the country). Others, still, argued that what was sought was to discredit the work of the Truth and Reconciliation Commission.

All of these interpretations have some or a lot of truth in them. But I think that if the debates discussed above hide political manoeuvres they also reflect, more interestingly, conflicting interpretations regarding Peru's recent violent past. In this section, I will attempt to elucidate these interpretations, focusing first on how the causes of violence are understood, then turning to examine how responsibilities and culpabilities for the violence are assigned, and, finally, evaluating what post-violent panoramas present themselves in the light of these interpretations. I think it is necessary to understand these different and, as we will see, irreconcilable interpretations in order to get a better understanding of the current debates. As I noted in the introduction to this paper, these interpretations do not correspond strictly to ideological positions or political interests, even when coincidences exist. They are extrapolations from the debate whose function is to establish the outside boundaries of the debate; its extreme and containing limits but also, for this very reason, its enabling limits. As the analysis below suggests, the polemic I have narrated in the first section reveals, beyond particular ideological positions or political interests, two distinct ontologies of violence, that is to say, two underlying discourses on the nature or the very essence of violence in Peru.[42]

Let us examine the interpretation of the causes of 'the violence' in Peru. According to a first interpretation, the violence was a product of the actions of a criminal gang of terrorists. Although this interpretation admits that some of the violence can be attributed to the actions of the State, actions that in some cases were framed within the legitimate exercise of state violence and sometimes not, in the final analysis, according to this view, there would not have been political violence in Peru had it not been for the fact that Shining Path initiated an armed struggle in 1980. The violence was caused therefore by the decision of Shining Path leader Abimael Guzmán, seconded by his followers, to initiate a revolution in the country. The causes of the violence must therefore be sought with Shining Path itself, i.e. in its ideology and in its military-political structure, which are understood as expressive of the personalities of the members of Shining Path, and in particular, of that of its leader. According to this interpretation, violence is, in its nature or essence, a product of the very nature of the violent actors: that is to say, this interpretation suggests that violence was a product of the inherently violent character of those who perpetrated that violence. If there was violence in Peru, this interpretation suggests, it was because, in their very essence, the *senderistas* were violent.

This interpretation is contradicted by a second interpretation which argues that violence was a consequence of the unresolved rifts that divide Peruvian society. Violence according to this interpretation is expressive or indeed a product of structural conditions intrinsic to Peruvian society, perhaps its very 'mode of production'.[43] Violence can only properly be understood within a broader analytical framework that necessarily takes into account factors such as economic inequality, racial and gender discrimination, the weakness of the nation-state, the predisposition to authoritarianism, among other factors (to some extent this interpretation aligns political violence with other forms of 'daily', 'common', 'endemic' or 'unbound' violence) (Moser and McIlwayne, 2004: 3).[44] In its most extreme formulation, this interpretation suggests that had Shining Path not emerged when it did, the prevailing conditions in Peru would have brought about the emergence of another organization with similar goals to those of Shining Path with similar consequences for the country. The violence, this interpretation suggests, was not a consequence of the fact that the *senderistas* were in essence violent but of the structural conditions that were favourable to the emergence of a violent order. Although this interpretation allows for a differentiation with regard to the legitimacy of *senderista* violence or state violence, in the final analysis it sees both as a product of a structure favourable to the expansion of violence as the grammar of social relations in Peru.

From these two interpretations of the causes of political violence result two understandings of the responsibilities and culpabilities of the violent and non-violent actors. According to the first interpretation, the responsibility and culpability lies entirely with Shining Path, since this organization, and this organization alone, initiated the violence. If the state, through the armed forces, committed acts of violence that led to the death of innocent people in the context of the war against Shining Path, then the responsibility for these acts also lies with Shining Path since these deaths would not have occurred had it not been for the need to combat the *senderista* insurgency. The responsibility and the culpability for violence lie exclusively with one of the violent actors. The non-violent actors, according to this interpretation, are mere victims while the non-*senderista* violent actors (the forces of order) are also victims.

This analysis is countered by a second, which argues that the responsibilities and culpabilities for the violence are broader. If the violence was expressive of structural problems intrinsic to Peruvian society, then it follows that, in the final analysis, the responsibility for the violence lies with Peruvian society. Given that the violence, in this interpretation, is seen as a grammar that articulates social relations, the violence perpetrated by Shining Path becomes one form of violence among many. However, this interpretation allows for a greater censure of *senderista* violence, because although it sees violence as a structural phenomenon, it does not fail to establish criteria for the legitimacy of different forms of violence. In other words, this interpretation does not justify *senderista* violence (as could be inferred) but rather inserts the censure of *senderista* violence within a broader censure of the society that produces this violence, establishing a differentiation as regards the severity of the violence but in no way minimizing it. At the same time, although state violence in this interpretation also appears as expressive of a violent structure, it is not for this reason justified or minimized.

At the same time, this structural interpretation of violence extends the responsibility and culpability for the violence beyond the violent actors to encompass Peruvian society as a whole. And this extension presents a very problematic ambiguity. On the one hand, the responsibility and culpability of non-violent actors is necessarily inferior *stricto sensu* to that of the violent actors. But, on the other hand, the responsibility of non-violent actors is absolute, given that it is society as a whole which produces the grammar of violence through its inability to resolve the problems that give rise to violence, that is, to repeat, economic inequality, racial or gender discrimination, the weakness of the nation-state, the predisposition to authoritarianism etc. In a sense, this interpretation posits that if violence occurred it was not because, in their essence, the *senderistas* were violent but rather because, in its essence, Peru is violent. In other words, what differentiates these two discourses is the identification of the individual social body (albeit limited to the *senderistas*) or the collective social body (extensive to all Peruvians) within which resides the source of violence.

Finally, two distinct conclusions regarding how Peruvian society must face up to the recent violent past in a post-violent context arise from these interpretations of the essence of political violence and the associated responsibilities and culpabilities for the violence. According to a first interpretation, given that the source of violence resides exclusively within Shining Path, the post-violent scenario is straightforward: the *senderistas*, who bear sole responsibility for the violence, must be subjected to judicial and moral punishment. According to a second interpretation, given that the source of the violence resides more generally within Peruvian society, the post-violent scenario is more complicated: on the one hand, all violent actors who perpetrated forms of non-legitimate violence must be subjected to judicial and moral punishment. But since the violence according to this second interpretation cannot be reduced to the violence of the violent actors, then it befalls upon the whole of society to take part, first, in a collective process of atonement, and second, in the development of a non-violent grammar to articulate Peruvian society.

I believe that this reading, whose purpose is to lay bare the ontologies of violence that underpin each interpretation of political violence in Peru, allows us to understand better the polemic that arose regarding the monument of Lika Mutal. Clearly, from the perspective of the first interpretation the presence of the names of *senderistas* among the stones that represent the victims of the violence is nonsensical. If the monument is a tribute to the victims of the violence, then it is absurd to include the names of the victimizers, of those responsible for and culpable of the violence. However, seen from the perspective of the second interpretation, the presence of the 41 stones with the names of the *senderistas* murdered in the Castro Castro penitentiary is insufficient. If the purpose of the monument is to pay tribute to the victims of the violence, then it follows that, from this perspective, the names of all *senderistas*, and not just those of the *senderistas* illegally murdered by the state, should be included. If the violence was structural, if the source of the violence resides within all Peruvians, then all Peruvians were both victims and victimizers. The degree of responsibility may have varied depending on the concrete actions perpetrated by each Peruvian but, in the final analysis, all Peruvians were both victims and victimizers.

Clearly, these are conclusions that arise from a somewhat abstract analysis and that reflect extremes that do not correspond, as I have already noted, to actually existing interpretations (although, again, there may be some coincidences). It may be worth stressing that the second interpretation is not germane to the conclusions of the Truth and Reconciliation Commission as some may hurriedly conclude. More generally, I agree with the anthropologist Kimberley Theidon that an effective approximation to the violence that Peru experienced requires us to abandon the binary logic that dominates both academic production and political activism and to, instead, listen to 'the polyphony that interrupts the metanarrative' (2003). The binary (re)construction of interpretations of violence performed in this section is not intended to suggest that these are the only possible or extant metanarratives on political violence in Peru. Doubtless, the vast majority of the Peruvian population interprets the violent past in ways that cannot be reduced to one or the other interpretation delineated here. But the analysis offered does allow a different and perhaps more complete understanding of the polemic that surrounded *The Eye that Cries*. In focusing exclusively on how the polemic reflected various hidden political manoeuvres, political commentators failed to see the deeper and more complex dimension of this controversy (at the very least they tended to fail to take it into account in their analyses or to articulate them in a sufficiently clear way): that is that the polemic reflected, and in so doing, (re)constituted, the differentiated and irreconcilable interpretations of the essence of violence in Peru.

Conclusion

In July 2008, as the Fujimori trial entered its eighth month, Vladimiro Montesinos, the former president's intelligence chief and, for many, the mastermind of the regime's repressive policies, was called to give testimony. After denying that his former boss had any responsibility for the human rights abuses of which he was accused, he responded to the questions posed by the prosecutor by saying that he could not remember every detail, 'even though I have a great memory'.[45] We should probably not read too much into this comment, but it does neatly illustrate how selective forms of remembering and forgetting are central to the ways in which Peruvians continue to engage the recent violent past. Although Montesinos, who faces a long stint in prison, has personal reasons to favour forgetting, many in Peru share the idea that, as the polemic surrounding *The Eye that Cries* illustrates, the violent past is best forgotten. This is not as easy to achieve as some would like. In May, forensic scientists began to excavate a mass grave in the hamlet of Putis, in Ayacucho, where some 420 villagers, including a number of children, were executed by the armed forces after having been made to dig their own mass grave in late 1983. In June 2008, another mass grave containing 37 bodies was uncovered in neighbouring Huancavelica. Some had been executed by Shining Path and others by the armed forces in 1991.[46] The current García administration, with various human rights abuses skeletons in the closet of its own (García was in power in the period 1985–1990 and various documented human rights abuses occurred under his watch), is doing its very best to hinder the work of human rights organizations in the country and, in so doing, is articulating its own project of remembering and forgetting. It is a project in which the memory promoted by *The Eye that Cries* has no role.

I tried to visit *The Eye that Cries* in mid April 2007. Looking for the monument, I was struck by the fact that when I asked people who were out for a stroll or simply resting in the Campo de Marte where I would find the sculpture the answer invariably was that they had never heard of it. After a short walk, I came upon an area closed off with six-foot-high railings and a padlocked door. Through the railings I could make out the large central rock and the labyrinth of small stones that surround it. I was unable to confirm whether the offending stones had been removed or turned over. A few months later, of course, the attack on the monument momentarily put *The Eye that Cries* again at the centre of public debate in Peruvian society. I suspect, however, that today, and despite the memory jolts that each new unearthed mass grave represents, most of the people out for a stroll or resting in the Campo de Marte still may not have much of an idea where the monument is located, let alone be concerned with what it stands for. *The Eye that Cries*, I would argue, seeks to promote a memory which some Peruvians reject as false and others admit as true but care little for. It is not so much a site of memory as a para-site of memory, both because it fails to function fully as a shared site of memory or remembrance, but also because for many its real purpose is to infect and weaken the collective body by promoting a collective memory that, so it is claimed, is tantamount to a eulogy for terrorism. But the Fujimorista attack on the monument of November 2007 suggests that in spite of this *The Eye that Cries* remains a threat to the politics of forgetting and the 'memory of salvation'. It represents a kernel of a democratic and inclusive project that may still form the basis of a more solidary and just Peru. It is therefore a source of hope even as, or rather precisely because, it forces us to confront memories of violence that continue to divide Peruvians.

Notes

1. This is a revised and updated version of the article '*El ojo que llora*, las ontologías de la violencia, y la opción por la memoria en el Perú', in *Hueso Húmero* 50 (2007), pp. 53–74.
2. On Fujimori's government, see, among others, Conaghan (2005) and Carrión (2006).
3. On Shining Path and Peru's recent violent past, the best introduction remains Stern (1998).
4. Until that point, most estimates suggested 20,000 to 30,000 victims.

5 See http://www.cverdad.org.pe/informacion/discursos/en_ceremonias05.php.
6 For reactions to the report, see the weekly bulletins of press cuttings produced by APRODEH, a Peruvian human rights organization. http://www.aprodeh.org.pe/sem_verdad/ydespues.htm.
7 For a different reading of the polemic see Hite (2007). For an intelligent analysis of the various ways in which Peru's recent violent past has been represented, see Milton (2007).
8 Although the present Peruvian government and sectors of Peruvian society, and particularly the right-wing press, are broadly supportive of George Bush's foreign policy, the use of the term 'terrorist' in this context has little to do with the post-9/11 'war on terror'. The use of the term 'terrorist' to refer to the Shining Path, the Movimiento Revolucionario Tupac Amaru (MRTA), or, indeed, to a number of other perceived threats to the status quo (such as human rights organizations, trade unions and students) has been a constant since the 1980s, as has resistance to its use by several Peruvian human rights organizations and left-wing intellectuals.
9 *Expreso*, 3 January 2007. I would like to thank Victor Vich, who made available to me his collection of press cuttings on this topic.
10 http://www.aprodeh.org.pe/ojoquellora2006/index.html.
11 A quipu is an Inca tool, made up a series of knotted strings, which was used to keep record. On the quipu's traditional use see, among others, Quiter and Urton (2002).
12 The concept 'culture of memory' is used by Huysen (2000); 'industry of memory', among others, by Klein (2000); and 'empire of memory' by Juliá (2006).
13 See, for example, Montero (2006); Jiménez (2005), Durand (2005), Romero (2005), Lerner (2004), Hamann (2003), Degregori and Jelin (2003), Croci and Bonfiglio (2002), Millones and Kapsoli (2001), Kaulicke (2001), Watanabe, Morimoto and Chamba (1999).
14 For a general perspective on the uses of 'memory' in the social sciences and in history, see, among others, Olick and Robbins (1998), Klein (2000), Kansteiner (2002).
15 This is the key idea contained in the concept *lieux de mémoire* introduced by French historian Pierre Nora and his collaborators. See Nora (1989) for an introduction to the broader project of historical re-writing of the French past through the lens of memory; a project which produced some 5000 pages of print, 133 articles, and involved 103 collaborators.
16 See, for example, Nelson and Olin (2003).
17 On Holocaust memorials, see Young (1993) and Carrier (2005). On the Twin Towers, see, for example, Zuber (2006).
18 As I have already remarked, one of the characteristics of this literature is a rather prolific generation of competing concepts. See, among others, Gillis (1994) and Winter and Sivan (1999).
19 http://www.aprodeh.org.pe/ojoquellora2006/index.html.
20 On historical consciousness in Peru, see Drinot (2004).
21 A study of this massacre is included in the Final report of the Peruvian Truth and Reconciliation Commission; see: http://www.cverdad.org.pe/ifinal/pdf/TOMO%20VII/Casos%20Ilustrativos-UIE/2.68.%20Penal%20CASTRO%20CASTRO.pdf.
22 Inter-American Court of Human Rights, Case of the Miguel Castro-Castro Prison against Peru, Judgment of November 25, 2006, p. 167. Available at: www.corteidh.or.cr.

23 Inter-American Court of Human Rights, Case of the Miguel Castro-Castro Prison against Peru, Judgment of November 25, 2006, p. 167. Available at: www.corteidh.or.cr.
24 *Perú21*, 31 December 2006.
25 *Perú21*, 10 January 2007.
26 *Perú21*, 2 January 2007.
27 *Perú21*, 31 December 2006.
28 *Correo*, 8 January 2007.
29 http://martintanaka.blogspot.com/2007/01/comunicado-de-responsables-de-el-ojo.html.
30 See 'Concurring Opinion of Judge A. A. Cançado Trindade'. Available at www.corteidh.or.cr.
31 *Perú21*, 9 January 2007.
32 *El Comercio*, 5 January 2007.
33 *La República*, 5 January 2007.
34 *Correo*, 11 January 2007.
35 *La República*, 18 January 2007.
36 *Correo*, 20 January 2007.
37 *La República*, 15 January 2007.
38 *La República*, 17 January 2007.
39 *La República*, 17 January 2007.
40 *El País*, 16 January 2007.
41 *El Comercio*, 16 January 2007.
42 An excellent introduction to the study of violence is Scheper-Hughes and Bourgeois (2007). For a somewhat different use of the concept of ontologies of violence, see Kalyvas (2003).
43 On violence as a 'mode of production', see Taussig (1987).
44 On the everydayness of violence, see, among others, Scheper-Hughes (1992) and Koonings and Kruijt (1999).
45 *Washington Post*, 1 July 2008.
46 See http://www.aprodeh.org.pe/fosas/index.html.

References

Bourke, Joanna. 2004. Remembering War. *Journal of Contemporary History* 39 (4): 473–85.

Carrier, Peter. 2005. *Holocaust Monuments and National Memory Cultures in France and Germany Since 1989: The Origins and the Political Function of the Vél d'Hiv in Paris and the Holocaust Monument in Berlin*. Oxford: Berghan.

Carrión, Julio. 2006. *The Fujimori Legacy: The Rise of Electoral Authoritarianism in Peru*. University Park: Pennsylvania State University Press.

Conaghan, Catherine M. 2005. *Fujimori's Peru: Deception in the Public Sphere*. Pittsburgh: Pittsburgh University Press.

Croci, Federico, and Giovanni Bonfiglio. 2002. *El baúl de la memoria: testimonios escritos de inmigrantes italianos en el Perú*. Lima: Fondo Editorial del Congreso del Perú.

Degregori, Carlos Iván. 2004. Heridas abiertas, derechos esquivos: Reflexiones sobre la Comisión de la Verdad y la Reconciliación. In *Memorias en conflicto: Aspectos de la violencia política contemporánea*, edited by Raynald Belay, Jorge Bracamonte, Carlos Iván Degregori, and Jean Joinville Vacher. Lima: PUCP/IEP/IFEA.

Degregori, Carlos Iván, and Elizabeth Jelin, eds. 2003. *Jamás tan cerca arremetió lo lejos: memoria y violencia política en el Perú*. Lima: Instituto de Estudios Peruanos.

Drinot, Paulo. 2004. Historiography, Historiographic Identity and Historical Consciousness in Peru. *Estudios Interdisciplinarios de América Latina y el Caribe* 15 (1): 65–88.

Durand, Anahí. 2005. *Donde habita el olvido: Los (h)usos de la memoria y la crisis del movimiento social en San Martín*. Lima: Fondo Editorial de la Facultad de Ciencias Sociales.

Gillis, John R., ed. 1994. *Commemorations: The Politics of National Identity*. Princeton: Princeton University Press.

Hamann, Marita. 2003. *Batallas por la memoria: Antagonismos de la promesa peruana*. Lima: PUCP/IEP.

Hite, Katherine. 2007. The Eye that Cries: The Politics of Representing Victims. *Contracorriente* 5 (1): 108–34.

Huyssen, Andreas. 2000. Present Pasts: Media, Politics, Amnesia. *Public Culture* 12 (1): 21–38.

Jiménez, Edilberto. 2005. *Chungui: Violencia y trazos de memoria*. Lima: COMISEDH.

Juliá, Santos. 2006. Bajo el imperio de la memoria. *Revista de Occidente* 303–304: 7–19.

Kalyvas, Stathis. 2003. The Ontology of 'Political Violence': Action and Identity in Civil Wars. *Perspectives on Politics* 1 (3): 475–94.

Kansteiner, Wulf. 2002. Finding Meaning in Memory: A Methodological Critique of Collective Memory Studies. *History and Theory* 41: 179–97.

Kaulicke, Peter. 2001. *Memoria y muerte en el Perú antiguo*. Lima: PUCP.

Klein, Kerwin Lee. 2000. On the Emergence of *Memory* in Historical Discourse. *Representations* 69: 127–50.

Koonings, Kees, and Dirk Kruijt. 1999. *Societies of Fear: The Legacy of Civil War, Violence and Terror in Latin America*. London: Verso.

Lerner, Salomón. 2004. *La rebelión de la memoria: Selección de discursos, 2001–2003*. Lima: IDEHPUCP.

Majluf, Natalia. 1994. *Escultura y espacio público. Lima 1850–1879*. Lima: IEP.

Millones, Luis, and Wilfredo Kapsoli. 2001. *La memoria de los ancestros*. Lima: Fondo Editorial Ricardo Palma.

Milton, Cynthia E. 2007. At the Edge of the Peruvian Truth Commission: Alternative Paths to Recounting the Past. *Radical History Review* 98: 3–33.

Moser, Caroline O. N., and Cathy McIlwaine. 2004. *Encounters with Violence in Latin America: Urban Poor Perceptions from Colombia and Guatemala*. London: Routledge.

Nelson, Robert S., and Margaret Olin, eds. 2003. *Monuments and Memory, Made and Unmade*. Chicago: Chicago University Press.

Nora, Pierre. 1989. Between Memory and History: les Lieux de Mémoire. *Representations* 26: 7–24.

Olick, Jeffrey K., and Joyce Robbins. 1998. Social Memory Studies: From 'Collective Memory' to the Historical Sociology of Mnemonic Practices. *Annual Review of Sociology* 24: 105–40.

Quilter, Jeffrey, and Gary Urton, eds. 2002. *Narrative Threads: Accounting and Recounting in Andean Khipu*. Austin: University of Texas Press.

Romero, Raúl. 2005. *Identidades múltiples: Memoria, modernidad, y cultura popular en el Valle del Mantaro*. Lima: Fondo Editorial del Congreso del Perú.

Scheper-Hughes, Nancy, and Philippe Bourgois, eds. 2004. *Violence in War and Peace: An Anthology*. Oxford: Blackwell.
Schepher-Hughes, Nancy. 1992. *Death Without Weeping: The Violence of Everyday Violence in Brazil*. Berkeley: University of California Press.
Stern, Steve J., ed. 1998. *Shining and Other Paths: War and Society in Peru, 1980–1995*. Durham: Duke University Press.
Taussig, Michael. 1987. *Shamanism, Colonialism and the Wild Man*. Chicago: University of Chicago Press.
Theidon, Kimberly. 2003. Disarming the Subject: Remembering War and Imagining Citizenship in Peru. *Cultural Critique* 54: 67–87.
Watanabe, José, Amelia Morimoto, and Oscar Chamba. 1999. *La memoria del ojo: Cien años de presencia japonesa en el Perú*. Lima: Fondo Editorial del Congreso del Perú.
Winter, Jay, and Emmanuel Sivan, eds. 1999. *War and Remembrance in the Twentieth Century*. Cambridge: Cambridge University Press.
Yauri Montero, Marcos. 2006. *Laberintos de la memoria: Reinterpretación de relatos orales y mitos andinos*. Lima: Fondo Editorial del Pedagógico de San Marcos.
Young, James E. 2003. *The Texture of Memory: Holocaust Memorials and Meaning*. Yale: Yale University Press.
Zizek, Slajov. 2008. *Violence: Six Sideways Reflections*. London: Profile Books.
Zuber, Devin. 2006. Flanerie at Ground Zero: Aesthetic Countermemories in Lower Manhattan. *American Quarterly* 58 (2): 269–99.

Mariano Mestman

THE LAST SACRED IMAGE OF THE LATIN AMERICAN REVOLUTION

> 'In certain rare cases, the tragedy of a man's death completes and exemplifies the meaning of his entire life.'
> (John Berger, 1967/1968)
>
> 'Che's brutally eloquent ending was like a flash of lightning that suddenly illuminated his whole admirable trajectory.'
> (John William Cooke, 1967/1968)

Some of the most widely circulated political images of recent years are those of Ernesto Che Guevara. And much has been said about the constantly renovated significance that those images acquired over the time and spaces within which they were disseminated. With regard to the iconic photographs, comment has focused on the enormous gulf between the political and cultural topography of the epoch in which they were captured and that of the subsequent periods in which they were (and are) deployed or received. Similarly, criticism has concentrated on the ideological emptying of the Guevara epic as a result of contemporary consumption of the posters, T-shirts, cups, stamps and postcards that have proliferated as part of the culture industry's uses and abuses of Che Guevara's image.[1]

Although a multitude of these images spread to many parts of the world, there were two which, for fundamentally different if not openly opposed reasons and political motives, were particularly widely distributed in the years immediately after Che's death. One is Alberto (Díaz Gutiérrez) Korda's famous photograph of Guevara wearing a beret with a five-pointed star and staring fixedly into the distance; the other, the photograph of Guevara's corpse lying in a stretcher atop a large concrete sink in the laundry room at Vallegrande Hospital, to where it was taken after his execution in La Higuera. There are many versions of the latter photograph, but the most well-known is Bolivian press photographer Freddy Alborta's shot, in which Guevara's body is surrounded by Bolivian soldiers and other journalists (figure 1).

Whereas the first was embraced by an entire generation as a symbol of the rebellious spirit of Revolution, appeared on the flags and banners of anti-establishment movements and was incorporated within the collective visual memory of political struggle from the 1960s onwards, the second (in its various versions), although not so durable, was equally as significant in that it was instantly transmitted as a radiophoto and hit the front pages of the world's press immediately after Che's demise; indeed, its intention was to prove that Guevara had been captured and killed.

FIGURE 1 Fotograph by Freddy Alborta, 1967.

Two documentaries made some time after what could be called the 'Che epoch' (or the extended sixties) utilized these photographs. Although stylistically different, they share the merit of recording the testimonies of the photographers who took those iconic images.

In *Una foto recorre el mundo* (*A Photo Travels the World* – 1981), filmmaker Pedro Chaskel examines the photograph Korda took at a 5 March 1960 event in Havana to commemorate those killed when the boat 'La Coubre' was sabotaged. At the very beginning of the documentary, Korda tells of the moment in which he took the picture: as he scanned those present on the podium, Che's face (in the second row) suddenly loomed large in the viewfinder, causing such a profound impression that Korda jumped backwards, as if in fright, pressing the shutter as he did so. This was the profound impact caused by an already legendary figure.

Similarly, when Freddy Alborta photographed the corpse in October 1967, Che was in many ways an already 'mythical' figure, says the photographer, known all around the world. In this case, the impact on the photographer is bound up with the context within which the picture was taken: at the public presentation of the body to the national and international press, in an event staged by the Bolivian authorities. And it is on this image that artist and filmmaker Leandro Katz focuses in *El día que me quieras* (*The Day You'll Love Me* – 1997), fracturing it to thus comprehend its potency.

Through his research for the film, Katz rediscovers the authorship of an image that circulated for many years as news agency property but which, even having fulfilled its allotted function as a press shot within the mass media's rules and regulations of organization and distribution, remains the work of one photographer, Alborta, who reclaims his role and reveals other photographs taken at Vallegrande. Katz's camera reconstructs the labour behind the iconic image: the quotidian ritual of the photojournalist revealing carefully preserved negatives, but no longer to sell them for $75 dollars to an eager agency hoping to be the first to hit the headlines, but rather to explore the more obscure elements of that infamous event.

On the basis of the testimony of Alborta as a prime witness (the value of which is heightened further by his recent death), the film re-examines some of the least well-known and unexplained aspects of Che's final hours to which the photographic focus inexorably draws the eye. Because of their explicitness, many of these aspects had until then not formed the principal focus of any previous investigations, at least not visual studies.[2] Katz's exploration of the margins and minute details of this image unlocks the photographer's memories of that transcendental moment in his (and world) history: the glances exchanged between those present, Che's mysteriously covered left hand, the bodies of other guerrillas on the floor, the staging of the event for journalists, the photographer's perspective, the aesthetic resonance with great works of universal art.[3]

Umberto Eco[4] included the photograph of Che's corpse amongst his selection of 'photos that made an age'; images transformed into myths and multivalent discursive metaphors; images that echo with other images, from both the past and the future; photos, paintings and posters that transcend their protagonists and subjects to express broader concepts, which function not as description, but as explanation; symbols engendering reality and moving fluidly between the politico-public and private spheres; a type of image which, 'at its very genesis, commences its communicative mission'.

In this analysis, the 'genesis' occurs in the moments following Che Guevara's death and in the final years of the 1960s, the period on which we will concentrate, seeing the significance of these images oscillate, in the case of Argentina, between the insurrectional impetus of revolution and the repressive logic of the security forces in Latin America.

I.

A few short hours after the capture and execution of Ernesto Guevara (8–9 October 1967), Vallegrande Hospital's laundry was transformed into an improvized third-world-style morgue. The next day reporters arrived to certify the death, fulfilling an essential function of press *photography*, with its truth effect and reality effect that, once converted into a press *photo*, inform about and verify the events.

This, as we already know, was the objective of the Bolivian government and the US agents; hence the swift conveyance by airplane of journalists, photographers and cameramen; hence the careful preparation of the corpse, the open eyes, the elevated head, the placing of a magazine shot of Che's face in life next to the dead body to facilitate an unequivocal comparison. These methods of public authentification fell short of the official identification that an event of such magnitude called for, but they nevertheless bore worldwide witness to Che's demise and thus, it was believed, signalled the end of insurrection in Latin America.

It is within this cramped cloister that Alborta moves with such care, looking for propitious angles and appropriate perspectives with which to frame a body that had made such a profound impression upon him. The gaze seemed almost alive and Alborta was overcome with the sense that he was looking at the body of a Christ-like figure.

We could argue that this figure, a Che referring to a Christ, does not emerge only from the composition of the film and photographic images taken at Vallegrande, such as Alborta's, but also, and fundamentally, from the referent itself, from the body's arrangement, its method of display, the preparation of both body and face; despite the fact that those interventions were designed with wholly different objectives in mind.

There are other images, taken just a few hours before the execution at La Higuera, in which Che appears standing, solemn, somewhere between crestfallen and furious, with dishevelled and dirty clothes and hair, part of his face obscured by a shadow that seems to extend his beard down his open shirt, being led with his hands cuffed before him. This is Che portrayed as a criminal or a bandit, not a political prisoner or a revolutionary. And then in the laundry at Vallegrande, next to his stretchered body lying prone on the concrete sink, are the corpses of two other guerrillas who were captured alive and then murdered at La Higuera: Willy and 'el Chino'. Inevitably, their presence is barely registered, but in some photographs and films they can be seen dumped on the floor, one beside the other, with the same dust and dirt on their faces and tattered clothes as when they were captured.

In contrast, Che had been carefully prepared by his captors before being displayed to the press. His body had been washed, his hair combed, his beard had even been trimmed and, as we have already mentioned, his eyes were opened to aid identification. But in that moment an unexpected effect was observed: 'A total metamorphosis' says Castañeda: '[Che] was transformed into the Christ of Vallegrande, reflecting in his limpid open eyes the utter peace of a willing sacrifice. The Bolivian army committed the only error of its campaign after it had already secured the most prized war trophy; it transformed the trapped and vanquished revolutionary, the indigent of la Quebrada del Yuro, utterly beaten, wrapped in rags and with shadows of rage and defeat obscuring his face, into a Christ-like image of life after death. By taking his life, Che's executioners imprinted a body a face and a soul on the myth that would travel the world (…)'.[5]

Castañeda and other biographers have commented on the swift spread of the physical comparison with Jesus Christ by those local people who had come before the corpse. This primary testimony would accompany the photographic and film images on their journeys around the world.

The images of the corpses of Willy and 'el Chino' seem to offer testament to the victims of war, anonymous entities frozen in a moment in time without, in this case, the least semblance of bureaucratic order to guarantee individuality. In contrast, the image of Che's body, although fulfilling the testimonial function we have already mentioned, also assumes an important evocative power.

II.

In later years a number of authors recovered the resonance, initially proposed by John Berger immediately after the execution, between the radiophoto of Che's corpse (figure 1) and Rembrandt's *The Anatomy Lesson of Doctor Nicolaes Tulp* and Mantegna's *Lamentation over the Dead Christ*[6] (figures 2 and 4).

Martine Joly,[7] for example, placed it alongside other examples of the deployment of allegory within press photography. In this case, the fundamental iconographic

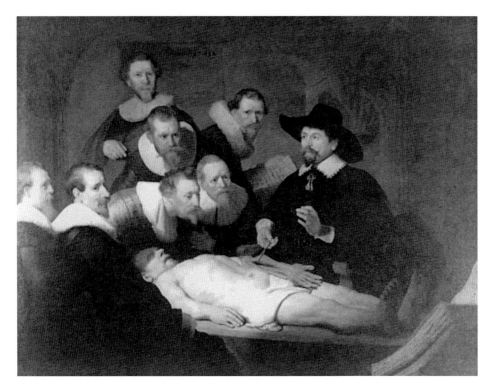

FIGURE 2 Rembrandt. The Anatomy Lesson of Doctor Nicolaes Tulp.

contradiction between the paintings cited leads to a more complex reading of the contemporary image: 'Between sacrifice and dissection, the analysis of Che's death is made more sophisticated by photographic allegory'.

Rocco Mangieri[8] proposes the interaction in the image of three fundamental themes (the mystical-Christian body, the medical-anatomical body, and the body and hunting), which elucidate three meanings: the fallen body of martyrdom, the pious body; the functional body of rational science, the body exposed to autopsy; and the hunted body or trophy. Similarly, Mangieri relates the Bolivian official's signalling of the body in the photo with three types of gaze, corresponding to the themes and meanings cited (the gaze of pity and pain, the analytical gaze and the possessive gaze), which he claims are deployed by many great painters of Western art.

Susan Sontag[9] also comments on the accidental resemblance between these two paintings and the image of Che's body. In her study of photography Sontag observes that, although a photograph's meaning and moral and emotional impact depend upon the context within which it is disseminated, the image's significance will never be fixed; every new contextual use (and particularly political use) of the image unravels the original and previous uses and contexts, which are eventually 'supplanted by subsequent uses – most notably, by the discourse of art into which any photo can be absorbed'. In this context, Sontag cites the radiophoto of Che's body as an example of images that 'right from the start' refer to other images, observing that 'what is compelling about the photograph partly derives from what it shares, as a composition, with these paintings'. Moreover, 'the very extent to which that photograph is

FIGURE 3 Así (magazin), Buenos Aires, October 24, 1967.

unforgettable indicates its potential for being depoliticized, for becoming a timeless image'. In this sense, Sontag recalls Walter Benjamin's interest in the function of the photo caption as an instrument to 'rescue it from the ravages of modishness and confer upon it a revolutionary use value', and portrays Berger's text as an extended caption that seeks to 'firm up the political associations and moral meaning of a photograph that Berger found too satisfying aesthetically, too suggestive iconographically'.

It is pertinent, therefore, to return once more to Berger's text as probably the first attempt to re-interpret the significance of the image in question. Despite the representative intentions of the authorities, Berger suggests that the image's impact was other. By interrogating its significance and establishing the comparisons already mentioned, Berger postulates certain compositional similarities between the photo and the two paintings and, in the case of Rembrandt's painting, also registers a 'functional' resemblance with the photographic image. But alongside the functional, facial and corporeal similarities, Berger also posits an emotional echo between the photograph and Mantegna's painting (figure 4). The sensations that invaded him upon seeing the photograph in the newspaper were very close to what he had imagined a contemporary believer might have felt before Mantegna's *Dead Christ*, adding that:

> When I look at the photograph now, I can only reconstruct my first incoherent emotions. Guevara was no Christ. If I see the Mantegna again in Milan, I shall see in it the body of Guevara. But this is only because in certain rare cases the tragedy of a man's death completes and exemplifies the meaning of his whole life. I am acutely aware of that about Guevara, and certain painters were once aware of it about Christ. That is the degree of emotional correspondence.[10]

These observations on the reactions and reflections of artists and believers – conducted, the author admits, with the help of historical imagination – are interesting because they transport the normal process of pictorial referencing towards a more multi-faceted experience. In other words, a reading focused on the allegorical echoes between the secondary significance of this picture and the paintings already mentioned,[11] fundamentally connected to their compositional (and functional) similarities, could provoke a fundamental reorientation of the photograph's essential sense towards a wholly artistic discourse, thus inhibiting its broad social scope. The cultural fluency required to successfully navigate the allegorical path traced by Joly (calling for the apprehension of a broad swathe of texts that bring known images, comprehended codes and familiar intertextual iconographs into play) is only available to a small part of the world's population, a small section of enlightened individuals with access to universal culture and to a cultural capital that includes, at the very least, knowledge of art history. Nevertheless, alternative readings of the same photograph (or others) in the same context by other receptors, even where these were unfamiliar with the paintings cited, could still engender similar sensations and emotions to those described by Berger. For example, Christian traditions and iconography were elemental influences within Latin American popular culture; hence, the photograph's resonance with representations of the Christ figure could call upon, but fundamentally transcend, knowledge of any particular works of art, tapping instead into the more generalized and extensive iconographic legacy of an imaginative tradition for which the adoration of saints and of the wounded or flagellated Christ was central.

Beyond any possible physical resemblance between an image of Che's body and that of the historical and cultural Christ figure familiar in Western representation, therefore, it is possible to discern the evocation of a more faith- or gospel-inspired Christ and his messianic role and mission.[12]

In this sense, without ignoring the fact that the religious images are redolent with the kind of pain suffered by godlike figures and Christian martyrs, as opposed to the 'just' pain or 'deserved punishment' experienced by 'infidels',[13] it could nevertheless be argued that, within the historical context of public expressions of progressive and even revolutionary tendencies within the Catholic Church, the image of 'Che-Christ' incorporates the necessary features to thus be adopted as a symbol of the fight for regional liberation. I refer here to a possible late 1960s re-signification of this photograph (and its other versions as disseminated by the global press) at the very moment when the life (and death) of Christ was being exposed to a similar re-reading. This period was characterized by political radicalization (Algeria, Cuba, Vietnam, the Third World and May 1968), and a not unrelated religious radicalization that sought to articulate the Church's pastoral mission with revolutionary practice. A decade of dialogue between Catholics and Marxists gave rise to such phenomena as the 'worker priests' and the emergence in Latin America of what would soon be known as Liberation Theology. In 1968, the Latin American Episcopal Conference was held in Medellín. In 1967, the Latin American bishops published their 'options for the poor' and the Colombian guerrilla-priest Camilo Torres was killed in action. Torres, like Che, would soon be converted into a regional symbol (although not of the same magnitude as Guevara).[14] In Argentina, for example, this process crystallized in May 1968 in the union of priests and lay members in the 'Movement of Priests for the Third World', whose message had been articulated and promoted since late 1966 in the pages of *Cristianismo y Revolución* (*Christianity and Revolution*) magazine, edited by ex-seminarist Juan García Elorrio.

At a time when another well-established popular figure – the bandit as the hero of social causes – made his politicized reappearance, it is not surprising that in several Bolivian villages, at the very moment when Che was conducting his guerrilla campaign nearby, a small poster appeared of a Christ-like figure, with matted hair and beard, gazing solemnly and piercingly out and accompanied by a text describing this Christ as an ill-fed working man of the common people who was hunted as a subversive and conspirator against the government of the day.[15]

Within this context, the image of a young, rebellious/revolutionary and even guerrilla Christ[16] takes on great symbolic strength, thus provoking a necessary re-analysis of the conditions in which the images of Che's body were received in Latin America.

Of course, this remains only one of the possible imaginative horizons along which to trace the diverging interpretations of the significance of these photographs. It will always remain difficult to establish with any degree of precision the actual interpretation(s) applied to the image of Che's body, but a more viable analytical option is to examine the different ways in which that image was re-appropriated, for both cultural and political ends in, for example, Argentina in this same period.

III.

During the 1960s the figure of Che Guevara, with his associations to the Cuban Revolution, was an essential reference point for a broad spectrum of progressive or leftist cultural exponents and his execution had an immediate impact upon the work of Argentinean plastic artists.

This was a moment of artistic and political encounter which since the mid-1960s had given rise to, amongst other things, demonstrations again the US intervention in Vietnam, the infamous censorship of León Ferrari's entry for the 1965 Di Tella prize, *La civilización occidental y Cristiana* (*Western Christian Civilization*), and, between April and May of 1966, the collective exhibition in the Van Riel Gallery *Homenaje al Vietnam* (*Homage to Vietnam*) that brought together more than 200 artists from various aesthetic and political positions.

The military regime came to power in Argentina in June 1966 in the so-called 'Argentinean Revolution'. From the end of 1967 onwards a number of works, performances and collective exhibitions focused on the figure of Che were carried out with the participation of artists from many different aesthetic tendencies. These often presented images of Che in life, as a leader of the Cuban Revolution, as a 'heroic guerrilla', and were often interrupted by the censors.

As well as inspiring the first of two important collective exhibitions dedicated to Che held at the Sociedad Argentina de Artistas Plásticos (SAAP – Argentinean Association of Plastic Artists) in 1967 and 1968, Korda's image (or similar or allusive images, often put together *ad hoc*) was utilized (often in textiles or poster form) by divergent creators of political art at the time such as León Ferrari, Carlos Alonso, Ricardo Carpani, Antonio Berni and Roberto Jacoby.

In contrast to many of the other artists, Jacoby permitted himself a subtle provocation: within a special publication consisting of a 'magazine-envelope' containing leaflets, documents and comics on the contemporary political and cultural situation, Jacoby inserted an 'anti-poster'. Against a red background in the uppermost third of the poster, the artist placed a black and white reproduction of Korda's photograph accompanied by a simple but ingeniously challenging white text: 'A guerrilla doesn't die so you can stick him on the wall'.

Beyond this exceptional deployment (with all its precocious perspicacity), it is understandable that these images of Che were the most widely used in social struggles and political art of the period. But the image of Che's dead body was also utilized, both allusively and directly, as homage and as denunciation, with the work of Carlos Alonso offering some particular interesting examples.

By the end of the 1960s Alonso had incorporated the main themes of Argentina's social and political reality into his work and had been actively involved in collective exhibitions such as those organized by SAAP, on whose executive committee he sat. Having followed the path of committed art in the 1950s and 1960s, 1967 saw Alonso distance himself from the Communist Party, of which he had been a member for many years, in the wake of the polemic stirred up by his daring look at the mangled body of the final phase of his one-time teacher Lino Enea Spilimbergo, who had died three years previously.

In subsequent years, and particularly in 1969 and 1971, Alonso returned often to the images from Vallegrande. He remembers being particularly drawn to photographs that appeared in Buenos Aires magazines such as the sensationalist *Así*, notable for the prominence it gave to the images and whose 24 October 1967 edition included, on both the front cover and the interior pages, three photos of Che's body at Vallegrande alongside either local villagers or military agents (figure 3).[17]

Unlike other artworks dealing with Che's death,[18] Alonso does not focus on the Christ-like dimension of those images. Although the representation of Che's body is

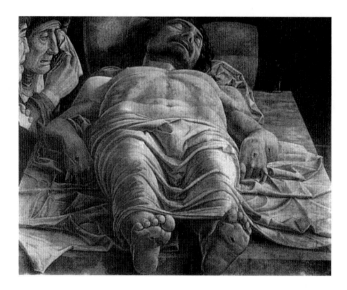

FIGURE 4 Mantegna. Lamentation over the Dead Christ.

sometimes evocative of the physical positioning of Christ's corpse, in general it is the analytical gaze that predominates, related to the reinterpretation of Rembrandt's 'anatomy lessons' already mentioned.[19] A number of Alonso's paintings, studies and sketches (pencil drawings, watercolours, inks, acrylics and collages) are testament to this exploration towards and encounter with Rembrandt's legacy in the series that Alonso entitled *La lección de Anatomía* (*The Anatomy Lesson*).

Along this trajectory, a number of works engage directly with the scene at Vallegrande, placing emphasis on its testimonial dimension and recording the media images taken there: Che's body, the soldiers and villagers, coming either closer or further away than they appeared in the original press photographs, such as in the drawing entitled *Che Guevara* (1970)[20] or in some of the more sophisticated paintings of those and subsequent years in which a heavily armed soldier accompanies Che's body (as if registering responsibility for the death) or in which the space is split between two opposing poles: soldiers and villagers, the latter portrayed on the frontier between lamentation and agitation (figure 5).[21] In *Che*,[22] despite the fact that the setting and the positioning of the principal characters is different from those in the photographs, the reference to Vallegrande remains significant.

Emerging from this exploration is an explicit link between the studies of Che's body and Alonso's series on meat.[23] In the drawing *Carne Argentina* (1970 – *Argentinean Meat*), for example, we see a cargo container (stamped with the words 'CARNE ARGENTINA') within which the inert body of Che lies on a stretcher with head raised and gaze meeting that of the spectator (figure 7). His hair is held by one soldier, who points at the body as if at captured prey, whilst alongside the body another two soldiers hold a photo of Che's face in life to enable unequivocal identification.[24]

By far the most disturbing renditions of the images of Che's body are achieved through deployment of the Rembrandtean legacy, the principal inspiration being *The Anatomy Lesson of Doctor Nicolaes Tulp*. In some instances there are no references to the incidents in Bolivia (the body is not that of Che, but of other, anonymous individuals

FIGURE 5 Carlos Alonso. Che Guevara (1970).

who are alive, are being tortured, or simply lie prone; the body of a woman in a sensual pose, a sick and malnourished child), in others – even where the body is still not Guevara's – other characters around Tulp and his disciples (such as soldiers) or landscapes (a line of mountains on the horizon) do have a clear resonance with the Bolivian scene.

Amongst those works in which the bodies and faces are more easily identifiable as Guevara's and, amongst the numerous sketches (from 1969–1970) in multiple techniques that were shown in the Buenos Aires (1971) and Rome (1977) exhibitions already mentioned, two large canvases merit further comment.[25]

In the first (figure 6), the foreshortened and naked figure appears in the foreground, upon the stretcher and sink, open and bleeding from chest to waist. Behind the stretcher, the phantasmagorical silhouettes of Dr Tulp (who is lifting Che's legs) and five of his disciples, (dressed in clothes and taking up poses analogous to Rembrandt's painting) lean over the body. In the centre of the painting, Alonso introduces a contemporary figure: a nurse wearing the customary cap and surgical mask. The silhouettes' positions are redolent of the theatrical poses captured by Rembrandt, but Alonso makes them almost caricaturesque, with pop influences and bright comic-like colours.[26]

In the other painting the position of the body is different and the overall scene shares more similarities with that of Vallegrande. The characters circle the lacerated and bleeding body of Che, with the viscera exposed as in *The Anatomy Lesson of Doctor Nicolaes Tulp*. The nurse appears once more, although more hidden behind Dr Tulp, wearing the same cap and mask and carrying a scalpel. Alongside, a medical machine connected by hosepipe to the tap on the sink circulates the blood of the body that lies

FIGURE 6 Carlos Alonso. La lección de anatomía.

prone in the stretcher. The clothes of two of the other figures identify them as Tulp's disciples but, unlike in the previous painting, these do not simply observe, but rather carry out the tasks of identification conducted by the Bolivian security forces in Vallegrande: one holds up a photo of Che's face in life (alluding to one of the images of Che's death that appeared in the press), another takes fingerprints from Che's right hand. Tulp also fulfils a similar role. Unlike in Rembrandt's canvas, in which Tulp uses pincers held in his right hand to extract the viscera, here Tulp holds the pincers in his left hand, raised towards his hat in a pompous gesture, whilst the index finger of his right hand points towards the wounds on the body, much like the Bolivian colonel in the press photo. Moreover, Alonso brings in other characters from Vallegrande: soldiers appear in the background and, next to Dr Tulp, a photographer is caught in the very act of taking the infamous shots.

Within this fascinating dialogue with Rembrandt and with the media images of Che's body, Alonso makes overt reference to the latter by framing his composition within a kind of television screen upon which can be seen part of the stretcher and the sink, Che's feet and the nurse's white apron in the foreground and part of one of the disciple's hats and the photographer's shoes at either side. In a similar vein, Antonio Berni made reference to the TV transmission of the scene at Vallegrande in a collage-painting produced in the same period. Che's body (accompanied in the background

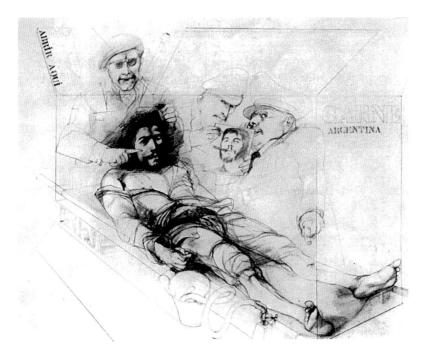

FIGURE 7 Carlos Alonso. Carne Argentina (1970).

by the prostrate body of one of the other executed guerrillas) appears on a TV screen in the centre of the piece highlighted with garish fuchsia and orange contours and surrounded by the cadaverous and monstrous faces and profiles of armed soldiers and authority figures.[27]

As was to be expected, one of the first pieces from the *Anatomy Lesson* series, presented in 1969 at the 'Panorama de la Pintura Argentina II' (2nd Panorama of Argentinean Painting), organized by the Lorenzutti Foundation, was censored on the orders of the Ministry of Culture.

1969 also saw Alonso taking an active part in collective pieces and exhibitions such as the 'Hambre, basta' (Stop Hunger) mural and the 'Villa Quinteros también es América' (Villa Quinteros is America Too) and 'Malvenido Rockefeller' (Unwelcome Rockefeller) exhibitions. All are examples of artists tackling political topics at a time when the articulation of both spheres was widespread. But Alonso's Anatomy Lesson series goes much further, placing the aesthetic dimension at the very hub of the nexus between art and politics. Through its incorporation of the political pulse of the day into an ongoing dialogue with art history (as with his introduction of elements that evoke both the Holocaust and the war in Vietnam whilst also echoing the representation of hell in The Divine Comedy) and its anchorage in the solidity of a classic (in terms of theme, compositional strength, dramatic arrangement and the narrative of Rembrandtean group portraits), thus stimulating the kind of cultural mediation and concomitant cathartic distance necessary to 'comprehend' the representation of Che's death as an enunciatory image of the fundamental tensions in Latin America, Alonso's series is revealed as by far the most systematic and meritorious aesthetic examination of those infamous images of Che Guevara's dead body.

IV.

It is somewhat difficult to measure the social importance of these works of art in that period; their impact was simultaneously inhibited and stimulated by the prevalent censorship of the day. What can be analysed with more ease, however, is the clandestine circulation in the years immediately following Che's death of a masterpiece of political cinema: *La hora de los hornos* (*The Hour of the Furnaces*) (1968) by Fernando Pino Solanas and Octavio Getino, which includes some of the images taken at Vallegrande at a critical moment in the film.

The film last more than four hours and is divided into three parts, distinguished by their structure, theme and even purpose. The title comes from a quote by the Cuban national hero, José Martí, adopted by Che Guevara in his message to the Tricontinental: 'Now is the time of furnaces and only light shall be seen'.

The images of Che's body and face, which in this instance are televisual images 'recuperated' for use in political cinema, appear at the end of the first part of the film and fulfil a pivotal role, illustrating the most viable option for an impoverished and dependent Latin America. The final scene of this section begins with hand-held camera footage of the funeral procession of a poor peasant in northern Argentina. Suddenly, the screen goes black and the voice-over – fulfilling the fundamental narrative role, as in an exposé documentary – asks the viewer: 'What is the only option left to Latin Americans?' The camera then scans over Che's body in the stretcher, moving upwards from the feet to the head to then pause and switch to a montage of Che's face which lasts for several frames. The next image shows half of the room (the upper part of Che's body and his face remain visible), with two soldiers in the top corners, as if on guard, and the centre occupied by local villagers who circle around the body. In the next scene the camera pans away from the lifeless bodies of Willy and 'el Chino' lying on the floor and moves towards Che's body on the concrete sink; there it freezes in a pan shot which shows a photographer (not Alborta) standing on top of the sink, as if on Che's body itself, taking pictures of the corpse. The voice-over answers its own question: 'Choose, with rebellion, its own life, its own death. When joining the fight for liberation, death ceases to be the final destination; death becomes liberation, conquest. He who chooses his own death also chooses a life'. Finally, the image of Che's dead face appears, looking forwards, occupying the full screen and staying for several minutes as if staring at the camera as the soundtrack plays the final phrase ('With rebellion, Latin America recovers its very existence') before ceding to a persistent percussion that accompanies the image of that face, interrogating the viewer with its gaze (figure 8).

For the directors – one-time leftist intellectuals who, by the time the film was made, had moved towards the political position of revolutionary Peronism – these images of Che occupied a pivotal point between the first part of the film (a denunciation of Latin American dependence) and the second (the history of what they considered to be Argentina's liberation movement, Peronism, and particularly the experiences of the so-called 'Resistance').

In a late-1969 letter to Alfredo Guevara (then head of the Cuban Film Institute – ICAIC), Solanas explains some of the messages that those scenes were intended to transmit and makes suggestions about the film's screening in Cuba, in what seems to be the Argentinean filmmaker's response to an earlier suggestion from the Cuban that the images of Che's corpse be removed for the Cuban screening.[28]

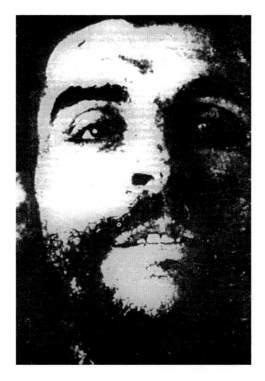

FIGURE 8 La hora de los hornos/The hour of the furnaces (Solanas y Getino, 1968).

The complete excision of the sequence was impossible, the director insisted, since its message was fundamental to the film: 'the choice facing Latin America is the possibility of saving itself by choosing its own life and death'. In this sense the scene would deliver 'a provocative shock' in those countries where images of Che's body had been widely distributed as the kind of evidential tokens already mentioned. The image of the photographer straddling the corpse would have a particularly potent impact, clearly demonstrating 'the total dehumanization of the enemy in the face of the total humanization of Che, who stares out at us with a vivid gaze, even after death. An expression that synthesizes the phrase "WHEREVER DEATH SURPRISES US, WELCOME IT WILL BE", etc.'. Hence, the sequence would have 'fundamental importance' and 'far from oppressing or depressing, it will LIBERATE, STIMULATE, *MOBILIZE*, CHALLENGE PASSIVITY'.

These themes of provocation and accusation of spectatorial passivity resonate with experimental cultural tendencies at the time, in Argentina and internationally, which included debates on cinematographic form and took inspiration from 'manifestation-appeals' such as that contained in Frantz Fanon's phrase: 'Every spectator is a coward or a traitor'.[29] Fundamentally, however, as is perceived in the voice-over narration that accompanies this part of the film or as can be read in the letter from Solanas, the meaning attributed to those sequences is constructed upon imaginative foundations, upon an epochal discourse that brings guerrilla heroism and Christian martyrdom together.[30] In light of this, and bearing the conditions described in section II of this article in mind, therefore, we can conclude that the figure of *Che-Christ* remained valid within political cinema's exhortation to Latin American viewers (both real and potential) to launch revolutionary action.[31] And although at the end of the letter Solanas concedes that the image of the photographer standing over Che's body could be cut for the Cuban screening, he insists on leaving the rest of the sequence in place as 'the conclusion towards which the whole film flows'.

We are witnessing the introduction of a highly emotional and profoundly passionate dimension from where this film engages with the debate about the significance of those images and about the actual details of Che Guevara's death. Unlike other artistic-political uses of or references to the film footage or photographs of Che's body, this film opted to completely exclude any images that could add weight to the interpretation of this event as 'a defeat for that struggle and a victory for the *gorilas*' (anti-Peronists) (as stated in Solanas's letter), such as those of the Bolivian soldiers alongside the body. Instead, the film emphasizes those images of the peasants circling the body, caught between simple curiosity and outright veneration. Although displaying a quite different spatial logic, the body of Christ is similarly surrounded by peasants in the Mantegna painting with which Berger established the aforementioned compositional and emotional resonance.

At the end of the 1960s and within the context outlined above, therefore, the use of these images in Solanas and Getino's film does not invite viewers to venerate the figure of Che in its own right, but rather pay homage to him as a viable example to follow, despite his death, at a time of resurgent class struggle in Argentina and across the region.

Nevertheless, this remains only one visual option amongst many. Whereas these images may well have served the Argentinean directors' aims to do nothing less than inflame regional insurrection, and, in this sense, share a broad platform with the Cuban Revolution, Caribbean filmmakers were interested in promoting a different image of Che, convinced that the footage of the photographer straddling his body and indeed any images of his corpse could become a powerful symbol of defeat. But this was not the only reason for these divergent deployments of the images.

Documentary maker Santiago Alvarez[32] recalls the 'fierce discussions' that leading figures in Cuban cinema had about the Argentinean film, suggesting that most did not agree with the way in which the images of Che's body had been utilized: 'We're talking about ideas we had about displaying images of Che's corpse and the way it was presented at the end of the first part of the film. That deathly face, the open eyes, staring at the camera; it all seemed very violent to me.' Alvarez, who reported from some of the bloodiest areas of conflict of that period, (particularly Vietnam) remembers many discussions in those years about images of slain martyrs and fallen heroes, suggesting that there were basically 'two positions'. The Vietnamese, he says, utterly abhorred those images, the Cubans did not. And yet, back in Cuba and involved in the arguments about the projection of pictures of Che's body, Alvarez found himself using many Vietnamese-type arguments: 'When we were in Vietnam with the news service (ICAIC), they used to ask us why we insisted on showing images of the wounded or of dead bodies, that it wasn't appropriate [...]. They were very reluctant to let us film even a single dead body. And we would try to convince them that those images would be very useful in the forums at which the Vietnam War was being discussed [...]. But later, when we discussed the images of Che's body, although the circumstances were different, it seemed as if we had come around to the Vietnamese way of seeing things.'[33]

Other Cuban filmmakers, directly and indirectly involved in the debates of the time, believe that the images of Che's corpse could provoke confusing sensations of defeat, aggression and violence which, far from mobilizing viewers, would do much harm. Director Octavio Cortázar, for example, suggests that: 'the images of the photographer who, with such utter irreverence, had climbed astride Che's body and was taking photos of him, and that terrible image of Che with his eyes open, could actually do real damage to the sensibilities of the Cuban people. Those images were too violent to show even in countries where Che had no special connotation [...]. For us Che was a symbol of revolutionary triumph, a beautiful man who was deeply cherished and respected by our people. That image was so violent; you have to understand that it was very important for us to treasure other memories of him.'[34]

To comprehend this attitude we must bear in mind that other images of Che Guevara held pride of place in the Caribbean imagination: those of René Burri and Alberto Korda, and many of the others that are known around the world and on which we have already commented. Moreover, Cuban cinema had accumulated many moving images of Che during the 1960s. According to director José Massip, commenting in early 1968 in *Cine Cubano* magazine (no. 47), held in the archives of ICAIC and of the Cuban Radio Institute (ICR), there were three principal groups of cinematographic material about Che: speeches, overseas travel and images of his life in Cuba. It was these types of images and representations that were screened in Cuba in the years following Che's death.

It is understandable, therefore, that the conclusion of the first part of *La hora de los hornos* was uncomfortable for filmmakers and senior officials in Cuba both as a symbol of defeat and as a catalyst for aggression, as discussed above.[35] They were able to reject the film's conclusion because of the reservoir of alternative images in which Che appeared as a vital force, a man who, from the very outset, worked in word and action for and on behalf of the Cuban Revolution. This Che as 'leader', 'builder'[36] and 'heroic guerrilla', as portrayed in Korda's photograph so charged with symbolic power, was an appropriate foundation from where to promote Revolutionary continuity, notwithstanding Che's own death.

Although Korda's photograph was also widely and consistently used in Argentina, particularly in the spheres of cultural production, in no way does this overshadow the prevalence and potency of the image of Che's corpse in important works of Argentinean art, such as those we have already discussed.

V.

It was also during those years that some voices were raised about political risk involved in delegating responsibility for necessarily collective processes of social transformation to individual heroes. Discussing his story 'Un oscuro día de justicia' ('A Dark Day of Justice'), completed just one month after Che's death, writer and journalist Rodolfo Walsh[37] recalls the references in the text to the supreme lesson for 'the people': finding themselves alone and burdened with the concomitant duty to fight against the hope for salvation deposited in 'external heroes'. Walsh considered this lesson applicable in the Argentinean context where salvation was sought either in Peronism or through figures such as Che. Walsh recalls the lamentation following Che's death and the belief that, if only he had still been alive, all would have joined his cause. 'A totally mystical notion [argues Walsh] a myth of one person or one hero making a revolution instead of an entire people coming together in revolution. The supreme expression of the people may well be a hero figure, such as Che Guevara, but [...] no isolated individual, regardless of their stature or standing, can do anything if alone'. Instead, Walsh proposed a search for a 'collective hero': the people, which in many ways he had been elucidating throughout the two previous years on the pages of *Semanario CGT* (*CGT Weekly*), the official publication of the workers' union opposed to the dictatorship of General Onganía.[38]

Myth, sanctity, heroism, sacrifice, the people: the threads of an imaginative tapestry dominated by the figure of Che Guevara; the image of his corpse that resists the simple symbolism of defeat with which the authorities tried to bind it, illuminating instead the praxis of transformation, in the style of a Sorelian myth, perhaps.

John William Cooke[39] began some notes on Che Guevara immediately after the execution at La Higuera, but had not completed them one year later when he himself died in September 1968. The notes are of interest as another skein pulled into the tapestry and alluding again to the image that concerns us in this article. Cooke, a senior official and principal ideologue of revolutionary Peronism, heard of Che's death in London, to where he had travelled after leading the Argentinean delegation in the OLAS (Organization of Latin American Solidarity) Conference in Havana.[40]

In these pages Cooke portrays Che as a common man who rejected heroism as an 'aristocratic prerogative', favouring instead a democratic understanding of the concept based on collective action. Cooke rejects all kind of canonization, seeking instead to insert Che's legacy within ongoing struggles: 'It is our task to ensure that the admiration and respect of the common people is transformed into true knowledge and empathy and is not channelled into any kind of legendary or historical sterility that robs Che of his present truth in favour of the stale immortality of a wax museum.'

Cooke rejects all portrayals of Che as a man 'entranced by death' as interpretations that distort the facts and blur Guevara's true historical importance. Recognizing that Che's experiences of guerrilla warfare meant that death was not unfamiliar, Cooke argues that a true revolutionary (Che or Cooke himself) doesn't look for death, but for victory.

Whilst recognizing that the immediate consequences of Che's death are 'very serious' for revolutionary movements, Cooke elucidates a novel facet of this event that is worth examining: the reaction of the Argentinean working classes to the 'murdered compatriot'. Walsh believes that the emotional impact of the events at La Higuera could lead to Che's incorporation within certain codes of popular culture ('the cult of courage, the disparaging of the law as something alien, imposed on common people "from above", the identification with rebels') along the same lines as 'those heroes from plebeian traditions who live on in memory across the generations'. Cooke recovers, therefore, the 'common approach', turning to it for explanation within 'the models that form part of his cultural baggage' and invoking 'the notion of sanctity applied to the secular' or the characterization of Che by Father Benítez as 'a Christian hero'. In this sense, Cooke believes that 'Che's brutally eloquent ending was like a flash of lightning that suddenly illuminated his whole admirable trajectory, infilling his still diffuse image with the features of a saint or of a hero and establishing thus the intimate link that binds both archetypes with the common people, who recognize in them their own likeness'. For Cooke, therefore, the popular intuition of the common people immediately comprehended the historic gravity of the events at La Higuera.

Alongside these and other observations made before Cooke's death are some notes that the author was never able to elaborate upon. As Horacio Ganzolez has already noted, these demonstrate Cooke's interest in 'the paradoxical themes of destiny and action: the abstraction of historical myth and the praxis with which it is deployed in the interaction of sensibility and death'.[41] In this list of themes one is entitled 'corpse'.[42] Although references to this are scant,[43] it seems likely that if Cooke had been able to conclude his notes, he too would have pondered the significance of the last sacred image of the Latin American revolution.

Acknowledgement

The original version of this text appeared in the review 'Ojos Crueles', *Temas de fotografía y sociedad*, no. 3, Buenos Aires, October 2006.

Notes

1. The Swiss photographer René Burri rediscovered his famous 1963 portrait of a 'triumphant' Che printed on cushions for sale in shops along the Champs-Élysées (cited in: Michel Guerrin, 1988. *Profession Photoreporter*. Paris: Gallimard, 167).
2. These aspects do appear in some biographies, however; see, for example, the brief commentary on some of the photographs in the illustrated book *Che, sueño rebelde*, Buenos Aires: Planeta, 1997, pp. 188–95, text by Matilde Sánchez.
3. Alborta's detailed memories and Katz's careful edition effectively lead the spectator into the scene at Vallegrande: through the scant, but exceptional film clips incorporated into the documentary, through the subtle 'animation' of the image achieved through the overlaying of photos of those surrounding the corpse, through the image of a nurse that 'turns' towards the soldiers, through the picture of Che's face that 'moves forwards' as Alborta recalls the impression the scene made upon him.
4. Umberto Eco. 1986. *La guerre du faux*, in the 'Lire les choses: un photo' section. Paris: Grasset. Cited in: Martine Joly. 2003. *La imagen fija*. Buenos Aires: La Marca, 160–1.
5. Jorge Castañeda. 1998. Muero porque no muero (I die because I won't die). *Cinémas d'Amérique latine* (Toulouse) 6.
6. *Aperture*. 1968. Che Guevara Dead, 13 (4): 36–8.
7. Martine Joly, op. cit., p. 169.
8. Rocco Mangieri. 1998. El cuerpo del Che: el gesto que muestra, el dedo que apunta (Che's body: the gesture that suggests and the finger that aims). *Cuadernos de Investigación y Documentación* 1: 34–9 (Mérida: Universidad de los Andes). My thanks to Gustavo Aprea for pointing me towards this text and for his gracious reading of and comments upon the present article.
9. Susan Sontag. 1996. *Sobre la fotografía* (1977). Barcelona: Edhasa, 116–9 (2002. *On Photography*. London: Penguin Books, 106–8).

10 John Berger, 'Che Guevara Dead', op. cit.
11 Others could include Holbein the Younger's *The Body of the Dead Christ in the Tomb* (see *Che, sueño rebelde*, op. cit., pp. 194–5), Rembrandt's *The Anatomy Lesson of Dr Joan Deyman*, which evokes Mantegna's *Christ*, or others referred to in Mangieri, op. cit.
12 Peter Malone. 1997. Jesus on Our Screens. In *New image of religious film*, edited by John R. May. Kansas City: Sheed and Ward. My thanks to Ricardo Yañez for supplying this text.
13 A point referred to by the artist León Ferrari in his ethical interrogation of the representation of Biblical violence in the frescoes, sculptures and paintings of the great masters of Western art.
14 This opinion was shared by *La Prensa* (Argentine conservative newspaper) (11 October 1967), which compared both deaths in an editorial signed by Carlos Villar-Borda.
15 Poster discovered by Leandro Katz during his research for *El día que me quieras*.
16 According to Beatriz Sarlo, the image of a guerrilla Christ achieved such iconographic status in *Cristianismo y Revolución* that in 1971 the magazine published a small drawing of Christ carrying a rifle. Sarlo describes 'a very young Christ, straight from a Pasolini film (...), a stylized icon or *art deco* drawing, with long straight hair, a perfectly symmetrical beard, head crowned with a saintly halo, face fixed in a steely gaze from squinting eyes (a wholly contemporary image, pop-inspired, heavy on the hippie and rock prophet); he bears an ultra-modern rifle on his shoulder, the geometrically perfect barrel of which forms the clear straight frame of the whole illustration' (2003. *La pasión y la excepción*. Buenos Aires: Siglo XXI, 166–87).
17 Not necessarily taken by Alborta. Following Che's death, most Argentinean newspapers and magazines did not publish the Alborta photo upon which this article focuses. The exception is *La Razón*, which published it (or a similar version) as a United Press radiophoto on 11 October 1967.
18 Juan Carlos Castagnino, in a version of his 1967 *Homenaje al Che* (*Homage to Che*) and in a 1970 poster-homage entitled *Octubre* (*October*), painted a frontal view of Che's foreshortened body and face not as prone, but rather in clear allusion to the crucified Christ. See the catalogue from the *Arte y política en los años sesenta (Art and politics in the 1960s)* exhibition, curated by Alberto Giudici (Palais de Glace, 2002), pp. 107–13.
19 In 1965, Alonso exhibited his *Homenaje a Rembrandt* (*Homage to Rembrandt*) in the Nice Galería de Arte.
20 Included in an Alonso exhibition in the Galería Giulia in Rome in 1977. A preliminary version also appeared in a 1971 exhibition at the Galería de Arte Esmeralda, Buenos Aires. Both catalogues were consulted in the Fundación Espigas.
21 See, for example, details from *Lección de anatomía* (*Anatomy Lesson*) no. 2 (acrylic on canvas, 1970) and from *La muerte del Che* (*Che's death*) (acrylic and oil on canvas, 1978), in: VVAA, *Carlos Alonso (Auto)biografía en imágenes* (*Carlos Alonso: (Auto)biography in images*), op. cit., pp. 98–9.
22 An etching and aquatint shown at the 'Carlos Alonso. Hay que comer' (Carlos Alonso: One Must Eat) exhibition (Museo de la Universidad Nacional de Tres de Febrero, 2004). Although dated 1977 in the exhibition, the date on the canvas is 1971.
23 The corporeal theme came to the fore during different periods of Alonso's career. With initial explorations in *El Matadero* (The Slaughterhouse) and *Hay que comer*, meat as an aesthetic theme came to prominence in Alonso's work after 1972.

24 Galería Giulia's catalogue (op. cit.)
25 Both from 1970. Reproduced in: VVAA, *Carlos Alonso. (Auto)biografía en imágenes*, op. cit., pp. 96 and 97. Also see María Teresa Constantin's text 'Un espacio para el dolor' ('A Space for Pain'); pp. 91–4.
26 Alonso also has one of the disciples asking: 'What did he die of?', to which Tulp replies: 'VERMOORD DOOR CIA' (murdered by the CIA).
27 Tempera on paper and collage, reproduced in Giudici, op. cit., p. 92. Although less well known, Berni produced other pieces on Che's death, most in paper.
28 The letter (a typed copy of which is archived in the Cuban Film Library) is dated 3 November 1969. The quotations, including capitalizations and underlining that follow, are taken from that typed copy.
29 Utilized in the film and on a banner that was hung underneath the screen during showings.
30 Sarlo (op. cit.) refers to the 'sacrificial ethic' of the revolutionary that she believes was embodied in Che. She identifies the image of his corpse with an image of Christ, 'the synthesis of immobile beauty and fatal determination'. 'In a Christianity of the poor, a Christianity of rage and violence [she adds] the image of the slain revolutionary was imbibed with sanctity as his death came about through a conscious and welcomed search for sacrifice.'
31 Although there is no suggestion here that these tendencies were consciously and explicity adopted by Solanas y Getino, they undoubtedly contributed to the 'epochal' atmosphere and should be considered amongst the contributing elements of the film's discourse.
32 Who directed *Hasta la victoria siempre* (*Ever Onwards to Victory*) that was screened on 18 October 1967 on a giant screen in Plaza de la Revolución in Havana when the official announcement of Che's death was made.
33 Author's interview with S. Alvarez, Havana, 1996.
34 Author's interview with O. Cortázar, Havana, 1996.
35 We should not underestimate the 'disagreeable', 'aggressive' (in its more quotidian sense), 'hurtful' and 'depressing' qualities of the image of Che's corpse for many Cubans who share this attitude towards him.
36 See: Pedro Chaskel. 1998. Rostros del Che (Faces of Che). *Cinémas d'Amérique Latine* (Toulouse) 6: 98–100.
37 Article by Ricardo Piglia (March, 1970), published in: *Un oscuro día de justicia*. Buenos Aires: Siglo XXI, 1973. In his search for an appropriate form of testimonial literature, Walsh had considered (in late 1968) Solanas y Getino's film as one possible avenue of exploration (R. Walsh. 1996. *Ese hombre y otros papeles personales* (*That Man and other Personal Papers*). BuenosAires: Seix Barral, 92, 94 and 95).
38 See: M. Mestman. 1997. Semanario CGT. Rodolfo Walsh: periodismo y clase obrera (CGT Weekly. Rodolfo Walsh: journalism and the working class). *Causas y Azares* (Buenos Aires) 6: 193–208.
39 Published at the time by his wife and comrade Alicia Eguren, and later re-edited in *La escena contemporánea* (*The Contemporary Scene*), Buenos Aires, no. 3 (1999).
40 Cooke had developed close ties with the Cuban Revolution and a political and personal bond with Che, whom he had seen for the last time in Cuba in 1965.
41 Horacio González. 'Fotocopias anilladas' ('Ringed Photocopies'), *La nación subrepticia* (*The Surreptitious Nation*). Buenos Aires: El Astillero, 37–8.

42 The citation of the presence of this 'impestuous word' in Cooke's notes as well as the expression used in the title of this article are taken from González (op. cit.).
43 Reference is made, for example, to the disappearance of Che's body (because of 'an imbecilious *gorila* fetish') which Cooke compares to the fate suffered by Eva Perón's corpse.

Hemispheric Domains: 1898 and the Origins of Latin Americanism

JULIO RAMOS

Worldings

Today, many of the barracks and military commissaries that line Gailard Avenue are almost empty, cleared of the supplies and soldiers that once occupied them. A humid breeze brushes by, pregnant with resignation and abandonment. Until recently, Fort Clayton had been one of the centres of the North American military presence in the Panama Canal. Now neither the corps of military engineers nor the high officials of the Southern Command are accountable for the buildings and remnants of military supplies strewn along Gailard Avenue, archaeological pieces of another time.

The cut-off date for the US Army to fully comply with the conditions stipulated by the Carter-Torrijos Treaty in 1977, i.e. 1999, has come and gone. These stipulations effectively transferred this property—not to mention the inter-oceanic administration of the Panama Canal—to the Panamanian government.[1] At the time of the treaty's conception, General Omar Torrijos feared that the very sovereignty of the national (Panamanian) state was at stake. Perhaps this is the reason he failed to consider certain details of the transfer: what his government would have to do, for example, with the useless weight of the trucks and military jeeps parked on the side streets of the old Clayton base. One needs to bear such details in mind to imagine why the Southern Command rendered US$370 million dollars to the Panamanian economy in repayment for the US withdrawal, a whopping 8% of Panama's gross national product.[2] Even more uncertain (and less ascertainable) is the fate of the local and informal economies—the cottage garment industries, food production, domestic services and prostitution, to take a number of examples—that have proliferated around the military complex since 1900. It was then that Theodore Roosevelt identified the Panama Canal as the very heart of a new aperture for the United States into the Caribbean, South America, the Pacific, and a new planetary order.[3]

The times have changed; and the maps have changed colours. After the end of the Cold War, the military presence in the Canal no longer had the same meaning that it might have had throughout the first decades of the twentieth century, when it was in effect considered essential to both the 'security' of North American hegemony in the central zone of the Caribbean, and to the expansion of finance capital and global trade. Hence the marked contrast between the Utopian dreams elaborated around the techno-medico-military-financial apparatus of the Canal at the time of its inauguration in 1914, and the recent abandonment of Fort Clayton, where the grass grows to almost seven feet today. Perhaps the traveller who reported such a sight meant to suggest that after the North American withdrawal from the Isthmus of Panama, the same forest that had been contained for almost a century—dominated without respite by engineering and tropical medicine in a permanent war against the mosquitoes, yellow fever and malaria—has impetuously returned.[4]

It was in Panama that the new colonial science of tropical medicine was institutionalized, committed to proving to the world that 'even the most remote tropical localities would soon be centers of white civilization, as powerful and cultured as every other that exists in the temperate zones'.[5] Of course, the genealogy of this science brings us to the Spanish American War, particularly in Cuba, where the insect bites and terror of contagion wreaked more havoc and caused more deaths among the North American soldiers than the weapons of the Spanish army. The taking of San Juan Hill in Santiago, Cuba, may have brought into relief the symbolic dimension of military heroism but it distracts us from that more minimalist (and certainly in the long run more decisive) scenario involving the war against the mosquitoes in the history of medico-military colonization inaugurated in the Spanish-American War. For this war was also a bio-war without precedent in the history of imperialism, in that it placed hygiene and public health at the very heart of colonial discourse, deploying new forms of domination based on the administration of bodies.[6] It was this war that continued long after Roosevelt and the Rough Riders victoriously withdrew from Cuba. The medico-military complex founded new Departments of Health in Cuba, the Philippines and Puerto Rico, and immediately extended its dominion to Panama. Here, the construction of the Canal was made possible (at least in part) by the intense and successful intervention of tropical medicine under the charge of Colonel W.C. Gorgas, an 1898 war veteran.[7] Colonel Gorgas is thus an emblematic figure of a complex colonial apparatus, a point of intersection among financial and technological interests, military and medical knowledges—all of which lead us to place both the war of 1898 and the construction of the Panama Canal in the wider context of a new *worlding* of the world, a new planetary order, reconfigured by the modern turn-of-the-century *techne*.[8]

As an inter-oceanic passage and point of articulation between the North and South, the Canal was as much an effect as a condition of possibility for such a worlding. In fact, it was constructed by migrant labour formed by nearly forty thousand workers hailing from Jamaica, Martinique, Costa Rica, Guatemala, Trinidad, Guadalupe, not to mention China, Scandinavia and Galicia: a heterogeneous or *discrepant* cosmopolitan force (as James Clifford would say) that inhabited and laboured in a profoundly transnational zone of contact. That zone of contact was maintained under the strong-arm control of an elaborate police apparatus that monitored and partitioned the area in accordance with a strictly stratified order of castes. The violence of imperial racism can thus be found at the very base of the modern project of worlding, undermining any other libertarian or dialogical assertion of global(izing) 'contact'.[9] Henry Franck, a member of the police force during that time, candidly recalls the racial and linguistic hierarchies in the small world articulated and compacted by the project of constructing the Canal:

> Here are the Basques in their Goinas, preferring their native 'Euscarra' to Spanish; French 'niggers', and English 'niggers', whom it is to the interest of peace and order to keep as far apart as possible; occasionally a few sunburned blond men in a shovel gang, but they prove to be Teutons or Scandinavians; labourers of every colour and degree—except American labourers, more than conspicuous by their absence. For the American Negro is an intractable creature in large numbers ... .[10]

In the epoch of its construction, the Canal was called *the Cut* by its engineers. In accordance with its namesake, the Canal inscribed and coordinated the intersection of forces, tensions and articulations in a codifying network of a new world. 'The history of wars for humanity', Peter Sloterdijk writes, 'are seen in a different light when certain wars or kinds of war are placed in relation to the crisis of changes in the larger forms of the world'.[11] In the almost immediate aftermath of the 1898 war, the pronouncements of President William McKinley in 1899 and the drive to construct the canal after the Panama secession in 1904, the military-financial-medical-technological complex elaborated a large-scale programme of *shrinking* the hemisphere by condensation and compression. Such a programme would permanently disrupt those maps and routes traversed by the circulation of capital: the cartography of transcultural currents, and the very conception and self-representation of America. In its wake, we see both the Utopian ebullience in the multiple celebrations of the canal, 'the new [world] wonder' that would unite the North with the South, the East with the West; and the fear of certain critics who remarked on its expansive power—a power that was intimately linked to the emergence of a new empire. These attitudes were best represented by, on the one hand, Theodore Roosevelt, with his peculiar Pan-Americanist ideal, and, on the other hand, those *Latinoamericanistas*, Latin-Americanists, committed to keeping watch over the borders of 'Our America'. Hence, the marked contrast between the Utopian mission to shrink the hemisphere at the turn of twentieth century and the reconfiguration of coordinates and maps—the form of the world—at the turn of our own. For now, let it suffice to say that the gradual withdrawal of North American troops from Fort Clayton and the handing over of the Canal to the Panamanian government in 1999 closed the history of an entire epoch, and with it a specific mode of colonial domination.

New problems have since emerged. For example, there is the question of what to do with the abandoned buildings strung across Gailard Avenue and where to relocate all the seemingly useless military surplus. Some of the scrap metal, recycled or perhaps re-semanticized, might travel north, where it could possibly serve to add height and thickness to the Tortilla Wall: a wall designed to contain the immigratory flux along the US–Mexico border. At its terminal point in California, one finds tons of recycled scrap metal, re-functionalized remnants of the Gulf War, as if blown there by magic by the terrible wind of the Desert Storm.

The solution proposed in 1994 by Panamanian president Ernesto Pérez Balladares and his administration would have been costly—$50 million at the outset alone. But at least it would initiate a new beginning to a new stage in the life of a post-Cold War Panamanian society beset with, among other things, the challenge of recovering the now missing 8% (by conservative estimates) of the gross national product. One profound believer in the Pan-Americanist network of power and intervention, minister Gabriel Lewis, proposed a new *Universidad Americana*, similar to that of Cairo or Beirut. 'We hope to replace North American soldiers with an international army of students and professors', he said in an interview. 'Where before troops were trained for battle, we hope soon to educate the best Latin American academics and professionals. I can't imagine a better use for these operations.'[12] The military barracks would be reoccupied and converted into student housing; the old club for military officials would be transformed into a comfortable faculty club for the distinguished professorate of a new university complex. Such a complex would easily accommodate more than 2500 students from the North and the South; their future *alma mater* would be Fort Clayton, where throughout the terrifying decade of the 1970s the North American army trained South and Central American military officers. Yet without entirely abandoning the Utopian resonance this central zone has held since the turn of the century, the university was to be called the *Ciudad del Saber* [City of Knowledge], a new point of conjuncture in the reconfiguration of inter-American hemispheric space. It would provide a new hinge that would affirm regional unity—but not as an effect of engineering, hygiene or military intervention, as Theodore Roosevelt would have had it at the turn of the last century. Rather, its integrity would be based on what is perhaps a more solid foundation in the long run—academic exchange and the formation of Pan-Americanist subjects in the City of Knowledge.

Of course, the source of funds to finance the new Pan-American university remains unclear, which leads one to doubt the viability of such a project in this period marked by a profound crisis in higher education. In any case, the City of Knowledge situates us at once before the present discussion of the political roles of inter-American intellectual exchange in the context of the changing relations between North and South. Such a discussion seems imperative today, now that the system of domination inaugurated at the turn of the past century, in the emblematic moments of the 1898 war and the invention of the state of Panama in 1904, seems to be drawing to a close.

Globalization of Knowledge and the Present Crisis of *Latinoamericanismo*

This exergue brings us to the contemporary discussion of the difficult place of knowledges and discourses of regional identity, as well as the dislocation of Latin-Americanist subjects confronted with the impact of gradual denationalization and the globalization of knowledges from or about Latin America at the end of the twentieth century. Inspired by the now classic genealogy of Orientalism proposed by Edward Said, the present discussion of Latin-Americanism reflects on its conditions of production and the possibility of articulating a specific set of discourses.[13] Such an investigation would begin not only with the rhetorical texture of discourses on Latin American difference but also with their institutional and disciplinary foundations.[14] The present discussion of the crisis of Latin-Americanism marks a moment of self-reflection and self-critique in the history of a discursive and disciplinary field that questions the very territorialized categories and geopolitics that sustain it. As in the case of Said, the investigation of the Latin-Americanist archive in itself implies the critique of the inescapable relationship between, on the one hand, the discourses and knowledges of difference—including the identification of the Latin American 'other'—and, on the other hand, the insertion of such heterologies into the specific formations of metropolitan power.

The analogy between Orientalism, as Said understands it, and Latin-Americanist discourses has generated many discussions and self-critiques of the field. Yet transplanting Said's thesis to the field of Latin American studies also obscures the multiplicity of subjects and discursive positions that intersect with the concept of *Latinoamericanismo*, Latin-Americanism. For example, the critique of Latin-Americanism as a field of knowledge tied to the history of international studies in European or North American universities neglects the *also problematic* history of vernacular *Latinoamericanismo* as an interpellative discourse produced by Latin American intellectuals.[15] Perhaps for strategic reasons, Said concerns himself primarily with delimiting his object in the archive of knowledges and discourses that have constructed and placed 'the Orient' on the maps of European identity. He concerns himself less with the interwoven network of intersections between the multiplicity of orientalisms produced in cultural institutions and the 'occidental' European social imaginary, not to mention in the Arab countries themselves. To put it another way, the history of Nasser and a pan-Arabist cultural nationalism constructs its own archive apart from the European imaginary, as well as tropes and strategies of geopolitical differentiation and identification. In the same way, the present concern with the nature of Latin-Americanist knowledge and power frequently obscures the key distinction between metropolitan formations and those vernacular identificatory discourses that—at least since José Martí and even more importantly, the Spanish-American War—have postulated either various defences of the local, of one's 'own' specificity, or emancipatory programmes of 'Our America', at different conjunctures of globalization and the 'worlding' of the world. Such are the formations of vernacular Latin-Americanisms, crisscrossed by multiple wills to power and framed by claims to authenticity that seem problematic to us today.

And yet, by making the distinction between a metropolitan Latin-Americanism and the vernacular defences of regional specificity, in no way do I attempt to dissolve the grey areas that relativize the borders separating the 'metropolitan' and the 'vernacular'—borders that are at once porous, well traversed and perforated by continuous migrations and the exile of vernacular intellectuals. Historically, the exile has played a constitutive role in metropolitan Latin-Americanism, contributing (from different angles and diverse political positions) to the invention of Latin America as an object of Latin American studies in the universities of North America. Such grey areas destabilize any facile attempt to essentialize the differences between those knowledges from or about Latin America and continue to problematize the very category of 'vernacular' discourse, even as they radically undermine the homogeneity of the metropolitan territories that feel the impact of transnational flows of globalization and contemporary migrations.

Alert and lucid until his final days, Antonio Cornejo Polar was a friend and colleague at Berkeley who faced the present disjuncture of Latin-Americanism in a sustained reflection on the borders and frontiers of the contemporary field. I refer particularly to 'Mestizaje y hibridez. Los riesgos de las metáforas. Apuntes', his final contribution to the Latin American Studies Association (LASA). The paper was read *in absentia* at the international convention celebrated in Guadalajara in March 1997, just two months prior to Cornejo's death in Lima.[16] What follows is a brief reading of this text that, in more than one sense, concerns the tropes of 'ending'. As the last piece written by a crucial author whose influence was felt in both vernacular and metropolitan expressions of Latin-Americanism, it alerts us to the possibility of 'the unhappy and undignified finale of *hispanoamericanismo*'.

It is not by chance that the concerns raised in 'Mestizaje e hibridez' connect with the wider historical background of 1898, particularly in the sense that Cornejo's essay can be read as one of the possible closures to a variety of discursive positions that have been posed in the field. In a sense, 'Mestizaje e hibridez' broaches the closure of a concept of Latin American culture and a way of conceiving the tasks of regional knowledge, including the defence of its borders. One may recall that these tasks were laid out precisely a century ago, with the same set of strategies and responses to the shrinkage of hemispheric space brought to a head in the 1898 war and the construction of the Panama Canal. It is in this respect that Cornejo's essay reflects doubly on closures: its autobiographical dimension appears to identify the last scene of writing for the author with the closure of an entire discursive field.

Such an association is not an exaggerated one. In various respects, Cornejo can be considered a humanist intellectual of a philological formation, placed in the tradition of Latin-Americanism, the legacy of the essayists, and the tradition that sustained the work of figures who narrativized the canon and the historical memory of the field that we inhabit today. These figures include Pedro Henríquez Ureña, Alfonso Reyes, and Angel Rama—'public intellectuals', to borrow a phrase, whose activities were not limited to the university, and whose wide field of intervention and political authority presupposed certain ties between culture and the public sphere that are perhaps no longer viable in contemporary neo-liberal societies. Cornejo's own reflection on 'the end of Latin-Americanism' thus assumes and reiterates a history of intellectual and academic labour, yet places it in the context of the present crisis characterized by the liberal-republican state in the orbit of globalization. The mere suggestion of a closure to this legacy is one effect of erosion in those models of cultural integration frequently posed by the humanities and the modern university. At least since Andrés Bello's time, the university has legitimized the production of humanistic knowledge and its pedagogical interventions by defining its function(s) in terms of constructing citizenship in the sphere of interpellations and education in literacy and culture. It would seem that the social formations of *our* turn of the century, marked by the globalization of perpetually 'developing' societies, no longer require the legitimizing intervention of those narratives that were taught as tools for national integration. Perhaps the cultural models of national integration—or the notion of integration itself—are no longer necessary at all, inasmuch as the state has reneged on its 'social contracts' to represent the common good. At the same time, systems of mass communication and consumption (to follow García Canclini's argument) continue to produce alternative parameters for defining one's citizenship—by both the exclusions it implies and the awareness of new and growing areas of abandonment.[17] As Beatriz Sarlo reminds us, in the field of cultural institutions (and their successive transformations) tied to the republican state, the very concept of the public intellectual has come under question.[18] The study of literature and culture, in turn, runs the risk of becoming the simple profession of experts, frequently based in the United States, who increasingly replace the evanescent figure of the public intellectual and the traditional Latin-Americanist humanist.

'Mestizaje e hibridez' questions the destiny of Latin-Americanism, 'the unhappy and undignified finale of *Hispanoamericanismo*'. In the process, Cornejo Polar's essay summarizes various key positions in the present debate on the transnational channels or 'canals' of production and the circulation of knowledge from or about Latin America. Written in the shadow of the discourse whose end he explores, Cornejo's text paradoxically reinscribes various tropes of origin, the borders of territoriality and the continual presence of a legacy—all of which, historically speaking, have been central aspects of Latin-Americanist rhetoric. The essay explores the changing frontiers of the field by considering the *proper* and *improper* ways in which the field borrows, translates and incorporates concepts from other disciplines, even as it questions the legitimacy of exchanges and contacts between itself and other languages and traditions. Cornejo ends by proposing a defence of the borders: he expresses alarm at the risk to the field's identity or immanence before those forces at the present conjuncture, that threaten the field's constitution, from the 'outside'—forces generated by the contact, commingling and hybridization of discourse itself.

Not coincidentally, in Cornejo's essay, the Althusserian *problematic* of contact and the porosity of borders is first and foremost posed as a question of linguistic order. According to Cornejo, Latin-Americanism in the present suffers from a condition of *diglossia*—a profound split that antagonistically separates those studies of Latin America produced in Latin American countries from Latin American studies produced in the United States. Creating a rupture between the interior and the exterior, between the proper and the improper, between the authentic and the inauthentic, diglossia manifests itself first and foremost in the growing prestige of English among Latin-Americanists in the United States, and the supposed crisis of Spanish teaching in North American pedagogy. The passage to English in and of itself would not be a problem, were it not accompanied by the increasing marginalization of vernacular Latin-Americanist knowledges produced in Spanish, in a cultural and ideological circuit entirely distinct and each day more precarious. Moreover, in the context of this linguistic divide Cornejo reiterates the trajectory of an even more profound and dangerous fracture—the division of labour that converts Latin American cultural objects into raw material exported to the United States and Europe, while metropolitan academic institutions produce epistemological models for theoretical elaboration and the consumption of that cultural raw material.

One need not agree with Cornejo to recognize that 'Mestizaje e hibridez: los riesgos de las metáforas' touches the very heart of the contemporary debate on the globalization of Latin American cultures, including the present discussion of the effects of the globalization of knowledge produced about these cultures. Cornejo identifies the crisis of cultural discourses and vernacular institutions in this neo-liberal era, and advises caution before the growing influence, *even in* Latin America, of metropolitan theoretical paradigms: cultural, postcolonial and subaltern studies. Cornejo's essay thus sets off a chain of associations and oppositions that can be abbreviated to the antagonism between the local and the global—between the interior field and the 'outside' of culture—and the contradictions that render problematic the possibility of 'regional' knowledge (or discourse of identity) in an increasingly homogenized world. One may add that even intellectual production becomes subordinated to the levelling demands of the market, penetrated by the velocity of transnational travel, and impacted by the consequent, rapid turnover of ideas. By reiterating the classic question regarding the specificity and originality of American knowledge, 'Mestizaje e hibridez' projects itself into the very historical and discursive network of vernacular Latin-Americanism that had motivated Cornejo's essay from the beginning, to announce an ending. How does one write at this liminal point of closure? How does a discourse assume the authority to reflect precisely on the crisis that calls all mechanisms of validation and authorization regarding its field into question? From what location and position does one write?

1898: Origins of Latin-Americanism and the Question of Local Knowledges

Beginning with José Martí's foundational essay, 'Nuestra América', and the series of texts on Pan-Americanism that prepare and anticipate the writing of that essay in 1891, vernacular Latin-Americanism has often been invoked as a defence of the local in diverse instances of globalization and worlding. Hence our assertion that 1898 and the reconfiguration of the hemispheric domain at the turn of the last century marks a decisive moment in the history of Latin-Americanism.[19] Although Martí died in the early months of that same war (which began in 1895 and *not* with the sinking of the US ship *Maine* in 1898), his *Latinoamericanista* essays can indeed be read as an early response to the reconfiguration and displacement of those borders produced by North American expansion following the Civil War and the colonization of the West facilitated by the Mexican-American War in 1848. It is no coincidence, for example, that the points of departure for Martí's Latin-Americanist discourse in 'Nuestra América', as well as his *Versos sencillos*, would be the intense debate over inter-American relations and, specifically, the official pan-Americanism generated around the Pan-American Congress in Washington and its culmination in the 1891 International Monetary Conference.[20] Indeed, I do not believe that the relationship between Martí's texts on the dangers of pan-Americanism—the risks of hemispheric compression—and his own compaction of a 'mestizo America', 'our America', has been sufficiently emphasized. It should suffice to recall that the speech entitled 'Madre América', a direct antecedent of 'Nuestra América', was dedicated as the welcome greeting on behalf of an exile (Martí) to the South American delegates participating in the inter-American conferences, some of whom he met during their stay in New York.[21]

As early as the late 1880s, the North American government, represented by Secretary of State James G. Blaine, proposed a series of inter-American commercial and industrial agreements that would spur the construction of railway and telegraphic networks, along with the relaxation of customhouse and border controls. These pan-American projects were also motivated by the ideal of a common currency that would at long last unite the American nations. The new map was to erase once and for all the obstinate boundaries separating North and South. Such an erasure would make possible the creation of an American power capable of undermining the hegemony of the European powers in the world order.[22] Yet Martí was unmistakably critical of this vision. In this period he identified the condition of modernity with the internationalization of not only capital but also cultural flows. His telluric Americanism thus set forth an alternative vision of modernity—one guided by the knowledge of the *earth*. According to Martí, such a knowledge would 'guide' and 'unite' an alternative hemispheric dominion. Martí's Latin-Americanism operates as a reversal of hegemonic modernity and its 'worldings'. It emerges, however, from the same historical conjuncture; it becomes displaced in the same space under compression; and the same networks of modernity—the market, the intensification of transnational contacts, and the inevitable cultural exchanges of a new cosmopolitan order—articulate it. Hence, Latin-Americanism in its turn would give way to the importance of journalism and the chronicle, texts of those travellermediators who traversed the new order, often serving as mediators between the metropolitan cultures and the Latin American reader.[23] It is thus no coincidence that the founders and inheritors of Latin-Americanism begin as travellers and/or exiles: such was the case for Martí, Pedro Henríquez Ureña, Rubén Darío, Alfonso Reyes and Gabriela Mistral.

In this new, disputed and unequal space, and in an epoch that historians generally identify with the gradual incorporation of Latin America into the world, the positions of intellectuals became redefined. Their new task was to ascertain the specificity and limits of a field dedicated to their 'own', 'proper' identity; to propose models for cultural contact and translation; and to determine the possibilities and risks of transcultural exchange in a global, cosmopolitan order. Hence the defence of local knowledges and vernacular cultures in Martí may be considered both a critical response to and an effect of the compression of hemispheric space, produced by the intense re-worlding of the Americas. The seizures of Cuba, Puerto Rico and the Philippines in 1898, as well as the succeeding invention of the state of Panama and the construction of the Canal, are events that emblematize that re-worlding. The construction of the canal in particular was at once a trope and a real effect of pan-Americanism—a strange and wondrous emblem, sprung from the new articulations between North and South.

Might it not be said, then, that Latin-Americanism—up until and including Cornejo and our turn of the century—is a field of investigation into the precarious balance among cultural formations of international capital and vernacular cultures? Attentive to the varied conjunctures of worlding, the Latin-Americanist subject emerges and institutionalizes his topographic and territorializing imaginary on the frontiers of mediation: separating the zones of contact from the danger zones and deciding the norms for a 'sanitary' cultural exchange. 'The haughty villager believes that the entire world is his village', Martí once said.[24] Confronting this perspective, the Latin-Americanist subject deploys two interrelated gestures: first, looking 'outside' ('the tiger from outside', as Martí would say) and then reflecting on the process of globalization; second, looking 'within' ('the tiger within') and then reflecting on the internal contradictions that sought to prevent the consolidation of political and civil institutions that would provide the democratic foundation of a virtual American order. Both positions call for mediation and translation. The authority of the emergent Latin-Americanist subject relies on the translation of foreign models, of course, but also on the translation of those obscured and subaltern voices—the 'mute masses of *indios*', the 'despised Negro' and the 'peasant, creator'. The gesture of incorporating and representing the other authorized and legitimized the aesthetic and intellectual project in the otherwise wide-open field of modern Latin American literature. One might argue that this is still true today. 'Speak through my words and my blood', Pablo Neruda writes in 'The Heights of Macchu Picchu' ['Alturas de Macchu Picchu'].[25] Yet beyond Neruda, Martí or (more recently) Miguel Barnet, the claim to representativeness is one of the foundations of the literary institution and its testimonial vocation: literature endows the other with the 'gift' of speech. The Latin-Americanist intellectual thus performs a dual task: she/he mediates between the world and the local on the one hand, and provides the internal translation necessary for the *construction* of the local on the other. The latter task involves the invention of vernacular tradition, along with its alternative legacies.

Yet this gesture of mediation defines only one ostensible pole of Latin-Americanism. José Enrique Rodó's *Ariel* occupies the other. For Rodó, the war of 1898 and the compression of hemispheric space provided the incentive for a new point of departure. In its polemical and immediate insertion into the emergent field of Latin-Americanism, *Ariel* is a cultural-aesthetic critique of '[North-]Americanization', which Rodó placed in opposition to the alternative of a legacy and archive inspired by the invention of Euro-American Latinism.[26] Of course, Rodó largely avoided the term *cosmopolitan*; when he did use the word, he used it in a pejorative sense. In *Ariel*, cosmopolitanism is synonymous with foreign influences and related to a popular and working-class immigration that threatened the very integrity of Latin American 'high culture'.

Without attempting to minimize the differences, one can nevertheless see how in both Martí and Rodó—whose models are frequently opposed in the historiography of Latin-Americanism—the reflection on the border and the practice of mediation(s) also responds to globalization and the necessity of constructing a Latin American legacy, memory and archive. Of course, the archives and notions of legacy proposed by Martí and Rodó were on the one hand radically distinct. While Rodó and his followers, at war with 'Americanization' and modernity, proposed a Euro-Latin-American legacy, Martí founded his identity-narrative on a fiction propelled by subaltern, 'autochthonous' or vernacular 'voices'. Nevertheless, the practices of Latin-Americanist mediation in both cases are based on the varied inflections of a cultural-aesthetic authority that privileges the role of literature in the construction of citizenship, or what Schiller has called 'the aesthetic education of man'.[27] The intellectual subject in both is called into being and given authority as the one responsible for reflecting on the necessary conditions for a democracy in which cultural-aesthetic representation would satisfy a regulatory principle. Such a role would, for Martí, contribute to the representation of particularity under the stigma of subalternity; for Rodó, it would provide the 'aesthetic of conduct' necessary for the self-administration of the soul and the constitution of disciplined subjects.[28]

Indeed, has not the reflection on democracy and the search for regulative principles extended all the way to our present? Would such a reflection not include even the distinctive registers of cultural-aesthetic authority in Beatriz

Sarlo and Nelly Richard, for example—both of whom take up, from different political positions, the defence of literature and the aesthetic? For both writers, the aesthetic retains the capacity to present alternative worlds to the instrumental logic of the market and the neo-liberal middle ground, both of which prefigure precisely in post-dictatorial contexts and democracies in transition. John Beverley has recently gone so far as to refer to these and other reconfigurations of the aesthetic subject in terms of a 'new Arielism'.[29] Without a doubt, one must qualify the almost epic heroism ascribed by Sarlo to artists as defenders of an autonomous and critical space in the postmodern scenario, on the one hand, as well as the (political) radicalization of the aesthetic subject in the anarchist-avant-garde discourse of Nelly Richard, on the other.[30] But there is no doubt that both Sarlo and Richard, who arise from theoretical and writing practices that are quite distinct, assign a certain privilege to aesthetic authority in the ongoing debate on democracy.

Without avoiding the obvious differences, in Martí and Rodó the question of delimiting boundaries of the 'proper' in modernity is inescapably tied not only to North American expansionism but also to the 'internal' problem of democracy. Modernity brought about the emergence of new political agents—women, workers, as well as unforeseen social alliances—that pressured the public sphere and forced a rethinking of the intellectual's place, as well as the place of high culture, in societies on the road to modernization. In this respect, it is not coincidental that for many of the new social subjects identified with the relative aperture produced by modernization, the war of 1898 would not necessarily represent a trauma or disaster. As many of the more radical working-class intellectuals of the epoch thought (particularly in the case of Puerto Rico), North-Americanization would, paradoxically, make possible the democratization of the public sphere and the creation of certain conditions and guarantees for the constitution of an anti-capitalist working-class movement. Such movements would have certainly held suspect many of the aesthetic-cultural discourses that privileged the mediating and representative role of the intellectual in the defence of nationalism and the Latin-Americanist registers that multiplied after 1898. I refer, for example, to Luisa Capetillo and the libertarian discourses tied to the emergence of the Puerto Rican workers' movement lucidly studied and anthologized by Angel Quintero Rivera.[31]

The working-class intellectuals at the beginning of the century, that ever-changing and voluble epoch, also intervened in the debate on globalization, producing local knowledges (albeit quite cosmopolitan in nature) and alternative libraries. Taking into consideration the Uruguayan and Argentine context of a nascent vigorous working-class movement at the time, one sees how in *Ariel* the proletarian immigrant subject lies at the unspoken and terrifying margins of the cultural-aesthetic subject in formation. Martí, on the other hand, became deeply involved with the most politically radical sectors of tobacco-workers and immigrants—many of them anarchists—who constituted the social and financial base of the Cuban Revolutionary Party (PRC) during the period of its establishment.[32] Without a doubt, the grounds of aesthetic authority were profoundly transformed in these arenas. As Martí headed for war (and his death), he cleared new paths for the aestheticization of politics.

1998

As we have seen, 'Mestizaje e hibridez' reinscribes and recalls the tone, the subject-positions and some of the rhetorical strategies of vernacular Latin-Americanism and its defence of local knowledges. It is organized around the binary of the global and the local; and it traverses and retains the borders that distinguish its 'own' territory, advising caution when faced with the borrowings of other disciplines (characteristic of cultural studies and its transdisciplinary passion) and other languages (especially English). But, in contrast with its antecedents, a certain pessimism in this essay leads the author to suggest that the present impact of globalization may well be decisive in drawing the final curtain on Latin-Americanism. This is perhaps because for Cornejo, as for Sarlo, the current crisis felt in cultural institutions (and the republican pedagogical apparatus) tends to cancel both the intellectual's representative role and the privilege granted to the cultural-aesthetic project, as two forms of authority central to the interpellation of subjects as citizens. Hence the organizational and legitimizing bases of vernacular Latin-Americanism—the representation of subaltern voices, the construction of models for translation, and the appropriation of foreign materials for the nation's benefit—have definitively lost their viability. To reiterate, this loss comes by way of the crisis of the liberal notion of representativeness, as well as the difficulties confronted by any and every reification of the local, of the *proper*, in this epoch of intense globalization.

The globalization of culture is not necessarily new. It may well be considered constitutive of the logic of capital. Yet what has certainly changed is the authority and the institutional basis of those discourses that once (at least until the 1970s and the beginning of the crises of the *Latinoamericanista* left) vigorously responded to the new worldings. As late as 1971, it was still possible for Roberto Fernández Retamar to believe that the cultural-aesthetic realm, the sphere of arts and literature, could satisfy a central, organic role, in a territorial defence of culture in so far as it could generate the necessary mediations for the formation of a national-popular culture.[33] In his late classic of Latin-Americanism *Calibán*, this national-popular culture represented no less than the crystallization of class warfare.

Still, the categorical oppositions of the metropolis and the periphery, the global and the local, the interior and the outside, the authentic and the inauthentic, are radically impacted by the acceleration and intensification of globalization. The phenomenon of continual travel, for example, or the migration of intellectuals and ideas or, more recently, the critical interventions of Chicano, Puerto Rican and Latino critics and students in the field of Latin-Americanism, shake the foundations of territorial representation. These are subjects whose vital experiences and intellectual labour either introduce new tensors or at times cross paths with the old, cutting diagonally across those territorializing notions of roots, linguistic purity, fixed origins or continuous legacies that still manifest themselves today as tropes of vernacular Latin-Americanism. If we believe that Latin-Americanism is after all a complex archive of discourses on territoriality and locality, discourses that attempt to define the specificity of its objects in terms of regional or geopolitical difference, we can today question the efficacy and viability of those modes whose task it once was to draw lines and boundaries over the field of identity. Such a project is particularly imperative in an epoch wherein the transnational flows of flexible capital have violently thrown open zones of contact and exchange, while the mass migrations of Caribbeans, Mexicans and Central Americans have produced enclaves of speech and Spanish culture at the very heart of the key metropoles in the United States. Perhaps it might not be entirely imprudent for us to ask, along with Tato Laviera, if Manhattan is not after all an island in the Antillean archipelago; or if Loaiza is a barrio of the Lower East Side. Perhaps it may not be inappropriate to wonder where Latin America, a locality mapped and protected by discourses of territorial identity, is now.

Neither is it extraneous to recall today, in Washington, DC, that one hundred years after the invasion of Cuba and Puerto Rico in 1898, the relative Caribbeanization and Latinization of the very urban area that situates our discussion on North and South rearticulations challenges any facile, monolingual notion of juridical citizenship, as well as any attempt to perpetuate the maps and inflexible territorial categories institutionalized by the discourses of vernacular identity.

Notes

1. For the full text of the 1997 Panama Canal (Carter-Torrijos) Treaty, see website http://lcweb2.loc.gov/frd/cs/panama/pa_ appnb.html.
2. Colin Woodard, 'In a Swap of Sword for Pen, Panama wants US Base to Be Knowledge City', *ChristianScience Monitor* (10 June 1997).
3. For a history of the Canal's construction and its representations, see David McCullough, *The Path Between the Seas: The Creation of the Panama Canal 1870–1914* (New York: Simon & Schuster, 1977).
4. Calvin Sims, 'Filling the Void and the Bases in Panama', *New York Times*, 30 October 1994 (IV:5; 1). Stella H. Nida has an interesting series of historical anecdotes on the war against the mosquitoes in *Panama and Its 'Bridge of Water'* (Chicago: Rand McNally, 1913).
5. Report of Colonel Dr W.C. Gorgas, who was a member of the Isthmanian Canal Commission and later head of the Department of Health in Panama. Cited by Charles F. Adams, *The Panama Canal Zone: An Epochal Event in Sanitation* (Boston: Proceedings of the Massachusetts Historical Society, 1911), p. 27. For a suggestive exploration of the body—technology relationship–as well as technologized bodies–in the imperialist discourses at the turn of the twentieth century (particularly throughout the construction of the Canal and during the Panama-Pacific Exposition celebrated in San Francisco, 1915), see Bill Brown, 'Science Fiction, the World Fair, and the Prosthetics of Empire, 1910–1915', in *Cultures of United States Imperialism*, eds Amy Kaplan and Donald Pease (Durham: Duke University Press, 1993), pp. 129–163.
6. I refer to the concept of 'noso-politics' and 'bio-power' in Michel Foucault: see 'The Politics of Health in the Eighteenth Century', in *Power/Knowledge: Selected Interviews and Other Writings 1972–1977*, ed. Colin Gordon (New York: Pantheon Books, 1980); and *The History of Sexuality, Volume I: An Introduction*, trans. Robert Hurley (New York: Vintage Books, 1990), pp. 139–143. For an analysis of the politics of health as a series of devices for ordering society and the nation, see J. Ramos, 'A Citizen Body: Cholera in Havana (1832)', *Dispositio*, 19:46 (1994), pp. 179–195. Special issue on 'Subaltern Studies in Latin America', ed. José Rabasa (published 1996).
7. Gorgas recounts his experiences in Cuba and Panama in William Crawford Gorgas, *Sanitation in Panama* (New York: Appleton, 1915).
8. On *techne* as an operation of inscription and the creation of 'worlds' as discursive constructs, see M. Heidegger, 'The Question of Technology'; and his critique of the category of the 'conception' or 'vision of the world' in 'Comments on Karl Jaspers's Psychology of World-Views', *Pathmarks*, ed. W. McNeill (Cambridge: Cambridge University Press, 1998), pp. 1–38.
9. See Michael Taussig's brief analysis of the construction of the Canal in *Mimesis and Alterity: A Particular History of the Senses* (New York: Routledge, 1993).
10. Harry Franck, *Things as They Are in Panama* (London: T. Fisher Unwin, 1913), p. 119.
11. Peter Sloterdijk, *En el mismo barco* (Madrid: Ediciones Siruela, 1994), p. 81.

12. Cited by Calvin Sims (see note 4 above).
13. See Edward Said, *Orientalism* (New York: Vintage Books, 1979). For Said, Orientalism involves 'a *distribution* of geopolitical awareness into aesthetic, scholarly, economic, sociological, historical, and philological texts; it is an *elaboration* not only of a basic geographical distinction (the world is made up of two unequal halves, Orient and Occident) but also of a whole series of "interests" which ... it not only creates but also maintains; it *is*, rather than expresses a certain *will* or *intention* to understand, in some cases to control, manipulate, even to incorporate what is a manifestly different ... world; it is, above all, a discourse that is by no means in direct, corresponding relationship with political power in the raw, but rather is produced and exists in an uneven exchange with various kinds of power' (12, emphasis in original).
14. Some recent studies of this field include Alberto Moreiras, 'Fragmentos globales: latinoamericanismo de segundo orden', in *Teorías sin disciplina (latinoamericanismo, poscolonialidad, y globalización en debate)*, eds Santiago Castro-Gómez and Eduardo Mendieta (México: Miguel Ángel Porrúa, 1998) (this text is available online: see http://ensayo.rom.uga.edu/critica/teoria/castro/moreiras.html); Román de la Campa, *Latin Americanism* (Minneapolis: University of Minnesota Press, 1999); and Julio Ramos, *Divergent Modernities: Culture and Politics in Nineteenth-Century Latin America*, trans. John D. Blanco (Durham: Duke University Press, 2001 [forthcoming]).
15. Vicente Rafael explores the politics of knowledge in constructing geopolitical difference: see 'The Cultures of Area Studies in the United States', *Social Text*, 41 (Winter 1994), pp. 91–111. See also A. Moreiras (note 14 above). For an analysis of vernacular Latin-Americanism as a discourse of identity, see Ramos, 'Mass Culture and Latin-Americanism' and '"Our America": the Art of Good Government', in *Divergent Modernities* (see note 14 above).
16. This essay appeared in *Revista de Crítica Literaria Latinoamericana*, 24:47 (1998), pp. 7–11. I examine this text more fully in 'Genealogías de la moral latinoamericanista. El cuerpo y la deuda de Flora Tristán', in *Nuevas perspectives desde/sobre América Latina: el desafío de los estudios culturales*, ed. Mabel Moraña (Santiago: Cuarto Propio, 2000).
17. Nestor García Canclini, *Consumidores y ciudadanos. Conflictos multiculturales de la globalización* (Mexico: Grijalbo, 1995).
18. Beatriz Sarlo, *Escenas de la vida posmoderna: intelectuales, arte y videocultura en la Argentina* (Buenos Aires: Ariel, 1994), p. 181.
19. Arcadio Díaz Quiñones has shown how the crisis of Spanish imperialism that culminated in 1898 was also decisive for the formation of Hispanism and its literary histories. In fact, up to this day Hispanism maintains a certain acceptance in US Hispanic studies, wherein Latin American literature frequently appears as one of many offshoots of a Spanish Castilian and imperial history inaugurated by *El Cid Campeador*. See A. Díaz Quiñones, '1898: Hispanismo y guerra', in *1898: su significando para Centroamérica y el Caribe*, ed. Walther L. Bernecker (Berlin: Vervuert Verlag), pp. 17–35.
20. I am referring here to the texts on the International and Monetary Conferences held in Washington, DC (1899), included in the volume *Nuestra América* (Caracas: Biblioteca Ayacucho, 1977), pp. 35–132.
21. José Martí, 'Madre América' in *Nuestra América* (see note 20 above), pp. 19–26.
22. José Martí (see note 20 above).
23. On the role of the traveller-mediator and the import journeys conducted by them, see Julio Ramos, *Divergent Modernities* (see note 14 above), esp. 'Limits of Autonomy' (ch. 4).
24. José Martí, 'Nuestra América', in *Nuestra América* (see note 20 above), pp. 26–33.
25. Pablo Neruda, *Alturas de Macchu Picchu* (Santiago: Ediciones de Librería Negra, 1947), pt. 12.
26. J.E. Rodó, *Ariel* (Caracas: Biblioteca Ayacucho, 1976). First published in 1900.
27. Friedrich Schiller, *On the Aesthetic Education of Man in a Series of Letters*, trans. Reginald Snell (New York: Frederick Ungar, 1983). First published in 1795.
28. On the other hand, one must not reduce the complexities of the aesthetic subject. Rodó himself, for example, maintains a very ambiguous relationship with the aesthetic and the rhetorical 'excesses' of literature, which he opposes at times to the priority of a desired 'manhood' ['energía viril'] for the citizen-subject. See note 26 above, p. 51.
29. John Beverley, comment at the symposium 'New Perspectives on/from Latin America: the Challenges of Cultural Studies', University of Pittsburgh (29–31 March 1998).
30. Beatriz Sarlo, *Escenas de la vida posmoderna* (see note 18 above); Nelly Richard, *Residuos y metáforas: ensayos de crítica cultural sobre el Chile de la transición* (Providencia, Santiago [Chile]: Editorial Cuarto Propio, 1998).

31. A. Quintero Rivera, *Workers' Struggle in Puerto Rico: A Documentary History*, trans. Cedric Belfrage (New York: Monthly Review Press, 1976); Luisa Capetillo, *Amor y anarquía: los escritos de Luisa Capetillo*, ed. Julio Ramos (Río Piedras, Puerto Rico: Huracán, 1992).
32. See in particular Martí's two speeches delivered in Tampa (1891), popularly known under the titles 'Con todos y para el bien de todos' and 'Los pinos nuevos'. José Martí, 'Discursos', in *Sus mejores páginas*, ed. Raimundo Lazo (Mexico City: Editorial Porrúa, S.A., 1985), pp. 54–64.
33. R. Fernández Retamar, *Calibán: apuntes sobre la cultura en nuestra América* (México: Editorial Diogenes, 1971).

Patagonia as Borderland: Nature, Culture, and the Idea of the State[1]

GABRIELA NOUZEILLES

Concluding his famous narrative of the *Voyage of the Beagle*, Charles Darwin states:

> In calling up images of the past, I find the plains of Patagonia frequently cross before my eyes; yet these plains are pronounced by all to be most wretched and useless. They are characterized only by negative possessions; without habitations, without water, without trees, without mountains, they support only a few dwarf plants. *Why, then— and the case is not peculiar to myself—have these arid wastes taken so firm possession of my mind? . . . I can scarcely analyse these feelings, but it must be partly owing to the free scope given to the imagination.* (p. 374, emphasis mine)

Darwin is not the only one whose imagination has been ignited by the seemingly boundless and eternal plains of Patagonia. From colonial times to the present, sailors, photographers, scientists, military men, writers, and tourists have been seduced by the eerie experience of infinity. Patagonia's lack of limits connects it to the myth of vanishing into the end of the world. *'Travelling to Patagonia is like going to the limit of a concept, the end of all things*. I have been to Australia and the American desert, but I sense that Patagonia is the desolation of all desolations . . . a region of exile, a place of deterritorialization', says Baudrillard (quoted in Hosne, 1997, pp. 281–282, emphasis mine). Baudrillard's perception of Patagonia, based entirely on the interplay of his imagination with the geographical myths created by master narratives like Darwin's, makes explicit, beyond the repetition of commonplaces, a widespread and fundamental articulation: that the images of Patagonia are always connected both to the idea of 'world' (hence the 'end of the world') and to the idea of a chronotopical infinity stretching between modernity and barbarism. Seen from this perspective, Patagonia is a paradoxical zone whose very lack of limits confounds a Reason dependent upon limits and scales. This explains why, according to some, the experience of the Patagonian space implies the risk of 'stepping out', of becoming civilization's Other. In *Idle Days in Patagonia* (1892), William Hudson describes such an experience: 'It was elation of this kind, the feeling experienced on going back to a mental condition we have outgrown, which I had in the Patagonian solitude; for I had undoubtedly *gone back*; and that state of intense watchfulness, or alertness rather, with suspension of the higher intellectual faculties, represented the mental state of the pure savage' (p. 205). If, in accordance with the historical assumptions of the West, moving through space implied moving forward in time (colonization as progress), then the experience of

Patagonia was, on the contrary, 'to go back', 'to recede', to veer off the path of history.

These images of Patagonia as the uttermost part of the earth and as a primordial, pre-historical space were both created by the imperial geographical imagination. As the last frontier, Patagonia played a significant role in the definition of imperial modernity. Magellan's discovery of a southern passage connecting the oceans was, among other things, the pragmatic beginning of a new spatial order that led to the imposition of a global economy and the hierarchical ranking of the peoples that inhabited the world. In discovering its ultimate frontier, Magellan stumbled upon the modern notion of 'the world'. Patagonia also played an important role in the production of modern patterns of knowledge involving history and nature. The very theory of evolution was born from the visualization of geological history in the Patagonian landscape. In his prologue to *The Origin of the Species* (1859), Darwin locates the epistemological scene of his *eureka* in Patagonia, where he 'discovered' the workings of evolution while observing its wild coasts and savage inhabitants (p. 65). As the outer limit or the origin of a global order, the liminal image of Patagonia has survived until today. At a time when natural spaces are shrinking and on the verge of disappearing as a direct result of massive urbanization, industrial pollution and global warming, Patagonia has become the concern of environmental organizations and a powerful fetish for adventure tourism.

The perception of Patagonia as last frontier, and its imperial characterization as pure negativity, problematizes the spatial production of the State as a territorial entity in the area. How, one might ask, can sovereignty be imposed over a space that resists the rational idea of limit? And moreover, why bother? What would be the economic, political, and social advantages of incorporating a hostile emptiness?

In this essay I would like to peruse some of the ways in which the Argentine State sought to 're-invent' Patagonia and questioned the imperial fictions that represented it as unconquerable space. My main interests are the mechanisms the State activated to produce space in its various forms, that is, the spatial practices through which Patagonian space became a place endowed with national value, and the set of spatial representations that would become the core of the hegemonic vision of the region.[2] It is my belief that the very difficulties that have consistently blocked the complete incorporation of Patagonia into the State make the spatial manipulations of the latter more visible. Such difficulties are both real and imaginary. On the one hand, there are practical limitations imposed by geography and climate in a vast area, two thirds of which is a cold desert. To this we should add the constraints placed on a peripheral State lacking the economic and technological resources to develop such a hostile environment. On the other hand, there is the power and authority of the imperial definition of Patagonia as 'accursed land'. There can be no definitive answer as to which obstacles have been most decisive. The invention of Patagonia as a place is an excellent example of how nature is part of culture, in the sense that every experience of the natural world is always mediated and shaped by rhetorical constructs such as photography, narrative, advertising, and aesthetics, and by institutions such as schooling, tourism, science, and the State (Wilson, 1992, p. 12). In saying that space is imagined I am in no way implying that its effects are inconsequential. As David Harvey has observed, social constructions of space and time 'operate with the full force of objective facts to which all individuals and institutions necessarily respond' (1996, p. 211). From this theoretical perspective, Patagonia is both empirical reality and idea.

As the hegemonic producer of locality, the Argentine State has promoted two central images of Patagonia: the illusion of a promised land, full of riches (even if not immediately apparent), always in danger of being taken over by foreign enemies; and the illusion of a landscape embodying the very idea of the national State. Both illusions were anchored in the fundamental articulation between peripheral State and nature that Fernando Coronil brilliantly discusses in *The Magical State* (1997). As with other Latin American countries that export raw materials in a context of economic and technological dependency, Argentina has also made nature the centre of its political, economic, and cultural self-representations.

The Geographical Imagination and the Creation of National Space

'The master of space is the State' says Lefebvre. Sovereignty implies space, and moreover, it implies a space against which violence is directed—a space established and maintained by violence. The first target of this violence is nature itself (Lefebvre, 1997, pp. 279–280). The modern State provides and manages the mechanisms through which nature, conceived as pure exteriority, is internalized within the process of social production, according to a technological utopia that dictates the absolute subordination of nature. Such a violence imposes a specific rationality, that of capital accumulation and of the rational and political principles unifying bureaucracy and the army. During this process, the State necessarily suppresses alternative forms of seeing and experiencing natural space.

The national State relies for its legitimacy on the intensity of its meaningful presence in a continuous body of bounded territory. Thus, in order to exist and survive, the State must find ways of creating a sense of locality and common space (Appadurai, 1996, pp. 177–199), and of producing and reproducing its citizens (Balibar and Wallerstein, 1991). Hence, among the first tasks of the State's agents are the mapping of national soils and waters, the effective occupation of land, and the construction of sites of memory and commemoration, such as museums and monuments, that will help to inculcate the Idea of the national State into its citizens. Such a project also requires mechanisms of discrimination against both competing nations and segments of the State's own population. Making maps, policing borders, and the regulation and displacement of bodies within and across the nation's boundaries are classical manifestations of the need for surveillance.

During the process of nation-building in Argentina and Chile, both countries claimed Patagonia as fundamental: the region's control and occupation were crucial not only for the economic future of each country, but also for defining their political and cultural communities. The first antagonists of these national claims were the numerous and diverse Amerindian tribes (Onas, Yamanes, Tehuelches, Araucanos, and others) that populated the area and fiercely opposed Western intervention. From then on, in the Argentine imagination, Patagonia would always be associated, on the one hand, with war, as a struggle against nature or against a common enemy for control of the area,[3] and on the other hand, with the frustrated fantasy of a utopia of progress whose success depends on the exploitation and development of the southern region.

One of the fundamental tasks in the spatial production of the State is to subdivide the space over which it reigns, or to utilize smooth spaces as a means of communication in between striated spaces (Deleuze and Guattari, 1987, pp. 385–386). To produce national space while suppressing the nomadic forces of Amerindian tribes, the Argentine State combined the technical accuracy of the scientific expedition with the disciplined violence of the military campaign. Thus, science and the army came to share similar goals and methodologies. While producing maps and inventories to expand the State's geographical archive, scrupulous engineers, naturalists, and geographers were also accumulating strategic information about roads and passages as well as the availability of food and water—data that the army could then use when advancing against the Amerindian settlements, if necessary, or to defend the frontier with Chile. For their part, military men not only protected the scientists travelling with them, but also had the capacity to implement by force the legal implications of scientific representations.[4] The hiring of the French engineer Ebelot by the minister of war, Adolfo Alsina, in 1875, is one of those occasions in which the imbrication between military and scientific agendas was almost absolute. Acting on the prerogatives given by his rank of Sergeant Major, Ebelot supervised the establishment of a permanent and irrevocable frontier with the nomadic Amerindians in the South, who frequently attacked the forts and towns of the Buenos Aires province. The new 'frontier' was a literal inscription into the Patagonian landscape of the geometrical representation of space in the scientific and military map: a 400 km long trench, 2.6 m wide and 1.75 m deep, that would run along the northern limit of Patagonia from the Atlantic coast to the Andes.[5]

The most famous case of juxtaposition of scientific knowledge and military discipline is the work of the naturalist and border expert Francisco P. Moreno, who travelled throughout Patagonia making maps and classifying its fauna, flora, soils, and native inhabitants. The pragmatic function of his work is apparent. While his maps served to establish scientifically the political boundaries with Chile, his travel logs gave density to geometrical representation by pointing out the economic potential of the lands to be conquered. In the prologue to *Travels to Austral Patagonia* (*Viaje a la Patagonia austral*), published in 1879 with state funds, he states:

> It is necessary then for us to find out, beyond any doubt, how and with what elements Patagonia can contribute to the prosperity of our country, and this can only be done by studying its geography and its natural resources. We must go there and study its geological and climatic conditions, its geography, its products, and the advantages it can offer to colonization . . . . I am contributing to this national duty with this work. (p. 6)

As was the case in colonial travel, written and graphic representations of space were a practical map for those who would come later to occupy the territory being described. But the fact that Moreno's text was oriented towards the future should not diminish the performative efficiency of his writing. Writing about Patagonia was in itself a symbolic way of taking possession of its space and its inhabitants on behalf of the State. The representational force of the letter bestowed the new territories with virtual legality. Moreno not only manufactured pragmatic representations of Patagonia; he also infused them with positive meanings and values. One of the central goals of this semantic adjustment was the modification of the imperial image of Patagonia as 'accursed land'—an idea extensively popularized through colonial narratives such as those by Pigafetta and Sarmiento de Gamboa, and reinforced by observations made by scientific travellers like Darwin, among others, that Patagonia has thousands of miles of uninhabitable desert, with a coast slashed by endless storms, without secure ports, and traversed by the most savage tribes on earth. Natural resources and the docile nature of its natives were the two pillars of Moreno's reinvention of Patagonia. Traces of this struggle for meaning are still present in the tensions between the apocalyptic toponymy left behind by the imperial travellers (Desolation Bay, Desired Port, Hunger Port, and so on), marked by disenchantment and the frustration of imperial desire, and the celebratory, almost chauvinistic names imprinted by Moreno (Argentine Lake, San Martín Lake), which inscribe onto the surface of Patagonian cartography the heroic enterprise of the State advancing into a promising expanse.

The Conquest of 15,000 Leagues. A Study of the Displacement of the Southern Frontier of the Republic to the Río Negro (*La conquista de las 15,000 leguas*, 1878), by Estanislao Zeballos, is another pragmatic effort directly associated with General Roca's successful military campaign against the indigenous tribes of Patagonia. Despite its title, Zeballos' text is not a tale of military conquest in the strict sense of the word, but rather the design—and the political and economic justification—for an occupation plan. The Conquest of 15,000 Leagues represents a virtual expedition, the reading of which made requisite its realization. Even though he had never visited the region, Zeballos assembled an archive, containing all the available information on Patagonia at the time, to provide Roca with not only a playing board (the topography of the terrain, the navigability of rivers) on which to envision a plan of operations, but also a historical genealogy through which Roca's actions could be legitimized. Roca's campaign would complete the slow advance of modernity that began with the arrival of Europeans in America. The appraisal and exaltation of regional riches again served as the primary inducements to conquer Patagonia and thereby advance the last frontier southward. Within this conceptual framework, the numerous botanical classifications in the text are simultaneously scientific descriptions and a commercial catalogue complete with price tags. Besides the generic identification, the location and the size of each specimen, Zeballos invariably underlines its economic potential: 'Muesno (*Euricriphia cordifolea*), a large tree, which grows from 38° of latitude south and can be up to 12 m high, whose cortex can provide boards of very good quality'; 'Lingue (*Persea lingue*) reaches 18 m, and its cortex is used to treat leather'; 'Molle (*Litrea moye*), a medium-sized tree whose wood is excellent for making farming tools'; and so on (pp. 171–173). One of the most surprising features of Zeballos's text is the methodology he proposes so as to defeat Amerindian nomadism. To prevail in the war against barbarism, he suggested, the army had to go beyond its usual recourse to geometrical movement based on the rational principles of positivism. Sometimes it was necessary to imitate nature by appropriating local knowledge about the land and even the tactics used by Amerindian in battle. Thus State apparatuses could strategically adopt nomadic rhythms to increase their effectivity.

But such mimesis was never more than a transitory strategy subordinated to the ultimate goal of dominating and transforming nature. In the geographical utopias of the scientific travellers, once Patagonia had been completely incorporated into the national territory, a new frontier of economic enterprise would take form, with pioneers and settlers as its protagonists. Döering, one of the geographers accompanying General Roca in his military campaign, imagined this frontier as a new kind of french, similar to Alsina's and Ebelot's, but in the form of an aqueduct that would exorcise forever the imperial ghost of a condemned land:

> Thus it would be possible to employ all the energy here for the establishment of colonial life; and the ditch of the new frontier line in the form of an aqueduct, in opposition to the old form, will distribute the blessing of its fertilizing waters over the peaceful domain of thousands of men, happy with the harvesting of the treasures that the virgin terrain of the former desert provides them with as a deserved reward for the powerful benefits of their laboring hands. (Döcring and Lorentz, 1939, p. 169)

Through the life-giving effect of water and agricultural life, the apparently barren land would reveal the treasures that only modern technology and the bourgeois values of work and discipline could extract; and thus, little by little, the desert would yield to the continuous advance of thousands of industrious citizens.

Gradually, the idea of Patagonia as an unconquerable desert gave way to the utopian vision of an endless abundant land waiting to be turned into national wealth. Not even the most contestatory and critical interventions against the oligarchic State questioned this belief. In concluding his *Argentine Australia* (*La Australia argentina*, 1898)—a series of journalistic reports harshly criticizing land speculation and military authoritarianism in the region—Roberto Payró could not help celebrating the transformation of the meaning and value given to the austral territories:

> The general belief that it was a sterile and ungrateful land is, fortunately and fairly, gradually disappearing. The magnificent cereal of Chubut, the secular woods on the Eastern side of the Andes, the green and rich prairies of its valleys; the wool and meat of Santa Cruz; the gigantic sheep of Tierra del Fuego; the gold-yielding sands; the inexhaustible deposit of beech-trees; the thermal springs; the ocean reverberating with fish, amphibians, whales, molluscs ... the extension, the incommensurable and solitary expansion, that offers and opens itself to fertilization. (p. 122)

Thus for Payró, the critique of a specific modality of the State, the oligarchic regime, did not at all imply a radical questioning of national production of space; what was at stake was the struggle for a more democratic political system that would give equal access to the natural resources of Patagonia.[6]

Over the years, the myth of Patagonian productivity grew in power. Mines, ranches, the fishing industry, sawmills, and, more recently, oil distilleries and hydroelectric generating plants would replace the aqueduct as symbol, yet retaining the primary theme of Patagonia as economic frontier. In every case, the program of transformation supported the hope for a better national society.

But the curse of the Patagonian desert would return many times with its threat of annihilation. The irreversible aridity of vast areas of Patagonia, the sparse population, and the lack of a coherent national plan for development have led some to question more than once those first programs of utopian transformation: 'Life in those places demands a sacrifice that perhaps an individual could fulfill in actions of supreme resignation, but the species has to reject that land which belongs to the ocean and not to man', wrote Martínez Estrada in 1933 (p. 144). In these pessimistic interludes, Patagonia's rugged nature is again seen as an insurmountable obstacle to a peripheral modernity based on the extraction and export of natural resources. At the beginning of this century, however, a new type of spatial production arose that enabled the State to incorporate Patagonia more effectively. This new strategy preached not transformation, but rather the fetishistic preservation of landscape and natural beauty.

Patagonia as Spectacle: Landscape and the Naturalization of the State Idea

In 1911, the Argentine minister Ramos Mejía asked the American engineer and geologist Bailey Willis to study the topography, geology and economic resources of northern Patagonia. The report, published in 1914, used essentially the same descriptive categories as previous scientific studies of the area, though with a more rigorous methodology and under more favourable conditions. Again the goal of the specialized report was to identify potential uses of nature and the most productive ways to exploit it. There was a novelty, though, in Section IV of his work, where Bailey discussed the viability of a centre for tourism in Bariloche, next to the National Park Nahuel Huapi at the base of the Andes. With the development of tourism and national parks, the symbolic dimension of the Patagonian landscape would acquire the *status* of a national spectacle, and the tourist and the sportsman would become the models of the new traveller.

A valorization of Patagonian landscape was already present in the writings of nineteenth-century scientific travellers. For Moreno, even though he avoided distractions to concentrate on his scientific observations of space, aesthetic contemplation of the landscape was clearly linked to a celebration of national iconography centred on natural images. In his writings one can find the two kinds of local landscape that would define from then on the perceptions of Patagonia's aesthetic and political meanings. The first kind corresponds to the arid mesetas of the eastern half of Patagonia, along the Atlantic coast. The second, in contrast, refers to the astonishing scenery of high mountains, deep forests, and the crystalline lakes of the Andes. One empty and the other full, each landscape elicits an aesthetic experience, different but complementary to the other. As in many cultural traditions, the primary meaning of the arid landscape is the idea of passage, of a journey through hardship that leads to a better destination. Thus, in nineteenth-century travel logs, the crossing of the mesetas functions within the narrative as a rite of passage by which the traveller acquires a right after exhausting all his energies.[7] The mountain landscape, which represents the reward of such a journey, provokes then in the traveller the powerful experience of the sublime. As in the Kantian interpretation, the intellect, dazzled by the sense of the sublime, confronts a nature whose magnitude and force defy the power of representation.[8] Indeed most descriptions of the Patagonian mountains are framed by the writer's apologies acknowledging helplessness in the face of the task of reproducing what his or her eyes are seeing. One could not describe such places as the Nahuel Huapi lake in northern Patagonia; one could only admire them. Words could only give a 'faint idea of that plaque of burnished cobalt' or of the lake's enormous amphitheatre, framed by tips of the austere Andean pines, their 'solemn image for centuries reflected' on the surface of the waters (Onelli, 1998, p. 21). Only nature was able to represent herself on the lake's mirror, in a mimetic circle that dwarfed and excluded human perspective.[9]

As cultural medium, landscape has a double function regarding the ideology it comes to serve. By representing an idea as if it were something given and inevitable, it naturalizes cultural constructions; and by making that representation operational, it interpellates its beholder (Mitchell, 1994, p. 2). In Argentina, the Patagonian landscape in both its arid and sublime versions has been particularly persuasive as a natural embodiment of the State Idea by making it palpable and inaccessible at the same time.[10] While the majestic scenery of the Andean landscape naturalizes, with its physicality, the presence of the national State, the accompanying sense of the sublime makes it eerie and untouchable. Its efficiency derives from the fact that, in appearance, it is not just a natural scene but also the 'natural' representation of a natural scene, as if we were dealing with an icon of nature in nature itself. The mixture of empirical perception, respectful contemplation and lack of understanding in front of what is absolutely unrepresentable—the 'thing' of the sublime experience—is translated to the political relationship between citizen and the State.[11] Along with the sense of passage, the desert-like landscape evokes the equally powerful idea of an absolutely empty expanse upon which man can build everything from nothing. Here the image of the desert is associated with the most extreme of all founding myths, that is, a national community that takes biblical genesis and absolute creation as its model.[12]

The ratification of the national parks law in 1902 institutionalized a movement, also initiated by Moreno, by which the State put aside lands with the objective of protecting natural sites for the enjoyment and education of its citizens. Following the American model, the spatial order of the park would juxtapose the functional logics of the museum with those of the gymnasium and the laboratory. In 1903, Moreno prophesied that the brand new Nahuel Huapi National Park would effectively preserve national nature for the education of coming generations, and also provide a secure place in which they would find 'a healthy and adequate view' and the 'rest and solace' to recover from the demands of modern life (1997b, pp. 281, 283).

Their promoters stressed the democratic character of public space in national parks. The parks' accessibility to all citizens was imperative to their efficient functioning as artefacts of the State. 'What is a national park?' Bailey Willis would ask rhetorically in his report, 'A wild region for the pleasure of the huntsman or occasional mountain climber who may have a desire to confront the difficulties of desolate peaks? This is a common conception but one entirely without reason. A national park is an area reserved by the State for the pleasure and welfare of the people' (1914, p. 412).

Despite this declaration of principles, the affluent classes and some cosmopolitan travellers were for many years the only ones with the means and the time to visit the distant parks of Patagonia. Some of these first distinguished tourists left detailed accounts describing their first encounters with the Patagonian landscapes and the overwhelming feelings they allegedly elicited.[13] Even some active members of the elite, known for their resistance to nationalistic claims, felt interpellated by the majesty of Patagonian nature. In 1939, on returning from the Nahuel Huapi area, Victoria Ocampo described the civic conversion she had gone through in the south:

> I have discovered that my trip to Patagonia, where I thought I had nothing to do, has not been just travel. I went there to take possession of a piece of land that belonged to me, for I have loved it with that special love that pays the price of things better than money. Now I have lakes, forests, falls and mountains whose beauty I had never imagined. The mysterious lake country is mine. I should like to see it belong to all those Argentines who do not know it yet, and since it is now mine, my first impulse is to share it with them. (1944, p. 122)

In Ocampo's account, experiencing the Patagonian landscape generated common ties of such magnitude that she felt compelled to use her own writing to bring the images of that landscape nearer to other Argentines not fortunate enough to see it. Patagonia provided unique experiences that no other landscape in the world was able to produce. Even though the woods, lakes, and mountains of the Nahuel Haupi were similar to those of Switzerland, or of the lake district in England, the Patagonian landscape had the power to transport the traveller to a primordial scene, a different geological age, where it was possible to glimpse a virgin space, unaltered by modernization (pp. 121–122). The 'Argentine' specificity of the land was based on a paradoxical connection: the Andean Patagonia evoked in the traveller a time that was pre-State and pre-history, but whose eternity was immediately absorbed by the Idea it represented, that is, that of the State as an atemporal and absolute entity.

Far from transcending the laws of the market, as Ocampo believed, landscape is, like money, a sign that obscures the real basis of its value. Beginning in the 1930s, tourist transactions would fetishize the Patagonian landscape by turning it into an object for consumption, whose commercialization would support an economic circuit of national and international dimensions, involving hotels, restaurants, sports centres, new roads, travel guides, postcards, and so on.

In *The Awakening of Bariloche* (1971), a testimonial account of the transformation of Nahuel Huapi National Park into one of the most successful tourist enterprises in the country, the conservative ex-public official Exequiel Bustillo underlines, with pragmatic cynicism, the founding imbrication of capitalist accumulation, cultural hegemony and border policy in the production of national space. From the beginning, he writes, the primordial functions of Argentine national parks had been to foment the colonization of underpopulated areas by creating bases for demographic support; to make the nation's natural beauty available to the people by promoting tourism and sport activities; and to protect national sovereignty by affirming the material presence of the State. The main difference between Bustillo's position and others' was that for Bustillo landscape was by far the most valuable natural resource in the region. This change of emphasis produced important modifications in the representations of landscape and travel experiences in Patagonia. In Bustillo's account of his first trip from the Patagonian coast to the mountains in 1934, the sequence of events in the narrative—the slow traversing of the desert followed by the sublime encounter—is structured by the logics of consumption. As a search for the object purchased by the tourist prior to departure, the first stage of the trip is long and uncomfortable, and arouses the anxiety felt by those who fear fraud: 'The worst part is that, after 40 hours on the train—25 of which were in Patagonia—the landscape is almost the same. ... That's why some time ago I said that this stage ought to be named "the stage of deception", because the traveller feels disenchanted after not finding the beauty he has heard talked about so much'. The traveller is now a tourist who collects landscapes and who expects gratification in exchange for his or her money and the inconvenience suffered while travelling. Although the rhythm of the journey has been accelerated by the train and the car, the increase in speed only exacerbates the tourist's impatience. Once the desert has been left behind, the following stages of the trip are still perceived by Bustillo as excruciatingly slow and partial revelations of the desired object, an agony that fortunately concludes with a flow of sensorial pleasure when he reaches:

> the meridian of beauty, because it is here where the soul is seized by a mixture of pleasure and apprehension at the sight of the Patagonian woods, where one can distinguish *coihues*, cypresses, *radales* and *maitenes*. Suddenly, one does not know what to say, nor how to express one's admiration for a scenery in which one sees the large blue basin of the lake and, in the background, straightening up with majesty, the snowed peak of the Tronador.

Reading such a description of the Patagonian landscape, we are struck by the conventionality of its representation. Beyond their differences, Bustillo, Moreno, and Onelli seem to have 'seen' the same thing. But this effect derives not so much from a common point of view as from the fact that the Patagonian landscape gradually became a textual convention that ultimately generated similar readings of nature, in the same syntactic order (woods–lake–summit). And even though in Bustillo's version the sense of the sublime is already mixed with the pleasure of consumption, the Idea of the State continues to be an important part of the cultural effect of the Patagonian landscape as fetish ('I couldn't believe that this was in Argentina, in the country of the endless *pampas*. Because *this patriotic sentiment, suddenly awakened, is one of the strangest feelings one experiences* upon first contact with our lake district' (p. 3, emphasis mine)).

In 1934, the writer and journalist Roberto Arlt resorted to the same images to narrate his first trip to Patagonia in a series of pieces for the newspaper *El Mundo*. After long hours on a dusty train, traversing a desert enervating in its repetitions ('This landscape pisses me off. I have already begun to consider it a personal enemy. It is unbearable, garrulous, as one who repeats himself endlessly' (Arlt, 1997, p. 57)) and on a car ride along irregular roads that once in a while let him see fragments of distant mountains, Arlt finally encounters the landscape he has been waiting for. Again the contemplation of the desired object creates immediate pleasure and amazement. But, suddenly, in the middle of this initial fascination, the cynical eye of the chronicler discovers the tricks of the commercial fetish:

> We go meandering up and down, from one picturesque valley to another, surrounded by mountains. Suddenly, an unexpected phenomenon

takes place. As if a marvellous cinematographic trick had raised the backdrop, a valley opens up and falls into an immense plain of cobalt. A voice next to me interrupts my ecstasy: 'The Nahuel Huapi!!' Contemplating it like this, before my eyes, I understand why people call it the most beautiful lake in the world. Any other description would not suffice. My eyes, once they have been able to pull out of the suggestion produced by that incredibly blue water, get fixed on the background. The Andes look familiar. The silhouette of the indented and snowed summits, lying on an indigo sky; I have seen them in photographs. With my hand I point toward the chain of rocky peaks, stained with patches of snow. I believe I have seen them before.

By 1934 it was already impossible to avoid the circuit of clichés about nature that the rapid series of images from movies, photographs, and tourist paraphernalia were producing. This saturation of cultural mediation quickly turned the landscape of the Patagonian mountains into a *kitsch* object, altering forever the aura of the natural. In an article written just a few days later, entitled 'The Enchanted Valley of Traful', Arlt slyly adopts the perspective of the merchant to suggest to his urban readers the endless possibilities of the Patagonian landscape. Imagination could turn the rocky formations of the Traful valley into the representation of anything the reader—or the tourist—wanted:

> What do you want to imagine in these circles made of cones of smooth stone, covered by a green tapestry and long rows of pines and cypresses, among which, isolated, are monuments of volcanic rock that adopt shapes as fantastic as any the imagination could create? . . . What do you want to dream or imagine, you, Sir, in the enchanted valley? Don't be frugal or shy. Everything is possible here. (Arlt, 1997, p. 73)

Arlt's demystifying and parodic gesture reveals the cultural mechanisms through which the images of the natural are constructed and given value in modern societies. In this sense, with his cynical intervention, Arlt not only unmasks the touristic illusion but also the naturalization of the State Idea and its effects on the meaning of a nation always divided by social injustice and political violence. But hegemonic forces still twist Arlt's radical positioning. His Patagonian *aquafortes* are not completely critical of the State *simulacrum*, nor of the commercialization of Patagonia in the market of cultural goods. On the one hand, a questioning of the landscape's authenticity does not prevent Arlt from complaining in other essays about the abandoned condition in which the Argentine State kept the southern provinces, over which it barely affirmed its sovereignty, leaving the region exposed to foreign ambitions and its inhabitants without support. On the other hand, the perspective that deconstructs the workings of the fetish landscape in Arlt's essays is not so efficient when it comes to celebrating the legendary characters of the Patagonian frontier. Arlt enjoys retelling in detail heroic tales of frontier life in which courageous men and women struggle with nature to impose the laws of modernity, tales he then 'sells' to his urban readers with the persuasive glow of an exotic merchandise, all within a narrative of conquest in which the journalist from Buenos Aires collects objects for a public tired of the same.

Conclusion

The production of space has always been essential to the formation and masking of the modern State, whose subsistence implies the suppression of alternative forms of conceptualizing and experiencing nature (Lefebvre, 1997, p. 280). Patagonia's geographical fictions demonstrate specific ways in which peripheral countries produce national space: as jurisdictional territory; as natural resources; and as an object for consumption and aesthetic contemplation. The particular difficulties that the territorialization of Patagonia has presented not only make the attempts to shape space on behalf of the State more obvious, but also reveal how the very ungovernability of Patagonian space can also become a natural resource—landscape—able to generate both national income and cultural cohesion.

In this interplay of reflections in which nature comes to embody the State Idea, the State is not the reality which stands behind the mask of symbolic representation. Rather, as Abrams insightfully argues, the State is itself the mask which prevents our seeing political practice as it is (1988, pp. 58–60).[14] Thus, there is no essence of the State hidden under the natural mask of ideology (Coronil, 1997, pp. 114–116). The reification of the State would be as much an effect as a condition of its multiple objectifications. As is the case with the images of itself that Patagonian nature reflects in its own lakes, the Idea of the State has no original.

Notes

1. I wish to thank Jon Beasley-Murray for his insightful comments on this essay and Stephen Hiltner for his editorial assistance with its English version.
2. For a classification of the main types of spatial production, see Lefebvre, 1997, pp. 33–46. Although fundamental for their oppositional character *vis-à-vis* spatial practices carried out by the State, for reasons of space and focus, I will not discuss here alternative geographical imaginations of Patagonia, such as the representational spaces created by the Amerindians, the Welsh in Chubut, and certain forms of anarchism.
3. War as the dominant form of border politics includes both the raids against the Amerindians, which were sometimes seen as an extension of the struggle against nature, and the territorial conflicts with Chile and Great Britain. A third form of war corresponds to the violence that the State directs against dissident behaviour. Patagonia as a frontier was also a place to exile those individuals that openly or tacitly endangered the stability of the State, such as criminals and political dissidents. The State defended itself by sending them to the margins of the national territory. This tendency is clear in the history and location of prisons in Usuhaia, Neuquén, and Trelew, which at different times in Argentine political history became the forced destination for 'degenerate' criminals, anarchists, communists, Peronists, and political prisoners. Chile's dictator Pinochet chose Dawson Island, in southern Patagonia, for the same end.
4. A particular modality of territorial occupation in Patagonia was the activities of the Salesians, who 'colonized' the region with missions, technical schools, and boarding houses for the assimilation and education of the Amerindians. Although their programmes did not always agree with the goals of the State, on many occasions they reinforced each other's projects. It is not mere coincidence that, besides scientists, military expeditions always included one or two priests. One of the main Salesian contributions to the geographical imaginary of Patagonia is the figure of Ceferino Namuncurá, son of the last rebellious Amerindian chief, who died in Rome in 1912, and who now is one of the most popular 'national' saints in Argentina. His remains are in a crystal box at the national monument 'Fortín Mercedes', located on the old military frontier between the national State and Amerindian lands before the occupation of Patagonia in 1879.
5. Another example of this mathematization of space are the cartographic descriptions of the engineer Emilio Frey, who was sent by the national government to map northern Patagonia. He classified more than 70 lakes. Tired of having to come up with new names for them, he decided, with the pragmatic spirit of the scientist, to just name them 1, 2, 3, 4, and so on.
6. The promises of Patagonian emptiness and its apparently unfinished nature have more than once inspired utopian and liberational thinking opposed to the authoritarian forces of the State. My point here is not to deny the existence of alternative geographical imaginations but to show to what extent the hegemonic visions of Patagonia have permeated all kinds of political discourses, even Payró's socialist thinking. On the radical nature of Payró's writings on Patagonia, see Andermann.

7. The representation of the desert as a spiritual crossing or rite of passage, through which the traveller becomes more deserving, is also part of the geographical imagery of the American West. See Nelson Limerick, 1985, pp. 166–167.
8. In his interpretation of the sublime in Kant, Lyotard concludes that 'in the sublime feeling, nature no longer speaks to thought through the coded writing of its forms. Above and beyond the formal qualities that induce the quality of taste, thinking grasped by the sublime feeling is faced, in nature, with quantities capable only of suggesting a magnitude or a force that exceeds its power of representation' (1994, p. 52).
9. The shores of the Patagonian sea could also activate the experience of the sublime at night, with the overwhelming spectacle of the austral skies hanging over them, this time duplicated on the mirror of the ocean instead of the lake: 'Before the sublime manifestations of Creation that man sees in the sky, he starts hearing voices that reveal Life in other worlds, and the memories that that grandiose view makes grow in his soul accumulate and become as numerous as the luminous points radiating from the large star clusters, nuclei of new worlds. . . . At first everything is confusing; chaos reigns in my being, produced by the violent transition that I have experienced when moving from my Self toward the Whole from which we humbly evolved. I cannot find words with which to express what happened within me' (Moreno, 1997a, pp. 231–232).
10. Obviously, the pampa is the landscape that has most tightly articulated the spatial expression of the national State, above all because of its relationship with the figure of the *gaucho* (see Montaldo, 1993). However, Patagonia and its landscapes have been a major element in the national imagination of the frontier, inwards and outwards, and in the contemporary debates about ecological policies and national and international tourism.
11. I am grateful to Alberto Moreiras for pointing out the possible connection between the experience of the sublime and the cult of the State Idea in symbolic landscapes.
12. In *Facundo* (1845), Sarmiento identified the desert as the main obstacle to Argentina's progress and the constitution of a solid modern State. In general, in the nineteenth century, the idea of the desert was applied to the large expanse of the pampas, meaning that it was an uncivilized and open space, although not necessarily beyond being tamed. As has been argued by Viñas (1983) and by Montaldo (1995), in contrast to the sense of emptiness that the image of the desert evokes, the pampa had rivers, cattle, abundant plant life, and a heterogeneous population of *gauchos* and Amerindians. It was the civilized traveller's point of view that 'emptied' the pampas in order to justify modernization. Patagonian mesetas also were traversed by Amerindian nomadic tribes, but in contrast to the pampas, its geographical features were closer to the traditional definition of a desert as an unproductive and arid region, with no plants or water. Thus, the effective occupation of Patagonia in 1879 did not imply the disappearance of its image as desert, which still survives today.
13. Perhaps the first testimonies of a tourist experience in Patagonia are two essays written in 1914 by Paul Groussac, 'De Punta Arenas a Mendoza' and 'À la terre de feu' (Groussac, 1920). Here, Groussac narrates his travel experiences to the Argentine public and the French respectively, in a period when a trip to the region still presented the risks and inconveniences of adventure travel and exploratory expeditions.
14. Abrams distinguishes between the Idea of the State as a juridical entity, and the State as a set of coercive and administrative apparatuses. As an administrative order, the State has no permanent 'essence,' and is rather the object of political struggle. The continuity of the Nation State, though, requires the postulation of a transcendental juridical force, the State, that would be the permanent element through political change. It is this side of the State that nature comes to represent.

References

Philip Abrams, 'Notes on the difficulty of studying the state', *Journal of Historical Sociology*, 1 (March 1988), pp. 58–89.

Jens Andermann, 'Instantáneas fronterizas: Paisaje, progreso y horror en las crónicas viajeras de Payró y Arlt', unpublished manuscript.

Arjun Appadurai, *Modernity at Large: Cultural Dimensions of Globalization* (Minneapolis/London: University of Minnesota Press, 1996).

Roberto Arlt, *En el país del viento: Viaje a la Patagonia* [1934] (Buenos Aires: Ediciones Simurg, 1997).

Etienne Balibar and Immanuel Wallerstein, *Race, Nation, Class: Ambiguous Identities* (London: Verso, 1991).

Exequiel Bustillo, *El despertar de Bariloche: Una estrategia patagónica* (Buenos Aires: Casa Pardo, 1971).

Fernando Coronil, *The Magical State: Nature, Money, and Modernity in Venezuela* (Chicago: University of Chicago Press, 1997).

Charles Darwin, *The Origin of the Species* [1859] (London: Penguin, 1985).

Charles Darwin, *Voyage of the Beagle* (London: Penguin, 1989).

Gilles Deleuze and Félix Guattari, *A Thousand Plateaus: Capitalism and Schizophrenia*, trans. by Brian Massumi (Minneapolis: University of Minnesota Press, 1987).

Adolfo Döering and Pablo Lorentz, *La conquista del desierto: Diario de la comisión científica de la expedición de 1879* (Buenos Aires: Edición de la Comisión Nacional Monumento al General Roca, 1939).
Paul Groussac, *El viaje intelectual: Impresiones de naturaleza y arte* (Buenos Aires: Jesús Menéndez, Librero Editor, 1920).
David Harvey, *Justice, Nature and the Geography of Difference* (Oxford: Blackwell, 1996).
Roberto Hosne, *Barridos por el viento: Historias de la patagonia desconocida* (Buenos Aires: Planeta, 1997).
William Hudson, *Idle Days in Patagonia* [1892] (London and Toronto: J. M. Dent & Sons Ltd, 1923).
Henri Lefebvre, *The Production of Space* (Oxford: Blackwell, 1997).
Jean-François Lyotard, *Lessons on the Analytic of the Sublime* (Stanford: Stanford University Press, 1994).
Ezequiel Martínez Estrada, *X-Ray of the Pampa* [1933], trans. by Alain Swietlicki (Austin: University of Texas Press, 1971).
W. J. T. Mitchell, 'Imperial Landscape', in *Landscape and Power*, ed. by W. J. T. Mitchell (Chicago: University of Chicago Press, 1994), pp. 5–34.
Graciela Montaldo, *De pronto el campo: Literatura argentina y tradición rural* (Rosario: Beatriz Viterbo Editora, 1993).
Graciela Montaldo, 'Espacio y nación', *Estudios. Revista de Investigaciones literarias* 3, 5 (Caracas, ene-jun, 1995), pp. 5–17.
Francisco P. Moreno, *Viaje a la Patagonia Austral* [1879] (Buenos Aires: Ediciones Elefante Blanco, 1997a).
Francisco P. Moreno, *Reminiscencias* (Buenos Aires: Ediciones Elefante Blanco, 1997b).
Patricia Nelson Limerick, *Desert Passages: Encounters with the American Deserts* (Alburquerque: University of New Mexico, 1985).
Victoria Ocampo, 'The Lakes of the South', in *The Green Continent*, ed. by Germán Arciniegas (New York: Alfred A. Knopf, 1944), pp. 116–122.
Clemente Onelli, *Trepando los Andes* (Buenos Aires: Ediciones Elefante Blanco, 1998).
Roberto J. Payró, *La Australia argentina* [1898] (Buenos Aires: Eudeba, 1963).
David Viñas, *Indios, ejército y frontera* (México: Siglo XXI, 1983).
Bailey Willis, *Northern Patagonia: Character and Resources. Report for the Ministry of Public Works. Bureau of Railways of the Argentine Republic* (New York: Scribner Press, 1914).
Alexander Wilson, *The Culture of Nature: North American Landscape from Disney to the Exxon Valdez* (Oxford: Blackwell, 1992).
Estanislao Zeballos, *La Conquista de Quince Mil Leguas: Estudio sobre la traslación de la frontera sur de la República al Río Negro* [1878] (Buenos Aires: Hyspamerica, 1986).

Jean Franco

THE RETURN OF COATLICUE: MEXICAN NATIONALISM AND THE AZTEC PAST

Tucked in at the end of Raimundo Lida's *Letras hispánicas* is a story by Rubén Darío that was first published in the *Diario de Centro-America* in 1915 with the title 'Huitzilipoxtli' (Lida, 1958: 301–6). Set in Mexico, during the Revolution, the first-person narrator is a journalist who has been given safe conduct to travel in the areas controlled by Pancho Villa. His travelling companions are a North American citizen, John Perhaps, and a certain Reguera, a colonel and priest who had supported both Maximilian and Porfirio Díaz. At night, kept awake by howling coyotes and too much marijuana, and like all true protagonists of mystery stories, the journalist lets curiosity get the better of him and walks in the direction of the uncanny noise. He finds himself in a clearing in which stands a monumental idol and a sacrificial victim – none other than the gringo, Mr Perhaps – lying under the statue of the great Teoyamique, one of the avatars of Coatlicue. Except for the pearl necklace, the description corresponds to the statue now in the National Anthropological Museum – 'Two serpents' heads, like arms or tentacles that belong to the block, come together in the upper part, on a kind of immense fleshless head surrounded by a string of amputated hands on a pearl necklace'. When the shaken journalist returns to camp, he is told that Colonel Reguera is away, supervising an execution squad, apparently acting in accordance with his conviction that the 'Aztec mystery is in every Mexican'. Darío's story can be said to have inaugurated a corpus of writing on the Latin American heart of darkness, a corpus that includes Cortázar's *La noche boca arriba*, Carlos Fuentes's *Chac Mool*, Gustavo Saínz's *Fantasmas Aztecas* and Carmen Boullosa's *Llanto*, in all of which dark pre-Columbian forces lurk under the surface of modern life. This particular corpus, however, is only a fraction of the long, complex and varied meanings that accrued around this one particular icon. The post-conquest history of the statue of Coatlicue is connected to the ideology of Mexican nationalism, to the history of aesthetics, to surrealism and to Chicano feminism. It has been an object of horror, extolled as a thing of beauty hidden from view, exhibited as a masterpiece, and is the subject of endless speculation, far more than any other single pre-Columbian artefact.

Coatlicue was buried in the vicinity of the Temple complex constructed after the Aztecs had consolidated their hold over the valley of Mexico and far-flung provinces a century before the Spanish conquest (see Matos Moctezuma, 2002).[1] Once established as the supreme power in the valley of Mexico, they had burned their records in the painted books in order to clear the way for a full-scale revision of the

Werner Forman Art Resources, New York

past. The Temple and the space around it was the symbolic centre and material representation of that revision, at once the sacred snake hill, the place where conquest was ritually re-enacted through sacrifice, the place where they established their legitimacy as heirs to the Toltec civilization and where the narrative of their patron warrior-god, Huitzilopochti, and his mother Coatlicue were on display. Octavio Paz rightly described it as simultaneously 'a charade, a syllogism, and a presence that condenses a tremendous mystery', a block of stone that he describes as 'a metaphysics' (Paz, 1997: 17). In this sense it is comparable to medieval depictions of the life of Christ and the saints, which tell a story and add meaning through symbols – the cross, the dove, the lamb.

Buried during the conquest of Mexico, the statue Coatlicue, 'she of the skirt of snakes' and 'mother of the gods', was unearthed from the Zócalo along with the Calendar Stone in 1790, at a moment when some of the colonial elite had begun to envisage Mexico as a mestizo homeland in which antagonistic races would be fused. Mestizaje or racial mixture became the crucial formula to achieve what the twentieth-century thinker, Antonio Caso, envisaged as 'the collective soul' (Caso 1973: 289). As José Emilio Pacheco had pointed out, it was a line of thought 'which sought its legitimacy ideologically in producing a *mestizo* culture' (Pacheco, 1983: 11–50 and Clavijero, 1971: 191–201) which, in turn, involved a re-evaluation of pre-Columbian civilizations in order to stress the importance and sophistication of their culture. The discovery of Coatlicue and the Calendar stone was thus an event of some importance and León y Gama's *Historical and chronological description of the two stones*), published first in 1792, was intended to preserve evidence of the discovery in case the stones were ever damaged or destroyed. But the fate of the two stones was quite diverse. Whereas the much admired calendar stone was placed on view in the cathedral wall as an example of the sophistication of pre-Columbian civilization, the statue of Coatlicue – described by León y Gama as 'this horrible simulacrum' (León y Gama 1990: 42) and which by no stretch of the imagination could be compared to Greek and Roman statues – was despatched to the patio of the university and then re-buried in 1805 on the orders of Bishop Moxó y Fernández because 'for some unknown reason foreseen by no one, the Indians, who looked at the monuments of European art with such stupid indifference, came to contemplate the famous statue with anxious curiosity'. The Indians were expelled from the patio, 'but with their fanatic enthusiasm and their incredible astuteness they outwitted this ploy. They spied on the monument in the empty yard, especially in the afternoon, when classes finished and the classrooms were closed. Then, taking advantage of the silence that reigned in the Muses' dwelling place, they left their hiding places and quickly went to adore their God Toyaomiqui.'[2] Reason enough it would seem to bury the dangerous statue. The statue was also briefly disinterred in 1803 for the benefit of the German scientist, Baron von Humboldt, who had expressed an interest in seeing it. But it was immediately buried again (Matos Moctezuma, in his 'Introduction' to León y Gama, 1990). Once more disinterred just after Independence the statue was confined to a corner of the university patio where it was partly hidden from view and when eventually put on display it was as an object of scientific curiosity in the National Museum, founded in 1825, although even in the museum it was hardly respected. The British scholar, Edward B. Tyler, visiting Mexico in 1856, described how an enterprising soldier had built a rabbit hutch out of idols and sculptured stones 'against the statue of the great Teoyamiqui herself and kept rabbits there'. Certainly, the statue of Coatlicue, with its references to human sacrifice, was difficult to incorporate into a national ideology that was then in its incipient stage. In her, analogies with Roman or Greek civilization broke down and the twin serpent's heads did not invite humanistic comparisons. The statue defied every aesthetic standard of the Renaissance and the Enlightenment that made human proportions the measure for beauty and the face the mirror of self-contemplation.

As for her mythic status as mother of the gods, this too was scarcely a usable past. When viewed not as an isolated statue but as an important element in the totality of the Templo Mayor, which synthesized the political hegemony of the Aztecs and of Tenochtitlan, the economic benefits of tribute and the rituals of sacrifice, she was progenitor of the warrior god, Huitzilipochti, to whom thousands of warriors were sacrificed. In the story, related by Bernardo Sahagún, Coatlicue, while sweeping the floor as a penance, was impregnated by a white feather that had fallen from the sky and which she had placed in her breast. Because of her unexplained pregnancy, the four hundred brothers (stars) who were her children and their sister Coyolxauhqui (the moon) planned to kill her. In León Portilla's translation:

> Cuando supo esto Coatlicue
> mucho se espantó
> mucho se entristeció.
> Pero su hijo Huitzilopochtli, que estaba en su seno,
> la confortaba, la decía
> – No temas,
> yo se lo que tengo que hacer.
> Los cuatrocientos Surianos se preparaban: ...
> Iban bien ataviados
> guarnecidos para la guerra.
> Se destribuyeron entre si sus vestidos de papel,
> su anecúyotl, sus ortigas,
> sus colgajos de papel pintado
> se ataron campanillas en sus pantorillas.[3]

The story told in this song is as exciting as a western or a police chase as it goes on to describe the advance of the rebel army and the birth of Huizilopochtli who emerged, fully grown, from the womb, in his warrior dress and paint. He wounded his sister Coyolxauhqui, who fell down the mountain and was shattered into fragments, and pursued the four hundred brothers to their death.

> Y cuando Huitzilipochtli le hubo dado muerte,
> cuando hubo dado salida a su ira
> les quitó sus atavíos, sus adornos, su anecúyotl,
> se los puso, se los apropió
> los incorporó a su destino
> hizo de ellos sus propias insignias. (León-Portillo, 1971: 480–4)[4]

This is a fine description of assimilation through conquest and of any imperial mission in which the conquered lose their very souls (their destiny) to the imperial power.

The Temple area was, as the archaeologist Matos Moctezuma describes it, the material depiction of a living myth, a reproduction of the sacred hill crowned by Temples to Huizilopochtli and to Tlaloc (Matos Moctezuma, 1995: 57). The recent rediscovery of a large stone representing the dismembered Coyolxauhqui and the subsequent thorough excavation of the Templo Mayor between 1979 and 1984 enabled archaeologists to trace two centuries of construction on the site that culminated shortly before the conquest (Matos Moctezuma, 2003: 48–55). The Templo and its surroundings were representations of Huitzilipochti's triumph and a simulacrum of the sacred snake hill. Though Coatlicue was not found in the Temple the statue certainly belongs to this narrative, which overlays and reinterprets more ancient representations of the goddess, although, as the historian Enrique Florescano has pointed out, the netting design on the head is a citation, linking Coatlicue to an earlier Mayan iconography of devouring agrarian earth gods (Florescano, 1999: 191).

But even seen in isolation the statue of Coatlicue is a field on which a fluid symbolism is distributed over a serpent-headed human body. The statue is covered on the front, back, sides and underside (that is, on a part invisible to the viewer) with figures and codified allusions to death and resurrection. Crowned by two fanged serpent heads on a severed and bleeding torso, it has eagle claws for feet on which there are eyes, a skirt of serpents buckled by a human skull and an adornment of hearts. At the base and invisible to the viewer is a god squatting in the attitude of the earth monster and interpreted either as Mictlantecutli, the god of death, or as Tlaloc, the god of rain. Because this figure is invisible, it suggests that Coatlicue was not there to be contemplated but was an embodiment of forces and an esoteric text.

In formal terms, the statue is constructed as a cross when viewed from the front and a pyramid when viewed from the side. The art critic Justino Fernández divides the body into four zones: the clawed feet, the skirt of serpents, the thorax and the flaccid breasts and, finally, the dual head, and points out the significance of the numbers – the two serpents round the waist, the two feathers hanging, the two breasts, the two snakes of the head, all of which also symbolize the dualism that is the axis of the Aztec universe; and the four hands and hearts, the four nails and the four eyes on the eagle's claws, four being the number of the cardinal points, the divisions of the day and the number of ages of the earth. Viewers could also read the story of Huitzilipochtli the eagle warrior and sun god engaging in the daily struggle for life, for which human sacrifice was necessary. According to myth, his journey takes place in four phases of the day with different guardians accompanying him. In the late morning, he is carried on a litter to the centre of the sky by warriors. When the sun sets, mothers lead the sun to its resting place in the earth. So the bottom of the statue with the eagle's feet and the feathers refer to his death and disappearance, a process that is sealed by the squatting but invisible god in the base (Fernández, 1959: 210–56).

In the second zone of the statue are the writhing snakes that identify Coatlicue as she-of-the-skirt-of-serpents. The serpents are poison and remedy, death and renewal and the change of skin is a resurrection. The waistband is formed by two serpents who may represent the earth gods and it is fastened by skulls at the front and the back.

The third and fourth zones of the statue denote the sacrificial body – the severed heads and the hearts over the flaccid breasts that Fernández construed as a flayed human skin and others interpret more prosaically as the tired breasts of a mother who has suckled four hundred children. The upraised arms are covered with jaws of eagles and the severed neck is crowned by the heads of two fierce snakes, possibly representing Ometecultli and Omecihuatl, the two gods who created the earth, and signifying both duality and renewal.

The flexibility of the pantheon, the polysemy of the images, the wealth of citation and the symbolism of the numbers make Coatlicue as complex as a baroque poem, while the repetitive theme of death and sacrifice, the intertwining of animal and human, and the skulls, the hearts and the severed hands leave the viewer in no doubt that human destiny is death that nourishes the renewal of nature.

As can readily be appreciated, there was no obvious message here that could be used by the modernizing Mexican intelligentsia of the nineteenth and early twentieth century. In contrast with the Maya who were, until recently, thought of as the Greeks of the New World before archaeologists revealed that they were as obsessed with sacrifice, the Aztecs were seen as derivative and cold (Schele and Miller, 1986). And on the periphery, where there was an aspiration to be part of the universal measured by the aesthetic standard's of Michaelangelo's David or Mona Lisa, Coatlicue could only be seen as aberrant or primitive.

The beauty or lack of beauty of Coatlicue continued to be debated throughout the nineteenth century (see Fernández, 1959). It was not until the Mexican Revolution of 1910 to 1917 brought about a thorough re-evaluation of the indigenous and of the pre-Columbian past that Coatlicue could be viewed as something other than the document of barbarism or the blood-soaked figure represented in the 1915 frieze by Saturnino Herrán (Herrán, 1994, plates 47–49). In the wake of the Revolution, however, scholars began to rewrite Mexican history, so that gradually the statue took on a new significance both in relation to the ideology of *mestizaje* and in art history as artists and art historians, following the European avant-garde's embrace of the arts of Africa Oceania and pre-Columbian America, began to revise their own indigenous tradition.

'The blueprint for incorporating the Indian in the construction of a national identity in the aftermath of the 1910 revolution' was, as María Josefina Saldaña-Portillo points out, Manuel Gamio's *Forjando Patria*, which differed from earlier theories of *mestizaje* in its celebration of the '"Indians" spectacular contributions in realms historical, artistic, cultural, and scientific' (2003: 206). Gamio famously concluded: 'To incorporate the Indian let us not try to "Europeanize" him all at once: to the contrary, let us "Indianize" him a bit, to present to him our civilization already diluted with his own, so that he will not find [it] exotic, cruel, bitter, and incomprehensible. Naturally, we should not exaggerate to a ridiculous degree our closeness with the Indian' (in Saldaña-Portillo, 2003: 206). Realizing that the bias towards European cultural models prejudiced the reappraisal of indigenous culture Gamio devised an experiment to illustrate the relativity of artistic taste. He showed photographs of a number of pre-Columbian sculptures and artefacts to art lovers who described as beautiful those pieces that were nearest to the European ideal, 'but amongst those to which they were indifferent or repulsed was the Goddess of Death, Mictlantecutli, and the Goddess with the skirt of snakes, Coatlicue' (see Toscano, 1952: 5). Clearly, if artistic taste depends on education and habitus, there is no question of inferiority or superiority or rigid standards of beauty and ugliness. Such was the conclusion of Edmundo O'Gorman in an essay on art and the monstrous in which he argued that, to appreciate Coatlicue, Greek perfection must be abandoned and the viewer must accept the monstrous as outside the natural order: 'Coatlicue is a consubstantial expression of the animal and the human, a crossroads at which all that order reason had worked so hard to produce was run over, and where all that is possible is the sovereign indifferent fluidity of myths' (quoted in Fernández, 1959: 101).

Coatlicue now became a key figure in two divergent causes: on the one hand, artists, many influenced by surrealism, read into the statue a prehistory of the human and, on the other, art critics, with a nationalist agenda, argued that she represented a beauty superior to that of Greek and Roman sculptures. Among artists there was a growing interest in the pre-Columbian past, and not only among the muralists but also thanks to the arrival of Europeans searching for alternatives to what they saw as the deceptive surface rationalism inherited from the Enlightenment. Antonin Artaud arrived in Mexico 'to search for the roots of a magical culture it is still possible to unearth in Indian soil' (quoted in Schneider, 1978). And, of course, there was D.H. Lawrence in a quest for the pulsating lifeblood destroyed by Western civilization, and later Lowry's *Under the Volcano* with its sacrificial ending. European immigrants or temporary residents, such as Wolfgang Paalan who published the journal *Dyn* from Cuernavaca and the French poet Benjamn Péret, contributed to this revisionism. Peret's essay 'Notes on Pre-Columbian Art', published in *Horizon* in 1947, argued that, contrary to rational Greek sculpture, pre-Columbian art corresponded to the deep intentions of art, although he also recognized that the Aztecs had transformed horror into the material instrument of domination as was manifest in the statue of Coatlicue, whom curiously he describes as a virgin goddess (Peret, 1947: 364). The presence of the past was, of course, reflected in painting – most strikingly in the non-figurative paintings of Gunther Gerzso, which depict overlapping layers with cuts and incisions that suggest both discontinuities and at the same time the lurking but hidden presence of the past before humanism. His 'mythological character' appears to correspond to Coatlicue.[5] In a rather different style, Diego Rivera's Detroit mural of the motor industry completed in the 1930s depicts the metal press as a citation of Coatlicue who thus becomes a goddess that overlooks and celebrates the post-humanist industrial age.[6]

New excavations and research into pre-Columbian sites led to more accurate dating and periodization as well as new insights into Aztec religion, art and poetry, which allowed art critics to celebrate a past that now rivalled anything produced in Europe. The brilliant critic Salvador Toscano, in a 1944 essay, described Coatlicue as 'a masterpiece of American sculpture. It is the most hallucinating sculpture conceived by the Indian mind and a work of art that cannot be judged according to the serene criteria of Greek art, nor the piety of Christian art: the Goddess expresses the dramatic brutality of Aztec religion, its solemnity and magnificence' (Toscano, 1952: 277). This was followed in 1954 by Justino Fernández's *Coatlicue*, in which he described the statue as a gem of world art. His careful description of the symbolism of the statue and its basis in Aztec myth and cosmology was the underpinning for his argument that it had all the formal qualifications to count as a great work of art. In the introduction to the book he refuted the idea of progress in art that had condemned some art as 'barbaric' or 'primitive' but invented a new hierarchy of value by claiming that tragic beauty is superior to beauty of any other kind.

Fernández's reading offers a humanistic account of the statue's meanings that attempts to understand the way the Aztecs might have viewed the statue as well as its impact on his contemporaries. He argued that 'the being of Beauty' for the Aztecs 'is the being of the warrior. It was beauty that gave meaning and justification to life and death, since one lived to die and died to live so as to maintain a dynamic order that was, in the end, provisional.' But his primary interest is in showing that it is a work of art that still moves viewers in the present and he argues that 'the contemplation of tragic beauty in any work of art that expresses it must always move us because it ultimately leads us to the most disquieting of issues: the final meaning of our own existence' (Fernández, 1959: 251, 269–70). If, as he claims, the tragic beauty of Coatlicue 'is the most profound of all beauties created or imagined by man, then Mexico's past splendour trumps that of Europe'.

In order to make this claim, Fernández had to tread lightly over the historical and the political significance of Coatlicue. His fine work of re-evaluation is, after all, also a contribution to cultural nationalism that obfuscated the politics of the Aztec empire at a time when the mystique of Mexico's corporatist state was still unchallenged. Its limitations became glaringly apparent in 1968 when demonstrating students were killed in the Plaza de Tres Culturas, Tlatelolco – a place where the inhabitants of Tenochtitlan made their last stand against the Spanish conquistadors, and an epochal event that exposed the time lag between economic, cultural and political modernization. Two prominent intellectuals – Octavio Paz and Carlos Fuentes – now made Coatlicue the symbol of a repressive order that had not been superseded. In *Postdata* ('The Critique of the Pyramid') Paz (1972) argued that the Aztec power structure

Werner Forman Art Resources, New York

still shaped national politics, and that the 1968 killing of demonstrating students at Tlateloloco was a repetition of Aztec sacrifice whose full horror Coatlicue represented. Without mentioning Justino Fernández by name, Paz attacked the aestheticization of the monument:

> [O]ur art critics wax ecstatic about the statue of Coatlicue, an enormous block of petrified theology. Have they ever *looked* at it? Pedantry and heroism, sexual puritanism and ferocity, calculation and delirium: a people made up of warriors and priests, astrologers and immolators.... And in all the manifestations of that extraordinary and horrifying nation, from the astronomical myths to the poets' metaphors, from the daily rites to the priests' meditations, there is always the smell of blood, the obsessive reek of it. The Aztec year, like those wheels-of-torture circles that appear in the novels of Sade, was a circle of eighteen blood-soaked months, eighteen ceremonies, eight ways of dying: by arrows, by drowning, by beheading, by flaying.... And what obfuscation of the spirit is responsible for the fact that no one among us – I am speaking, not of our

outdated nationalists, but of our philosophers, historians, artists, poets – wishes to see and admit that the Aztec world was one of history's aberrations.... Mexico-Tenochtitlan has disappeared and what concerns me, as I gaze upon its fallen body, is not the problem of historical interpretation but the fact that we cannot contemplate the cadaver face to face: its phantasm haunts us. (Paz, 1973: 93)

For Paz this dead civilization is a dangerous ghost.

In *Tiempo Mexicano* ('Mexican Time') Fuentes goes further, claiming the superiority of Western culture over that of ancient Mexico. The openness that makes Greece the cradle of democracy stands in contrast with the monolithic Coatlicue, who is the antithesis of all democratic aspirations. In Greece the gods had human attributes:

> Venus and Apollo are Gods that can be fissured: vaginal and testicular, they penetrate and can be penetrated by man. Coatlicue – the God Mother of the Aztec pantheon – cannot allow any fissure at all: she is a perfect monolith, an intense totality – self-contained and omnicontinent. Significantly, she is headless and renounces anthropomorphism. She is a Goddess, not a person, and a deity cut off from all vacillation, all temptation, needs or human freedoms. The square, decapitated Coatlicue, with its garlands of skulls, its skirt of snakes, its open lacerated hands, wants to be impenetrable: monolithic. Like all gods of the Aztec pantheon, it has been created in the image and likeness of the *unknown*, and its decorative elements, although they may separately be called skulls, serpents, hands, in truth mesh together to compose the unknown: seen together, they do not want to be named. Coatlicue is the symbol of a ceremonial culture: a culture of sacred repetition that excludes historical renewal. Quetzalcóatl flees in the knowledge that, while he is absent, he will be desired. The monolithic, impenetrable, faceless Coatlicue remains. (Fuentes, 1971: 19)

Whereas Paz fears a haunting, Fuentes embraces the post-Enlightenment secular individual over the sacred and the unknown, and chooses to overlook the fact that the statue does have a head – though it is not a human one. Both writers turn Coatlicue into a scapegoat for Mexico's restriction of democratic freedom.

Tlatelolco marked the beginning of a crisis of the Mexican state that was deepened by the debt crisis of 1982. The signing of the NAFTA treaty between Mexico, the US and Canada in 1994 ushered in a period of neoliberal reform, dividing the nation between those who benefited and those who suffered. Two years earlier, and in preparation for the NAFTA treaty, the Museum of Modern Art in New York had put on display the exhibition that was suggestively named *Mexico. Splendors of Thirty Centuries*, which once again made culture the cover story for a political and economic deal. The exhibition was sponsored by, among others, Emilio Azcárraga, head of the television company *Televisa*, and the introduction was written by Octavio Paz (Paz, 1990). To be sure there was still the awkward fact of the conquest to be explained, but the very title of the exhibition measured the distance travelled from Clavijero's modest claims for pre-Columbian civilization in the eighteenth century (see Clavijero, 1971). The exhibition proudly asserted that Mexico was the sum of 30 centuries of civilization reflected in great and unique art.

The weight of the catalogue alone called for training in weightlifting to read it. In an about-turn from *Postdata*, Octavio Paz, who wrote the introduction, now embraced the aestheticization of the Aztec civilization he had once attacked. Taking as his theme 'The Will to Form' he distinguishes between the marvellous that attracts us because it is fantastic and magical, and horror that, while inducing fear and repulsion, also reflects respect and veneration for the unknown and the sublime. Though human sacrifice does not seduce him 'it is impossible not to admire it'. Although he only mentions Coatlicue once, when he does so it is to make a surprising transformation of the Aztec story: 'Coatlicue, she of the skirt of serpents, from whose decapitated trunk Huitzilopochtili sprang fully armed, like Minerva from the brow of Jupiter' (Paz, 1990: 18–19). The hideous god and goddess of *The Critique of the Pyramid* undergo a startling change of gender with Huitzilipochtli feminized as Minerva and Coatlicue turned into the father of the gods. The analogy is so bizarre that one can only surmise Paz's desperate need to absorb the Aztecs into Western culture. Although the sculptures of the ancient gods cannot be considered beautiful, he argues, they:

> ... are works that are at once marvelous and horrible. By that I mean works that are impregnated with the vague and sublime sense of the sacred. A sense that wells from beliefs and images issuing from very ancient and radically *other* psychic depths. In spite of their strangeness, in an obscure and almost never rational way, we recognize ourselves in them. Or, more exactly, we glimpse through their complicated forms a buried part of our own being in such strange objects – we contemplate the unfathomable depths of the cosmos, and we peer into our own abyss. (Paz 1990: 5)

He thus ends up making exactly the same claim as Fernández. What has made this re-evaluation possible is that Paz has separated politics from culture and identified the latter with the sacred, that is, with the sacred rescued from any social organization and confined to the individual experience. We have moved beyond the romantic and modernist irony that Paz had described in *Children of the Mire*, beyond the dire inheritance of pre-Columbian Mexico outlined in *The Critique of the Pyramid* and into the realm of the sublime: 'The sublime and not the beautiful is the sentiment called forth in these works', Paz writes. The sublime restores the sacred to the individual subject, to the viewing subject, the atomized individual.

For Paz the dualism of the eagle and the jaguar, 'manifest in many ways throughout our history', is transcended by mediation – and the mediators are Quetzalcoatl, in whose being 'the earthly and celestial principle are joined', and the Virgin of Guadelupe, who is described as 'more mysterious, more profound and complete'. It is the Virgin who now becomes the bridge between Christianity and ancient religions, between the male and the female. 'Now there is no longer ideological conflict but the dialectic, the three figures – what better than eagle and jaguar in opposition with the Virgin as transcendent mediation, as advocates/intercessors for an exhibition of Mexican art' (Paz, 1990: 37–8). The unexpressed message is there in the final sentences: the clash of male deities is superseded by the feminine, which is a sign of reconciliation, acceptance, negotiation and non-aggression at a time when Mexican culture was crossing boundaries as a global post-national spectacle and showcase, abstracted from the dark realities of the NAFTA accord that, two years later, the neo-Zapatistas would bring to light.

But Paz was not finished with Coatlicue. In an essay for a multilingual edition dedicated to 'Arts rituals', he summarized the history of the statue and the change in Western sensibility that made pre-Columbian civilizations contemporaneous with our own. La Coatlicue Mayor, as she is now called, 'surprises us not only because of her dimensions – two metres high and two tonnes in weight – but also because she represents a petrified concept. If the concept is terrible – to create, the earth must devour – the form of its expression is enigmatic: each devine attribute – canine teeth, bicefalous tongue, snakes, skulls, cut hands – is represented realistically, but as a whole they become an abstraction' (Paz, 1997: 17). What had been a symbol of totalitarianism for him is now 'a tragic vision of human existence'. This leads him to an extraordinary inversion of his former evaluation. Sacrifice is now creative; man is both cruel victim of the gods but also the axis of the universe. 'Without their blood life would cease flowing and the universe would be extinguished', the exact reverse, Paz argues, of our view of life based on the exploitation of nature. 'We have destroyed the natural environment and endangered the survival of our species. Mesoamerican civilization is an example of the reconciliation of man with nature, even in its most terrible aspects. It is a lesson in solidarity with the universe' (Paz 1997: 17–18). Coatlicue is now ecologically correct.

This is by no means the end of the Coatlicue story. She now illustrates the museum catalogue of the Anthropological Museum and presides over the Mexico City mortuary. A website links Coatlicue to Ted Hughes: 'a demonic pile of *mana*, a petrified mass of grotesque music, equivalent to an irruption of the electrons that vibrate in our sensual world' and quotes Carlos Monsiváis's devastating dismissal: 'La Coatlicue sigue callada porque está pasadísima' ('Coatlicue remains silent because she is out of it').[7] The performance artist Jesusa made an attempt to popularize her by making her a puppet adorned with palpitating hearts (see Franco, 1992). In a special issue of *Debate feminista* on 'Identidades', Coatlicue's body becomes a figure on which is inscribed Mexico's tourist identity. A theatre group of indigenous women in New York calls itself *Teatro Coatlicue*. This feminist version of Coatlicue owes a lot to the Chicana feminists who set out to rescue the goddess from her Aztec imprisonment. In *Borderlands, La Frontera*, the Chicana writer Gloria Anzaldúa identified Coatlicue with deep creative and feminine forces, 'the consuming internal whirlwind, the symbol of the underground aspects of the psyche. Before the Aztec conquest, the gods of Mesoamerica had represented a balance between masculine and feminine forces. Azteca-Mexica culture drove female deities underground giving them monstrous attributes, substituting male deities in this place, thus splitting the female Self and the female deities (Anzaldúa, 1987: 27). Anzaldúa describes herself as breaking down the barriers between human and non-human in order to rapturously reconfigure her identity in which she is devoured by the serpent goddess and reborn into the 'Coatlicue State'. The severed hands are now reinterpreted as the act of giving life and the hearts represent 'the pain of Mother Earth giving birth to all her children'. It comes as no surprise that Coatlicue's very ambiguity opens up the possibility of appropriating that frontier place inhabited by the 'prohibited and forbidden'. Coatlicue has become the cultural icon of New Age Chicana feminism (Anzaldúa, 1987: 47, 5; see also Castillo, 1994).

Octavio Paz wrote that after her rediscovery at the end of the eighteenth century, Coatlicue 'passes from being a crystalization of the powers of another world, to become an episode in the history of human belief. On leaving time for the museum, it changes in nature if not in appearance' (Paz, 1997: 12). While true enough, this does not quite explain the ever-increasing fascination with the figure in the post-national and post-humanist age. Perhaps it is that Coatlicue is a body whose parts do not add up to a discrete wilful unity, to the whole person that we have long deified. In Aztec belief, the energies she graphically represents, energies located in the head, the heart and the liver, disperse and go in different directions after death. We might think, then, of the limbs and organs of Coatlicue not as parts of whole but as variable functions of a temporary unit of the great cosmic machine. I would further argue that the image of the dispersed and fragmented body that is alien to humanist thinking may now represent a reality that in an era of global trafficking in body parts and of organ transplants becomes eerily relevant. Sculpted as the terrible mother of an imperial machine, Coatlicue was imagined before the beginning of humanism and now stands watch over its end.

Notes

1. Esther Pastorzy (1983) believes it may have been carved around the year 1506, possibly in imitation of an earlier sculpture.
2. Letter of Bishop Benito María Moxó y Francoly, published in 1805 and cited by Eduardo Matos Moctezuma in the introduction to the facsimile edition (no page numbers).
3. 'When Coatlicue came to know/she was so shocked/she was so sad./But her son Huitzilipochtli, lying in her breast/comforted her, saying/–Do not fear,/I know what must be done./The four hundred Surians ('surianos') readied themselves…/They were well-dressed/decorated for war./They shared their paper dresses,/their anecúyotl, their nettles,/their bunches of painted paper/and tied bells to their calves.'
4. 'And when Huitzilipochtli had slain them,/when he had vented his rage/he took their clothes, their decorations, their anecúyotl,/he put them on, taking them/he icorporated them into his destiny/and made emblems of them.'
5. See for example, 'Personaje mitológico', in *Risking the abstract: Mexican modernism and the art of Gunther Gerzso* (Santa Barbara Museum of Art, 2003).
6. Thanks to Dawn Addis for pointing this out.
7. On the probably irrecoverable web page, serpiente.dgsca, that includes a mind-blowing variety of topics from Antonio Skármeta to Windows 95.

References

Anzaldúa, G. 1987. *Borderlands. La Frontera. The new Mestiza*. San Francisco: Aunt Lute Books.
Caso, A. 1973. *Obras completas XI. Sociología*. Mexico, UNAM.
Clavijero, F.X. 1971. Sobre las artes de los mexicanos. In *De Teotihuacán a los Aztecas, Antología de fuentes e interpretaciones históricas*, by M. León-Portilla. Mexico: Instituto de Investigaciones Históricas, UNAM.

Castillo, A. 1994. *Massacre of the dreamers. Essays on Xicanisma*. Albuquerque: New Mexico Press.
Fernández, J. 1959. *Coatlicue. Estética del arte indígena antiguo*. Mexico: Instituto de Investigaciones Estéticas. Mexico: UNAM.
Florescano, E. 1999. *The myth of Quetzalcóatl*, translated by Lysa Hochroth. Baltimore: Johns Hopkins University Press.
Franco, J. 1992. The profane Church of Jesusa Rodríguez. *Tulane Drama Review*.
Franco, J. 1996. Identidad gráfica: México turístico', *Debate Feminista*, Año 7, 14 (Octubre).
Fuentes, C. 1971. *Tiempo mexicano*. Mexico: Joaquín Mortiz.
Herrán, S. 1994. *La pasión y el principio*. Mexico: Bital.
León y Gama, A. 1990. *Descripción histórica y cronológica de las dos piedras que con ocasión del nuevo empedrado que se está formando en la Plaza Principal de México se hallaron en el año de 1790*, 2nd edn. Mexico: Instituto Nacional de Antropología e Historia (facsimile edition; first published Mexico: C.M. Bustamante, 1832).
León-Portillo, M. 1971. Nacimiento de Huitzilopochtli. In *De Teotihuacán a los Aztecas, Antología de fuentes e interpretaciones históricas*. Mexico: Instituto de Investigaciones Históricas, UNAM.
Lida, R. 1958. *Letras hispánicas*. Mexico:Fondo de cultura económica.
Matos Moctezuma, E. 1995. *Life and death in the Templo Mayor*, translated by Bernard R. Ortiz de Montellano and Thelma Ortiz de Montellano. Boulder: University Press of Colorado.
Matos Moctezuma, E. 1998. Las piedras negadas. De la Coatlicue al Templo Mayor. Mexico: Consejo Nacional para la Cultura y las Artes.
Matos Moctezuma, E. 2003. The Templo Mayor, the great temple of the Aztecs. In *Aztecs*. London: Royal Academy of Arts.
Pastorzy, E. 1983. *Aztec art*. Norman: Oklahoma University Press.
Pacheco, J.E. 1983. La patria perdida. Notas sobre Clavijero y la 'cultural nacional'. In *En torno a la cultura nacional*. Mexico: Fondo de cultura ecónomica.
Paz, O. 1972. *Postdata*, translated by L. Kemp. In *The Other Mexico: Critique of the Pyramid*. New York: Grove Press.
Paz, O. 1990. Introduction. In *Mexico. Spendors of Thirty Centuries*. New York: Metropolitan Museum of Art.
Paz, O. 1997. Introduction. In *Arts Rituals de Nou Continent. Amèrica Precolumbina*. Barcelona, Instituto de Cultura.
Peret, B. Notes on pre-Columbian art. *Horizon*, No. 89 (June).
Saldaña-Portillo, M.J. 2003. *The revolutionary imagination in the Americas and the age of development*. Durham, NC: Duke University Press.
Schele, L. and M.E. Miller. 1986. *The blood of kings. Dynasty and ritual in Maya art*. New York: George Braziller Inc and Fort Worth: Kimbell Art Museum.
Schneider, L.M. 1978. *México y el surrealismo. 1925–50*. Mexico: Arte y Libros.
Toscano, A. 1952. *Arte precolumbino de México*, 2nd edn. Mexico Instituto de Investigaciones Estéticas, UNAM.

John Kraniauskas

A SHORT ANDEAN HISTORY OF PHOTOGRAPHY: *YAWAR FIESTA*

José María Arguedas's (1911–1969) first novel, *Yawar fiesta*, is full of unexpected, culturally overdetermined, political alliances, and sudden shifts in those alliances.[1] As in many of his subsequent works, economic contradiction and racialized class hatred, at times violently expressed, seem paradoxically to feed and sustain historically given forms of cultural identification, as well as to strengthen the structures of landowner power in republican Peru known as *gamonalismo*, rather than to tear them asunder.[2] The sense of a postcolonial Andean culture that the novel portrays, one that is resistant to government-sponsored modernization, emerges as a particularly resilient and even dynamic reaction-formation as it, moreover, feeds on – or cannibalizes – constituent Indian forms. From this point of view, *Yawar fiesta* presents itself as a study in what Mirko Lauer (Lauer, 1997: 25–9) calls indigenist 'reversion', the cultural work of a paradoxically conservative and nationalist modernism that, in his view, strengthens Peru's feudo-capitalism.[3] The problem thus becomes: how to read the novel, its cultural and political drama as well as its radical and critical contents?

In a historical context of cyclical *gamonal* crises caused by successive waves of Indian rebellion and capitalist modernization – and, most importantly, their containment – Arguedas's novels actively experiment with cultural and political possibility: what might happen, for example, if we ally migrant student followers of the recently deceased founder of the Peruvian Socialist Party, José Carlos Mariátegui, with representatives of the state attempting to 'civilize' the Indian population of an Andean town, Puquio – a town they had all left for Lima, but to which they now return on an anti-*gamonal*-landowner mission? And, what would be the significance of the 'barbaric' failure of both alliance and mission? Since all appearances in this novel are deceptive, including its own apparent 'reversion', another way of asking the question dramatically posed in *Yawar fiesta* is: how are dominant structures reproduced by those who fervently oppose them, and, how might such a situation be rendered critically in a novel? Here lies the enigmatic – and dramatic – core of the text.[4] The answers to these questions are to be found in the political and economic logics of subalternization, and in its cultural forms.

Published in 1941, *Yawar fiesta* looks back on historical experiences associated with two key figures of Peru's then recent political history: on the one hand, the modernizing design of a 'new fatherland' (*Patria Nueva*) during the government of Augusto B. Leguía between 1919 and 1930; and, on the other, the idea of a possible Indianized communism as set out tentatively by Mariátegui (who, having been sent by Leguía into the European exile where he learns his Marxism, dies the same year as the Leguía government is overthrown). It is the 'estudiante Escobar', Arguedas's militant character in *Yawar fiesta*, along with his comrades from the *Centro Unión Lucanas* (a regional migrants' club based in Lima whose members come from Puquio and other towns in the province of Lucanas), who represent the peculiar alliance between state and communist opposition in the novel, brought together under the banner of Mariátegui (his portrait hangs in the Centre) to free Indians from the yoke of *gamonalismo*.[5] Now modernized, theirs is an enlightenment project: 'Nosotros', insists Escobar, 'que ya tenemos los ojos abiertos y la conciencia libre, no debemos permitir que desuellen impunemente a nuestros hermanos...' (68). This is the subalternizing enlightenment view that, paradoxically, seems to lead to the reproduction of *gamonalismo* in opposing it – the mirror-reflection of the student's belief that the Indians of the town, on not being conscious of their own interests, are captured (and sacrificed) by dominant 'Andean' ideology. Thus, as we shall see below, in their political actions the students both attack and uphold aspects of the constitutive fact of *gamonalismo* – the racist (or racialized) exploitation of the Indian population – at the same time. The novel's key fictional gesture in this regard is to transpose the Leguía-like modernizing gesture – the reformation of a 'savage' local bullfight – into the post-Leguía 1930s so as to represent dramatically a practical misreading of Mariátegui *qua* modernizing developmentalist; that is, a one-sided distortion of his possible de-subalternizing legacy (given in the attempt to think the possibility of an Indianized communism). In other words, *Yawar fiesta* is a novel about Mariátegui after Mariátegui (in this case, the 'wrong' Mariátegui).[6]

Insistence

'Antes, Puquio entero era pueblo de indio' (14), says the narrator of the novel. But the narrator will also go on to insist that it remains so. The story told in *Yawar fiesta* is a simple one. Interpreting its significance, however, is not. Which is why, as many critics have pointed out, the first two chapters of the work are so important:[7] they constitute a kind of prehistory of the novel, the spatio-temporal conditions of its story, offering, on the one hand, a description of the town's layout – the social and ethnic distribution of its population around the town centre and local state apparatus run by the ruling creole landowning class (known as '*mistis*') – and, on the other, a history of its origins as a provincial capital and now, apparently, *misti* town.[8] *Misti* control of Puquio is real, and materialized in the town's architectural layout. However, and this is the novel's decisive point, this control is only apparent because, as the narrator insists, from a certain perspective the town may still also be interpreted and conceived as an Indian town:

> en las cascadas, el agua blanca grita, pero los mistis no oyen. En las lomadas, en las pampas, en las cumbres, con el viento bajito, flores amarillas bailan, pero los mistis no ven. (17)

The sound of the river, and the colourful dancing movement of the flowers: sight and sound, both are crucially related to perspective and to the politics of experience in *Yawar fiesta*.[9] The landowners may have property in the land as a factor of production (that is, as capital), but, as a 'body without organs' – in Deleuze and Guattari's terms – the land also speaks and waves to the Indian population, identifying itself to them thus beyond existing property relations (a miraculating fetishism of the 'earth' rather than of the commodity). Although for some critics, Arguedas's vision of Puquio may appear nostalgic – introducing a sentimentalized and regionalist perspective on the past in which, amidst the mountain tops, the town becomes a nest (that is, a simple idyllic image)[10] – such a reading arguably reduces and flattens the text and thus reads it too 'recto' – and as we are told, '[c]alle de misti es siempre derecha' (13) – and thus too focussed on established patterns of power. Puquio is rather represented as a kind of palimpsest, produced in a series of historical and cultural overcodings in which the broken and blurred traces of the past – an 'other' (non-capitalised) land – can still be glimpsed or heard; if, that is, unlike the *mistis*, you can see and hear them.[11] The main story of the novel, told from chapters three to eleven, tells of another – this time *national* – historical overcoding: the attempt to synchronize (and 'civilize') the *time* of the 'patria' (to make it one as well as 'nueva'). But, on emplotting the past into the story as an 'antes', in such a way that its traces are still visible and audible to those who can see and hear, Arguedas installs temporal dislocation, and the memory of dislocation, into the heart of the present such that it suggests future possibility (that is, another 'tierra'/'earth'). The idea of dislocation thus functions in the text in two of the senses foregrounded by Ernesto Laclau: firstly, as the constitutive effect of the non-synchronous, or of uneven and combined development, on the social and, secondly, as the condition of possibility of the political (of the impossible) – opening the present up to its past and to its future. It is as if, in *Yawar fiesta*, there was a surplus of reality, in reality, an excess of 'savage' territory ('tierra'/'earth') overflowing capitalized territory (landed property).[12]

On the one hand, the novel, as a written form, acts as a recording machine, registering the co-existence of other semiotic systems and environments at its edges, to which it appeals for critical perspective and internalizes productively (as song and dance, for example, or as we shall see below, as the photographic enhancement of light): they tell other stories. On the other, by resorting to the experience of pictorial sight and sound, *Yawar fiesta* becomes inter-medial; photo- and phono-graphic, the text demands that its readers not only read, but look and listen beyond its pages too: it provides other perspectives. The novel thus de-reifies the literary text by hinting at its outside, not only as a wider cultural domain of patterned surfaces, but also as a necessary interpretative frame.[13] In this respect, *Yawar fiesta* clearly does not want a slightly mesmerized contemplative reader, typical of instituted literary forms and 'auratic art' (*modernismo* and *indigenismo*, perhaps), but a wary, 'distracted' one, whose attention moves (or, is made to move) from the text to its inter- and con-texts.[14] Thus dislocation also has a formal moment in the composition of *Yawar fiesta*, as it does in many of Arguedas's subsequent novels: the introduction of a quasi-conceptual dimension into the work, the better to think it – small interpretative machines that are semi-autonomous and re-usable. In *Yawar fiesta* this machine is an 'opening' – 'el abra' – to which we will turn below (but which, in truth, I am already commenting upon); in *Los ríos profundos*, it is the anthropological reflection on the spinning top; and in *El zorro de arriba y el zorro de abajo*, Arguedas's diaries – all reflexive quasi-conceptual, or epistemological, interruptions of literary convention inside the text.[15]

Yawar fiesta begins by briefly figuring its narrator as an informant and guide who dialogically addresses both readers and travellers (and readers as travellers), the 'visitors' he is guiding through the mountains (and text) to Puquio. This doubling of narrative voice soon ends, however, and the visitor-travellers disappear from view as the narrator turns towards and focuses upon his objects and their history. At this point his voice becomes monological and the figure of the narrator as native informant is subordinated to a much more conventional and disembodied – but mysterious – third-person narrative voice.[16] Nevertheless, the initial doubling is crucial to the first two chapters of *Yawar fiesta*, and for the interpretation of the novel as a whole. The narrator-as-guide informs us (readers and travellers): 'Llegando de la costa se entra al pueblo por estos ayllus', the *ayllus* (Indian communities) of Pichk'achuri, K'ayau and Chaupi. 'Pueblo indio!' (12) a voice responds, and does so repeatedly, just in case we have not quite got the message the first time, folding the story around a sound produced in astonished realization, but which also doubles as an insistent affirmation: *yes*, indeed, '¡pueblo indio!'. The exclamation marks the appearance of the *ayllu* in the text, a social institution important to Arguedas (and Mariátegui). Indeed, one might even adventure the proposition that the *ayllu* emerges here to become the subject of Arguedian (literary) history. The exclamation '¡pueblo indio!' is thus a split dialogical enunciation, signifying in two opposing directions at once. If, for the visitors from the coast the narrator is guiding to Puquio, the exclamation is one of aversion, for the narrator who repeats it, it is, in contrast, both a historical truth and a matter of pride on which he will insist, now for the readers' benefit – that is, for those visitors to the text (readers) who may be open to other perspectives (this, in a sense, is where the politics of the text begins).[17]

The exclamation '¡pueblo indio!' thus arguably constitutes the literary origin of what I would like to call Arguedas's *insistence* (he insists on the *ayllu*), important for a number of reasons. Firstly, because it becomes constitutive of the cultural politics of his artistic practice of transculturation in all his novels to come: confronted with persistent historical forms of de-Indianization, he will counter with permanent – that is, insistent – re-Indianization. At one level, there may be something voluntaristic about Arguedas's ethical stance. At another, however, it introduces and maintains a *transcultural torsion*, or an 'out-of-place', within the 'structured place' (of *gamonalismo*) whose story the novel relates – in other words, it provides the various forms adopted by its strategy of dislocation with specific social content. Secondly, Arguedas's insistence is also what provides his continuous experimentation with literary form with its particular cultural content: re-Indianization now as an evolving modernist combination of lyrical expression (his literary-political passion and suffering), on the one hand, with its highly conceptualized and constructed negation (evident in his varied orchestration of Indian cultural materials), on the other. Indeed, this combination of expression and construction (how Adomo construes artistic mimesis) is what gives Arguedas's work its formal dynamic over time, and the reason why his texts are so highly composed.[18] Finally, here also lies the political drama of *Yawar fiesta*: having affirmed the Indian character of Puquio at the outset, the novel goes on to show its historical improbability. Let us, therefore, look more closely at the parameters of Arguedas's insistent affirmation (which, of course, is also a *negation* of the given).[19]

The opening

Arguedas, who was later to carry out anthropological research in the town of Puquio (where he lived as a child), has his narrator present the travellers (and readers) he is guiding over the mountains with a detailed map of the town. To begin with they (we) look down on Puquio from above, through a mountain opening, the 'abra de Sillanayok', as it is called by the narrator. The town is divided, and in all kinds of ways: ethno-socially and politically. There is the *mestizo* part ('ni comuneros ni principales' [13], and represented in the novel by the migrant students[20]), the *misti* 'jirón Bolívar' – 'en esa calle corretean, rabian y engordan los mistis, desde que nacen hasta que mueren' – and the 'plaza de armas', the ruling centre of the town (13). In this sense, the mistis are represented in *Yawar fiesta* as the embodiment of what Deleuze and Guattari call 'anti-production': the moment of non-production (within the *socius*, here capital) that, however, appropriates and regulates all production.[21] But there is also the older Indian part of Puquio, different from the rest. As you enter the town, past the river and through the *ayllu* of Pichk'anchuri, the narrator informs us, '[n]o hay calles verdaderas en ningún sitio; los comuneros han levantado sus casas según su interés, en cualquier parte...' (12). The lines of *ayllu* architectural arrangement are not straight ('recto' or 'derecho' – a line, of course, which suggests the establishment of the law; specifically, colonial law in the area). The narrator goes on to describe the houses, both inside and out. He clearly belongs and has access. This is the Indian town, the 'pueblo indio'; and this is also the kind of information travellers and readers want, especially the detail of architectural difference. In itself, however, the fact of difference is not important; it is rather a question of the *difference of difference*, that is, the difference that difference *makes*. *Yawar fiesta* is concerned specifically with the difference the 'pueblo indio' makes – a phrase, as we have seen, which is first uttered 'con desprecio' when the disorganized lines of the Indian *ayllu* come into view. The first two chapters of the novel are concerned with overturning such a view whilst producing another: the *ayllu* perspective (which, in the students' mistaken enlightened view, is no perspective) that emerges from the 'abra', a veritable Indian *dispositif* (a technology and a knowledge).

Yawar fiesta begins by staging an indigenist scene: the crossing by travellers and readers – with the assistance of the narrator – of the imaginary line that marks the ethno-racial division constitutive of the post-colonial symbolic map of Peru, and of *indigenismo*, as set out analytically by Antonio Cornejo Polar (1978; 1980) amongst others.[22] The importance of *indigenismo* in his critical version is that it reveals the geo-political co-ordinates of a literary formation whose principal referents (for which, here, read 'Indian societies and cultures') lie *outside* the socio-cultural domain – that is, the circuits – of the writing and reading of the texts that constitute it. Cornejo Polar refers to this binarized disjuncture of elements as 'heterogeneity'. This subalternizing disjuncture is what also splits the utterance '¡pueblo indio!' into the opposing meanings noted above, making it simultaneously heterogeneous – it repeats the structured place – and a critical turn against such heterogeneity – it 'twists' the structured space: *Yawar fiesta*'s transcultural torsion. From the point of view of the politics of culture, heterogeneity here means that the Peruvian literary institution constitutes its writing- and reading-subjects *in opposition to* Indian social and cultural forms. These forms may be necessary to it; they are, however, disavowed: contained and objectified by the indigenist text to become its mere 'referential' support, an inside-outside, significant as civilizational background or decor to be consumed elsewhere or, alternatively, as an obstacle to be overcome or 'educated' (later 'developed') into citizenship as enlightenment is spread (for example, by the students).[23] Here, the 'other' is not just given, but produced and reproduced in an ongoing post-colonial transcultural encounter. In this sense, *indigenismo*, as a heterogeneous literary-artistic formation, may be considered a particular instance – a 'regime' – of what Rancière refers to as the 'division of the sensible'. The 'other' that is constitutive of heterogeneous literature – of the '*indigenista* regime' – does not participate in the political or literary nation: it is a part 'without a part'; a 'nothing' which, however, is 'everything'.[24] This is the subalternizing *social form* taken by the heterogeneous referentiality (of the Indian) of *indigenismo*.

At the beginning of *Yawar fiesta* Arguedas gives this literary scene a visual – almost photographic – inflection, offering travellers and readers a comprehensive panaroma of Andean otherness from the mountain 'abra' (opening or aperture). Puquio, in other words, is described as if from a panopticon. Associated with the emergence of a rising provincial middle class, *indigenismo* depends on such a totalizing site – provided by the divided symbolic map of republican Peru referred to by Cornejo Polar – from where it becomes involved in the anxious production of fetishistic stereotypes (the reduction, that is, of Indian subjects and cultural forms to mere 'referents'), one of the key means, insists Lauer, for the territorial extension of the Republican state's creole imaginary. Deborah Poole (1997) has also shown that in Peru this cultural fetishism was commodified too as, for example, postcards of Indians, Andean landscapes and villages – some, perhaps, taken at the 'abra de Sillanayok' – circulated in a vast, urban-based, 'visual economy' sedimenting ideas and images of 'race' and nation that (re-)produced the divided symbolic geography on which the *indigenista* regime is based.[25] This is the formation – with its writers and readers, photographers and viewers ('visitors' all) – that *Yawar fiesta* addresses... so as to 'dislocate' it.

From chapter three onwards, the novel reduplicates the indigenist gesture in its interventionist, nation-making mode: it is a question of synchronizing the nation, subordinating its space to the ('new') time of the 'patria', on the 28th July, the 'day of the nation'.[26] A state edict arrives – copies of which its local representative, the 'Subprefecto', has had pinned around the centre of town – demanding the reformation and professionalization of an Andean practice of bullfighting which is perceived as 'savage' and, from the point of view of Escobar and his *mariateguista* followers (who have been charged with contracting a professional bullfighter in Lima), as strengthening the power of local *misti* landowners over the local Indian population. This differentiation between the *gamonal* landowners and the Indian communities of the Andes established by the students is important, a difference often elided in both the post-colonial symbolic map of Peru (that privileges the ethno-racial) as well as in the homogenizing idea of 'Andean culture' itself. And bringing this class conflict to light is their principal function in the novel. It is also what endows *Yawar fiesta* with its cultural and political drama: the students' critical gesture that paradoxically *re-*subalternizes the very subjects they intend to rescue (because, like the Communist International with which Mariátegui was in conceptual struggle – which was also a struggle against himself – Escobar and his comrades are developmentalists, still looking for a modernising bourgeoisie to carry out its historical anti-feudal task of creating a national citizenry, a 'pueblo').[27] The portrayal of such a modernizing gesture in *Yawar fiesta*, and its apparent failure, as an initially split *misti* community is recomposed around the traditional Andean practice – the 'savage' and bloody bullfight (the *turupukllay*) – might even be read as another, pessimistic, indigenist narrative. Which poses the question: is *Yawar fiesta* itself another example of *indigenismo* in which the local landowners *and* Indians ('Andean culture') are represented as obstacles to the modernization of the nation? Arguedas, however, will spoil this view of things (and of the text), the one-sided *inidigenista* view from the 'abra' (which is also too 'recto'), because the opening onto Puquio provides much more than a simple, one-way perspective.

Here is where the potentiality of the division produced in the dialogic exclamation '¡pueblo indio!' – and the split it produces between readers, on the one hand, and travellers (who show 'desprecio' at what they see), on the other – is realized. What follows in the rest of the first chapter of the novel is a lesson in reading and interpretation: the first two chapters of *Yawar fiesta* reveal not only the Indian historical background crucial to the story of the bullfight so as to dislocate the present of the main narrative, as we shall see below, but also the *subjective conditions for its reflection*: that is, the Indians of the *ayllu* communities need to be understood, Arguedas insists, not only as indigenist 'referents' but as technicians of the visual as well as a reflexive (and potentially political) subject too. This constitutes the ethical and social contents of Arguedas's transcultural insistence (his '¡pueblo indio!'), and is what makes reading the narrative so compelling. Arguedas's transcultural insistence is also what forces his text, as it turns against *indigenismo* (its torsion), beyond it. In this sense, what might be considered the transculturating aspect of literary heterogeneity according to Cornejo Polar – the semiotic effect of what he calls 'the materiality of the referent', that is, of Indian culture (for example, the presence in the novel of the sounds of a predominantly oral culture) in literary texts – is, for Arguedas – following in the tentative footsteps of Mariátegui – an opportunity to epistemologically recompose and transform the *ayllu*. It becomes a literary site, not only of cultural production, but also of conceptual and reflexive subjectivization: it sees and thinks, thinks what it sees, and sees what it thinks – it knows. *Yawar fiesta* is a writing-out of *indigenismo*: in its composition ('montaje'), the novel de-composes ('des-monta') the *indigenista* regime, inaugurating a far-reaching 'minorizing' literary project.[28]

Having shown the view of the town from the 'abra', the narrator also adds that each house – which, we have been told, has been built in 'cualquier lugar' – has a 'seña', 'para conocerla bien desde los cerros' (12). This is an important piece of information. In a characteristic Arguedian moment of comparative anthropological commentary, the narrator has already suggested that the urban dwellers of the coast, 'viajeros' who come to visit the town, 'no conocen sus pueblos desde lejos'; 'los presienten', but they do not know them. The narrator continues, now transported and enthusiastically identified with those he describes, for the benefit of the reader-traveller:

> ¡Ver a nuestro pueblo desde una abra, desde una cumbre donde hay saywas de piedra, y tocar en quena o charango, o en rondín, un huayno de llegada! Ver a nuestro pueblo desde arriba, mirar su torre blanco de cal y canto, mirar el techo rojo de las casas... mirar en el cielo del pueblo, volando, a los kilinchos y a los gavilanes negros... oir el canto de los gallos y el ladrido de los perros.... Y sentarse un rato en la cumbre para cantar de alegría.

'Eso', he concludes, 'no pueden hacer los que viven en los pueblos de la costa' (11–12). The 'seña' is thus crucial for, as it is variously aligned with the 'abra', it visually and aurally internalizes and particularizes the knowledge of the 'pueblo' in the form of a 'happy' science (in, that is, a 'fiesta' of seeing and hearing). As a 'pueblo indio' of *ayllus*, Puquio has thus built into its very architecture and dwellings a kind of self-reflexivity, its own enactment (I know that I see, I see what I know) from the 'abra', that introduces negativity (and the thought of particularity) into identity (the identity of this town) as an everyday happy experience – but, of course, only from a particular perspective, that of the 'abra de Sillanayok'.[29]

This is, I think, the perspective of the novel: an opening ('una abra'), in which distance is brought close at the same time as it is historicized. The spatial 'desde lejos', which combines the 'allá' with the 'aquí', overlaps with the temporal 'antes', and the sentimental image of the nest is transformed into the literary equivalent of a concept. And this conceptual site now has a history, a history of dislocation and accumulation (an 'antes') which can be seen and heard, from the right place (an 'allá) – if you know where to look (an 'aquí'). It is as if Puquio were endowed with a historical 'optical unconscious', photo-graphically enhanced. What can be seen and heard from the 'abra'? The answer is to be found in the second chapter of the novel.

Primitive accumulation: the bull-machine

'Puquio es pueblo nuevo para los mistis' (12). They came to stay, and occupy the town, when the regional mining industry collapsed, attracted, we are informed, by the possibilities of 'muchos indios para la servidumbre' in the 'pueblo grande'. So 'comenzó', the narrator goes on to tell, 'el despojo de los *ayllus*' (15). Like the word '*ayllu*', which connotes the power-knowledge of the common – and, as we have seen, the social and cultural conditions of the transcultural torsion of Arguedas's novels – the word '*despojo*' is also a keyword of *Yawar fiesta*: the 'abra' reveals its history in Puquio. Indeed, the second chapter is called 'El despojo'. Before the main story of the novel actually begins in chapter three, this one briefly sets out an account of what Marx refers to as 'so-called primitive accumulation', the process through which *misti* domination of the town was consolidated in the past. It is a story connected by the narrator to a boom in cattle farming, the subsequent capitalisation of the land, and a transformation of social relations of production in the area – and thus, also, later in the novel (its narrative present), to the mythical figure of the bull 'Misitu', its capture, as well as to the bullfight or *turupukllay* (the *yawar fiesta* or 'bloody feast'), in which the bull is sacrificed, with which the novel concludes.

Amongst the Indian population of the *ayllus*, the *comuneros*, there are many who have become landless, the *punarunas*. Years before, the Indian communities had lands in the hills outside the town: 'La puna grande era para todos. No había potreros con cercas de piedra, ni de alambre... era de los indios.' We are even told that 'los mistis le tenían miedo... – Para esos salvajes está bien la puna – decían' (18). The demand for cattle products, however, spurred the *mistis* on to invade and expropriate the 'savage' lands for cattle rearing: 'Año tras año, los principales fueron sacando papeles, documentos de toda clase, diciendo que eran dueños de este manantial, de ese echadero, de las pampas mas buenas de pasto...' (19). In official rituals, communal lands were capitalized and passed over to *mistis*, legalized by the law (with its judges) and blessed by the church (with its priests), symbolically replicating age old, absolutist acts of colonization. The private appropriation of the land is thus accompanied by a process of state territorialization, making its presence increasingly felt throughout the country in a dual process of economic and political 'primitive' (or 'originary') accumulation: the origins of *gamonalismo*. From this point of view, *Yawar fiesta* marks Arguedas's first attempt at producing a literary critique of Peruvian political economy: it narrates the bloody ('*yawar*') – that is, 'anything but idyllic' – process of so-called primitive accumulation described by Marx, the Peruvian enclosures – here of the *puna*.[30] 'Los comunales, que ya no tenían animales, ni chuklla, ni cueva, bajaron al pueblo. Llegaron a su ayllu como forasteros...' (they were now 'other') – in other words, as potential commodities:

> Y en Puquio había un jornalero más para las chacras de los principales, o para 'engancharse' e ir a Nazca o Acarí, a trabajar en la costa. (25)

As in Marx's *Capital*, where images of vampirism abound, the effect on the bodies of the newly dispossessed workers is as if they had been attacked by *pishtacos* ('vampiros serranos', in Flores Galindo's words[31]), their energy and souls drained by the violent process of dispossession first, and super-exploitation later:

> Allí servían de alimento a los zancudos de la terciana. El hacendado los amarraba cinco o seis meses más fuera del contrato y los metía a los algodonales, temblando de fiebre. A la vuelta... si llegaban todavía al ayllu, andaban por las calles, amarillos y enclenques... y sus hijos también eran como los tercianentos, sin alma. (22)

Some *punarunas* are incorporated back into the *ayllus*, whilst others – now proletarianized – remain on the land, servicing the new lords of the *puna*, suffering – and this is the key moment in the composition of Arguedas's novel – the disappearance of the domesticated cattle as it is transported away 'al "extranguero"', especially the bulls: 'Entonces venía la pena grande.... Cantaban a gritos los punarunas....' *Despojo* here thus becomes articulated as sound, and centred on the bull, as it is disseminated far and wide in the mountains:.

> ... y en las hondonadas, en los rocales, sobre las lagunas de la puna, la voz de los comuneros, del pinkullo y de la tinya, lamían el ischu, iban al cielo, regaban su amargo en toda la puna. (24)

The broken spectral bodies and the bitter sounds of primitive accumulation, its living memory, so to speak, constitute *Yawar fiesta*'s primary artistic material, making it a multi-media text in which the effect of the sound of *punaruna* suffering reduplicates the historical process it narrates: literary composition, 'primitive' accumulation of the land, and exchange value (including the now abstract and commodified labour of the *punarunas*) in 'the letters' of Arguedas's work of transculturation.[32] This is what can been seen and heard from the 'abra' – if, that is, you can see and hear, and thus read the signs of the history Arguedas establishes as the perspective on what is to follow: a political narrative of an attempt to synchronize the nation.

What is seen and narrated from the perspective provided by the 'abra' is, in Benjamin's words, of 'another nature': 'other in the sense that a space informed by human consciousness gives way to a space informed by the unconscious' – what he calls the 'optical unconscious'.[33] In other words, what is revealed from the opening in the mountain tops – with the help of the *ayllu* technical invention of the 'abra' at the 'abra de Siilanayok' (which, like Benjamin's photography, is also optical) – are the historical determinations invisible to *misti* or indigenist eyes, which, as we have seen, see too 'recto'. More specifically, the 'abra' provides the perspective from which a culturally overdetermined political conjuncture, defined by the figure of the mythical bull 'Misitu', is narrated. The latter gathers together and condenses all of the conjuncture's constitutive histories and spaces (it is their point of narrative articulation) and maintains them, as if in a cubist montage, in permanent tension so as to finally negate – or better, *dislocate* – them.

Misitu lives high up in the mountain highlands, in the *puna*, the 'savage' lands of the *ayllus* that are now property of the *mistis*, as well as the source of don Julián's power in the international cattle market (he is the wealthiest of the local *mistis* and, according to the student Escobar, 'el cabecilla de los gamonales más atrasados' [88]). In an act of what Flores Galindo refers to as the 'reciprocidad asimétrica' characteristic of *misti* rule, don Julián donates 'his' Misitu to the *ayllus* to celebrate the *turupukllay*. But the savage ('*sallk'a*') bull lives high up in the lands dominated by the magic mountain – the *auki* – K'arwarasu, and don Julián cannot capture it. The Indian *comuneros* of the K'ayua *ayllu* can, however, and on doing so provide the novel with its most important image – of the entrapped and lassoed Misitu – produced over a short, quasi-cinematic passage in the novel which narrates his capture:

> Tiró su lazo, bien, midiendo, sobre seguro, y lo enganchó en las dos astas, sobre la frente misma de Misitu. Cuando los k'ayuas abrieron bien los ojos, el Misitu se encabritaba saltando alto ... ¡Yastá carago! Él también, midiendo tranquilo, ensartó su lazo en las astas del toro, cuando Misitu estaba saltando, como loco.... Sintiendo el otro lazo bramó el Misitu, bramó feo.... Los k'ayuas se acercaron para mirar bien al Misitu. Era gateado, pardo oscuro.... No era grande, era como toro de puna, corriente; pero su cogote estaba bien crecido y redondo, y sus astas gruesas filudas, como raukana de tejedor.... Todo el claro del k'eñwal se llenó de indios .... Los k'ayuas lo miraban, tristes. Era un animal de puna no más.... En ese instante alumbró el sol desde lo alto de la quebrada ... iluminando los matas de ischu que crecen al filo de la quebrada; aclaró el verde oscuro del k'eñwal; y de frente cayó sobre los ojos de los comuneros que estaban mirando a Misitu.... Una tropita de k'ayuas ... escojidos por el varayok' alcalde, se acercaron al Misitu. Cinco agarraron cada lazo. Eran seis lazos, tres para el arrastre y tres para el tiemple.... Mientras, el Misitu esperaba. De frente y de atrás le templaban los lazos.... A saltos lo bajaron hasta la hondonada; le hicieron llegar al camino. De legua en legua se reemplazaban para arrastrarlo. (101, 102, 103)

The account Arguedas gives of the roping and capture of Misitu reminds us that the *punarunas* had domesticated the cattle (including the bulls). They were a fundamental part of their land/'earth', the 'savage' – pastoral – economy of the *ayllus* whose capitalization they mourn in their songs – producing, as we have seen above, the transculturating sounds of dispossession ('el despojo') that occupy so much space in the text: '¡Ay Misitu, /te vas a ir; /ay lloramos/ las mujeres!' (98). From the point of view of the 'abra', 'el despojo' constitutes the most important connotative domain of the novel, which here first passes through the almost 'elasticated' image of the roped bull, to arrive later at its final sacrifice (as we are about to see). By the light of the sun, the communal Indians of K'ayua, having been charged with the organization of the *turupukllay*, re-appropriate the savage bull, and thus the *ayllu* land and the cattle economy, now in the hands of don Julián, too. Entrapped and pulled in different directions by the ropes, the moving image of Misitu functions as the specular moment of the text — in which it sees and reveals itself — at the same time as its reader-visitors witness it from the 'abra'. Escobar and the students recognize this 'fuerza de los ayllus, cuando quieran' (111) in the feat carried out by the K'ayuas, and ally themselves with them as they celebrate. But not totally: the students still insist that the Indians should not participate in the bullfight, and so, in their eyes, subject themselves to the power of the most 'backward' of the *mistis*.[34] On the contrary, the developmentalist (and one-sided *Mariátueguista*) students still insist on imposing the professional, hispanized bullfighter (called Ibarrito) they have brought from Lima to 'educate' the 'fuerza del ayllu', revealed now as the self-valorizing communal power of their labour power.[35]

Pulled at from all sides (and interests) in the conjuncture narrated by Arguedas — that is, by its different constitutive historical and social temporalities[36] — Misitu is also, as we have seen, the object of the state's modernizing mission. This project insists on civilizing the *turupukllay* — and hegemonize the conjuncture — celebrated in Puquio on the day of the nation: that is, to professionalize and 'extirparla' (in the words of the 'Vicario' in the novel) of its constitutive bloody violence that opens ('abre') a disjunctive breach in the desired statist conjugation of the nation — to which the majority of the less powerful *mistis* of the town momentarily (and opportunistically) ally themselves.

The turupukllay

What happens at the end of the novel? The bullfight takes place in the presence of the 'principales' of Puquio, the students and the 'Subprefecto'; but also of the Indians of the *ayllu* communities (many of whom, however, cannot get inside the recently built 'civilized' arena in which it takes place). When the professional bullfighter withdraws from the 'plaza' (he is afraid of the 'savage' Misitu), at the precise moment when the students also (the increasingly excited narrator tells us) 'perdían confianza' (131), the 'corrida' is reconfirmed as a *yawar fiesta* (a 'bloody feast') and *turupukllay*. Suddenly, the modernizing project to synchronize the nation on the day of the 'patria' — such that all might celebrate the same 'now' — falls apart. And does so to the music of the *wakawak'ras*, the bullhorns, in an echo of the sounds that recall originary ('primitive') dispossession. The novel concludes when one of the K'ayua 'capeadores' (the 'Honrao' Rojas) seems to obey an order from the Mayor of Puquio, don Antenor (sitting beside the 'Subprefecto'), to enter the arena and face the bull. Which is what he does, seemingly as a sacrificial victim. According to the Mayor, 'la autoridad' — and, one supposes, *misti* power — is re-established:

> El Wallpa se hacía el hombre todavía. . . . Estaba frente al palco de los principales. Casi todas las niñas y los mistis lo estaban mirando. De repente, se hincharon sus pantalones sobre sus zapatos gruesos de suela, y salió por la boca de su wara, borboteando y cubriendo los zapatos, un chorro grande de sangre; y empezó a extenderse por el suelo. Un dinamitazo estalló en ese instante, cerca del toro. El polvo que salió en remolino desde el ruedo oscureció la plaza. Los wak'rapukas tocaron una tonada de ataque y las mujeres cantaron de pie, adivinando el suelo de la plaza. Como disipado por el canto se aclaró el polvo. El Wallpu seguía, parado aún, agarrándose de los palos. El Misitu caminaba a pasos con el pecho destrozado; parecía ciego. El "Honrao" Rojas corrió hacia él. – ¡Muere, pues, muérete, sallk'a! – le gritaba, abriendo los brazos. – ¿Ve usted, señor subprefecto? Estas son nuestras corridas. ¡El yawar punchay verdadero! – le decía el alcalde al oído de la autoridad. (132)

At first glance, the Mayor would seem to be right. But, how should we interpret the conclusion of *Yawar fiesta* from the perspective opened to us by the 'abra'?

According to Cornejo Polar, it is clear that at the end of the novel 'los *chalos* alimeñados [that is, the student-followers of Mariátegui] fracasaron y el mundo andino se recompone bajo su modelo tradicional'. And what is recomposed in this interpretation of the novel's sudden ending is the dualist vision inscribed in the symbolic map of Peru that subtends the heterogeneous indigenist regime – but in which, according to Cornejo Polar, Andean culture remains opposed, in 'aguda contienda', to the modernizing project of the state. His conclusion would thus seem to imply that on insisting on re-Indianization in the face of the state's de-Indianizing (and 'civilizing') policy, Arguedas's Indian sacrifice (his *yawar fiesta*) in fact reproduces – that is, both feeds and guarantees – *misti* domination. The majority of the *gamonal* class had allied themselves with the state, which they depend upon to stay in power; but, on witnessing – and enjoying – the violent deaths of the bull and of El Wallpu, they change position, and now celebrate the *ayllu* version of the *turupukllay* – because they also depend on the Indian labour and *ayllu* power they appropriate (exemplified here in the Mayor's use of the first person plural of the possessive when he says to the 'Subprefecto': 'Estas son *nuestras* corridas' – my emphasis). More recently, Horacio Legrás has added that the most important conflict of the story of the *turupukllay* told in *Yawar fiesta* is not between the Indians and the *mistis*, but between the Indians and the students – the *chalos* – who also refer to the Indians of Puquio in the first person plural: '*nuestros* hermanos' (68 – my emphasis).[37] As we have seen, the students recognize the Indian 'fuerza' of the *ayllus*, their powerful historical subjectivity – indeed, as Legrás underlines, this 'fuerza' is their own condition of existence: it was the Indians from the *ayllu* that built the road between the mountains and the coast along which they first travelled to Lima, and along which they later returned, politicized[38] – but disavow it as they, like the *mistis*, ally themselves with the state's modernizing project (represented in Puquio by the 'Subprefecto'), which they interpret as being consistent with Mariátegui's thought. The 'fuerza' of the *ayllus* must be 'educated' if it is to be political (because it bears no active principle of futuricity *in the present*). The students thus regard those they want to free as the *objects* of a developmentalist history (in this sense, they de-subjectivize them *qua* possible subjects of emancipation). Indeed, such enlightened objectivization – the re-subalternization of the *ayllus* against which Arguedas writes – is the condition of possibility of their alliance with the state (more: it is what allows for and facilitates the momentary hegemony of the state's project in the novel).

Read from the perspective of the 'abra', however, as if the scene of the *turupukllay* were a historical palimpsest, the 'fuerza' of the ayllu remains present as an agency or collective subject of the history narrated, rejecting both the state-student project of 'civilization', and the *misti* appropriation of land and labour the event represents: when the 'Honrao' Rojas throws himself, as if taking flight – with his arms wide-open, like an eagle – at Misitu, the *comunero* Indians *insist* that *all* (the land, the animals, the *turupukllay*) is, in reality, part of the 'savage' order of the 'earth' which the *mistis* cannot hear nor see. Equally, the memory of 'el despojo' is also maintained, dislocating the structured place and present of the *gamonales* – its 'hegemony', in Mariátegui's words – with a past that persists (and which is more than merely 'residual'), opening it up (from the 'abra') to its negated other: its historical unconscious. In other words, sacred violence is here (like the laughter produced by Chaplin's movies) an example of what Benjamin calls *Jetztzeit*: Arguedas 'does not mean to recognize' history "'the way it really was'" in *Yawar fiesta*, but rather 'means to seize hold of a memory as it flashes up at a moment of danger'.[39] What can be seen from the 'abra' is that very moment when the non-contemporaneous becomes suddenly contemporaneous (and the harbinger of a future that is 'other'): '¡pueblo indio!'

As we have seen, the perspective of the 'abra' on which the novel insists is an invitation to the reader-visitor: it asks that it be applied in the reading of the text, *including its conclusion*. *Yawar fiesta*'s readers have seen and heard things in the story that the *mistis* have not witnessed. In this sense, they too constitute an 'inside-outside': although absent from the narrative, readers are necessary to its textual signification. The novel thus uses and deploys the irony that constitutes it as a form: the surplus knowledge that the narrator and reader possess, compared to that of its main characters, *divides* the celebratory and homogeneizing utterance of the 'nuestra' used by the Mayor as it also rejects the developmentalist historical project of the students – and its 'nuestro' – as well as the 'Subprefecto' to which it is addressed. The experience of the 'abra' thus provides readers with continuity in the action of the narrative – and of its meaning – between past dispossession, the (re-)capture of Misitu in the mountains, and its sacred sacrifice. Another first person plural is produced which, for its part, insists, like Arguedas, in re-Indianization. Thus the *turupukllay* can be interpreted according to its historically reflexive logic: it interrupts the scene of *misti* celebration to stage there – in the newly 'civilized' arena – an act of 'savage' re-appropriation and re-constitution of an 'other' land/'earth'. Indeed, what is also installed in the continuity between the acts of capture and sacrifice established by the narrator and reader is another space – or arena – entirely: the magical land of the *auki* mountain K'awarasu. And in doing so, moreover, the legacy of Mariátegui that is at play in the novel is reconfigured: rather than privileging its positivist side, like the students, the novel concludes foregrounding its de-subalternizing, mythical side, in which Mariátegui(-Arguedas) foreground(s) the importance of the moment of mythical 'enchantment' for the constitution of possible subjects of 'la revolución social'.[40]

Finally, at the same time as *misti* cannibalization of the 'fuerza' of the *ayllus* (that is, the constitution of Andean culture, 'bajo su forma tradicional' in Cornejo Polar's words, its 'nuestro') is interrupted, the structured space of the 'indigenist regime' is opened up to the future so as to inaugurate another politics of literature: maintaining its transcultural torsion, but without resolving it. In other words, *Yawar fiesta*, with its historically reflexive 'abra' (its small interpretative machine), *is* an 'abra', an opening that retrospectively constitutes itself as a point of departure for the rebellions (in *Los ríos profundos*) and revolutions (in *Todas las sangres*), as well as the industrial reconfigurations of the 'fuerza' of the *ayllus* (in *El zorro de arriba y el zorro de abajo*) of Arguedas's novels to come.[41] 'What is aura, actually?', asks Benjamin. And he answers: 'A strange weave of space and time: the unique appearance or semblance of distance, no matter how close the object may be.'[42] Like the photographs Benjamin is commenting upon, Arguedas's novels also attempt to destroy the heterogeneous distance that structures the indigenist regime: 'they pump the aura out of reality [through the 'abra', JK] like water from a sinking ship.'

Notes

1. José María Arguedas, *Yawar fiesta* (1941), Editorial Horizonte, Lima, 2010. All references to the novel will be to this edition and included in parenthesis in the text.
2. *Gamonalismo* and the struggle against *gamonalismo* is fundamental to Arguedas's literary production. What is it? According to Mariátegui: '[e]l término "gamonalismo" no designa solo una categoría social y económica: la de los latifundistas o grandes propietarios agrarios. Designa todo un fenómeno. El gamonalismo no está representado sólo por los gamonales propiamente dichos. Comprende una larga jerarquía de funcionarios, intermediarios, agentes, parásitos, etc. El indio alfabeto se transforma en un explotador de su propia raza porque se pone al servicio del gamonalismo. El factor central del fenómeno es la hegemonía de la gran propiedad semifeudal en la política y el mecanismo del Estado.' Mariátegui, 1978, p. 37.
3. See Lauer (1997: 25–9).
4. 'Enigmatic' in the sense that, apart from what it may say about reality, this is also the site of the text's own demand to be interpreted.
5. If we take note of Mariátegui's use of the notion of 'hegemonía' to describe *gamonal* rule, *gamonalismo* might best be thought of as a hybridized *state*, reproducing and subordinating underdeveloped forms of rural capitalism to the localized personal rule of the landowner (or *misti*) class. Emerging from the collapse of the colonial state, according to Alberto Flores Galindo (1988: 290–1), it constitutes a postcolonial form in which 'la privatización de la política, la fragmentación del dominio y su ejercicio a escala de un pueblo o de una provincia' – that is, 'poder local' – is paradoxically institutionalized as dominant. This is why Mariátegui insisted that capitalism in Peru was the work of the 'feudo' rather than the 'burgo'. From this perspective, Leguía's *Patria Nueva* government represents something like a belated revenge of the 'burgo', a US – capital and government loan – sponsored programme of state modernization aimed at the economic and political power of the landowning 'feudo'. The character of Leguía's government is thus best understood as a statist modernization programme – involving the simultaneous expansion and centralization of both repressive and ideological state apparatus: strengthening the armed forces and the civil guard, as well as creating and expanding state education. See Flindell Klarén (2000: 241–88).
6. Indeed, *Yawar fiesta* is a novel that dramatizes the constitutive tension between (developmentalist) positivism and (mythic) romanticism in Mariátegui's thought. See Kraniauskas (2005).

7   See Elmore (1993: 99–144) and Paoli (1985: 165–87).
8   'En teoría eran blancos, o por lo menos se consideraban como tales; lo más frecuente es que en términos socioeconómicos se tratara de propietarios o terratenientes, dueños de un fundo, una hacienda o un complejo de propiedades ... ejercían su poder en dos espacios complementarios: dentro de la hacienda, sustentados en las relaciones de dependencia personal, en una suerte de reciprocidad asimétrica; fuera de ella, en un territorio variable que en ocasiones podia comprender ... la capital de un departamento, a partir de la tolerancia del poder central. El Estado requería de los gamonales para poder controlar a esas masa indígenas excuidas del voto y de los rituales de la democracia liberal ....' Galindo (1988: 290–1. This describes the social relations of *Yawar fiesta* quite well.
9   See the important essays contained in Rowe (1996).
10 For example, see Paoli (1985) – although this does not exhaust the interest of his account.
11 Deleuze and Guattari's use of the idea of 'the body without organs' is notoriously difficult and slippery, whilst also developing over time. Here I will refer to it in the sense suggested by the following passage: 'Its one purpose is to point out the fact that the form of social production, like those of desiring-production, involve an unengendered non-productive attitude, an element of antiproduction coupled with the process, a full body that functions as a *socius*. This socius may be the body of the earth, that of the tyrant, or capital. This is the body that Marx is referring to when he says that it is not the product of labor, but rather appears as its natural or divine presupposition. ... It falls back on ... all production, constituting a surface over which the forces and agents of production are distributed, thereby appropriating for itself all surplus production and arrogating to itself both the whole and the parts of the process, which now seem to emanate from it as a quasi cause. Forces and agents come to represent a miraculous form of its own power: they appear to be "miraculated" ... by it.' See Deleuze and Guattari (2004: 11). What is up for grabs in *Yawar fiesta* is the 'earth' before and after being capitalized (that is, 'miraculated' by capital).
12 In Deleuze and Guattari's periodization of history, the idea of a 'savage' territoriality principally refers to nomadic societies. Here I am using it – that is, the idea of 'earth' – to refer to the non-capitalist and non-feudal territoriality of the '*ayllu*' as deployed by Arguedas in *Yawar fiesta*. It would be important to see to what extent it is a fictional construction made out of materials produced both by his experience and by his anthropological and historical studies – all subordinated here, however, to his own literary-political project. Laclau discusses 'dislocation' in Laclau (1990: 39–59).
13 Arguedas thus uses the novel form to expand, firstly, the archive, as a counter-history, to include other voices ('air-writing', in Cornejo Polar's sense) excluded by established history-writing, and secondly, the idea of legitimated reading, to include non-literary patterning (dance) and surfaces (land, buildings, sky). See Rowe (1996) and Cornejo Polar (1994).
14 Arguedas has evidently learned from the avant-gardes and the experience of mechanical reproduction. On 'distraction', see Walter Benjamin (1979), 'The Work of Art in the Age of Mechanical Reproduction'.
15 This inclusion of documents of reality into literary space – like in conceptual art – prefigures the compositional practices of writers like Rodolfo Walsh, Augusto Roa Bastos and Ricardo Piglia: the artistic use of the non-artistic and the non-artistic use of the artistic.

16 For the mysterious identity of the third-person narrator who says and sees everything, but from an inaccessible point of view, see Jameson (2007: 380–419).
17 It is important here to note the difference between the exclamation of the author-narrator of *Yawar fiesta* and the colonial institution 'pueblo de indios' – the product of the colonial 'reduction' of the Indian population. A discussion of these as well as of their postcolonial republican transformation can be found in Thurner (1997).
18 See Theodor W. Adorno's discussion of the contradiction between expression and construction in art as developed in Adorno (2004).
19 For the ideas of 'structured place', 'out-of-place' and ethical 'torsion', I have freely adopted from Badiou (2009) and Rama (1982).
20 For the different positions adopted by Arguedas with regard to 'mestizaje' from the beginning of the 1950s on (that is, after the publication of *Yawar fiesta*), and which range from optimism to disappointment, see Manrique (1993: 85–98).
21 For the notion of 'anti-production', see note 11 above. For an account of the social contents of the novel see Rodrigo Montoya, '*Yawar* fiesta: una lectura antropológica', *Revista de crítica literaria latinoamericana*, Año 6, No. 12, 1980, pp. 55–68; and for the significance of the urban design of Puquio, see François Bourricaud (1958), reproduced in Carmen María Pinilla (2011: 87–99) as well as Arguedas's 'The Novel and the Problem of Literary Expression in Peru' in the English-language translation of *Yawar fiesta*, translated by Frances H. Barraclough, Waveland Press, Prospect Heights, pp. xiii–xxi (this edition also contains Arguedas's study of the town, '*Puquio*: A Culture in Process of Change').
22 Cornejo Polar (1978: 7–8) and (1980).
23 According to Laclau, the 'constitutive outside' is constitutive of social antagonism, 'an "outside" which blocks the identity of the "inside" (and is, nonetheless, the prerequisite for its constiution at the same time)' (Laclau: 1990: 17).
24 '... the system of self-evident facts of sense perception that simultaneously discloses the existence of something in common and the delimitations that define the respective parts and positions within it. ... This apportionment of parts and positions is based on a distribution of spaces, times, and forms of activity that determines the very manner in which something in common lends itself to participation. ...' 'However,' continues Rancière, 'another form of distribution precedes this act of partaking in governement: the distribution that determines those who have a part in the community ....' See Rancière (2004: 12). Rancière goes on to describe and periodize a number of 'aesthetic regimes'. In this regard, one might say that what could be called the 'indigenist regime' described by Cornejo Polar from the point of view of literature traces a diagram of the *foundational* 'disagreement' of post-colonial Peru. See Rancière (1999: 9).
25 See Lauer (1997); Poole (1997).
26 As Marx says of capital: it 'strives ... to annihilate this space [the 'whole earth'] with time ... ' – its time. Marx (1977: 539).
27 See Oscar Terán (1985) and, for the subalternizing aspects of the concept of 'development', my 'Difference Against Development: Spiritual Accumulation and the Politics of Freedom', *Boundary 2*, 32, 2, 2005, 53–80.
28 For 'minor literature', see Deleuze and Guattari (1993: 16–20). In their view, minor literature has three characteristics: the *deterritorialization of language* (of both the Spanish and the Quechua in *Yawar fiesta* – like Kafka, Arguedas is a bilingual writer), the *political immediacy* of every individual act and utterance (the political overdetermination of the

actions of all in the novel's story), and the *collective assemblage of enunciation* (on the one hand, the dissonant mixing of languages dramatized in *Yawar fiesta* – there is no attempt to create a 'mestizo' language that would reconcile the conflicts in and between the languages, or to search for equivalence in their translation – and, on the other, their dramatization from the perspective of the 'abra' and *ayllu*). In this sense, the *dissonance* of the languages reduplicates the *dislocation* of the novel's form.

29 In this sense, the *ayllu* – or community – subject of Arguedian literary history emerges from the 'abra' as a kind of 'open' and 'exposed' subject, as it is set out, for example, by Jean-Luc Nancy in his reflections on Roberto Esposito's idea of 'communitas-immunitas'. See Nancy (2003: 9–19). This topic is addressed in a set of further essays on the work of Arguedas and Augusto Roa Bastos in development.
30 Marx (1976: 874).
31 Flores Galindo (1988: 295). See also my essay on Guillermo del Toro's vampire film *Cronos*: '*Cronos* and the political economy of vampirism: notes on a historical constellation', in Francis Barker, Peter Hulme & Margaret Iverson (eds.) (1998: 142–57).
32 'And this history, the history of their expropriation, is written in the annals of mankind in *letters* of blood and fire.' Marx (1976: 875) (my emphasis).
33 Walter Benjamin, 'A Small History of Photography', in (1979) *One-Way Street*, New Left Books. London, 243.
34 In truth, as François Bourricaud points out, the modernizing plan to which the students are allied involves substituting the Indian *tutupukllay* with a 'civilized' bullfight (or 'corrida'): Bourricaud (1991), included in Carmen María Pinilla (2011: 103–21). And, to resist this transformation is to insist in the 'savage' domestication of the bulls, including the mythical Misitu: ¡Indian cattle!
35 'Only the standpoint of bodies and their power can challenge the discipline and control wielded by the republic of property', write Antonio Negri and Michael Hardt in their recent book; Hardt and Negri (2009: 27). In this sense, Arguedas's insistence – like that of another exemplary writer in this regard, José Revueltas – is similar to the rhetorical and theoretical insistence of Antonio Negri, whose Ideas on the common I am adapting here. For a negative review of *Commonwealth*, see Kraniauskas (2010: 39–42).
36 This is what Néstor García Canclini calls a 'hybrid' conjunctural formation: a fragmented unity of a variety of historical temporalities, such as those represented by misti *gamonalismo*, the Lima-mediated cattle economy, the state, and the ayllus (amongst others) – and the figure of Misitu articulates them all. See García Canclini (1989).
37 Antonio Cornejo Polar (1973: 79, 93) and Horacio Legrás (2008: 207–11).
38 The story of the building of the road is told in the context of the law pertaining to the *conscripción vial* imposed by the Leguía government in 1920: all men between eighteen and sixty years of age had to work for six to twelve days a year on the building of roads. In the novel, this becomes a kind of *neo-mita* that the Indians of the provincial towns *invert* in local competitions (Elmore, 1993). For its social consequences (such as migration and the creation of clubs of migrants in Lima), see Flindell Klarén (2000: 250–1).
39 Walter Benjamin, 'Theses on the Philosophy of History' (1940), *Illuminations*, Fontana, London, 1979, p. 257. Benjamin is quoting Ranke.
40 As is well known, Arguedas also insisted that 'el socialismo no mató en mi lo mágico', 'No soy un aculturado...'; Arguedas (1975: 281–3). See also Mariátegui (1979: 23–8). The key question here would be whether, for Mariátegui, the mythical quality

of the 'social revolution' needs to be historically mediated by the cultural experience of secular disenchantment or de-mythification for its own political efficacy. For François Bourricaud (1991) the deaths of the bull and of the K'ayua 'capeadores' are 'auto-destructivos', and symptoms of Arguedas's own melancholy (Bourricaud is writing after the author's suicide). From the point of view of the 'abra', however, sacred destruction can also be productive: it dislocates and reveals.

41 For the latter, see William Rowe (1975: 117–28) and Jon Beasely-Murray, '*Arguedasmachine*: Modernity and Affect in the Andes', *Iberoamericana*, 30, 2008, 113–28.

42 Walter Benjamin (1979: 250), 'A Small History of Photography'.

References

Adorno, Theodor W. 2004. *Aesthetic Theory* (1970). translated by Robert Hullot-Kentor. London: Continuum.

Arguedas, José María. 1975. No soy un aculturado.... In *El zorro de arriba y el zorro de abajo.*, 281–3. Buenos Aires: Losada.

Arguedas, José María. 2010. *Yawar fiesta* (1941). Lima: Editorial Horizonte.

Arguedas, José María. 1985. The Novel and the Problem of Literary Expression in Peru. In *Yawar fiesta*. translated by Frances H. Barraclough. Prospect Heights: Waveland Press.

Arguedas, José María. 1985. *Puquio*: A Culture in Process of Change. In *Yawar fiesta*. translated by Frances H. Barraclough. Prospect Heights: Waveland Press.

Badiou, Alain. 2009. *Theory of the Subject* (1982). translated by Bruno Bosteels. London: Continuum.

Barker, Francis, Hulme, Peter, and Iverson, Margaret, eds. 1998. *Cannibalism and the Colonial Order*. Cambridge: Cambridge University Press.

Beasely-Murray, Jon. 2008. *Arguedasmachine*: Modernity and Affect in the Andes. *Iberoamericana* 30: 113–28.

Benjamin, Walter. 1979. The Work of Art in the Age of Mechanical Reproduction. In *Illuminations*. London: Fontana.

Benjamin, Walter. 1979. Theses on the Philosophy of History (1940). In *Illuminations*. London: Fontana.

Benjamin, Walter. 1979. A Small History of Photography. In *One-Way Street*. London: New Left Books.

Bourricaud, François. 2011. Sociología de una novela peruana. (1958). In *Itinerarios epistolares: la Amistad de José María Arguedas y Pierre Duviols en dieciséis cartas*, edited by Carmen María Pinilla. Lima: Fondo Editorial, Pontificia Universidad Católica del Perú.

Bourricaud, François. 2011. *Yawar fiesta*: violencia y destrucción. (1991). In *Itinerarios epistolares: la Amistad de José María Arguedas y Pierre Duviols en dieciséis cartas*, edited by CarmenMaría Pinilla., 103–21. Lima: Fondo Editorial, Pontificia Universidad Católica del Perú.

Cornejo Polar, Antonio. 1973. *Los universos narrativos de José María Arguedas*. Buenos Aires: Editorial Losada.

Cornejo Polar, Antonio. 1978. El *indigenismo* y las literaturas heterogéneas: su doble estatuto socio-cultural. *Revista de crítica literaria latinoamericana* : 7–8.
Cornejo Polar, Antonio. 1980. *La novela indigenista: literatura y sociedad en el Perú*. Lima: Lasontay.
Cornejo Polar, Antonio. 1994. *Escribir en el aire*. Lima: Editorial Horizonte.
Deleuze, Gilles, and Félix Guattari. 1993. *Kafka: Towards a Minor Literature*. Minneapolis: University of Minnesota Press.
Deleuze, Gilles, and Félix Guattari. 2004. *Anti-Oedipus: Capitalism and Schizophrenia 1972*. London: Continuum.
Elmore, Peter. 1993. Lima y los Andes: caminos y desencuentros. In *Los muros invisibles. Lima y la modernidad en la novela del siglo XX*. Lima: Mosca Azul Editores.
Esposito, Roberto. 2003. *Communitas: Origen y destino de la comunidad*. Aires: Amorrortu Editores.
Flindell Klarén, Peter. 2000. *Peru: Society and Nationhood in the Andes*. Oxford: Oxford University Press.
Flores Galindo, Alberto. 1988. *Buscando un Inca*. Lima: Editorial Horizonte.
García Canclini, Néstor. 1989. *Culturas híbridas. Estrategias para entrar y salir de la modernidad*. México: Grijalbo.
Hardt, Michael, and Antonio Negri. 2009. *Commonwealth*. Cambridge, MA: Harvard University Press.
Jameson, Fredric. 2007. A Monument to Radical Instants. In *The Modernist Papers*. London: Verso.
Kraniauskas, John. 1998. *Cronos* and the political economy of vampirism: notes on a historical constellation. In *Cannibalism and the Colonial Order*, edited by Francis Barker, Peter Hulme, and Margaret Iverson., 142–57. Cambridge: Cambridge University Press.
Kraniauskas, John. 2005. Laughing at Americanism: Benjamin, Mariátegui, Chaplin. In *Walter Benjamin: Critical Evaluations in Cultural History* (Vol. III), edited by Peter Osborne., 368–77. London: Routledge.
Kraniauskas, John. 2005. Difference Against Development: Spiritual Accumulation and the Politics of Freedom. *Boundary 2* 32 (2): 53–80.
Kraniauskas, John. 2010. Remake, the Sequel. *Radical Philosophy* 160: 39–42.
Laclau, Ernesto. 1990. *New Reflections on the Revolution of Our Time*. London: Verso.
Lauer, Mirko. 1997. *Andes imaginarios: discursos del indigenismo 2*. Lima: Centro de Estudios Regionales Andinos Bartolomé de las Casas, Cuzco, and SUR Casa de Estudios del Socialismo.
Legrás, Horacio. 2008. The End of Recognition: Arguedas and the Limits of Cultural Subjection. In *Literature and Subjection: The Economy of Writing and Marginality in Latin America*., 207–11. Pittsburgh: University of Pittsburgh Press.
Manrique, Nelson. 1993. José María Arguedas y la cuestión del mestizaje. In *La piel y la pluma: escritos sobre literatura, etnicidad y racismo*. Lima: SUR Casa de Estudios del Socialismo.
Mariátegui, José Carlos. 1978. *Siete ensayos de interpretación de la realidad peruana*. Lima: Editorial Amauta.
Mariátegui, José Carlos. 1979. El hombre y el mito. (1925). In *El alma matinal*., 23–8. Lima: Obras Completas 3, Editora Amauta.
Marx, Karl. 1976. *Capital: A Critique of Political Economy*. Vol. 1, translated by Ben Fowkes. Harmondsworth: Penguin Books.

Marx, Karl. 1977. *Grundrisse*. translated by Martin Nikolaus. Harmondsworth: Penguin Books.

Montoya, Rodrigo. 1980. *Yawar* fiesta: una lectura antropológica., *Revista de crítica literaria latinoamericana* Año 6, No. 12

Nancy, Jean-Luc. 2003. Conloquium. In Roberto Esposito, *Communitas: Origen y destino de la comunidad*. Buenos Aires: Amorrortu Editores.

Osborne, Peter, ed. 2005. *Walter Benjamin: Critical Evaluations in Cultural History* (Vol. III). London: Routledge.

Paoli, Roberto. 1985. Mundo y mito en *Yawar fiesta*. In *Estudios sobre literatura peruana*. Firenze: Stamperia Editoriale Parenti.

Pinilla, Carmen María, ed. 2011. *Itinerarios epistolares: la Amistad de José María Arguedas y Pierre Duviols en dieciséis cartas*. Lima: Fondo Editorial, Pontificia Universidad Católica del Perú.

Poole, Deborah. 1997. *Vision, Race, and Modernity: A Visual Economy of the Andean Image World*. Princeton, NJ: Princeton University Press.

Rama, Angel. 1982. *Transculturación narrativa en América Latina*. México: Siglo Veintiuno Editores.

Rancière, Jacques. 1999. *Disagreement: Politics and Philosophy* (1995). Minneapolis: University of Minnesota Press.

Rancière, Jacques. 2004. *The Politics of Aesthetics: The Distribution of the Sensible*. translated by Gabriel Rockhill. London: Continuum.

Rowe, William. 1975. Deseo, escritura y fuerzas productivas. In *El zorro de arriba y el zorro de abajo.*, 117–28. Buenos Aires: Losada.

Rowe, William. 1996. *Ensayos arguedianos*. Lima: Universidad Nacional Mayor de San Marcos and SUR Casa de Estudios del Socialismo.

Terán, Oscar. 1985. *Discutir Mariátegui*. Puebla: Universidad Autónoma de Puebla.

Thurner, Mark. 1997. *From Two Republics to One Divided: Contradictions of Postcolonial Nationmaking in Andean Peru*. Durham, NC: Duke University Press.

Guillermina De Ferrari

CUBA: A CURATED CULTURE

> What is art is not only an aesthetic question; we have to take into account how it responds at the intersection of what is done by journalists and critics, historians and museum writers, art dealers, collectors and speculators.[1]

While the popularity of Cuba on the international culture circuit is self-evident, the aesthetic and social impact of this phenomenon has yet to be decoded. Until now, few critical texts treating cultural production in post-Soviet Cuba are more telling than the short story 'La guagua' ('The Bus') by Alexis Díaz Pimienta. The story recounts the seemingly banal experience of riding in a crowded bus in downtown Havana. It begins in a realistic tone: it is hot, it is hard to breathe, the rain outside prevents the passengers from opening the windows on the bus, bodies keep piling in. Just when it seems as though no other person could possibly fit in the bus, the driver takes pity on a passer-by, allows him to climb in, and closes the doors after him. The passengers suddenly realize that they are trapped, and 'that at the next stop ... there would be no room for [the doors] to open' (2000: 159). The bus reaches the end of its run and the driver, who has been kept cool thanks to a little fan, realizes what has happened, jumps out of his window and calls the fire department. The firefighters are unable to pry the doors open and are forced to cut the bus in half. When both sides fall off, it appears that:

> The mass of people was still compact. The bus had moulded the group, which was now a block of faces, backs, profiles; a painting in 3-D of terribly open eyes and mouths. It looked like the sombre work of an artist, carved in marble or ice.
>
> Some of the people, those on the periphery, appeared to be in one piece. Others were only an arm, or an ear, or a right shoe, just like me. From above, it was a collection of hair, bald spots, unfinished shoulders, shadows.... Each side deserved to be signed by Velázquez, Rembrandt, Picasso: The faces! The chiaroscuros! The angular figures! (2000: 160)[2]

So far, the story invites an allegorical reading of Cuba's recent history. As a closed space, the bus can be read as the blockaded island; the driver as a leader who is blind to the needs of his passengers; the bus's route as the journey of a revolution that has lost its capacity to serve the people. Yet, this reading is complicated by the meta-referential aspect of the story's denouement. The story resolves the ontological confusion of the bodily mass of passengers by placing the object, first in the gardens of the Department of Transportation (Mitrans), and finally at:

The Museum of Fine Arts, where the public can enjoy it Tuesday to Sunday, from 2 to 9. Some of the visitors, mostly foreigners, inquire after the author of such magnificent work, or they leave thinking that it is someone called Mitrans, because they confuse the author with the donor. (2000: 160)

In part, the story's ending offers a parodic view of postmodern art, which is often based on questioning the very boundaries of what is art and what is not. At the local level, this meta-referential comment amounts to a complaint. As the text suggests, the crisis in which Cuba is now immersed has become in itself a form of art. This view is not very popular in literary circles, where it has often been suggested that the novels that focus on contemporary living conditions only seek to feed the curiosity of a foreign readership.

The story, however, hides more than it actually tells. While 'La guagua' proposes that new Cuban art is a combination of circumstance and error, the presence of the human mass in the museum obeys someone's active decision to place it there, a decision that helps determine the foreigners' 'misreading' of the object.[3] In this essay, I contend that it is possible to consider that decision as a legitimate cultural act; that is, one that responds neither to market nor to political pressures, but to assumptions shared in the cultural world regarding the way in which objects are labelled, exposed and circulated as art. Understanding how that decision was possibly made will tell more about contemporary Cuban culture than the accident theory offered by Díaz Pimienta.

Behind the story is the international popularity of the art produced in Cuba during the crisis that became known as 'Período Especial en Tiempos de Paz' (Special Period in Times of Peace). The term 'Special Period' refers mostly to the time that followed the dissolution of the Soviet Block, when Cuba lost its subsidies and its Eastern European commercial network, succumbing to a violent economic crisis. This crisis, which was 'a lot more than a mere crisis', in Kevin Power's words, reached unimaginable levels of intensity in the early 1990s (1999: 24). The hunger and indignity were such that, in fact, Cuban reality often appeared more interesting than fiction. It is not surprising then that one of the most distinctive aesthetic projects to take place in Cuban culture since 1990 consists of presenting reality 'as it is', presenting objects and telling stories in an exhibitionist, 'unmediated' manner.

In literature, the following titles are self-explanatory: *Trilogía Sucia de La Habana* (*Dirty trilogy of Havana*) and *Animal Tropical* (*Tropical Animal*) by Pedro Juan Gutiérrez, *El hombre, la hembra y el hambre* (*Man, Woman, Hunger*) by Daína Chaviano, *La nada cotidiana* (*Yocandra in the paradise of nada*) by Zoé Valdés, among others. These texts are devoted to the explicit portrayal of prostitution, of lack of food, water and transportation, and of an acute state of hopelessness. Other writers have produced more elaborate, less transparent narrations, but with ultimately a similar effect. Antonio José Ponte's story 'Un arte de hacer ruinas' ('An Art of Making Ruins'), for example, elaborates a conspiracy theory about the overwhelming collapse of buildings in Downtown Havana due to negligence and overcrowding. Ponte, who is an engineer by training, found inspiration in an article published in an urban studies journal that used the term 'miraculous statics' as a way to explain the survival of many buildings in Centro Habana that should have already collapsed by all scientific calculations.

In film, it is quite common to come across hybrid examples that are aestheticized variations on the documentary film. The most revealing ones are, perhaps, *Si me comprendieras* (*If you only understood*) by Rolando Díaz (1998) and *Suite Habana* by

Fernando Pérez (2003), both of which use non-actors as their protagonists. These 'actors' offer their own lives, their dilapidated houses, their complicated family stories, and their frustrated dreams to create the very texture of the film. *Si me comprendieras*, the less visibly mediated of the two, starts as meta-fiction but soon becomes completely absorbed by the real-life stories of the aspiring actresses, their families and houses. Interestingly, the director made a point of never interviewing the actresses off-camera so as to preserve their spontaneous, emotional reactions for the final film. In turn, *Suite Habana* can easily be dubbed a 'visual poem' that intertwines (artificially, in fact) the daily lives of various families. The unexpected silences (the film has no dialogue), the slow camera, the extended repetition of familiar movements and domestic tasks, and, particularly, a very fine editing job help make this film intensely realistic and highly mediated at the same time. As in the literary cases mentioned above, the appeal of both films seems largely to emanate from an exhibitionistic presentation of real life with apparently minimal authorial intervention.

As the short story 'La guagua' suggests, international demand has been an important force behind this type of art production. With the insolvency of Cuban state publishing houses and the virtual collapse of the once booming local film industry, the dissemination of Cuban art and culture has passed into foreign hands, mostly to Spanish publishers and film producers. The result has been the proliferation of Cuban art outside Cuba, allowing for a reinvigorated and redefined cultural production that has been the focus of much critical attention. *Suite Habana*, made with European funds, won several international awards including the Goya award for best foreign film (Spain 2004); Chaviano's novel *El hombre, la hembra y el hambre* won the Azorín award in Spain 1998; and Gutiérrez's *Animal tropical* obtained the Alfonso García Ramos award in 2000, also in Spain. The success of Cuban art in the international cultural circuits has led critics to discuss the existence of a cultural boom (Jesús Díaz) that addresses the ethnographic curiosity of a foreign public (De Ferrari), often serving as dictionaries of an attractive reality to the literary tourist (Whitfield), and which is ruled by an international market that has effectively replaced state guidance about what Cuban art should be like, or even about (Buckwalter-Arias).[4] Indeed, as Sujatha Fernandes and others have noted, the marketing of Cuban culture in the 1990s cannot be separated from a new economy of export and exchange, one in which art is traded across nations in the absence of traditional export goods. I also agree with Fernandes, however, when she suggests that 'the insertion of the Cuban culture industries into global markets . . . has opened up the site of culture to new contradictions', and, I may add, to unexpected redefinitions (2006: 10–11).

As the story 'La guagua' seems to suggest, the literary boom based on the material reality of the Special Period, which has been named 'literatura del desencanto', is seen as problematic within literary circles on the island.[5] This may be traced at least in part to the commercial success of this trend. Traditionally, a work with commercial appeal is deemed to be of lesser quality, equating the idea of 'selling' with that of 'selling out'. Similar is the case of the political malleability of a given text.[6] In fact, the association that has been established between these works and a 'minor' genre such as testimony, on the one hand, and the socialist realism of the early years of the Revolution, on the other, has clouded the perception of these works. In addition, art that traffics in the current state of affairs on the island – and thus depicts the far from beautiful reality of hunger, scarcity and filth – does not categorically conform to the aesthetic notions that are upheld by, and indeed define, the artistic and intellectual class as a whole. I have to admit that, though I don't share most of these assumptions, I would agree that a realist type of aesthetic in postmodern times seems somewhat suspicious. The apparent ingenuousness of these texts becomes all the more dubious when we consider the fact that they have been produced in Cuba, a country that takes pride in its sophisticated cultural tradition, and which has recently benefited from the generous cultural politics of the Revolution.

Inspired, in part, by the story 'La guagua', and convinced that art critics have had a much better grasp of the function, mechanisms and, certainly, the aesthetics of cultural production in this period than literary critics, I want to use the model of the visual arts to shed some light on literary production during this time. I would like to justify this comparison based on the higher visibility of the circulation of art than of literature – it is easier to know who exhibits a painting and who buys it than to know who buys a book, how it travels and who reads it. Similarly, the institutional apparatus of biennials, international exhibitions and mixed-capital foundations that disseminate Cuban art throughout the world render more visible the cultural mechanisms that I think also affect the literary world.[7]

As new Cuban art illustrates, to say that realism is the natural expression of the difficult living conditions is to say only half the truth.[8] This trend has also been made possible by a series of agents who evaluate, select and group these works according to both aesthetic and commercial criteria. Using the art world as a model, I suggest that Cuban culture since the 1990s can be thought of as a 'curated culture'. In using this term, I do not seek to minimize the intrusion of the marketplace in the socialist utopia but to focus on the cultural processes, both in Cuba and abroad, that condition the management of art. In other words, I seek to view the Cuban trend as a complex process that, though inserted in an uneven international financial system, obeys its own laws and reasons that speak not so much of Cuban politics but of First World cultural paradigms. Concretely, I will propose two ideas: first, I will argue that the type of art I have been making reference to should be seen not so much as forms of testimony, but as a cynical realism that amounts to an avant-garde, which I will call hyperrealism. Second, I propose to view the administration of Cuban contemporary culture as an imaginary space between centre and periphery, art and market, self-exoticization and neo-avant-garde, which reflects Cuba's active participation in a postmodern world that is fascinated by difference.

In his essay 'Reporte del hombre en La Habana' ('Report by Our Man in Havana'), the eminent Cuban art critic Gerardo Mosquera alludes to a real story in order to explain the art production of the 1990s. 'No discourse speaks more eloquently to the contradictions in which Cuban art production is immersed today, than what happened in the recent V Biennial', during which elements such as toilet paper, soap, cigars, crucifixes and toy guns were stolen from the installations. According to Mosquera, these unexpected social interventions comment lucidly on the acute state of necessity of the general population during these years (presumably, of 'violence, religion, pleasure and hygiene'). Mosquera concludes:

> The crisis is so deep, and simple survival so trying, that it is impossible for most Cubans to respect the line that separates aesthetics from reality – a reality dominated by scarcity and neglect. This situation affects how people react to the work of art when it contains objects that are badly needed, even when such work is located in an auratic space.[9] (1995: 131)

The anecdote mentioned by Mosquera took place in 1994 — at the peak of the crisis — during a biennial that has been considered a landmark in the history of Cuban art. The event was described by Rachel Weiss as both an alternative aesthetic lab, and a professional platform for the international market. In turn, a review that appeared in the Spanish newspaper *El País* celebrated the presence of renowned museum curators and prominent collectors from around the world.[10] Although the biennial, which included 171 works by artists from 41 countries, promoted itself as a natural venue for Third-World art, it was Cuban art that met with the most enthusiastic acclaim. Considered to be simultaneously 'daring and critical', 'harsh and heart-breaking', these works focused on prostitution and the generalized desire for emigration that dominated Cuban society at this time (in fact, the biennial took place two months before the summer of 1994, when about 40,000 people left the island in precarious boats hoping to reach the Florida shore, although it is not clear how many succeeded). It is not surprising that the work that caused the most impact according to *El País* was the installation 'Regatta' by Alexis (Kcho) Leyva (figure 1). This piece, which re-creates the shape of a boat, is composed by objects found on the shore, such as shoes and toys, but particularly by 'testimonial objects' and materials (cork, wheels, chocolate wraps and candles) that attest to the process by which Cubans make 'an object that floats and allows them to leave the country'.[11]

The international success of Cuban art in this biennial is mainly due to the originality of a type of art that, according to Mosquera, 'has brought the street into the gallery' (1999a: 37). In his anecdote, however, Mosquera seems to disapprove of the reaction such art had produced among the Cuban public, who had been unable or unwilling to respect the line separating art and life, even to the point of performing social interventions in the work of art (denying perhaps the fact that such interventions can become part of the works themselves). Although this realism derives from the fusion of the social and the aesthetic, such fusion must be conceptual, not accidental. This is why Mosquera seems worried that a literal reading of the work of art may negatively affect the aura of a piece whose very originality emanates precisely from its literality.

Both Mosquera's anecdote and the short story 'La guagua' promote the idea that there are incorrect approaches to a given work of art. And both are partly right because, ultimately, these works work precisely to the extent that they allow for a double reading that is not always easy to sustain. For instance, while 'La guagua' promotes the need to read the material and to be suspicious of the aura, Mosquera's anecdote promotes the importance of trusting the aura of the piece, and disengaging from its materiality. In my view, the resistance to the double reading can effectively be traced to a 'structural' notion: Claude Lévi-Strauss made the distinction between primitive art, which stresses the material, and Western art, which stresses the model (1992: 27). According to this paradigm, the intense referentiality of the new Cuban art would help label it as primitive art and, therefore, minor. This would explain why critics have been more receptive to realist Cuban art and literary works when these establish an explicit dialogue with themes and tropes familiar to Western art history.

For the most part, new Cuban art is referential in the same way photography is referential. Although referentiality is an inevitable aspect in photography, not one referent is intrinsically preferable to any other. For instance, images by Carlos Garaicoa, like the novels by Abilio Estévez, expressly combine a bleak view of Havana with Western traditional notions of beauty. Garaicoa's installation 'Primer sembrado

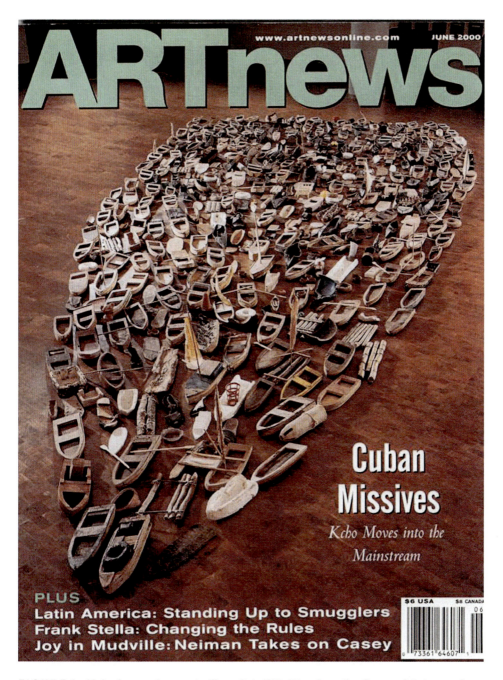

FIGURE 1   Kcho Leyva, La regata (Regatta), 1994. Mixed media. Cover of *Artnews*, June 2000. © 2000 ARTnews, LLC. Reprinted by courtesy of the publisher.

de hongos alucinógenos en La Habana' (figure 2) places a photograph of downtown Havana in its current state of ruin on top of an architectural drawing of a similar yet classic landscape. The ruins in the photograph are, in the words of Abilio Estevez in *Los palacios distantes*, 'not like Roman ruins, which attest to man's presence in history, but,

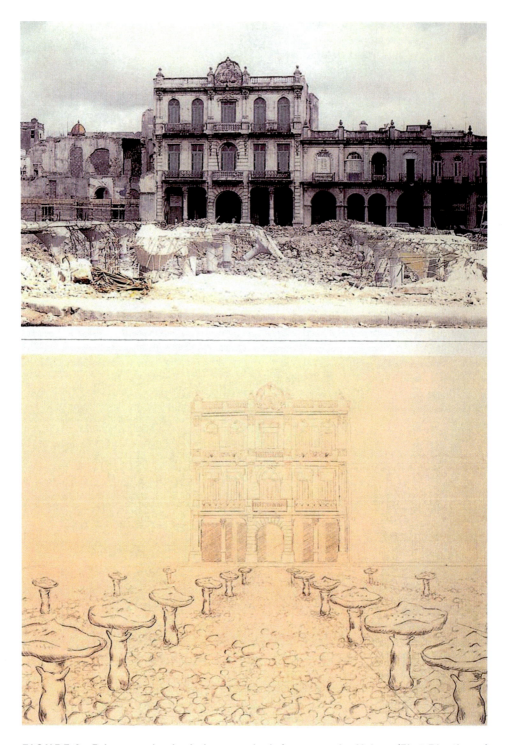

FIGURE 2 Primer sembrado de hongos alucinógenos en La Habana/First Planting of Hallucinogenic Mushrooms in Havana, 1997. Color photograph (50 × 60 cm), pencil and ink drawing on cardboard (57 × 76 cm). © Orlando J. Hernández Collection, Havana.

much to the contrary, they attest to history overwhelming man' (2002: 64). By contrast, the architectural drawing placed underneath offers a 'poetical intervention', to use the artist's words. It is a hallucinatory view of the ruins that points either to the desire to escape such reality, or to the fantastic character of such landscape. The combination of these two images further reminds us of Estevez's protagonist, to whom 'the city provokes two impressions: that of a bombarded city, that awaits the slightest breeze to become a mere pile of stones, and that of being an eternal city, always new, always offering itself to future immortalities. Havana is never and is always the same' (2002: 21). The double structure of Garaoicoa's work has been seen as an attempt on the part of art to 'cure' the city.[12] While the juxtaposition of ludic fantasy and harsh reality offers a humorous, medicinal take on Cuban reality, it still forms part of an 'aesthetics of frustration', as it has been dubbed in painting, or of an 'aesthetics of disenchantment', the term most commonly used in literature. Similarly, Estévez's novel casts the themes of ruins, hunger and prostitution within an elaborate, highly poetic Neo-Baroque prose. The search for literary beauty in the text mirrors the search for worldly pleasures in characters that are exhausted by decades of forced heroism and austerity. Estévez's characters, much like Estévez himself, feel that only a good dose of beauty can redeem Cubans' exhausted souls.

I believe that the double aesthetic convention found in Garaicoa's work and in Estévez's writing produces two simultaneous effects. First, its commitment to a modernist idea of beauty clearly helps furnish the object with a recognizable 'aura'. Second, the exhibitionism of some of these pieces amounts to an ethical statement, since they explicitly denounce the toll revolutionary heroism has taken on the Cuban people. However, duplication can be seen as duplicity when aesthetics turn into ethics without fully abandoning a traditional code of beauty that can be comforting to the spectator. By this I mean that the highly artistic elaboration that accompanies the testimonial aspects of the work softens its impact on the spectator's sensitivity. At a political level, then, this type of work is somewhat compromised. For if we consider the Cuban Revolution as a typically modern political act, we can say that the modernist notion of beauty present in the text expresses only partial disenchantment with the ideals and the utopias of modernity. At an aesthetic level, however, the explicit contrast between pure art and pure reality emphasizes the role played by the gaze – here, a second gaze offered by the artist himself – in lending the work its artistic status.

Another type of realism features prominently in this period, one that is much more violent to the spectator. This trend elaborates on the same sort of problematic that we see in the works by Garaoicoa and Estévez mentioned above, but without appealing to the dignifying effect of the Western tradition. It is an austere rendering of a desolate society, one that shuns any expectation of originality, coherence or beauty. Poorly constructed narrations, unclear plots, dirty streets, cruel characters populate the novels by Pedro Juan Gutiérrez. This is also the subject of the photography series 'Ojos desnudos' by Abigail González (figures 3 and 4). In Gutierrez's novel *Dirty Trilogy of Havana*, his narrator, who is also called Pedro Juan, justifies his writing in the following way:

> I was disappointed with journalism and started to write some very crude short stories. You can't write softly in times as heartrending as these .... I write in order to needle and to force others to smell the shit. (1998: 85)

FIGURE 3 AND 4 Abigail González, from the series *Ojos desnudos* (Naked Eyes). Black-and-white photograph. © Abigail González, published by permission of the author.

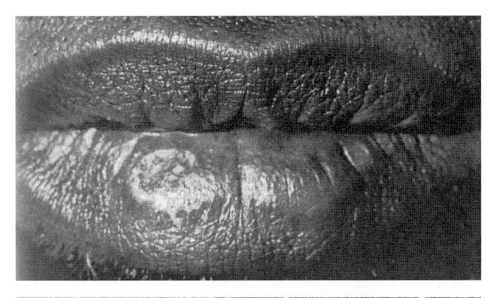

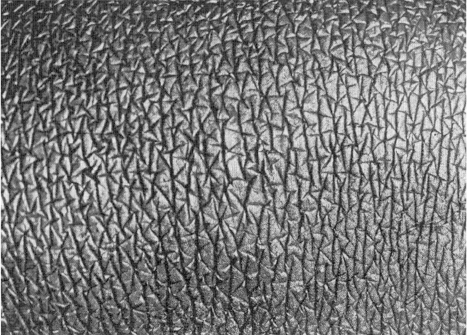

FIGURE 5 AND 6 René Peña, from the series *Man Made Materials*, 1998–1999. Black-and-white photographs. © René Peña, published by permission of the author.

Sure enough, Gutierrez's writing elaborates on topics such as collective bathrooms, as well as prostitution, cruelty, hunger and frustration. However, as the narrator also points out:

> Nothing is made up. It is just that I gathered enough strength to grab the pile of reality and let it drop at once on the white page. (1998: 103–4)

Because of their crude themes and raw manufacture, this type of art can be defined as a sordid rendering of reality that can be violent to the spectator. Often, the use of the human body becomes a privileged subject, which can in part be attributed to its availability – bodies are free. However, when the human body is cast in a way that it produces neither beauty nor desire, it usually forces the spectator to confront his or her own 'animality'. This type of artistic representation amounts to a political statement in that both the subject and the spectator are debased, humiliated. It makes the spectator, especially the liberal intellectual, question the real consequences of our idealism.[13]

The exhaustion of ideology explains, in part, the intense referentiality of this type of art. As poet, critic and curator Orlando Hernández states in his essay 'The Pleasures of Reference':

> The tumultuous social and cultural atmosphere of the 1990s, in which the majority of these artists developed, has proved to be a more provocative and nourishing subject matter for their work than the usual wellsprings of the subconscious and the individual imagination. I am not sure if it constitutes a methodology, but the majority of these artists has explored the labyrinths of external reality to a much greater extent than their own inner depths and have preferred to take their ideas directly from everyday life rather than from the moldy archives of tradition, including the history of art. The focus is on the *here* and *now* rather than on historical legacies, which makes for a curious philosophy of the immediate – as though the natural distrust of promises for the future were united with disappointment and disillusionment with the past. (2001: 25, emphasis in the original)

Hernández suggests that referential art in the 1990s in Cuba amounts to a neo-avant-garde defined in opposition to the psychological incursions of past avant-gardes, as well as to the 'moldy archives' of Western artistic traditions. Animated by a 'philosophy of the immediate', this aesthetic reduces the ludic dimension of art to the minimum, which serves the purpose of communicating the artist's exhaustion vis-à-vis official rhetoric more aggressively. In other words, these hidden layers of conceptualization help build the aura of a realism that seems to purposely avoid the presence of any recognizable auratic elements in its structure.[14]

There is no doubt that the most provocative case among these is that of Angel Delgado, author of a San Lázaro made of soap in 1991. The fact that Delgado recreated this religious icon using a non-traditional medium attests to the scarcity of objects and materials in Cuba in these years, but it also evokes prison art. From this perspective, the piece can be seen as a metaphor for the double siege that defined the situation on the island in the 1990s. In this case, however, it is not really a metaphor, since Delgado made this piece during the six-month sentence he served in 1990 for an artistic intervention with another type of non-conventional material. Notoriously, Delgado had defecated on a newspaper as part of an exhibit called *El objeto esculturado*

(*The Sculpted Object*) that took place at the Centro de Desarrollo de las Artes Visuales in Havana in 1990. According to critics, Delgado sought to demonstrate that excrement is a human-sculpted object; naturally, 'the police saw it differently' (Hernández, 2001: 25). For the police it was key that the newspaper used for the occasion was *Granma*, the official daily publication of the Communist party. Delgado was accused of public indecency and sent to jail. While evoking the irreverent statements often made by the avant-garde artists of the early twentieth century, Delgado's gesture forcefully expresses the demoralization of an exhausted society.[15]

In fact, Delgado's performance anticipates the dirty narratives of collective bathrooms of Pedro Juan Gutiérrez's Trilogíou, whose protagonist shamelessly declares that 'en el baño la mierda llega al techo' (1998, 81). Not only do these provocations seek to 'épater le communiste', as it were, but they also act as social criticism. Borrowing Joshua Esty's words, we can say that '[e]ven when understood according to the representation codes of realism ... shit has a political vocation: it draws attention to the failures of development, to the unkept promises' of revolutionary dignity (Esty, 1999: 32). The intervention by the police in Delgado's case underlines Mosquera's opinion that 'new Cuban art has been able to play a unique function as a place for social discussion in a country where these places are nonexistent' (1999b: 49). In other words, these 'artistic' gestures and works act as substitutes for the critical role usually expected from the press in non-authoritarian places — as Delgado seems to suggest in a none too subtle way, and as the police seem to have understood quite well.

Like the short story 'La guagua', Delgado's performance and its aftermath can also be seen as a story of readings and misreadings. On the one hand, there is the reading by the police, who have technically confused art with crime — thus reverting the irony in Díaz Pimienta's story, in which foreigners see art when facing 'sculpted objects in non-conventional material'. Again like 'La guagua', Delgado's act underlines the determining role played by critical conceptualization in the process of labelling art as art. In Delgado's so-called artistic intervention, legitimacy is granted by his position as a known young artist, by the auratic space in which his act took place, and by the implicit dialogue established with the title of the exhibit. In turn, the exhibit of the mass of passengers in the Museum of Fine Arts that appears in the short story by Díaz Pimienta is in fact guaranteed by the mention of a donor and of spectators, as well as by the explicit comparison the story makes to the work of canonical painters and sculptors. In turn, the legitimacy of the novels mentioned above is granted by the fact that they are published by well-known publishing houses in Spain, and that are reviewed in *Babelia*, the cultural supplement to the newspaper *El País*. From a sociological point of view, we can say that Delgado's performance, the story 'La guagua' and Mosquera's Biennial anecdote effectively underline the particularly determining role of the 'reader' in referential art. For while all three instances promote the idea that there are incorrect readings, they insist on the fact that such readings have consequences (be it fame, sales, jail, ostracism), and hence the importance of a professional reader with authority to grant 'aura' to a given object. This person is, of course, the curator.

A curator is usually defined as the person in charge of selecting the works that will be included in an exhibition of one or more artists, and of articulating the discourse that will lend identity to the exhibit. In Spanish, the word 'curator' is very new — in fact, Mosquera defines himself as a 'crítico, *curator* y narrador', using the word in English (1995: 140; emphasis added). Etymologically speaking, the Spanish word 'curador' suggests a 'curandero', a witchdoctor. Although this connotation is partly in keeping with Garaicoa's idea of 'curing' the city with humour, the practice itself is only tangentially related to medical discourse. The official translation of the word curator is 'restaurador', a word that designates the person in a museum whose role is to preserve, or conserve, a given cultural patrimony, not to contest it or to initiate new discourses. By contrast, in Spain, the freelance curator is usually referred to as a 'comisario', literally a sheriff, which doesn't suggest innovation either.[16] The word used in Latin America is 'curador', an Anglicism, which, by virtue of being a new word, seems more attuned to the task of propitiating new discourses, thus becoming a true 'author' in the sense given by Foucault. What I find interesting about the freelance curator is that, by providing the work with its own metalanguage almost at the very moment of its production, the curator anticipates and even pre-empts the critics' work. At the same time, however, because his mission is to design a discourse capable of producing immediate meaning in a given society, the curator resembles the marketing agent. I don't want to imply here that the curator does not belong to the art world but that his methods can place him in the hybrid role of being both the producer and the promoter of avant-garde art. What is more, because of the lack of an internal art market in today's Cuba, the curator is also, essentially, an exporter of avant-garde art.

The phrase 'curated culture' appears in an essay by Kevin Power entitled 'Cuba: One story after another' (1999). Power, an American professor at the Instituto Superior de Arte de La Habana, uses this term to refer to the determining role that the foreign public plays in Cuban art production. Power affirms that the 'most dangerous corollary in the present situation is that curated cultures produce as a function of demands from the center', the centre being galleries, museums, publishers in some cities in the United States and Europe, which tend to prefer works that comment on the ideological and social tensions in Cuba (1999: 44). However, Power also locates the referentiality of Cuban art in a complex dynamic:

> What, you might ask, has this [prostitution, hunger, black market] to do with art? Well, nothing and everything! Everything in the sense that much of the content of Cuban art is specifically concerned with sociocultural commentary and with ideological tensions. Indeed, should the artist turn away from certain *legitimized* themes (legitimized from the outside, although at the same time indisputably *natural* to the inside), he may well find himself outside the pale of interests of the international art world, debarred, as it were, through his own choosing, and isolated from the consequent economic benefits. It is clear in the present climate social criticism is like breathing in, i.e., literally, 'in-spiration', even though the artist's attitude towards it may, in the harsh contradictions of the nineties, have acquired a hard-boiled, strategic, and cynical edge. (1999: 29)

Even though Power rejects the possibility that artists may be interested in making a political statement, he makes a welcome distinction between selling out, and selling. It is true that an artist can get up to US$5000 for one of his or her works, whereas a doctor usually makes US$17 dollars a month, which makes selling art a highly desirable activity. More importantly, Power thinks that the opportunity to sell offers artists an opportunity to create, even if this relegates them to certain thematic expectations.

Power traces the international interest in Cuba to its situation as an ultra-periphery: 'periphery functions best when it assumes its identity as periphery, and consequently, artists who leave for the center risk falling out of sight' (1999: 24). An artist who 'emigrates' in themes and methods that are usually considered his or her 'natural habitat' runs the risk of falling out of sight as much as an émigré artist. The main problem with catering to an international taste, however, is the simplification of the work of art: for a piece to travel well, it has to stick to themes that confirm their otherness and they must do so in a clear, reductive way so that the message doesn't get lost (1999: 29). When the consumer at the centre wants difference, he or she usually wants such difference to be authentic. Hence the importance that the artist stays put, on the one hand, and that the 'curators/explorers' from the First World work with local curators, on the other (1999: 44). Such mixed processes or institutions help make the relationship between periphery and centre more democratic, since they allow the periphery to own not just the work and the experience behind the work but also its hermeneutic discourse as well, at least in part. In the end, however, they also help confirm the traditional roles that centre and periphery usually play in cultural transactions given that their main objective is to certify the legitimacy of difference.

The titles chosen for Cuban exhibits around the world are clear indicators of the expectations of Cuban authenticity: 'Made in Havana' (Australia 1989), 'Nacido en Cuba' (Caracas 1991), 'Comment peut-on être cubain?' (Paris 1998). This situation is even re-created on the island itself, where a 1995 exhibit organized in an alternative space called 'Espacio Aglutinador' was entitled *Inside Habana*. On the one hand, the English word 'Inside', an invitation for the voyeuristic foreign spectator, contradicts the exceptionality and reveals, instead, the desire not to let the message get lost. On the other, the 'b' in Habana acts as a certification of origin while suggesting the primitive charm of the native who is unable to translate himself. Even the title of one of Mosquera's essay that I mentioned earlier: 'Report by our man in Havana', re-creates a similar situation. Not only does it evoke Graham Greene but it also confirms that both exhibition and publisher are located outside Cuba, in this case in Barcelona, and that Mosquera lends the exhibition his stamp of authenticity. The fact that many Cuban critics mentioned in this article are quoted in English is probably the most curious piece of evidence. The words of many artists and critics quoted here appear in English as 'originals in translation'. This is due to the fact that these essays are usually requested, translated, compiled and published by critics in the United States and Europe for the first time. Even the catalogues and art criticism that are published in Spain often include an English translation at the end of the text. It would be wrong, in my view, to see this situation merely as an absolute indication of a colonizing pattern, since Cuban voices need these international mediators in order to be heard, although they are heard mostly by the mediators' public.[17] Ultimately, the international interest in this art helps ensure the survival of a cultural activity that surpasses the island's capacity to absorb it.[18]

At the local level, the control over the artist's voice gives rise to other mixed cultural processes. More concretely, a curious effect on Cuban art production is determined by censorship. Those in charge of censorship in Cuba are bureaucrats in the cultural sector who are themselves artists, and whose main role is to mediate between the artist and the state. Mosquera explains that during these years:

Art has become more radical since it is ritually protected behind layers of metaphorical density and a cynical attitude. I say 'ritually' because, ultimately, everyone knows what the works mean, but what matters is that they are not explicit. This gives cultural bureaucrats – the ones in charge of censorship – a way to protect themselves vis-à-vis those who control their work. (1995: 133)

In other words, in order to publish material that could be considered politically dangerous, the artist-bureaucrat needs to make sure that he or she can promote a non-political reading. The artist-bureaucrat, then, is censor and curator at the same time, juggling labels and redefining aesthetics on the basis of its ambiguities. In contrast with the foreign curator, the censor needs the message to be lost. After all, it is important for the artist to be on good terms with the state, given that official institutions manage artists' right to travel – travelling to foreign institutions and universities being one of the main sources of income in hard currency for artists and scholars.[19]

When we speak about money, we always imply a market. However, what has determined this market and not any other is a state of mind in international intellectual circles that values alterity and is willing to pay its price. In her introduction to the book *Art Cuba*, Holly Block, former director of Art in General in New York City, states that 'Remembering why Cuba is different remains important; in this global age, changing societies often undervalue what makes them distinctive' (2001: 11). What makes Cuba distinctive is a combination of characteristics that are both unique to the island and particularly attractive outside it. For starters, Cuba combines a racially and culturally Afro-Latin make-up, with a political structure that is as heroic as it is anachronistic – for decades, it has defined itself as an Anti-American utopia. What is more important, it produces exceptionally well-trained artists. Indeed, the cultural politics of the Revolution created many art schools and institutions that train artists and promote art production. Thanks to the Revolution, Cubans are highly educated and, since the early 1990s, their subsistence is mostly made possible thanks to international sponsorship. That Cuban artists try to sell their art in international circles is hardly surprising at all. That international markets appreciate Cuban affordable yet original art is even less so.

As the art critic Luis Camnitzer said, Cuba uses capitalism without letting itself be totally used by it (1994: 150).[20] Cuban curators such as Magaly Espinosa and Meyra Marrero, Gerardo Mosquera and Corina Matamoros considered the importance of the role of the curator in a symposium entitled *La curaduría, un laboratorio para el arte*, which took place at the UNEAC (Unión Nacional de Escritores y Artistas Cubanos), and parts of which were published in a special dossier entitled 'El oficio de curar' in the journal *Artecubano* in 2001. The presentations show a certain anxiety to define the role of the curator, who is simultaneously seen as an activist, i.e. as an agent for change, and as the provider of a language with the capacity to make such change both possible and meaningful. In these texts, one notices a familiar anxiety over the meaning of multiculturalism. The curators in this symposium seem eager to better understand their working material in a world in which art, society and culture are not only inseparable but are also analysed in similar ways. In other words, Cuban curators seem to share preoccupations with other non-Cuban colleagues around the world.

The curators and critics in the UNEAC symposium seem to be somewhat concerned about the role that the international market plays in the production of art in Cuba. Some are proud of the prevalent notion that 'the most innovating discourses in art' are produced in the periphery. It is not clear, however, if they are innovative because they are peripheral or if this situation helps redefine the traditional relationship between centre and periphery. Divergent opinions on the connection between art and market are also apparent. For instance, while Llilian Llanes, director of the legendary V Biennial, thinks biennials respond to the need to create alternative spaces for those who 'have not yet had access to "universality"' (Llanes, 1997: 18), others undermine them as events designed for cultural tourism (Espinosa, 2001: 7). I, in turn, cannot help but wonder if it is productive, or even possible, to distinguish between spectator, consumer and cultural tourist. At the same time, and somewhat paradoxically, Espinosa finds that 'the boom of international exposure of our artistic production has increased the aesthetic quality of the pieces, and it has opened us to other forms of art such as installations, performance and environment' (Espinosa, 2001: 7). We can conclude from the various comments included in the dossier 'El oficio de curar' that the problems and questions faced by the local managers of Cuban art can be remarkably similar to those of other cultural critics and agents in the art world in general, and in peripheral societies in particular. I think, then, that these comments ultimately suggest that the Cuban boom may be less Cuban than it seems.

In a way, the relation centre/periphery that Cuba embodies is symptomatic of the place Latin America occupies in the First World imaginary not just as primitive space but, most importantly as an 'intelligible' primitive space. As Mosquera pointed out in an earlier essay, Latin America produces a hybrid alterity, one that allows the centre to value difference without ever having to abandon Western sensitivity (Power, 1999: 44). Behind Mosquera's comment is a warning against the 'paradoxical self-exoticization' of peripheral societies that wish to fulfil the 'expectations of alterity dictated by Postmodern exoticism.' (2002: 626). Furthermore, Mosquera rightly condemns those:

> ... so-called international cultural phenomena and institutions that not only consider themselves contemporary and universal, but also reserve themselves the right ... to determine what should and should not be included in those categories. They constitute a conceptualizing system of power, one that legitimizes itself while failing to understand that 'international' and 'contemporary' are relative and relational terms. (2002: 626–7)

The situation described by Mosquera summarizes an international cultural practice whose methods need to be made evident. And this is, in my view, what new Cuban art does really well, at least when in the right hands.

A paradigmatic institution of the new era is the Fundación Ludwig de Cuba (FLC), a non-government institution created in 1995 by German collectors Peter and Irene Ludwig as a result of their fascination with the V Biennial. The FLC is managed by its local president, Helmo Hernández, who has put his stamp on the art trends that have circulated during these years. The FLC 'programming manager', Luisa Marisy, affirms that the Foundation:

> ... is interested particularly in artists who are researching new expressive languages without abandoning their own identity.... Because of the foundation's status as a non-governmental organization and its simple structure, the

Foundation's work represents a new, experimental way of promoting and administering culture within Cuba. (1999: 48)

Not only does the foundation promote local artists through the organization of international exhibits and festivals but it also organizes conferences, seminars, academic courses and international exchanges. In other words, the FLC is an active (or rather, activist) agent in the international cultural exchange, promoting local art while educating its receivers. In this sense, FLC works as a mediator between centre and periphery from the periphery. It is not surprising, then, that the art promoted by FLC reflects on the very same themes the foundation redefines in its managing role.

In its early days, the FLC organized an exhibit entitled 'Una de cada clase' ('One of each type'). In the video-catalogue of the exhibit, New Cuban art is explained in these terms:

One can today imagine a new realism centered precisely on the spectator, [on the quest] to make visible the relations that take place in the space of art between emitters and receivers, buyers and sellers, values, auras, prestige, groups and experiences.

Judging by this comment, then, one can understand Cuban hyperrealism as an art that not only describes the society of origin, but also the society in which it inserts itself, and whose mechanisms it keeps in function from its very intervention.

The complex critical spirit cited by the FLC exhibit is palpable in the two forms of hyperrealism that I mentioned earlier, even though they elaborate their critical position in different ways. The type of hyperrealism that is in explicit dialogue with Western artistic tradition, such as that of Garaicoa, Ponte, Estévez, Fernando Pérez, among others, offer an aesthetic project that is conscious of both their innovative and their peripheral conditions. Making this paradox possible is the artists' cultivated, ludic spirit, which helps them evaluate the many aspects of their own historical and artistic situation. One of the effects resulting from the counterpoint between reality and sublimation in these cases is to render more evident the distressing living conditions of Cubans today. At the same time, however, because these works propose their own conceptualization more or less explicitly, we can describe it as 'curated' art from its inception.

In contrast, the novels by Gutiérrez and Valdés, as well as the film *Si me comprendieras* and the photography by Abigail González, offer a raw type of hyperrealism. In these texts, both represented world and the representation itself appear as naturally chaotic. In a way, they act as open invitations for someone to organize, classify, elevate them. A type of art that so overtly insists in its 'curability' is understandably popular among curators. In spite of its appearance, however, this is not an innocent type of art. Its referentiality seeks more than to stress the material, as Levi-Strauss had it, but, rather, to mimic the transparency of photography instead. As critic and curator Meira Marrero suggests, photography creates the illusion that reality imprints itself on the paper. That is why photography is a naturalistic artistic medium, one in which reality appears to be written 'by God himself' (2001: 12).[21] We may conclude, then, that in its emulation of photography – that is, in its adoption of methods and expectations external to it – literature reinvents its own functions and mechanisms. Its realism, then, is highly conceptual. Paraphrasing Lévi-Strauss, we can say that Cuban hyperrealist art and literature are conceptual and primitive at the same time. We can go further and propose that hyperrealism is conceptual *because* it is primitive. By embodying its geographical and critical position in the world, new Cuban art forcefully unveils the pitfalls of both the global cultural spirit and the financial processes that condition Third World art production today. Hyperrealism, then, is a poetic intervention in post-utopian, postmodern societies. In this regard it is important to note that postmodernism is an acquired sensitivity in Latin America. In the Cuban case, in particular, postmodernism is not a natural consequence of either of the two most common features associated with this trend. For it does not found itself either on the exhaustion of grand narratives or on a disengagement of art from history.[22] The most interesting aspect of such complex cultural development may very well be that, by creating a postmodernism that is emptied of its sole historical justification, Cuban art has rendered postmodernism more genuinely postmodern.

Acknowledgements

The author would like to thank Desirée Díaz, Lillebit Fadraga, Marcela Guerrero, Courtney Lanz and Carole Rosenberg, president of the *American Friends of the Ludwig Foundation of Cuba*, for helping her find material and obtain copyright permissions. She would also like to express her gratitude to James Buckwalter-Arias and Mario Ortiz-Robles for their comments and suggestions.

Notes

1. See Néstor García Canclini (1995: 5). The discussion that follows shares some of Canclini's preoccupations regarding the national and global management of Latin American art. However, the historical context of this article could not have been envisioned by Canclini when he wrote *Culturas híbridas*, first published in 1989.
2. All translations are mine unless otherwise specified.
3. The foreigner's inability to tell the donor apart from the author, however, would suggest an inherent inability on the part of the non-local reader or spectator to understand Cuban reality. This idea undermines the power of art to convey meaning regardless of experience.
4. See 'De fiesta' by Jesús Díaz (1998), 'Reinscribing the aesthetic' by James Buckwalter-Arias (2005), 'Aesthetics under siege' by Guillermina De Ferrari (2003), and 'The novel as Cuban lexicon' by Esther Whitfield (2003).
5. For the term 'literatura del desencanto', see Jorge Fornet's 'La narrativa cubana' (2001). For some of the reactions mentioned in these sections, see the essays by Odette Casamayor Cisneros, Waldo Pérez Cino, Margarita Mateo Palmer and Jorge Fornet included in an issue of *La Gaceta de Cuba* that was devoted to the literary production of Cuba in the 1990s. It is remarkable that these essays often ignore works by Pedro Juan Gutiérrez, among other 'hyperrealist' writers.
6. See Buckwalter (2005) and De Ferrari (2003).
7. A historical fact can also help explain the different views held by the artistic and literary worlds. Cuban artists who gained international fame in the 1980s emigrated at the beginning of the 1990s due to the rigid state policy that prevented them from

being paid in dollars. Consequently, the generation that followed, and which Gerardo Mosquera calls 'Mala Yerba' for their capacity to survive in unfriendly circumstances, tend to share aesthetic views that are both generational and historically conditioned (see Mosquera, 2001). This is not necessarily the case in literature, where younger writers may be overpowered by the authority of the previous generation.

8   I use the phrase new Cuban art as a way to refer to all art produced in Cuba since the early 1990s, regardless of its medium. I should clarify, however, that I am borrowing this term from the visual arts, which has used the term 'New Cuban Art' to refer to a more or less homogenous work produced in this period. This gesture is justified by the fact that I explicitly seek to look at literature in the light of the processes and language of the visual arts.

9   'Auratic space' is my translation of Mosquera's phrase 'espacios auráticos'. This phrase refers to places that produce or attest to the artistic 'aura' of an object (in the sense attributed to it by Walter Benjamin).

10 The newspaper article lists notable figures such as 'Nelson Aguilar, the curator of the Sao Paulo Biennial; Milton Esterow, the director of the art magazine *Art News*; María Corral, the director of the Museo Nacional Reina Sofía; [and] the American Alex Rosenberg, who has represented artists such as Dalí and Henry Moore'.

11 A version of Regatta was used as the cover of *Art News* in 2000 (see figure 1).

12 See Torres del Sol and López Saborit (2006).

13 See also René Peña's photographic series entitled 'Man Made Materials' (figures 5 and 6), although Peña seems to suggest racial issues as well.

14 This trend is notably very similar to a hyperrealist trend in contemporary American drama as described by Carol Gelderman. According to her, American hyperrealist drama consists of representing the world as it is, with the least possible degree of connotation. It is an art that emulates the mechanicity of photography, and seeks to avoid moral hierarchies (more below). The idea is, precisely, that social criticism is all the more effective because it lacks ethical commitment. For this type of art is motivated, at least in part, by the desire to undo false ideological promises (Gelderman, 1983: 358 and 365). In my view, the similarities between the American and the Cuban artistic projects support my understanding that there is a philosophical, postmodern motivation behind this type of art production that is not determined by history alone. See De Ferrari (2003).

15 Delgado's gesture is slightly more daring than Marchel Duchamp presenting a urinal to be exhibited under the title 'Fountain' at the Society of Independent Artists in 1917. Although Duchamp's urinal was rejected for not being art, it soon became canonized as an example of Ready-Made Art, Neo-Dadaism, Surrealism, pop art and even New Realism. Recently, one of its replicas sold for three million euros.

16 When consulted on this matter through its website 'Spanish today', the *Real Academia Española* categorically denied the existence of the word 'curador' in Spanish. This response is clearly oblivious to the fact that the word appears frequently in both oral and written expression throughout Latin America, and that it even appeared in the Spanish daily *El país* (see quotation in note 8, which includes the word 'curador' in the Spanish original).

17 An interesting case is the use of the Internet by Cuban artists and critics to disseminate their work. Virtual spaces allow the dissemination of material through channels that are less intensely controlled by either the state or foreign agents. It is to be expected that the use of this medium affects the circulation and readership of the art and

18 commentaries that are distributed in this way, making them more direct. However, the fact that individual use of the Internet is legally forbidden in Cuba turns such practice into a challenge to the state, and makes its impact hard to measure.
18 International fame can also ensure the social survival of a certain artist or intellectual. Mosquera himself has stated that 'If it weren't for the demand that my work has abroad, the regime would have made me a *desaparecido cultural* (cultural disappeared)' (1999b: 49).
19 In his comments on the V Biennial, Luis Camnitzer lists examples of state interventions on the exhibits that forcefully illustrate the impossibility of distinguishing between censorship, aesthetic judgment and 'curation'.
20 A notable (or notorious) exception is offered by *Buena Vista Social Club* (the film, the CDs, the phenomenon). 'El Tosco Cortés', a musician and creator of *timba*, echoes a generalized opinion when he refers to Ry Cooder as a Columbus-like figure: 'I believe in reincarnation. Christopher Columbus was reincarnated as Ry Cooder. Ry Cooder arrived and said, "I am Christopher Columbus." He came to discover Cuba.... He discovered [Compay Segundo and Elíades Ochoa] and he made a record and sold it to the world. That's all good and I am really happy, because in the end they are Cuban and their music is real Cuban music. [People think] there has been no new music in Cuba for forty years. That's not the music of Cuba. That's the old music of Cuba. That is the music of the Republic' (Cortés, 2003: 128). I think it is a mistake to see Cooder and Wenders's promotion of the Cuban 'flea market' aesthetic as emblematic of the overall process of cultural exchange that has taken place for the last decade and a half. They were unable to negotiate Cuban tradition, on the one hand, and Cuban artists' capacity for innovation. Ultimately, they failed to create a new discourse. Theirs is an isolated, or at least seriously exaggerated, example of the inequalities of this type of cultural exchange.
21 See Gelderman's comment in note 14.
22 For more on postmodernism in the Cuban political context, see Power (1999: 41–8.)

References

Block, Holly. 2001. Remembering why. In *Art Cuba: The New Generation*, translated by Cola Frantzen and Marguerite Feitlowitz. edited by Holly Block. New York: Harry N. Abrams, 7–12.

Buckwalter-Arias, James. 2005. Reinscribing the Aesthetic: Cuban Narrative and Post-Soviet Cultural Politics. *PMLA* (120:2), Mar, 362–74.

Bourdieu, Pierre. 1984. *Distinction: A social critique of the judgement of taste*. translated by Richard Nice. Cambridge, MA: Harvard University Press.

Camnitzer, Luis. 1994. Review of The Fifth Biennial of Havana. *Third Text* Autumn–Winter: : 147–54.

Casamayor Cisneros, Odette. 2002. Cubanidades de fin de siglo o breve crónica de ciertos intentos narrativos por salvar u olvidar la cubanidad. *La Gaceta de Cuba*. November–December: 36–40.

Cortés, José Luis. 2003. El tosco. Interview by Hugo Pérez 'The Babalawos of Cuban Music'. In *Cuba on the Verge: An Island in Transition*, edited by Terry McCoy. Boston, New York and London: Bulfinch Press, 126–39.

Chaviano, Daína. 1998. *El hombre, la hembra y el hambre*. Barcelona: Planeta.

De Ferrari, Guillermina. 2003. Aesthetics under siege: Dirty realism and Pedro Juan Gutiérrez's *Trilogía sucia de La Habana*. *Arizona Journal of Hispanic Cultural Studies* 7: 23–43.

Delgado, Ángel. 2001. In *San Lázaro. Art Cuba: The new generation*, edited by Holly Block. translated by Cola Frantzen and Marguerite Feitlowitz New York: Harry N. Abrams, 25.

Díaz, Jesús. 1998. De fiesta. *Encuentro de la cultura cubana* 8–9: 3–4.

Díaz Pimienta, Alexis. 2000. La guagua. In *Nuevos narradores cubanos*, edited by Michi Strausfeld. Siruela: Madrid, 157–61.

Espinosa, Magaly. 2001. Curaduría por qué y para qué. Dossier 'El oficio de curar'. *Artecubano* 1: 2–9.

Estévez, Abilio. 2002. *Los palacios distantes*. Barcelona: Tusquets.

Esty, Joshua. 1999. Excremental postcolonialism. *Contemporary Literature* XL.1: 23–57.

Fernandes, Sujatha. 2006. *Cuba represent! Cuban arts, state power, and the making of new revolutionary cultures*. Durham, NH and London: Duke University Press.

Fornet, Jorge. 2001. La narrativa cubana entre la utopía y el desencanto. *La Gaceta de Cuba* September–October: 38–45.

Foucault, Michel. 1977. What is an author? In *Language, countermemory, practice: Selected essays and interviews*, edited by Donald F. Bouchard. translated by Donald F. Bouchard and Sherry Simon, Ithaca, NY: Cornell University Press, 113–38.

Garaicoa, Carlos. 1997. *Primer cultivo de hongos alucinógenos en La Habana*. In *Art Cuba: The New Generation*, edited by Holly Block. translated by Cola Frantzen and Marguerite Feitlowitz, New York: Harry N. Abrams, 28.

García Canclini, Néstor. 1995. *Hybrid cultures: Strategies for entering and leaving modernity*. translated by Christopher L. Chiappari and Silvia L. López. Minneapolis and London: University of Minnesota Press.

Gelderman, Carol. 1983. Hyperrealism in Contemporary drama: Retrogressive or avant-garde? *Modern Drama* 26 (3): 357–67.

Gutiérrez, Pedro Juan. 1998. *Trilogía sucia de La Habana*. Barcelona: Anagrama.

Gutiérrez, Pedro Juan. 2000. *Animal Tropical*. Barcelona: Anagrama.

Hernández, Orlando. 2001. The pleasures of reference. In *Art Cuba: The New Generation*, edited by Holly Block. New York: Harry N. Abrams, 25–9.

Lévi-Strauss, Claude. 1992. *The savage mind*. Chicago, IL: University of Chicago Press.

Regata. Kcho Leyva. 1994. *Artnews*, June 2000, cover.

Llanes Godoy, Llilian. 1997. Presentación. In *El individuo y su memoria: Sexta Bienal de La Habana*. Paris: Association Française d'Action Artistique, 18–23.

Marrero, Meira. 2001. Se hace camino al andar. Dossier 'El oficio de curar'. *Artecubano* 1: 10–13.

Luisa, Marisy. 1999. Luisa Marisy: Programming manager, Ludwig Foundation of Cuba. *Flash Art* January–February: 48.

Mateo Palmer, Margarita. 2002. A las puertas del siglo XXI. *La Gaceta de Cuba* November–December: 48–52.

Mosquera, Gerardo. 1995. Reporte del hombre en La Habana. In *Cuba: la isla posible*. Centro de Cultura Contemporanea de Barcelona. Barcelona: Ediciones destino, 131–41.

Mosquera, Gerardo. 1999a. La isla infinita: Introducción al nuevo arte cubano. In *Contemporary Art from Cuba: irony and survival on the utopian island = Arte contemporáneo de Cuba: ironía y sobrevivencia en la isla utópica*, edited by MarilynA. Zeitlin. Arizona State University Art Museum, New York: Delano Greenidge Editions, 31–7.

Mosquera, Gerardo. 1999b. Gerardo Mosquera: Independent curator and critic. *Flash Art* January–February: 49.

Mosquera, Gerardo. 2001. New Cuban art Y2K. In *Art Cuba: The New Generation*, edited by Holly Block. translated by Cola Frantzen and Marguerite Feitlowitz, New York: Harry N. Abrams, 13–16.

Mosquera, Gerardo. 2002. Sobre arte, globalización y culturas. In *Ensayo cubano del siglo XX. Selección, prólogo y notas de Rafael Hernández y Rafael Rojas*. México: Fondo de Cultura Económica, 620–37.

Pérez Cino, Waldo. 2002. Sentido y paráfrasis. *La Gaceta de Cuba* November–December: 22–9.

Ponte, Antonio José. 2000. Un arte de hacer ruinas. In *Nuevos narradores cubanos*, edited by Michi Strausfeld. Madrid: Siruela, 123–39.

Power, Kevin. 1999. Cuba: One story after another. In *While Cuba waits: Arts from the nineties*. New York: Smart Art Press, 23–65.

Quiroga, José. 2005. *Cuban palimpsests*. Minneapolis: University of Minnesota Press.

Si me comprendieras. Dir. Rolando Díaz. Luna Llena Producciones. 1998.

Suite Habana. 2003 Dir. Fernando Pérez. Wanda e ICAIC.

Una de cada clase: Arte joven cubano. 1995 La Habana: Fundación Ludwig de Cuba.

Torres del Sol, Ludmila y Yusleydy López Saborit. 2006. Construir entre la realidad y la utopía. El proyecto visto desde la plástica: un acercamiento al tema de la ciudad. *Arteamerica* 28 July. Available from http://www.arteamerica.cu/5/dossier/ludmila.htm; INTERNET.

Valdés, Zoé. 1995. *La nada cotidiana*. Barcelona: Emecé.

Vicent, Mauricio. 1994. Una gran balsa llamada Cuba: Artistas cubanos exponen obras críticas y denuncian el drama migratorio de su país en la V Bienal de La Habana., *El País* 15 May, Cultural Section.

Weiss, Rachel. 1995. Review of Quinta Bienal de La Habana. *Review: Latin American Literature and Arts* 50: 95–8.

Whitfield, Esther. 2003. The novel as Cuban lexicon: Bargaining bilinguals in Daina Chaviano's. In *Bilingual Games: Some Literary Investigations*, edited by Doris Sommer. New York: Palgrave Macmillan, 193–201.

Argentina's Secret Poetry Boom

NESTOR PERLONGHER

It is well known that poetry does not sell a great deal. What fewer people realize, however, is that it does circulate well, that it has a very particular mode of circulation, like a network of stamp-collectors exchanging the typographical minutiae of verse. The end of the 70s saw the emergence in Argentina of an interesting phenomenon: the proliferation of poets. At first this phenomenon seemed to be attributable to the enforced fall in political activism, due to the necessarily clandestine nature – imposed by the bloody military coup of 1976 – of mass militancy typical of the Argentina of the seventies. But with the advent of democracy – which in Argentina has not been and is not a smooth process, but one paved with shadows and threats, with the former dictatorial big shots still active in political life – the phenomenon of the multiplication of bards continued. . . and continues to gather pace. This can be dangerous: in Buenos Aires one can be talking to anyone and suddenly find oneself subjected to the reading of a poem when, at the carefully orchestrated high point of the conversation, the other produces from among his clothes a crumpled manuscript. It can be good or bad, but it is a poem, a sublime oasis of nothing in the midst of the giddy rush of everyday activities.

This is not mere wishful thinking, but something which acquires consistency when seen in the context of certain facts, which are real phenomena. I shall mention two: the first being the energetic existence of the publishing house Último Reino, which has published hundreds of books of poetry and must be, in the absence of evidence to the contrary, the biggest publisher of poetry in Latin America. True, these books, bitter reflections of the crisis, are financed for the most part by their authors, who combine the seriousness of poetic inspiration with the more prosaic payment of publication costs. In any case, despite this unpleasant detail, the little authors' editions have an enormous readership; there are all kinds of networks of poets in which the most heterogeneous forms of poetry are cultivated, with certain predominant tendencies – for example, that of the neobaroque movement. Último Reino, while the most prominent, is by no means the only minority or alternative publishing house. In fact, a myriad of them, sometimes extremely small, are appearing and disappearing. What is unusual about this particular one, Último Reino, is its vitality and staying power (it is now more than ten years since it was opened).

The second phenomenon is the survival of *Diario de Poesía*, published quarterly with a circulation of more than 40,000, and entirely dedicated to poetry. I shall not comment on its quality, but wish to stress that it has a significant role to play, and that in view of the fact that we are dealing with such a minority, hermetic activity, there is large public support for this publication, which contains much work by our own national bards.

It is curious that this volume of output does not translate into commercial success. The thing is that books are lent and swapped, their proliferation is not matched by the market.

There are few book shops in Buenos Aires with decent poetry sections. Another current phenomenon is the appearance everywhere of poetry workshops, which is part of a process now taking place all over Argentina, with the formation of study groups for all subjects. These are attended by people who have not necessarily had a university education but who do have intense intellectual or aesthetic curiosity. Courses on Lacan are (or were) the fashion these days, but poetry workshops, generally presided over by a coordinator who is a reasonably well-respected poet, are part of that massive wave of interest in cultural practice. Each participant pays to take part in these cultural gatherings. There are also free poetry workshops subsidized by the town councils. I know of a case, in Avellaneda, of a lady of over seventy who discovered her talent for writing sonnets in slang... Truly admirable (and the poems are good!).

One could not say the same of, for example, Brazil, where it seems that poetry interests no-one, or almost no-one... There are state-financed literary workshops. Even so, little attention is given to the subject, and readings (unless they are given by acclaimed lyricists) are only attended by a hard core of university students of literary criticism; university absorbs everything... I saw an example of this at the Poetic Word Seminar held in the magnificent Latin-America memorial in São Paulo in December 1990, for which poets were brought from Argentina, Mexico, the United States, Europe... Despite this lavish initiative, the event was a failure in terms of audience: more people attended the presentation of papers than the poetry reading. That is, academic interest took priority over aesthetic appreciation (and does so in Brazil in general).

To return to Argentina, it is not easy to identify the consequences of that 'poetic inflation' we were discussing. Poetry directly affects the *plane of expression* (Deleuze and Guattari take the term from Hjemslev). In that case, a quiet revolution could be taking place, with signs of a profound change in modes of expression on the broadest social level. Could it be that poetry is sufficiently powerful to spark off that transformation? Some indications – certain changes in the language of journalism, visible in the playful sarcasm of a daily like *Página 12* and in the sophisticated style of a magazine like *El Porteño*, in the context of the high quality of the language of journalistic essays – can be noted, but it is no simple matter to assimilate them into the miracle of the proliferation of poets. When all is said and done, partly due to a certain tendency towards hermeticism which in reality is like successive layers or roots of linguistic experimentation which superimpose themselves on and refine one another and combine together, poets are read only in their own group. The radius of action is intense, but quite limited. There are practically no links between poetic writing and the masses, and certainly not through television. At the most a subtle, remote and indirect influence, like that of surrealism on advertising.

It would seem that the poet is the stranger, the one who has placed himself on the margins. Segregated by the difficulty and difference (separatist?) of their babblings and constantly on the look-out for an ear which will be able to stand their radiant outpourings, poets (especially beginners) tend to gather together in conspiratorial huddles and carry out delicious rituals of serialized reading, like animated wine and cheese parties. I remember one I had the privilege of attending in the late 70s in Buenos Aires, with the poet Hilda Rais. Solitude was defied and the creation of a web of sensitive sonorities was advanced; one was stimulated to find a clear path in the midst of the turmoil of poetic inspiration.

Another important element in this current abundance is the solitude imposed by the destruction of the political and micropolitical networks of contact achieved by the dictatorship of 76; a strong introversion which favoured the appearance of muses. In those years writing was an outlet. Writing poetry, then, favoured the cyphered and refined manner of the mannerist code.

Why has that tendency not disappeared with the end of the dictatorship? We must realize that mass-militancy has not been resumed under democracy. What is happening is that the tide of that poetic movement is being consolidated and affirmed.

It is not easy to detect the dominant tendencies inside this secret boom. There is space for everything to bloom and flourish. Diversity and pluralism are the hallmarks of this process of open-ended proliferation. The task of sketching a panorama would require a prolix and laborious investigation which would probably still be incomplete.

However, without claiming to be neutral, since I am a part of that growing poetic movement which I am talking about, I think it is possible to distinguish a new phenomenon: the eruption of the neobaroque. A real movement of 'baroquization' of the arts in the whole River Plate region, which is surprising if one considers, for example, Borges's condemnation of that over-wrought style. This emergence of the baroque is a new development which had never been seen before in Argentina, even if we take the experimentalism of people like Oliverio Girondo or Macedonio Fernández as precedents, or the epic surrealism of Francisco Madariaga and Enrique Molina as the foundations of this movement. The neobaroque is a post-Borges literature, which writes – excuse the daring heresy – *against Borges*. Osvaldo Lamborghini (born in 1940 in Buenos Aires, died in 1985 in Barcelona), a decisive catalyst in this revolt in the arts in the Plate region, launches the attack: he gives one of the bold poems in prose which make up his second short book *Sebregondi retrocede* (Buenos Aires, Noé, 1973) the following title: 'With an orthopaedic hand, the Marquis of Sebregondi has written his poem'. The poem written by the Marquis (in whose person we can see some subtle sympathetic allusions to Gombrowicz) is a glorious homosexual narrative, in the course of which moods are mixed and roles are inverted, upturning everything. And everything is a provocation which ironizes (sodomizes?) the unhappiness assumed by Borges, who, it will be remembered, wrote: 'And still you have not written the poem'.

Osvaldo Lamborghini's baroque is curious. It is not an elegant or frivolous baroque, like the Cuban version. On the contrary, we are dealing here with a muddy, entrenched baroque, where all kinds of material of dubious origins are inextricably mixed. The aberration prepares the way for the joke: we could speak, in relation to this uncertain current, of *neobarroso* (barroso—muddy) instead of *neobarroco*. This creates a reference to the shallowness of the estuary of the River Plate, which is never fully renounced, as if it would not do to throw oneself into the pure game of extravagant words, as if one were afraid of confusing *ludismo* (=playfulness) with *boludismo* (=stupidity/thickness).

In the shadow of the maestro Lamborghini, the paths of the neobaroque rhizome diverge into a wealth of specific experimentations. It is worth mentioning the playful baroque, linked with the work of Severo Sarduy, of Arturo Carrera, who evolves in the direction of a certain simplicity in his later works, the tango baroque of Tamara Kamenszain, most noticeably in her latest collection of poems, *Vida de living* (Buenos Aires, Sudamericana 1991), elements of a gauchesque baroque present in the writing of Leónidas Lamborghini, Osvaldo's older brother (I am thinking in particular of the poems in *Episodios*, 1980) and, among the younger poets, the ecstatic suspense of the Peruvian resident in Buenos Aires Reynaldo Jiménez, notably in his recent double volume *Ruido incidental/El té*, published by Último Reino.

The list is manifestly incomplete, seeking only to give a sketchy idea of this baroquization, which is also strong in Uruguayan arts, in the poetry of, for example, Roberto Echavarren, Eduardo Milán, Eduardo Espina, Marosa di Giorgio. . . An interesting detail is the evolution of Último Reino, which from being a neoromantic literary group has become an organ sensitive to the most audacious experiments, baroque or otherwise, but at any rate close to a *literature of language* (the expression is Hector Libertella's) and far removed from intimism.

This advance in the neobaroque provokes reactions which are aired in the great organ of expression of the criollo poets, the *Diario de poesía*, whose editors prefer to align themselves with what has come to be known as *objectivism*, that is, in approximate terms, with a certain type of poetry which concerns itself more with meaning than with game or linguistic resonance. The objectivists' attacks on the baroque poets are usually very scathing. It would seem that the neobaroque eruption has gone too far for their liking, in its demand for sophistication and complication in the act of writing, and at the level of poetic form, and thereby caused severe resistance, not always justified, on the part of a more provincial and coastal aesthetic (given that several of its practitioners are from the Argentine province of Santa Fé). Anyhow, this controversy is enriching and creates poles of identification for the new bards, nourishing the secret boom in Argentine poetry.

Magazines, author's editions, photocopies, stencilled or even carbon-copied texts, all resources are valid as a channel for this need for expression. I felt this when I coordinated, during the conference on Young Art in Buenos Aires, a literacy workshop, an opportunity which left me pleasantly surprised by the eagerness and dedication of the young people who were stubborn in their determination to write (and to show and discuss what they wrote!). In the melancholy of disaster with which this critical *fin de siècle* seems to be tinged, one trembles slightly in allowing oneself even this faint glimmer of optimism.

Translated by Margaret Smallman

Tin Tan: The Pachuco*

CARLOS MONSIVÁIS

In my view, the secret of Tin Tan's continued appeal lies in an extremely effective combination of language and attitude. More specifically, in the way he condenses an attitude into language. With Tin Tan, anarchism and disorder do give way to solemnity, but only so as to immediately make way for more chaos. Dressed to the nines when his first films came out, he represented, then, a faint transcultural glimmer of modernity. Today, to those for whom Tin Tan is mainly a television experience, he represents the uncontrollable laughter of an otherwise grey epoch, when jokes circulated like memorial plaques, and respect had become society's death mask.

Tin Tan: the great comic actor that a tamed film industry was loath to accept, hardly understood, and ruthlessly exploited. Nothing foreshadowed his explosive appearance in 1943, the year of his debut. Whilst Cantinflas, dominating a film comedy that was more verbal than visual, remained trapped in the prison of his one great disovery, and the rest were mere variations on themes adapted from the Frivolous Theatre, Tin Tan was a leap in the dark: he had not escaped from the circus, nor was he the standard crook softened by the insignificance of his crimes; he was, simply, a young man who walked, talked and loved as if he carried a sinfonola brimming over with boogie-woogies and boleros in his head.

The Comedians

In Mexican cinema established comedians stick to a few variants on few themes. The following is a list of their main duties:

– they must belong to the popular classes, expressing them in word and in movement (not to speak of appearance). The comic must be both sympathetic and obedient, lascivious and controllable, a scoundrel but honest. (An upper class comic or ladies' man is inconceivable);

– they must shy away from any idea of class conflict so as to rather represent the limitations of the dispossessed: their timidity, their false arrogance and mythomania. The function of such comedy is to make of social resentment a folklore of gratitude, and of humour, a means of stifling all signs of rebellion;

– they must foreground the 'essence of comedy' (especially in love stories) purely in the industry's terms – as the prolongation of sentimentalism: when it comes down to it, laughter and tears are the same thing. Jokes, meanwhile, mould and temper the emotions. You laugh so as not to cry, and you cry because it hasn't occurred yet to anyone at this funeral to put an end to the wailing with a few good jokes;

– the comic actor must maintain his original cultural capital, that is, the personality that took him onto the screen in the first place. If, for whatever reason, they change and lose their well-worn tics and techniques, spectators cry foul. In a medium in which what counts is tame verbal jokiness and an appreciation of the most simple of gags (the visual joke) the comics' initial resources (expressions, voice, gestures) tend to be their final ones;

– they must remain located, no matter what, within the popular domain: the comic character may experience unexpected success, wander through bourgeois mansions, travel, and even become famous, but in the last roll he will return, vanquished but victorious, to the wealth of poverty;

– comedians must put up with the most abject use of their talents. The function of even the most famous and gifted comic is to provide humorous relief in melodramas, to be the foil of successive Perfect Couples. Even if it had wanted to, the Mexican film industry could never have produced a Groucho Marx, or even a Bob Hope. This is because humour was a degraded form in the 1940s and film (an instrument that can actualize and change its spectators) a magic with eyes for melodrama alone – considered significant at the time because it was the place where the resources of the industry and the public coincided;

– they must accept becoming the vehicle of puerile, mainly idiomatic, gags that legitimize a culture of submission through inversion (the reproduction of Indian, peasant and, most often, urban popular speech as the expression of a child-adult);

– they must respect the dogma that the joke – memorized and finely tuned – is the only redoubt of prestige in popular entertainment. Verbal wit, on the other hand, the spontaneous spark of light that opens out onto entirely new situations, is considered to be non-transcendent, just fun ('relajo'). Such a devaluation of inventiveness actually enthrones the joke – laughter at something which declares itself to be funny *in itself*, because it has always been there: the same words, occupying the same time;

– they must resign themselves to the stasis in comic roles imposed by trade belief: throughout his career a comic develops one character, and one character alone;

– they have to accept 'natural' limits: Hollywood levels of production and the myth of Cantinflas. A successful comedian may become an idol, but he will rise no further in the identification stakes. It is not for him to represent the People – with a capital P – only examples of the 'popular'. This is because Cantinflas has monopolized the emblematization of the People to such an extent that audiences now amuse themselves in recognising what they see and what they already know of the idol's 'proverbial ingenuity', laughing at the jokes they hear or, alternatively, at those they just imagine – all of which they will then ecstatically repeat for their friends the following day. The weight of the legend is such that, in the memory of the spectator, even the most pitiful of films becomes enshrined as yet another example of the 'national sense of humour'.

What sumara con la baisa?

Es el pachuco un sujeto singular
pero que nunca debiera camellar
y que a las jainas las debe dominar
para que se sientan veri fain para bailar.

Toda carnala que quiere ser feliz
con un padrino que tenga su desliz
vaya a su chante y agarre su veliz
y luego a camellar pa'mantener al infeliz.

Tin Tan's Song, written by Marcelo Chávez

Tin Tan (Germán Genaro Cipriano Gómez Valdés Castillo) was born on September 15, 1915 in Mexico City. In 1927 the family moved to Cuidad Juárez where his father was a customs officer and his mother a housewife. He was brought up in a neighbourhood that was later to become a pachuco bastion, did odd jobs and – something he often forgot – became a tourist guide. According to his brother Manuel, Germán's biggest influence was the city of Los Angeles, but the neighbourhoods of Cuidad Juárez and El Paso (full of with-it 'cool cats' with quiffs, their hands buried in deep pockets and shoulders slouched as they rhythmically strolled the streets) were also important.

'My first job', says Tin Tan in an interview, 'was to stick labels on the entire record collection of a radio station. To save spit, I found a street dog and taught it to stick its tongue out so I could wet the labels manually. Then I was an errand boy and later a sweep. But I owe my first real opportunity to a broken microphone. This is how it happened: I always liked playing jokes, and at the radio station I enjoyed imitating my friends and the bosses. Agustín Lara was fashionable at the time – I'm talking about the end of the 1930s – and I also imitated him. One day the microphone broke. When it was mended, Mr. Meneses asked for someone to test it. They asked me. So I started imitating Lara. Mr. Meneses thought someone had put one of Lara's records on, but it was me, fooling around! One week later I was starring in a show called Tin Tan Larara, scripted by Mr. Meneses . . . Then, I wanted to be a singer, but I ended up becoming an announcer and impersonator. I impersonated everyone, and did it quite well. Then I was given my first stage name – Topillo Tapas – and I toured with it.' Not long afterwards he became a comedian (and singer) in Paco Miller's company – which toured Mexico and the Southern U.S.A.. Another comic, Donato, also worked with Paco Miller. His sidekick – the one who represents high seriousness amidst the custard pies – was Marcelo Chávez, who became Tin Tan's 'buddy' ('carnal') for more than 20 years. 'One day we just started rehearsing, out of the blue. We went on stage that night, and it went down very well. We decided to stay together, write songs, and rehearse.'

The stories about Tin Tan usually leave out one important detail: his bewilderment at events in Los Angeles. Between approximately 1938 and 1942, in the Mexican-American neighbourhoods of Texas and, especially, California, the pachuco emerges as the first important aesthetic product of migration, the bearer of a new and extremist concept of elegance – he is a dandy living on the outskirts of fashion – that in the eyes of the Anglos (and the fathers of the pachucos) is an outright provocation. The pachucos' audacity in clothing and in gesture permits them to mark out their new territory with mobile signs and, like their model, the Harlem dude, challenge discrimination too. The pachuco is thus affiliated to the American Way of Life only eccentrically, and becomes a part of Mexican culture by confronting racism. Pachucos eventually become (not very voluntary) symbols of cultural resistance, and end up cornered and persecuted in the segregation campaigns that culminate in the Los Angeles Zoot Suit Riots.

By the time Tin Tan acquires his name, pachucos had disappeared from the scene in the US, whilst in Mexico they had become synonymous with the idea of a vagabond with radical taste and, what is more, associated with the suburban pimp, or even the embodiment of a new neighbourhood masculinity – as it is played, for example, by Victor Parra in

El Suavecito (Fernando Méndez, 1950) and Rodolfo Acosta in Emilio 'el Indio' Fernández's films *Salón México* (1945) and *Víctimas del pecado* (1950). In *El Suavecito* the father scorns his son, the pachuco, and eventually expels him from the family and society with the words: 'That's not a man but a hairdresser's dummy'. A traditional society – the only one that existed in Mexico at the time – can only see such an unrestrained wardrobe – jacket down to the knees, tails, incredibly wide lapels, a watch chain that hangs dangerously close to the ground, fantasy braces, a feathered hat, flowery shirts whose sleeves are long enough to cover the hands, and a sense of combination that sets the memory of decent clothes ablaze – as an inflammatory provocation.

Ever since the Porfiriato, Mexicans who became 'gringified' have been the object of disdain and fun. From the point of view of this dimension of popular culture, whoever so renounces the 'national condition' (dressing and behaving like grandads) is amusingly found lacking. In his well-known novel *Al filo del agua* set in 1909, just before the outbreak of the Revolution, Agustín Yañez lists villager reactions to such 'Northerners' – those who had gone to North America, and returned:

> 'Poor people, poor country.' 'The're the cleverest, the bravest; just because of a handful of words they can mouth in a Christian tongue – even tho' they don't know how to read, like when they left.' 'And just because they've got those gold teeth they pick all the time.' 'Because they wear those big, thick boots, felt hats, wide trousers and cuffed shirts and shiny cufflinks.' . . . 'And what about the way you talk? You've even forgotten the language your fathers taught you.'

With marvellous impudence Tin Tan undoes, without appearing to know it, such a lack of understanding and rejection. His dress and style announce, for the first time, a popular modernity.

Guilty Conscience

In Mexico City during the 1940s, Tin Tan triumphantly became the archetypical 'pocho', a category that was demonized both linguistically and socially. 'Pocho': a person who has lost caste ('descastado'), who has forgotten their roots, and exchanged the vigour of idiosyncrasy for the plate of beans of superficial Americanization. In his column of 20 June, 1944, Salvador Novo remembers an article of his on 'The Purity of Language':

> It is a good article, really. I was inspired by all that talk about Tin Tan, who stands accused of corrupting the language with 'pochismos' which the young repeat. Of course, I did not have the space to develop the whole theory as I should have, but essentially, and the intelligent reader would have understood, it rests on making of Cantinflas the representative of the Mexican unconscious, whilst recognizing that Tin Tan, when he bothers us, does so because he embodies the guilty conscience of our own voluntary or passive loss of caste ('descastamiento').

Tin Tan elaborates to perfection the linguistic collage in which all those Anglo-Saxon words imposed by the necessity to name the new, a rural Spanish full to the brim with archaisms, and sayings and expressions from the whole country, participate. Tin Tan asks Marcelo, for example, about 'the "jale" that you got as "guachador"', and 'do your "relativos" still "forgetean" you?' One has to immediately translate: 'jale' is job and 'guachador' is 'velador' (watchman), and the 'relativos' that 'forgetean' are parents that forget. Nevertheless, Tin Tan does not emblematize loss of caste ('descastamiento'), as will become obvious in the years that follow, he only interprets the synchcretism that marks the second half of the century. Many a reprimand still awaits the 'pocho', and will appear later in films, plays, radio programmes, sermons and editorials. The steady increase in migration, however, will eventually 'normalize' them: there are so many 'pochos' that the use of the pejorative collapses.

Tin Tan articulates a script opposed to known convention. He is the pachuco: a word that in Mexico City oscillates between friendly irony and insult. There is a considerable leap from the riots in Los Angeles to the dance halls of Mexico City, and the pachucos of the capital – who do not offend the 'other', the North American, but rather the 'other', the man of respect – bet everything they have on this character that makes an adventure of dressing and an urban fantasy of the migrant's challenge.

'Turirurá tundá tundá tundá'. But even this is too much. A classicism that feigns concern for correct syntax rejects innovations in the name of linguistic purity. And if Cantinflas is accepted in the name of an incoherence proper to the crowd, Tin Tan is rejected for his offence against immutable speech, the ideal property of the elites. Tin Tan is denounced by journalists and academicians of the Language who lay siege to his prefigurative attitude. More or less by force, however, producers and scriptwriters begin to incorporate the comic, the pachuco, into their big-city neighbourhood scenes; and although they do not supress the 'Americanisms' in his style entirely, they do lighten his linguistic experimentation.

Tin Tan's career was not as linear as it is usually presented. In fact, just as he was inspired by the Los Angeles pachucos, his most recognisable influence was Cab Calloway, singer and director of the *Harlem Orchestra* and a huge star in the 1930s. Tin Tan takes his gestures of optimistic ecstasy from Calloway, his dress, a sense of movement on stage, and a syncopated malice that distorts, elevates and magnifies his songs. *Stormy Weather*, for example, reveals Cab Calloway definitely to be Tin Tan's model, with his circus humour, the labial exaggeration that 'swallows' and ironically recreates his songs, and the architectonic suit that makes all preambles unnecessary ('Let my clothes introduce me so that I can just get on with it.') To this Tin Tan adds his experience of the circus and music hall, his use of the cinematographic scene (the sketch), his ability to improvise and his enormous confidence: apart from the spectators, no one else is looking.

On November 5, 1943 Tin Tan makes his debut in the Iris Theatre in Mexico City with a salary of 40 pesos. Cantinflas was the star of the show; and Tin Tan was only moderately successful. Which is not surprising: only gradually would the dynamism, the fun and the offensiveness associated with Tin Tan be understood. His side-kick ('carnal') Marcelo, was an old-fashioned comic, the interlocutor who takes all the jokes or who offers his physique up for ritual derision (in his case, fatness and baldness; whilst in the complementary case of the dwarf José René Ruiz *Tun Tun*, closeness to the ground). Whilst acknowledging the real differences, Marcelo is to Tin Tan what Margaret Dumont is to Groucho Marx: the ideal victim of jokes and humorous situations. The receiver of blows aimed originally at the comic, he represented offended respectability, his face swollen by the surprise of either gratuitous verbal or physical abuse.

Tin Tan and Marcelo are contracted to work in the Follies Theatre, The Patio – a fashionable night club – and to do a weekly radio programme on XEW. Tin Tan is also given a part in René Cardona's film *Hotel de verano*: 'They paid me 350 pesos for a number, which was nothing, but what the hell, I was still very green as far as film was concerned!' In fact, Tin Tan's first films were not very good. He is not a humourist either, although he resorts to North American vaudeville humour when on the offensive and improvising. He has no hierarchical repertoire of jokes, nor has he timed the rhythm of his punch lines, but he does have other allies: ferocity of gesture, verbal aggression, an enthusiasm for chaos, sentimentalism dissolved by irony, and a lack of respect for solemnity and its sense of propriety (property). From such a balancing act, and the continuous sense of impending catastrophe that accompanies it, he mocks decorum without demolishing everything that surrounds him, unlike the Marx Brothers, because of a hatred for institutions – nor does he call for universal ruin, like Buster Keaton. The results are, nevertheless, equally apocalyptic. Tin Tan passes by and nothing remains standing, no one escapes the chaos.

From the series of films made by Humberto Gómez Landero – *El hijo desobediente* (1945), *Hay muertos que no hacen ruido* (1946), *Con la música por dentro* (1946), *El niño perdido* (1947) and *Músico, poeta y loco* (1947) – Tin Tan's character already possesses the characteristics that he will then go on to endlessly hone (despite the director's lack of imagination): impudence, cynicism, amorous frivolity, and an ineptitude balanced by destructive efficiency. Tin Tan's verve leaves an immediate impression: he acts as if he had transported the audience itself right into the screen.

¡Qué mené, carnalita, qué mené!

Tin Tan leaves no word in peace, he twists them, stretches them, discovering their sonorous interrelations. He emancipates urban speech. In Gómez Landeros's films the story and dialogue credits go to Guz Águila (Guzmán Águilera). But Guz Águila, an able scriptwriter in the Frivolous Theatre for two decades, is inadequate when it comes to the linguistic vitality of Tin Tan. In a dialogue in *Músico, poeta y loco*, Tin Tan, working in a shop that sells windows, says to a client:

> Orejas, sabe que esta chompeta (*ear*) me falla un poquetín . . . Y su guaifo (*husband*) ¿cómo está por ahí? . . . (*Looking at his suit*) Usa muy buena garra. Fijón. ¡Qué mené, carnalita, qué mené! (*Fantastic!*) . . . No, no, no, jainita (*honey*) . . .

And Marcelo responds: 'Se me hace que le pusiste de a feo a la yesca y te anda girando la chompeta.' And so on. Tin Tan 'jazzes' up speech, he improvises, contriving neologisms on the move.

In 1948 Tin Tan begins his collaboration with Gilberto Martínez Solares (director) and Juan García 'el Peralvillo' (scriptwriter). In an interview published in *Cuadernos de la Cineteca (4)*, Martínez Solares says, somewhat contemptuously:

> Tin Tan was an extraordinary comedian. At first, I didn't have much confidence in him. I didn't feel like working with him either. He was a bit common, both in the characters he portrayed and in the places he worked, right? Tents, theatres . . . I wrote stories, although I've never been good at street talk, especially neighbourhood talk, which was my collaborator Juan García's strength.

Calabacitas tiernas, the film that begins the collaboration between Tin Tan, Martínez Solares and Juan García is enjoyable today for its energy, despite breakdowns in plot. Tin Tan sings, dances, seduces, pretends to be what he isn't, doubts being who he is, and confronts himself in the mirror like Harpo Marx in *Duck Soup* – audaciously performing on the tightrope that separates theatre from film, he walks to the rhythm of the city suburbs, from danzón to swing. In *Calabacitas tiernas* the modern urban comic appears, largely emancipated from sentimentalism, installing the logic of survival into the domain of fun ('relajo') whilst acknowledging that he is condemned to fail. Without his pachuco clothing, and that touch of contemporaneity provided by Anglo words, Tin Tan is as irreverently up to date as times permit. He improvises, entrances the camera, speaks to the audience ('the Lord of A Thousand Brains'), gets obviously bored with old-fashioned dignity, refuses to protect his honour, pays no tribute whatsoever to linguistic serfdom and, furthermore, does not care if he offends the audience.

Listen Marcelino, play one that makes me cry from here to the next song

Inevitably, Tin Tan's real environment is the picaresque – which I define here quickly as the gift to take advantage of all circumstances except for the really advantageous ones. He is a good-for-nothing who has no room for either justice or injustice, he is no one's fool and everybody's fool. His character perfectly combines extremes: adulation and lechery, sentimentalism and daylight robbery, solidarity and plunder. And in this coming and going from heroism to anti-heroism (from radical failure to fleeting victory), Tin Tan displays a modernity which – loyal to the circular resignation of the circus – Cantinflas, Palillo, Monolín and Shilinsky, Polo Ortín, El Chaflán, el Chicote and even Resortes (who is only modern when he dances) never knew.

The Tin Tan who matters, and who speaks to us now, is the product of fifteen years of filming and recording between 1945 and 1959. What follows this period is almost unbearable: the sadness that comes from watching a great but wasted comic actor, a comic who is misunderstood and abandoned by an industry that exploited him without recognizing his brilliance. But from *El hijo desobediente* to *El violetero* (1959), Tin Tan is that extraordinary figure who marks a generation (in ways that were only understood much later), transcends the lamentable scripts, redeems through improvisation the badly planned scenes, democratizes relations with the public, and opens the door to a modern humour that will influence not only a whole generation of television comedians (Héctor Suárez, The Polivoces, Alejandro Suárez and, of course, the Loco Valdés) but also, through the mythical evocation of his figure in the trade, recent ones like Andrés Bustamente, Ausencio Cruz and Víctor Trujillo.

Tin Tan never completely distances himself from the Frivolous Theatre. He is a film comedian – no doubt –! with a gift for speedy repartee and a facility for acrobatics, dance, extreme facial plasticity, and the insult as a form of relationship. He is also a creature of the sketch (to which he resorts whenever he feels lost). In his terrific hullabaloos, amidst the destruction of a house or a shop, it suddenly appears:

'Now, yes, Marcelino, you're going to have to work with UNESCO.'
'With UNESCO?'
'Yes, with a broom.'[1]

For years Cantinflas's strategy of appearing in only one film a year was praised. During the 1950s, on the other hand, Tin Tan limited himself by filming every two or three months. Now, however, the majority of Cantinflas's films are almost unwatchable (except, in my view, *Aguila o sol, El signo de la muerte, Ahí está el detalle, El gendarme desconocido*, and *Ni sangre ni arena*). But even the worst of Tin Tan's films contain memorable scenes, songs, and jokes. His vitality enables him to overcome the limitations imposed by the industry on his character, the mediocrity of the screenplays (when they exist), the idea that film is defined by speed and forgetfulness, and the alarming ineptitude of the young 'starlets' (with one exception: Sylvia Pinal in *El rey del barrio*). If the scorn of the critics hardly matters, the partial incomprehension of the public that celebrates him, without knowing the contemporaneity of his lack of inhibition, is overwhelming – an inhibition, moreover, that enjoys very little support: the freedom to improvise from Martínez Solares (who on seeing him, according to Wolf Ruvinskis, laughed and just carried on filming), his popular register provided by Juan García 'el Peravillo', and the discretion and efficiency of his sidekick Marcelo.

And his successes are not meagre. In the 'Golden Age of Mexican Cinema', only one other actor breaks down the rigid barriers of convention: Joaquín Pardavé, who preserves and transmits the accumulated knowledge of actors in the tradition of Frivolous Theatre – whose ceremonial and measured diction acts as the architecture of irony, and whose voices are, almost literally, decorated with the epoch. On saying this I am not forgetting the contributions of Resortes, Mantequilla, El Chaflán, El Chicote, Oscar Pulido, Amelia Wilhelmy and Delia Magaña, but none of these managed to satisfactorily transcend the inertia of screenwriters and the haste of directors. Whilst Pardavé achieves his success thanks to his complete understanding of traditional sensibility, Tin Tan does so through his lack of inhibitions – Germán does not bow before the film camera, he rather makes it his accomplice, his witness, his immediate applause, part of his own environment.

Tus besos se llegaron a recrear/aquí en mi boca

I believe that *El rey del barrio* (1949) is Tin Tan's best film. On saying this I am not forgetting *Simbad el Mareado, El Revoltoso, El Ceniciento, Ay amor ... cómo me has puesto, El sultán descalzo*; but in *El rey del barrio*, Tin Tan reaches his apogee: he is flexible, ironic, sentimental and destructive, and his character, fruit of both the astuteness of the industry and his own biography, is perfect, as defenceless as a catastrophe, and with the eloquence of someone with nothing to lose. Tin Tan is the most joyous product of urban neighbourhoods, someone who explains himself in the light of the devastation he disseminates. He is, at one and the same time, contemporary in attitude and as anachronistic as the neighbourhoods that will soon be demolished, as the pool hall crooks, and as the methods used for injecting the past with actuality and a night at the movies with dance hall rhythm. *El rey del barrio* contains some of Tin Tan's best sequences: the humiliation of detective Marcelo in the house they are painting, the fabulous duet with Vitola (in a 'cirivirivi' that pursues the grotesque by celebrating the ridiculous), and the bolero 'Contigo' that Tin Tan, drunk and in love, sings whilst taking charge of the block he lives in and in doing so transforming it into a set from *Romeo and Juliet*.

Singing – be it rancheras or boleros – Tin Tan's humour is extremely effective. His style is naturally exaggerated. Nevertheless, he successfully manages to neither distort the meaning of the joke nor the virtues of romance. Dancing, Tin Tan is the pachuco who adds spice to the choreographic fun. He is the neighbourhood dandy, and when it comes to the bolero, he celebrates the 'pick-up', and falls 'madly in love' – which is the invasion of machismo by lyricism – without a hint of vocal pretension. His style thus provides an alternative outlet for the transcultural tang that censorship pursued in his speech. Tin Tan is the crooner and the bolero singer, impregnated with the onomatopoeia of boogie-woogie. He sings with his whole mouth ('my drooling snout'). And if he cannot be solemn like Juan Arvizu or Emilio Tuero, nor sensual like Frank Sinatra, Tin Tan does manage to both parody a variety of styles and unify them into his own ironic and openly affected ('cursi') one. As a singer, Tin Tan is, unusually, parodic and orthodox at the same time.

Chaos within chaos

How do you put a Tin Tan film together? For the most part, they are dismal distortions of classics or of contemporary successes. Their names bear the mark of the immediacy of the joke: *The Mark of the Fox* ('La marca del zorrillo'), *The 3½ Musketeers* ('Los tres mosqueteros y medio'), *Cindarello* ('El Ceniciento'), *Seasick Sinbad* ('Simbad el Mareado'), *Sleeping Beau* ('El Bello Durmiente'), *The Viscount of Monte Cristo* ('El Vizconde de Montecristo'), *The Blue Beard* ('El Barba Azul'), *Look What Happened to Samson!* ('Lo que le pasó a Sansón'), *Rebel Without a Home* ('Rebelde sin casa'), *Puss-without-Boots* ('El gato sin botas'), *The Phantom of the Operetta* ('El fantasma de la opereta'). Even *El violetero* is, in part, a caricature of *María Candelaria*, a humorous bow on Tin Tan's part, happy to imitate the 'Indio' Fernandezque way of speaking Castillian in Xochimilco (and to then immediately move on to Spanglish).

To the weakness of the plots and the irresponsibility of the producers, convinced that cinema is the art of the immediate recovery of their investments, Tin Tan opposes his obsession for parody and hatred of boredom. From this point of view, improvisation is the only way to escape memorising the script – the film industry's equivalent to the prison-house of boredom. The task of 'nationalizing' the delirium then falls to folklore, and there is plenty of it; whilst reality becomes whatever happens before or after each comic scene. In such a cinema, parody involves much more than the transformation of situations that are already in themselves grotesque or ridiculous. Parody is the continuous, knockabout invention of the world just as it should be, where satire is the mistress of ceremonies for historical times-gone-by, melodrama, passionate affairs, incomprehensible plots. Nothing is serious, except for death – but that only occurs in the film showing next door.

Tin Tan is, in the main, the product of his youthful energy dramatized in dance, leaps in the air, irreverence, and frenetic escapes. Tin Tan sings mambo and cha-cha-cha, shouts, knocks over and destroys whatever is in reach, sings serenades, fails as if his life depended on it and sets everything around him going. With the passing of years, he concentrates on verbal humour. But without a competent team in his later films, and impotent and disenchanted when it came to routine (although there are always magnificent moments: see *El Quelito*, for example), Tin Tan looks as if he has had enough. People admire his charm, he is honoured and always working, but no one thinks he will last. He is like he is, and best not dedicate another minute to the matter: he is, or was, a pachuco embattled by linguistic censorship; he is, or was, a product of neighbourhood and small-town vaudeville; he is, or was, a comic who refused to allow himself to be intimidated by the cinema. From our own privileged perspective today, there is no real point in quarrelling with the stupidity of the Mexican film industry, which also wasted Resortes and Mantequilla, and buried Pardavé, Pedro Armendáriz, Fernando and Andrés Soler, David Silva, Tito Junco, Roberto Cañedo and other excellent actors in abominable melodramas. Tin Tan was used and abused by a booming industry, but thanks to this very situation Tin Tan was also able to work free from the intimidation suffered by the established and 'sacred' stars. He did what he wanted as often as he could, and became, for the generations that followed, the emblem of a kind of urban vitality which still, when it's time for fun ('relajo'), moves us today.

Translated by John Kraniauskas

* First published as 'Es el pachuco un sujeto singular: Tin Tan', in *Intermedios*, No. 4, October, 1992.

Notes

1 'Un esco' + 'ba' = 'un escoba' = a broom! (Translator's note)

(Queer) Boleros of a Tropical Night

JOSÉ QUIROGA

The tropics have assumed a unique space in terms of the construction and reconstruction of Latin American subjects at various points in the twentieth century. From political faith in Pan-Americanism at the turn of the century, through the revolutionary struggle in the thirties, the 'modern' nightlife of the forties, and again with revolution and the 'new man' in the sixties – the site of the tropics in Latin American culture forms a complex circuit of desire that would take considerable time to deconstruct. What I intend to do as a modest first step in that process is meditate on the current revival of the sad, sentimental, tropical boleros of the 1940s and 1950s in the context of a contemporary rearticulation of the Latino and Latin American subject. What is important for me at this point is how the indeterminate politics of the subject at the threshold of a new era are represented by means of the homosexual male or the drag queen in different artistic modes. In movies, in literature, in popular culture, the gay man (or the transvestite) not only carries the burden of nostalgia but is given the added mandate of representing and resolving the very indecisiveness that seems to result out of the present moment of Latin American societies – torn between the demands of a savage neo-liberal order and the equally savage demands of maintaining at least some kind of tenuous links to an 'authenticity' that is seen in terms of the past. Tropical music, the tropical night – these are the sites chosen by some contemporary Latin American subjects as they undergo the processes that accompany the triumph of the neo-liberal order, under the guise of a singular intimacy given by the embodiment of a sexual choice in the form of the melancholic homosexual.

Of course, boleros appear as a point of reference in the work of artists that are not necessarily gay. But at least in the examples that will follow, the revival of the bolero is accompanied by a representation of the homosexual as a polemical figure that mourns and celebrates. As such, and given the sometimes limited confines of the representation, the gay man becomes the most visible emblem of a modern paradox, posing a question that stops short of eroticizing the dissolution of the nation: what part of Latin American identity is in flux and what part of it remains in spite of changes over time? The very ambivalence of the question is embodied in the figure of the gay man and in his connection to the bolero as a form, and this is why it is important to understand that behind the genre's revival, there is something other at stake than merely nostalgia or 'camp' sensibility. Nostalgia, in this case, has chosen to represent its very ambivalence, at this time, via the gay man.

What is the cultural context for the rearticulation of the bolero? Outside the more direct gay milieu, the Venezuelan writer Rafael Castillo Zapata introduces his *Fenomenología del bolero* (1990) by naming as mentors Roland Barthes (particularly *A Lover's Discourse*) and then Werther, Proust, Adorno, psychoanalysis – all as part of the psychological baggage of a certain (left) aesthetics that any inhabitant of Latin American urban centers would recognize. Talking about the origins of his own book, he explains that:

> ... listening to boleros had become an adventure of cultural self-knowledge in a passionate period associated with the Grupo Tráfico and street poetry, with conversationalism, and with a sentimentality recuperated for the sake of reflection and writing – that Latin American sentimentality which has been cast aside by disdainful modernizing, wrapped in anachronisms that, in the end, has proved to be beneficial, for it has actually saved that uninhabited milieu of passion from the barbarism of modernity characteristic of this part of the world and whose loss European modernity is now lamenting. Slowly, however, I realized that Barthes had never in his life heard a bolero, that he died without the experience of listening to Olga Guillot singing Luis Demetrio's 'Bravo', and that this lack of knowledge – crucial, without a doubt, – was reflected whether he wanted it or not, in his extraordinary book (Castillo Zapata 1990,10).

What is interesting in this passage is not that it names the particular milieu for the recuperation of the bolero, or that it does so by claiming to be the addenda, the supplement to Barthes' discourse – a supplement, furthermore, that in true Derridean fashion would decentre the privileged status of the original. This rhetorical ploy has been, after all, a Latin American constant since Borges if not certainly before him. What is more interesting is that this supplement (the anachronistic bolero) is presented as part of a kind of 'virginal' space (as Zapata names it, at a later point) that European postmodernity now wishes it possessed. Never mind that Barthes was also intensely aware of his vaguely anachronistic stance vis a vis European cultural trends – Castillo Zapata, as befits his Heideggerian origins, is also projecting his self onto a genre that, as he confesses, is the most self-reflective of all – what is more significant is that Castillo Zapata's ambivalence manifests itself as a resistance to theorize the space of the bolero, as if theory will immediately undo the magic, will disrupt 'the stability of a free zone of the world' (Castillo Zapata, 16) a stability which is precisely given by the resistance to theory and intellectualism. Castillo Zapata's mode of theorizing, engaged in a battle whose most visible emblems are given in the opposition between authenticity on the one hand and intellectualism and theory on the other, can be linked to the representation of the homosexual within the space of boleros, for the homosexual embodies the relation between the bolero and the critic – as a double helix of resistance to, and beckoning of, theorizing. In other words, gay men, as they appear indissolubly linked to boleros in other artistic products, embody Castillo Zapata's reluctant or resistant theoretical act. The recent visibility of gay men in Latin American film and in literature, is predicated upon this ambivalent gesture.

How can we theorize outside of the parameters of resistance given by Castillo Zapata? Indeed, is it possible or even necessary, to theorize or to write from outside of this space? I am not sure that I have an answer, or even if there is *one* answer, to this question, but I think it is a necessary question to pose at this time, in order to remotivate the discussion and lead it outside the realm of temporal, regressive and proleptic nostalgia. Let us recall, first of all, that the bolero as a genre had already appeared, in a non-gay context, in Guillermo Cabrera Infante's *Tres tristes tigres (Three Trapped Tigers)*, and in Pedro Vergés *Sólo cenizas hallarás*, among others, but that it is sung in a different register in the tropicalia of the Argentinian Manuel Puig, and in Luis Rafael Sánchez's *La importancia de llamarse Daniel Santos*. These works recuperate a mode, a time and a place, they bridge the tangible borders between high and low culture, in order to voice a certain dislocation from a time gone by. If la Estrella allows Cabrera Infante to mourn a lost Cuba, in Puig or in Sánchez the bolero signals the beginning of a new voice that reappears from the past in order to seduce readers into a meta-Caribbean (and even transnational) space, where the present is but the prelude to a future that will not come in the guise of an eternal return. Because one of my premises is that the bolero as a recuperated genre demands that we break the tenuous border between the self and the other, between objective and subjective discourse, I will mimic Castillo Zapata's appeal to a kind of phenomenological and Barthesian theorizing of the personal, in order to remotivate the discussion along parameters that might be dissimilar from his.

A mí me pasa lo mismo que a usted

I should mimic, first of all, the role of bolerista, in order to quote and rupture the seamless discourse of the critical essay with boleros themselves. But then, what kind of boleros should I quote? 'No es falta de cariño, te quiero con el alma, te juro que te adoro y en nombre de este amor y por tu bien te digo adiós' (*It's not that I don't love you/I love you with all my heart/I swear that I adore you/and for the sake of this love I must say goodbye*). And maybe not that bolero but others, in different registers – for in all of these the critic is able to leave the realm of distance and find at least a tenuous place of habitation for his or her own pleasure with the succint elegance of Tito Rodríguez, the allure of Carmen Delia Dipiní, the perturbed desire of Bola de Nieve, and an ill-defined pantheon that certainly includes, and is not limited to, the bolero as a form, but rather to a time and a space and a possibility: Chavela Vargas, Toña la Negra, Olga Guillot, the self-conscious (almost ridiculous sublime) of Agustín Lara, the portly elegance of Lucho Gatica, the epidermic *frisson* of the composer Lolita de la Colina and the melancholic, bohemian moons of Sylvia Rexach. The sheer mass and volume of cultural production over-powers the pretenses of objectivity, but the pantheon is crowned, of course, by the Queen of them all, La Lupe, and her renditions of Tite Curet Alonso's 'La tirana' and 'Teatro.' Although I will write on, instead of sing, boleros, like all true boleristas I will talk about myself, perhaps in a sentimental mode, but always with a sort of indirection.

This something or other, this private and public lip-synching of boleros, will be my theoretico-bolerista space, and I will enter into this space not via Puig or Sánchez, but by means of two films where gay characters reappropriate the stage of popular culture by means of boleros or rancheras. The first is *Doña Herlinda y su hijo*, by Jaime Hermosillo. The scene that I think is most important in order to understand what Barthes called the 'punctum' of an image, occurs after Doña Herlinda's son, Rodolfo, marries Olga, the woman chosen by Doña Herlinda for her very gay son. Aware of the fact that Rodolfo has left his lover Ramón behind, Doña Herlinda takes Ramón to a spectacle where a singer (female) sings a ranchera of spurned love. At this point, Ramón cries, and his tears are meant to elicit the laughter but also the silence of the viewing public, aware that what we are seeing is, in effect, a crying game. Whereas the implacable normality of the whole cinematic affair (son, lover, mother, wife) gives the film a kind of perverse strangeness but also a curious sense of *ananké* – as if what happens is but what *should* happen in the best of all possible worlds, where the social conventions are repeated like the plot of a movie seen by an indifferent (and thoroughly entertained) public – the circulation of events beckoned some kind of catharsis brought about by the ranchera a la Chavela Vargas. At this musical point in the film, some kind of silence sets in via the gay man, listening to the ranchera, crying, as if precisely the waning of the affect of the sequence of events had to stop for emotion to appear. But underscoring the postmodern gaze that is implied by her role in the whole affair, Doña Herlinda (à la Frederic Jameson) simply takes a white handkerchief from her purse and passes it on to Ramón, who wipes away his tears. The ranchera, which in this case I equate with the bolero, ruptures the postmodern gaze, it beckons some kind of authenticity that appears paradoxically via the gay character.

The second film that needs to be mentioned in the context of the bolero is María Novaro's *Danzón*, where Julia's search for Carmelo is aided by a transvestite in a postcard Veracruz – quoted from Agustín Lara as rendered by Toña La Negra. But the transvestite here is not just another element in the search for a new space. Nostalgia – for the particular order, for the universe of the danzón – reconfigures the characters of María Novaro's film, but nostalgia never obliterates the fact that these characters want to live within the safety of an order regulated by them, and not necessarily by a return to heterosexual male dominance. Where the return of the ranchera in Doña Herlinda, and the boleroized transvestite in *Danzón*, intersect with the bolero as used in the context of gay culture, is in this aspect of looking back in order to ground the present without the undertow of all of its previous silences (this past as present and as possible future, the movie implies, will not silence women, will not deny the presence of gay men).

It is obvious that the recuperation of the boleros that these films announce (with their attendant regression into the 1940s and 50s) arises from within a context of a new appropriation of the public sphere. If these are the cultural products of NAFTAist and savagely capitalistic Latin America, where the certainties of the left have collapsed and apparently allow an open and malleable cultural space, then how can we recontextualize this move as something other than nostalgia and something other than camp?

The angels of history in Latin American cinema are now gay, and they deface the past within the present, they allow tragedy to fissure the parodies of the postmodern canvas, while remotivating tradition. The queer is now placed at the border, while the bolero itself speaks about the border of stage, of gender, and of culture. It is imperative to examine these now, without ever losing sight of the queer.

Ya conozco ese teatro

The first border that is posited by the bolero itself is a kind of border *of the stage*. To sing a bolero (one always sings it at the moment of despair) beckons the luminous erasure of the subject: an abandoned, plaintive, destitute, or defiant subject, rebellious or intransigent, but always engaging in the shared memory of a loss reconstructed from within its ruins. 'Hoy mi playa se viste de amargura, porque mi barca tiene que partir . . .' (*Today my beach is dressed in bitterness, because my boat must leave*). Arias may tap into the virtuosity of the throat and they may flesh out the mimicry of the possibility of voice. But in boleros, the subject and the public are positioned within a complex web where a confession is always overheard. This is why even taking into account different kinds of boleros, these are sung to no one, or rather, to somebody outside: their voicing is given beyond the public, so that somebody else can take stock of the afflictions of the present.

If in terms of form the bolero stakes out a certain borderline territoriality of performer and audience, in terms of content the bolero borders and delimits the notion of gender roles. Women may be defiant or aggresive, men may be forlorn, destitute or disinterested. Gender roles may switch, they may be renegotiated, but the very fact that there should be gender roles is renegotiated although never put into question. 'Falsedad bien ensayada, estudiado simulacro. Fue tu mejor actuación destrozar mi corazón, y hoy que me lloras de veras recuerdo tu simulacro. Perdona que no te crea, me parece que es teatro' (*Well-rehearsed falsity, well-studied pretence. Your best role was destroying my heart, and now that you cry for me I remember your pretence. Forgive me if I do not believe you, it all seems like theatre to me*) as written by Tite Curet Alonso for La Lupe. But once the theatrical mask has been ripped apart, what we have is the same man and the now furious, destitute woman. The simulacra that the bolero entertained was to believe that this did not have to be so. Performer and audience, gender switches that speak of intransigent gender roles, also have to be seen within the vast array of the very border that the bolero seems to erect in terms of culture. And this is, I believe, the border that will allow us to go back to the queer affection for the bolero, as well as to the representations of the queer within the genre.

Boleros appeared within the moment of maximum diffusion of that golden age of mambos, danzones and chachachá – as part of a transnationalization of a Latin American urban popular culture whose primary locales were the bar or the bedroom. Because, as Carlos Monsiváis has acutely perceived (Monsiváis, 1977), boleros recirculated the word 'romántico' and gave it a prestige no longer to be had by the word 'modernista', they created the possibility of a marginal nightlife that gave Latin Americans a sense of modernity by virtue of the possibility of 'living in sin'. But this, I should add, was the most paradoxical modernity of it all, for unlike the Desi Arnaz kind of rhythm-is-gonna-get-you mambos, rumbas and chachachá, boleros are ill-suited for translation – among other reasons, because they are too dependent upon a sense of poetry and lyric that, even when translated, shows its obvious inheritance from the sentimentality of the *modernista* space. In the sixties, for example, when aggressive salsa moved from the barrios of San Juan and Venezuela to the barrios of New York, boleristas never quite made it in the U.S.. New York, a city that could guarantee the survival of jazz or salsa singers, would in moments of financial despair have them go back to the bolero, as a way of tempering the aggressivity and the ferocity that their salsa already did not possess. Even so, none of the boleristas, like Vicentico Valdés, or Santitos Colón, could definitively triumph in New York. Only Tito Rodríguez, Cheo Feliciano, or La Lupe could sing boleros and survive, but that was because they had the salsa link.

These three borders that are present within the bolero as a form – borders that have to do with performance, with gender and with culture – need to be reconfigured by examining the role of gay men within the present anxieties given in Latin American neoliberalism. My point of entry into this discussion is, once again, the lucid work of Carlos Monsiváis on Agustín Lara:

> Sin el contexto de lo que lo volvió necesario, Agustín Lara se va mostrando progresivamente anacrónico y patético. Su cursilería aislada es una catástrofe sólo recuperable a través de técnicas importadas como el camp. Pero estas técnicas o trucos de los sesentas más sepultan que redimen...la indefensión literaria de las improvisaciones de Agustín Lara se esencializan si se les aplica la visión camp. [Lara no es] una opulencia de la forma a expensas de la ridiculez del contenido, sino la postrer defensa de un contenido primitivo que ve en lo exagerado su acceso a lo sublime. No es delirio de la forma, sino de las urgencias expresivas, del amor que se volverá "¡Cuna de plata de la mañana / que en la montaña se hace canción!"
> (Outside the context that made him necessary, Agustín Lara looks increasingly anachronistic and pathetic. His now isolated "affectation" ("cursilería") becomes a catastrophe that is only recuperable through imported forms as camp. But such 1960s techniques in fact bury more than they redeem...Agustín Lara's literary improvisations – which are defenseless – are essentialized by camp. [Because in Lara] you will not find opulence of form at the expense of ridiculous content, but rather the last defense of a primitive

content that sees in exaggeration its path to the sublime. Nor is there delirium of form; it is rather a matter of expressive urgency, of a love that will become "¡ Cuna de plata de la mañana/ que en la montaña se hace canción!" (Morning's silver cradle/ that in the mountains becomes a song!) (Monsivais, 1977; 86).

Monsiváis argues against the recycling of Lara as camp – camp understood not only as an imported aesthetics, but also as a kind of defense against the very sublime given in those quoted lines. Camp, then, with its regressive mode, essentializes the catastrophe of Agustín Lara's absence – the catastrophically bad aspects of Lara's style. For Monsiváis, camp may only be understood as the glorification of opulent form, whereas Lara himself understood that it was the content that allowed for access to sentimentality. For Monsiváis, until we no longer understand the very content and idealism of Lara's work, we will keep returning to him with a paternalistic and a melifluous sense of nostalgic sentimentalism for an old time and place that has transformed itself into almost a pre-modern essentialist 'sensibility'.

Whereas I agree with Monsiváis' assessment, particularly in relation to the essentialism that is masked by means of camp, I would like to mediate or, if I may, refine it- for camp seems to be involved in a sentimental economy that also accounts for Monsiváis' fascination with a catastrophe that flirts precisely with the possibility of essentialism. In other words, the ruins of Lara's style are precisely given as a tease, but Lara is not buried or redeemed by camp, nor is his 'bad' style necessarily essentialized by it. The recuperation of Lara, of La Lupe, of Bola de Nieve may be, in some context, the recuperation of nostalgia as camp, but in others it may not be. To laugh and cry at the formal excess of La Lupe as she sings 'Qué te pedí que no fuera leal comprensión' implies, in a sense, a gesture whose effect is given by means of contrast: one that heightens the very undecidability of the sentiment expressed. That same recuperation within a transvestite show – subject to constant police searches, harassment, and barely tolerated clandestinity in the docks of the port city of Valaparaíso, in the midst of the very Catholic Pinochetista Chile, where Madonna, Isabel Pantoja, Whitney Houston and Olga Guillot share a stage made by the performers themselves out of cardboard and rhinestones – is not given as camp, even if the audience of open and closeted queens, bugarrones and university faggots screams and laughs at the performers. *Who* is speaking here of course matters in terms of class, social status and context. The catastrophe of the bolero, and of Lara, becomes a mode of articulation for defiance. And this defiance can only be expressed by means of paradox.

The use of boleros as a genre by gay men has exposed the marginalization given within borders staked out by society as a whole. In other words, boleros allow gay men to deploy, suspend and remotivate borders according to their own wishes and desires. By mimicking the constitution of the borders, by erecting them again and again, gay men reveal that the only possible essentialism lies precisely in the hybrid arbitrariness of the border, one that conspires to further marginalize them within a national space that they in fact constitute and create (by being perhaps some of the most avid consumers and creators of what in Latin America is known 'la farándula' or 'la clase artística nacional'). It is precisely because this recuperation within the context of camp has to be seen in terms of positionality, that a certain kind of indirection is always at play, for in rescuing for themselves a voice, in taking over and subverting a space, the bolero and the queer will manipulate the very spaces that they put under control. When Almodóvar uses Los Panchos and Bola de Nieve in *Law of Desire*, or La Lupe in *Women on the Verge of a Nervous Breakdown* this use implies, at least for certain latino gay men, a kind of *validation* not given within the national space itself, as a quoted gesture of recognition sought after, delayed, displaced.

The queer will use the borders employed by the bolero in order to jump out and appeal to other imagined communities for at least a tenuous sense of recognition.

Because the bolero involves some sort of inviolate space circled over and delimited by culture, performance and gender, the essentialist gesture implied by camp turns into a performance of something else. And in the context of a Latin America pursued and marginalized by its own sense of tenuous border, this act acquires a decidedly defiant mode, for the queer will not hesitate to manipulate the border, and attempt to be recognized by another space beyond the national, when the national does not offer the validation that it seeks.[1] In other words, the queer in the bolero house of essentialism will allow the house to collapse in order to gain the voice that is denied, and this position is inscribed upon the sadness that the bolero itself will perform. The bolero speaks not of heroics, but of a sense of a past and future betrayal. Who has been and will be betrayed? Whoever stands at the margins of the center given by the imaginary community of the nation. Logic would seem to dictate that the emergence of a suppressed entity would create new forms of expression, a new aesthetics not necessarily conditioned by the catastrophes of the past. But what is interesting in this context is that the bolero is precisely a thing of the past – within its lucidity, it forecloses the possibility of innocence. In a sense, it implies, it warns, it even desires and knows, that the catastrophe will return, once again.

Según tu punto de vista, yo soy la mala

What kind of authenticity is at play here? The uncomfortable fact of a fissure thrown at us, precisely beckoning, insisting, demanding, hyperventilating, but also shouting, screaming, for an equally impervious resistance? Only in manipulating this border may queers point out the tenuous construction under which we labour: looking back, seeing, discovering ourselves in others, quoting.

I will end this essay with a fable and an emblem. Even if she had been almost completely detroyed and obliterated by the record industry, and had fallen into the wreckage of drugs and booze and men – La Lupe, La Yiyiyi, the Queen of Soul – decided to crossover and sing for a U.S. public. If we truly want to hear ultimate sadness, we only need to go back to *Llesterdei*, La Lupe's version of *Yesterday*, sung not in English but in some kind of esperanto that has the ability to touch a nerve beyond confession and that has nothing to do with the Beatles' ballad, which is now turned, by means of a language that is not Spanish and is definitely not English, into the crying anthem of a Lady Macbeth with sunglasses, a silk turban and a knife in her right hand. Her rendition speaks of a certain *ananké* of migration, from the past and into a future which is faced with resignation, with the kind of shattered voice given only to those that can possess no voice, and that may only sing in English with a white handkerchief in her left hand, in order to wipe the tears streaming with eyeliner down her cheeks. The space of sentiment that is recuperated by means of this figure is Benjamin's angel of history, but now contemplating the catastrophes of the past as the simulacra of a Latin America turned into a cabaret. The past is but an endless series of destroyed baccarat piling upon satin sheets and lamé curtains, and the storm is a cheap perfume that blows from paradise and gets caught in her turban and that threatens to reveal her tousled and unmade hair. She is propelled 'into the future' to which her back is turned, while the catastrophe of the cabaret keeps piling on, as she sings in an absolutely incomprehensible language, for another hand to rescue what the previous hand forsook. And every time this angel of history tries to pick up the pieces from the cabaret s/he allows us to understand that the curtains are always already ripped, but that the storm of progress may demand us to rip them once again, and that if we do not have this figure to pick up the pieces the storm will keep on blowing from paradise and the angel will never look back to the past or to the future, but always to the present. When all these queens do La Lupe in drag, it seems that the past that is related, seems to have been, and may be, always already retold.

Notes

1 However, in the more recent Colombian film *La estrategia del caracol* (1993), director Sergio Cabrera's use of a transvestite character (a nostalgic male who dresses as woman and is steered back into 'masculinity' and then used as a seductive, 'feminine' pawn) as the central piece in a defiant struggle with insensitive authorities that try to evict a social community from its dwelling already presages what the boleros themselves seem to foretell: that once the social order is able to regain its bearings, the queer and the boleros will once again become part of the ruined landscape of modernity.

References

Carlos Zapata, R., 1990: *Fenomenología del Bolero*, Caracas
Monsiváis, C., 1977: 'Agustín Lara' in *Amor Perdido*, 61–86, México

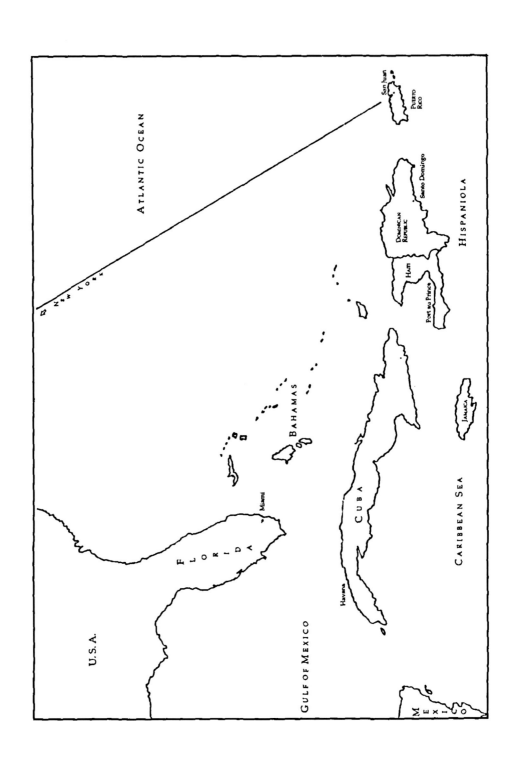

Heavy Metal Music in Postdictatorial Brazil: Sepultura and the Coding of Nationality in Sound

IDELBER AVELAR

Preamble: 'you censor what we breathe/prejudice with no belief' (Sepultura, 1993)

Heavy metal is a postdictatorial genre in Brazil, one whose musical and cultural significance is best grasped by mapping the various meanings acquired by metal music amongst urban youth during the decline of the military regime in the mid-1980s.[1] As in most countries, speed, thrash and death metal evolved in Brazil primarily as working-class urban youth genres. Unlike their Anglo-American and continental sisters, however, Brazil's pioneer metal bands began to craft their art under a heritage of intense censorship and repression, courtesy of a two-decade-long dictatorship (1964–85). Brazilian metal not only had to face the usual aesthetic and moral reprimands flung against it in the North, but also a political accusation that as a form of protest it was not socially aware enough. Never mind, of course, that bands or fans themselves rarely phrased their own agenda in such crude terms as 'protest' or 'resistance.' Once a certain orthodoxy defined that such a function was the only one to be attributed to popular music—and the only meaning a phenomenon like heavy metal could have in Brazil—the debate was already framed in a no-win situation for the genre. In order to establish itself heavy metal had to *implode* the terms of that debate and show how inadequate they were to account for the genre's sound, writing and iconography. The band I will follow here, Sepultura, has been for 18 years (1985–2003) largely responsible for the genre's victory in that *national* cultural battle, one that they could only win by rephrasing it as an *international* debate.

In Brazil not only did headbangers have to prove to the usual guardians of musical standards that theirs was genuine music and not sheer noise; not only did they have to prove to the usual guardians of morality that their message was not immoral and did not incite violence; they also had to prove to then-influential guardians of political meaning that theirs was not a futile and alienated form of protest against the country's still grim political reality. Although also in Europe and North America metal bands faced the charge of being a 'force of political indifference' (Cashmore, 1987, p. 263), in peripheral postdictatorial countries such as Brazil that critique was particularly ferocious and potentially damning, especially when legitimized by the 'good taste' in popular music associated, amongst the country's middle class, with the heterogeneous ensemble of harmonically and lyrically sophisticated acoustic musics known as

MPB (*Música Popular Brasileira*).² Squeezed between the moral/aesthetic Right and the cultural/political Left, heavy metal was always intensely interpellated by contradictory demands from several sides at the same time. The history of the genre's elaborations, responses and parodies of those attacks in Brazil remains to be written, but there is no doubt that the genre fared extraordinarily well in those cultural battles—and thanks solely to its musicians and fans. Forced into a corner between the demand for moral or aesthetic positivity and the demand for cultural or political negativity, heavy metal crossed both avenues and parked nowhere. It took a line of flight, and did it its own way.

The Genre: 'we who are not as others/we who are not as others' (Sepultura, 1993)

Of all ill-informed generalizations flung at heavy metal, the charge of nihilism seems the funniest to me. Whenever that word is used as an accusation one can be sure that the accuser has at best a vague idea of its meaning. In its rigorous philosophical sense (constituted in the Nietzschean transvaluative genealogy), nihilism designates the *epochal* horizon in which all higher values, i.e. those of life-affirming power and joy, are defeated by the negative, guilty slave morality of self-commiseration and pity inaugurated by Socratism and continued by Christianity. The fall of the slavish Socratic-Christian paradigm, captured by Nietzsche in the 'death of God' formula, brings us to the abyss where all values appear as equally fallen and voided. Although Nietzsche's critique of nihilism is present in his work since *The Birth of Tragedy in the Spirit of Music* (1967/1872), it would only begin to be explicitly named as such after *The Gay Science* (1974/1888), where nihilism is associated with (1) the universal realization that 'the way of this world is anything but divine' and that 'even by human standards it is not rational, merciful, or just'; (2) the epochal perception that one can no longer transform this disillusionment or this 'unbelief into a new belief, a purpose, a martyrdom' (1974, p. 286).³ Nihilism is therefore not one among other ideological positions that we might to choose to occupy or not, in any case not something one can be accused of so easily, but rather the framework against which we all operate as subjects. Taking the word 'nihilism' in its rigorous sense, in fact, few popular music genres are *more critical* of nihilism (i.e. more celebratory of the intensity and power of life) than heavy metal. If the first effect of nihilism, according to Nietzsche, is the loss of the ability to evaluate and discern, heavy metal is a carefully constructed code for establishing *sound hierarchies*. If nihilism leads us, negatively, to treat all values as fallen, metal music invariably counters this fall into impotence with an affirmation of strength, expressed not only in lyrics or iconography but most importantly in its music, organized around the trope of *power*.

Robert Walser's *Running with the Devil* provides us with an illuminating analysis of the musical production of power in heavy metal. Without forgetting the social contingency affecting the drawing of genre boundaries in popular music (in fact in all music and all art), Walser delimits the formal specificities of the genre. Among them the *power chord* stands as a unique reference: 'produced by playing the musical interval of a perfect fourth or fifth on a heavily amplified and distorted electric guitar' (Walser, 1993, p. 2) the power chord is used by all metal bands and 'until heavy metal's enormous influence on other musical genres in the late 1980s, by comparatively few musicians outside the genre' (ibid.).[4] Simultaneously a musicological category and a cultural metaphor, power is mapped by Walser's reading onto the *music* of metal: its particular timbre, captured in the use of long unarticulated sustains and distortion on guitars, often replicated by extended vocals that dwell on long notes; the genre's preference for Aeolian and Dorian modes (most speed metal preferring in fact Phrygian or Locrian modes); its reliance on technology for radical effects with volume; its melodic preference for long notes at the end of phrases and syncopation in the singing (which places syllables between beats and thus solves the problem of intelligibility of lyrics in metal, a genre with high instrumental volumes); its rhythmic structure, based on the traditional 4/4 rock time, but often organized around a pulse rather than a meter. Walser also explores the significance of the frequent guitar solos by relating them to a dialectic of freedom and control. This dialectic also informs his analysis of metal's harmonic variations—exemplified in a detailed reading of Van Halen's anthem 'Running with the Devil'—one that gives a decent burial to ill-informed generalizations on the 'simplicity' of rock harmonies.[5]

In his mapping of the axiologies that organize popular music, Simon Frith has pointed out that there is no reason to suppose that 'the accumulated knowledge and discriminatory skill' (1996, p. 9) underlying value judgements in popular forms differ in any significant way from those consecrated by erudite culture. As anyone who has devoted attention to heavy metal can confirm, the genre's value-laden acts of self-definition include a myriad of subtle and complex distinctions that have evolved for over 30 years.[6] Although all metal fans will produce positive statements about which bands best represent the genre for them, the most common entrance into self-definition is a negative assertion about what heavy metal is not. Heavy metal fans coincide, for example, in setting one of the genre's borders up against one particular neighbour: for most fans metal is *that which is not hard rock*—of course where one thing starts and the other ends is always a heated point of contention. Ask a Metallica fan, and chances are that Poison will not qualify as a metal band, although Poison fans might think otherwise. Likewise, Metallica's later, more melodic work might be the one that does not qualify as metal in the eyes of Sodom or Slayer fans. I point it out not to set up a search for 'objective' criteria that would allow us to define where the genre starts and ends but rather to approach the genre's language within the discursive battles through which it is constituted. Critical, theoretically inflected ethnomusicology reminds us of the point not to be missed here: it is precisely *because* boundaries are socially contingent that the rigorous musicological analysis of melody, harmony, volume, mode, rhythm, pitch is strictly necessary. As Susan McClary points out, 'given the tendency in cultural studies to stress the radical idiosyncrasy of each listener's musical perception, we need to find ways of understanding the socially grounded rhetorical devices by means of which music creates its *intersubjective* affects; otherwise the medium remains privatized and mystified, impervious to cultural criticism' (1994, p. 32). In other words, the theory of the social contingency of meaning cannot function as excuse to give up formal analysis.

Heavy metal is a genre that takes to its ultimate consequences the will to rupture, break, negate that underlies all rock music. In metal, more than in most rock genres, self-definition takes the form of a negation accompanied by a claim that a faster and louder brand is in fact heir to rock music's true spirit, coming to negate elements in the tradition perceived as pop or commercial betrayals of the radical spirit of rock music.[7] Harris Berger's ethnomusicological research explains the genre's preference for the depiction of 'the history of their music in a progressive fashion' (1999, p. 56). This depiction is often cast in narratives organized around tropes of *radicalization* (associated with operations on volume, tempo and pitch as well as with darkened iconography, stripped-down performance and anguished, aggressive or apocalyptic lyrics) and tropes of *negation* (what heavy metal *is not* being a crucial component, for most fans, in any explanation of what *it is*).

It is around a vocabulary that stresses negativity and superlatives—fastest, loudest, dirtiest—that metalheads ground their value judgements not only about their favourite bands but also about the non-metal traditions they inherit. Although their syntax is relatively simple, the codes governing such judgements can acquire considerable complexity. Most Brazilian metal fans would claim, for example, that Bahian rocker Raul Seixas's juxtapositions of north-eastern accordion music (*baião*) and Elvis-inflected, '50s style rock'n'roll is 'heavier' and 'more authentically true to the spirit of rock music' than all of the theatrical electrified 'hard rock' that circulated in Brazil until the mid-1980s, some of which was even classified as 'heavy metal' in the specialized press at the time.[8] In metal's intensely contested terrain, Brazilian band Sepultura combines two unique accomplishments: for 18 years their music has *been changing consistently*, yet they are universally recognized by metal fans as a premier and uncompromising *death/thrash metal* band. This has allowed them continually to redefine their relation to their national origins as well as to the industry and to their multinational fan base. Sepultura have methodically invented ways to introduce difference within the genre's strict codes, a move made possible by their understanding of the negation/radicalization dialectic that underlies heavy metal music. I shall not only make an argument about Sepultura's music but also suggest that their casting of this tension can help us unsettle a few frozen oppositions in the cultural studies of popular music.

Many of the formal traits mapped by Harris Berger's analysis of death metal apply to early Sepultura music, and with variations in different degrees to their late albums as well: experimentations with 'extremes of tempo' (1999, p. 59), efforts 'to avoid the diatonic or blues-based harmony' in favour of 'unexpected half steps or tritones' (ibid., p. 62), distinctive 'noisy, unpitched vocals' that replicate the distorted guitar timbres (ibid., p. 57), and 'variations of the harmonic vocabulary that break up the minor tonality and obscure the tonal center' (ibid., p. 58) that move away from the vocabulary of minor chord progressions typical of earlier metal. These musical operations go hand in hand with a new performative ethic/aesthetic, as metal acts opted for 'stripped-down stage moves' as a reaction against the 'phony theatricality of commercial hard rock' (Saladin quoted in Berger, 199, p. 70). In Sepultura the sheer intensity of their sound establishes a strong tension with that contained style of performance. Like most heavy metal (and especially its faster, speed/thrash varieties) the art of Sepultura depends on a careful balance between energy (power, intensity) and control (containment, enclosure).

Founded in 1984 in the early days of a national heavy metal boom particularly strong in their hometown, the south-eastern state capital of Belo Horizonte, Sepultura's first line-up consisted of the brothers Max and Igor Cavalera (guitar/vocals and drums), Paulo Jr (bass), and Jairo T (guitar). Picked up by emerging metal label Cogumelo Records, they recorded *Bestial Devastation* (1985) and *Morbid Visions* (1986), still grounded in a quite traditional death metal recipe. In 1987 Jairo T left the band and was replaced by Andreas Kisser. A superior guitarist, steeped in the blues and in traditional metal, Kisser brought an entirely new texture to their sound. The Max and Igor Cavalera brothers, Paulo Jr and Andreas Kisser remained as the line-up from their qualitative leap *Schizophrenia* (1987), through the international breakthrough *Beneath the Remains* (1989), the unorthodox yet unmistakably metallic *Arise* (1991), the enraged experimental protest record *Chaos AD* (1993), to the metal-Afrodiasporic sound feast of *Roots* (1996). After *Roots* a disagreement over management caused Max Cavalera's exit, in an episode that his brother Igor has described as 'a wound that will never heal'. Max was replaced in Sepultura by Derrick Green, the African-American lead singer (and former pianist!!) heard on *Against* (1999), *Nation* (2001), and *Roorback* (2003). Since then Max Cavalera has gone on to form Soulfly and record the albums *Soulfly* (1998) and *Primitive* (2000). With excursions into reggae, hip-hop and Afro-Brazilian rhythms, the latter record, especially, expands on the cross-genre experiments of Sepultura's *Roots*.

For over 18 years Sepultura's uniqueness has resided less in the maintenance of a presumably pure and original 'authenticity'—the band changes its music consistently—than in the ability to *think and act ahead*. Underlying their thinking is the understanding that the coding of their music by journalism, record companies, academics and moralists has always tended to be one step behind the music itself. Before the defenders of (musical, cultural, national) territories can stake them out, their music has already crossed these territories on a line of flight into an elsewhere. By the time the detractors of 'heavy metal Satanism' discovered Sepultura's *Morbid Visions* (1986), the band was no longer doing that but rather an anguished critique of social alienations and pathologies, as in *Schizophrenia* (1987) and *Beneath the Remains* (1989). Before moralists could misunderstand that and accuse the band of 'inciting violence or suicide,' Sepultura was somewhere else, putting forth *Arise* (1991) and *Chaos AD* (1993), a record that framed a radical, internationalist social critique within rhythms unmistakably Brazilian. When they reached worldwide success and became an international band, the defenders of national purity did not have much time to condemn them, as Sepultura effected a political and musical rediscovery of Brazil in the cross-genre experiments of *Roots* (1996). The success of *Roots*, especially given the album's courageous incorporation of a host of non-metal references, led many metal purists to discard the band as irrevocably crossover and lost to the genre. They did not have much time to formulate their attack either, as Sepultura returned, with new vocalist Derrick Green, by recording two unmistakable metal records, *Against* (1999) and *Nation* (2001). These two records, although in more coded ways, continued the band's rediscovery of Brazil begun on *Roots*. The band now faces attacks from some who associate internationalization with inevitable and unconditional sell-out. Everything indicates that detractors are arriving late again.

The Scene: 'we're growing everyday/stronger in every way' (Sepultura, 1996)

As the Brazilian military regime ceded power to the first civilian, albeit still undemocratically elected government in 1985, heavy metal bands in Belo Horizonte, Santos, São Paulo, Rio de Janeiro and other metropolises were beginning to brew a cultural phenomenon of considerable proportion. Influenced by Motörhead, Iron Maiden, Slayer, Metallica, Megadeth, they took the genre known in the 1970s as *rock pauleira* [hard rock] to a new level of distortion, loudness and aggressiveness. Out of the most unlikely Amazonian state of Pará, far removed from the country's cultural centres, a band named Stress had travelled to Rio in 1982 to record the eponymous album that fans would later acknowledge as a foundational moment for national metal (Dolabela, 158). In Belo Horizonte bands such as Sepultura, Sarcófago, Sagrado Inferno, Morg, Armaggeddon, Holocausto, Chakal and Overdose (in addition to Minotauro from São Paulo), participated in either one or both editions of the BH Metal Festival, events that catapulted most of those bands to record singles, EPs and/or LPs. The city's intense metal scene congregated around Cogumelo Records, a store founded in 1980 that evolved into an independent label in 1985, date of the Sepultura/Overdose split album *Bestial Devastation–Século XX*. This is an underground legend, a record that helped turn Cogumelo into Brazil's first successful metal label. In São Paulo a compilation entitled *Metal SP*, released by independent rock label Baratos Afins, featured Salário Mínimo, Avenger, Vírus and Centuria. In the neighbouring coastal city of Santos, the pioneers of Vulcano climbed from the *Om Pushne Namah* single (1982) to a Live LP (1985) on their way to the landmark *Bloody Vengeance* (1986) that is still a cult object among Brazilian fans. In Rio de Janeiro, for interesting reasons, heavy metal always had a smaller following than other international youth genres like funk and hip-hop but the city is home to one of the country's most respected metal bands, Dorsal Atlântica, who has been around since their *Ultimatum* EP (1985) and their debut LP *Antes do Fim* [Before the End] (1986).

The national scene was given greater impetus by the megafestival Rock in Rio (1985), a 10-day event where all metal acts were international: Iron Maiden, Ozzy Osbourne, White Snake, Scorpions and AC/DC, the latter four packed into one long metal night.[9] Speed and thrash metal giants such as Metallica, Slayer and Venom soon began regularly to include Brazil in their tours. Magazines such as *Heavy* or national editions of international fanzines such as *Rock Brigade* began to pop up. Following Belo Horizonte's Cogumelo, other stores invested in low-budget, independent record producing. Among the ones that consistently produced metal records are São Paulo's Baratos Afins and Devil Discos, as well as Rio's Heavy and Point Rock, all of them responsible for the first releases of dozens of new bands. The blockade against metal on radio was weekly lifted for one hour on a few stations, with the emergence of metal shows such as *Comando Metal* (on São Paulo's 89 FM), *Metal Massacre* (on Belo Horizonte's Liberdade FM), and *Guitarras para o Povo* [Guitars to/for the People, a deliberate Lennon quote for sure] (on Rio's Fluminense FM). All of that contributed to constitute a scene later described by a critic as an 'anthill of black shirts exchanging information all over Brazil' (Alexandre, 2002, p. 349).

By the late 1980s metal was as important a cultural phenomenon in Brazil as it was an entity continually misunderstood by rock journalists, moralists and popular music stars alike. Wasn't their music invariably repetitive, noisy and bereft of any artistic merit? Weren't they after all copying a foreign genre and doing a disservice to Brazilian popular music? Weren't they involved in strange Satanic rituals? Weren't they renouncing the most important task of popular music, the conscious political protest? Didn't their music convey a nihilistic and negative message that could prove to be a dangerous influence on youth? Never mind that such questions often contradict one another, all of them betraying ignorance about the genre. Given Brazil's context in the 1980s, these hostile interrogations took a very politicized spin, one that continually besieged the genre. As late as 1995, when Sepultura was already one of the world's most successful metal bands, the Hollywood Rock festival that brought Megadeth, Judas Priest, Slayer and Queenshrÿche to Brazil had to face an intense letter-writing campaign from metal's ever-loyal fans to be convinced that Sepultura had to be included on the bill. As often happens, the marketing-oriented organizers (more in tune with statistics of radio airplay than with the social reality of concert going) could not see that even *Slayer* or *Metallica* would not understand how a metal night in a rock megaconcert in Brazil in 1995 could possibly be held without Sepultura.

Metal Languages between the City and the Jungle: 'war for territory' (Sepultura, 1993)

Outside the English-speaking world heavy metal bands patiently concocted a vocabulary through *translation*. Even though one can find much metal music sung in other European languages, heavy metal means, to an extent unparalleled in most other youth genres, music sung primarily in English, even when composed in Brazil, Sweden or Germany. It remains as a task for Latin American criticism to understand these operations of translation in terms more complex than either the simple lament for the adoption of foreign models or the tired, facile celebration of the 'subversive' or 'resistant' hybridity of peripheral appropriations of metropolitan languages. The choice of language for Brazilian metal bands in the mid-1980s was not casual and did not go undiscussed among musicians and fans. Rio de Janeiro power trio Dorsal Atlântica was one of the genre's few acts singing only in Portuguese, on *Ultimatum* (1985), *Antes do Fim* (1986), and *Dividir e Conquistar* [Divide and Conquer] (1988), before their definitive switch to English on *Searching for the Light* (1990). On the historic Sepultura/Overdose *Bestial Devastation–Século XX* shared LP (1985), Sepultura filled their side with songs in English, while Overdose preferred Portuguese. By Overdose's first full-length LP *Conscience* (1987) the band had adopted mostly English lyrics. Although most metal bands choose English, Witchhammer (*Mirror, my Mirror* 1997) and other examples show that Portuguese lyrics popped up preferentially on punk/hardcore collaborations, or cross-genre experiments with other youth musics. In its relationship to language—and in many other respects—Sepultura defined early on what would later become a paradigmatic choice for the genre: a momentary flight from the Portuguese that would allow for both a critique of the nation and a very particular entrance into the international market. The irony was that, unlike Brazilian bands that chose English names (Witchhammer, Vulcano, Viper), the name *Sepultura* was itself the product of a translation *not from but into Portuguese*. It was thanks to his habit of translating songs that Max Cavalera came up—while rewriting Motörhead's 'Dancing on your Grave', in Portuguese—with the name for the new band being formed with his brother Igor, not suspecting he was creating a seal that would arguably match anything Motörhead ever accomplished.

Sepultura's lyrics on their first albums feature apocalyptic *theatres* (on *Bestial Devastation* and *Morbid Visions*), schizo-paranoid dismantling of societal hypocrisy (on *Schizophrenia*) and images of ruins that synthesize their earlier, anguished work (the masterpiece *Beneath the Remains*). The cover and liner art dialogue with music and lyrics, as covers evolve from an aesthetic of darkened, nightmarish monstrosity (inaugurated by Iron Maiden's unique blend of expressionism, surrealism and comic book codes on their cover art) to the focus on individual psychic pain, expressed by drawings rather than photographs or paintings (*Schizophrenia*, 1987). *Beneath the Remains* (1989) featured a reddish skull set on a dark background; the close-up focalization from below humanized the skull by turning it into an allegory of the caging, enclosure and suffering embodied in lyrics and music. Marked by their growing awareness of the workings of violence in Brazil and abroad, Sepultura released *Arise* and *Chaos AD*, albums that consolidated the band as a worldwide reference for vigorous, socially aware heavy metal. At that moment they initiated a decade-long history of collaboration with Brazil's foremost punk band, Ratos de Porão—a collaboration that marked them ideologically and culturally more than musically. Sepultura's turn to a radical internationalist politics—inspired by both punk and reggae—included videos where the fast tempo of metal dialogues with the fast montage of images of violence (shot with a low, handheld camera) in places such as Palestine, Belfast and Brazil. Exemplary of this aesthetic is the video to 'Territory', winner of Brazil's MTV Video Awards in 1994. Accompanying the transformation in the music, their cover art would increasingly highlight a focus on nationhood, as in the painted Indian face on the cover of *Roots* (1996) or the return of symbolic political statements, as in the raised dark fists against the bright orange background of *Nation* (2001).[10]

Much like Brazilian Cinema Novo's 'aesthetics of hunger'—which turned the poverty of technical means into an auteurist and politicized statement about filmmaking in the Third World—Sepultura's first records use the lack of technological resources to intensify the raw and harsh character of their sound. Throughout 1983–84 Igor Cavalera developed his playing counting on no more than a snare drum, a floor tom and a cymbal. *Bestial Devastation* (1985) was recorded without bass drums, as he did not own drum pedals and had never used any. Those were the times when the Cavaleras' broomsticks were often enlisted as support for the cymbal. By then, however, Igor had enjoyed long percussive training in jams with *charangas*, the polyrhythmic, 30-plus-member percussion combos that lead fan chanting in major Brazilian soccer games.[11] *Bestial Devastation* and *Morbid Visions* were recorded in an eight-track studio with overdriven amplifiers. Having self-produced their three first records on Cogumelo Records, for *Beneath the Remains* (1989), their first album with international label Roadrunner, the band had to be convinced that a producer could enhance their sound. *Beneath the Remains* was recorded in nine days in a Rio de Janeiro studio—or better said nine *nights*, as Sepultura still needed to use nightly studio time, at cheaper rates, and sleep during the day in the stifling, 100-degree Rio summer. *Beneath the Remains* circulated as a cult object in Europe and was chosen by several fanzines as the best thrash/death metal album of 1989. By the following year Sepultura was playing in front of 26,000 fans in Holland's Dynamo Open Air Festival and mesmerizing metal and non-metal fans alike in Rock in Rio II. By the early 1990s they were playing shoulder to shoulder with bands that inspired them such as Metallica and Kreator, as well as opening for heavy metal legend Ozzy Osbourne. With *Arise* (1991) and *Chaos AD* (1993) they established a routine of gold or platinum records and legendary tours, not only in Europe and the US but also in places like Indonesia and Japan. By the time they travelled to the occupied territories of Palestine to shoot the video for 'Territory', Sepultura had achieved feats hitherto unthinkable for a thrash metal band. They had become the most widely, globally known Brazilian musicians ever, overcoming a certain Antônio Carlos Jobim who, although still alive back then, was not fully equipped to understand what was going on (perhaps unable to see the striking analogies between the irruption of his own music into American Jazz in the early 1960s and Sepultura's globalization as a Brazilian metal band in the 1990s).

Throughout their career Sepultura has sped up even further the fast tempo inherited from their influences—Slayer, Metallica, Motörhead, Venom. Crucial to that operation is Igor Cavalera's powerful drumming style, based on 'dry,' brief and repetitive hits. His career is marked by increasing use of unexpected variations and syncopation well learned in the polyrhythms of *charanga* soccer percussion combos. Distortion on Max Cavalera's and Andreas Kisser's guitar is likewise raised to a limit. Following Igor's lead in the rhythm section, Paulo Jr's bass lines have evolved from the 'louder and faster' ethic of death metal to more recent variations of Brazilian/Afrodiasporic inspiration, which have usually remained, however, faithful to the fast *tempo* of the metal bass. Early on Max Cavalera developed a hoarsened, low-note style of vocalization that would become one of the band's trademarks and inaugurate a school in Brazilian heavy metal. The syncopated syllables growled by Max Cavalera into the intervals of his brother Igor's aggressive drumbeats not only made the lyrics minimally intelligible, as Robert Walser shows to be a trait of the genre, established by Anglo-American metal vocalists who sing in their native language. The syncopation further allowed Max to change accentuation and intonation as he developed a singing style in a language that he would beautifully master only a few years later. Sung in low notes, but in as high a volume as possible, his vocals battled with the 'wall of sound' created by not one, but *two* highly distorted guitars.

If, as Walser has pointed out, the dialectic of freedom and control is an apt metaphor to describe metal, in the early art of Sepultura (and in most metal bands in postdictatorial Brazil) that dialectic perennially tilted away from freedom into the pole of control, asphyxia, enclosure. For this reason it is hard to find in an early Sepultura song anything resembling a drum solo, a feature not uncommon in other brands of heavy metal. The drum solo (with its own dialectic of freedom and control) would not have fitted the asphyxiating atmosphere that Sepultura wanted to create on their first albums, where the metaphor of *enclosure* was the dominant one. In their later work, as collaborations with other genres developed, drum solos, funky bass lines and instrumental syncopation would increasingly appear.

On 'Territory' and 'Propaganda', powerful protest songs on *Chaos AD*, Andreas Kisser provided the listener with longer guitar solos, lines of flight that offered some breathing room away from the enclosure suggested by the oppressive and suffocating wall of sound. Likewise, 'Territory' featured one of Igor Cavalera's first studio drum solos, dialoguing with Andreas's as yet another line of flight offering escape. As a whole *Chaos AD* was the first true registering of Igor's experiments with unexpected tempo variations inspired in Brazilian/Afrodiasporic polyrhythms. This would lead to the 'explosion of sounds' heard on *Roots*, where the band enlisted collaboration from Brazilian multipercussionist Carlinhos Brown and relied on recordings from the Amazonian Xavantes, collected by the band during a visit to their reservation. *National* contents that earlier had represented a cage, a suffocating territory for the band, were now being incorporated in the band's own terms, as the nation became a source that would allow them to tilt their musical dialectic toward the pole of freedom again. The evolution of Sepultura's music is, then, coherent with an interesting transformation: the nation is initially a hostile territory, coded in ways that by definition excluded the genre. It was thus a territory to traverse and transgress. Thanks to the band's intelligent thinking and incessant musical learning—as well as to an international success that allows them to rediscover Brazil from another angle—the nation progressively becomes a source for musical and cultural lines of flight, unexpected experiments and collaborations. They continually redefine the genre's very boundaries at the same time as they refine what one had hitherto understood as *Brazilian* music.

'Ratamahatta' as National Allegory: 'Amazonia burns/can you hear them?' (Sepultura, 1996)

I will spell out this movement with a brief reading of the music, lyrics and iconography of track 4 of Sepultura's *Roots*, 'Ratamahatta', the song that most powerfully evokes Sepultura's recent rediscovery of Brazil. This is a song that features not only the usual metal rhythm section, distorted guitars and hoarse loud vocals but also Amazonian Xavante singing and a percussion ensemble made up of large bass drums (the *surdo*, used in samba, maracatu and other Brazilian/Afrodiasporic genres), cans, djembes, water tanks and rattles, all played by Brazilian percussion wizard, multimedia figure and activist, Carlinhos Brown. The track opens with Xavante vocals over drumming in 2/4 time, accompanied by the metallic sound of a shaker. Performed in low notes, the singing is highly vocalic and privileges closed vowels /o//e/, and is known among the Xavante nation as a healing chant. The context of this drumming—its presence on a Sepultura album—produces anticipation for the entrance of the distorted guitars and the loud/fast rhythm section typical of heavy metal. The listener's feeling of anticipation gets produced and frustrated again on 0:12, as the Xavante drumming is interrupted not by a metal rhythm section but by an introductory *maracatu* phrase, performed on the bass drum by Brown. The *maracatu* line barely remains long enough to establish a tempo and is immediately cut short, this time by silence.[12]

Following Brown's 'one two three' call, the metallic expectation is again created and denied, as the *maracatu* phrasing on the drums picks up where silence had left off. Only at 0:31 do Max's and Andreas's distorted guitars come with a major chord melody, and phrasing in Aeolian mode. The bass and snare drums continue dictating rhythm, as for 10 seconds the song combines the time of *maracatu* and the guitar phrasing of heavy metal. At 0:41 Max begins to intersperse hoarse growled vowels in the intervals to the beat, announcing that the metal ensemble will gather in its totality soon, as Igor's 4/4 drumming comes in as loud as ever. The metal ensemble is in place at full speed, but the *maracatu* rhythm continues underneath, on Brown's *surdo* and snare drums, dialoguing with Igor's rock drumming and producing a polyrhythmic effect not only original but full of cultural and political meaning in Brazil (given the social distance between *maracatu* and metal). By 0:50 into the song two of Brazil's loudest and richest percussive machines—Brown's unique synthesis of Brazilian/Afrodiasporic rhythms and Sepultura's fast thrash metal—are dialoguing polyrhythmically to great effect. Brown accompanies his drumming with vocal effects that recall the hip-hop art of scratching, while Max continues to build up the vocals with a high-pitched 'o' at intervals between the beats. After a full minute of build-up, Brown's and Max's syncopated and grave vocals storm in with lyrics that dialogue with Brazilian minimalist, 'dirty' poetry, shouted in the form of call and response:

> C.B. 'biboca/garagem/favela' [shithole/garage/slumtown]
> M.C. 'biboca/garagem/favela'
> C.B. 'fubanga/maloca/bocada' [hodgepodge/hut/hideout]
> MC: 'fubanga/maloca/bocada'
> [repeat 2 times starting from 'maloca' and 'favela']

The call and response pattern in a vocal duo is a feature unknown in Sepultura's previous work, and further connects the song with an Afrodiasporic sensibility. More than simply summoned for their meanings, words come in here primarily due to their *rhythmic power*. They are all highly vocalic words, where every consonant is followed by a vowel, thereby creating the 'typical' Portuguese sequence of two-letter syllables. All words in the stanza are trisyllables accentuated on the second-to-last vowel, also the 'default' accentuation pattern in Portuguese. The stanza features an alternation of voiced and voiceless bilabial stops—[b] and [p]—and an alternation of voiced and voiceless velar stops—[g] and [k]. Building on these four highly percussive sounds, Max and Brown's vocal art dialogue replicate the instrumental syncopation going on between Brown's ensemble and Igor's metal drumming.

Much like the Indian chanting and Brown's *maracatu* drum phrasing in the introduction, the lyrics in Portuguese (uncommon in Sepultura's earlier work) come in *to signify Brazil*. Not only are their phonology and rhythm quite typical of the Portuguese language but their semantics is unmistakably Brazilian, as most words are of indigenous origin. Of these six words *garagem* is probably the only one comprehensible to a non-Brazilian speaker of Portuguese. *Biboca* comes from the Tupy and its original meaning of 'excavation or valley' was later expanded to designate a poorly built shack, before becoming urban slang for 'shithole'. *Favela* is an internationally known term for the urban Brazilian slums. *Fubanga*, a word still not found in dictionaries, suggests to most youth a rag, a nothing, a worthless piece. *Maloca* is an Araucanian word that reached Portuguese through Spanish and means 'indigenous hut'. Over time it also came to designate urban shacks, and amongst youth urban tribes in Brazil the noun gave birth to the verb *malocar*, meaning to hide, especially drugs or an illicit object.

Malocar is an art invariably associated with oppressed groups, and always alludes to the act of hiding something from the eyes of a repressive authority. *Bocada*, coming from *boca* ('mouth') is also a word that few outside Brazilian youth tribes would understand, as it designates a faraway, hidden and dangerous place most often associated with drug dealing. The chorus's overall effect is a pan-national youth-inflected portrayal of Brazil from the jungle to the city, one that emphasizes oppression and struggle.

The symmetrical accentuation pattern (as all words are composed of three consonant–vowel pairs, and all stressed on the second-to-last syllable) allows the lyrics to follow neatly the beat of Igor Cavalera's drums, forcing the usually soft-singing Carlinhos Brown to a pitch and volume he probably had never attempted. At 01:13 Max's and Andreas's short and fast phrases on the guitar return. Although one can hear Carlinhos Brown's north-eastern-inflected percussion in the background, Paulo Jr's metal bass and Igor Cavalera's metal drumming come to the forefront. Accompanying the return of metal-style distorted guitars, Brown's vocals fade and give way to Max's hoarsened [ôs], growled in the intervals to the beats. By the time they reach the bridge Igor's furious drumming has turned to syncopated beats, announcing the return of the call-and-response pattern in the vocals, this time devoted to Brazilian folk legends or anti-heroes:

C.B. Zé do Caixão/Zumbi/Lampião
MC. Zé do Caixão/Zumbi/Lampião
[repeat 2 times]

Zumbi, the leader of the largest American maroon state in the seventeenth century (the *Quilombo of Palmares*, in north-eastern Brazil) has become a symbol of black struggle for freedom and a national hero widely respected among whites as well. It is not surprising that his name would be evoked in 'Ratamahatta', a song devoted to rescuing sounds associated with oppressed populations. Neither is it surprising to see his name in a genealogy continued by Lampião, the north-eastern outlaw hero who became a Robin Hood type of legend in the backlands, until the police and the army concluded a decades-long drive to destroy his gang in the 1930s. The illustrious gallery of underground heroes is joined by Coffin Joe, a horror-film director who endured ridicule in Brazil from the 1950s to the 1970s, before seeing his parodic, comic-book horror cinema revered internationally as a cult object. These are three highly national figures, united by their struggle against official (racist, oligarchic or colonized) versions of their country. Nationality is also foregrounded formally, as these three highly vocalic words are sung in such a way that the highest pitch coincides with the nasal rhyme in [ão], the phonological trademark of the Portuguese language.

At 01:48 the tempo begins to be dictated by Brown's percussion again, with the guitar sound being suspended for a while. This time the beat is a loud funk led by bass, drums and Brazilian percussion instruments. In the background the snare drums continue phrasing in recognizable *samba* rhythm. Brown now shouts English lyrics, breaking the words in autonomous syllables, fitting one per interval between the funky beats. By now the song has established a dialectic that it will follow until the end: metal and Afro-Atlantic rhythms coexist, dialogue with each other and take turns leading the way. The alternation generates diverse sets of expectations and is coded differently depending on the listener's genre of preference. When the guitars return they take with them Igor's drums, which resume playing fast metal tempo as Brown and Max take turns playing gutturally with the sounds of the chorus word, 'Ratamahatta'—not a Portuguese word but a suggestive sound combo full of associations, as 'rata' means *rat*, *Mahatta* cannot but evoke, given the song's themes, Mahatma Gandhi, who also names one of the famous Rio de Janeiro squares that punks first called their home. Furthermore, Cavalera and Brown play with the word also to make it suggest *mata*, the familiar command form for the Portuguese verb 'to kill' and at same time a noun meaning 'the woods' or 'jungle'. Overall, the chorus crowns the thematic of violence, struggle and oppression constructed musically and lyrically by the song. The call-and-response pattern, initially limited to vocals, takes over also in the dialogue between Brown's Afro-Brazilian ensemble and Cavalera's and Kisser's guitars, which alternately suggest enclosed territories and lines of flight away from that enclosure.

'Ratamahatta', the song, made use of material recorded during Sepultura's stay with the Xavante tribe in the northern state of Mato Grosso but for the video they opted for a futuristic computerized animation signed by Fred Stern. Images of drunkenness, visits to Afro-Brazilian *candomblé* priestesses, flirtation in the slums, incarcerations, are all portrayed in fast succession amidst an atmosphere that evokes black magic, voodoo and tribal ceremonies. Featuring 'little creatures' coming out of jungles and urban slums at a faster and faster pace to accompany the music, the animation quite consciously suggests a complete loss of consciousness in the speed of a futuristic darkened scenery. Masked beings descend first upon the jungle, then the ghettos, and find an ethnographic collection of objects that chronicle the 'darker' side of both the jungle and the city. In the jungle a tribal ceremony honours a tycoon type in a tuxedo, while in the city a collective ceremony foregrounds a passive multitude moving their heads to a leader, in a darkened variation on Pink Floyd's classic images to *The Wall's* 'We don't need no education'. The video concludes with the masked beings appropriating some of the behaviour they find (such as the drinking), as the metal and Afrodiasporic rhythms slowly fade to give way to the Xavante healing chant that returns as a coda to the song. 'Ratamahatta' is, then, conceived *as a totality*: its operations on rhythm, melody, harmony, pitch and volume, its minimalist lyrics, its unique form of production, its featuring of a highly symbolically partnership, and finally its innovative and caustic video, are all elements that help ground our final reflections, devoted to Sepultura's revolutionizing of the representation of nationality in sound.

Distortion and Mixing against World Music: Sepultura's Routes to the Nation

Reflecting back on the band's early days in the 1980s, Sepultura lead guitarist Andreas Kisser recounted: 'we listened to heavy and black metal and found everything made in Brazil to be shitty. We didn't like *samba*, we didn't like national rock, we didn't like any of that crap' (quoted in Alexandre, 2002, p. 347). For large sectors of the urban youth of postdictatorial Brazil, heavy metal became at the same time a metaphor for the absence of a nation with which they could identify *and* an antidote against that exclusion. Unlike metropolitan bands that emerged in opposition and negation of other *genres*, Sepultura arose by initially negating the *totality* of the nation's music—quite a courageous gesture if you are playing in musically rich Brazil. It was not by chance that it was national music that had to be negated for metal to establish itself. The array of musics coded as 'Brazilian' by the 1980s ranged from several varieties of the national genre, *samba*, to traditional instrumental genres such as *choro*, to rhythmic verbal arts such as *embolada*, to percussion-based *maracatu* or *coco*, to piano- or guitar-based bossa and postbossa sounds, to accordion music such as *baião* and *xaxado*, and even what was then beginning to be called 'national rock'.[13] The codification of nationality in sound was not only effected through discourses that linked one or more of these genres with the authentically national. Paralleling these discourses was the remarkable operation by which certain musics (evolving either out of *samba* or fusion with regional musics) acceded to a status increasingly identified with good taste in music: the malleable category of MPB [*Música Popular Brasileira*, a term that, as pointed out above, does *not* designate the totality of the country's popular music but certain forms associated with sophistication]. The sociocultural category MPB operated in the 1970s–80s primarily as a measure of distinction in Bourdieu's sense: it projected the fable of exceptionality of one particular social class. Theoretically, music of any kind can *become* MPB by erasing its regional origins if it derives from a regional genre, by trimming its rough edges if it is too electric or too percussive, by complexifying its harmonies or arrangement if it draws on popular forms. When the heavy metal revolution was initiated in the mid-1980s, the elastic throat of MPB had already engulfed and neutralized rock music's outsider aura, as Brazilian rock bands such as Titãs, Paralamas do Sucesso, Legião Urbana and Blitz were slowly ushered into the MPB pantheon of middle-class good taste.

Regardless of how the young Sepulturans phrased their anti-national cry back then, their conscious gesture of refusing national music as such *called attention to the exclusionary practices governing the coding of nationality in sound*. Long after the 1960s debates against folkloric and mythical conceptions of nationhood in music had been won, 'national' music—though no longer coded in terms of authenticity—was still produced through mechanisms that left unrepresented a large portion of youth not identified with either MPB or 'Brazilian rock'. Instead of struggling for a particular position within the universal concept at stake ('Brazilian music'), Sepultura denounced the concept in its totality. In refusing the term *tout court*, they in practice exposed its false universality, its dependence on a previous exclusion, its reliance on a constitutive abjection.[14] Naturally, even when they were playing straight thrash metal from first to last track, all of them (most especially drummer Igor Cavalera) were already unmistakably 'Brazilian' musicians. The pursuit of these musical traits of nationality only started in conscious fashion much later, however, as Sepultura's *internationalization* allowed them to refract to Brazil's musical establishment an image of the nation that such establishment was not ready to recognize. Their internationalization also allowed them to carry out the 'rediscovery' of Brazilian rhythms that led to the sound feast of *Roots*, while in the process crashing the codes by which the nation had learned to project itself in sound.

As the *Arise* (1991) and *Chaos AD* (1993) tours gathered multitudes everywhere from Holland to Japan, Sepultura began to be known among European fans as 'the jungle boys'. The great irony is that they were from a metropolis, Belo

Horizonte, and most certainly got to see London and Amsterdam before they ever saw an Amazonian parrot. In acceding to the international market Sepultura is led to *become* a Brazilian band, and their national origin would increasingly be highlighted in their concerts and records. Of course, the international music market also coded the nation in ways that Sepultura did not recognize as their own: 'jungle? What jungle? It's easier to get to New York than to the Amazon from here.' In this broken mirror where internal and external images of the nation get reflected, it is to Sepultura's credit that their journey into their nation's sounds was never phrased in the tired vocabulary of authenticity.[15] After the collaboration with the Xavante tribe on *Roots*, Igor Cavalera stated that 'we did not do a world music record'. His insistence that 'everything is mixed and distorted' was not only an attempt to highlight the album's heaviness but most importantly to set their collaboration with the Xavante tribe in terms irreducible to the Paul Simon or Peter Gabriel style 'recoveries' of indigenous musics, marked by an exoticizing that in practice denies those musics any coevalness with the artist doing the gathering. Stressing upfront the work of mixing, Igor removes the discussion from the terrain of preservation, authenticity, recovery, that is to say he removes it from the language of world music. Implicitly asked to become 'boys' of a 'jungle' they had never known, Sepultura indeed goes Amazonian but brings back not an 'anthropological document' but a politicized, electrified and polyrhythmic counterethnography.

Anthropologist Hermano Vianna noted the irony that Sepultura, Brazil's most international band, should release a record entitled *Roots* (p. 5). He is quick to add that the Xavante–Sepultura alliance makes sense, as it is 'the encounter of tribes inimical to an ideal of national homogenization that determines that "whoever doesn't like samba/can't be a good type" ' (p. 5).[16] The most 'primitive' and the most 'international' are both excluded from the dominant coding of nationality in sound. They would find in their musical kinship (especially in the strong percussive energy of both) the key to cracking open an exclusionary definition of national identity in music. In the process, they also engaged the international market's coding of 'Third World' musical nations, and such coding did not go unaffected by their intervention. It is not a question of assuming they can romantically subvert the production of exoticism in the world music arena.[17] Sepultura's awareness of the terrain on which they operate—and most importantly their constant reinvention of their sound—suggests, however, that they are framing these debates in terms that fit neither the preservational paradigm of authenticity nor rock music's tired dialectic of self-marginalization versus sell-out. Constantly engaging international references in debates around nationhood (and conversely reframing the nation in ways unexpected by the global arena), Sepultura brought a genre into a nation. In that process they turned the Brazilian musical nation into something as of yet unknown; as they rediscovered the nation they were transforming, the rediscovery would not leave the genre unchanged. By the hands of Sepultura Brazil met metal and metal met Brazil. After this encounter neither the place nor the sound would remain the same. The complexity of this clash forces us to rethink not only previous conceptions about heavy metal and about constructions of Brazilianness through music. It can also help us rethink a number of frozen oppositions that still plague the cultural studies of popular music.

Notes

1. This article is particularly indebted to Ana María Ochoa's interlocution. The author also thanks Christopher Dunn and Charles Perrone for insightful and careful readings of an earlier version, and Paulo Henrique Caetano for crucial references on metal in Brazil. A shorter version of this paper was presented at Birkbeck College at the University of London in June 2003. The author thanks most especially John Kraniauskas for the invitation and interlocution. He is also grateful to Philip Derbyshire, David Treece, Jens Andermann, Ana Álvarez, Jon Beasley-Murray, Lorraine Leu, Sean Stroud, Andrea Noble, Bill O'Connor and Cristina Nordenstahl for their comments during the round table at Birkbeck. He also gratefully acknowledges Sepultura's permission to reprint excerpts of lyrics.
2. Best grasped as a sociocultural category rather than a musical genre, MPB began to circulate circa 1966 as a term to designate a set of acoustic musics, based primarily on the guitar/voice duo (mediated or not by the bossa nova revolution). In a period of highly politicized TV festival/contests those musics developed as nationalist alternatives to the first experiments with rock'n'roll, which were viewed with suspicion by sectors of the Left. In the 1970s, somewhat freed from the constraints of that debate, MPB became the acronym for a 'sophisticated' spectrum of popular music in Brazil, associated with figures such as Gilberto Gil, Caetano Veloso, Chico Buarque de Hollanda or Milton Nascimento–all known for complex harmonic progressions, multiple operations with rhythm, innovative melodies, and highly poetic, 'literary' lyric writing. For an indispensable English-language study of MPB, see Perrone (1989).
3. Nietzsche's most complete and radical autopsy of nihilism, 'this uncanniest of all guests' (1967, p. 7) would later be developed in the posthumous collection of fragments *The Will to Power*.
4. 'The power chord can be percussive and rhythmic or indefinitely sustained; it is used both to articulate and to suspend time. It is a complex sound, made up of resultant tones and overtones, constantly renewed and energized by feedback. It is at once the musical basis of heavy metal and an apt metaphor for it, for musical articulation of power is the most important single factor in the experience of heavy metal' (Walser, 1993, p. 2).
5. Walser shows how metal's well-known connections with the heterogenous ensemble that the twentieth century came to call 'classical music'–for example in a cult of virtuosity and classical training that sets it apart from, say, punk music–rely on *specific* appropriations of 'Bach, not Mozart; Paganini rather than Liszt; Vivaldi and Albinoni instead of Telemann or Monteverdi' (1993, p. 63), all of them evoking in metal a particularly *baroque* sensibility. Walser's formal analysis has the further merit of grounding a definitive debunking of aestheticist, moralist or political attacks on metal, as well as grounding a rereading of the genre's pronounced masculinism.
6. The year of 1970 is commonly referred as a foundational moment, with the release of *Deep Purple in Rock*, *Led Zeppelin II* and especially Black Sabbath's *Paranoid*. A year later Deep Purple released another classic landmark for the genre, *Machine Head*, and the sound later codified as heavy metal began to take definitive shape.
7. Heavy metal has often appropriated the commonplace 'rock music is dead' (which in a fan's mouth invariably means that it has abandoned or betrayed its rebel spirit) in order to claim metal music as its true heir. Twisted Sister's Dee Snider was one of many who stated that 'heavy metal is the only form of music that still retains the rebellious qualities of 50s rock'n'roll' (Halbersberg, p. 41 quoted in Walser, 1993, p. 16). Likewise, Sepultura's Max Cavalera affirmed to *Rock Brigade* that 'rock has died' and that 'thrash metal carries more of rock music's original spirit than rock itself' (quoted in Alexandre, 2002, p. 348).
8. Among the 1970s/1980s bands associated the *rock pauleira* genre are Made in Brazil, Tutti Frutti and Joelho de Porco. Made in Brazil, a national rock music legend founded in 1968, incorporated heavy metal musical codes sporadically in the early 1980s; Tutti Frutti, once the support band for Rita Lee's bluesy rock'n'roll, evolved into poppier forms in their solo career. Joelho de Porco, an extremely original band devoted to a theatrical collage of musical genres, used metal codes sporadically as well but in their case their appropriation was a parodic one. For full discography and indispensable information on these bands and on Brazilian rock until 1986, see Dolabela (1987).
9. In the history of rock music in Brazil, it is virtually impossible to overestimate the significance of Rock in Rio: coinciding with the return to democracy, Rock in Rio marked the country's definitive entrance into the international circuit of megaconcerts. It also provided proof that such things could be carried out professionally in Brazil and, to large sectors of the national

music public, the confirmation that the enormous rock movement was something with which to reckon. In addition to the metal bands the eclectic international lineup of the 10-day event included Rod Stewart, James Taylor, Go-Gos, B-52s, George Benson, Yes, Al Jarreau, Queen, Nina Hagen. For a good account of the festival see Alexandre (2002, pp. 190–205).
10. This highlighting of nationality is coherent with the role that it ended up playing in the choice of Cleveland native Derrick Green to replace Max Cavalera. Green, later baptized 'Predator' due to his six-feet-plus figure, was increasingly welcomed by the Sepultura fan base as he passed tests of both heaviness but also Brazilianness of spirit, as detected in his passion for national cultural markers such as soccer.
11. About the powerful soccer charangas, Max Cavalera would respectfully say in an interview on British radio: 'they can get louder than a metal band'.
12. Particularly popular in north-eastern Brazil (especially in the state of Pernambuco), *maracatu* is an Afro-Atlantic dramatic dance that relates the crowning of a king and a queen. It is performed over percussion, uses quite stylized costumes, and features a host of characters and several plot lines. Relying on large percussion ensembles and utilizing a variety of tempos, *maracatu* has recently evolved from a semi-folkloric regional dance to a fundamental component and inspiration for a variety of new hybrid genres in Brazil.
13. The Portuguese bibliography on most of these genres is relatively abundant, and quite daunting, in fact, in the case of *samba*. For an English-language introduction to these genres, see Olsen and Sheehy (2000).
14. Highly critical of varieties of feminism that unreflexively assume traits assigned to women and then attempt to turn them into sources of 'subversion', Judith Butler has suggested that feminism privilege the undoing of the very dichotomies where the codes of maleness and femaleness are produced. This critical operation invariably reveals that the opposition itself needed a previous exclusion in order to be constituted. See Butler (1993).
15. One of the important tasks of popular music criticism is to understand 'authenticity' for what it is, namely a fable, a narrative that, in the case of rock music, provides a 'reenchantment of the world mediated by the grand apparatuses of mass media and technology' (Ochoa, 1999, p. 174). See Ochoa for an insightful critique of the ways in which the fable of authenticity has been reproappriated in the 'simultaneous movement of transnationalization and regionalization of the record industry' (p. 176) coded circa 1991 as 'world music'. For an indispensable analysis of 'world music', see Taylor (1997).
16. The original lines (*quem não gosta de samba/bom sujeito não é*) appear in a song that celebrates *samba* as the national genre, and have since then become vox populi in the country. The song was composed by Dorival Caymmi, since the 1930s a key figure in the canonization of *samba* as well as in the irruption of his Afro-Brazilian state of Bahia into the center of national music. On Dorival Caymmi the indispensable reference is Risério (1993).
17. For a forceful reflection on how 'world music' has become a terrain where even the most seemingly 'horizontal' collaborations are traversed by a multinational corporate establishment of considerable power–one in which even concepts of 'oral tradition' are instrumentalized for further exploitation and production of profit–see Feld (2000).

References

Ricardo Alexandre, *Dias de luta: o rock e o Brasil dos anos 80* (São Paulo: Dórea Books and Art, 2002).
Idelber Avelar, 'Defeated Rallies, Mournful Anthems, and the Origins of Brazilian Heavy Metal', in *Brazilian Popular Music and Globalization*, ed. by Christopher Dunn and Charles Perrone (Gainsville: University of Florida Press, 2001).
André Barcinski and Silvio Gomes, *Sepultura: toda a história* (São Paulo: Editora 34, 1999).
Harris M. Berger, *Metal, Rock, and Jazz: Perception and the Phenomenology of Musical Experience* (Hanover, NH: Wesleyan University Press, 1999).
Judith Butler, *Bodies that Matter: On the Discursive Limits of Sex* (New York and London: Routledge, 1993).
Janice Caiafa, *Movimento punk na cidade: a invasão dos bandos sub* (Rio de Janeiro: Jorge Zahar, 1985).
E. Ellis Cashmore, 'Shades of black, shades of white', in *Popular Music and Commmunication*, ed. by James Lull (Newbury Park, CA: Sage Publications, 1987).
Coffin Joe ' Banda é o segredo da origem do tudo', 1994 [11 June 1996].
Marcelo Dolabela, *ABZ do rock brasileiro* (São Paulo: Estrela do Sul, 1987).

Steven Feld, 'A Sweet Lullaby for World Music', *Public Culture*, 12/1 (2000), pp. 145–171.
Simon Frith, *Performing Rites: On the Value of Popular Music* (Cambridge, MA: Harvard University Press, 1996).
Susan McClary, 'Same as it ever was', in *Microphone Fiends: Youth Music and Culture*, ed. by Andrew Ross and Tricia Rose (New York and London: Routledge, 1994).
Friedrich Nietzsche, *The Birth of Tragedy in the Spirit of Music*, trans. by Walter Kaufmann (New York: Random House, 1967[1872]).
Friedrich Nietzsche, *The Gay Science*, trans. by Walter Kaufmann (New York: Random House, 1974[1888]).
Friedrich Nietzsche, *The Will to Power*, ed. by Walter Kaufmann, trans. by Walter Kaufmann and R.J. Hollingdale (New York: Random House, 1967[1901]).
Ana María Ochoa, 'El desplazamiento de los discursos de la autenticidad: una mirada desde la música', Antropología, 15–16 (1999), pp. 171–182.
Dale Olsen and Daniel E. Sheehy, *The Garland Encyclopedia of Latin American Music* (New York and London: Garland, 2000).
Charles Perrone, *Masters of Contemporary Brazilian Song: 1965–1985* (Austin: Texas University Press, 1989).
'Queremos ajudar a pôr o Brasil na história', entrevista com Igor Cavalera', *Folha de São Paulo*, Caderno Mais! 14 April 1996, p. 5.
Antônio Risério, *Caymmi: uma utopia de lugar* (São Paulo: Perspectiva, 1993).
'Sepultura', in *Rock: The Rough Guide*, ed. by Christopher Buckley et al. (London: Rough Guides, 1999), pp. 868–69.
'Sepultura conquista súditos na Inglaterra', *Folha de São Paulo*, Caderno Ilustrada, 7 June 1999, p. 5.
'Sepultura e Ramones percorrem o país em turnê inédita', *Folha de São Paulo*, Caderno Folhateen, 7 November 1994, pp. 6–7.
'Sepultura: Legends in the Making' [http://www.angelfire.com/rock/sepulturatron/history.html].
Timothy Taylor, *Global Pop: World Music, World Markets* (New York: Routledge, 1997).
Robert Walser, *Running with the Devil: Power, Gender, and Madness in Heavy Metal Music* (Hanover, NH: Wesleyan University Press, 1993).
Deena Weinstein, *Heavy Metal: A Cultural Sociology* (New York: Lexington Books; Toronto: Maxwell Macmillan Canada; New York: Maxwell Macmillan International, 1991).

Select Discography

Dorsal Atlântica, *Antes do Fim*, 1986.
Overdose, *Século XX*, EP Cogumelo.
Overdose, *Circus of Death*, Pavement, 1999.
Sarcófago, *Rotting*, Cogumelo, 1989.
Sarcófago, *INRI*, Pavement, 1999.
Sepultura, *Bestial Devastation*, EP, Cogumelo, 1985.
Sepultura, *Morbid Visions*, Cogumelo, 1986.
Sepultura, *Schizophrenia*, Cogumelo, 1987.
Sepultura, *Beneath the Remains*, Roadrunner, 1989.
Sepultura, *Arise*, Roadrunner, 1991.
Sepultura, *Chaos AD*, Roadrunner, 1993.
Sepultura, *Roots*, Roadrunner, 1996.
Sepultura, *Against*, Roadrunner, 1999.
Sepultura, *Nation*, Roadrunner, 2001.
Soulfly, *Soulfly*, Roadrunner, 1998.
Soulfly, *Primitive*, Roadrunner, 2000.
Witchhammer, *Mirror, my Mirror*, Cogumelo, 1990.

Sabina's Oranges: The Colours of Cultural Politics in Rio de Janeiro, 1889–1930

TIAGO DE MELO GOMES AND MICOL SEIGEL

The Spectacular Sabina

Sabina was an orange-seller. For thirty years she hawked her wares at the door of Rio de Janeiro's School of Medicine, acquiring legendary status for several generations of Brazilian medical students. In 1889, a year after the abolition of slavery, Sabina became a player in the intense political debates then raging over the fate of the monarchy. Apparently, from behind the shelter of her fruit stand, 'the students of the Medical School … had directed some Republican irreverence to the occupants of the carriage of the Imperial Regent Princess'.[1] In response, a local police official prohibited the sale of oranges at the door of the School of Medicine.

However, Sabina's clientele was not going to take this lying down:

> … after having used up all the arguments they could think of to the subchief of police to bring about the orange-seller's return, [the medical students] resolved to plan a protest march against the authorities to avenge Sabina. Therefore, days after the incident, Rio de Janeiro watched, amused, an unexpected spectacle: more than 200 medical students, in formation and with oranges skewered on the tips of their canes, left in the direction of Ouvidor Street—the most elegant street of Rio de Janeiro at the time—cheering Sabina and yelling 'Down with the subchief of police!'.[2]

The marchers were careful not to articulate any political positions during the parade, but it was perfectly clear to everyone involved and to observers that the message was Republican.

This wonderfully carnivalesque protest was also highly effective, in both the short and the long term. The minor police official was removed from his post; orange-vending resumed at the School of Medicine's front gate; and a few months later, the Monarchy ceded to Republican government. Not that the pro-orange manifestation was decisive in altering Brazil's political system, but it did constitute a small part of the Republican movement that soon achieved its overall goal.

Participants in the winning side in these large and small debates, the medical students and Sabina had hit upon some of the representational strategies that would continue to entertain, convince, compel and coerce over the course of the

First Republic. The figure of Sabina, it turned out, eloquently communicated some of the political and social messages people in early twentieth-century Rio de Janeiro most wanted to convey. Over some forty years following the Medical School protest, members of elite, middle and eventually, marginal classes would embrace the icon of Sabina to present their respective visions of social hierarchy, pleasure and possibility. This paper traces a handful of the uses of this icon in popular culture and public venues between 1889 and the 1930s.

The various historical actors who deployed Sabina's image reveal, through their actions and words, the landscape of social possibilities in which they moved, and their hopes for altering that landscape. Their actions demonstrate the extent to which popular cultural terrain was considered as a site of struggle. While the first and the bulk of these mobilizations were those of elite and middle-class actors, their representations of Afro-Brazilian and marginal figures in popular culture opened spaces that Afro-Brazilian and marginal people could and did occupy with explicitly political intent. Subaltern agency irrupted into and upset even elite, stereotypical representations of blackness in Brazilian popular culture.[3] This discussion aims to consider the radical potential of popular-cultural politics, and specifically of urban Afro-Carioca (Rio de Janeiro) popular culture prior to the 1930s. It hopes to make this politics, too often occluded by comparative perspectives, fully visible in its own right, through an analysis that provides a full ideological context for everyday life under the First Republic.

This research also suggests that categories of social identity such as race, gender and sexuality are more profoundly interrelated than is suggested by the many (and often excellent) studies that focus on each of these categories separately. It uncovers a great degree of fluidity in racial terminology, finding many terms used in ways other than that assumed by historical memory, and many which have primarily to do with social categories other than race (sex and gender, in particular). It finds terms divorced from their explicit meanings, such as geographically based terms divorced from geography, racial terms that have little to do with race, or with surprising definitions, or connoting primarily sexuality. Within this confusing tangle of texts and contexts lie rich veins of meaning and possibilities.

* * *

The strategy employed by Sabina and the medical students was well judged. The glorious carnivalesque of their action caught the fancy of the attending populace, and might intrigue even a cynical twenty-first-century observer:

> ... all armed with oranges driven over the points of their canes and umbrellas, they left the Academy two by two, preceded by the *man with seven instruments* and the woman who accompanies him, forming a most unusual procession. A standard opened the march, with a crown on a pole made of bananas, chayotes and other vegetables, and hanging from the standard, two large banners, engraved with the following inscriptions. On one: *Offered to the subchief of police of the district of the neighborhood of S. José by the School of Medicine*; and on the other: *To the Eliminator of Oranges.*
>
> Leaving Misericordia Square, the boys followed the street of the same

name, passing along First of March [Street], among banks of the people, who hailed them, while from the windows the ladies, laughing, saluted them with their handkerchiefs.

In Ouvidor Street, where greetings were proffered to all the editorial staff of newspapers with headquarters there, the procession stretched itself out, from First of March Street to Uruguayana [Street], forming an enormous serpent, slithering among the population, the oranges giving the whole thing an immensely festive aspect.

Walking among a constant retinue of cheers and applause, when they arrived in front of the building occupied by the editorial staff, offices and workshops of this newspaper [the *Diario de Notícias*], the youths offered up clamorous cheers for [the paper's editor, the Republican politician] Ruy Barbosa and all his colleagues, directing themselves next to the [offices of the newspaper] *Gazeta da Tarde*, and from there to the building of the Polytechnical School, where they were received with all honors by their fellow-students at that institution.

Incorporating the Polytechnic students to their ranks, they quickly made a large harvest of oranges, bought from the first street-vendor they encountered, and the procession, thus swelled, crossed St. Francisco Lane and September Seventh and Gonçalves Dias Streets, where the students saluted the editors of the newspapers *Novidades*, *Dia*, and *Revista Illustrada*. ...

Back at the School of Medicine, the academics convened in solemn session, saluting the Polytechnic students with an oration interrupted periodically by applause from the entire audience.[4]

The pro-orange protest drew its eloquence from several sources, as the savvy participants played to a variety of contemporary expectations. First among the event's fans were the enthusiastic journalists who recorded the event, who shared the protest's Republican leanings or perhaps allowed themselves to be flattered by the procession's pointed bow in their direction. Besides currying favour with journalists directly, the protestors relied upon a traditional leniency towards student protest, and the harmless entertainment of elite carnival play.[5] A *Gazeta de Notícias* reporter rejoiced that 'the academic bohemians of twenty years ago reappeared yesterday', congratulating the 'procession of the oranges', as a 'rejuvenation of the academic spirit that is today almost entirely absent'.[6] Most critical to the eloquence of this action, however, was the foregrounding of a particularly useful vehicle for the expression of political dissent: the body of Sabina herself.

The axis of the protest was Sabina's physical presence, or even physical excess: 'Sabina, the black [woman], in a white turban, a shirt with lace trim, round skirt, jewelry trinkets, and sandals, "hugely heavy, waddled between two freshmen, who brought her along on their arms".'[7] Replete with symbols of marginalization (blackness, the taint of the condition of slavery, the subordinate gender category, physical excess and poverty), Sabina's body offered an eloquent statement of social protest in and of itself.

Positioning themselves as acting on Sabina's behalf, the students made good political mileage out of this self-portrayal as gallant champions of socially subordinate, marginal citizens. The esteemed tradition of elite abolitionism made this posturing easily identifiable, and was especially useful for future politicians interested in communicating their intentions and ability to construct a unified, democratic nation—what better demonstration of their gallantry than embracing the cause of a poor, old, female, black ex-slave?

Contemporary reporters and the two historians of this event, Tinhorão and Ferreira da Rosa, have accepted the medical students' version of their relationship to Sabina, namely that she was an individual to whom they were deeply emotionally attached, and that at least some part of their protest was intended to protect her position from official sanction. The newspapers presented the march in part as a manifestation of affection for Sabina herself, and one even remembered that the procession collected money and remunerated Sabina directly for the losses caused by the prohibition.[8]

To see the march as direct support for Sabina overlooks a few nuances. First, it was the students who had caused the problem in the first place, by hiding from the target of their 'irreverence' behind her voluminous starched skirts. Second, Sabina was not actually present at the march. Sabina had died in early 1889.[9] It was an orange-seller who had set up in her place, another Afro-Brazilian woman, who 'waddled' along on the arms of her fellow marchers and received any cash that might have come her way. So much for the oft-touted love for Sabina.

However fictional, Sabina and the medical students' ostensible affection for each other was critical to the attractiveness of the protest. In the wake of the long process of abolition, which had culminated the previous year, many Brazilians were enthusiastic consumers and producers of images of black 'cordiality', of Afro-Brazilian acceptance of and gratitude for white patronage, no matter how meagre or forced. Black gratitude would have been a great comfort to whiter elites, who shared their urban quarters (most markedly prior to turn-of-the-century urban reforms) with a swelling population of people with good reason to feel bitter over past and continuing injustices. Brazilians repeatedly reminded themselves how lucky they were to have established amicable race relations, unlike the United States, where the racial question had come to 'ignite deadly hatred among brothers'.[10]

If the students made a powerful statement by positioning themselves on behalf of Sabina, they made another, veiled, and therefore perhaps even more powerful statement, by positioning themselves *against* Sabina. While the privileged status of their own bodies ensured their physical safety at the hands of the state, Sabina served as foil against which the students could emphasize and revel in the contrasts: they were younger and whiter, with access to healthcare, the promise of a prosperous future, and they were male. In highlighting the difference between Sabina's body and theirs with ridicule and pomp, the medical students reflected and reproduced these differences. Making Sabina an object of ridicule as well as sympathy, the medical students borrowed her large, dark figure to constitute their privilege, by highlighting the contrasts between their bodies and hers.

The dynamics of this use of a black, female body by whiter, elite young men, oppositional only within a very limited ambit, would characterize many of the subsequent re-articulations of Sabina's image. It is far, however, from the end of the story, especially given that Sabina had her own ideas about her relationship with students and staff at the medical school. Most of Sabina's personal opinions are inaccessible from our twenty-first-century vantage point, but not all. Sabina was a street-smart, independent entrepreneur, the sign of her success the secure market niche she had carved out for herself over thirty years of catering to the needs of the medical school.[11] She did not express a vision of herself as socially inferior to her clientele, reminding them in terms that they understood of her parity. A *Gazeta de Notícias* journalist reported that Sabina 'never left off bragging about her *apprenticeship* in the school, affirming that she had matriculated even before Dr. Pizarro, and that Dr. Martins Teixeira, with all of his pot-belly, had been a freshman in relation to her'.[12] This writer's patronizing tone cannot hide Sabina's inclination to talk back, her casual adoption of medical school jargon ('apprenticeship', 'freshman'), and her complete disinterest in treating students or graduates with humility.

The significant strength of Sabina's personality emerges again in the adjectives used to describe her: 'unforgettable', in the journalist's view, and in the opinion of the editor of the country's most widely read medical journal, 'legendary' and 'well-known and well-regarded'. Her death in a public hospital, he claimed, was a fact of interest to the entire medical community—and if it wasn't already, his claim made it so when he published it in the pages of the professional journal addressed to that community, O *Brazil-Médico*.[13] As the first journalist noted, it was only after Sabina's demise that the police dared raise a hand against the selling of oranges in her locale: 'the police authority, which couldn't bring itself to rebel against Sabina, revolts now against the institution, attacks its second reign and prohibits the sale of oranges!'[14] If, perhaps particularly in her advanced years, Sabina did indeed cut an imposing enough figure to intimidate the police, we might wonder: had Sabina herself still been alive, would the medical students have dared to manipulate and ridicule her as they did her successor? While we cannot know whether Sabina herself would have participated in the protest had she still been alive, it is worth noting that the students were saved from that confrontation by her death in their mentors' care.

Although historians can deduce certain things about her, the ultimate absence of Sabina's own voice is a crucial part of this story. Historical sources are inherently more articulate about elite perspectives than those of non-elites, leaving gaps unbridgeable even by reading between the lines, as we have attempted here.[15] Indeed, the impassable barriers to Sabina's 'real' voice were erected alongside and at the same moment of Sabina's greatest public exposure; her voice was silenced by the same dynamics that allowed for the recording of its traces. Journalists and historians simultaneously recorded and erased Sabina's speech, because her viewpoint was unimportant to the messages they wanted her body to convey.

For example, reporters barely noticed that the post Sabina deserted when she died had been occupied by a new orange-seller. Not assimilating the change of cast, many reports insisted that the march had featured 'the fruit-vendor herself', 'Sabina', or 'the old black woman Sabina'. Newspapers who noticed the change described Sabina's successor only as 'the *parda*, Geralda'.[16] Others expressed their disregard for the individuality of street vendors directly, with such labels as 'Rosa-Sabina-Geralda', or worse, 'Sabina II'.[17] Sabina's story, in part, recounts the transformation of an individual named Sabina and an unknowable number of colleagues into 'Sabina', a social symbol and cultural trope sheathed in quotation marks, enmeshed in a process of cultural signification beyond any single person's control.

Nevertheless, underlying even the most coercive representation is the agency of the actors whose lives provided the basis of these representations. Their agency would endure to provide a handle to later observers, looking for purchase on the slippery surface of a popular cultural symbol. In other words, even on occasions when the elites made use of popular-cultural blackness, insights can be gained into those whose symbols they appropriate. Returning to Sabina and the medical students, events surrounding the appropriation of the body of the marginal, black woman, by privileged young men would soon get out of hand.

Orange and Black

The festive colour of this enticing spectacle was not only orange, but also black. The orange-lovers' procession seduced observers by invoking and reproducing already-familiar implications of blackness and Afro-Brazilian women in *carioca* public space and popular culture. These implications were woven into narrative images used by elites to discipline and disenfranchise, but which also marked the irruption of non-elite agency into elite social and public spaces, compelling elite recognition.[18] These images carried, therefore, a quite ambiguous charge. Three in particular appear of noteworthy significance.

First among the narrative images underlying the march's success must be the figure of the *quitandeira*, or street vendor. Streetvending in Rio de Janeiro over the nineteenth century and through the First Republic (1889–1930) was an occupation predominantly held by free and enslaved, mostly older, Afro-Brazilian women.[19] Carving out a space in Rio's informal economy was one of the few ways older, Afro-Brazilian women could support themselves and their (inter)dependents, especially as racist immigration policies and hiring practices constricted economic opportunities for Afro-descended city-dwellers, displacing them from even those economic sectors they had previously made profitable.[20] If the struggles in which female street vendors in the nineteenth century engaged to maintain their public presence and the profitability of their enterprises are any indication, this was no easy task.[21] These vendors fought their way into the consciousness of the city, where they would later be nostalgically recalled in caricature and prose as typically *carioca*.[22] So the medical students, in drawing on the 'typical' figure of an older, female, Afro-Brazilian street vendor, were paying inadvertent tribute to the determination and competence of her colleagues and predecessors, as well as to the individual who sparked the event.

Over the course of the First Republic, the image of the *quitandeira* would lend its qualities to another narrative image, the *baiana*. Literally, '*baiana*' means simply a woman from the north-eastern state of Bahia, but the term would come to carry a heavy burden of signification. Eventually this narrative image would evolve into the *baiana* recognizable today, the dark-skinned woman incarnating 'authentic' Afro-Brazilian culture in dress (starched white skirts and lacy blouse, bangles and trinkets, head-wrap), occupation (a street vendor of traditional sweets or snacks, particularly *acarajé* or bean fritters), and religion (generally *candomblé*). The *baiana* is a figure now ensconced in the pantheon of Brazilian national types and essential to contemporary street culture, carnival, Afro-Brazilian culture and politics, and Brazilian popular culture in general, at home and abroad. It was as a *baiana* that Carmen Miranda became Brazil's first Hollywood mega-icon, singing 'O Que é Que a Baiana Tem' ('What the *Baiana*'s Got') at the Urca Casino in 1938 to US promoters.[23] In Carmen Miranda's *baiana*, whitened beyond recognition by the Portuguese-born performer, Sabina travelled very far from home.

Prior to the First Republic, the *baiana* was a figure recognizable primarily in Rio as a representation of the African traditions brought to Brazil by slaves.[24] At the turn of the century, few Bahians (especially elites) considered this essentially *carioca* invention to be an appropriate self-reflection. Nor did Brazilians in general. Their resistance to this figure would be somewhat extenuated after the First World War, amidst the search for both national and regional identities.[25] The *baiana* stands at the crossroads of that dual search, which yielded such paradoxes as the reinterpretation of the *quitandeira*, a figure recognized as deeply *carioca* throughout the nineteenth century, as a *baiana*. *Acarajé*-vendors dressed for success in starched white skirts, ubiquitous and indispensable on Rio's tourist beaches even today, extend and exploit the legacy of this mild ideological contradiction.

The transition from *quintandeira* to *baiana* during the First Republic passes through the figure of Sabina. The quintessential *quitandeira*, she would become the occasion for the first mass-culture showing of the *baiana*. Her evolution helps reveal some of the social and political contests played out in popular cultural terrain.

The second narrative image underpinning the appeal of the Medical School protest was that of the '*Mãe Preta*', the Black Mother of slavery times. The romanticized Black Mother figure would soon be widely acclaimed to memorialize a fictional affection between slaves and masters. Sabina provided some of the material that would constitute her image, in the supposedly affectionate relationship she enjoyed with her young patrons. Consider this journalistic eulogy for Sabina, which described her as an emblem of interracial familiality, sanitarily circumscribed by the country's foremost institution of scientific medical authority (the hospital in which Sabina breathed her last): 'Sabina died, she died in a hospital room, at home, with her family, for Sabina's family consisted of all the students, and because her home, her true home, the one she lived in heart and soul, was that great house of charity'.[26] The image of the hospital as home was striking in part because the comfortable, respectful death in a genteel 'home' that it invokes was a far cry from the humiliation and anonymity of death in the unsanitary, crowded hospitals in which the poor died, as likely from a disease contracted there as from any pre-existing condition.[27]

Discussions of Sabina's supposedly familiar relationship with her clientele revealed the contours of the nostalgia for the social arrangements of a previous era that the *Mãe Preta* would also invoke. The journalist who eulogized Sabina congratulated her for her 'generous heart', which 'never permitted her to compare the common commercial punctuality of today's customers with the remittances, the adorable remittances of the youth of yesteryear' who bought on credit.[28] From a post-abolition perspective of the debt owed the ex-slaves, 'buying on credit' is a fine description of slaveowners' purchases of the labour of their captives. Sabina's 'generous heart' towards these 'adorably' self-centred youths anticipated the Black Mother's famous indulgence.

The third narrative image underlying the pro-orange procession's triumph was the figure of the lascivious *mulata*. The eroticization of women of African descent in general, and most markedly of mulattas, was already a venerable tradition in Brazil by the final abolition of slavery.[29] The sexual attributes of the mulatta were so central that in some cases they came to overshadow the racial meaning of the word's etymological origin. In Rio during the First Republic, particularly in theatrical contexts, '*mulata*' could mean a woman who used her body in a performative, sexualized way, regardless of her racial mixture. Actresses such as Margarida Max, the daughter of Italians, and Otília Amorim, daughter of Portuguese immigrants, played *mulata* roles throughout their careers, alongside actresses of self-declared African descent, such as Araci Cortes and Zaira Cavalcanti. In a similar vein, today, Brazilian women of any physical appearance working (especially abroad) as erotic dancers often call themselves professional 'mulattas'. Like the *baiana* divorced from geography, the mulatta was distanced from racial mixture by the more important narrative elements her image came to convey.

Nobody saw Sabina as *mulata*, but the mulatta accompanied Sabina's narrative journey in several ways. First, Sabina communicated pleasure. Despite the de-sexualization of the journalists and historians who described the Sabina of 1889 as dark, old and unattractively large, they could not (nor did they want to) divorce from her the abundant pleasurable connotations of blackness in an elite-circumscribed public space, from the everyday luxuries of service to the annual blast of carnival. Furthermore, if the Sabina of 1889 was reiteratedly '*preta*', her subsequent appearances would represent her as variously indeterminate—mulatta, and even white. As Sabina whitened, her narrative could be used to tell a story of national progress in racial terms, a story the mulatta also soon came to convey.

The mulatta's social symbolism shifted over the course of the First Republic. In the late nineteenth century, many Brazilians placed their hopes in the idea of *embranquecimento*, or whitening, as a way to avoid their nation's relegation to the dustbin of degeneracy.[30] The mulata in this view, a vehicle of whitening, deserved more tolerance than that accorded her by nineteenth-century scientific racism.[31] This modification of European scientific racism laid the groundwork for the embracing of the mulata as a sign of the superiority of Brazil's racial mixture, a posture that would emerge later, during the search for national popular symbols.[32] Sabina served first as a counterpoint to, and later as expression of the evolving representation of the mulatta.

In her first appearance, Sabina and the mulatta would be juxtaposed to tell this tale of progress, via the orange-seller who took Sabina's place. Sabina's successor, when recognized at all, was described only as 'the *parda*, Geralda'. The adjective *parda*, literally the feminine inflection of 'brown', is an intermediate category between Sabina's blackness and the likely paleness of her clientele. But the dictionary definition was not the one in use in late nineteenth-century Brazil, or not the only one. In the post-abolition period, *parda* indicated an Afro-descendant of *any* skin shade who had never endured the condition of enslavement. In contrast, '*preta*' or '*negra*', both of which were used to describe Sabina, became synonyms for '*liberto*', a slave freed in 1888 or at any moment prior.[33] The term that indicated Geralda's social status, although it designated a colour, reveals nothing about the shade of her skin. It shows, instead, how Brazilians mapped the yearned-for 'progress' of the transition from slavery to wage labour and profitable democratic capitalism with racial terms, peering through the lens that the ideology of *embraquecimento* held up to the social landscape.

The figures of the *quitandeira*, *Mãe Preta* and *mulata* would animate new arenas as popular culture became mass culture, amidst the urbanization and industrialization of the early twentieth century. In Rio de Janeiro, the narrative images that had propelled the 1889 protest to wide attention would suffuse the three intertwined branches of *carioca* popular culture: carnival play, musical theatre revue and popular music.[34] Afro-Brazilians would find spaces for self-expression there as well, as composers, musicians, playwrights, directors and scenographers, actors, dancers and carnival performers. While the extent of their participation was undeniably circumscribed, this did not prevent people from using the tools available to them to expand the constrictions on their lives. One such tool turned out to be the legacy left by the 'unforgettable' Sabina.

As an amalgam of *quitandeira*, *Mãe Preta* and *mulata*, Sabina caught the *zeitgeist* of her moment. She combined the recognition factor of a popular urban denizen; an emotional play to the desire for black cordiality and familiality; and a hedonistic address, all clothed in the marvellous garb of the comedic and the carnivalesque. The striking performativity of the protest she animated was not lost on contemporary observers. One journalist offered 'a cheer for the boys, who have just written the best scene of the upcoming annual theatre revues'.[35] Though the attribution of authorship is a little narrow—just who wrote the scene?—the reporter was prescient.

The Star of the Stage

In November 1889, four months after the manifestation on Sabina's behalf, Republican government replaced the Brazilian monarchy. (Although Sabina and the medical students' protest was striking, it is probably safe to characterize the progression as chronology, not causality.) Another four months later, in March of 1890, the musical theatre revue '*A República*', or 'The Republic' debuted to great success. Its playwright, Artur Azevedo, the best known and most prolific theatre revue author of the period, lauded Sabina and the medical students' protest with a tango, '*As Laranjas da Sabina*', 'Sabina's Oranges', 'the biggest hit of any song from theatre revue at the end of the [nineteenth] century', set to remain a *carioca* favourite for years.[36]

In this period of minimal opportunities for dark-skinned actors, the role of Sabina was sung and performed by Greek soprano Ana Menarezzi. Just as the Sabina of 1889 relied upon the mediation of the freshmen to mitigate her dazzling girth, Sabina's presence on this public stage was mediated by Azevedo's authorial decisions, and Menarezzi's precious European whiteness, which softened Sabina's excessive marginality (*so* fat, *so* black). If the *parda* Geralda, performing the role of Sabina in the procession, symbolically whitened her character, this actress advanced along the explicitly racial progression envisioned by the dictates of whitening. Yet if Menarezzi whitened Sabina, Sabina blackened Menarezzi, who adopted the 'typical' accent of an uneducated Afro-Brazilian, and the typical clothing. Menarezzi did not want to erase Sabina's blackness entirely, for it was the source of the entertainment that the actress, the playwright and the audience wanted the performance of her character to convey: humour, pleasure, leisure.

The narrative elements of this Sabina character underlie critic and music historian José Ramos Tinhorão's location of 'The Republic' as the first incidence of the figure of the *baiana*.[37] While calling 'The Republic's' Sabina a *baiana* in the contemporary sense may be anachronistic, Tinhorão is certainly correct in identifying Sabina as a proto-*baiana* figure, one that would shoulder the narrative elements of the *baiana* as soon as struggles over that national/regional narrative image made them available.

So a year after her death, Sabina emerged as star of the stage, darling of the theatre-going public—and in an era when theatre revue enjoyed considerable public influence.[38] In a decade or so, as theatre revue expanded its audiences, the genre would reach an even wider public outside the theatre. As soon as technological advances permitted, '*As Laranjas da Sabina*' the hit song of the revue 'The Republic', would be recorded. This took place in 1902 and at least two more times thereafter, twice by Baiano, the most popular singer of the day.[39]

Thanks to the recording, we know the words of the song today:

> I am Sabina
> I can be found
> Every day
> There on the sidewalk
> Of the School
> Of Medicine
>
> A sub-chief of policemen
> Very pinched and stingy man
> Sent two soldiers
> To take away my fruit-tray, ai!
>
> Without bananas, monkeys get by
> And kings are ok without *canja*[40]
> But medical students
> Can never
> Go without Sabina's oranges!
>
> The boys planned
> A big procession
> And thereby showed
> How ridicule can kill, ai![41]

In translation the song loses its comedic elements—puns, slang, the accent Azevedo thought 'characteristic', period references, etc.—and in any language, lyrics in print are severed from the meanings conveyed by melody and rhythm. Still, the words illuminate the rich storyline that the event provided; by remembering that story, the recordings show its endurance in popular memory even as they contributed to its further survival.

With its recording, the song transcended the genre of theatre revue, restricted to middle- and upper-class audiences until about the second decade of the twentieth century.[42] Popular music drew listeners from a greater range of social positions, and so if the song was a hit, it must have appealed to some who identified with as well as against Sabina (regardless of their racial, gender or class positions). Perhaps it helped that the ridicule that the song explores flowed in several directions. If the song offered the character of Sabina as an object of ridicule, with her ignorant accent and funny lines, it also made her the observer of ridicule inflicted on others, and the beneficiary of the disturbance it produced.

The Unpaid Debt

The recording of a song that had been a revue or carnival hit often served to prolong its popularity. In 1915, less than a decade after 'Sabina's Oranges' was recorded, and with *cariocas* still humming the chorus, Sabina emerged in a new venue. That year, the Brazilian Treasury defaulted on a series of bank notes. For some reason, the bad notes were nicknamed 'Sabinas'.[43] These Sabinas, like the earlier ones, made their blithe way into popular culture thanks to theatre revue.

In a musical theatre revue that year, author J. Brito presented '*A Sabina*' ('Sabina'). The title character represented both 'the 'Sabina' of the oranges and the other, of current events'.[44] Dressed as 'the celebrated *baiana* of the oranges, at the door of the Medical School', the famous actress Maria Lino pleased reviewers and audiences 'with her natural grace'.[45] The 'natural' grace of this white actress took several more steps away from the ridiculous, decidedly ungraceful nature of the Sabina of 1889. Perhaps she conveyed less ridicule on purpose, since by then theatre revue had to cater to audiences both humble and privileged in order to enjoy commercial success. The conditions of mass cultural production required this Sabina to be a figure of wide appeal.

Interestingly, this is the first time that Sabina is called a '*baiana*' in the material that we discovered. Although no one in 1889 applied this label, when the *baiana*'s conjunction of characteristics coalesced into a legible narrative image Sabina moved into that category as if she had been made for it, which in part, of course, she had.

Why were the Treasury notes named after the Sabina of orange-selling fame? While the existing sources permit no definitive answer, one possibility suggests itself. In contemplating the state's various unpaid debts, mentioning an Afro-Brazilian who may have been a slave brings one particular debt immediately to mind: the reparations owed for the crippling experience and legacy of slavery. While reparations were not explicitly under discussion in this period, they seem to have been on people's minds in a less conscious way, as in the following decade, Brazilians who identified themselves as white would discuss this debt in no uncertain terms: 'the black race ... gave us in bitter effort during slavery times: the immense labor which made our economic wealth and began to erect the gigantic edifice of our *Patria* [fatherland]'.[46] Brazil ought to make good on this debt, they wrote, 'one of its most sacred obligations', 'a debt of gratitude', 'a responsibility of gratitude'.[47] Writers in the São Paulo black press agreed with the characterization of the relationship as a debt, and urged Brazil to 'redeem its debt to the Black Race'.[48]

Whether the reference to the debt owed to Afro-Brazilian ex-slaves and their descendants was intentional or an implication hovering just below the surface in the case of the Treasury notes, the nickname, a personified political caricature, clearly expressed political dissent. Sabina, once again, lent herself to an expression of protest, still by fairly privileged sectors of the society. Despite its multiple mediations, Sabina's icon retained enough of the markers of marginalization to express dissatisfaction, and would continue to do so into the first few decades of the twentieth century.

The Carnival Chicks

In the 1910s and 1920s, at least two different groups evoked Sabina during carnival. The first was the *Sociedade Dançante Carnavalesca Familiar Kananga do Japão* (Kananga of Japan Family Carnival Dancing Society), an association based in the poor, heavily Afro-Brazilian *Cidade Nova* neighbourhood of Rio. Kananga housed a group called the '*Sabinas da Kananga*' or the '*Grupo das Sabinas*' ('Kananga Sabinas' and 'Sabina Group'), coached by the future samba giant Sinhô, who despite his music's success lived precariously, dying of tuberculosis at the age of 42.[49] Sinhô's life reflects the difficult conditions that beset most of Kananga's working- and lower-class members. Their actions, like those of so many non-elite subjects, trod lightly upon the historical record, leaving us little to decipher of their Sabinesque performance. The other carnival Sabinas, better able to display themselves, left a few more clues.

The second carnival group to play at Sabina was the '*Fenianos*', one of the three large 'societies', then made up largely from the middle and upper classes, especially upwardly mobile European immigrants and their Brazilian-born children or families.[50] The *Fenianos* boasted a sub-group called the '*Sabinas do Poleiro*', whose exploits were recorded in several venues. Composer Antônio R. de Jesus e Lezut lauded the Fenianos's Sabinas in the form of a carnival march:

> The *Sabinas do Poleiro*
> are not daughters of Bahia
> They're from Rio de Janeiro
> From the kingdom of carnival
>
> Shake it *baiana*
> you've got *munguzá* [a sweet cooked-corn dish]
> Shake it like you do
> Don't be cruel
>
> They are lovely they are dainty
> distracting, impudent mulattas
> they are coquettes they are foxy
> as they enchant you
>
> There is no group as beloved
> in this Rio de Janeiro
> or more applauded
> than the *Sabinas do Poleiro*.[51]

'Poleiro' was the name the Fenianos gave their dance hall, the private space that in this period they increasingly preferred to the street for their carnival celebrations. The word means roost, as in roosters. It conjured up the *galinha*, or hen, slang for an easy woman. These 'Sabina chicks' were out for the sensual pleasure of carnivalesque revelry. The song focused on these Sabinas' sexual desirability, the product of their fine performance of Afro-Brazilian female sensuality, or mulatta-ness. Sexuality and race inextricably performed this coveted identity.

These partygoers were enjoying the classic carnival upset, taking positions opposite from those they occupied in their everyday lives. Blacking their faces was only half of the cross-dressing their Sabina performances entailed, for these Sabinas were men. A photograph published in the popular magazine *Careta* in 1920 shows about thirty men carnivally festooned in dresses, encaptioned 'The *feijoada* of the Group of Sabinas'.[52] Gender transvestism during carnival is a long and cherished tradition, often *not* intended to convey same-sex practices or identities.[53] These Sabinas performed femininity with deliberate excess, as artifice, and performed masculinity as 'real', carefully ensuring that markers of the latter (hairy legs, steady leers, squarely solid posture, etc.) would protrude 'through' their costumes as if revealing the truth beneath.

This cross-dressing enhanced its performers' aggressive, conventional heterosexuality. It worked to represent the objects of the performers' desire rather than of their identification, although the seams of any such performance are far from watertight. Overall, consumption is perhaps the best way to characterize the relationship these Sabinas expected to have with the identities they performed. Consider the place of food in their acts. The corn, cane sugar and milk dish *munguzá*, typical of Bahia, flavoured their pelvic gyrations, while *feijoada* was the centrepiece of their celebratory feast. These metaphors were unremarkable iterations of the time-honoured tradition of eroticizing *mulatas* via culinary metaphors.[54]

Feijoada is black bean stew, a modest dish long associated with slave diets, and today a symbol of Brazilian national culture. The year 1920 was near the beginning of the period in which many different types of people would work to transform symbols of Afro-Brazilian culture into national symbols. The Sabinas do Poleiro provide us with a privileged glimpse of this process. They consumed with gusto, via *feijoada*, the African and Afro-Brazilian traditions associated with the figure of the *'baiana'*, just as they smacked their lips over the dainty morsels their costumes summoned to mind.

But the Sabinas did not just cook for themselves; this was a feast offered to others. This carnival group seized upon a racially marked cultural item for its value in conveying the sensual pleasures of carnival, and put it into slightly wider circulation. Out of many such small actions, elements of Afro-Brazilian traditions widened their appeal. And widen it they did; in 1927, the entire Fenianos society enjoyed a 'victory *feijoada*' after carnival.[55] Is there evidence of the influence of the Sabinas do Poleiro over carnival groups on the whole? Was this a sign of the sexualization of carnival in general? It is impossible to know, and ultimately, perhaps unimportant. This erstwhile symbol of racial particularity became a national symbol, thanks to sex. Its sexual charge made it interesting and valuable to the *Sabinas do Poleiro*. The nationalization of racial particularity cannot be understood by looking only at ideas and practices involving race, for social categories make sense only in context, in conjunction with each other.

The Fenianos Sabinas' 'typical' clothing and the lyrics of their carnival march reveal how this group toy with the notion of the *'baiana'*—actively negotiating, making claims about, but also simply playing with this narrative. This Fenianos group was adamantly *carioca*, but even born far from Bahia, the song claims, *these* Sabinas still had the moves and the *munguzá* to qualify as *'baiana'*. Furthermore, those same qualities designated them delicious *mulatas*. Their *baiana* qualities, divorced from geography, brought them closer to the figure of the dedicatedly sexy *mulata*.

This might surprise observers in the late twentieth century, for whom there is a great distance between the two figures in the popular imagination. Today's mulatta, young, light-skinned and sexualized, a common representation of Brazil (especially abroad) and of sensual femininity, is very far from the dark-skinned, older *baiana*, quintessential repository of 'authentic' Afro-Brazilian culture. Following the trajectory of the separation of these two narratives in popular culture and activist discourse would surely reveal a fascinating tangle of negotiations over national representation. This paper gives only the barest of nods in that direction, but perhaps it can provide signposts for future research.

For example, a 1923 effort to re-direct Sabina's story suggests that one of the projects at stake in the formation of the distinct narrative images of *mulata* and *baiana* would be that of forming Brazil's mixed-race mass into a disciplined labour force, to contain class conflict and assure Brazil's prominence in the developing capitalist world.

Grace of the Fruit

In 1923, the Rio newspaper *A Noticia* told another version of Sabina's story, confirming its durability by assuming that readers were still familiar with the song and its referent. This mainstream, liberal paper made Sabina's story into a morality tale concerning a new fruit-vendor named 'Engracia das Frutas'. In awkward translation, this means 'Grace of the Fruit'—not intentionally, but also not coincidentally, a personification of actress Maria Lino's 'natural grace'. Engracia was a Portuguese immigrant who, 'placing her tray or basket full of fruit here and there on the avenue, reminds one of old Sabina. Though she was black, and this one white, that matters little. At the end of the day, we have the same sentiments, running parallel.'[56] Sabina, the essayist maintained, had laboured in Rio to send money for the education of a son in Bahia, never letting him know she was black. Ashamed of her 'blood' and her work, Sabina represented for this storyteller a past generation. The hardworking *portuguesa*, on the other hand, was not ashamed to show her children how hard she worked, nor the kind of work she did. An exemplary worker, Engracia provided 'proof of the great truth that in Rio, the parasites are only those who want to be'.[57]

With this twist, the writer turned Sabina's story to address post-Abolition changes in the status of work and workers, a process several generations of Brazilians self-consciously confronted in the transition from slave to free labour. The writer of this tale here applied himself to the task, arguing for a view of work as no longer debased, humiliating, or black, but instead a sign of individual self-worth, familial progress and Brazil's gradual sloughing-off of its poor, African-descended population. Offering, as a metaphor for epochal progress, the replacement of a humble black woman by an ambitious white one, this version of Sabina's story explained Brazil's 'progress' in terms of the 'graceful' extinction of black subjects.

The article's ultimate message reveals the limits of the liberal universalism expressed in its anti-racist bromide ('Though she was black, and this one white, that matters little ...'), and highlights the use of 'colour-blindness' to obfuscate the continued salience of race in economic terms. Its smug congratulations to the social status quo places the blame for poverty on the poor themselves, claiming that the solution to poverty (hard work) is available to all. This writer tweaks the stereotype of the happy poor, popularized by contemporary chroniclers of *favela* life such as Benjamin Costallat or João do Rio.[58] The poor were happy not because they *didn't* work (as the chroniclers implied), but because they *did*—like the lucky *portuguesa*, 'Poor, but happy in her life of work'. Any cantankerous malcontent, in this view, would have only herself to blame.

Sabina's whitewash via the persona of Engracia, like her transition from *preta* to *parda* in the person of her successor, Geralda, and the varying degrees of whitening imposed and imagined by her early twentieth-century interpreters, all followed the eugenic wishful thinking of the ideology of *embranquecimento*. But Sabina still had other things to say. In the 1920s, Afro-Brazilians were increasingly taking to the stage, showing some of the ways producers of culture could bring figures such as Sabina to realize a measure of their oppositional potential.

All Black

Blackness made its way to the popular stage because the qualities in narrative images of black people were precisely those that popular theatre wanted to convey. The black stock figures that white actors increasingly represented onstage in the 1920s—*malandros*, or rogues, *capoeira*-players, *mulatas*, and others—were mocking, patronizing reproductions of racial stereotypes, or else representations of racial mixture and conviviality useful to plaster over social conflict in the interest of good clean nationalist fun.[59] Yet that is not the end of their story. These images were signs of Afro-Brazilians' irrefutable claims to public space, noteworthy traces of resistance in a city bent on 'sanitizing' its streets and its image into a pale, European order. Further, these stock characters eventually brought Afro-Brazilians themselves to the stage. Black actors found themselves increasingly (type)cast in theatre revue productions as the decade progressed. With their feet in the door, some of these actors were able to take another step.

The typecasting of the early twentieth century made possible a range of self-representations by Afro-Brazilian performers thanks to the congruence of a few critical historical conditions. Local changes such as urbanization and the rise of mass culture offered stage performers a measure of autonomy and opportunity. Transnational factors weighed in as well: post-First World War modernisms and nationalisms throughout the Americas and Europe encouraged even elites to embrace indigenous and folkloric cultural forms. The contempt in which racial 'science' and *embranquecimento* had held cultural traits associated with Afro-Brazilians began to be tempered by admiration and protectiveness. It is not clear what came first,: intellectual movements, demographic changes or subaltern resistance. What is clear is that all of these developments opened a tiny fissure of possibility, which Afro-Brazilian artists split wide open.

In 1926, a group of experienced theatre revue writers, musicians and actors founded the *Companhia Negra de Revistas*, or Black [Theatre] Revue Company. Made up entirely of self-identified *'negros'*, its cast and crew included such prestigious figures as Miss Mons, Rosa Negra, Jandira Aimoré, Bonfiglio de Oliveira, the music teacher and composer Sebastião Cirino, the flautist, teacher and composer Pixinguinha, and the playwright De Chocolat, who wrote their debut play *Tudo Preto* (All Black). Only scenographer Jayme Silva did not identify himself as Afro-Brazilian. Since many of these same actors would make up the *'Companhia Mulata Brasileira'* (Brazilian Mulatta Company) in 1930, the troupe's definition of *'negro'* seems very close to capital-N 'Negro' as used then in the United States: a general denomination for anyone who was identified as being of African descent. If that is so, that definition would have coloured even the word in the play's title, as *'preto'* was usually used to refer to very dark skin, minus any political intent. The *Companhia Negra* recognized language as a site of struggle, and occupied it bodily.

Sabina the orange-seller made no cameo appearance in *Tudo Preto*'s skits or songs, at least not in a way recorded in the script submitted to the government censor and therefore preserved in the National Archives. But the *Companhia Negra* invoked her precedence and the durability of her legacy via the three images that made up her popular cultural presence: the *quitandeira/baiana*, the *mulata* and the *Mãe Preta*. The *baiana* was there largely by inference, as when actors discussed the value of Bahia as a source of theatrical black *'originalidades'* (novelties).[60] Proving their assertions, the play's original song 'Cristo naceu na Bahia' (Christ was born in Bahia) became a huge hit.[61] The limelight in *Tudo Preto*, however, focused largely on the *mulata*. *Mulatas* were the lovely stars of the show, the 'Black Girls all in Bathing Suits', singing 'we are lovely celebrated ... futurist bathers'.[62] As to the Black Mother, the play concluded with an 'apotheosis' celebrating the *Mãe Negra*.

A play contemporary to *Tudo Preto* suggests that the black troupe's mulatta stars evoked Sabina directly for some viewers. The title character of J. Sousa's *Ai... Sabina!* was a lovely mulatta who decided to become an actress. She quickly found various Portuguese men (famous for their penchant for mulattas) willing to finance her venture by forming a theatre troupe in which she would be the star.[63] The choice of name for the star could be a coincidence, reflecting perhaps the popularity of the name 'Sabina' among Rio's popular classes, but that too might be a sign of Sabina's enduring popular-cultural presence. In any case, the bow to *Tudo Preto* is unmistakable. It marked a moment in which Afro-Brazilian women could dream of successful theatre careers.

Tudo Preto was self-reflexive. It began as a meta-play about the formation of an all-black theatre company that could later, presumably, put on a play; then it turned to skits and sketches. It offered stock images of black people, detailing, within the humoristic conventions that characterized the genre, their transformation into a successful theatre troupe. It joked, for example, about the greater stage illumination such a troupe would require, and about recruiting cast members from the street flux of maids and other domestic workers leaving their white employers' homes. Embracing the conventions of popular theatre, *Tudo Preto* was uninterested in deviating from the recognizable types and predictable slapstick humour proven to draw and satisfy audiences. Even so, the play offered profound ideological interventions, including a pointed critique of the absence of blackness on the popular stage and advocacy for the restitution of that lack. Furthermore, it opened to discussion questions which were previously rarely entertained, brought Afro-Brazilians together in a context in which those questions were made possible, and, most simply and perhaps most powerfully, articulated an Afro-Brazilian identity in an ideological context that powerfully discouraged such identification.

Certainly the troupe's contemporaries found it amply political. Articulate observers who identified as both black and anti-racist thought that ground had been gained by the *Companhia Negra*'s efforts. In the small black press of São Paulo, for example, contributing writers who perforce identified as being of African descent and who sought to fight racism through their contributions happily discussed the cultural politics of the *Companhia Negra*. They felt it would bring Brazilians nationwide to recognize and applaud Afro-Brazilian talent, positioning them at the heart of an 'authentic' national art form—and what greater performance of national inclusion could there be? When *Tudo Preto* travelled to São Paulo, the Afro-Brazilian newspaper *O Clarim d'Alvorada* rejoiced:

> We, *Paulistas* and *Paulistanos*, sensible Brazilians, today more than ever are satisfied ... [with] the brilliant show of the Black Theatre Revue Company, at the Apollo. ... So we have our consecration, although it is still crucial that we struggle on, with great enthusiasm, to further progress. The era is ours, as so many confirm; this theatrical novelty arose in the City of Light—Paris, with Josephine Baker, and today, among us Brazilians, is already being celebrated. We must all, willingly, go applaud our countrymen who with ardour and good will are struggling courageously.[64]

This writer placed Afro-Brazilian struggles in multiple, concentric contexts. He defined his opening 'we' in four ways: as *Paulistas* (people from São Paulo state); *Paulistanos* (from the city of São Paulo), Brazilians, and witnesses of a grand moment ('the era is ours'). Local, regional, national and transnational identities were all in play in his celebration, for he and his fellow urban Brazilians lived their lives on all of those levels. *Tudo Preto* participated in a drama of national representation played out on several stages at once, in Rio de Janeiro, São Paulo, Paris, New York and elsewhere.

Not content to let this drama unfold however it might, this reviewer struggled to guide the interpretation of *Tudo Preto*'s implications for questions of nation and race. The reviewer, and *Tudo Preto*'s cast, were some of the many Brazilians of colour struggling to turn their fellow citizens away from the contempt for blackness and race mixture evident in North Atlantic racial theories that relegated Brazil to the dustbin of 'degeneracy'. They hoped that a dramatic performance of Brazil's embracing of blackness on an international stage could encourage the nation to accept the historical and cultural legacy of slavery, and along with it, ideally, the people who wore its 'badge'. French opinion was particularly useful in that task, for France had long been the Brazilian elite's final arbiter of cultural prestige and value. Thus the reviewer's pleasure in making Paris the site of origin for the cultural revalorization that he hoped would spread to Brazil. *Tudo Preto* offered a similar reminder: 'In Paris, doesn't Douglas have his Negro Revue company?', asked one of the protagonists in the opening scene.[65] In 1930, one of the stars of the *Companhia Mulata Brasileira* would adopt the French-sounding stage name Jacy Aimoré, in reference to the foreign acceptance of performers of African descent. 'My dream today', enthused the starlet, 'is to be a great artist and to go abroad ... to Argentina, to Europe. They say they really like *mulatas* there, so I want to go see if it's true.'[66]

As these references to Josephine Baker and to African-American choreographer and dancer Louis Douglas suggest, black North Americans abroad were particularly interesting to Afro-Brazilian cultural activists. Despite their acute awareness of North American racism, readers of the black Brazilian press assigned to African-Americans the most positive of US national characteristics: industry, practicality, cleverness, and above all, wealth. Josephine Baker's global success, supposedly evidence of the best of US national qualities, offered a gratifying riposte to ideas of biological racial inferiority. *Tudo Preto*, the journalist hoped, would translate Baker's message into a parable of the value of blackness, and bring that message home.

Such local interpretations and applications are the bricks in the edifice of the concept of a global African diaspora, then circulating in Pan-African, Garveyite and emigrationist discourse. Note that as the *Clarim* writer contemplated other diasporic subjects, he used not a single racial term, other than the title of the theatre troupe. This very effectively gets around the discrepancies among racial categories in different cultural contexts. This refusal to engage racial categories also conveyed the writer's wistful hopes for the racelessness premised in the idea of whitening. This is a desire, but also a demand; given the frequent notice that writers in the black press took of the vehemence of racial 'hatred' in the USA, their assertions of Brazilian racelessness and of the relative absence of racial conflict there reveal their intent to set an example to the world.

Tudo Preto and its fans and exegetes (such as the *Clarim* reporter), asked *Paulistas*, *Paulistanos* and Brazilians in general to recognize the great cultural value of blackness in France, the accomplishments and qualities of black people in the USA, and the world's gaze on Brazil's racial relations. They brought these intrusions of transnational contexts into local contexts, where they would charge the language of whitening, and what would later be called 'racial democracy', with unexpectedly radical overtones.[67] If their language then sounded to their neighbours like acceptance of the social contours of the status quo, all the better for its recognizability and efficacy in their specific ideological contexts.

If any doubt remains that author De Chocolat intended his play to carry anti-racist political overtones, and that the cast shared his activist priorities, *Tudo Preto*'s final act should dispel it. This 'apotheosis' celebrated the *Mãe Negra*. Its details, alas, have not been preserved, but we can surmise its content from other clues. The figure of the Black Mother was in the news at that time because in April of 1926, roughly three months before De Chocolat submitted his script to the censors, a proposal to construct a monument to the Black Mother had ignited great enthusiasm in the capital and other urban areas. This was an action on conventional political grounds, which *Tudo Preto* joined, as a photograph published about a month after the play's debut reveals. In this photograph, the cast and crew of the *Companhia Negra* posed at a Mass on behalf of the monument held by the black church in Rio, the *Irmandade de Nossa Senhora do Rosario e São Benedicto dos Homens Pretos* (Brotherhood of Our Lady of the Rosary and Saint Benedict of the Black Men).[68]

The *Companhia Negra* actors were only a tiny portion of the popular, Afro-Brazilian support for the Black Mother monument. The Mass, for example, was attended by hundreds of supporters of all colours. Contributors to the São Paulo black press picked up the news soon after its proposal in Rio de Janeiro, discussing it at great length and in largely glowing terms; when white interest, along with funding, lagged, their support surged.[69] While we do not know the course of events in the 1930s, Afro-Brazilian support was probably important to the eventual construction of the monument, which was built in the 1930s and

Figure 1. Credit: Denise Botelho.

stands to this day in a plaza outside the Church of São Benedito in São Paulo (Figure 1).

Encore: Yellow, Green, and Black

The Black Mother may have been embraced by elites to make nostalgic a fictional aristocratic past, but she was re-signified in subaltern discourse into a source of racial affirmation. Perhaps in retrospect the cultural politics of the Black Mother monument movement, and *Tudo Preto* as well, have been of dubious value in the long run in challenging racial inequality in Brazil. Readers familiar with the US context may be tempted to compare these Afro-Brazilian cultural politics with African-Americans' more open challenges to US racism, or to equate the *Mãe Preta* and the North American 'Mammy'.[70] In that light, they seem poor political choices. Yet simply to say that these activists were misguided would fail to take into account the alternatives available at that historical moment, and the logic guiding their choices.

The context in which these cultural politics made sense in the Brazil of the First Republic was multi-layered and global. Afro-Brazilians who did find explicitly political value in the centrality of blackness in national popular culture in the 1920s were performing for local observers, but also for a transnational audience. As the original proposal explained, public monuments such as that of the Black Mother were the means through which 'a country's "people" [*povo*] truly "express" their soul, revealing its intimate structure and affirming its particular individuality in the eyes of foreigners'.[71] The monument's supporters hoped that the statue would show that Brazil's global uniqueness lay in its exceptionally peaceful race relations. Brazil's loving racial mixture had 'placed us, *in the world*, in a unique position vis-à-vis the black race. Acting on the profound chimera of our sentiments, it stripped us of racial prejudice, as it did no other people *on the planet.*' The result, the monument proposal happily concluded, 'distinguishes us *above all other nations* of the Earth'.[72] By embracing its own blackness, this proposal suggested, Brazil could position itself favourably among the nations.

Afro-Brazilian supporters of the monument (and of *Tudo Preto*) hoped that a genuine embracing of blackness would make Brazil a better home for its citizens of African descent. They worked to circulate their cultural centrality in a transnational arena, in which images of 'good' Afro-Brazilians and of racial harmony as a deeply national characteristic would flatter and exhort their fellow-citizens to move closer to their stated ideals. Their nuanced grasp of their ideological context is apparent in the success that this strategy enjoyed: not only did supporters who did not identify themselves as black abound, but foreigners, too, applauded the idea of the monument. Portuguese journalist Mario Monteiro found the idea to be of 'an elevated nationalist significance which can only be pleasing to the Portuguese'.[73] Chicago *Defender* editor Robert Abbott, who loved Brazil and had travelled there in 1923, received news of the monument and splashed a huge headline across the *Defender's* front page, offering US readers nationwide news of the generous benevolence with which Brazilians considered their black fellow-citizens.[74]

Brazilians of all shades played to both domestic and transnational audiences when they represented black characters such as Sabina or the *Mãe Preta*. Fully aware of the value of fraternal harmony in the wake of the First World War's devastations, they directed highly performative cultural politics to the task of showing other nations its national value. Aware too, that the weight of the world's gaze could guide domestic social policy, they sought to influence their fellow-citizens with the promises implied in their stagings of the centrality of blackness to the Brazilian nation.

Acknowledgement

Tiago de Melo Gomes thanks FAPESP for support for this publication through his doctoral fellowship.

Notes

1. José Ramos Tinhorão, *Música Popular: teatro & cinema* (Petrópolis: Vozes, 1972) pp. 17–20, citing in part Ferreira da Rosa, *Memorial do Rio de Janeiro* ... in the magazine of the Arquivo do Distrito Federal, Vol. II, 1951, Departamento de História e Documentação da Secretaria Geral de Educação e Cultura do Rio de Janiero, p. 91. Translations are Micol's unless otherwise noted.
2. Tinhorão. *Música Popular* ... , p. 18.
3. Homi K. Bhabha, 'A questão do 'outro': diferença, discriminação e o discurso do colonialismo', in *Pós-modernidade e política*, ed. by Heloísa Buarque de Hollanda (Rio de Janeiro: Rocco, 1991).
4. 'Mettem-Se Com Elles... Manifestação ... A Laranja', *Diario de Noticias* (Rio de Janeiro), 26 July 1889, p. 2; emphasis in the original.
5. Vieira Fazenda, 'Vida Acadêmica', *Revista do IHGB*, 93/147 (1923 [1907]); Ana Maria Rodrigues, *Samba negro, espoliação branca* (São Paulo: Editora Hucitec, 1984); Maria Isaura Pereira de Queiroz, *Carnaval Brasileiro: O Vivido e o Mito* (São Paulo: Brasiliense, 1992); Maria Clementina Pereira Cunha, *Ecos da Folia: Uma História Social do Carnaval Carioca entre 1880 e 1920* (São Paulo: Companhia das Letras, 2001).

6. 'As Laranjas', *Gazeta de Notícias*, 7/26/1889, p. 1.
7. Tinhorão, *Música Popular* ... , 18. Tinhorão manages to call Sabina 'fat' three times in as many pages. If Sabina was indeed a former slave, and if she had indeed sold oranges for thirty years, a substantial portion of a poor woman's life in this place and period, then she must have done this work while enslaved. This would not have been unusual; a substantial number of urban slaves performed wage labour in the nineteenth century, periodically turning their wages, or a certain set amount, over to their owners. On these 'escravos de ganho' (wage slaves, roughly), see Sidney Chalhoub, *Visões da Liberdade: Uma História das Últimas Décadas da Escravidão na Corte* (São Paulo: Companhia das Letras, 1990); Luis Luís Carlos Soares, 'O Escravo de Ganho no Rio de Janeiro do Século XIX', *Revista Brasileira de História*, 8/16 (1986), pp. 107–142.
8. 'As Laranjas', *Gazeta de Notícias*, 26 July 1889, p. 1; 'a quitandeira foi delirantemente aplaudida', 'Manifestação Original', *Jornal do Commercio*, 27/7/1889, n.p.; Tinhorão, *Música Popular* ... , p. 18, citing Ferreira da Rosa. His is the only chronicle that mentions money, however.
9. 'A.S.' [probably Azevedo Sodré, the editor], 'Boletim da Semana', *O Brazil-Medico*, Ano 3 (15 January 1889), p. 9; 'As Laranjas', *Gazeta de Notícias*, 26 July 1889, p. 1.
10. 'Pr.' [= proprietario, Argentino Wanderley?], 'A Formula Igualitaria Para Resolver a Questão Racial Americana', *Progresso*, 2/24/29; Urban Afro-Brazilian populations grew before abolition as well as after, as flights, manumissions, self- and family purchases, and other factors increasingly eroded the numbers of people enslaved. The actual number of slaves freed by the 1888 act was therefore quite small. Robert W. Slenes, 'The demography and economics of Brazilian slavery, 1850–1888', PhD dissertation, Stanford University (1976), pp. 697–698; Maria Helena Machado, *O Plano e o Pânico. Movimentos socias na década da Abolição* (Rio de Janeiro: Ed. UFRJ, 1994).
11. 'Thirty years', in 'As Laranjas', *O Paiz*, 26/7/1889.
12. Anon., 'Crônica da Semana', *Gazeta de Notícias*, 28 July 1889, n.p.
13. 'Inolvidável' is anon., 'Crônica da Semana', *Gazeta de Notícias*, 28 July 1889, n.p.; next two are both 'A.S.' [probably Azevedo Sodré, the editor], 'Boletim da Semana', *O Brazil-Medico*, Ano 3 (15 January 1889), p. 9. Sodré wrote: 'It has been quite some time since we have had cause to register a week as fertile in events of interest to the medical community as the week that has just ended. From the recurrence of the paroxystic recrudescence of the lethal endemic which for many years has desolated and undermined trust in this city, to the visit the noble Minister of the Empire paid to the hospital in Jurujuba; from the unexpected disappearance of the legendary Sabina, the well-known and well-regarded fruit seller at the door to the School, to the supposed poisoning of children in Niterói, all that has greatly drawn the concern of the medical community and is justly here inscribed.'
14. Anon., 'As Laranjas', <u>Gazeta de Notícias</u>, 26 July 1889, p. 1.
15. Gayatri Spivak, 'Can the subaltern speak?', in *Marxism and the Interpretation of Culture*, ed. by C. Nelson and L. Grossberg (Urbana, IL: University of Illinois Press, 1988), pp. 217–313; Florencia Mallon, 'AHR Forum: the promise and dilemma of subaltern studies: perspectives from Latin American history', *AHR*, 99/5 (December 1994), pp. 1491–1515.
16. 'Notas de um Simples (fato da semana)', *Novidades*, 27/71889; 'Importante Manifestac ͺão', *Gazeta da Tarde*, 25/7/1889.
17. 'Rosa-Sabina-Geralda', in 'As Laranjas', *O Paiz*, 26/7/1889 (we have not been able to discover why 'Rosa' was included here); Sabina II in 'Mettem-Se Com Elles... Manifestação ... A Laranja', *Diario de Noticias* (Rio de Janeiro), 26 July 1889, p. 2.
18. Although elaborated in a significantly different context, we find very useful the concept of the narrative image as developed by Wahneema Lubiano in 'Black ladies, welfare queens, and state minstrels: ideological war by narrative means', in *Race-ing Justice, En-gendering Power: Essays on Anita Hill, Clarence Thomas, and the Construction of Social Reality*, ed. by Toni Morrison (New York: Pantheon Books, 1992), pp. 323–363. Lubiano examines images of Black women charged to convey 'a constellation of ideas' (p. 332): 'Categories like "black woman," "black women," or particular subsets of those categories, like "welfare mother/queen," are not simply social taxonomies, they are also recognized by the national public as stories that describe the world in particular and politically loaded ways–and that is exactly why they are constructed, reconstructed, manipulated, and contested. They are, like so many other social narratives and taxonomic social categories, part of the building blocks of "reality" for many people; they suggest something about the world; they provide simple, uncomplicated, and often wildly (and politically damaging) inaccurate information ...' (pp. 330–331). Her astute observations on

images in which 'black women function as the narrative means by which the country can make up its mind' (pp. 336–337), translate well to the Brazilian case in question here, not due to some transnational, ahistorical similarity among Black women, but because her insightful description of the ways narrative images function to preserve or contest power happens also to describe their function in this particular context in Brazil. Like Lubiano, we search in these narratives for a silver lining, for ways to read them 'that allow us to see genuine gendered and racialized challenges to the successful and multifacted operations of power' (p. 349n). In the case of the Hill-Thomas hearings, Lubiano can offer only wistful optimism ('power is never completely successful', p. 361). The Carioca First Republic stage offers somewhat better prospects.

19. Roberto Moura, *Tia Ciata e a Pequena Africa no Rio de Janeiro* (Rio de Janeiro: FUNARTE/Instituto Nacional de Música, 1995); Maria Odila Leite da Silva Dias, *Power and Everyday Life: The Lives of Working Women in Nineteenth-Century Brazil*, trans. by Ann Frost (New Brunswick, NJ: Rutgers University Press, 1995 [1984]).
20. Moura, *Tia Ciata*.
21. Silva, *Power and Everyday Life*.
22. Seth [aka Álvaro Marins], 'Flagrantes Cariocas: Caricaturas de Costumes, 1930 a 1935', in *Exposição. Desenhos a Pena de Seth, 1929–1936* (Rio de Janeiro: Edição do Atelier Seth, 1927); Raul Pederneiras [aka Raul], *Scenas da Vida Carioca. Caricaturas de Raul*, vol. I (Rio de Janeiro: Officinas Graphicas do 'Jornal do Brasil,' 1924); vol. II (Rio de Janeiro: Jornal do Brasil, 1935); João do Rio (Paulo Barreto), *A alma encantadora das ruas: cronicas* (São Paulo: Companhia das Letras, 1997); Benjamin Costallat, *Mistérios do Rio* (Rio de Janeiro: Secretaria Municipal de Cultura, Turismo e Esportes ... , 1990 [1920]); *Mademoiselle Cinema: novela de costumes do momento que passa* (Rio de Janeiro: Casa da Palavra, 1999 [1922]); *Mutt, Jeff & Cia (chronicas)* (Rio de Janeiro: L. Ribeiro, 1922); *Depois da meia-noite: as novellas nocturnas* (Rio de Janeiro: Flôres & Mano, 1931 [1923]).
23. Tinhorão. *Música Popular ...* , pp. 19–20; *Carmen Miranda: Bananas is My Business*, dir. by Helena Solberg, prod. by David Meyer and Helena Solberg (International Cinema, 1995).
24. Wlamyra R. de Albuquerque, *Algazarra nas ruas: Comemorações da Independência na Bahia (1889–1923)* (Campinas: Editora da UNICAMP, 1999), and electronic personal communication, May 2001.
25. Albuquerque, *Algazarra nas ruas*.
26. 'As Laranjas', *Gazeta de Notícias*, 26 July 1889, 1.
27. Julyan G. Peard, *Race, Place, & Medicine: The Idea of the Tropics in 19th-Century Brazilian Medicine* (Durham & London: Duke, 1999); Micael Herschmann, Simone Kropf and Clarice Nunes, *Missionários do Progresso: Médicos, Engenheiros e Educadores no Rio de Janeiro, 1890–1937* (Rio de Janeiro: Diadorim Ed., 1996).
28. Anon., 'As Laranjas', *Gazeta de Notícias*, 26 July 1889, 1.
29. Affonso Romano de Sant'Anna, 'A mulher de cor e o canibalismo erótico na sociedade escravocrata', in *O Canibalismo Amoroso* (Rio, Ed. Brasiliense, 1984), pp. 17–60.
30. E. Roquette-Pinto, *Impressões do Brasil no século vinte. Sua historia, seo povo, commercio, industrias e recursos* (London: Lloyd's, 1913); Roquette-Pinto, *Seixos Rolados* (Rio de Janeiro: Mendonça, Machado, 1927); João Batista de Lacerda, 'The *metis*, or half-breeds, of Brazil', in *Papers on Inter-Racial Problems Communicated to the First Universal Races Congress*, ed. by G. Spiller (London: P.S. King & Son, and Boston: World's Peace Federation, 1911), pp. 377–382; Aline Helg, 'Los intelectuales frente a la cuestion racial en el decenio de 1920: Colombia entre Mexico y Argentina', *Estudios Sociales* (FAES), 4 (March 1989), pp. 37–53; Giralda Seyfirth, 'Construindo a Nação: Hierarquias Raciais e o Papel do Racismo na Politica de Imigração e Colonização', in *Raça, Ciência e Sociedade*, ed. by Marcos Chor Maio e Ricardo Ventura Santos (Rio: FIOCRUZ/CCBB, 1996), pp. 41–58; Nancy Leys Stepan, *Beginnings of Brazilian Science* (New York: Science History Publications, 1981); Stepan, *'The Hour of Eugenics': Race, Gender, & Nation in Latin America* (Ithaca: Cornell University Press, 1991); and Thomas Skidmore, *Black into White: Race and Nationality in Brazilian Thought* (Durham & London: Duke University Press, 1993 [1974]).
31. Sueann Caulfield, *In Defense of Honor: Sexual Morality, Modernity and Nation in Early-Twentieth-Century Brazil* (Durham & London: Duke University Press, 2000), p. 146.
32. Tiago de Melo Gomes, 'Lenço no Pescoço: o malandro no teatro de revista e na música popular–'nacional,' 'popular', e cultura de massas nos anos 1920', MA thesis in Cultural History, IFCH-UNICAMP, Campinas, São Paulo (1998).
33. Discussing the first half of the nineteenth century, Mary C. Karasch reports that lighter-skinned Afro-descendants struggled to substitute the term 'pardo' for 'mulato', the slaveowners' pre-

ferred term; *A Vida dos Escravos no Rio de Janeiro, 1808–1850* (São Paulo: Companhia das Letras, 2000), pp. 36–41; on the terms in the second half of the century, see Hebe Maria Mattos de Castro, *Das Cores do Silêncio: os significados da liberdade no sudeste escravista–Brasil, séc. XIX* (Rio de Janeiro: Arquivo Nacional, 1995). When 'pardo' came to denote social status (e.g. never having been a slave) rather than colour, it was in part a representational victory, taking the people it named another step away from the degradations of racism, but also a reinforcement of the link between lightness and social progress.

34. On the relationship of these three forms, see Gomes, 'Lenço no Pescoço …'.
35. Anon., 'Crônica da Semana', *Gazeta de Notícias*, 28 July 1889, n.p.
36. Tinhorão, *Música Popular: teatro & cinema*, 17.
37. Tinhorão, *Música Popular: teatro & cinema*, 20.
38. Fernando Antônio Mencarelli, *Cena Aberta: a absolvição de um bilontra e o teatro de revista de Arthur Azevedo* (Campinas: Ed. Unicamp-Cecult, 1999).
39. The recordings are Bahiano on Zon-o-Phone Disco No. X-1036; Bahiano again on Zon-o-phone Disco No. 10.012; and Pepa Delgado on Odeon No. 40.350, Rx-452. Alcino Santos, Gracio Barbalho, Jairo Severiano and M.A. de Azevedo (Nirez), *Discografia Brasileira 78 rpms, 1902–1964*, vol. I (Rio de Janeiro: Funarte, 1982), pp. 1, 10, 46.
40. *Canja*, a kind of chicken soup, was a favourite of the Emperor D. Pedro II. Thanks to Beatriz Resende for help with this translation.
41. Tinhorão, *Música Popular: teatro & cinema*, p. 19. Proof of the song's success is available in the theatre revue *Bendegó*, by Oscar Pederneiras, which in 1900 included a new version of 'As Laranjas da Sabina', renamed 'O Tango da Quitandeira', 'The Tango of the Street-Vendor'.
42. Gomes, 'Lenço no pescoço …'.
43. *A Noite*, 4 May 1915; 24 and 25 August 1915; *O Paiz*, 25 and 28 August 1915; J. Bocó, 'Chronica', *O Malho*, 21 August 1915, p. 2; Anon., 'O Quinto da Emissão …', *O Malho*, 28 August 1915, n.p.
44. *O Paiz*, 29 August 1915.
45. *Jornal do Commercio*, 29 August 1915.
46. Unsigned (Candido Campos), 'O Brasil Deve Glorificar a Raça N. Erguendo Um Monumento á Mãe Preta. A Significação desta figura Luminosa. Appello de "A Noticia' á imprensa brasileira", *A Noticia*, 4/5/26. The occasion was Campos's suggestion, discussed below, that a monument be built to the glory of *a Mãe Preta*, the enslaved Black Mother.
47. Jorge Pinto, reported in 'O Brasil deve glorificar a raça negra erguendo Um Monumento á Mãe Preta. Fala-nos o Dr. Jorge Pinto …', *A Noticia*, 4/16/26, p. 1; no author or title noted, *A Noite*, 4/13/26, n.p., reprinted in 'Monumento á Mãe Preta', *A Noticia*, 4/24/26, p. 3; no author or title noted, *A Energia Nacional*, 4/22/26, reprinted in 'Tribuna Publica', *A Noticia*, 6/4/26, p. 3.
48. Moyses Cintra, 'Justiça e Gratidão', *O Clarim*, 1/15/27, p. 3; Anon., 'O Dia da Mãe Preta', *O Clarim*, 9/28/28, p. 1.
49. Maria Clementina Pereira Cunha, personal communication, for which we would like to express thanks; Edigar de Alencar, *Nosso Sinhô do Samba*, 2nd edn (Rio de Janeiro: FUNARTE, 1981), pp. 23, 29.
50. Cunha, *Ecos da Folia*; Queiroz, *Carnaval Brasileiro*.
51. Antônio R. de Jesus e Lezut, 'As Sabinas do Poleiro', *marcha carnvalesca* (carnival march) dedicated to the '*rainha das sabinas*' (queen of the sabinas). Arquivos da Empresa Pascoal Segreto–Divisão de Música da Biblioteca Nacional, Rio de Janeiro, caixa 102.
52. *Careta*, 606 (1/31/20); further photos appear in 661 (2/19/21); 709 (1/21/22); 762 (1/27/23).
53. James Green, *Beyond Carnival: Male Homosexuality in Twentieth-Century Brazil* (Chicago and London: University of Chicago Press, 1999); Cristiana Schettini Pereira, 'Nas Barbas de Momo: os sentidos da presença feminina no carnaval das "grandes sociedades" nos últimos anos do século XIX', undergraduate thesis, IFCH-Unicamp (1995).
54. Sant'Anna, 'A mulher de cor …'.
55. *Careta*, 714 (2/25/22).
56. 'A Engracia das Fructas …', *A Noticia*, 4/16/23, p. 1.
57. Ibid.
58. João do Rio, *A alma encantadora das ruas*; Costallat, *Mistérios do Rio*; *Mademoiselle Cinema*; *Mutt, Jeff & Cia*; *Depois da meia-noite*; *Mistérios do Rio*.
59. Gomes, *Lenço no pescoço …*.
60. De Chocolat, *Tudo Preto*, playscript, 1926, Arquivo da 2a Delegacia Auxiliar de Polícia, Box 40, no. 891 (Arquivo Nacional, Rio de Janeiro), p. 4.

61. Jairo Severiano and Zuza Homem de Mello, *A Canção no Tempo*, vol. I: 1901–1957 (São Paulo: Editora 34, 1997), p. 77.
62. *Tudo Preto*, p. 35.
63. J. Sousa, *Ai... Sabina!*, playscript, 1926, Arquivo da 2a Delegacia Auxiliar de Polícia, Box 37, no. 796 (Arquivo Nacional, Rio de Janeiro).
64. 'Tudo Preto', *O Clarim d'Alvorada*, 10/24/26, p. 1. The following month, the paper printed, in homage to the company, the photos of 'Rosa Negra, Star', two other actors, and the director. 'Homenagem do 'Clarim' á Cia. Negra de Revistas', *O Clarim d'Alvorada*, 11/14/26, p. 1.
65. *Tudo Preto*, p. 2; also p. 4; 'Le Roi s'Amuse', 4th q.; 'Moda Parisiense', p. 31; 'a Mistinguette Brasileira', p. 34.
66. 'Chegou a Companhia Mulata Brasileira que vai trabalhar no República', *O Globo*, 17/12/30, n.p.
67. See Caulfield, *In Defense of Honor*, p. 153.
68. 'Companhia Negra de Revistas. A homenagem do "Centro dos Homens de Côr". Missa em acção de graças na igreja de N.S. do Rosario', and accompanying photo, captioned, 'Aspecto tomado á porta da igreja de N.S. do Rosario, vendo-se entres os presentes varias figuras da Companhia Negra de Revistas', *A Noticia*, 8/19/26, p. 4. The better-known Black Brazilian theatre movement of the 1940s, the *Teatro Experimental do Negro* (Black Experimental Theatre, usually abbreviated TEN), might well recognize its political kinship with the vulgar, comedic, politically ambiguous *Companhia Negra de Revistas*.
69. 'O monumento á Mãe Preta e o presidente eleito da Republica', *Getulino*, 5/13/26,. 1; Ivan, 'Monumento symbolico á Mãe Preta', *Getulino*, 5/13/26, p. 3; Moyses Cintra, 'A Mãe Preta', *O Clarim*, 4/25/26, p. 1; *O Clarim*, 6/20/26. In *Clarim*, to take only the longest-lived Black newspaper, pro-*Mãe Preta* material appeared in 1/15/27; 5/13/27; 6/3/28; 7/1/28; 8/12/28; 9/28/28; 10/21/28; 11/18/28; 1/6/29; 5/13/29; etc.
70. The elite version of the Mãe Preta narrative was nostalgic for slavery, paternalist, condescending, quiescent, sexist, limiting–in short, as racist and reactionary as its North American counterpart, the Black Mammy, lucidly and repeatedly criticized by anti-racist North Americans. Micki McElya, *Monumental Citizenship*, PhD dissertation, New York University (in progress); M.M. Manring, *Slave in a Box: The Strange Career of Aunt Jemimah* (Charlottesville and London: University Press of Virginia, 1998); Michele Wallace, *Black Macho and the Myth of the Superwoman* (London: Verso, 1990 [1979]); Doris Witt, *Black Hunger: Food and the Politics of US Identity* (New York and Oxford: Oxford University Press, 1999).
71. Campos, 'O Brasil Deve ...'.
72. Ibid. (emphases added).
73. Mario Monteiro, 'Monumento á Mãe Preta', *Clarim*, 9/28/28, p. 5, reprinting an article from the mainstream Rio paper *A Notícia*, 12/8/26, n.p., itself reprinting from the *Primeiro de Janeiro* (Porto, Portugal), n.d., n.p.
74. 'Brazil Pays High Honor to Dark Citizens. Brazil to Honor Her Women', Chicago *Defender*, 5/22/26, p. 1. The *Defender* was the African-American paper of greatest circulation in this period. For a discussion of this monument in transnational context, see Micol Seigel, 'Black Mothers, Citizen Sons', Chapter 6 in 'The point of comparison: transnational racial construction in Brazil and the U.S., 1918–1933', PhD dissertation, New York University (2001).

Luis Duno Gottberg

MOB OUTRAGES: REFLECTIONS ON THE MEDIA CONSTRUCTION OF THE MASSES IN VENEZUELA (APRIL 2000–JANUARY 2003)

Turba: Fossil fuel formed by the accumulation of plant remnants in swamps, of dark brown colour, earthy consistency, not heavy, and producing a dense smoke when burned. (*Diccionario de la Real Academia Española*) (Spanish Royal Academy Dictionary)

I. From 'fossil fuel' to 'dangerous people'

In Spanish, the first meaning of the term 'turba' is that of a residual, dark substance used for fuel ('peat' in English) and were it not for this marginal utility it would be a synonym for the abject. It is only in its second meaning that it refers to the idea of a confused and disordered mass, standardly translated into English as 'mob'.[1] But this shift in meaning in Spanish from 'fuel' to 'dangerous mass' turns out to be useful for thinking about the political contentions of contemporary Venezuela.

This essay will investigate the cultural and political meaning of media representations of a number of the popular sectors allied with Chavism, which have been disseminated by the privately owned Venezuelan media. By looking at journalism, press photography and TV, we can 'see how the media produces the crowd', unpicking and analysing media strategies for constructing the collective as an undesirable, rebellious multitude.

I have chosen a quite restricted time frame, looking at the representation of the masses during a few days in April 2002, when Venezuela was shaken by a dizzying series of events: a huge mass demonstration, and then a *coup d'état* and counter-*coup* which followed on from each other in a matter of hours, ejecting President Chávez from power and then restoring him.

There are three basic claims underlying this approach. First, I want to engage with the work of the Colombian theoretician Jesús Martín Barbero, to emphasize that 'mediation' does not designate a neutral space through which discourses pass but is rather a space of hegemonic struggle. Second, despite the obvious differences, I have been inspired by the reflections of Ranajit Guha on Indian peasant rebellions and the studies of E.P. Thompson and Eric Hobsbawm on primitive forms of protest, to show that the construction of collectives in terms of mobs or rabbles constitutes a strategy to remove political legitimacy from marginalized social subjects. Finally, I want to suggest that the so-called 'mob' also reveals its character as social movement when it demands a space of representation in the media, in order to stage *its* rationality and political agency.

II. Civil society and the mob: us and them (the others)

A group of toothless, deformed grotesques are dismantling the Venezuelan national coat of arms (Figure 1). They are making off with everything: the sheaves that represent the states and the interlocked arms that celebrate the Republic's victories over its enemies. We are present just as a white horse, an obvious symbol of freedom, is caught hold of. An upturned horn of abundance spills and scatters the fruits of the fatherland. To the left, there is a character with a gun sticking out of his shorts – and all the participants are wearing shorts, hi-tops without laces and vests. They are running off grimacing and staring wild-eyed, all of them having the same vampire look about them, perhaps because they are illegitimately removing the very stuff of what it is to be Venezuelan. They embody what in the early decades of the twentieth century the philosopher Ortega y Gasset called 'social idiocy' (Ortega y Gasset, 1981: 67), expressing his own stunned reaction to the processes of modernization, democratization and revolution in Europe.[2] In the Venezuelan case, the undifferentiated and violent cartoon characters are the masses who pose a threat to the basic values of the nation and its future stability.

What a difference from the representation in a photograph published a few days earlier, in the context of the *coup d'état* (Figure 2).

As opposed to the image of the mob, we have a different image that elicits much greater sympathy: a group of women, 'civil society', moves forward decisively, holding up another patriotic symbol – the flag. They are dancing, smiling, waving, their features relaxed as they nevertheless move forward in a decisive manner. They walk in unison but without losing their own identity. In the background, various people are extending their arms, as if incorporating and lifting the viewer. The captions confer legitimacy on the group: these are clearly families on the march.

Let us set up a counterpoint between the images. In the first, patriotic symbols are perverted and violated at the hands of an amorphous, violent multitude. In the second, we have brave families demonstrating in honourable fashion, worthy of protection. In the first, we are present at an act of pillage and destruction of nationhood: in the second, we participate in a sort of national exaltation.

The edifying photograph comes from the front page of the daily *El Nacional*, a few hours after the coup on 11 April 2002. The cartoon was published in the daily *El Universal*, after Chávez was reinstated, thanks to a number of different factors, including the willing and organic involvement of large numbers of people from the shantytowns of Caracas. With only a few days difference, the images register a situation where large masses of people came out into the streets to defend different political projects and models of the country. On the radio and television and in the press, one of these groups became known as 'civil society', the other 'the mob'.

This production of audiovisual discourses constitutes an attempt to construct subjectivities through the means of communication, interpellating certain collective

'The masses dismantling the Venezuelan coat of arms'.

FIGURE 1 Source: Rayma Suprani, El Universal, Caracas, 20 April 2002.

'A group of women striding purposefully with the Venezuelan flag'
FIGURE 2 Source: El Nacional, 12 April 2002.

groupings as organized political subjects, or on the other hand, as dangerous masses. The press and TV not only played a fundamental role in the elaboration of a narrative that gave meaning to the events that took place in the streets but also reinforced a social imaginary that sought to legitimize certain subjects and disqualify others.

Sarmiento's dichotomy, embedded in Venezuelan culture through the novels of Rómulo Gallegos, re-emerges when the media show events moving from barbarism to civilization, and then back again.[3] In the image that follows, the opposition to the Chávez government are celebrating their political gains, and are placed on the side of civilization. The animals in the cartoon look discontentedly at the TV screens, where in effect, and as the present study tries to show, part of the struggle for political power is unfolding.

Between the 11 and 12 April 2002, as the coup developed, it became obvious how a certain sort of collectivity – understood as mob, horde, rabble, lumpen – was displaced by contrast to acceptable, democratic and organized political rationalities.

Images taken from Venezuelan TV during the night of 10 April are extremely revealing in this respect. In one of them, one can see an opposition deputy speaking on a podium in front of the principal office of the state oil company.[4] In his speech he stated: 'There are only two ways out of our present situation: the arbitrariness and violence created by the government, or the reconstruction of the republic with decent people, people gathered together here at PDVSA'. But who was there that night? Or rather, who was not there? Must we suppose that the people who were

'Cartoon showing animals watching the struggle for political power unfold'
FIGURE 3 Source: Rayma Suprani, *El Universal*, Caracas, Thursday 5 December 2002.

not there were those whose 'decency' was in question, the mob that could not be constituted as 'civil society'? In any event, a headline from the day after the coup made manifest the project of part of the 'decent people' (Figure 4).

On 13 April, the government installed by the coup was overthrown and Chavism progressively returned to power. Though events were confused, one of the clearest factors involved was the way in which a multitude of inhabitants from the shantytowns came out onto the streets demanding the return of the deposed president. However, the mass media chose to render this contingent invisible. Some days later they did get around to 'registering' the return of the undesirable, rebellious people

'Newspaper headline the day following the coup.'

FIGURE 4 Source: *El Universal*, 13 April 2002.

but this was due to otherwise external factors – for example, the actions of a sector of the army – or because of the strength of the people's growing, pre-political power. Nevertheless, the media still suggested that the mob did not really know what it was doing: it was swayed by its leader, or moved by base emotions, failing to exercise its will in rational fashion. This last element is significant and is connected to a recurrent rhetoric used to demean the political rationality of popular sectors that support the government.

This refusal to accept that the masses can possess political agency is common in the media, and not just in the present situation. It is worth recalling what Carlos Monsiváis mentions in another context, when discussing the media representation of the masses during the 1985 Mexican earthquake, and the media's incapacity to recognize the demonstrations of self-management and solidarity: 'the producers of TV programmes cannot conceive of a society that moves on its own account'.

In the Venezuelan case we have another type of shock and the mass media tell the same sort of story: 'those people' go on marches because they get paid to, or because it gives them a chance to get drunk. In the cartoon shown in figure 5 we see demonstrators surrounded by what appear to be flies, with pig-like faces flushed with booze.

'Cartoon of two demonstrators'
FIGURE 5 *Source:* Rayma Suprani, *El Universal*, Caracas, Friday 24 January 2003.

These representations have numerous important precursors. An extremely offensive example was published in an editorial in the newspaper *El Nacional*, some months before the events we are discussing, when a Chavist demonstration was criticized in the following terms:

> The response of the President and his entourage to the concerns of Venezuelan society about the grave crisis we are experiencing ... consisted of bringing the usual lumpen in from the interior of the country once again, bussing them in with their lump of bread and bottle of rum.[5]

Another example of this media construction of social subjects in exclusionary terms is apparent in a headline of *El Nacional* on 19 July 2002. On the front page, we read

'Civil Society Bangs its Casseroles'. The headline refers to a group opposed to the Chávez government, who had expressed their discontent on this occasion by banging their pots and pans in the streets. However, some readers were irritated by what they perceived as an attempt to define 'civil society' in restricted terms, given that the headline appeared to take for granted that government sympathizers could not form part of the so-called 'third sector'. The response of the newspaper was even more symptomatic, defending itself from criticism with the argument that it was increasingly difficult to work out who was part of 'civil society'. This reply might suggest that what is really problematic is the visibility of a new social subject: 'the mob', whose political action is unrepresentable or inconceivable in terms of a legitimate project. In this sense, it is interesting to recall Ortega y Gasset again, and his reference in a different context to the new visibility of the masses and their 'invasion' of spaces previously reserved for select minorities:

> The individuals who make up these throngs had a previous existence but not as crowds. Scattered across the world in little groups or on their own, they carried on with their lives in divergent ways, dissociated and distant from each other. Whether individual or small group, each occupied their own place – in the countryside, in the village, in the town, or in the *barrio* of the large city. Now suddenly, they appear in agglomerations, and our eyes witness throngs everywhere we look. Everywhere? No, no: precisely in the best places, in the relatively refined domains of human culture, previously reserved for smaller groups and certainly for minorities. The throng, suddenly become visible, has occupied the preferential sites of society. Previously, if it existed, it passed unnoticed and was the backdrop of the social stage.... (1981: 67)

The pieces that I am bringing together do not in fact constitute isolated examples but are part of a wider design, an imaginary widely transmitted on Venezuelan TV and in the press: an imaginary that marks off a legitimate 'us' which restores the interests of the nation in the face of a barbaric other which undermines them. And this could all be inscribed in a sequence of historical representations that run from the colonial representation of runaway slaves to the looting of the Caracas uprising in 1989.

III. The colours of the mob

Turba (*Mob*): '*Fuel … dark brown in colour, earthy,* not too heavy, producing a dark smoke when burned.

It is difficult to discuss the subject of racism in Venezuela. We are convinced that the '*mestizo* motherland' and the 'café con leche people' are strangers to this kind of discrimination.[6] So that we can assume the issue to have been resolved we do not talk about it. However, this comforting discourse on Venezuelan *mestizaje*, articulated through what I call the ethno-populist imaginary, must be carefully dismantled.[7] The study of the media representation-production of the mob seems to suggest that contemporary political conflicts undergo subtle forms of racialization and that the consensus that preceded the Chavist regime was based on covering over the prejudices that have underlain the design of the nation.

In an article published in the paper *El País* in 1944, Andrés Eloy Blanco, poet and founding member of the Venezuelan social democratic party, compared the racial composition of Venezuela with 'café con leche'.[8] The article was a response to a letter from a friend, who told him that the Brazilian government was thinking of resolving 'the Negro problem' by offering whites a stipend if they married Afro-Brazilian people. Eloy Blanco thought the proposal offensive and unrealistic, particularly for his compatriots who had reached a 'racial balance' after several centuries of *mestizaje*.

Later in his article, Eloy Blanco recalls a conversation with a North American professor, to whom he said: 'you have never worked out how to make coffee or how to treat the Negroes. Your coffee is too light and your Negroes too black.... If America has to be white, I prefer our method of making coffee ... [a]nd our way of making *café con leche*, which will be a bit slower, but better.' By using these words, the author of 'Little Black Angels', a founding member of a party that had a number of people of Afro-Venezuelan origin in its lower echelons, managed to articulate the hoary old notions of 'whitening' and cultural assimilation with a supposedly anti-racist discourse. African components are thus gathered to the national bosom, only in so far as they are on their way to becoming 'white'.

It is interesting in the light of these ideas to look at a novel like *Pobre Negro* by another founding member of Acción Democrática, Rómulo Gallegos, where the freeing of the slaves is seen to bring conflict in its wake if it is not accompanied by the complete integration, or assimilation of the Negro: 'That very freedom had complicated his life, promising him a narrow road which promptly led to the *impasse* of tyrannical necessity' (1937: 117), the narrator says.

Conflicts seem to be attenuated toward the end of the novel. The rebellion of the main character, Pedro Miguel, wanes under the influence of Luisana's *mestizo* love. The foundational romance thus confirms the whitening of a nation where in theory the races have found their natural balance. Gallegos writes: 'No longer a battlefield between irreconcilable races, as he previously came to fear it, but quite the opposite, the constructive harmony of a nation which will face its future with decisiveness and courage, accepting in full consciousness the *fait accompli* of *mestizaje*' (1937: 89).

This brings us back to the words that the narrator places in the mouth of another character, Cecilio. These show how a certain teleology is imposed on the Afro-Venezuelan, who seems to be conceived in the text as a subject in process of 'perfection' through *mestizaje*: 'Pedro Miguel is not the common, opportunistic fruit of blind appetites, nor of the disturbance of a pure soul, *but the dramatic offspring of a plan that had to be accomplished, of an idea in search of its form*' (1937: 51). That form – constituted as fate and celebrated by liberal intellectuals such as Blanco and Gallegos – emerges from the dissolution of the African element.

Gallegos and Blanco, the founders of Venezuela's most important populist party, thus celebrate the synthesis of the national based on the erasure of the Black subject. Is there not an equivalence here with the celebration of a racial democracy which has displaced discussions about racism and discrimination? The synthesis of what it is to be Venezuelan, our condition as 'café con leche' subjects, makes such a discussion

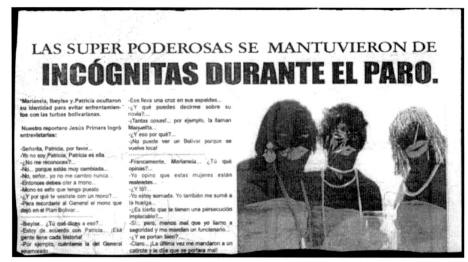

'Three journalists disguised'
FIGURE 6 Source: El Camaleón, El Nacional.

seem absurd given the *mestizo* reality of a country that guaranteed the participation of all Venezuelans in national affairs.

Nevertheless, a reading of messages transmitted by the mass media during the period we are studying throws up clear evidence that part of the national political imaginary is articulated on the basis of racist thought. In the pages of the supplement *El Camaleón*, which appears in the daily *El Nacional*, there appeared a cartoon showing three well-known journalists opposed to the Chávez government disguised as a 'mob'. In the drawing, these professionals appear as rag dolls, painted black, so as to pass unnoticed by 'those violently opposed to them'.

Inter alia, the text puns on the meaning of 'mono', which in Venezuela also refers to a debt that is due as well as designating a humble person of colour (in addition to meaning 'monkey'). In this string of meanings, it is pointed out that the permanent use of disguise means that the characters must start to smell 'like monkeys'. What is really interesting here is that the cartoon assumes that the mob is in some way dark, like the first meaning given in the *DRAE*, and that 'civil society' has a light skin. If not, what sense would it have for the journalists to wear camouflage to escape from what the text calls the 'Bolivarian mob'?

Let us look at another example. An image repeated on innumerable occasions by Caracas TV stations was that of a protest outside the newspaper *El Nacional*. The most widely seen segment showed a very agitated Afro-Venezuelan. The manipulation of the image, that is the editing and the use of paratexts to accompany it, was such that it seemed to 'register' violence unleashed by a subject surrendering to 'atavistic impulses'. The cameras repeatedly showed drums, cutting to a close-up of the subject, whilst the commentators made reference to 'violent elements' apparently carrying out a witchcraft ritual. On this occasion, however, there was no violence directed against the newspaper. For his part, the demonstrator was simply yelling slogans and the drums were nothing more than part of the country's own culture.[9]

Another eloquent example was presented by the broadcast on 19 December 2002 of the TV programme 'Today's Headlines' by Globovisión. On this occasion, the linkman, Orlando Urdaneta, gave a long disquisition on what he called 'ugly people', where the populist gesture of the discourse of *mestizaje* was linked to a series of subsequent commentaries that were openly racist.

> Why aah? A country full of beautiful Black women and men, of impressive Indian men and women, of people of mixed blood, proud of the best master brewer, for the quality of that marvellous mix, ahh, the best European produce with that Creole magic, why then so many ugly people? Where do they get them from? It's like a Fellini film, but without the Italian's talent….

In the first part we can see ideas linked to what I have called ethno-populist discourse, building on *mestizaje* to give acceptability to the ethnic components that flow into the national subject. In this case, the responsibility for mixing falls on the 'master brewer' who joins 'the best produce of Europe' with 'Creole magic'.

Urdaneta makes no reference to the violent processes of assimilation that Blacks and Natives were subject to but only to something incidental to *mestizaje*, charmingly characterized as 'magical'. We should not get caught up in this problematic image but who is this master who does the mixing, what does all this have to do with magic, and where does this leave Black and Indigenous people? Let us pass on to another fragment of Urdaneta's discourse, which clearly demonstrates how this rhetorical and paternalist gesture becomes a frankly offensive posture.

> Aristóbulo, for example, remember when he was working here? Didn't he look better? Now this is really pronounced (*indicates his mouth*). He looks like he's suffering from gorilla jaw. Now that I've said gorilla, haven't you analysed the gestures I was telling you about? There's some Cro-Magnon influence, Neanderthal, 'monastic' then, almost at the level of banana.[10] If you don't believe me, try and watch Vale TV, which every once in a while shows really interesting documentaries about these jewels of the animal kingdom.[11]

We could use other examples of the racialization of the mob taken from Venezuelan humour, where there is a remarkable amount of real prejudice in between the laughs[12] – for example, the jokey commentaries of the journalist Marianela Salazar on that dangerous mixture of Black and Native, the *zambo*. But nevertheless we will go straight on to the subject of the decontextualization of violence.

IV. The mob on fire

Turba: … *producing a dark smoke when burned* (ibid.)

The Spanish Royal Academy Dictionary indicates that, despite its light consistency, peat gives off a black smoke when it burns. This appears to coincide with what the media report when they show us a disordered, violent collective, moving through the spaces of the city. The image of *chavistas* on motorbikes has been recurrent and links up with memories of the Caracas uprising in 1989, when the lootings as well as the

'A large group of motorbikes wreathed in smoke'
FIGURE 7 Source: *El Nacional*, 12 April 2002.

resistance to police repression were organized by people on motorbikes.[13] Let us look at an image from the days of the coup, from 11 April 2002.

It is often said that a photograph is worth a thousand words, indicating the eloquence and realism of this privileged form of representation. However, Barthes has questioned the medium's 'reality effect'. He points out that the analogical character of photography, its capacity for denotation, coexists with procedures for connotation, which codify the analogical photograph through resources like cropping and selection (Barthes, 1986: 11–17). In the case of press photography there are also other resources to fall back on, such as captions and headlines, that define lines of reading and determine the meaning of the image.

The page of *El Nacional* that we reproduce here is a good example of the former. This refers to an incident when there was an exchange of gunfire and shows a large group on motorbikes wreathed in smoke – the black smoke of the mob – riding through the streets in the centre of Caracas. Without the headline, what would be violent about the image? Are we meant to think that these people are somehow involved in the shootout? This was not the case, but the composition of the text and photograph seem to suggest it.

Another fantasy that was revived in the Venezuelan media was that of looting: violence against private property carried out by the resentful or envious mob.

> The throng, with passive soul, lets itself be carried to the worst excesses.... (In) the city there were riots and reprisals. Innocent machines and other more useful ones were dragged out from a printing works, where a servile gramophone recorded its flattery of the fallen government, and scattered throughout the city by drunken looters, to the joy of watching rogues. Revenge ... was

taken ... against defenceless houses. That human torrent swollen with hate, rancour and envy respected nothing.... Portraits, furniture and pieces of art, when not completely destroyed by sticks, swords and knives, were thrown into the ravines. Intimate objects, destined normally never to emerge from the discrete penumbra of the alcove, were brought into the harsh light of the streets.... Drunk with vertigo, taking courage from the confusion, shielded by the dense, disordered multitude, certain treacherous, vile hearts began to exact their personal revenge. (Díaz Rodríguez: 1981: 202)

One or two anachronisms reveal that I am playing a trick on the reader by introducing a fragment from *Broken Idols*, a novel published in 1901 by the Venezuelan writer Manuel Díaz Rodríguez, where he describes the violence of a mob given over to looting. As Venezuela struggles to modernize at the beginning of the twentieth century, the writer gives a horrifying representation of the barbarous throng that the national project had to control.

The anachronistic counterpoint serves to point up the spectacular character of the representation of looting in Venezuelan media. The fictional and mass media imaginaries of looting unfold an irrational and gratuitous violence that occludes the historical character of these demonstrations.[14]

Eric Hobsbawm refers precisely to the omnipresence of violence in the mass media and to its character as spectacle. The author discusses the particularity of different manifestations of social violence and suggests that a lack of determination in the phenomenon has consequences of a political order: 'It is altogether useless, except as a juridical excuse for repression or as an argument in the debate about "not giving in to force", to treat these different types and degrees of violent action as essentially indistinguishable' (1999: 195). The violence of the 'common people', historians like Hobsbawm and Thomson have shown us, can be constituted by the political actions of 'uncommon people'. With regard to Venezuela, studies like those of Yolanda Salas and Margarita López Maya have tried to uncover the political articulation of such actions in the context of the Caracas uprising. The same has to be done with the events of April 2002. It is not sufficient to say that the violence that characterizes looting is a product of resentment.

V. Media, mediation and hegemony

Gramsci's reflections on hegemony opened the way to an explanation of the relations between social control and the processes of symbolic production and distribution. In this sense, hegemony is a form of power that derives from intellectual or moral leadership and is different from the openly coercive forces of military power, for example. A ruling class seeks to ensure its control by creating forms of political and cultural consensus by means of diverse institutions: unions, political parties, schools, churches, and of course the media. The latter are today fundamental to the production of reality, as they traverse different social spaces and normalize the dominant ideology. Nevertheless, this model has to be understood in dynamic terms, as the Venezuelan case demonstrates, given that the consumers of the media are not passive subjects.[15]

'Cartoon describing looting as a product of resentment'
FIGURE 9 Source: Rayma Suprani, *El Universal*, Caracas, Sunday 21 April 2002.

Along these lines, Jesús Martín Barbero has issued a call to rethink the mass culture industry from the point of view of hegemony, and points out that in doing so there would be a repositioning of 'problems in the space where cultural practices and social movements connect, that is, in the *historical* space of the displacements of social legitimacy which leads from the imposition of submission to the search for consensus' (1991: 94). The author then goes on to show how the mass media 'construct their discourse with a basis in the *continuity* of the imaginary of the masses with narrative, dramatic, and popular-iconographic memory' (1991: 177). This interpellation of the popular creates spaces of recognition that articulate the national on the basis of an imaginary and sensibility that derive from the subaltern classes. According to this argument, the people can see themselves portrayed in the media, and thus, the definition of the national is widened. But what happens when a particular social group does not see itself represented? If today social mediation passes through mediatic mediation, then the suppression and stigmatization of particular subjects in this latter circuit constitute forms of social exclusion.

In subsequent work, Martín Barbero recognizes that 'the communication media today constitute spaces that are decisive for social recognition' and that mediation 'has come to constitute, to be part of the web of discourses and political action itself' (1999: 50). Nevertheless, with its marked emphasis on the possibilities of agency by the consuming public, Martín Barbero's theory cannot help us understand the phenomena at issue in the case of Venezuelan communication media, where the imaginary of consensus stops functioning for a period of time, and a curious exercise of exclusion is put into practice, operating through stigmatizing representations of a sector of national life designated as 'the mob'. Here the media have come to constitute a preponderant political force that outlines the profile of the citizen and the nation in terms of exclusion.

This hiatus in the function of mediation was slowly suspended towards December 2002, when a new TV company began to incorporate popular subjects from the shantytowns of Caracas in television propaganda against the Chávez government. In this instance, the imaginary tried once more to establish a space of recognition that in populist terms would cover a larger number of Venezuelans. From the point of view of hegemony, this strategy could be seen as a readjustment. This is how Fiske sees it in his study of TV culture: 'hegemony is a constant struggle against a multitude of resistances to ideological domination, and any balance of forces that it achieves is always precarious, always in need of re-achievement' (Fiske, 1987: 41).

In one of the videos financed by the organization 'Civic Alliance', we can see a dark-skinned woman saying that the government is starving poor people to death; in another, financed by 'Solidarity', a man with indigenous features says that the country is in crisis and is on the road to Communism. These media images once more give coverage to excluded sectors. The 'people' is redeemed in this new mode of representation, offered up in terms that are in line with the interests of the media themselves.

Here I would go back to the reflections by Santiago Castro Gómez in order to rethink the connections between hegemony, media and mediation. Castro Gómez is responding to the turn taken by media theory after its questioning of the determinist aspects of the Frankfurt School. Without retreating to such positions, Castro Gómez points out that we cannot go to the opposite extreme and ignore the relations of power that determine the circulation of discourses and the formation of imaginaries (or to use Althusserian terminology, the reproduction of ideology).

> ... I disagree with those cultural analysts for whom the media have extended the space of the public, and have thus become instruments of democracy. The media would thus be something like the postmodern agora where all opinions could be discussed, where all interests could be contested and all ideological positions could be engaged with. The media appear as *neutral spaces* for the formation of the citizenry.... But then they reveal themselves incapable of laying out the links with political economy and demonstrating that information is just that: a process of in-forming, giving ideological form to a pre-existent material. ('Althusser, cultural studies and the concept of ideology', http://www.campus-oei.org/salactsi/castro3.htm)

Thus the celebratory theories of the media, like that of Martín Barbero, need to be rethought so that they show the degree of conflict inherent in the process of mediatic mediation and social mediation. The production of the imaginary of the mob in the Venezuelan press and TV is an example of the strategies of the formation of national citizens in exclusionary terms.

VI. Mediation negotiated (with rocks)

On 13 April 2002, towards nightfall, groups of demonstrators on motorbikes and on foot lay siege to the various TV channels in the capital. They threw rocks and broke windows. The images that the TV channels under attack put together were disturbing. Or perhaps not. In the days after the coup, the media decided not to represent the adverse reaction of the popular sectors to the overthrow of President Chávez. The people who raced out into the streets had no existence in the Venezuelan press or on Venezuelan TV. The TV stations showed cartoons, whilst a multitude rose up against the replacement government headed by Pedro Carmona Estanga, the president of the country's bosses' organization.

A notable incident took place in front of Radio Caracas Televisión, when a group of citizens demanded that the station inform its audience of what was going on in the country. After the mediation of the Ombudsman, the channel's director of information, Eduardo Sapene, agreed to transmit the demonstrators' communiqué. However, the latter were incensed when they found out that the images went out on air without sound.[16]

Something similar happened with Venevisión, when a cameraman made a copy of a transmission that never went out on air. When the channel's representatives agreed to transmit the demonstrators' messages, they were accompanied by an image with a rubric that said that the transmission was a consequence of pressure exerted by these people. Once again there was a dispute with the demonstrators, who threw stones at the building.

The media's motives in taking such decisions are not so important; what is interesting is the reaction of the 'mob', which demanded that it be represented. I think that this reveals the consciousness of these social groups of the importance of what Bourdieu has called 'media arbitration' (1997: 87). It would appear that in this instance 'the mob' knew that mediation through television guaranteed social and political existence.

A notable example of this was reluctantly picked up by the Televén channel. In this instance, the camera was looking out from inside the building and focused on a silhouette leaning on a metal grille that separated the figure from the journalists. A voice said:

> We want you to listen to us. Because we have had more than a week, more than a week, listening to this terrorism by the media, OK, and here we are a huge section of the people, the popular sectors, who don't have the money that the powerful do, who you allow to transmit what they want every day, something else. But the people expressed themselves through the vote, putting President Chávez in power and we demand that this be respected. Respected, because we are Venezuelans too. And we also want to be listened to, and that [our voices] be transmitted via TV.[17]

VI. Conclusion: the media counter-insurgent imaginary

Despite the differences, this counterpoint of images leads me to read the representation of the masses by the Venezuelan press and TV, along the lines that Ranajit Guha has suggested, looking for what we might call 'a media counter-insurgent imaginary'.

I am referring to that discourse which, through the mass media, attempts to abolish the political rationality of rebellious social subjects through their representation in terms of atavism, boundless violence, lack of will, ignorance and so on.

This process, revolving around the delegitimization of a certain popular political rationality, prepares the field both for exclusion and for repressive violence. In this sense, it is worth recalling articles published in *El Nacional*, a little after the coup against Chávez, which posed the question as to what to do with the demands of those who wanted to restore the government. One of the article headings, which made use of the opinions of academics and social scientists to lend an air of authority, seems to respond to the question: 'It will be necessary to employ violence, if you want the poor to keep quiet'.[18] It is always easier to repress 'the mob' than 'civil society'.

If we begin with the existence of this discursive mechanism that I have called the media counter-insurgent imaginary, then we can understand that *mob outrages are really the expression of a political will which obeys its own, legitimate rationality*. In a word, what has been labelled mob, rabble, lumpen has often been a political actor that has challenged power.

Notes

1   The English 'mob' doesn't have the same double sense. However, the idea of the 'mob' as 'mobile vulgus', 'an excitable crowd bent on lawless violence', is appropriate. Here the issue is the restless nature of the collective. In French the word 'tourbe' has the double meaning that we find in Spanish.
2   In the first part of *The Rebellion of the Masses,* Ortega y Gasset states that the most important fact about contemporary European public life 'is the coming of the masses to full social power' (1981: 65), and this constitutes a grave crisis inasmuch as they 'by definition cannot *and ought not* to control their own existence' (1981: 65, emphasis added).
3   In particular, the novel *Doña Bárbara* (1929), which has come to embody the grand Venezuelan narrative of civilization versus barbarism.
4   The state oil company, PDVSA, was a crucial site for the events of those days. The opponents of the Chávez government gathered there and it was the starting point for the march to the government palace, near which took place some of the bloody incidents that preceded the *coup* on 11 April.
5   *El Nacional*, 'The Government's Response', 14 October 2002.
6   A good study of the problem is Wright (1996).
7   Our starting point is Laclau's concept of populism (1979), according to which: 'what transforms an ideological discourse into a populist one is a *peculiar form of articulation* of the popular-democratic interpellations in it ... *populism consists in the presentation of popular-democratic interpellations as a synthetic-antagonistic complex with respect to the dominant ideology*.... Populism starts at the point where popular-democratic elements are presented as an antagonistic option against the ideology of the dominant bloc. Note that this does not mean that populism is always *revolutionary*. It is sufficient for a class or class fraction to need a substantial transformation in the power bloc in order to assert its hegemony, for a populist experience to be possible' (Laclau, 1979: 172–73, emphasis in the original). Ethno-populism would

constitute a form of popular interpellation that begins from a determinate configuration of subjects that supposedly share certain biological or cultural features. The discourse essentializes the constitution of the people, inventing its past and predicting its future as a cohesive project. I have studied this problem in more detail in *Solventar las diferencias. La ideología del mestizaje cubano*. Frankfurt, Madrid: Veuveurt-Iberomamericana, 2003.
8   *El País*, 25 April 1944.
9   Here we can see one of the discursive strategies that Bourdieu discusses in his well-known essay On television: hiding by revealing. That is, the strategic selection of actions and happenings that surround an event and its consequent fabrication on the basis of the interests which constrain the news media (1997: 24–9). The demonstration occurred, there is no doubt, but what was more complex to work out was how it happened.
10 He is referring to Aristóbulo Istúriz, the Minister of Education, who had a programme for while on this channel. The joke is about the minister's looks, a consequence of his being Afro-Venezuelan. Then he refers to Chávez, who is made fun of for being a *zambo*. We can see another allusion to 'mono' (monkey) with the joke word 'monastic', which properly refers to monastery but is turned by the presenter's fury into an allusion to apes.
11 Archive images, 19 December 2002, 'Today's Headlines', Globovisión.
12 See appendix.
13 These references are to messengers on motorbikes who undertake various errands for very poor pay. They live in the poorest parts of the city.
14 A second aspect requires more wide-ranging studies. It suggests the possibility of a link between the perception of an 'undocile' and 'uncivilized' people spread after the revolts that shook Venezuela during the Federal wars and the uncomfortable visibility of a new social subject that took public space and which the media have called 'the mob'.
15 'Whether and to what extent hegemony is achieved by the dominant class in a specific period is a matter for investigation. The use of the term hegemony to suggest the unending and unproblematic exercise of class power, and the complete incorporation of the subordinate classes into the dominant class culture, sacrifices the capacity for historical specificity that the concept possessed in Gramsci's usage' (Thomson, 1986: 123).
16 Archives of the Ombudsman. Witness statements. Report on the events of 11–14 April 2002.
17 Archive image, 13 April 2002, Televén.
18 El Nacional, 21 April 2002. One of the specialists consulted in this article states: 'the State yielded the monopoly of violence to anarchist groups, and the only way to re-establish control is through the repression of those groups'.

References

Primary sources

El Nacional, Caracas, Venezuela, 1998–2003..
El Universal, Caracas, Venezuela, 1998–2003.
Así es la Noticia, Caracas, Venezuela, 2002–2003.

Globovisión, April 2002–January 2003.
Radio Caracas Televisión, April 2002–January 2003.
Televén, April 2002–January 2003. *Theory.*
Barthes, Roland. 1986. *Lo obvio y lo obtuso. Imágenes, gestos, voces.* Barcelona: Paidós.
Bennett, W. Lance, and Robert, M. Entman. 2001. *Mediated Politics. Communication in the Future of Democracy.* Cambridge: Cambridge University Press.
Bourdieu, Pierre. 1997. *Sobre la televisión.* Barcelona: Anagrama.
Castro Gómez, Santiago. 'Althusser, los estudios culturales y el concepto de ideología'. Available at http://www.campus-oei.org/salactsi/castro3.htm
Fiske, J. 1987. *Television culture.* London: Routledge.
Hobsbawm, Eric. 1999. *Gente poco corriente. Resistencia, rebelión y jazz.* Barcelona: Crítica.
Hobsbawm, Eric. 1959. *Primitive Rebels: Studies in Archaic Forms of Social Movement in the 19th and 20th Centuries.* New York: Norton.
Laclau, Ernesto. 1979. *Politics and Ideology in Marxist Theory. Capitalism, Fascism, Populism.* London: Verso.
Martín-Barbero, Jesús. 1991. *De los medios a las mediaciones. Comunicación, cultura y hegemonía.* México–Bogotá: Ediciones G. Gill..
Martín-Barbero, Jesús. 1999) El miedo a los medios. Política, comunicación y nuevos modos de representación. *Nueva Sociedad* No. 161, Caracas.
Ortega y Gasset, José. 1981. *La rebelión de las masas.* Madrid: Espasa-Calpe (1st edn 1930).
Thomson, K. 1986. *Beliefs and Ideology.* London: Tavistock Publications.
Wright, Winthrop. 1996. *Café con Leche. Race, Class, and National Image in Venezuela.* Austin: University of Texas Press.

Venezuelan narrative.

Díaz Rodríguez, Manuel. 1981. *Ídolos rotos.* Caracas: Vadell Hermanos Ed.
Gallegos, Rómulo. 1937. *Pobre negro.* Caracas: Editorial Elite.
Gallegos, Rómulo. 1954. *Doña Bárbara.* Mexico: Fondo de cultura económica.
http://www.producto.com.ve/224/notas/informe.html (*Revista Producto*. An account of the April events that gives the media's response to accusations of partiality).
Monsiváis, Carlos. 1988) Los días del terremoto (Earthquake days). In *Escenas de pudor y liviandad.* México: Grijalbo.

Appendix

The following text was widely circulated on the Net and was then commented on in various media, as something amusing:

APPLICATION TO JOIN THE BOLIVARIAN CIRCLES

Name:...Age:... Alias:... Charges Pending:... Sentences Served:...

COURSES TAKEN
( ) none
( ) primary school
( ) secondary school?!

PLACE OF BIRTH
( ) public jeep
( ) in the bushes
( ) in jail
( ) on the banks of the Güaire
( ) in a brothel

NAME OF PARENTS
( ) don't remember
( ) haven't got any
( ) found in the streets when I was little
( ) they died in a settling of accounts

MOTHER'S PROFESSION
( ) prostitute
( ) collects cans
( ) sells sausages
( ) drug tester
( ) glue sniffer

FATHER'S PROFESSION
( ) crook
( ) pusher
( ) drunk
( ) kidnapper
( ) carjacker
( ) corrupt
( ) all of the above

PROFESSION
( ) unemployed
( ) convict
( ) rock thrower
( ) paid motor biker
( ) marcher (if they pay)
( ) corrupt
( ) all of the above

OTHER SOURCE OF INCOME
( ) bus crier
( ) moonlighter
( ) odd job man
( ) child prostitution
( ) selling babies
( ) marching for the robolution

ILLNESSES
( ) cerebral paralysis
( ) schizophrenia
( ) St Vitus Dance

( ) Berri-Berri
( ) all at the same time

HOBBIES
( ) burning tyres
( ) throwing rocks
( ) getting pissed
( ) producing kids
( ) smoking crack
( ) all of the above

PETS
( ) ticks
( ) lice
( ) crabs
( ) house rats
( ) all of them

NOTE:
IN CASE THE CHAVISTAS FIND THIS ON A MARCH, DON'T WORRY, THEY'RE ILLITERATE

Translated by Philip Derbyshire

The City Cross-dressed: Sexual Rights and Roll-backs in De la Rúa's Buenos Aires

ANA GABRIELA ÁLVAREZ

> The license and immunity that were enjoyed during those three awful days were cruelly felt by the cultivated classes. Revenge was taken in many ways: houses were broken into, women assaulted, the tails of frock-coats were cut off and the arrogance and pride of gentlemen were punished. (Jose María Ramos Mejía, *Rosas and his Time*)

When the city of Buenos Aires regained its political independence, it was seen as a victory for Porteño civil society, and received universal support from progressive intellectuals and the media. Buenos Aires, as the national capital, had from the beginning of the nineteenth century had its head of local government appointed by the president of the Republic. The reform of the national constitution that President Menem carried out in 1994 so as to allow him to serve a second term in office also granted political autonomy to the city of Buenos Aires. It was stipulated that the city would have a 'system of independent government, with its own jurisdiction and mechanisms for legislation, and its head of government would be directly elected by the people of the city'.

In June 1996, the Porteños duly elected a head of government for the city, as well as 'representatives who would promulgate the founding statutes for the municipal institutions'. Just as in the previous national elections, FREPASO,[1] led by Graciela Fernandez Meijide, the mother of one of the disappeared, gained a majority of the Constituent Assembly. However, the executive office fell into the hands of the Radical candidate, Fernando de la Rúa.

The sessions held by the Constituent Assembly in the August of that year seemed to promise a political future that, by contrast with the dark ages of Menem's administration, held out great hopes for change. During that month, human rights organizations and sexual minorities groups[2] held round the clock vigils in the park surrounding the National Library, where the Assembly was holding its sessions, and pushed for their demands to be included on the agenda for discussion. This had results that would have been unthinkable a few months before. It was agreed that the established police ordinances should be repealed and that new legislation should be enacted, at the latest three months after the assumption of office by the new city council, otherwise the old ordinances would be automatically repealed.

From the city government taking office in May 1997, then, it was clear that Buenos Aires would once again be a 'laboratory', a showcase for 'what ought to be'. Reforms that would benefit the winning coalition would be tried out in the city, before being extended to the country at large.

Some months later in August, the leading lights of the Radicals (UCR), Alfonsín, his former economics minister Terragno, and De la Rúa met with Chacho Alvarez and Graciela Fernandez Meijide and agreed a programme for the forthcoming presidential elections of 1999. Thus the Alliance for Labour, Justice and Education was forged (Alianza), and it was Buenos Aires that was to be the first place where the accords would be worked out.

Thus in the course of the debate on the repeal of the police ordinances there was a modification of the balance of power between both parties, and an important part of the strategy of the Radical leadership (with the more or less grudging approval of FREPASO) could be read in terms of a reterritorialization of urban sovereignty, an operation which looks to the production of a new bearer of new civic virtues: the 'neighbour', or 'resident'. The resident was a figure that reterritorialized urban space according to certain values associated with property and morality (and with moral propriety). As the articulating figure of a new hegemonic it was distinguished by its use of the rhetoric and forms of representation that had emerged from social movements (protest marches, collections of signatures, public meetings etc.). At the same time its production created a new legitimacy for the repressive forces now charged with the protection of the space of the neighbourhood (district) against those who do not belong. It is thus an attempt to displace liberal discourse for which everyone is a citizen (albeit if often only at the level of rhetoric).

It was the repeal of existing police ordinances and their replacement by a Code of Co-existence (Código de Convivencia) that would become the main media scenario for this redefinition of the city as resident-space, as an aggregate of neighbourhoods besieged by undesirables who did not belong, who, that is, were not residents.

In March 1998, the City Legislature approved the new Co-existence Code, which was nevertheless open to amendment. There was a period of 150 days during which different opinions might be heard before the Code received its final form. What constituted a contravention of the code was not established in any conclusive manner, only what would be *considered* as such, what would potentially constitute conduct with an impact on peaceful social coexistence. Up to this point, the passing of the new Code had only been touched on in the political sections of the newspapers. But now it entered centre stage. A previously minor piece of political news was suddenly the front page story and the main item on TV news programmes. De la Rúa proposed that both aspects of soliciting for prostitution (the offer and the buying) should be penalized and was seen waving opinion polls carried out by his own executive office which confirmed that 'the great majority of the citizens of Buenos Aires' agreed with his project. The recently elected progressive city legislators, who a few days earlier had been talking up the legislature as a new Greek polis, now stood facing the cameras having only been informed of matters minutes before going on air. The legislators now cast doubt on the whole procedure, having to explain exactly what the police ordinances were and having to apologize for the lack of debate prior to their repeal.

Suddenly it was the 'residents' who were the new protagonists, though in fact what the media presented in all innocence as 'residents' turned out to be the leading lights of an *ad hoc* organization called the, ACACPCD (the Co-operative Association of Residents of Campaña del Desierto Plaza). When the city ratified the first Code, there were street demonstrations by Palermo[3] 'residents'. These, however, were made up mostly of middle-aged men and women, accompanied by lots of children carrying placards that read 'Protect our families, our property and our way of life. It is your duty!', 'We don't want Buenos Aires to be an independent city of Drag Queens!'. The demonstrators complained loudly to the cameras about the decline in value of their houses, and made a show of lifting up their children, saying that the kids had to see the meat market that the pavements and hallways had become. Somehow it was always the parents who spoke, never the children. But there would also be other activists there—travesti,[4] gay, lesbian, female prostitutes—defending the first version of the Code that had been ratified.

What was being fought over in this media event? Essentially whether female and *travesti* prostitutes should be allowed to trade in sex on the city streets. The debate was thus centred on two main actors: the 'residents' and the 'travestis', the 'drag queens'.

In the following months the Code was modified several times, and each time it became more strict and more punitive. First, in June of that year, Alianza representatives agreed to an amendment whereby it was expressly stated that 'the city of Buenos Aires does not prohibit nor regulate prostitution' but did penalize 'disturbances of the peace outside residential buildings, educational establishments or churches' caused by concentrations of female or travesti prostitutes, and 'noise, insults, threats or preventing the right of way' of vehicles or pedestrians. The agents of enforcement would be city officials, and the police would only be there as back-up. This was proposed as a compromise between De la Rúa's proposal to completely prohibit the sex trade on the streets and the first version of the Code. There was much horse-trading with the Menemist senators and deputies, who accused the Alianza of 'promoting prostitution', lack of morality and other outrages. But when De la Rúa gained the Alianza nomination for president, he and the right-wing elements of the UCR rapidly came to dominate the UCR and the Alianza as a whole, and eventually during the sweltering month of March 1999, the leaders of both parties 'required' the legislators to vote for a final version of the Code. Article 71 of the New Co-existence Code made it an offence 'to offer or to request sexual services in a public place, either for oneself or on behalf of another'. There were only four votes against.

The National Penal Code does not criminalize prostitution, which makes Argentina one of the most progressive countries in the world with respect to its norms on prostitution. However, the Buenos Aires City Legislature now prohibits what the National Constitution does not.[5]

The once progressive legislators now defended themselves by aligning themselves with the changes of the summer: on behalf of the 'legitimate' inhabitants of a neighbourhood, and against those subjects who were portrayed at best as noisy and militant, and at worst as perverts and corrupting elements they had to obey the 'popular demand'. Those who had been the main losers in the repeal of the ordinances thus succeeded in keeping themselves out of the limelight: the police, faced with a seemingly obvious need to impose order and security, could thus recover from the absolute loss of prestige they had previously suffered. As far as the media were concerned, the difference between the old ordinances and the new code was whether or not it regulated street prostitution. Only very secondarily, and only in terms of 'security', was there any concern expressed over powers of arrest for 'verifying previous convictions' or for 'suspicious behaviour'.

In fact, both the Police Ordinances and the new Co-existence Code regulated something more than street prostitution.

A Short History of Ordinances

The Police Ordinances, or Codes of Offences, were powers deployed by provincial police forces and the Federal Police in order to repress acts which had not been foreseen by the the laws of the National Penal Code.

Although they had been in force since 1870, it was only towards the beginning of the twentieth century that the police had the task of the repression and control of the lower classes delegated to them. The geometrical growth of the population that had resulted from immigration, and the corresponding expansion of an Argentine working class with its organization into trade unions controlled by anarchists and socialists, required that the Criollo oligarchy, who had taken charge of the state apparatus in 1880, create new instruments of repression.

By 1899, violators of the law would be, then, not so much those subjects who committed crimes as those whom power suspected had done so: 'subject(s) of doubtful honesty, of whom it was known that they had no fixed abode nor employment, who raised suspicions or had committed some offence without there being sufficient evidence to prove it' (Salessi, 1995, p. 153).

A category of 'dangerousness' comes into use, that is to say, a notion of the intention behind the crime, which allows the large urban masses to become subject to state control. This notion of dangerousness as potentiality, that is to say as desire, can perhaps be related to other potentialities and other desires that lead to ideas of control over the alien soul, over others. At the same time as the other's desire is constructed as intelligible (that is, the desire to rob, to kill), it is named and circumscribed. But that dangerousness is never quite graspable, it always escapes into perpetual spirals of pleasure and power, as Foucault would say. Power which tries to grasp desire and desire which is nourished on escaping from power. Medicine and the police were the main players in this game.

This construction of Others also serves to educate the nascent middle classes in the norms of bourgeois respectability. These norms are constructed as self-evident truths by displaying the disruptive otherness that lies outside. Reproductive heterosexuality (given this is what is grounded here) appears as constructed and besieged in the same gesture, from outside by simultaneously the working masses and the sexually abnormal, and from inside by the very body of the nouveau bourgeois where any moment the marks of an overflowing sexuality might be revealed. What is necessary then is an attitude of perpetual vigilance towards oneself and towards others.

In 1958, under Aramburu's miltary dictatorship, a decree was promulgated which established a new Law for the Federal Police, which remained in force, albeit with modifications, until the repeal of the Police Ordinances. In it the police discretionary powers to prosecute under the ordinances was ratified (Article 6). Even at that point the police also had the power to generate ordinances. Subsequent civilian governments legitimized the murky origin of the ordinances: they were transformed into congressional law during Frondizi's presidency. By a decision of the Supreme Court the unconstitutional manner of their origin was rectified, and in 1985, through law 23.184. Congress created seven new types of delinquency (*figuras contravencionales*), which the police were given discretionary powers to prosecute. The inspiration behind this law was none other than the current president, Fernando de la Rúa.

The Police Ordinances or Code of Offences, now in force across the country, act as mechanisms of control as much by the behaviours and actions they penalize as by their procedures. Types of delinquency 'constitute an unlimited classification of personal ascriptions rather than prohibited acts' (Palmieri, 1995, p. 22). The most frequently used for purposes of arrest are: Vagrancy and Beggary where minors are concerned, under which provisions minors can be fined or imprisoned if 'found wandering in the streets or other places away from their homes' (Article 12); Outrage, which provides that, amongst others, 'those who appear in public in the clothes of the opposite sex' can be arrested (Article 2F), a power used to detain transvestites of either sex, and 'those persons of either sex who in a public place encourage or offer sexual acts' (Article 2H), which is used against female prostitutes. Much more quotidian acts are regulated as well, such as picking up confetti, singing or playing music in the streets, playing hopscotch etc. But the police also have other powers. Paragraph 11 of Article 51 of the Federal Police Law establishes that 'if there are grounds for suspecting that someone who cannot reliably prove his identity could have committed a criminal or illegal act then he be required to go to a police station'. The potential 'could have committed' allows suspicion to fall not merely on something that happened but on a possible, future event.[6]

These procedures have been insistently challenged by human rights organizations as anticonstitutional: it is the police themselves who are charged with collecting and evaluating the evidence and 'proof'. It is also the police who prosecute and judge the offence. The accused makes his plea in the sole presence of an officer, without a lawyer being present. The confession of the accused plus the report of the officer concerned are sufficient to find the accused guilty. Although appeal is possible so long as it is made within 24 hours (which makes it difficult for someone who has gone through the awful experience of having been locked up in a cell for at least ten hours to rush off to court to lodge an appeal), this rarely happens since such cases have only a small success rate. More importantly, the person involved will often find themselves face to face with the same officers, since he might live or work in the same neighbourhood as the officers involved.

In the police ordinances and in the power of arrest to establish proof of identity, the present day police force has a legal instrument which is central to the legitimization of its function. It has an internal role, since local stations have to present their superiors with statistics on arrests. It is therefore important to have 'good figures', that is to say, a large number of persons arrested for crimes solved. Of course, this ties up with the fact that illegal income is the rule rather than the exception. The control and exploitation of important illegal activities such as drugs and arms trafficking, bank robberies etc, and of lesser activities such as illegal gambling and prostitution rely on the absolute discretion with which the police deploy their legal instruments—centrally, the ordinances and the power to check previous convictions—granted to them by civilian and military governments.[7] These serve in turn to show the threatened middle classes that the populations which they perceive as dangerous are in fact under control. Mostly, these are the poor, the young and migrants. Finally, the female and travesti prostitutes, illegal gamblers, migrants without papers etc. are shown that they must carry on lining the coffers of the neighbourhood police station.

It is young people and 'cabecitas negras'[8] who swell the police statistics, filling the station cells on a daily basis. After ten hours in some station cell in the Capital they will leave without a fuss. Or perhaps some over-zealous officer will leave them with a couple of bruises, or needing a trip to the hospital, or even leave them dead. These are the principal victims of the repeal of the ordinances, and they constitute a majority in the country as a whole, albeit a minority in the city of Buenos Aires, yet they were only of secondary importance in the discussion of the City Code.

Why was the media spectacle built around the issue of street prostitution, and more specifically around travesti prostitution? Why were the majority of the participants excluded from the media soap-opera? Superficially, because 'drag queens' sell: for weeks on end junk TV shows kept their ratings up by showing the whole range of travesti types. There were angry militants and others who seemed to come from the pages of some perverse sexology textbook, who when faced with the gross and aggressive questions of the interviewers, asserted their difference from 'those who do the streets', shouting that they were real women. 'Serious' programmes took up the issue as well, showing prostitution but also making a point of showing the police on the take and the misery of marginalization.

At the other end of the social and media pyramid, the new goddesses of review theatre like Cris Miro (who died some months ago) and Florencio del Vega displaced the starlets of the 1980s. Gossip romances with the famous (like Luis Miguel) put Florencia on the covers of the third world showbiz magazines. Even in prostitution the image of the travesti sells: many men, who go by the glorified name of clients, have daily relations with travestis. There are hundreds of men, young and old, solo or in company cruising in their cars or just on foot, wanting to possess the sex of a travesti for just a few moments, and perhaps enjoying the risk of being discovered. Saunas and apartments where men can go for a discreet liaison are listed in the classified ads.

To complete the picture, there are families with kids, or groups of friends who spend their evenings watching the travestis through their car windows, perhaps slipping away in their *petit bourgeois* reverie to Amsterdam or Hamburg.

'We travestis never go unnoticed' was the terse way in which Nadia, a travesti militant, summed up the problem. The exhibition of the travesti body can awake disparate emotions in the onlooker: aversion, repulsion, rejection, fascination, desire. Never indifference. And perhaps this is even more the case when that body is partly clothed (and it is never shown naked) and becomes 'provocative'.

It is an alien body, with features of both sexes mixing chaotically. Ambiguity and mystery. The gaze shudders in the face of what cannot be apprehended. That gaze which has become hardened by insistent technological innovations that try to shock the consumer into the purchase of new commodities, suddenly discovers a primary emotion in the face of the alien body and seeks to recoil from the otherness that touches it. Let us put a mirror up to that look so that the primary fear can appear. It is a look that must not be itself observed because this would disrupt the fiction that it has no particular location and is universal. Only by constituting itself through logic and the natural order of things can it exercise with impunity its violent constitution of these beings as radically other.

Of Mirrors and Mirages

Foucault was one of the first and most trenchant theorists of this game of gaze and power. In his classic *History of Sexuality* (1977) he shows that sex came to be articulated in discourse at the beginning of modernity and definitively during the eighteenth and nineteenth centuries. The western subject is constituted as a desiring subject, and Foucault traces the genealogy of this modern subject back to the Greeks in his second volume. It is not just that the sexual field is regulated but that sex itself is thought of as something dark and omnipresent. 'The West has succeeded in making us pass in our entirety—ourselves, our body, our soul, our individuality, our history—under the sign of a logic of concupiscence and desire.'

As Gilbert Herdt notes, it is after the spread of Darwin's theory of natural selection that the principle of sexual dimorphism—that is the idea that male and female are innate structures in all life, including human beings, and that heterosexuality is teleologically necessary in that it serves the aims of reproduction—is set up as a self-evident truth, as a law of nature (Herdt, 1994, p. 26). Thus the opposition normal/abnormal is constructed on the basis of what is 'natural'. This central difference will be constructed taking as its 'natural' axis the institution of marriage. With the development of a medical science of sex in the second half of the nineteenth century, differences will be constructed that are founded in bodies and reified.[9]

Although those who are 'normal' (heterosexual adults) ought not to be problematic, the latency of sexuality requires us to be on our guard. That is the functioning of our being in terms of the dark mystery of desire, the incontrollable concupiscence embedded in all of us that can appear and take possession of us, making sexuality into a threatening force that requires us to question ourselves constantly, and to control those desires. Thus they are not simply other: the other(s) is already inside us.

As Butler suggests, 'I would assert that in principle nobody could embody this regulatory ideal, and at the same time the compulsion to embody the fiction of heterosexual coherence, in order to imagine the body in accord with its requirements is everywhere' (1992, p. 89). Perhaps it is also the very dark nature of sex which will never allow identity to be fixed. There is always the lurking risk that desire will burst out, overflow and take furious possession of us, sweeping those limits away.

The functioning of the West's sexual code thus turns out to be complex, by turns ambiguous and contradictory. How can we define the limits of good and evil, of what can and cannot be done? If sexual experience is an essential part of the growth of the human spirit and to expand the limits of sexuality is to expand the limits of our own knowledge of ourselves, how can one condemn the desire to construct a distinct identity through the male/female binary (qualities that reveal themselves as natural)? How do we account for the desire to possess (physically or spiritually) that gamut of other identities? How can the moral system be reorganized so as to condemn sexual identities whilst in the same gesture producing new sexualities which are then categorized as normal or abnormal?

But we need to be cautious here. This sexual system is not laid down once and for all, in the same way, everywhere. Theories that stress the performativity of symbolic constructions allow us to dismantle the idea of the Western sexual system as fixed. We could see the debate on the Code as a performance in which the multiple discourses on sexuality are expressed, put in to play and positioned. They appear to reconfigure the political and discursive field of Argentine sexualities at the *fin de siecle*. Furthermore, there is still the problem of how this alignment of a broad spectrum of problematic Others comes to pivot the question of repeal of the Police Ordinances around the issue of street travestis.

Mary Douglas gives us a useful critical point of entry to this question. In her *Purity and Danger* (1973), she makes 'ambiguity' synonymous with 'anomaly' and through a critical reading of Leviticus concludes that 'we can consider anomalous happenings as dangerous'. In a subsequent text (1976), making a comparative analysis with other societies, she recognizes that it is specifically in the West where these 'anomalous happenings' are taken as the source of power and danger. And just as the moral system is broad and at times contradictory, as in the above example, she observes that it will be the rules governing pollution (just as social as any others) that are charged with reorganizing the moral system where it undergoes any sort of weakening (1973, p. 178). 'Where, humanly speaking, outrage tends not to be punished, people call on beliefs about pollution to make up for the lack of other forms of sanction' (p. 179). This is even more the case when the risk of pollution falls upon the life not just of the transgressor but of some innocent. Here, the belief in the risk of pollution helps awaken moral indignation against the transgressor.

With this idea of Douglas' in mind we can read the debate on the repeal of the Ordinances and the ratification of a Co-existence Code as a discursive engagement (in the sense of a moment of some war of position) where the central problematic is whether travestis will be allowed to remain on the streets, and only secondly (and always listed after the issue of travestis) the issue of kerb-crawling. Such emphasis is laid on the travestis as anomalous and dangerous in as much as they unbalance the sexual order and introduce chaos within it. I will now go on to discuss some of the statements made by different major players in the media debate so as to evince the positions that form the problematic.

Of Leperhouses

On his fourth day in office as head of the city government, Fernando de la Rúa (the current Argentine President) declared that he would veto a FREPASO proposal in the Buenos Aires Legislature to allow 'same-sex couples' to use short-stay hotels, which had heretofore been reserved exclusively for heterosexuals. In a radio interview he said:

> ... they should go to hotels set aside for these affairs, otherwise everyone is going to get mixed up together ... I think the proposal has its drawbacks. You should go and talk to the residents of Palermo who have to put up with the outrage that they (travestis) cause in the streets. It's a mad idea ... FREPASO is always coming up with these things. I don't share them, we're trying to make a quite different world. Respect for everybody, equality for everyone, freedom, but there are certain rules that are laid down for a reason and we have to be careful about the risks involved. (*Página 12*, 31 May 1997, pp. 18–19)

It is a mad idea to mix up these 'affairs' with heterosexual couples, which then requires De la Rúa's interlocutor to explain the social rules. (In Spanish, De la Rúa is punning on the resemblence between 'alocada' mad, and 'loca' queen, or effeminate homosexual, and polluting FREPASO's political discourse with the street sexual argot.) Initially it is homosexuals who are a potential danger. But it is not just that those who are abnormal and sick belong on the wrong side: if you let them get closer, if you allow homosexual couples to go to the same hotels, sleep in the same beds, sweat on the same sheets, both 'worlds' will be superimposed and confused with each other. The risk of pollution and contamination is a spectral presence which cannot be uttered but which is omnipresent.

But why is the figure of the Palermo travestis deployed to point out the 'drawbacks' of a proposal allowing access by homosexuals to short-stay hotels? It could hardly be a question within heterosexist common sense itself to inquire what resemblence De la Rúa found between homosexuals and travestis. That is, what resemblence there is between persons who according to the fiction of sex have the right gender but an inverted sexual desire, who were demanding the right to the same private spaces (a room rented for a few hours for making love), and persons who had an inverted gender identity (since it is not appropriate to their sex, that is their nature) and who are engaged in prostitution, that is sex for money, making their contract on a public street. What seems to be in play is the idea of sexual abnormality or perversion as a non-specific field of disorder which allows quite dissimilar identities and behaviours to be placed in the same semantic space: but even inside this disorder the travestis are the most chaotic. Just as AIDS was called the 'gay plague' in the early days of the epidemic, prior to the discovery of the causal agent HIV, and this designation served to encourage proposals to ghettoize homosexuals, so nowadays it is travestis who are the apocalyptic figures that generate panic.

In the face of demands by lesbian and gay organizations, the fiction of heterosexual consistency stops functioning as something natural and therefore without need of justification, and now has to be made explicit: there are 'rules which are laid down for a reason, and we have to be careful about the risks they involve'. What also seems central is that these rules (that is the regulatory fiction of heterosexual consistency) are the basis of society and therefore more important than the political system. In the face of those discourses centred on the liberal fiction of the citizen which are then used to gain access to new political spaces (and contemporary lesbian and gay organizations hold fast to this strategy) De la Rúa poses the heterosexual norm as the basis of society. And in order to legitimate this move, he sends his interviewer off to ask the residents of Palermo about 'the outrage they cause in the streets'. Here there are various discursive operations: in the first place it legitimizes the Co-operative Association of Residents of Campaña del Desierto Plaza as the totality of the Palermo residents (they embody everyone, as Spivak would say), which obscures the violence of representativity and the falsity of this particular claim (since there were never more than two hundred people present on a demonstration). Secondly, talk of 'outrage' converts this sign into pure referentiality since its other meaning, that is as a type of violation set out in the Police Ordinances used to lock up travestis, is hidden. It thus succeeds in giving legitimacy to the offence addressed by the Ordinance which would then punish 'what goes on' in an appropriate manner.

Lastly, once these operations are established as the truth of the situation, what is heard and seen as representative is the resident, not the citizen. Thus we can see how the City executive shifts the terms of political debate through the dispute about travestis.

Corrupting Children

One image that was constantly brought up during the debate was that of children seeing 'naked' travestis in the streets. And here we are 'all' interpellated. Even given that some people were more or less sympathetic and did not demand that travestis be expelled from the city, to be kept out of sight, there remained the inevitable question: would you let your children see this spectacle? But what exactly ought a child not see?

Father Farinello, a progressive priest in the Catholic Church, spoke in an interview of how some travestis had visited him in Quilmes asking for help:

> They bore many scars, and I felt a great desire to show them love, to hug them, they had suffered so much and were so alone. I felt no disgust, you can see the loneliness, the insults, the betrayals. Once Mauro Viale (the frontman of a junk TV programme) asked me on a programme when I was defending them, 'But would you want them in your nursery school?'. When he asked me, 'Your children, the ones you bring up, would you want them to see these travestis at the gate?' And I felt so bad ... but it came out from deep inside: I said, no. And I knew that I was backing him up.

The speaker begins by sketching human features of the travestis, whom he genders as female: loneliness, insults, suffering. Perhaps even carrying Christian charity to the limit, he manages to express the fact that he did not feel disgust, that he a felt a desire to show love for them (though we are left in doubt whether he succeeded in doing so or not). He even begins his discourse speaking of them as females, breaking with the tone that refers to them as men. But in the face of the journalist's interpellation about what his children might 'see', he has to side with his interviewer, both in agreeing that they should not be at the gates of his nursery school (and in the context of the debate that they should not be in the streets) and in changing the gender with which he refers to them: they are now men. It is to this point that Christian morality leads.

A question that common sense (however doubtful we are about its existence) might put is: why would a travesti be at the gates of a nursery school, allegedly during the day? It is not even necessary to clarify how s/he would be dressed, since it is taken for granted. The image would be of a travesti, with a short red skirt, a tiny top, made up and making lewd movements in his/her high heels and ... making obscene propositions to children. That outfit and that pose reveal a corrupt soul, a soul that thirsts to corrupt the pure and innocent.

The first move is to construct the clothing and gestures as the essence of the being-travesti. Here is absolute otherness: they possess no human feature which they share with those who are normal. Is it really conceivable that anyone could spend 24 hours a day in six inch heels, tight-fit clothing that requires constant readjustment so that it can cover anything at all, make-up that has to be constantly touched up to keep it even, given that when one sweats it runs, etc.?

The speaker is thus blind to the obvious, that is, that the travestis are working, *engaged in prostitution* when they 'exhibit' themselves in this way. That is, the costume and gestural repertoire belong to the requirements of the market, of that transaction which we call prostitution. They are not going to hang around outside a kindergarten or a school acting out travesti prostitution because what they are doing is their work, or their profession. But perhaps their profession is not so invisible, since by equating the travesti operation with uncontrollable desire, prostitution is turned into a way of making money from their insatiable sexual desire. This violent operation that produces them and maintains them as radically other, on the margins of the human, has to exclude any feature of ordinary everydayness which might make them similar to us.[10] At the same time those discourses disclose and construct children as non-adult beings lacking reason, and unable to make decisions about what they like or don't like. Why should children not see a travesti engaged in prostitution? Hardly anyone questions the fact that children see news bulletins: seeing war on screen doesn't make them pick up a gun and go out and kill. But we assume that if children see a travesti outside their front door something terrible will happen, something so terrible that it can't be stated.

Changing Dangers

The figure of the travesti is not only dangerous in itself, as these statements attest, but becomes even more frightening when related to the men who make use of travestis in prostitution, who 'consume' them.

At the end of February 1998, the City Legislature ratified the first version of the Co-existence Code, which did not penalize prostitution, and created a criminal judicial power. There was an immediate campaign launched against this version by the City Executive Power (CEP) and by the ACPCD. Between February and March residents' associations sprouted in neighbourhoods like Saavedra, Flores and Constitucion, where there was also street prostitution, and made claims similar to the ones in Palermo.[11]

At the beginning of March I was present at a public meeting organized by the CEP through the neigbourhood council for the prevention of crime. The ACPCD had called on the media and on its own members and those close to them to attend. At times there were perhaps 150 people there. The meeting was composed of members of the middle class, but mostly of the lower middle class. The majority were women over the age of 50, dressed in cheap clothing and with badly dyed hair. By contrast, the officials in dark, expensive suits arrived with their personal assistants, blond, tanned, young women. The women from the neighbourhood behaved as if at some witches' sabbath: they screamed at the tops of their voices if anyone disagreed with getting the travestis off the street, and if they couldn't intimidate, they would clap loudly in the middle of a sentence until one of their leaders made a sign, and then they would remain docilely silent.

The meeting lasted a little more than two hours. At the beginning the then assistant head of the city government, Olivera, felt obliged to explain why they were dealing with the Code of Offences when they should be discussing the prevention of crime.[12] He would go on to say that it was about questions that 'had to do with life in the neighbourhood, with order in the neighbourhood and with keeping the peace', leaving Enriquez, who had drawn up the version of the Code that the Executive would present, to explain in more elegant and legal terms what their proposals consisted in. In their proposed version, in a section on 'individual feelings', were found the offences of accepting money on the streets, threatening appearance and offering sex in a public place. 'We would like to make residents feel safe, guarantee their right to go about freely ... without the open offer of sex on the public highway affecting their deepest and most cherished feelings.' And pointing to the underlying spirit of the proposed Code, he went on: 'the wider we make the field of anti-social offences, then the less we need to use the criminal law which is when we arrive too late after the murder or the robbery has already been committed. A code of urban co-existence (must) ... address itself to the issue of control that a society has to have so as to maintain social order'.

The idea is that residents should be able to go about freely through their streets without being disturbed by someone begging, someone on the game, or the dark-haired guy who is probably a thief. The right social order will have been achieved when those beings disappear from the good residents' sight. What is necessary to achieve this end is a widening of the list of types of delinquency extending the category of 'dangerous subjects' to cover the whole spectrum of those populations that constitute a nuisance (to be imprisoned for crimes and offences not yet committed).

Although what was central to the debate was how to eliminate the travestis from the streets of Palermo, someone living on the other side of Avenida Cordoba, where property is much cheaper, spoke about the houses that had been squatted: 'From Cordoba to Corrientes, I'm talking about Lerma, Jufre and Castilo Streets ...This area is full of houses that have been squatted by people—Peruvians, Paraguayans, Chileans and Bolivians. We go through constant dramas because muggings, robberies go on in broad daylight ... I've got a map that the authorities have given me where I'm going to mark all the houses that have been occupied ...'. In this case these 'people' who live in houses that have squatted, are not Argentinian: they are from surrounding countries and they are thieves.[13]

Even Enriquez replied that the authorities were taking more effective legal measures to speed up evictions from these squats. They were encouraging 'measures against squatting ... because we know that these places encourage marginal elements who are criminally disposed'.

One needs to remark that this statement is false, as became clear in the debate on the law on migration proposed by the Government. The police themselves had to deny this account as their own statistics indicate that the majority of robberies and minor thefts are committed by Argentines. What was central, however, was that Enriquez made the equation: squatters (mostly people without the money to buy a property) = marginals = criminals.

Levi-Strauss Would Have Been Delighted

The discourse that brought together all the opinions that had been discussed at the meeting was that of one of the leaders of the AC. Having apologised for not having spoken at the beginning when it was his turn, 'but I had urgent business and had to leave', he said:

> There is a constitutional right ... I refer to being able to go about freely anywhere in the country without interference, but our womenfolk have a problem in the neighbourhood, they can't leave their houses at nine at night, and they can't at half past six in the morning either. It's not the travestis, because really I have no problems with any of them, but the real problem is their clients, who are invading the neighbourhood, and they mistake our women for prostitutes or something worse. It doesn't matter who they are. I ask, I demand ... that you give us constant police help with these vile creatures who are their clients who have no compunction about treating our women as prostitutes or something worse. This is why we're making demands because we're denied our constitutional right, because our women can't go out because it doesn't say anything about moral interference in any code.

With his mid-quality suit, confident bearing, his lack of time, his statement at the beginning that he knew some of the officials who were present, he was clearly someone 'important' (and white, of course). It was the first time that night that anyone had discussed the clients of the travestis, and he did so at length. Calling them 'vile creatures' placed them in an ambiguous space since they are 'creatures', perhaps lacking humanity, and vile in that they know what the rules are but do not respect them. And their invasion brings confusion as well.

What is clear is that the clients cannot tell the difference between the good women (that is the wives of the neighbourhood male residents) and the bad, nor can they distinguish them from something worse, the unnameable, that is, the travestis. What underlies this expression is the idea that someone who desires a travesti is sick because he cannot tell the difference between real women and those who are only apparently so. Here we have once more the construction of the travesti as a practice which is imitative of an original, that is those who are born women. Thus there is an affirmation, and a raising to a higher power of the hegemonic sexual model with two sexes and real, normal genders versus abnormal ones. And perhaps the travestis themselves are the cause of the confusion, seducing by their arts of imitation.

Both in desiring them and by having physical contact and mingling bodies with them, the client becomes part of this other world. But what makes him dangerous is that he is also part of this world, of the normal. He is someone who moves between the two worlds, but when he is in his ordinary life he looks just like the rest of the men, even the speaker (which is perhaps why he stresses their condition of being contemptible, since he must position himself within the discourse as radically other to the client).

But it is the speaker who has the responsibility for expressing the problem of how 'our womenfolk' live in the neighbourhood. In the course of the meeting this problem came up several times, but always raised by men. Why is it only a man who can say this? Because if a woman were to raise the matter, if she were to say 'they mix me up with a whore' the accusation would rebound on herself, and there would be questions about what she was wearing, how she was walking and so on ... the suspicion that somehow she did something to 'provoke'. This social control of women is sustained and reaffirmed then by the speaker being a man. He speaks about our neighbourhood women indicating possession of women, territorial possession and a sense of masculine community.

Conclusions

Firstly, then, we have seen how the figure of the resident is being established, both by the practices of the political powers and by the practices of those who embody the figure, as the legitimate inhabitant of the Buenos Aires urban space, in the same act counterposing as illegitimate and dangerous a whole series of figures that had previously been at most nuisances.

The redefinition of the neighbourhood, appealing to old values and to a mythical community past, is affirmed on the basis of a strong sense of private property and propriety: men with good morals, houses, wives and children. This cannot be unconnected with the weakening of other identities, fundamentally the withdrawal from political identities, be they of party or organization, whose project had been the construction of a better society. With the idea of an Argentine community having disappeared, just as the desires for change have retreated, so desires have fallen back territorially. The neighbourhood, as the last bastion, is converted into a space positively constructed with a sense of absolute property/propriety. Its identity is constituted by a sedentary population, with a clearly established order that situates persons and things in clear, hierarchical relations. By contrast, the social groups towards which, barely a decade ago, the much maligned progressive middle classes felt a responsibility for their improvement and advancement, and who for the left were the potential subjects of change, have changed their status. They are now nomad populations defined as dangerous since they introduce chaos into the *petit bourgeois* order. They threaten others by trying to relieve them of their goods and property, and take over the streets conduiting stolen goods from their point of legitimate origin to places constituted by illegality.

The squatters, who are mostly poor and who are therefore forced to inhabit delapidated buildings, mostly ones abandoned for years without electricity or gas, are transformed into a mass of individuals who have set out to appropriate the belongings of the bourgeois: first their houses, then their goods.

But the streets and their traffic have always been controlled by the police and carry on being so. The repeal of the city ordinances was initially a threat to the power of the police, both political, in that it attempted to impose another power over it, that of the so-called democratic institutions, and economic, since it deprived the police of an important source of income.

Thus through discourses and practices emanating from these democratic institutions, at first the City Executive Power, then social groups who constituted themselves via these practices and legitimated them as such, and then the police, succeeded in imposing a particular emphasis on the debate on the repeal of the ordinances.

The establishment by the media of the issue as a moment where chaos was introduced into the city and into the neighbourhoods, centred the problem on street prostitution specifically on the figure of the travestis. They were characterized in ways that situated them as dangerous and as contagious carriers of disorder. This set-up reorganized with renewed force the sexual normativity that had begun to be checked (however marginally) by the growth of organizations of sexual minorities and a greater social tolerance towards these minorities. Thus in the construction of travestis as amoral and as potential perverters of children, the family as the fundamental space was reorganized: parents must protect the innocence of their children, and men must protect the virtue of their women. The image of all these dangerous subjects using the streets redefined the latter as the property of the residents, which required the police to keep watch on these populations, to keep 'danger' at bay, outside the limits of the neighbourhood.

The electoral triumph of the Alianza in the elections of October 1999, and De la Rúa's arrival in the Presidential office, raise the question whether there will be an attempt to extend these clearly repressive discourses and policies to the national level.

Translated by Philip Derbyshire

Notes

1. FREPASO came out of the Broad Front created in 1994 by Peronists (for the most part in office with the Menem government) who had left the Justicialist Party in government. The Broad Front got 5 million votes in the 1995 elections, when Menem was elected for a second term, and for the first time pushed the Radicals into third place. Their achievement was built on their appealing to voters, mostly in the cities, who had rejected the corruption of the Menem government, examples of which were continuously exposed in the press. The voters had also seen the necessity of acting against mafia corruption and had been repelled by the attack on the APIA. And finally parts of the electorate had seen the need to discuss human rights issues in the political sphere. Following on from this, ex-Justicialists like Chacho Alvarez and Octavio Burdón joined with smaller parties like Socialist Unity and the Christian Democrats and with independent activists, many of them, like Graciela Fernández Meijide, from human rights organizations, to create FREPASO (Countrywide Solidarity Front). From that time on, people began to talk about the need for an alliance to 'beat Menemism' which would include the UCR (Radical Civic Union).
2. These were types of organization seen to be concerned with different problematics. But after the strong travesti mobilization during the debate on the Co-existence Code (discussed below), human rights organizations, initially devoted to the disappeared and later to questions of political repression, took up the issues raised by sexual minorities' groups, and began to treat them as questions of human rights.
3. Palermo is a relatively central neighbourhood of Buenos Aires, with a predominantly professional middle-class population. As a residential area, there are few high buildings, and it is one of the most expensive areas of the city. But it is there in a ten-block area that street prostitution takes place, most of it involving travestis.
4. Translator's note: I use the word *travesti* here rather than transvestite, because the Spanish term often refers to not merely cross-dressing but to bodily transformation, often by surgery or

hormone use, which yields a body bearing the marks of both sexes: breasts and penis, for example. The English term is too weak, and hence I maintain the Spanish word throughout.

5. Currently, there is a legal action in process to throw out Article 71 as unconstitutional, on the grounds that it contravenes provisions of the City Constitution, such as the right to be different, and the recognition of freedom of sexuality as a basic human right, and rights established by the National Constitution, such as the right to free movement, and 'the right to privacy, and the right not to suffer penalties for actions which are not in fact penalized by the national criminal code'.

6. Martínez *et al.* (1996) analyse the total number of arrests for proof of identity made by the Federal Police during September 1995, concluding that the majority were men (83%), Argentine and between 21 and 25 years old. Suspicious behaviour, according to police statements, was 'walking and looking constantly from side to side as though looking for something, or as if looking out for the police' (Report to Subcommissioner Mantel, implicated in the Wilde massacre, in January 1994). The Chief of the Federal Police under Menem, Commissioner Adrián Pelacchi, stated during a radio interview 'I think that the power of arrest for identity checks should be not be used in an arbitrary way but against those who are under suspicion because they do not live in the neighbourhood, or who aren't close to means of transport that would get them home, or because they can't give clear reasons for what they are doing in the neighbourhood (*Rompecabezas*, 7 March, 1997, quoted in Martínez et al., 1996).

7. In the city of Buenos Aires there were 35,350 convictions under the ordinances in 1985, and in 1995 the projected figure will be 133,588 (Palmieri, 1995, p. 27). For identity checks, the figure was 150,000 in 1995. As for violence: in 1994 in the Federal Capital, there was one officer killed for every 39 civilians. The majority of the latter were killed for 'acting suspiciously', or 'demand for ID', assaults on taxis or banks. What was exceptional was confrontations with commando groups or bank robbers. In the Province of Buenos Aires, the ratio was one officer killed for every four civilians (Tiscornia, 1996).

8. The untranslatable 'cabecitas negras', literally 'little black heads' is a derogatory term that the urban middle classes, particularly those of Buenos Aires, use to describe people with mixed race features, or those who are not pure whites.

9. A paradigmatic instance of this emergence of sexual science and the constitution of sexualities is the publication and circulation of *Psychopathia Sexualis* by Krafft-Ebing, which came into print in 1887. The enormous success that it enjoyed throughout Europe and America, both inside and outside medical circles, led to numbers of editions. In the tenth edition, there were 238 clinical cases discussed and there was an exhaustive typology of pathologies constructed, which are still in current use: fetishism, masochism and homosexuality for instance. The pathology of these cases lies in their not satisfying the sexual instinct, given that this consists not merely 'in sexual pleasure, but also in a deep desire to perpetuate one's own transient existence by transmitting one's physical and mental characteristics to a new being' (quoted in Katz, 1996, p. 47). Katz remarks that in the whole of the book's 436 pages the term 'heterosexual' only appears 24 times, and is not in the index (Katz, 1996, p. 51). The heterosexual norm is constructed through a detailed description of pathological instances.

10. To think of them as human would also require that prostitution be considered not as the happiest of professions, and that many of the prostitutes might want to do something else. Generally, although there are no statistics on this, most travestis in Argentina begin their career as such in early adolescence, for which reason they are kicked out of home. When the physical transformations become apparent, it is common for them to be expelled from college or sacked from their work. Prostitution thus becomes the only occupation open to them. The police ordinances still in force throughout the country allow the police to detain them at any hour of the day in any place, which makes holding down a job impossible, even assuming they can find one.

11. The police kept a low profile during this time. The police lobby was at work, as so often before, on the sidelines. In the case of Palermo, some of the AC members had taken part in an ancillary organization of the 23rd Commissariat, which had one of the highest arrest rates for travestis, and had been accused of numerous instances of extortion and torture by travesti political organizations. They had publicly defended Commissioner Blanco, even after a hidden camera TV programme had revealed officers under his command extorting money from prostitutes and travestis.

12. Gentili claims that those who defend the police ordinances maintain that there are types of

offence that should not be punished by the penal code but by the ordinances, or by-laws. That is to say, that the difference should be maintained between crimes and types of delinquency.
13. The instances of xenophobia that show up in Argentine society and particularly amongst the urban middle classes are always supported by enormous but always anecdotal evidence. For example, in 1999 the head of the Office for National Migration claimed that the majority of thefts and muggings were committed by illegal immigrants, and in consequence proposed a law to control migrant populations.

References

Judith Butler, *Gender Trouble. On the Discursive Limits of Sex* (London: Routledge, 1990).
Judith Butler, 'Problemas de los géneros, teoría feminista y discurso psicoanalítico', in *Feminismo y Posmodernismo*, compiled by Linda Nicholson (Buenos Aires: Feminaria, 1992), pp. 75–95.
Mary Douglas, *Pureza y peligro. Un análisis de los conceptos de contaminación y tabú* (Madrid: Siglo XXI, 1973).
Mary Douglas, *Sobre la naturaleza de las cosas* (Barcelona: Anagrama, 1976).
Michel Foucault, *Historia de la Sexualidad, 1—La Voluntad de Saber* (México: Siglo XXI, 1977).
Rafael Gentili, *Me va a tener que acompañar, Una visión crítica sobre los edictos policiales* (Buenos Aires: El Naranjo, 1995).
Gilbert Herdt, 'Third Sexes and Third Genders', in *Third Sex, Third Gender. Beyond Sexual Dimorphism in Culture and History*, ed. by Gilbert Herdt (New York: Zone Books, 1994), pp. 21–84.
Jonathan Katz, *The Invention of Heterosexuality* (New York: Plume Books, 1996).
María Martínez, Gustavo Palmieri and María Victoria Pita, 'Detenciones por averiguación de identidad: policía y prácticas rutinizadas', forthcoming 1996.
Rosalind Morris, 'All made Up: Performance Theory and the New Anthropology of Sex and Gender', *Annual Review of Anthropology*, 24 (1995), pp. 567–592.
Gustavo Palmieri, 'El sistema contravencional, los edictos policiales y la detención por averiguación de identidad', *Informe Anual 1995 del CELS* (1995), pp. 20–33.
María Victoria Pita, 'Notas sobre la corrupción policial y cronología de hechos—1996', *Informe Anual 1996 del CELS* (1996), pp. 86–110.
Jorge Salessi, *Médicos, maleantes y maricas* (Rosario: Beatriz Viterbo, 1995).
Sofía Tiscornia and María Angélica Villarouel, 'La violencia policial en la Capital Federal y el Gran Buenos Aires', *Informe Anual 1995 del CELS* (1995), pp. 1–19.

Elaine Luck

CONSPICUOUS CONSUMPTION AND THE PERFORMANCE OF IDENTITY IN CONTEMPORARY MEXICO: DANIELA ROSSELL'S *RICAS Y FAMOSAS*

In 2002 Daniela Rossell published a series of photographs titled *Ricas y famosas* that depicted wealthy Mexican women, many of whom were close relatives of Partido Revolucionario Institucional (PRI) politicians. According to Rossell, herself from a wealthy family with close PRI ties, the women were photographed in poses and locations of their own choosing, with the majority opting to be photographed in their own homes in a conspicuous display of wealth that shocked many viewers.[1] The images, taken between 1994 and 2001, had been circulating in art galleries throughout Mexico, the US and Europe without drawing much attention from outside the art world. However, after the publication of the book, the Mexican media began to uncover the identities of those photographed, sparking polemics about government corruption, the wealth gap that continued to widen under the North American Free Trade Agreement (NAFTA), and the projection of Mexican 'bad taste'. With the exception of a few academic texts,[2] Rossell's photographs have been primarily approached from two perspectives: that of the Mexican media, which appropriates the photographs as documentary evidence of corruption and social inequality, and the international art press, which tends to view them as a comment on consumer culture and its construction of feminine identity.

These approaches fail to historicise the images in relation to Mexican photographic discourse and its imbrication in the construction of dominant national narratives, or to properly set them within the context of the economic transformation that has been redefining these narratives and has produced new conditions for the construction and expression of identities through consumption. I propose an analysis of *Ricas y famosas* that addresses gender performativity as culturally specific and intersected with class-based performance, and argue for the importance of consumption and material culture in understanding the projection of class and gender identity. Furthermore, I suggest that the series needs to be located at the intersection between global consumer culture and its projection of a sexualised femininity, and Mexican discourses of national identity, particularly as they are elaborated photographically, in a way that addresses the re-articulation of nationalism through consumer culture and the role of the visual in the construction and representation of subjects.

Rossell tended to avoid contact with the media, and has presented her images, in galleries and in her book, without contextual information that would guide interpretation or indicate her intentions, or those of her subjects.[3] What textual direction is provided is limited to the title, a short text at the end of the book by art critic Barry Schwabsky, and a caption preceding the images which reads: 'the following images depict actual settings. The photographic subjects are representing themselves. Any resemblance with real events is not a coincidence'. Both the title and the caption set an ironic tone for the series which may not be wholly shared by her subjects, and serve not to direct interpretation of the images but to accentuate their ambiguities by playfully complicating the boundaries between reality and fiction. The presentation of the catalogue in a coffee table format, with glossy, high-colour images that fill entire pages, seems to parody celebrity magazines such as ¡Hola!, as well as perhaps poking fun at the aspirations of her subjects (very few of whom are actually famous, with the exception of exotic dancer Lyn May and *telenovela* actress Itati Cantoral). While I am hesitant to draw conclusions as to the extent of self-awareness on the part of her subjects, it seems that they playfully parody the kinds of images they re-enact: those of consumer culture and the mass media.

Once the previously concealed identities of those portrayed became public, many were revealed to be wives and daughters of prominent PRI members, including Carlos Salinas de Gortari and Gustavo Díaz Ordaz.[4] Many of those photographed claimed that they had not given permission for their images to be published,[5] and Rossell has been involved in legal action, and, she says, has received threatening phone calls. Taken between 1994 and 2001, the project was initiated in one of the most turbulent years of Mexico's recent history: 1994 was the year in which Mexico joined NAFTA, the inauguration of which was accompanied by the armed uprising of the Ejército Zapatista de Liberación Nacional (EZLN) in Chiapas, and then later a severe financial crisis that led to a sharp increase in urban crime and violence.[6] Until 1994 Carlos Salinas had been building a reputation as an economic and political reformer, opening the country to foreign investment and democratic reform, and had been credited with producing unprecedented economic growth. However, the crises of this year revealed many of these reforms to be largely superficial, aimed at creating an impression of democracy and stability in order to attract foreign investment and maintain PRI power. The period in which Rossell's project was undertaken spans the PRI's final years in power, which ended with defeat to the centre-right Partido Acción Nacional (PAN) in 2000.

Appropriated by the media, an industry that posits the image as truth, the aesthetic motivations of Rossell's images, intended not as objective photojournalism but as an art project with ambiguous and contingent meanings, were overlooked. By omitting the textual pointers which often accompany photographs and guide their interpretation, Rossell's series cultivates photography's inherent ambiguities, and for the same reason is left open to appropriation. It is perhaps this absence of supplementary text that allowed its easy incorporation into the media, which provided a new context for the images. Rossell's photographs have become inscribed into Mexico's history as documents of PRI corruption and the uneven distribution of wealth, the gap widening as a result of economic liberalisation and the implementation of NAFTA. Their publication in 2002 seemed to reawaken and give visual form to the media uproar about government corruption that culminated during the mid-nineties with the trial of Raul Salinas, and were treated as proof of self-enrichment by government officials. For Lorenzo Meyer, Rossell's photographs are evidence of 'el México Feo', the generalised corruption and injustice that are at the heart of the country's institutions (Meyer 2002). The book also coincided with the publication of statistics that showed the wealth gap to have grown under NAFTA, thus prompting indignation at its subjects' grotesque displays of wealth.

The changes to economic and political structures that were taking place at this time were the culmination of a long-term cycle of transition that can be traced to the student movement of 1968, an event which marked a transformation in political culture and the government's failure to successfully incorporate opposition as it had done in the past, and have been accompanied by broad cultural changes that cannot be viewed simply as a result of globalisation or within the universalising discourses of postmodernism. Such theories can encourage the reductive labelling of cultural and socio-political processes rather than an analysis of the specific transformations of relations between the processes of production, distribution, and consumption of culture within local contexts that alter their relation to global contexts of production (Rowe 2003: 39). Since the 1990s there has been a radical reconfiguration of national identity, linked to changes in the demands of political legitimation, the importation of Western models of multiculturalism, and the redefinition of Mexico–US relations. For many, the uprising in Chiapas signalled a crisis of national identity: the model that has been dominant throughout the twentieth century is incompatible with neoliberalism, and brings to the surface deep contradictions between the myth of a common identity based upon indigenous culture and the reality of conditions for many indigenous groups.[7]

The realignment with the US promoted by NAFTA has disrupted the model of self-conceptualisation in which Mexico was defined in opposition to the US, replacing it on the one hand with a more urban and industrialised culture in keeping with neoliberalism, and on the other a neo-indigenismo that calls for indigenous autonomy (Morris 2001). The model of neo-indigenismo seems to fit with the rhetorical recognition of plurality at a governmental level, influenced largely by a global multiculturalist rhetoric which contrasts sharply with revolutionary nationalism's drive towards a homogeneous cultural identity through the incorporation and hispanicisation of the indigenous population.[8] The coexistence of these two opposing models has the potential to cause deep divisions, particularly as the wealth gap continues to increase. This move away from integrationist politics, and from its cultural corollaries which have helped to construct a sense of cultural unity, is accompanied within the field of cultural representation by a shift towards the representation of multiple subjectivities: recognition of the intersections of identifications such as class, ethnicity, gender, sexuality, generation. This is not to say that the nation ceases to influence and frame identity constructions, but that it is no longer presented as transcendent, and does not subsume all other forms of identification. Rossell's photographs present an attempt to assert the specificities of identity construction against totalising discourses which have construed the subject as national above all, and portrays a subjectivity which cannot be abstracted as a representation of an idealised national character.

The role of culture as a legitimising mechanism for the PRI throughout the twentieth century cannot be underestimated (Bartra 2002: 8–10); neither can the role of the visual in the construction of national culture and the definition of the ideal national subject (Noble 2005: 11). Photography in Mexico has been instrumental in defining national identity according to ethnic and racial logics (Debroise 2001: 132), and has been the site of convergence between ethnography and visual culture, as photographers appropriate anthropological discourse as a means of granting visibility to indigenous cultures. The tensions between the representation of specific identity constructions and their abstraction and appropriation by official culture are continually played out in photography. This issue has been well explored in Erica Segre's book

Intersected Identities, which examines the production of visual identities in reproductive media, emphasising the occularcentric vein in identity discourse and focusing on attempts to construct specific visual/visible identities against the totalising identities constructed from an allegorised indigenous past (2007). The capacity to be at once general and specific is a defining feature of photography as a medium, and while it can be employed as a means of opposing totalising discourses, it can equally be appropriated and repositioned by these same discourses. John Mraz divides Mexican photography into two camps (a binary that, by Mraz's own admission, may be too simple): the picturesque, defined by reification, which converts subjects into types (2001: 2); and the non- or anti-picturesque, which employs the same national symbols against the reification of the picturesque through contextualisation, using specificity against the idealised and dehistoricised abstraction of the picturesque (2001). It is within and against the history of photography in Mexico, and the uncertainties of identity brought about by a changing political culture, which in turn has created problems for photographic representation due to the recognition of photography's historical complicity with the functioning of power, that Rossell's series should be read. *Ricas y famosas* relies on the discursive role of images and presents an intersection of visual discourses: the construction of national identity and the universalising discourses of advertising, which in Mexico come together often in seemingly contradictory ways.

The crisis of identity in contemporary culture has led to a crisis in representation in both art and photography, and perhaps *Ricas y famosas* can be seen as an experiment into the role of photography after revolutionary nationalism: one which parodies the ethnographic conventions of Mexican photography; the practice of social documentary and its claims to objectivity; and the visual strategies of the media, advertising and fashion industries. It also makes clear the paradoxes of the assumptions that greater representational visibility equals greater social power, a notion problematised by Peggy Phelan, who argues that representational visibility in itself does not constitute more social power, as representation often entails objectification (Phelan 1993: 6). The over-representation of indigenous culture can lead to an over-familiarisation which obscures the 'real' lived conditions of indigenous groups (Pérez de Mendiola 2004), and reduces the indigenous body to signification as the indigenous image is abstracted as the basis for common identification, or as a means of countering official constructions. Those with the greatest social power are not simply those who are the most visible, but those who have control over when and how they are represented, having not only the social power to make themselves seen, but also to remain hidden. Rossell's subjects, most of whom live their lives hidden from public view behind high-security fences, expressed anger after the publication of the images and the hostile reaction received from the media, and perhaps this was a result of the perceived violation of the privacy deemed to be a basic right by people of their social class.

One US art critic has characterised *Ricas y famosas* as a reversal of the conventions of ethnography (Israel 2000), and indeed the anthropological/sociological dimension of Rossell's photographs has been noted by several critics, including Juan Villoro (2002). However, many of these critics fail to connect Rossell's quasi-anthropological portrait of the rich with the tradition of ethnographic portraiture that has dominated Mexican photographic history. While they note Rossell's anthropological approach, they continue to locate the series within the conventions of contemporary art, and overlook its relation to the genealogy of photographic practice and nation-building discourses that have traditionally appropriated anthropological discourse. This approach is characteristic of many art critics, who treat art photographs exclusively as art, disregarding the specificities of the photographic image and its particular histories. While I recognise the artistic motivations of the images, and it is important to remain aware of the original context of their presentation, I argue that they cannot be understood separately from the Mexican photographic canon and the identity discourses that have been played out within it, and need to be viewed in the context of the crisis of narratives that have defined the national subject not only as *mestizo*, but also as anti-Western and anti-capitalist (Bartra 2002: 10).

The generalising tendencies of photography result in the conversion of subjects into types, and this has been a function of photography since its emergence. These logics, which emerged from the Enlightenment and its desire to make the world knowable and classifiable, preceded photography and were also applied in colonial contexts: eighteenth-century *casta* paintings placed colonial subjects into a racial taxonomy in which all possible combinations of racial mixing were named and placed within a hierarchy. Late nineteenth- and early twentieth-century Mexican photographic practices also revolved around classificatory logics, drawing on the literary practice of *costumbrismo*, which documented idealised rural traditions thought to be on the verge of disappearance (Debroise 2001). As a photographic practice *costumbrismo* classified subjects according to ethnic categories or, as was often the case, occupation, reducing them to their place within the social order. From the outset, photographic practice in Mexico was employed as a means of classifying people according to a social hierarchy that was naturalised and made to appear stable through the apparently codeless medium of photography, and furthermore it elaborated a system of classification based upon visual markers of identity. Rossell's series extends this taxonomy of national subjects by focusing on the least represented sector of Mexican society, and the emergence of the *nouveau-riche* within a specific historical moment in which the dominant narratives of the twentieth century are being redefined.

As the division of reality into small consumable units, the world is atomised in photographs, becoming a series of 'unrelated freestanding particles' that are easily organised and reorganised according to the requirements of the discourse that appropriates them (Sontag 1979: 22). There have been two significant studies into the use of classificatory logics in photographic practice, both making classification and the archive central to the functioning of photography while each approaching the topic from a different perspective: Deborah Poole focuses on the construction of ideas about race in nineteenth-century Peru, and the role of photography in establishing race as a biological fact (1997), while Paul Frosh brings an analysis of the archival in photography outside of the obviously classificatory realm of anthropological images to examine the role of classification in the production of commercial photographs (2003). These studies not only make use of the concept of the archive as a means of organising and cataloguing images as units of meaning, but also revolve around a concept of the archive drawn from Foucauldian analysis as a system which actively defines and delimits discursive practice (Foucault 1972: 129), and focus on the particular subject constructions of racial discourse and advertising respectively.

Poole uses the term 'image world' to describe the relationship between images: images are given meaning by other images and their relation with image producers and consumers, and therefore none can be taken isolation (Poole 1997: 7). Poole's study makes classification central to photography's function as an archival technology, focusing in particular on *cartes de visite* as equivalent and exchangeable images to be classified and reclassified (132). Where both Poole's and Frosh's studies depart from other studies on photography's archival aspects is in their focus on non-institutional images (the tendency has been to focus on the construction of notions of deviance by focusing on specific institutional image archives and their relationship to the construction of notions of, for example, criminality), emphasising the archival tendencies of all photographic images and their role in the construction and naturalisation of identity categories, emphasising the visual bias of such categorisations. Paul Frosh brings a focus on the archival into the contemporary era, focusing on commercial photography and the stock image in particular. Like Poole, he argues for an approach to images as part of a network, arguing against the singling out of individual images for their particularities and proposing that commercial photography constructs a 'rhetoric of the overlooked': an all-encompassing visual environment of images that project a carefully constructed sense of ordinariness (45).

Produced to meet specific client demands, the stock image is catalogued according to key words that are incorporated into the production of the photograph, therefore the logics of classification that the image becomes subject to affect the very kinds of images produced. While stock photography provides an easy example of the structuring of the photographic image through classificatory logics, it is argued that all photography is both 'object and agent of classification': it demands to be classified while also constructing and reproducing a system of classification based upon stereotype and social hierarchy (Frosh 2003: 92). This incorporation of the logics of classification, usually thought to take place after the fact, into image production encourages the proliferation of stereotypes, which are themselves naturalised by the constructed ordinariness of the advertising image. Frosh draws connections between the archival foundations of the photographic image and performativity/performance, evoking both Judith Butler's concept of performativity, and Diana Taylor's notion of embodied performance. In presenting images of ordinariness, advertising images perpetuate and construct normative identities, reproducing gendered ideals which are transformed through time.

The classificatory aspect to Rossell's photographs needs little explanation: the absence of information that would allow an identification of the subjects as individuals, and the title of the book, indicate that we are looking less at a collection of images of individuals than a particular social group, ironically classified as the rich and famous. Furthermore, it suggests that the identity of her subjects is formed not only through the consumption of goods, but through the consumption and re-enactment of images and the ideals they project. In simultaneously evoking the performative in the Butlerian sense, and the theatrical notion of cultural performance such as that elaborated by Taylor, Frosh raises questions regarding photography's relationship to the performative: the relationship between the unconscious internalisation and repetition of norms (as conceived by Butler), and the more intentional performances or 'embodied behaviours' that often characterise photography, whether carefully staged like stock photography, or the more 'spontaneous' (although I use this word with some reservation, as spontaneity itself is often theatrical) enactments. According to Butler, 'gender is the repeated stylization of the body, a set of repeated acts within a highly rigid regulatory frame that congeal over time to produce the appearance of substance, of a natural sort of being' (1999: 43), yet Butler herself makes a distinction between performance and performativity, using the example of drag as a parodic performance which denaturalises all normative gender constructions. The obviously staged and 'performed' nature of many photographic images complicates this distinction, as staged images are used to naturalise and construct gender conventions rather than subvert them and highlight their artificiality, and hence the commodified images of mass culture are implicated as part of the regulatory frame that makes such constructions appear as natural. The act of being photographed is a performance, an embodiment of certain visual codes, which can be employed subversively to highlight the artificiality of all gender constructions as copies without originals, but also can be employed as a means of projecting and naturalising such constructions. Rossell's subjects self-consciously perform and parody visually constructed stereotypes, but as a form of visual consumption which does not necessarily amount to an awareness of their artificiality.

In a sense portraits are always authored by their subjects, who (re)present themselves to the camera. Portraiture is a form of identity discourse, in which the identity of the sitter can be transformed. The degree to which this process is controlled by the sitter (as a kind of self-portrait) or by the photographer (as is most often the case within ethnographic portraiture, an encounter that takes place around an unequal power relationship) often depends upon the social position of the sitter and the context of the photographic encounter. In any case, portraiture develops a semantics of the self (and/or other), a codification of the human body in which social categories such as class, gender, status and ethnicity are represented, naturalised, and at times transformed. This performance depends upon the relationship between photographer and subject, a relationship that has widely been acknowledged as one of the most problematic aspects of photography. As Phelan has argued, the relationship between subject and photographer always mirrors that of self and other (1993: 3), and necessarily entails a process of objectification.

Rossell's project was conceived as an exercise in self-representation, claiming that her sitters had complete control over how and where they were photographed. While it cannot be said that these images, which project their subjects' fantasies and desires, represent the 'real' lives of the depicted women, what they do document is a certain relationship with the camera that could be conceived as a particular interpretation of what it means to be photographed: what is apparent within these images is the absorption by Rossell's models of a certain visual code, an embodiment of the aesthetic values of consumer culture and its construction of feminine identity. Susan Sontag has described the relationship between people in industrialised cultures and the camera, stating that while people in non-industrialised countries often view having their photographs taken as a trespass, 'people in industrialised societies seek to have their photographs taken – feel that they are images, and are made real by photographs' (1979: 161). The photographic act is a cultural performance, in which the subjects not only exhibit themselves, but also re-enact the visual conventions of the photographic image.

As we have seen, Rossell's 'ethnology' of the rich necessarily intersects with reflections on the subject constructions of advertising and the media. Approaches towards gender performativity often focus on the body, yet identities are also performed through consumption and the subjects' material surroundings. The rich are depicted as being defined by material possessions and constructed by the consumable identities offered by consumer culture, while indigenous people are often portrayed as outside of and indeed anterior to these processes. This highlights the role of space in photography as a means of producing associations and stereotypes by constructing its subjects as extensions of their environments. The accumulation of objects within a domestic environment invites a museological interpretation, as Eileen Hooper-Greenhill has argued: 'the house, in many ways is a "collection". It holds an accumulation of imaging that is personal, yet social' (2000: 108). The house acts as a frame delineating the private from the public, marking out and defining the personal, and containing an intertextual collection of objects which work together in an 'artefactual framework' (116). Yet subjectivity cannot be constituted independently of the social, and the constitution of the subject takes place at the intersection of public and private narratives, between which lines cannot always be easily drawn. The intersection of public and private narratives displayed in Rossell's photographs makes clear the permeability of these boundaries.

The performance of class is expressed not only through the consumption of goods, but also of signification. Barthes has described the relationship between denotive objectivity and connotative symbolism in photography, arguing that a photograph appears as a 'message without a code', due to the literal relationship between the objects that appear in the image and their referents (1977: 46). The apparent codelessness of the photographic image serves to naturalise its connotative meanings, masking the signs of culture as nature, thus reinforcing views of photography as an 'innocent' and objective means of reproducing reality. Unlike the carefully constructed advertising images that Barthes deconstructs, Rossell's photographs reframe what is already framed by the house itself. This is not to say that they are objective, or 'codeless', but that the content of the image is not entirely under the control of the photographer, and is also authored by its subject whose accumulation of objects projects a certain representation of their subjectivity. There are two intersecting codes at work: the collection of objects, whose consumption is as much about the consumption of their meanings as for their use value; and that of the photographic image in which this collection is framed, often in a way that exaggerates the dimensions and grandiosity of the interiors, and emphasises those elements that serve as signifiers of wealth.

Susan Stewart's work goes beyond the model of semiological analysis of consumption and the visual developed by Barthes, to look at the ways that interactions with objects are construed metaphorically. Stewart's analysis revolves around metaphors of containment, with the gigantic representing exteriority, the public, and the social; and the miniature representing interiority and the personal (Stewart 1993). Unlike traditional semiological models, which attempt to make visual and verbal language superposable by conceiving objects as individual units of meaning, this model involves a consideration of objects' relations to the body and space, and the body's insertion into the material environment as another object, one that is constructed externally through images (1993: 125). On the construction of personal/domestic environments it is argued that the interior serves as a means of self-fashioning, with its boundaries (the house) representing its limits, thus positioning the house as a metaphor for the body and the self. The subject acts as a producer as well as consumer of objects through arrangement and manipulation, becoming the author of one's own collection

(159), blurring the subject/object binary as subjectivity plays a role in the construction of objects and how they signify, while the subject cannot be formed independently of the objects with which it attempts to define itself.

The notion that the body occupies 'one more position within a seriality and diversity of objects' (159), as Stewart argues, seems to be one of the central propositions of Rossell's work. The photographs are saturated in colour and bathed in light in a way that reduces distance between foreground and background, thus flattening the image and the spatial relationships between objects. This contrasts sharply with much portrait photography, in which the subject appears in sharp focus against a blurred background, focusing attention onto the subject. The women photographed in *Ricas y famosas* appear at times indistinguishable from the objects around them, and the images invite a reading that focuses less on the women as subjects than a focus on a collection of objects among which they are included, perhaps even as possessions of their absent fathers and husbands. This is reinforced by extreme camera angles, which at times reduce the size of the subject in relation to other objects, confining them within the limits of the interiors that define them (figure 1). Rossell's extreme use of colour is also important: while black and white photography is paradoxically used to signify reality despite its dissemblance with perception, as it is imbued with the authority of documentary modes of representation, Rossell's rather extreme use of light and colour, associated with the commercial image, is used to signify artificiality. Yet this sense of artificiality itself is appropriated as evidence of her subjects' extravagant materialism.

The rapid and uneven economic growth of recent years has led to the perception that there are now two Mexicos: that of the peso and that of the dollar, a division between those who have access to the dollar economy and global trade and

FIGURE 1 Daniela Rossell 2002. Untitled image from the series *Ricas y famosas*.

communication flows, and those who have traditionally made their income from the domestic market (Dawson 2006: 121). In contemporary Mexico conspicuous consumption not only serves as a measure of status, it also marks out consumers as belonging to the 'first world', involving not only a dissociation from Mexican commodities but also an obsessive taste for imported goods.[9] The consumption of imported brands as a measure of status is apparent in Rossell's images: there are two images in which champagne is foregrounded. In one of these, a woman is draped across a giant gold Buddha, surrounded by a very large ice cooler containing many bottles of Moet champagne, on top of which several banknotes are scattered (figure 2). The use of money in the image emphasises what is implicit in all of these images: the accumulation of commodities as the consumption of wealth itself. The primary function of luxury objects is rhetorical and social and serves a classificatory function, serving to mark out those who consume them as having high socio-economic status (Appadurai 1986: 38).

The determination to exhibit wealth through an excessive display of objects perceived to be representative of upper-class taste often manifests as kitsch, and Rossell's subjects have been attacked for their 'bad taste' and the negative image of Mexico that has been projected by these images when exhibited abroad. While Rossell is part of the social class she portrays, and indeed some of those she photographs are family members, she seems to attempt to distance herself from the baroque excess with which they surround themselves. Perhaps this is simply a result of the medium that she chooses: photography is inherently a distancing mechanism in which the photographer removes themselves from the depicted scene. However, Rossell's distancing techniques go beyond what is implicit in photography, and her objectification of the

FIGURE 2 Daniela Rossell 2002. Untitled image from the series *Ricas y famosas*.

women photographed through the visual techniques discussed above emphasises this distance. Rossell seems to be critical of her subjects' excessive materialism even while she avoids any explicit social criticism, and while she shares their social background, she appears keen to be distanced from the world of kitsch that they inhabit.

If it can be said that there are two Mexicos, it is clear that Rossell's subjects identify with the Mexico of the dollar, and perhaps this division is transposed onto the first/third-world binary. One image shows a dark-haired girl slumped upon on a sofa, dressed in a nightgown patterned with dollar bills. Behind her on the wall are displayed a collection of neatly mounted *huipiles*, which contrast sharply with her own attire. The contrast is not only between the objects themselves and what they represent, the dollar being emblematic of wealth and Western capitalism, and the *huipiles* representing an idealised and exotic indigenous heritage. There is also contrast in their presentation and relation with the subject: the night-gown is worn close to the body and therefore has a stronger identification with the self, while the *huipiles* are stripped of use value and reduced to decoration, serving to ameliorate the anxieties of capitalism where everything is mass-produced (like the nightgown), through consumption of the unique (and exotic) object. Paradoxically, while the idealisation of rural culture as the basis for a common identity is incompatible with neo-liberalism, indigenous objects find a new place within consumer culture as a measure of distinction in opposition to the increase in mass-produced commodities, even while this leads to the increasing commodification of these very objects, drawing them further into the logics of consumption.

The combination of objects and signs with diverse and seemingly opposing origins is not new in Mexico, and is characteristic of *mestizaje*. Néstor García Canclini's model of hybridity provides a more useful framework for approaching cultural mixing, not only because it does not share *mestizaje's* racial connotations, but also because it allows for a consideration of new forms of hybridity that emerge at distinct historical moments from new conditions of production, and accounts for the elite staging of popular culture. In the image described above it is manifested through the display of indigenous artefacts as a measure of distinction, which is itself, as García Canclini argues, constantly in the process of reconstituting itself as the boundaries between elite and popular culture become blurred (1995: 11).

The intertextual framing of objects in the domestic collection can produce juxtapositions which seem to empty signs of their meaning, reducing them to their iconographic status. In one image a blond dressed in a tight, partially unbuttoned leather shirt stands on the left side of the page, on the right side an image of the virgin of Guadalupe is displayed on a shelf beside an Oscar (figure 3). Besides the obvious contrast between national and imported cultural symbols (a division that is no longer sustainable), what their juxtaposition effects is an emptying of their cultural meanings and celebration of their iconic status. Rossell's framing of the image, one half of which is occupied by the posed subject, the other by the image of the virgin, also draws an opposition between the gender role designated by the virgin and the sexualised self-presentation of the image's subject, an opposition that can be transposed onto that of two Mexican archetypes: Guadalupe and the other Mexican mother, La Malinche.[10] There has been a tendency to construe deviance from the submissive model embodied in the virgin mother as a betrayal of national culture, with Malinchista being a term that has been given to women who have escaped such restrictive roles.

FIGURE 3 Daniela Rossell 2002. Untitled image from the series *Ricas y famosas*.

Whether such combinations were chosen by the subjects or directed by Rossell herself, as is most likely the case given the highly composed and aesthetic character of these images, it is impossible to say. The domestic surroundings provide the stage upon which the performance is enacted, and in many cases it is dependent upon these surroundings for definition. It should also be remembered that as wives and daughters of wealthy men they inhabit environments that may not be entirely of their own making. One image is particularly striking in this regard (figure 4): a dark-haired girl wearing a Stetson sits upon a saddle on a large desk, resting one foot upon a stuffed alligator, while staring directly at the camera and flicking cigarette ash on the desk in front of her. Behind her is a painting of Emiliano Zapata, and also on the desk is a photograph of a man (her father?) posed in front of an image of Pancho Villa, and a PRI election flyer with a photograph of the same man, highlighting the continued relationship between official culture and politics. The room in question appears to be the study of the photographed girl's father, and is filled with many symbols of masculinity and nationalism (stuffed animals as hunting trophies perhaps, revolutionary heroes, etc.). This room, apparently belonging to a PRI official, appears as a monument to the revolution and to masculinity, and Rossell's subject draws upon these surroundings for her own performance, which mocks the grandiose officialism of revolutionary nationalism, as well its patriarchal foundations.

There are many material expressions of nationalism within these interiors: revolutionary heroes, idealised portraits of indigenous people, landscape paintings, the national flag, and religious images and artefacts. Many of these objects constitute some of the most official and grandiose manifestations of nationalism, and appear as relics of an official culture that is becoming increasingly less relevant, and the populism many of

FIGURE 4 Daniela Rossell 2002. Untitled image from the series *Ricas y famosas*.

them imply often stands in stark contradiction to the lifestyles of those who identify with it; their presence in the homes of PRI politicians appears as an attempt to cling to the nationalism that has helped to sustain their power. Rossell's photographs affirm the continued presence of nationalism within contemporary culture and its increasing commodification, and the overlapping and coexistence of different cultural and political frameworks rather than the supplantation of the old by the new. Not only does *Ricas y famosas* present a portrayal of a group that has traditionally been able to resist objectification, and one that cannot be abstracted as the basis for an idealised national heritage, it also goes beyond a class-based representation to expose the identity construction and clannish affiliations of the PRI in its final days. Yet Rossell has been careful not to limit her portrayal to the PRI, and also focuses on PAN members, therefore exposing a power network that cuts across party lines (Brooksbank Jones 2007: 64), increasingly so as social power and status are redefined through the logics of the market.

As Jurgen Habermas has argued, globalisation involves the replacement of power with money (2001: 78), through a process of denationalisation opening nation-states to an economically driven world society (61). The PRI's gradual loss of power leading to the election of the PAN, whose political base is formed primarily from the business elite in Northern Mexico, completed this process with the convergence of the economic and political elite. The identification of wealth with status is clear in *Ricas y famosas*, particularly in those images taken in the houses of PAN members, whose homes are some of the most ostentatious of those photographed by Rossell, while the images of PRI politicians' homes taken in Mexico City retain the signs of official culture that symbolically link them to the revolution. Neoliberalism has been responsible for the transferral of many countries' national wealth into the hands of the top percentiles, and the redefinition of socio-economic stratifications: *Ricas y famosas* represents the emergence of a new stratum defined more through economic circumstances than genealogy, and emphasises consumption and material culture as the means through which they are produced and represented as an active process around which identities are formed. The classification and hierarchisation of subjects discussed earlier is at work not only in the photographic image, but also in the consumption of objects, particularly luxury objects, as signifiers of socio-economic status.

The invitation to voyeurism granted to the public by Rossell's photographs has been characterised by Brooksbank Jones as the opening of closed spaces characteristic of democracy (2007: 70), and it is certainly true that a great deal of debate was sparked by these images and their presence in the media. However, while these photographs seem to provide a glimpse into the hidden lives of the upper-classes, they are little more than a simulation of the 'real' lives that remain behind closed doors, and furthermore do not necessarily lead to an interrogation of the conditions that produce such extreme social differentiations. The use of media scandal for the staging of the political is symptomatic of the conversion of politics into spectacle in the contemporary era, and while the images provoked some debate about free trade and a renewed focus on political corruption, much of the attention was directed at the subjects' perceived bad taste, and singled out and ridiculed those portrayed. Brooksbank Jones has also suggested that by representing persons of her own social class Rossell has avoided complicity with the objectifying gaze (64), yet *Ricas y famosas* presents an exoticisation of wealth, which despite its contextual specificity is easily convertible into a stereotype of the rich, although in international contexts fascination is provoked by an element of surprise which counters preconceptions about the image of poverty by which Mexico has been characterised. The images were received with hostility in Mexico, but also with a voyeuristic fascination for a world that, through its separation in gated communities with high-security fences, remains remote from the majority of Mexicans (Sá 2007: 154).

As noted earlier, both Poole and Frosh have argued for an approach to images based upon their relations to other images, and Rossell's portraits of the rich cannot be understood separately from the many representations of both rural and urban poverty that have been emblematic of much cultural representation in Mexico, which Rossell self-consciously seeks to invert. This is emphasised by the structure of the book, which begins and ends with photographs of servants, whose images are implicated not only in their own identity constructions but also that of those who employ them (Brooksbank Jones 2007: 77). Rossell's series is symptomatic of a departure from totalising representations of the national subject, and as what Brooksbank Jones has called an individualist ethnography and one that departs from approaches based upon solidarity (2007: 74), *Ricas y famosas* emphasises the divisions, both material and cultural, of contemporary society. Such divisions are a result of both the fragmentation of identities within capitalist societies and the breaking of social bonds which its emphasis on individualism only exacerbates, as well as the breakdown of a hegemonic national culture based upon the exclusion of those who do not conform.

While these photographs, along with many other contemporary cultural products that consciously seek to undo the myth of an inclusive identity, depart significantly from the approaches that have tended to characterise the Mexican photographic canon or the uses to which photography has traditionally been put, identity and the nation are themes that continue to preoccupy cultural producers. Contemporary photographers employ experimental approaches towards image making, and draw upon a rich photographic canon that has played a fundamental role in the construction of ideas about race and identity, inserting their practices among both this national photographic tradition and the image-world of contemporary consumer culture, an image economy, to use Deborah Poole's term, that is shared globally.[11] Rossell's series is an example of an exploration of contemporary identity constructions, one that situates its subjects in relation to both national and global discourses, asserting the primacy of the visual in both the identity discourses that have underpinned the Mexican photographic canon and its ethnographic bias, and the 'universal' identities projected by consumer culture and the global market.

Notes

1 The photographer's editing processes cannot be overlooked here: it is possible that images not taken in domestic settings were excluded from the publication.
2 Ruben Gallo suggests that the project would have been more effective if the images had been presented alongside details of the sitters' identities as a kind of political expose. See Gallo, *New Tendencies in Mexican Art*, 68. Anny Brooksbank Jones approaches Rossell's images in terms of the tensions between personal and national imaginaries, and situates them in relation to both nationalist discourses and contemporary narratives, arguing for their coexistence rather than a replacement of the old by the new; see Brooksbank Jones, *Visual Art in Spain and Mexico*.
3 See article titled 'Ricas, famosas e irritadas' in *La Jornada*, 30 August 2002, for a rare interview with Rossell.
4 For a full chronology of the media scandal see Gallo, *New Tendencies in Mexican Art*.
5 See article in *Reforma* (Hernández 2002).
6 For a full account of these events see Dawson, *First World Dreams*.
7 For more on the relationship between the conflict in Chiapas and identity discourse see Bartra, *Blood, Ink and Culture*, chapter titled 'Tropical Kitsch in Blood and Ink', and Thelen, 'Mexico's Cultural Landscapes'.
8 The application of multiculturalist discourse to postcolonial societies is extremely problematic. Charles R. Hale has theorised the development of new political space for the articulation of indigenous cultural rights as 'Neoliberal multiculturalism'; see 'Does Multiculturalism Menace?'
9 Guadalupe Loaeza has also focused on conspicuous consumption and feminine identity in contemporary Mexico. Her 1993 novel *Compro, luego existo* focuses on a group of fictional characters who benefitted greatly from the period of growth during the Salinas sexenio.
10 The associations that come with the virgin of Guadalupe and La Malinche have often served to justify oppressive gender roles, and to construe any attempt at liberation from these roles as a betrayal against the nation. However, there have been many significant re-appropriations, particularly by Chicana feminists. See Norma Alarcon 2003. Traddutora, Traditora: A Paradigmatic Figure of Chicana Feminism. In *Dangerous Liaisons: Gender, Nation, and Postcolonial Perspective*, edited by Anne McClintock, Aamir Mufti and Ella Shohat, pp. 278–97.
11 Poole uses the term 'visual economy' over visual culture, emphasising networks of exchange over shared meanings and community (1997: 8).

References

Appadurai, Arjun. 1986. Introduction: Commodities and the Politics of Value. In *The Social Life of Things: Commodities in Cultural Perspective*, edited by A. Appadurai. Cambridge: Cambridge University Press.

Barthes, Roland. 1977. Rhetoric of the Image. In *Image, Music, Text*, edited by S. Heath. London: Fontana Press.

Bartra, Roger. 2002. *Blood, Ink and Culture: Miseries and Splendors of the Post-Mexican Condition*. Translated by M.A. Healey Durham: Duke University Press.

Brooksbank Jones, Anny. 2007. *Visual Culture in Spain and Mexico*. Manchester: Manchester University Press.

Butler, Judith. 1999. *Gender Trouble: Feminism and the Subversion of Identity*. London: Routledge.

Dawson, Alexander S. 2006. *First World Dreams: Mexico after 1989, Global History of the Present*. London: Zed.

Debroise, Olivier. 2001. *Mexican Suite: A History of Photography in Mexico*. Translated by S. de Sá Rego. Austin: University of Texas Press.

Foucault, Michel. 1972. *The Archaeology of Knowledge*. Translated by A.M. Sheridan. London: Tavistock Publications.

Frosh, Paul. 2003. *The Image Factory: Consumer Culture, Photography, and the Visual Content Industry*. Oxford: Berg.

Gallo, Rubén. 2004. *New Tendencies in Mexican Art: The 1990's*. New York: Palgrave Macmillan.

García Canclini, Néstor. 1995. *Hybrid Cultures: Strategies for Entering and Leaving Modernity*. Translated by C.L. Chiappari and S.L. López. Minneapolis: University of Minnesota Press.

Güemes, Cesar. 2002. Ricas, famosas e irritadas. *La Jornada*, 30 August

Habermas, Jurgen. 2001. *The Postnational Constellation: Political Essays*. Translated by M. Pensky. Cambridge: Polity.

Hernández, Edgar Alejandro. 2002. Ofende a Díaz Ordaz que publiquen sus fotos. *Reforma*, 30 August.

Hale, Charles R. 2002. Does Multiculturalism Menace? Governance, Cultural Rights and the Politics of Identity in Guatemala. *Journal of Latin American Studies* 34 (3): 485–524.

Hooper-Greenhill, Eilean. 2000. *Museums and the Interpretation of Visual Culture*. London: Routledge.

Israel, Nico. 2000. Daniela Rossell. *Artforum International* (April): 143–144.

Loaeza, Guadalupe. 1993. *Compro, luego existo*. Mexico DF: Alianza.

Meyer, Lorenzo. 2002. Agenda Ciudadana/ El otro México profundo. *Reforma*, 13 June.

Morris, Stephen D. 2001. Between Neo-liberalism and Neo-indigenismo: Reconstructing National Identity in Mexico. *National Identities* 3 (3): 239–55.

Mraz, John. 2001. Envisioning Mexico: Photography and National Identity. In *Mexican Literature and Culture for the Millenium*. UCLA: Duke University Press, Program in Latin American Studies.

Noble, Andrea. 2005. *Mexican National Cinema*. London; New York: Routledge.

Pérez de Mendiola, Marina. 2004. Mexican Contemporary Photography: Staging Ethnicity and Citizenship. *Boundary 2* 31 (3): 125–53.

Phelan, Peggy. 1993. Broken Symmetries: Memory, Sight, Love. In *Unmarked: The Politics of Performance*. London: Routledge.
Poole, Deborah. 1997. *Vision, Race, and Modernity: A Visual Economy of the Andean Image World*. Princeton: Princeton University Press.
Rossell, Daniela. 2002. *Ricas y famosas*. Madrid: Turner.
Rowe, William. 2003. The Place of Literature in Cultural Studies. In *Contemporary Latin American Cultural Studies*, edited by S. Hart, and R. Young. London: Arnold.
Sá, Lúcia. 2007. *Life in the Megalopolis: Mexico City and São Paulo*. London: Routledge.
Segre, Erica. 2007. *Intersected Identities: Strategies of Visualisation in Nineteenth- and Twentieth-century Mexican Culture, Remapping Cultural History*. New York: Berghahn Books.
Sontag, Susan. 1979. *On Photography*. Harmondsworth: Penguin.
Stewart, Susan. 1993. *On Longing: Narratives of the Miniature, the Gigantic, the Souvenir, the Collection*. Durham; London: Duke University Press.
Thelen, David. 1999. Mexico's Cultural Landscapes: A Conversation with Carlos Monsivais. *Journal of American History* (Special Issue: Rethinking History and the Nation State: Mexico and the United States).
Villoro, Juan. 2002. Ricas, famosas, y excesivas. *El País*, 9 June.

From Urb of Clay to the Hypodermic City. Improper Cities in Modern Latin America

MARZENA GRZEGORCZYK

Purity, fictitious as it is, was much on the mind of the nineteenth-century Latin American creoles. In founding the liberal project, they were eager to order, construct and maintain what they saw as necessary and progressive hierarchies. While observing rapid urbanization and industrialization, and dreaming of subsequent political centralization, the liberal leaders witnessed a period of decentralization due to the chaos of the wars of independence and their unsettled aftermath. As Richard Morse notes, the mid-nineteenth century was actually a golden age for rural elites and *caudillismo* in Latin America (Morse, 1992, p. 9).

The schism between the desired demographic and physical profile of Latin American space and the real one generated an impulse to reject the real space while contrasting it with an ideal: a locus of the future that ought to be constructed. Not unlike today, architecture and urban planning were conceived as an expression of, if not anticipated salvation, at least a means to eliminate the potential for disorder and to advance national progress. This normalizing tendency eventually led to utopian visions of Latin American cities like Sarmiento's *Argiropolis*. It is not, however, the utopian perspective that I will focus on here. Nor will I explore in detail the tension between the city and barbarism that was the primary critical paradigm established in nineteenth-century Latin America. As the urban reality became more varied and more contradictory, and the initially dynamic opposition between the city and what is outside of it was no longer the single defining category, alternative representations of the city appeared. I reflect here upon a particular one: a latent tradition that I call the 'improper city', that is, a city that does not fulfill the parameters set up by civilization.[1] Scrutinizing Canudos, Havana and the abstract cities that emerge from the paintings of Guillermo Kuitca, I argue that the main source of 'improperness' lies in the ways in which bodies relate to cities. To be more precise, this improperness comes about from the uneasy collapse of Cartesian dualism (in this case, the distinction between design and construction) upon which the idea of the Latin American city was founded. The discussion of the 'improper city' contributes to the reconceptualization of one of the most powerful critical paradigms of modern Latin American culture: the dichotomy of civilization and barbarism.

What is a 'proper city'? I forgo here a detailed definition, defining it implicitly through the representation of the improper city. In general terms, however, the proper city would be what Angel Rama describes in *La ciudad letrada* as the 'Latin American city'. Exploring the relationship between urban form, use, function and socio-economic structure, Rama sees the Latin American urb as product of the obsession with order that characterized the colonial enterprise. Thus, the city of the New World was conceived as a new city built from scratch but with a rigorous plan—a plan that did not necessarily arise from the organic needs of the community but obeyed an order imposed from outside or above.[2]

In orders to Pedrarias Dávila (a founder of Panama City in 1519) for the conquest of the New World, the Spanish King outlines the logic of the Spanish colonial expansion and, more specifically, its urban aspirations:

> Vistas las cosas que para los asientos de los lugares son necesarias, y escogido el sitio más provechoso y en que incurren más de las cosas que para el pueblo son menester, habréis de repartir los solares del lugar para hacer las casas, y estos han de ser repartidos según las calidades de las personas y sean de comienzo dados por *orden*; por manera que hechos los solares, el pueblo parezca *ordenado*, así en el lugar que se dejare para plaza, como el lugar en que hubiere la iglesia, como en el orden que tuvieren las calles; porque en los lugares que de nuevo se hacen dando la *orden* en el comienzo sin ningún trabajo ni costa quedan *ordenados* e los otros jamás se *ordenan* (my emphasis, quoted in *La ciudad letrada*, Rama, 1984, p. 6).
>
> Having ascertained what things are necessary for the settlements and having chosen the site most advantageous and abundantly provided with all things necessary to those who will settle therein, distribute town lots for the construction of houses, in orderly fashion, according to the quality of the recipients, so that once constructed, the town will appear well-ordered as regards the space designed for the central plaza, the location of the church, and placement of the streets; because where such orders are given from the outset, orderly results will follow without undue cost and effort, and in other places order will never be achieved (quoted in *The Lettered City*, Rama, 1996, p. 4).

If land inspired heroic visions and great ambitions in Spanish conquerors, the King's instructions for foundational procedures put these original fascinations in perspective. The King's words testify to the fear of contingency, uncertainty and dissonance. The faith in the power of order translates itself into an emphasis on *anticipation*. The order, if established before the city exists, will prevent disorder in the future. After all, as Rama suggests in his reflection on the King's notion of urban perfection, signs have a peculiar virtue of staying unaltered. The inalterable signs control the changing life within a rigid grid. With time, the inalterable symbolic order of urban existence ought to leave its imprint on the material reality (Rama, 1996, p. 8).

Whereas the function of this doubled Latin American city (existing symbolically and physically) was to perpetuate power and conserve the socio-economic and cultural structure that this power guaranteed, the 'improper city' testifies to the progressive demystification of this purpose. Rather than looking at the imprints that the symbolic realm leaves on the material one (a shorthand definition of Rama's project), I scrutinize conflicts that emerge when the symbolic urban lawmaker—the ordering Logos—crosses its path with material reality and lacks the power to mold it. 'Improper cities' are moments of eruption of the urban unconscious, zones of conflicts provoked by the persistent tension between the symbolic and material aspects of the city. These eruptions are caused by the bodies whose improper functioning unravels the ordering (European) mentality. With their apocalyptic endings, improper cities appear to be much more than just an aesthetic error arising from the problematic cult of the illicit. They point to an error of creole consciousness: its excessive desire for normalization.

In my reflection on improper cities, I introduce three different instances of these urban poetics. Although told in different styles and through different means, all of them have a dose of pathos, exasperation, nostalgia and irony. Like any improper figure, they are indeterminate and multifaceted. The first is the story of Canudos, an improper city in the Brazilian backlands monumentalized in Euclides da Cunha's celebrated text from 1902, *Os Sertões* (translated as *Rebellion in the Backlands*). Moving to Havana in 1941, one finds a more personal vision of impropriety in Guillermo Cabrera Infante's autobiographical novel *La Habana para un infante difunto* (*Infante's Inferno*). Here, the city becomes the sexualized body of the feminine other. For a third improper moment, I leave bodily cities for the city without bodies, examining the excess of order as represented in the paintings of the contemporary Argentine artist Guillermo Kuitca.

Process Against the City

Euclides da Cunha's *Os Sertões* is the dramatic history of the late nineteenth-century rebellion in Canudos, a city in northeast Brazil. This text is a demanding mixture of sociological treatise, biography, insightful analysis of a messianic movement and war reportage. Even though the title suggests the traditional tension between city and country—and its implicit corollary civilization and barbarism—the description of Canudos itself focuses on it as a disruptive urban space—an improper city. Thus, in part, the rebellion is a struggle over what the city—any city—is, can, and ought to be.

The main protagonist of *Os Sertões* is the Counselor, a messianic leader who vows to end the old world of misery and begin the new era of justice, which he in no way confused with the recently proclaimed Republic of Brazil (1889). Throngs of suffering people were attracted by his apocalyptic sermons, swelling a provincial town into a throbbing city, seemingly overnight. Soon this "dead society galvanized by a madman" (da Cuhna, 1944, p. 167) was seen as a threat to the newly instituted democracy. When the Counselor led a tax-revolt against the sinning cosmopolitans of the Republic, the Brazilian government moved aggressively to put down the insurrection. In a protracted military conflict far exceeding the government's prognostications, almost 30,000 inhabitants were killed, including the Counselor himself.

The purpose of my analysis is to unearth—by examining the representation of Canudos—what the city at the end of the nineteenth century was *not* supposed to be. As suggested before, one of the legacies of the nineteenth century was a normative view of the city. Angel Rama (1996) defines the idea of the Latin American city as "the offspring of intelligence" (p. 1) and "a dream of reason" (p. 5). This dream is governed by a rigorous centralist model tightening the relation between rules and everyday life. The concrete model of this structure is, for Rama, the checkerboard or grid that obeys the following regulatory principles: unity, planning, and rigorous order (p. 5).

The scandalous city of Canudos subverts this model of the Latin American polis at all levels. The picture that emerges in the Canudos of da Cunha's text is a disturbing distortion of the idyllic vision of citizen–subjects brought into glorious albeit hierarchical harmony. Instead of projecting order, the city materializes chaos. Canudos is a city, but it is not a proper city: it is old; it is invisible; it is "the work of insanity", and it is an inverted city, for it was not planned.[3]

The first of these characteristics—the fact that, as da Cunha writes, Canudos is not only an old city, but was "born old"—stands in direct conflict with the most fundamental element of the colonial urban dream, for it does not project into the future, does not encourage its inhabitants to participate in the advantages of the new: science, civilization, democracy—a whole new social order.[4] On the contrary, Canudos manifests itself as something anterior to humans, something that emerges from the interior of the earth as if forced to the surface by an earthquake. Yet it cannot capitalize on the historic past either. Its past is timeless rather than historical, with no conscious, founding act. The harmonious mixture of biological ('offspring', 'dream') and rational elements ('reason', 'intelligence') that, in Rama's conviction, characterizes the founding of the Latin American city, is replaced in da Cunha's text by the violation of the subtle balance between the precisely ordered civic geometry and the erratic motions of the human body. As a text, *Os Sertões* is a kind of desperate meditation on the inconceivability of Canudos' origin.[5]

Canudos is a monstrous chaos for da Cunha. It is also an invisible, clandestine city: *la ciudad-trampa*, perhaps more dream than reality. The proper city is the centre of a region or nation, a crossroads logically placed to take advantage of the natural means of communication. Canudos, however, is an enclosed extremity; it is walled in by mountains and easy to miss: 'Without the revealing gleam of its whitewashed walls and calcined roofs, it was invisible at a certain distance, indistinguishable from the earth on which it stood' (p. 146). ('Sem a alvura reveladora das paredes caiadas e telhados encaliçados, a certa distância era invisível. Confundia-se com o própio chão' (p. 165).) Without the pride of an ideal Latin American city that manifests itself as an indicator of its ordering principle, 'it was a parenthesis, a hiatus. It was a vacuum. It did not exist. Once having crossed that cordon of mountains, no one sinned any more. An astounding miracle was accomplished, and time was turned backward for a number of centuries' (p. 444). 'Canudos tinha muito apropriadamente, em roda, uma cercadura de montanhas. Era um parêntesis; era um hiato. Era um vácuo. Não existia. Transposto aquêle cordão de serras, ninguém mais pecava. Realizava-se um recuo prodigioso no tempo; um resvalar estonteador por alguns séculos abaixo' (p. 506). Although more than three centuries had passed since the Spanish King provided specific instructions for settling Latin America, in the post-independence period, the totalizing image of the ordered, progress-oriented city is still there, although the specific aura has changed. Canudos's invisibility and illegibility seriously undermines the persistence of the colonial conceptions that characterize post-independence cities: 'there was no such thing as streets to be made out; merely a hopeless maze of extremely narrow alleyways barely separating the rows of chaotically jumbled, chance-built hovels, facing every corner of the compass and with roofs pointing in all directions, as if they had all been tossed together in one night by a horde of madmen' (p. 144). ('Não se distinguiam as ruas. Substituía-as dédalo desesperador de becos estreitíssimos, mal separando o baralhamento caótico dos casebres feitos ao acaso, testadas volvidas para todos os pontos, cumieiras orientando-se para todos os rumos, como se tudo aquilo fôsse construido, febrilmente, numa noite, por uma mutidão de loucos' (p. 162)). Hidden, with germs of disorder and crime, it does not participate in the protection of colonial nor civic power nor in the execution of its order.

This disturbing Canudos is figured as the work of insanity and, as everything in-between, it generates powerful rhetoric. When da Cunha's code of reason fails, when neither social nor geographical determinism works, he tries to explain the social reality of Canudos with the most extreme accusation that can come from a man of reason: madness. Here, the concept of madness is related to the idea of race: the inhabitants of Canudos do not constitute a pure race, but three races that have blended into one type. They constitute an aberrant pastiche where piety and religious devotion coexist with assassinations and promiscuity, where honest mothers pray next to shameless concubines, where it is the same to wear a crucifix or a sword on the chest.

As an overall label, da Cunha refers to Canudos as an inverted city, the underside of civility and order.[6] The inverted character of Canudos is exemplified by an alteration in the reigning concept of justice: 'Inexorable where small offenses were involved, absolutely unconcerned with the major crimes, justice, like everything else, was an antinomy in this *clan* policed by bandits. It had in view one particular delinquency, representing a complete inversion of the concept of crime' (p. 158). ('Inexorável para as pequenas culpas, nulíssima para os grands atentados, a justiça era, como tudo o mais, antinômica, no *clã* policiado por facínoras. Visava uma delinqüência especial, traduzindo-se na inversão completa do conceito do crime' (p. 171).) According to 'the law of the dog' (as da Cunha ironically labelled the system, paraphrasing one of the poems that inspired the sect of the Counselor), it was not allowed, for instance, to drink liquor nor miss prayers—crimes punishable by imprisonment. The murderer, allegedly, might go free, and promiscuity was not punished. Thus, Canudos—like *la pampa* or the forest in the western imagination—provides asylum to people estranged from the hegemonic social order; it shelters an alternative society operating on a principle of social justice that significantly differs from that of the world outside.[7] In short, Canudos has the mesh of a city yet is denied urbanity. Whether we are looking through da Cunha's eyes at the funky fronts of the buildings with their windows askew or the topsy-turvy system of justice, Canudos equals chaos. But it is a chaos with its own order, a singular social organism with its own magnetic force. The inverse of the ideal city is not merely disorder, but an alternative, uncanny order: the power of the improper.

The aporia found in the clash of juridical systems has its material markers in the city's topography whose logic reflects rhizomatic unpredictability instead of teleological linearity. The absence of laid-out streets combined with fast, unplanned, uncontrollable growth emphasizes the paradoxical constitution of Canudos as an urban reality. The rapid proliferation of houses, which, for da Cunha, resemble gross parodies of old Roman dwellings, is the opposite of the compositional clarity that would characterize the rational utopia of harmony. The most graphic example of the improper nature of Canudos comes through da Cunha's reaction in front of the cathedral, the master piece of the feared Counselor. The church reflects the delirious spirit of the Counselor, for it exhibits an indecipherable style: a confusion of curves, incorrect forms—all out of proportion with the inversion of parts and the alteration of their natural use (da Cuhna, 1944, p. 161). Equally important, however, this cathedral has been built not by adult males but with the fragile arms of women and children, and the spent muscles of the old.

The eruption of the cathedral, and of Canudos as a whole, points to the primary source of urban impropriety: the city does not appear as a product of human consciousness. In da Cunha's text the operative word is 'extension': this city is the organic extension of the earth and the organic extension of the bodies—not their product. What is at stake here is not the city itself but the way in which people are engaged in the production and transformation of cities.[8] The plan—something that Canudos lacks—is, according to Rama, a powerful model that, by imposing an ideological frame, authorizes intellectual operations (Rama, 1996, p. 9). In Canudos the lack of binarism between design and construction not only produces a monstrous urb of clay but also spreads an unsettling message about the deep symbolic deregulation of the problematic *civitas*. While the split between the ordering mentality and its physical force presupposes the existence of the Cartesian subject (a conscious agent), the non-dualist conception of Canudos' inhabitants engenders a form of subjectivity unacceptable to the creole elite and its Republican army. These perverse and unacceptable citizens are marked by, to use Elizabeth Grosz's apt formulation, a body that "shakes itself free of statist investments" (Grosz, 1995, p. 107). 'Statist investments' (the constant demand for control, regulation and categorization) presuppose a body regulated by reason. In da Cunha's text, however, a confused, powerful lunatic emerges, replacing, to use the classic Cartesian analogy, the sober captain of the ship.

The captain's and lunatic's interests, motivations and agendas are in conflict. So are their pleasures and ideals. The narrative construction of *Os sertões* emphasizes this exasperation. Da Cunha's telling of the story of feverish construction is a failed attempt at normalization. The narrator gradually gives up the scientific language with which he described the backlands in the first chapters and makes use of the language of images, associations and allusions. This semantic change is clearly visible in the different names with which he tries to fix Canudos. They are very suggestive, mostly based on biblical and mythological images: the mud-walled Troy of the *jagunços* (p. 143); perverse Civitas of error (p. 150); sacred Canaán (p. 153); the unclean anteroom to Paradise (p. 155); Jerusalem of clay (p. 175); Babylon of huts (p. 425). Contradictory in themselves, these labels suggest the narrator's desperation at trying to order this improper city through words. While da Cunha proposed to himself to regulate the living disorder of Canudos through the word, by the end he is uncertain of his own convictions. In a larger sense, the text questions the evolutionary movement of Brazilian history toward perfection, a movement thought to be informed by the increasing role of reason. At the end, da Cunha is less ready to accept that there exist only two realities, the categories that he inherited from Sarmiento of civilization and barbarism.[9] The final two images of the book (the last four defenders facing the raging army of 5000 soldiers and the decapitation of Conselheiro's corpse) suggest, if nothing else, at least respect for the captivating paranoia of the Counselor and his followers.

The Bodily City. On Improper Pleasures

The next instance of the improper city is Havana in 1941. As in Canudos, the melding of the city and body erases the distinction between mind and body, between plan and action, between leaders and the body politic—divisions so important for 'la ciudad letrada'. In this case, however, gender distinctions become the motive force for the narration. Guillermo Cabrera Infante's novel *La Habana para un infante difunto* (*Infante's Inferno*, which could also be translated appropriately as 'Havana for a stillborn baby', 'Havana for a deceased infant', or even 'Havana for the dead Infante'—Guillermo Cabrera, that is) can be seen as an erotic mapping of Havana. The city is not only the setting for his unceasing search for erotic satisfaction but also the symbolic birthplace for the narrator. Sexually frustrated in the first half of the book and promiscuous during the second, the protagonist's increasing sexual experience is matched by his widening forays into a feminized Havana.

The book opens with the image of marble stairs. Arriving from the provinces to Havana on 25 July 1941, the narrator sees and conquers a set of stairs that mark the beginning of his adolescence. It is, the narrator admits, a 'vertical move': 'I had stepped from childhood into adolescence on a staircase' (Cabrera Infante, 1984, p. 1). The stairs, with their convoluted design and baroque banisters, are an image of challenge, mystery and danger. Once the narrator enters the long hallway with many doors, his anxious feelings become intensified in the impatient anticipation of his initiation into other things, like adult sexuality, urban poverty and cinematic fantasies.

In the last scene of the novel the imagery of vertical ascent is reversed: the narrator descends into the very depth of his sexual obsessions, the *vagina dentata*. While riding with a friend in a white convertible—all open air and innocence—he spies a flirtatious woman buying a ticket at the entrance to a movie theater. He immediately decides to follow her into the show, plunging into the darkness guided only by her white dress. Soon his ritual of seduction begins. As he nervously searches for mysteriously lost objects—his wedding ring, a watch, cuff links—he disappears in her vagina. In a blend of fascination and terror, he passes into another world of adventure, and, after a succession of images of ascent and descent, he falls 'freely into a horizontal abyss' (Cabrera Infante, p. 410). Like a teratological mini-treatise, the final episode associates monstrosity with femininity and erratic reproduction. Whether dead, reborn, or stillborn, Infante has finally been silenced by the woman/womb/vagina Havana.

But let's not pass over the multiple improprieties—the melding of so many bodies—too quickly. Throughout the novel, every time the narrator enters a woman, he is retelling and recasting his introduction into the city, the place where adolescence began and innocence was lost. It is not really the enigmas of femininity but his own pleasure that he investigates. Physically weak and often ill, the narrator spills a lot of ink and energy on describing women in terms of their approaching or retrogressing from his aesthetic standards. Whether it is wide hips, large breasts, long graceful noses or something more manly—like a pair of thick reading glasses that Honey, the apprentice writer wears (p. 234)—the discussion of female attributes invariably leads to detailed descriptions of the narrator's sexual accomplishments. Virgins or hookers, women usually are described in terms of their sexual disposition, while his own sexual performance is evaluated solipsistically.

Women are not only objects of desire for him but are also a spectacle inseparable from the movies: 'Rubén and I went often to the Fausto Theater and I discovered other Faustian phantoms, other shadowy loves, not other actresses but other women: Priscilla Lane, Anne Sheridan, Joan Leslie, Brenda Marshall, Ida Lupino, and the false and *fatale* Mary Astor: a girl in every part' (p. 41). Unable to distinguish between fact and fiction, the narrator solidifies this confusion in the course of his film adventures with his mother. Movies, besides proving him with memorable, highly stylized yet authentically alluring female beauties, are also a place of significant sexual negotiation for, as Rosemary Geisdorfer Feal notes, the narrator's early bond with cinema 'runs parallel to his attachment to his mother, for whom the movies represent much more than a mere diversion' (Geisdorfer Feal, 1986, p. 64). Often choosing between *cine o sardina* (the movies or sardines), the narrator sees himself as his mother's accomplice in fantasies that engage her movie idols. The very choice between food and movies suggests that both are for him a form of nutrition. Going to the movies, being a form of re-enactment of the primal oedipal scene, is a bodily experience.

Yet his mother does not only appear as a desirable figure. Her function is much more ambiguous. She often challenges her promiscuous son's curiosity by placing impossible obstacles in front of him. An insomniac herself, she entrusts the narrator with the task of waking up Etelvina, the 14-year-old, highly priced prostitute who lives on the same floor. He must not, however, enter Etelvina's room in performing this task. Active and searching as always, he wakes her but first climbs into her bed: 'I knocked once again and saw the door, as in mystery movies, was ajar ... She was lying face down on the bed—totally naked. I don't know what precisely led me to enter, either uncertain curiosity or definite desire. I went to the bed and touched her body (her shoulder) because, my morbid mind!, I thought she was dead, perhaps felled by the foul woman's disease' (Cabrera Infante, 1984, p. 33). Different forms of desire are connected in this passage with the open door functioning as the classical icon of curiosity and transgression: desire to see, desire to know but also desire to touch. In a prefiguration of the end of the novel, Etelvina's sexuality is represented as mystery and—in its cadaverous association—as threat. Although the narrator, fearing his mother, eventually leaves the room, he spends a few moments of intimacy with Etelvina, marked by an uneven combination of anxiety, timidity and excitement. It is not the only instance when the mother literally 'makes him open the door'. On another occasion, the narrator finds a pornographic book under his parents' mattress, which he suspects was acquired by his curious mother: 'That little book, which I read again and again, opened an erotic door through which I entered' (p. 68). One could conclude then that the house and the mother appears as much the scene for control of as for the production of sexuality.[10]

It is in Infante's home—the overpopulated *solar* on Zuleta 408, which is constructed as a site for promotion of sexuality—where the production of Havana, the bodily city, is initiated. Buildings (and architecture in general) are based on the principle of economy: they control, regulate and subordinate pleasure and sexuality by virtue of the placing of walls, roofs, doors, divisions. As Mark Wigley puts it, 'the propriety of place derives from elimination of excess' with excess understood as sensuality and improper pleasure, which are to be 'regulated and displaced into the intellectual pleasure of the regulations themselves' (Wigley, 1992, p. 352). In such buildings, the plans of the mind order the flows of the body and the flow of many bodies that make up the urban mass. In opposition to the Cartesian subject, for whom the mind is the main source of cognition, in Cabrera Infante's text the body teaches the mind, the sensuality of the city only later leading to consciousness. At one point, the narrator notes, 'the city was entering me not only through the eyes, but also through the pores, which are the eyes of the body—it was fascinating' (p. 22). Carnal experience, as Elizabeth Grosz characterizes it, 'is uncertain, non-teleological, undirected. While not entirely involuntary, it lacks the capacity to succumb wilfully to conscious intentions or abstract decisions. It upsets plans and resolutions; it defies a logic of expediency and the regimes of signification' (Grosz, 1995, p. 195). Yet in Infante's case, carnal pleasure provides an optic through which reorganization of the city occurs, with intensity being its main shaping force. Havana appears as a space that can be shaped according to the joy of the protagonist. The search for sexual pleasure recreates a new topography of the city through instances in which erotic games and sexual revelations compete against urban memories:

> I don't remember any ejaculations but I do remember wandering the streets parallel to Monte, from Rastro—a source of alcohol—to Cuatro Caminos (a city crossroads, not the town of the same name many kilometers away), not only a dangerous but a busy corner and, what's worse (I never before thought I would hate the lights of the Havana night), very illuminated, in a bewitched wanderlust, in complex surrender to sex, still incipient but already powerful, entrancing, enthralling, an invisible halo but no less radiant than the phosphorescence of the city. (Cabrera Infante, 1984, p. 21)

Urban landscape becomes an organic landscape in the sense that it is seen in terms of its capacity to produce centers for erotic pleasure. The lush lighting of Havana that initially fascinates the narrator becomes disturbing when it interferes with the possibility for pleasure. In another instance Infante complains about his too frequent and uncontrollable erections that he has while talking to women: 'I often ended up traveling to unknown regions of Havana, not at all included in my itinerary—Arroyo Arenas, El Diezmero, Nicanor del Campo—waiting vainly for the swelling to go down. The opposite, of course, occurred: the length of the trip increased in direct proportion the size of my penis, reaching shameful dimensions. I sometimes managed to leave the bus because my travel companion had gotten off first. Other times I risked the charges of gross indecency ... descending from the vehicle in motion at an unforeseen point of the route' (pp. 226–227). Again the sexual drive puts the productive apparatus into motion and formulates yet another version of Infante's city. Undomesticated women, adolescent girls, cousins, neighbours and prostitutes are his 'urban university' (p. 33) in which social analysis intersects with the space of masculine action. The narrator's sense of social class comes not through the mind's eye but the body's urges, as he searches out and learns from women across the Havana socio-economic strata. Cartographer of his carnal force rather than of geographical space, the narrator, while running errands for his mother and for the entire tenement, comes across countless 'heavenly bodies' which he 'enters' regardless of social status.

But as the bodies please the narrator so do the paragraphs he writes. Eventually he moves from the bodily charms and sexual charge of the city to his own role in signification, for it is also in the city that the narrator's literary career began. The city is thus an erotic center and a place of transition: a passage through the realm of carnal pleasure to arrive at the pleasure of the word. The progression city–woman–vagina, the three collapsing post-coitally in the movie theater, is a passage that starts with a promise of sensuality and ends with the announcement of productive creativity.[11] In a way, his sexed subjectivity becomes replaced with literary subjectivity, initiating a new relation between thought, life, experience and writing.

After conquering the city, sexually, the narrator can enjoy the pleasure of separation: ('My success would be my exit' (p. 404)), he announces. The smothering, mothering city is the Other, and he has to separate himself, now defining himself against the city. Having learned the word from his mother and explored the territory through the body, he is ready for the final gesture of re-ordering the past. The theme of maternal hegemony—the relation between caves, movies and womb—suggests a very particular way in which the form, structure and norms of the city have an effect on corporeality and subjectivity. The map becomes both the territory and the body: the subject is swallowed by it; there is no space for consciousness. This symbolic vanishing, however, could also announce itself as a preamble to a symbolic rebirth: this time with consciousness. The image of urban experience undergoes a significant change. Whereas throughout the novel the body appears to be in the privileged position, the conclusion suggests a shift in emphasis. The birth of a writer, though exacerbated by nostalgia, reinscribes the classical paradigm: the body is back in its old place; it appears as a source of negativity. Although it is associated with pleasure, it also indicates a certain kind of disfunction and otherness. In the duel between the 'narrating self' and the 'experiencing self' (Souza, 1996, p. 144), the former wins. Ultimately, the disembodied state appears to be highly valued. The writer comes to life again, this time with signs, ready for the production of a more intelligible world.

Hypodermic City

Yet disordering excess is not the most radical way of annihilating urban properness. A different kind of improper city, one marked by the excess of order rather than disordering excesses, emerges from Guillermo Kuitca's paintings. While Cabrera Infante's city is represented, impregnated and disoriented by the phallic signifier, Kuitca's urban landscapes are marked by the absence of signifying bodies.[12] Thus, there are different kinds of improper cities: in one kind, suggested by da Cunha and Cabrera Infante, there is an excess of bodies, movement, garbage—all going beyond the bounds of order, an entrancing vision of urbanity consuming itself. The other kind is an excess of order, or order that is excessive. In this vision, the urban spaces and institutions make people into machines, evoking images of company men in grey flannel suits boarding the same commuter train at exactly 7:17a.m. every morning. While not so overdetermined as that image, Kuitca's work suggests some of the improprieties of the rage to order.

From his early paintings of thorn-outlined apartment floorplans to his ongoing interest in the bed and the mattress; from his paintings of maps to his most recent representations of architectural drawings of public buildings, the body is gone, the human subject only hinted at. The spaces, mostly urban, are spaces built to process, control, and order human collectivity. Born into a family of Russian–Jewish immigrants, the 36 year old Argentine artist explores what might be called the sadness or happiness of not-belonging. 'Where do I fit into the universe?' is the question that drives his art. His paintings, although abstract, suggest very strong emotional content. In his early work, Kuitca displayed an intimate but still abstract perception of space. The bed was his favourite element: it is an ordinary yet ambiguous piece of furniture, the site of pleasure and pain, where everything starts and everything returns. His recent "Tablada Suite" is a series of paintings of public buildings— a theatre, a stadium, a hospital, a prison—where the paintings resemble architectural drawings. The title is a Spanish word for wooden panel, which is also the name of the Buenos Aires suburb that is the site of the city's main Jewish cemetery. To enhance the abstract quality, the paintings are untitled. Dense, detailed, and claustrophobic, these plans are extreme examples of the mind ordering bodies. The fright with which most viewers view the prison once they realize it is a prison just might carry over to the happy claustrophobia of the football stadium rendered in the same style.

Other recent work, in which he makes private use of maps, speaks to the improper as the excess of order by re-inserting some aspect of instability.[13] These paintings look like copies of maps. The disturbing order is combined with the physical dislocation of the bodies. As paintings, they denaturalize the ordering of the bodies that are not present, but their absence is a very eloquent way of evoking them.

"The red map of Germany" illustrates the tension between the organic and the ideal. While the underlying 'picture' is a stable map, there is an almost biological feel to it, especially from afar. It is not unlike micro-organisms that are stained in order to see them under a microscope. The red coupled with Germany brings an inevitable association with the Holocaust. Kuitca achieves the uneven organic red deliberately: when he works with graphite, he sometimes erases one part with his arm while he is drawing something else. The result undercuts the static ideal of map: the map is unable to represent action, process, change; it is always imposing order on what has developed with little overall planning. Kuitca's map, however, reveals itself as process for the eye that returns to the site of absent bodies.

"The green map of Maryland, Pennsylvania" has an X-ray feel to it. The colouring brings fluidity to the map: the green is not a solid tone as it would be in a regular map but always shading behind the yellow. Again, the organic erupts onto his maps; this one might also be taken for a veiny leaf. That it is mixed media on a mattress is crucial. A mattress is very personal, being one of the most important elements of domestic intimacy. At the same time, it is unchangeable, with little variation from one mattress to another. The buttons of the mattress look almost like bullet holes, thus tying the static map to the unpredictability of human experience in a roundabout way.

The dialectic between organic chaos and the self-contained ideal world that the maps project takes an interesting twist in 'Aerial views of fragments of city maps'. This urban text made up of sections of what seem to be city maps placed on a grid generates reflection on margins and confinements. The precision of the partial maps seems to conflict with the vitality that the entire work projects. While stabilizing social organization by containing it within a firm grid, these maps emphasize dynamicity, for they are traces of cities that have grown without an overall plan. At the same time, the white on black motif emphasizes the shapes as shapes, tracings that lead to multiple suggestive connections: one has the look of a complex cave painting; another seems to show heads; we see spiders and webs or twisted skeletons of unknown organisms. In short, there is tension between what you know (this is a map) and what you see. The map falsely freezes life, but in reading the 'map' one is never frozen or fixed.

While "Aerial views of fragments of city maps" evokes the human subject who observes, interprets and analyzes what one sees, in the next two paintings symbolically charged elements of daily life replace human figures and evoke existential drama. The streets of Edinburgh outlined in thorns in "Town of thorns" are an obvious allusion to redemption through pain, the humanizing element being painful transformation. Here, urban spaces appear as painful passageways, the thorns like barbwire. "Hypodermic needles" is the most unsettling of Kuitca's paintings and the one that best encapsulates the instance of the improper city where order is exposed as both excessive and as in a constant state of flux or tension. Although not clearly visible unless viewed from up close, it is a city plan marked by hypodermic needles instead of lines or building outlines. The painting projects tension between the order of the map and the idea of disease, which works by breaking down the order inside the body. One possible interpretation is that urbanizing tendencies are machines that produce disease (whether Middle Ages plagues or AIDS). Diseases are passed from one body to another through mysterious paths, transmitted by things we do not see (viruses, microbes, bugs). In other words, the city, which is planned to order bodies, is a machine producing its own destruction through the breakdown of the very bodies it is built to protect and process. The needle itself is a very powerful symbol of this ambiguous status. When one goes to the doctor for an injection, it is the order of science combating a disordered or diseased body. In the case of a drug user, however, the body has an insatiable appetite for something, overcoming one's good sense. The shorthand formula that emerges from these pictures is that the proper city is for the mind that properly controls the body; yet the planned ordering of bodies begets its own destruction.

Kuitca's paintings, like da Cunha's and Cabrera Infante's texts, remind us that rules evoked by architecture are in conflict with real dwelling. Yet when compared with *Os sertões* and *La Habana para un infante difunto*, Kuitca's art evokes a different kind of improperness. Da Cunha suggests that the non-ordered city is partially predicated on the mixing of races. Cabrera Infante's stress on the disruptive presence of the female body in the urban environment can be interpreted as a temporary assertion of a male's notion of inhabiting space that eventually—in the last scene of the novel—turns into an acknowledgement of the debt to the primordial maternal space. In opposition to these two versions of the improper city, which are built on a dualist notion of the subject, Kuitca presents us with the excessively ordered city—the one that subordinates the body to the mind and maintains a one way relation between the subject and the city—in which bodily differences (races and sexuality) are elided. Although the human figure is physically absent from the paintings, Kuitca's work exhibits an intense, albeit concealed, concern with the human body. His concern is paradoxical, for it seems to be both delicate and overarticulated at the same time. We see only traces of the body spread over what is a social fantasy of order and purity. The artist presents us with 'space' and not with 'place'. Place, as Casey observes, is always a result of experience. It can be defined as something that occurs between the body and landscape (29). Kuitca confronts us with the impossible: with the disembodied experience of place.

The abject, a milder form of horror, springs out of the surface of his paintings. A map shares with the abject an abstract yet primary concern with borders. Both the map and abjection show how a territory is shaped by some sort of authority. While maps delineate the geometry of buildings, streets, neighbourhoods and so on, abjection is the process of constituting the body's territory. In an essay on abjection, Kristeva comments on Céline's tendency to segment the sentences of his apocalyptic prose. She describes his fractured style as a 'worship of the depths, as resurrection of the emotional, maternal abyss' (*Powers*, p. 189).

His stylistic strategy—'the three dots' (the frequently used points of suspension)—often blends description with intense affective charge by simply indicating rather than stating a specific psychological attitude (*Power*, pp. 197–204). What is suspended—the three dots—marks the presence of deep emotion in language. In Kuitca's eerily eloquent paintings 'the three dots' of Céline's prose become the borders made of thorns and needles. The fact that in Kuitca's paintings accessories and things expelled during and from acts of defilement (thorns, blood, hypodermic needles) become part of the border itself suggests that the socio-symbolic territory formed through the process of abjection is not a product but rather an ongoing process. While experiencing repulsion and horror, we as viewers are engaged in an act of purifying the community from all sorts of forms of impurity: from waste, filth, from the corpse.[14] Through this sterile inscription of possible emotions, Kuitca's paintings suggest that the social contract is there even when there are no humans. If the abject, as Kristeva argues, is the condition for the constitution of the proper speaking subject, Kuitca's work can be seen as a reflection on the constitution of the proper community. The excessive order of that process is the dark side—the spectre—of collective genesis.

This particular form of collective abjection, formed by the unmediated conflict between the intimate and the abstract, is symptomatic of tensions that separate *la ciudad letrada* from the *improper city*. The core of these tensions could perhaps be captured best as the difference that separates two distinct ways of conceiving the city: the city as an *essay* and the city as a *tragedy*. These two conceptions of the city, as described by Italian historian of architecture Massimo Cacciari, are based on two different ways of mediating the contradiction between form and life. The *improper city* is *tragic* for it exposes and exploits this contradiction to its fullest (Cacciari 1993, p. 77). Although life is not identical to it, city conceived as tragedy is governed by the logic of experience rather than analysis. In all the modalities of tragedy that the improper city evokes (one could say that da Cunha's vision is a messianic tragedy, Cabrera Infante's text a consoled tragedy,[15] and Kuitca's paintings suppressed tragedy), city appears as a site of experience and a product of invention.[16] While mediating between the form and life, in the improper city the latter opposes itself to the former.[17] Being a product of experience, the improper city includes in its texture imagination, suspense, danger, disorientation and gratification.

In opposition, *la ciudad letrada*—the city as essay—is a product of what one might call 'second level experience': it is an analytical construct. While the locus of productivity in the improper city was experience, here it is thought.[18] According to Cacciari, who elaborates on the meaning of the 'city as essay', its central characteristics are the confirmation of the supremacy of the whole over separate parts and the synthesis of its various functions (synthesis of parts, that of nature and art). The main value of the insistence on synthesis, Cacciari argues *pace* Simmel, is the possibility of overcoming the city's regressive, unpredictable aspects (Cacciare, 1993, p. 89). Making a connection between the structure of value (in particular, the notion of civic duty) and the rationality of language, Cacciari, concludes:

> Language does not dominate any *thing*; it exists in relation to *nothing*. Its structure, the laws of its rationality, its form, have no specific *significations*; they do not communicate directly with anything. The rational is no longer the state of being to be gained, the goal of a duty the thing to be attained or dominated through a transcendental relation—it is given in the very structure of language, in its immanent constitution. As such—and not as signifying communicator—language is rational. Here the collapse of duty is the collapse of the whole structure of values: values become precisely that about which one is unable to speak. (p. 57)

This passage suggests that when language (its rationality) becomes the paradigm of order, values—being inherent in the language—are impossible to talk about. General and generalizing as this comparison is, the city-essay shares with *la ciudad letrada* its relation to power, namely, its synthesizing efforts to sustain and justify the existence of the whole. *La ciudad letrada*, with its semantic fixity and atemporality which makes its structure identical to that of the sign, sets in place a power structure and a structure of values. The hierarchical differentiation produced in this way is in constant opposition to the exigencies of the material city, which constantly undergoes reforms and changes. This duality—the specular existence of the city perceived before the city's actual existence, which echoes the distance that separates the immutability of writing from the fluidity of speech—evokes the presence of colonial authority. It offers a scenario of colonial difference, in which, as Bhabha suggests, the colonial scene is invention of historicity, mastery, mimesis, or as in the other scene of *Entstellung*, it is displacement, fantasy, psychic defense, and an 'open' textuality (p. 108). Its dual structure demands what Bhabha calls 'an impossible cultural choice: civilization or threat of chaos' (p. 133).

Canudos, that unplanned monstrous city, interrogates the volatile boundaries of these two concepts. As an interesting mix of fear, pessimism and attraction, da Cunha's text could be interpreted as an acceptance that the dream of order can never be concretized. A century after Canudos, however, after looking at Kuitca's paintings, we can read da Cunha's disenchantment from a different perspective and with a dose of relief. Kuitca's vision of the improper city helps us see more clearly the anxieties produced by the hegemonic imposition of norms that come from somewhere else. Rereading da Cunha's text, we see the persistence of hybrid forms. The improper and the proper speak to the possibility of coexistence in the same space of different visions of what that space ought to be. Most importantly, however, the improper city dissolves the opposition between civilization and barbarism, replacing it with a struggle over the definition of civilization. Civilization remains as a site of an unresolved paradox instead of exclusionary consensus. While the reader of da Cunha's text is likely to recall Sarmiento's definition of civilization (the one that emphasizes order, proximity, visibility and civic values), after looking at Kuitca's paintings, we might turn toward Lucio V. Mansilla's more comforting vision of the civilized, one that he came to inspired by his experience with *los indios Ranqueles*: civilization is where man has not lost the capacity to sleep well (Mansilla, 1984).

Notes

1. I employ the terms improper and proper in the psychoanalytical sense: the territory of the unconscious and of the repressed coincides with the improper while the clear speech of proper terms corresponds to consciousness (Agamben, 1993, pp. 144–145).
2. Puebla, Lima and Trujillo are examples of the classic model of the Spanish–American colonial city. The first Spanish cities established in the Caribbean and on the mainland did not adopt a regular urban plan. Nor did all the Spanish settlements in America adhere to the classic model after it had been adopted. Mining centers and ports were often exceptions (Hardoy, 1975, pp. 29–30).
3. An interesting colonial antecedent of the unplanned, improper city is Villa Imperial de Potosí, a city that did not have a founding decree nor order but was created by the passion, lust and ambition of the Spaniards. The improper character of Potosí comes across in Bartolomé Arzans' representation of the city: while big and powerful, the center of its life was neither the colonial project nor the law but the mountain. Being the source of wealth (silver) and colonial exploitation, it also became the producer of the symbols of time in the history of Potosí (García-Pabón, 1992, 'The Indian as Image and Structure', p. 540). Bodily disorder, crucial for the improper city, is manifested in Potosí through the fiesta: while the procession constituted and represented Spanish power, the Indians disrupted the flow of people. As Leonardo García-Pabón describes, since there was no space for Indians in the Spanish hierarchy, they were everywhere: next to the soldiers, close to the mineowners, in the carriage of the virgin (García-Pabón, 1995, 'Indios, criollos, y fiesta barroca', p. 430).

4. By treating Canudos in the broader Latin American rather than in the Brazilian context, I am following Angel Rama's continental perspective. There were, however, significant differences between Spanish–American and Brazilian cities. Argentine urbanist Jorge E. Hardoy, for example, considers Olinda—a city with a medieval plan, lacking straight streets and regularly shaped plazas—the prototype of the early colonial Brazilian city (Hardoy, 1975, p. 38).
5. Not only the origin but the end of Canudos is also timeless. As Roberto González Echevarría argues, the asynchrony between the time of *sertão* and the city (the proper city, that is) is persistently present in the text: 'It is, in fact, a war without end, for the citadel never surrenders, and even when the soldiers are busy ensuring that not a stone is left standing, resistance reappears. The time of Canudos expands into infinity, marked by the asynchrony of convulsive violence' (González Echevarría, 1990, p. 133).
6. The representation of Canudos brings to mind a similarly improper city, one coming from the mind of Jorge Luis Borges in his short story 'El inmortal' (Borges, 1989). The protagonist of the story learns of the existence of a city of immortals from a traveller. When he finally comes upon it, he describes it as an inverted city, the product of irrational or insane gods. Although isolated in a secret desert, the mere existence of this city is so horrible that it contaminates the past and the future. Faced with this the narrator wants to turn away, to turn from representation. In both cases, da Cunha and the narrator of Borges' story, the compulsion to destroy the cities and the analytical anxiety of the narrators are inspired by the intellectual horror that they feel facing an anomalous city hidden in the desert, whose very existence puts into question the happiness of the so-called civilized world.
7. Robert Pogue Harrison summarizes the role of forest in the Western imagination: 'If forests appear in our religions as places of profanity, they also appear as sacred. If they have typically been considered places of lawlessness, they have also provided havens for those who took up the cause of justice and fought the law's corruption. If they evoke associations of danger and abandon in our minds, they also evoke scenes of enchantment'.
8. This part of my argument is informed by Elizabeth Grosz's illuminating reflection on the relations between bodies and cities (Grosz, 1995, pp. 103–110).
9. For a long time the messianic movement was interpreted as a result of the parallel existence of two sectors of Brazilian society that were unrelated to each other; now a number of historians view 'messianism' as part of the national structure (see Cava, 1985).
10. On 'housing' and 'privatization' of sexuality see Mark Wigley, 'Untitled: The Housing of Gender' (1992).
11. Geisdorfer Feal explores the relation between acts of 'self-amusement' and 'self-stimulation', that is, the narrator's attempts to forge a sexual and linguistic identity for himself. Cabrera Infante himself remarked that the novel involves his 'erotic relationship with words', but it is a relationship that fails to reach consummation, for the identity of the narrator remains elusive (Geisdorfer Feal, 1986, p. 52).
12. While the interpretation of the paintings is my own, I relied on the following sources for background knowledge of Kuitca's life and work: Amor (1993), Ayerza (1993), Dona (1993), Filler (1994), Greenlees (1991), Horton (1994), Leibmann (1991), Merewether (1990) and Zabalbeascoa (1993). The reproductions are courtesy of Sperone Westwater Gallery in New York.
13. The Argentine essay of the late 1930s and 1940s (e.g. Ezequiel Martínez Estrada's *Radiografía de la pampa* (first published in 1933); Eduardo Mallea's *Historia de una pasión argentina* (1937)) is another important part of the corpus of the 'improper city'. The main notion here is the image of monstrosity, which, as in Kuitca's paintings, is the result of modernization.
14. Impurity as Mary Douglas defines it, is 'that which departs from symbolic order' (quoted in Kristeva, *Powers*, p. 91).
15. Consolation is a way of bringing the solitary experience of the hero back to the community. It is possible only where there is 'becoming', that is, where the subject decides, where there is an alternative (Cacciari, 1993, pp. 79–80).
16. I use the concept of experience as defined by Willy Thayer. At the core of Thayer's definition lies displacement from the 'usual' to the 'unrepresented', which puts into crises the 'habit' (Hume) or the *verosímil* (Todorov). Experience is something that deviates not only from the routine but also from the limits of the routine (p. 168).
17. An excellent example of this opposition is the experience of becoming lost in the city, an experience that can be seen in terms of a duel between the body and the map. It is the body—its mistake, its displacement—that appears as the originator of knowledge. Yet in order for the production of knowledge to happen, a certain psychological disposition is required. As Néstor Perlongher aptly puts it, self-dissolution has to occur: 'Quien se pierde, pierde el yo' ('Who loses himself, loses his I') (Perlongher, 1997, p. 143).
18. This separation is the very base for the distinction that Angel Rama makes between *la ciudad letrada* and *la ciudad real*: 'las ciudades despliegan suntuosamente un lenguaje mediante dos redes diferentes y superpuestas: la física que el visitante común recorre hasta perderse en su multiplicidad y fragmentación, y la simbólica que la ordena e interpreta, aunque sólo para aquellos espíritus afines capaces de leer como significaciones los que no son nada más que significantes sensibles para los demás, y, merced a esa lectura, reconstruir el orden. Hay un laberinto de las calles que sólo la aventura personal puede penetrar y un laberinto de los signos que sólo la inteligencia razonante puede descifrar, encontrando su orden' (*The Lettered City*, pp. 37–38).

'Although in some cities the tension between the discursive and material dimensions has become especially acute, all stand as the sumptuous embodiment of a kind of language composed of two different but superimposed grids. The first exists on the physical plane, where the common visitor can lose himself in increasing multiplicity and fragmentation. The second exists on the symbolic plane that organizes and interprets the former (though only for those with a certain affinity and the ability to read as signifiers what others might see merely as physical object), rendering the city meaningful as an idealized order. There is a labyrinth of streets penetrable only through personal exploration and a labyrinth of signs decipherable only through the application of reason' (pp. 27–28).

References

Giorgio Agamben, 'The Proper and the Improper' in *Stanzas. Word and Phantasm in Western Culture*, trans. by Ronald L. Martinez (Minneapolis: University of Minnesota Press, 1993), pp. 141–151.
Monica Amor, 'Guillermo Kuitca, Sperone Westwater', *ArtNexus* (1993), pp. 144–145.
Josefina Ayerza, 'Guillermo Kuitca, On the Map', *FlashArt* (1993), pp. 45–47.
Jorge Luis Borges, 'El immortal', *Obras Completas*, Vol. 1 (Buenos Aires: Emecé, 1989), pp. 533–544.
Guillermo Cabrera Infante, *Infante's Inferno* (New York: Harper & Row, 1984).
Guillermo Cabrera Infante, *La Habana para un infante difunto* (Barcelona: Seix Barral, 1979).
Massimo Cacciari, *Architecture and Nihilism: On the Philosophy of Modern Architecture* (New Haven: Yale University Press, 1993).
Ralph della Cava, 'Brazilian Messianism and National Institutions: A Reappraisal of Canudos and Joaseiro', in *Readings in Latin American History*, Vol. 2, ed. by John J. Johnson, Peter J. Bakewell and Meredith D. Dodge (Durham: Duke University Press, 1985), pp. 179–194.
Euclides da Cunha, *Os sertões* (Rio de Janeiro: Paulo de Azevedo, 1954).
Euclides da Cunha, *Rebellion in the Backlands*, trans. by Samuel Putnam (Chicago: The University of Chicago Press, 1944).
Lydia Dona, 'Guillermo Kuitca Interview', *Journal of Contemporary Art*, 6 (1993), pp. 53–63.
Martin Filler, 'Slightly Stateless, but at Home With Himself', *The New York Times* 8 May 1994, p. 34.
Leonardo García-Pabón, 'The Indian as Image and Structure. Bartolomé Arzans' *Historia de la Villa Imperial de Potosí', Amerindian Images and the Legacy of Columbus*, ed. by Nicholas Spadaccini and René Jara (Minneapolis: University of Minnesota Press, 1992), pp. 530–564.
Leonardo García-Pabón, 'Indios, criollos y fiesta barroca en la Historia de Potosí de Bartolomé Arzans', *Revista Iberoamericana*, 172–173 (1995), pp. 423–439.
Rosemary Geisdorfer Feal, *Novel Lives: The Fictional Autobiographies of Guillermo Cabrera Infante and Mario Vargas Llosa* (Chapel Hill: The University of Chapel Hill, 1986).
Roberto González Echevarría, *Myth and Archive. A Theory of Latin American Narrative* (Cambridge: Cambridge University Press, 1990).
Don Greenlees, 'Guillermo Kuitca: How to Map the Universe', *Artnews*, October (1991), pp. 94–95 and cover.
Elizabeth Grosz, *Space, Time, and Perversion. Essays on the Politics of Bodies* (New York: Routledge, 1995).
Jorge E. Hardoy, 'Two Thousand Years of Latin American Urbanization', in *Urbanization in Latin America: Approaches and Issues*, ed. by Jorge E. Hardoy (Garden City: Anchor Press, 1975), pp. 3–55.
Anne Horton, 'Kuitca at Sperone Westwater', *Art & Auction* (1994), pp. 84, 86.
Guillermo Kuitca, 'Aerial views of fragments of city maps' (76 × 117 in.).
Guillermo Kuitca, 'The green map of Maryland, Pennsylvania' (untitled, 80 × 80 × 4 in.).
Guillermo Kuitca, 'Hypodermic needles' (111 × 146 in.).
Guillermo Kuitca, 'The red map of Germany' (untitled, 80 × 80 × 4 in.).
Guillermo Kuitca, 'Town of thorns' (78 × 80 in.).
Lisa Leibmann, 'Guillermo Kuitca', *New Yorker*, 7 October (1991), p. 13.
Lucio V. Mansilla, *Una excursión a los indios ranqueles* (Caracas: Biblioteca Ayacucho, 1984).
Ezequiel Martínez Estrada, *Radiografía de la pampa* (Buenos Aires, Losada, 1991).
Charles Merewether, *Between Time, Between Places: The Passage of Desire in the Paintings of Kuitca* (Rome: Gian Enzo Sperone, 1990).
Richard M. Morse, 'Cities as People', in *Rethinking the Latin American City*, ed. by Richard M. Morse and Jorge E. Hardoy (Washington, DC: Woodrow Wilson Center Press, 1992), pp. 3–19.
Néstor Perlongher, *Prosa plebeya. Ensayos 1980–1992* (Buenos Aires: Colihue, 1997).
Angel Rama, *La ciudad letrada* (Hanover: Ediciones del Norte, 1984).
Angel Rama, *The Lettered City* (Durham: Duke University Press, 1996).
Raymond D. Souza, *Guillermo Cabrera Infante. Two Islands, Many Worlds* (Austin: University of Texas Press, 1996).
Mark Wigley, 'Untitled: The Housing of Gender,' in *Sexuality & Space* by Beatriz Colomina (Princeton: Princeton Architectural Press, 1992), pp. 327–389.
Anatxu Zabalbeascoa, 'Guillermo Kuitca, IVAM', *Artforum* (1993), pp. 93–95.

Justin A. Read

OBVERSE COLONIZATION: SÃO PAULO, GLOBAL URBANIZATION AND THE POETICS OF THE LATIN AMERICAN CITY

Globalization may be understood as a system of measurement. Any globe, after all, is a geometric unit with a finite volume, diameter, circumference. Likewise, the 'globe' of globalization is the world – or at least a certain version of it, one in which all usable spaces are known and demarcated so that movement from one point on the surface to any another can be calculated. ExxonMobil can calculate the cost of extracting crude oil in Nigeria, transporting crude across the African landmass and the Atlantic Ocean to refining facilities in New Orleans, until it reaches its final destination in your gas tank. And just as assuredly, ExxonMobil can also calculate whether it has actually met its prognostications after-the-fact, taking into consideration disruptions of supply-flow due to unforeseen circumstances such as civil war, hurricanes, famine, genocide or what have you. Everything on the globe has definable extension, length, distance, volume, *cost*. And by 'everything' I do indeed mean everything: cities, nations, dead or starving bodies, your gas tank, *you yourself*, all these things cost something, measure for measure.

The measurability of the universe – the fact that everything can be measured under globalization – fundamentally alters the relation of universals and particulars, which are now perhaps best understood as 'globals' and 'locals.' Globalization appears to operate simultaneously at the worldwide (global) and urban (local) levels, collapsing them into a singular scale-of-measurement. The local *is* global, at least in some cities – the global city.[1] As a consequence, the nation-state – an intermediary order between the local and the global – does not seem to be as stable as it once was, although global order does not seem to function without it. In any case, whereas the nation served as a dominant in cultural studies through the 1980s and '90s, over the past decade considerable critical attention has turned to sociocultural interpretations of urbanization, as urban and global networks have become increasingly intermeshed. This is, I believe, what Robert Davidson has in mind when he states that:

> As the breadth of critical inquiry in the humanities continues to expand, the use of geographical metaphors and techniques to analyze not only the imagined spaces of artistic production and theoretical discourse, but also the real, physical spaces of the built environment and the shifting coordinates of 'the national,' grows concomitantly. That there may exist new coordinates relating to these discourses insinuates the possible rearrangement of constellations or the taking of new bearings based on unused or overlooked beacons that actuate both the past (the already-mapped) and the future (willed trajectories that may or may not be realized; the possibility of drifting). Interdisciplinarity has shown that new

coordinates are not necessarily *off* the map but *of* the map, in that one need not seek out undiscovered country, *per se*, in order to offer a novel response to the continuing spatialization of disciplines, theory, and lived experience.[2]

Without question, deconstructive and poststructural critique expanded the notion of 'text' beyond poems and novels, providing us with the means to read city-spaces as textual representations with regard to continually modified coordinates of national and international order. As a field of inquiry, representation itself has been extended into larger social questions of how national ideologies come to represent subjects as citizens; how citizens gain political representation by means of a 'voice'; how city-scapes delimit the activities of city-dwellers; or how these same residents create alternative representations, alternative spaces and mappings of the city. Davidson rightly surmises that the turn to interdisciplinarity in the humanities hinges on globalization: since everything *can be mapped* (made to be measurable), it no longer matters whether space will be discovered. Rather, we must be concerned with how space will be 'spatialized,' how shifting historico-spatial coordinates can be mapped in increasingly complex ways, in turn requiring multivalent critical perspectives. As such, humanistic disciplines are attempting to carve out a space of relevance for themselves – spaces from which to articulate direct injunctions into how the globe will be mapped, configured and reconfigured by the forces of globalization.

This is particular true in studies of the so-called 'Third World', a concept itself in a state of re-articulation. Despite a common belief that globalization is still in the process of completion, an even more common belief holds that the Third World has yet to arrive fully into the New World Order. The 'Third World' seems caught in a time lag: an out-of-date concept that once denominated nations that did not quite fit into the world order ('non-aligned' nations), and that now denominates places that *have not yet* been completely folded into the global order. Whatever problems occur in this Third World would therefore be the result of the tragically imperfect replications of globalization's mappings and spatializations, most prescient in the horrendous poverty of Third World megacities. Yet such a view is fallacious.

My interest in this essay is to determine how to *read* the Latin American city – specifically São Paulo – as exemplary of the Third World's relation to globalization. In order to do so, I believe we must find means to eliminate the sense of 'time lag' thought to be constitutive of the Third World. To think of the Latin American city in terms of its *contemporaneity* to globalization is *not* to state that Latin America has finally arrived in the First World. Rather, it is to suggest that the globe operates as a singularity, or what I will call a 'unicity', in which the extant division between First and Third Worlds no longer suffices. Given that 'First World' and 'Third World' are really just euphemisms for 'rich' and 'poor', we will be well served to measure the globe in terms of distributions of wealth and poverty. Such distributions can only be measured coarsely at the international level but may be measured with much more refinement on the scale of neighborhoods and city blocks. Yet once we view wealth and poverty at the local level, we quickly realize that they may be present *in any city*. If any 'time lag' now exists, it is only that nominally 'First World' cities are catching up with nominally 'Third World' ones in the extent of their poverty. The Third World is no longer the colonized addendum to the First, but rather produces what I would call an 'obverse' colonialism. In order to understand what I mean by this, we need to read the city *poetically* – 'unicity' as a rather cruel *poetic structure* of globalization.

Global city/Fourth World

Angel Rama's final, posthumously published work, *La ciudad letrada*, is perhaps the most pervasive and influential humanistic theorization of Latin American urbanization and social history. For Rama, there may be no distinction between the constitution of Latin America as a geo-political/sociocultural region and the construction of cities in that region after 1492. That is, the 'discovery' of the new continent(s) by the Iberians not only held forth the promise of limitless wealth and social advancement for the colonizers but also the possibility of instantiating a new social order in harmony with the divine universe. The Latin American landscape therefore appeared to the Europeans as a *tabula rasa* upon which new cities – embodiments of social order – could be built with Platonic (or really Pythagorean) precision. Furthermore, this social order, which Rama dubbed the 'Baroque order of signs', was to be maintained by a class of literate functionaries (i.e. *letrados*) through the writing of ornate government decrees and rhetorically elaborate poetry. Although subordinated to *peninsulares* during the colony, this class of *letrados criollos* was to hold preponderant sway over social power well after national independence and into the twentieth century. Indeed, Rama notices a tendency among Latin Americans to forge an overdetermined link between literacy, citizenship and effective agency even into contemporary times (c.1980s). In sum, the city is *the* locus of sociohistorical and cultural order in Latin America but only if we admit that the Latin American city is double: at once *la ciudad real*, an actual, physical urban space; and *la ciudad letrada*, a class-specific, symbolic order.[3]

Such a reading appears to be at odds with prevalent social scientific views. The British/Argentine sociologist, Saskia Sassen, provides one of the most compelling concepts with which to understand urbanization during the time of globalization: the 'global city'. The global city is a concentration of corporate management headquarters, service-sector industries and intellectual labor that may be found in various metropolitan centers networked across the planet. In essence, the global city functions as a 'command center' for the globalized economy, allowing multinational entities to outsource important functions like accounting, IT and R&D from anywhere those entities do business. Global cities therefore operate as super-national spaces – at once located in national contexts, and yet functioning in tandem across national borders. In this sense, Sassen points to New York, London and Tokyo (along with, perhaps, Frankfurt, Bangkok and others) as now sharing more in common with one another than with other cities in their respective nations. The global city represents the creation of a truly *cosmopolitan* world order, one that in many respects operates beyond the control of national governments.

One of the commonalities among these global cities, however, is their incompleteness. Sassen herself recognizes that the global city is only really a *part* of the larger urban landscape. Specifically, it is located mainly in high-rise office complexes and the residential areas where those working in these complexes live. The global city is only those parts of Manhattan and central London and Tokyo where the global services economy is managed but it is not, say, the Bronx or Hackney. This situation is nowhere more evident than in Brazil's financial capital. As a finance, managerial and communications command center for much of South America, São Paulo may indeed justifiably hold claim to the title of global city, at least in part. Yet the 'global city' of São Paulo is largely concentrated in the Zona Oeste (West Zone), in the office complexes along the Avenida Paulista and Marginal Pinheiros, towards the Universidade de São Paulo and the upscale residential districts of Morumbi and the Jardins. In spite of its wealth, however, São Paulo is also the site of unbelievable poverty, with between 25% and 35% of its 17 million residents living in dire poverty. The city's poor are largely concentrated in the sprawling Zona Leste (East Zone) – home to some 4 million people (or double the size of Toronto) of whom 1 million are totally unemployed, without jobs in either formal or informal economies. Much of the Zona Leste, in other words, is *favela* without paved roads or running water or waste disposal. And so, despite the fact that the city has the most congested helicopter traffic in the world as the super-rich commute from skyscraper to skyscraper, the Zona Leste's 4 million residents have access to precisely *seven* hospitals.[4]

As João Sette Whitaker Ferreira has noted in his tacit critique of Sassen, the 'global city' concept often has more to do with local real-estate values and property development than it does with the creation of universal cosmopolitan culture:

> By this criterion can one understand the argument of those who are beholden to the idea of defining the city of São Paulo as a global-city. This is not, however, the most meaningful criterion, as seen in the disastrous results caused by international finance capital in the real estate market of Bangkok. Nobre demonstrates how megaprojects merely served as a means to attract investment by way of an urban design designed to please large corporations and the elites. Swayed by the example of the megaprojects executed in the 1980s in the U.S. and London, the author shows how this nevertheless augmented the risk-potential for real estate investments.... If the high risk of real estate investment already caused crises not only in Bangkok, but also in central nations like the U.S. and England, what does this say for the eventual risks for an economy that finds itself in a high degree of instability like that of Brazil? Would São Paulo, with its nearly 6 million excluded residents, have sufficient financial and economic wherewithal, within the restricted circle of its besieged elites, to guarantee the success of an economic boom promoted directly by speculative international capital?[5]

In Whitaker's critique, it is not so much that the global city does not exist, or that the 'global city' is a useless concept. Rather, the moniker of 'global city' can be utilized by elite civic leaders in order to promote speculative investment in high-end real estate, which in turn leads directly to the overdevelopment and overvaluation of already unstable markets in a weak position to withstand huge financial fluctuations. Those who suffer this boom-and-bust cycle the most, however, are not the global city's elites but rather those (miserably poor) residents who live in those areas of São Paulo that are evidently excluded from the global city per se. This is the case because wealthy investors in the global city have not only the financial wherewithal to withstand crisis but also the political capital to attract further infusions of capital in times when infrastructure investments should be allocated more broadly throughout other parts of the city. As a consequence, although they are evidently not integrated into globalization the poor are still disproportionately affected by it.

In fact, Sassen appears to recognize the problem broadly speaking. She ends *The Global City* by ruminating on what appears to be a paradoxical situation. As global power is concentrated into global cities, we will see 'the formation of a new territorial complex at the level of the spatial and institutional arrangements in cities dominated by corporate services and finance: a complex of luxury offices and housing, massive construction projects, and appropriation of urban areas that previously had gone to middle- and low-income households and to moderately profitable firms'.[6] Yet this intensification of 'high-end' gentrification is accompanied by the polarization of society both economically and spatially. Specifically, Sassen charts – both statistically and qualitatively – the expansion of low-end wage labor and the increasing informalization of the economy in New York, London and Tokyo. This appears to be a typical pattern that several sociologists have noted, particularly under the moniker of the 'dual city', in which the reduction of the middle-classes correlates to expansion of the upper and lower classes. In the end, Sassen clearly sees new phenomena of urbanization emerging:

> There is clearly a structural process at work here as well. Global cities are a key site for the incorporation of large numbers of immigrants in activities that service the strategic sectors. *The mode of incorporation is one that renders these workers invisible*, therewith breaking the nexus between being workers in leading industries and the opportunity to become – as had been historically the case in industrialized economies – a 'labor aristocracy' or its contemporary equivalent. In this sense 'women and immigrants' emerge as the systemic equivalent of the offshore proletariat.[7]

The consequences of what Sassen states here are quite stunning. Globalization *does* represent a structural shift in the world's political-economic order, one that results in an abrupt transformation of class–labor relationships. But, perhaps counterintuitively, the generation of great wealth made possible by the efficiency of global corporate services and production appears to result in the generation of great poverty.

Sassen provides a wealth of quantitative data (which she has been gathering since the late 1980s) that justify her claims, as well as an impressive qualitative narrative of gender and immigration demographics in the three 'First World' cities she studies. All the same, the question remains as to *why* all of this is happening. Sassen posits that the expansion of the lower end of the socioeconomic spectrum is the direct consequence of expansion at the top. To wit, the emergence of the global city leads to a change in high-end consumption and lifestyle habits that require greater amounts of labor in menial service and manufacturing (such as janitorial work and child care). Yet frankly, one is left to wonder whether high-class consumption alone is sufficient to explain the extent of low-class concentrations in global cities, as if we were witnessing a rather simple cause-and-effect relationship between the two. This is especially true of large Latin American cities in which the sheer size of severely impoverished classes would seem to far outweigh changes in high-end spending habits. Indeed, turning again to São Paulo (though we could also turn to Mexico City, Buenos Aires or Lima) the continued growth of poverty is just that – *continued*, a continuity of spatial distributions of wealth and poverty begun at least as far back as the nineteenth century. Without foregoing the possibility that globalization represents a decisive structural shift, then, we need to confront two questions: How does 'global' urbanization concentrate wealth and poverty simultaneously? And how does the Latin American city (in the so-called Third World) relate to sociospatial distributions in so-called First World cities like the ones Sassen so impressively analyzes? A daunting amount of quantitative data will be required to answer such broad questions. Yet we cannot even begin to ask these questions, let alone answer them, without imagining the world in new ways.

I will contend here that literary reading provides a more accurate means than is currently available for the concrete interpretation of social spaces, in a way that is *measurable*, precisely because literary/cultural critique provides an acute sense of the imaginary. The kinds of reading I am thinking through here are therefore inflected by both sociological and critical-theoretical perspectives on contemporary urbanization, which themselves have already surpassed any strict limitations of the 'real/imaginary'. That is, the division between the 'real' and the 'imaginary' (as formalized by Rama, for instance) has effectively been transposed onto a distinction between 'reality' and 'virtuality' — a distinction that has collapsed into singularity under networked globalization. (Incidentally, this 'reality/virtuality' collapse may signal another aspect of the structural shift posited by Saskia Sassen.) One of the most poignant reflections on this matter may be found in recent work by Joan Ramon Resina, with his concept of 'after-image'. Resina begins by working through a scenario in Michel de Certeau's *The Practice of Everyday Life* in which Certeau looks down upon New York City from the World Trade Centers, creating a false, almost voyeuristic image of an immobilized city. From such heights, the city appears frozen in time as an image so that it can be read like a map or a text; of course, Certeau impugns the validity of the static image by questioning how one would actually walk through the city at street-level. However, Resina's interest lies not in the ideological falsity of reading a static image (which would be the easy path among standard Marxist, psychoanalytical and poststructural critics) but in the process by which images themselves are produced. That is, there seems to be a cognitive gap between the time it takes for one to perceive a visual sensation and the time it takes for that perception to be recognized as such. Every image of a place, if this is the case, is in fact an 'after-image' of place; or as Resina states, 'Rushing in through this gap, stories, and above all, the story of the production of the image burst into the image. That gap is signified by the hyphen in the term "after-image." More a semantic placeholder than a place, the hyphen also expresses the gap in the after-image, itself a non-place, but one that re-places the image, restores it to place by infusing it with time and change.'[8] What one gains by thinking in this way is an acute sense that *space* and *place* are not static but *temporal* qualities that may dissolve and be reconstituted. There is always a 'virtual' time-gap in the image-production of the city as an after-image, a gap of time that enables change.

We may unpack certain possibilities of Resina's 'after-image' by reading it in conjunction with Manuel Castells's 'space of flows'. In *The Rise of the Network Society*, Castells holds that informational networks have fundamentally altered the globe's societies, and with them the very concept of social space:

> On the other hand, the new communications system radically transforms space and time, the fundamental dimensions of human life. Localities become disembodied

from their cultural, historical, geographical meaning, and reintegrated into functional networks, or into image collages, inducing a space of flows that substitutes for the space of places. Time is erased in the new communication system when past, present, and future can be programmed to interact with each other in the same message. The *space of flows* and *timeless time* are the material foundations of a new culture that transcends and includes the diversity of historically transmitted systems of representation: the culture of real virtuality where make-believe is belief in the making.[9]

In many ways, ideas such as these are an advanced form of network theories that have been emerging since 1950.[10] In Castells's view, the fact that information can be communicated virtually instantly over informational networks nearly annihilates spatial obstacles between peoples and cultures, and thus alters temporal relations (or at least cultural representations of these relations) between past, present and future.[11] As a result, we are almost compelled to view cities not as static *places* but as places where people and information *flow*. Or rather, the city becomes a network of networks, linking together the movements not only of residents and information but also of electricity, water, food, cars, planes, and so forth. The city is *not* houses, and cars, and buildings and elevators. Rather, the city is the *time* it takes for you to leave your house in your car, drive across roads to your building where you take an elevator to work; it is the time it takes gas and water to be purified and transported to the airport and onto the plane that will fly you to Bangkok or Buffalo; and it is the time it takes you to access satellite maps of Bangkok or Buffalo on Google Earth. And the greater the efficiency of the network, the more this time seems to be reduced to a minimum, a 'timeless time'. At the limit of such thought – with which Castells may or may not agree – *there may be no effective difference between one city and the next*. Cities are individuated places, of course, but once they are linked by transportation and communications networks, they may become functionally embedded into one another. At the very least, Castells sees the creation of 'mega-cities' consisting of conjoined urban areas and jurisdictions. The area from Hong Kong to Macau, for instance, functions as a single urban area even though it contains tens or perhaps hundreds of individual cities; or, as Castells puts it, the mega-city is 'globally connected and locally disconnected'.[12]

One should not take Castells's ideas, however, as heroic endorsements of global capitalism in the information age. If the entire globe has been networked into what is effectively a massive 'mega-city', the political-economic system maintaining this network nonetheless draws a division between who is 'in-network' and 'out-of-network'. In *End of Millennium* (the third in the *Information Age* trilogy that begins with *The Rise of the Network Society*) Castells writes that, 'overall, *the ascent of informational, global capitalism is indeed characterized by simultaneous economic development and underdevelopment, social inclusion and social exclusion*, in a process very roughly reflected in comparative statistics'.[13] Later, Castells proceeds to theorize this social inclusion/exclusion in spatial terms, under the concept of the 'Fourth World': 'The territorial confinement of systemically worthless populations, disconnected from networks of valuable functions and people, is indeed a major characteristic of the spatial logic of the network society....'[14] Although the concepts of 'Second World' and 'Third World' have faltered, the 'First World' has not totally filled the void in their wake, has *not* come to cover the entire globe. Instead:

> ... a new world, the Fourth World, has emerged, made up of multiple black holes of social exclusion throughout the planet. The Fourth World comprises large areas of the globe, such as much of Sub-Saharan Africa, and impoverished rural areas of Latin America and Asia. But it is also present in literally every country, and every city, in this new geography of social exclusion. It is formed in American inner-city ghettos, Spanish enclaves of mass youth unemployment, French banlieues warehousing North Africans, Japanese Yoseba quarters, and Asian mega-cities' shanty towns. And it is populated by millions of homeless, incarcerated, prostituted, criminalized, brutalized, stigmatized, sick, and *illiterate* persons.... In the current historical context, the rise of the Fourth World is inseparable from the rise of informational, global capitalism.[15]

Similar to the ways Sassen sees the dual expansion of wealth and poverty in 'First World' global cities, Castells views simultaneous 'First World' overdevelopment and 'Fourth World' underdevelopment as global phenomena of the network society.

Drawing on both Resina and Castells, then, we may devise a new way of measuring the global city. Both scholars point to a certain de-spatialization or virtualization of urban space. Space never disappears or dematerializes, of course, but it is no longer sufficient to measure space only in terms of extension (in meters, kilometers or miles). Instead, globalization compels us to imagine cities in terms of time and history, as the progressive flow of people, things and information. Imagined historically, the urban landscape is always the 'image-scape' of itself. Or, more precisely, we may think of the city as being at once a place *and* a 'collage' or 'flow' of after-images that unfolds historically. For the remainder of this essay, I would like to map São Paulo in its historical genealogy, in a way that accentuates the collapse between the real (the urban landscape) and the virtual (the urban image-scape, the flow of after-images). The point here, however, is not to utilize São Paulo merely as a specific case in order to prove general theories. Rather, I am interested in how reading São Paulo (and indeed Latin American cities in general) in terms of literary representation and culture critique allows us to modify, extend and even surpass the concepts just outlined.

Não Paulo: illiteracy/hyperliteracy

Each Latin American city has its own individual histories, shapes, patterns and problems. But we may take São Paulo to be emblematic of Latin American urbanization in general, to the extent that the city has emerged from a *long history* of simultaneous social inclusion and exclusion of the sort that Castells (and, tacitly, Sassen) only sees as a *contemporary* phenomenon. Indeed, Angel Rama correctly conceptualized the Iberians' construction of cities in the sixteenth and sevemteenth centuries as that which constituted the social divisions (such as urban/rural, European/Indian, educated/uneducated, and civilized/barbaric) that have always been constants throughout Latin American history.

São Paulo differs somewhat from Rama's *ciudad letrada*, however, in that the ascent of São Paulo as a site of global power has been shockingly rapid. Although founded in the sixteenth century by Jesuit missionaries, São Paulo remained something of a provincial backwater for much of its history, until, that is, coffee production boomed at the end of the nineteenth century. With the abolition of slavery in 1888, São Paulo became the primary end-point for the mass migration of wage-laborers from Europe, Asia and other parts of Brazil.[16] Agricultural wealth was re-invested into a burgeoning industrial sector in the early twentieth century, and from there into international banking and financial services, which have become dominant in the twenty-first century. Demographic growth figures for the city are simply staggering: from a population of 31,000 in 1870, São Paulo mushroomed to 240,000 by 1900, and then quintupled to reach a population of 1.3 million in 1940.[17] Obviously, the city grew much faster than its leaders could manage, as evidenced by the fact that São Paulo lacked *any* official urban plan until 1930, by which time it was about to top 1 million people.[18]

As Nicolau Sevcenko has stated, the super-rapid expansion of São Paulo has historically created serious difficulties in identifying the city in any meaningful way:

> In the end, São Paulo was not a city of blacks, nor of whites, nor of *mestiços*; not of foreigners nor of Brazilians; neither American, nor European, nor native; nor was it industrial, despite the growing volume of the factories, nor an agricultural emporium, despite the crucial importance of coffee; it was not tropical, nor subtropical; it wasn't even modern, yet it still didn't have much of past. This city that sprouted suddenly and inexplicably, like a colossal mushroom after the rain, was an enigma for its own inhabitants, perplexed, attempting to understand it as much as they could, while fighting to not be devoured.[19]

Indeed, this lack of identity seems to be reflected in our first 'after-image' [20] of São Paulo (figure 1), which shows a city that is fundamentally amorphous. How, then, can

FIGURE 1 São Paulo from space. Google Earth, used by permission.

we locate the design of the city, when historically São Paulo has never really had any, and now *looks* absolutely amoebic? Unlike Mexico City and other Latin American cities, São Paulo is *not* marked by history,[21] but by a fundamental modernity erasing the past. Thus, unlike what Rama said of the Latin American city, the idea of order in São Paulo is that of industrial modernization (or what we might call 'inhumane dehumanization'), not that of Baroque colonization ('inhumane humanism').

Accordingly, São Paulo has grown out of seemingly 'pragmatic' economic choices based on individual use and utility, rather than the establishment of an overarching sociopolitical or aesthetic order. As just mentioned, the rapid expansion of coffee provided capital for re-investment into the manufacturing sector. Industry was further promoted over the twentieth century by federal and local governments (who have been eager to 'modernize' the nation), and by foreign direct investment, principally from Britain, the United States and Canada. Factories first spread out along the (now highly polluted) Tietê and Pinheiros rivers, and then later along the city's rail lines and highways.[22] If we were to look at a map of São Paulo's industrial sectors, we would see that they correspond to a map of rivers and major automobile thoroughfares. Likewise, residential zones have tended to remain in close proximity to industrial zones, evidently because workers migrating to the city have sought to remain close to workplaces. Yet the majority of São Paulo's residences are technically illegal, lacking proper ordinances from the city. São Paulo has some 1600 *favelas*, of which half are located near the city's two rivers. And the majority of *favela* residents are *working-class* poor.[23]

In short, São Paulo has been constructed according to perceived economic necessities, a kind of 'free market' just beyond government regulation. But these 'pragmatic' choices have introduced chaos: São Paulo is a mixed-up patchwork of rich and poor neighborhoods, with wealth largely concentrated to the west (Zona Oeste) and poverty concentrated to the east (Zona Leste). But even though they might only be separated by a matter of meters, rich and poor areas remain largely out of sight from one another. Indeed one's ground-level perspective in São Paulo is largely marked by a *lack of vision*, left amidst a seemingly endless sea of 20- to 30-story concrete buildings that block out both sunrise and sunset.

Thus, despite the mantra of real-estate agents, 'Location! Location! Location!', there really is no location in São Paulo, since it is nearly impossible to orient or locate one's self in the city's space. Simply put, the space of the city does not provide clear benchmarks or indices of why or how São Paulo is as it is. Its space alone is rather immeasurable. Aesthetic representations of the city bear out this fact. Unlike Rio with its *samba*, São Paulo has no music to call its own. Paulistana music these days is really hip-hop, and before that it was *rock e roll*, and before that it was really *forró*. In other words, its music is always borrowed from somewhere else. Forró, for instance, is the music of Brazil's Northeast, of the rural *sertão*, yet it only became popular on a mass scale over São Paulo's radio waves in the 1940s as the music of poor northeastern immigrants to the city such as the king of *forró*, Luiz Gonzaga. In 'Asa branca', his first hit from 1947, for instance, Gonzaga sings:

> Hoje longe muitas léguas, numa triste solidão,
> Espero a chuva cair de novo pra mim voltar pro meu sertão.
> Quando o verde de teus olhos, se espaia na plantação,
> Eu te asseguro não chore não, viu, eu voltarei, viu, meu coração.[24]

[Now so many leagues away in sad solitude,
I hope for the rain to fall again so I can return to my sertão.
When the green of your eyes shoots from the plantation,
I promise you, don't cry now, see, I will return, see, my love.]

Here 'home' for Gonzaga is place where his cattle and crops and green-eyed lover live, but it is also far away. Obviously, Gonzaga sings from a 'here' that is not 'there' where his home is; framed another way, Gonzaga has traversed a network of problematic socioeconomic relations that have permitted, even compelled him to migrate, to exile himself to the place from which he sings. He has had to come 'here' to São Paulo out of 'pragmatic' economic choices based on his poverty but he wishes to leave as soon as he can, even if that is impossible and even if he *never mentions* where 'here' is. This *forró*, then, is São Paulo music, to the extent that São Paulo is the source of unspeakable sadness and privation that is nonetheless necessary to the song's production. São Paulo is present, but unspoken; São Paulo is *no place*, a place-holder.

Forró, just like other national musics of Brazil, is a lyrical mode of the illiterate. Not that Brazilian music is unintelligent, hardly so; rather, historically Brazilian music has emerged from the *favela*, the *sertão* and the *senzala*, and not the *casa-grande*. Moreover, while Brazil has had a literate *letrado* class, we always have to understand the Brazilian *letrado* with regard to Brazilian illiteracy, which now stands at around 30%, but which has historically stood at anywhere from 65% to 85% over the past 150 years. Although during this period Brazil has enjoyed a large reading public, one must remember that educational systems have always been limited, that the printing press and university were banned by the Portuguese crown until after 1800,[25] and that as a result Brazil's national 'imagined community' has not been transmitted through print media like newspapers and novels as Benedict Andersen would have it, but rather broadcast over radio and television.[26] In any event, my interest here is to examine what happens when we take the *letrado* out of the ideal Baroque order of signs, and place the *letrado* in the pragmatic modern-industrial order of signs. Surprisingly, a good number of elite, modernist and postmodernist aesthetic productions have focused on a very small locale in central São Paulo. A second 'after-image' (figure 2) shows the area known as either República or the Centro Novo (New Center), an area built up between 1890 and 1910, which begins roughly with the Viaduto do Chá (a steel bridge crossing the Anhangabaú Valley) past the Teatro Muncipal (a Beaux-Arts theatre based on the Paris Opera) down what is now the pedestrian walkway, Barão de Itapetininga, to the Prefeitura (or City Hall) on the Praça da República near the intersection of two main arteries, the Avenidas Ipiranga and São João. This area is the site of rather impressive list of aesthetic works: Oscar Niemeyer's modernist S-shaped Copan Building (one of the most distinctive in São Paulo); the setting for the modernist profane oratorio 'As enfibraturas do Ipiranga' by Mário de Andrade; the place where Mário de Andrade read his poetry during the Semana de Arte Moderna or Modern Art Week of 1922, which inaugurated Brazilian modernism from the Teatro Municipal; one of the main locales of the cubist novel *Parque industrial* by Patrícia Pagu Galvão; and also for Caetano Veloso's song 'Sampa' ('Alguma coisa acontece no meu coração/Que só quando eu cruzo a Ipiranga e a Avenida São João'); and recently Regina Rheda's collection of short stories *Arca sem Noé: Histórias do edifício Copan*, among others.

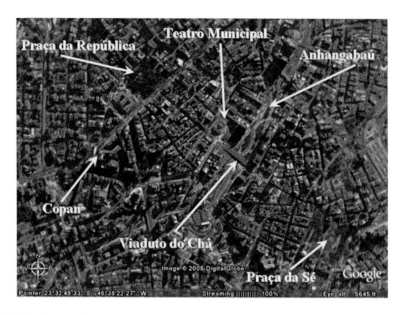

FIGURE 2 Centro Novo. Google Earth, used by permission.

With so many key works centered here, *why* the aesthetic centrality of the Centro Novo? Ironically, its *centrality* stems from the *de-centering* of São Paulo's urbanization. That is, the historical center of the city lies just to the east of República, around the Praça da Sé. However, mass immigration and demographic expansion placed incredible pressure on the Centro Velho, such that the Viaduto do Chá and the Centro Novo had to be constructed in the 1890s as a kind of 'urban release valve' so that people and trams could cross the Anhangabaú Valley and begin to settle westward.[27] Indeed this is exactly what the city's elite began to do, by building neighborhoods and subdevelopments like Higienópolis, Avenida Paulista, the various Jardim districts and Morumbi, all in the Zonas Oeste and Norte where one will find placed like Ibirapuera Park and the Universidade de São Paulo. Yet the movement from Old Center to New Center also seems to have created a dividing line, with the poor industrial working class and underclass, largely composed of powerless migrants flooding into the city, beginning to concentrate to the east of Anhangabaú. The line of the Anhangabaú Valley and the construction of the Viaduto do Chá, in other words, represent a key historical moment in the city's growth when the limits between old and new, east and west, rich and poor, and perhaps even white and black were irrevocably imposed on the landscape. This created what I call the 'city limit' of São Paulo, a border that is no longer to be considered a *boundary around* the city but an internalized crossing-point or border-crossing that has determined the shape of the city over time. And yet you would never recognize the historical importance of this place by looking at it, especially since the Centro Novo has literally been buried in modern concrete, glass and asphalt.

The Centro Novo, that is, is something of a *no place*, akin to what we saw with Luiz Gonzaga's *forró*. São Paulo (with its various centers) *is* a place, of course; yet aesthetic representations continually refer us back to a *no place*, a place of exclusion, within that place. And this *no place* is so powerful (as both a reality and an imaginary) that we should have some means of measuring it as such. In essence, we can come to a critical engagement with this evident paradox (place/*no place*), and with São Paulo as a 'space of flows,' by juxtaposing photographic after-images of the city (cf. the satellite images in figures 1 and 2) with poetic/lyrical after-images. To do this we may turn not only to *forró* and other popular forms but to a well-known work (figure 3) from 1963 by the São Paulo concrete poet, Augusto de Campos, entitled 'cidade/city/cité'.

As we read this linear 'after-image' left-to-right as a single lexeme of over 150 letters, we may not even be able to read at all except in fits and starts: perhaps 'atrocaduca' to 'ducapaca' to 'pacaustid' and so forth. The verses contain fragments, partial tokens of words that could possibly make sense but that ultimately fail to do so; and when these fragments are taken as a unified whole, they can only be seen as entirely muddled. In this sense, Augusto's poem is an 'illiterate' text, in that it foists upon the reader the inability to understand what has been written. The reader has to modify her/his reading practices entirely, by use of a 'key' that is provided in the poem's tripartite title appearing at the tail end of the work. Here, 'cidade/city/cité' does not refer to a city at all, although this meaning can never be totally evacuated. Instead, the title serves as a kind of 'transcriptor' that the reader utilizes to generate strings of lexemes: 'atro-cidade, cadu-cidade, capa-cidade, causti-cidade, dupli-cidade, etc.' In other words, the title refers only to its own material as typographic signal, in its role as a suffix used to nominalize a series of adjectives (stems of adjectives, that is) that are ordered (for the most part) *alphabetically*. As such, the poem is instantly translatable into Portuguese, English and French.

This illiterate reading practice effectively substantiates the *time* of words, just as it de-substantiates their space. Language literally has *no place* in Augusto's poem. As a physical thing in the space of the page, the poem is relatively unpronounceable (unless you have a lot of practice at it), and the only three complete words of the work ('cidade/city/cité') are only understood to be suffixes, that is *incomplete parts* of words. Complete words ('atrocity', 'caducity', 'capacity' etc.) can only be generated as a function of *time* (and not *space*), by 'transcripting' a string of terms that *do not exist* on the page but rather only exist as an *after-effect* of transcription. This inability to read what is actually *there* on the page, a peculiar form of illiteracy, therefore produces a kind of 'hyperliteracy'. Hyperliteracy because the poem is simultaneously triple and trilingual, a triple string of signifiers in three languages – but only when considered as *incorporeal, temporal* quantities. The poem *looks* as if it only has one line but in fact it has three: *three disembodied lines*. And these three lines, which only exist in time and not space, are further ordered by etymological history, since translation between Portuguese, English and French is only possible because of each language's historical relation to Latin, and indeed the conquests of the Roman Empire in Hispania, Britannia and Gaul. This idea of order is bolstered by the poem's alphabetical order (in the *Latinate* alphabet of course). But, by the same token, the historical origin, the tie-back to Roman conquest is rendered invisible: in the poem's generative transcription there can be no *original* words, just a triplicate set of *translations*.

'Cidade/city/cité' thus plants a problem of civilization, since the poem is marked by a simultaneous exaggeration of civilizing rhetoric (hyperliteracy) and the evacuation of civilizing rhetoric (illiteracy). This evident paradox is epitomized at the poem's end: 'veravivaunivora', which generates the string, 'veracity, vivacity, unicity, voracity'. Although it begins with notions of truth and life, this string surprisingly falls out of alphabetical order with the term 'unicity', which would seem to disrupt notions of

atrocaducapacaustiduplielastifeliferofugahistoriloqualubrimendimultipliorganiperiodiplastipublirapareciprorustissagasimplitenavelover aviva univoracidade
city
cité

FIGURE 3 Augusto de Campos. "cidade/city/cité" (1963). *Viva Vaia, Poesia 1949–1979* (São Paulo: Editora Brasiliense, 1986), 115.

singularity, unification and order in the poem at the very moment these notions are introduced. When the order of the alphabet is reasserted with the next term, we are given 'voracity', a term connoting wild bodily impulses, a term of 'savage' cannibalism par excellence, at which point the poem ends abruptly in the 'cidade/city/cité'. Clearly, then, Augusto's poem asserts a powerful temporal-historical ordering of its terms but just as quickly interrupts the very order it asserts, finalizing this interruption with a reference to violent bodily impulses. In terms of the body of the poem (the *corpus* of the text itself), what is *here* on the page of the poem is impossible to read or understand; and what is *there* in the generation of incorporeal linguistic units is ultimately undone by reference back to bodily impulses deemed to be primordial, pre-civilized, cannibal under the Eurocentric 'conception of Man'. The 'city' unifies Augusto's poem, yet this 'city' is hardly the city we would expect from the term itself. Augusto's 'city' has no place, but only time. And this time of the city must be seen as *modern* time: the time of France and England and the US and Brazil, not the time of Rome; the time of an 'illiterate literature' that de-composes the *letrado*'s Baroque order of signs of regular stanzas and rational geometric urban plans in harmony with the universe.

How does this reading of a poem entitled 'cidade' allow us to read an actual 'cidade' named São Paulo? We may take 'cidade/city/cité' as an imaginary virtualization of São Paulo. However, the mere fact of its virtuality does not negate the poem's reality but does precisely the opposite. First and foremost, the 'stuff' of the 'city' – the material of which cities are composed – is not space, but time. *Cities are composed of time, and de-composed in space*. This would confirm the conceptualization of the city as an organizational network based on the rapid flow of people, goods and information. But it would also suggest that as time is compressed by urban networks ('timeless time' as Castells called it), space does not disappear at all; rather, space dis-integrates, and grows into increasingly massive disintegration. We have seen São Paulo as a space of unchecked growth, a kind of metastasis across the landscape; we have seen it as a space with no orderly design, but something that has just accrued over time as people and businesses and governments have made seemingly 'pragmatic' economic choices in the moment.

If we follow from Augusto's one-line poem, however, we can begin to map the city – in all its massive disintegration – as a linear progression *over time* (figure 4). The ordering principle of São Paulo is dis-placement. Once the city crossed the line of the Anhangabaú Valley from Centro Velho to Centro Novo, São Paulo's city center began to follow a line to the southwest, first to the Avenida Paulista and more recently to the skyscrapers along the Marginal Pinheiros where one now finds the Latin American headquarters of Citibank and Microsoft and others. We must consider this line a border, since it is a demarcation or limit that determines the shape of the urban area as a whole; but here we would see the border as *internalized*, since it does not delimit the outer edge of a space, but points us to how the space will grow and develop outwards over time. This line I have drawn resembles nothing so much as a tectonic fault-line, in that this border marks what I call a *dis-location of culture* (to bastardize a line by Homi Bhabha). That is, the dis-location and dis-placement of the city center along a line has functioned as a kind of vector (figure 5) – a line of force that has propelled a concentration of wealth to the west and north, thus pushing a simultaneous concentration of poverty to the east where land is *cheaper*: rich and poor, west and east, hyperliteracy and illiteracy. This would show as a cruel kind of *unicity* undergirding the

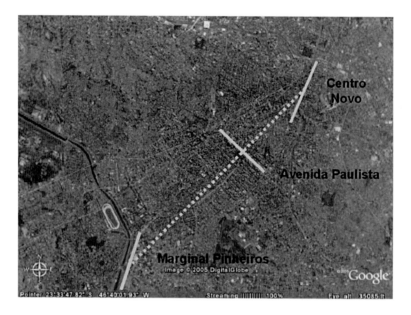

FIGURE 4 Google Earth, used by permission.

simultaneous development and underdevelopment of São Paulo. São Paulo has indeed grown into a global city, but we can also see in the after-image presented in figure 5 how the spread of poverty appears to result from the spread of globalization along the lines I have drawn as a massive, linear concrete poem: far from being excluded from

FIGURE 5 Google Earth, used by permission.

globalization, the poor are integral to it; or rather, as the rich earn their wealth, so too the poor earn their poverty. Unicity quickly moves to *voracity*.

But I cannot leave this essay without one final observation: if the border of the global city has been internalized, then *there can be no external limit* to the growth of the city. If this is the case, then we might begin to imagine – albeit *poetically* – that São Paulo *is the world* or that it *will soon cover the globe*, that there is now really only one city that operates as a reiterative network or global rhyme scheme from one place to the next. Returning to our poetic model, 'cidade/city/cité' translates instantly in English, French and (Brazilian) Portuguese. But, notably, it is *not* translatable into Spanish because, of course, the affix '-cidad' in Spanish does not 'rhyme' with the word 'ciudad' in a similar fashion to the other languages just mentioned. Evidently *not* by accident, then, Augusto's poem permits the instantaneous translation of Portuguese into prevalent languages of the First World but also simultaneously *blocks* translation into the prevalent language of other Latin American nations in the Third World. Perhaps we may take this as an attempt – not uncommon among Brazilian artists in the 1950s and '60s – to create an image of Brazilian culture as 'First World', so that we might be tempted to charge that this poem is 'infected' with a 'First-Worldism'. However, we have been reading globalization as a kind of 'one-worldism', a unicity that blurs distinctions between First and Third Worlds. Globalization does not erase the conditions of poverty marked as typical of the Third World, but merely dis-locates these conditions, inordinately relegating them to other zones of the world – 'rendering them invisible' to paraphrase Sassen, or creating what Castells dubs the 'Fourth World'. In this sense, 'cidade/city/cité' might just as easily attempt to accomplish the *obverse* of 'First-Worldism' – by attempting to 'transfect' the Third World into the First through translation.

Such a 'transfected' reading, paradoxically, would allow us to reintroduce a certain Latin Americanism (including Spanish-speaking America) into the political dynamics of the poem. Significantly, reading São Paulo through a poem has confirmed the existence of structural disequilibrium in sociospatial distributions of wealth and poverty – the same kind of disequilibrium posited by Sassen and Castells in other spaces/places. Yet, in the case of the Latin American city, this structure of social inclusion and exclusion has not resulted from a recent structural shift in the global political-economic order, even if the shift to globalization has exacerbated the Latin American city's problems. Rather, what I have just attempted to show – by means of literary analysis – is that far from being a new event, structural disequilibrium is the *historical constant* of São Paulo's urban growth. In essence, São Paulo has been generating its own 'Fourth World' for most of its modern history, long before the structural alterations of globalization. What has changed is that the 'First World' global city (e.g. New York, London, Tokyo) has merely lagged behind ('time-lag') São Paulo in terms of poverty growth and concentration. Into the global 'space of flows' of the network age, therefore, the space of the wealthy becomes an after-image of the space of the poor, the space of the colonizer an after-image of the space of the colonized. Now that São Paulo has been networked into the global order, its problems are being transfected and replicated by other global cities in the network, even in the 'First World'. Or, rather, we should cease thinking of First, Third or even Fourth Worlds as large national, geographic places, and instead begin to see how all of these worlds are distributed and interspersed at the local level, often on a block-by-block basis, regardless of whether the city lies in the US, Britain, Brazil or Bolivia. Can we not *measure* similar phenomena of migration, dis-placement, de-centering and socio-economic schism in Los Angeles, New York, New Orleans, Paris, Amsterdam, London, Berlin?

We might call this process of transfection 'obverse colonization', in which nominally rich nations will begin to replicate the (il)logic previously relegated only to nominally poor nations. Without anyone knowing it, or measuring it statistically, or even intending it, Latin America has finally begun its conquest of the new world.

Notes

1 An exact definition of the concept 'global city' will be provided in the discussion to follow.
2 Davidson, Robert A. 'Spaces of Immigration', 3.
3 Rama, *The Lettered City*.
4 Official statistics listed on the Prefeitura de São Paulo's (City of São Paulo's) website. Available from http://ww1.prefeitura.sp.gov.br/portal/a_cidade/urbanismo/zona_leste/index.php?p = 372&more = 1&c = 1&tb = 1&pb = 1; INTERNET.
5 Whitaker Ferreira, 'Globalização e urbanização subdesenvolvida', 17. My translation.
6 Sassen, *The Global City*, 357.
7 Ibid., 322. Emphasis added.
8 Resina, 'The Concept of After-Image and the Scopic Apprehension of the City', 22.
9 Castells, *The Rise of the Network Society*, 406.
10 Cf. Wigley, 'Network Fever', 82–122.
11 For a more comprehensive discussion of this 'annihilation of space by time', see David Harvey's discussion of Marx's Grundrisse in *The Urbanization of Capital*.
12 Castells (2000), op. cit., 436.
13 Castells, *End of Millennium*, 82. Emphasis in the original. Significantly for the purposes of the present essay, Castells cites illiteracy as the leading index of social exclusion.
14 Ibid., 164.
15 Ibid., 164–5. Emphasis added.
16 For a more complete account of the early history of the city, see Morse, *From Community to Metropolis*.
17 United Nations Department for Economic and Social Information and Policy Analysis, 'Population Growth and Policies in Mega-Cities: São Paulo', 3.
18 Ibid., 12.
19 Sevcenko, *Orfeu extático na metrópole*, 31. My translation.
20 I will refer to the satellite images in this essay, used by permission of Google Earth, as 'after-images' for several reasons. On the one hand, they are real-time images that give us an idea of what São Paulo actually looks like. On the other hand, they are virtual representations of reality obtained from an optical lens in space, beamed back to earth and digitized by a private corporation, accessed over the Internet on my home computer in Buffalo, and copied for use in this journal. In other words, we must always remind ourselves of the coincidence of reality and virtual-reality: the coincidence of the place, the image of the place, and the process by which that image has been produced.
21 By saying this, I am self-consciously trying to provoke. São Paulo is historical, of course, but this history *appears* to have been erased as a matter of place. In other

words, it seems that most 'historical' buildings in São Paulo were built in the nineteenth century, which is hardly historical at all. And this is something that is entirely typical in many other places of the Americas, such as my home town of Los Angeles.

22   United Nations, op. cit., 9.
23   Ibid., 16.
24   Gonzaga and Teixeira, 'Asa branca'.
25   Cf. Lajolo and Zilberman, *A formação da leitura no Brasil*, 122–45.
26   This idea of Brazil as a 'broadcast imagined community' is reinforced by Bryan McCann's new history of radio and popular music, *Hello, Hello Brazil: Popular Music in the Making of Modern Brazil*.
27   Cf. Sevcenko's discussion of urbanization projects in *Orfeu extático na metrópole*, op. cit., 106–27.

References

Andrade, Mário de. 1993. *Paulicéia desvairada*. In *Poesias completas*, edited by Diléa Zanotto Manfio. Belo Horizonte: Vila Rica [originally published in 1922].

Campos, Augusto de. 1986. cidade/city/cité. In *Viva Vaia, Poesia 1949–1979*. São Paulo: Editora Brasiliense [originally published in 1963]: 115.

Castells, Manuel. 1998. *End of Millennium*. Malden, MA: Blackwell.

Castells, Manuel. 2000. *The Rise of the Network Society*. 2nd edn. Malden, MA: Blackwell.

Davidson, Robert A. Spaces of Immigration 'Prevention': Interdiction and the Nonplace. *Diacritics* 33 (3–4): 3–18.

Galvão, Patrícia. 1993. In *Parque Industrial/Industrial Park, a Proletarian Novel*, translated by Elizabeth and K. David Jackson. Lincoln, NE: University of Nebraska Press [originally published in 1933].

Gonzaga, Luiz, and Humberto Teixeira. 1999. Asa branca. In *Focus: O essencial de Luiz Gonzaga*. BMG 7432169061-2 [originally published in RCA 'Luiz Gonzaga', 78 RPM 80.0510].

Harvey, David. 1985. *The Urbanization of Capital*. Baltimore, MD: Johns Hopkins University Press.

Lajolo, Marisa, and Regina Zilberman. 1996. *A formação da leitura no Brasil*. São Paulo: Editora Ática.

McCann, Bruce. 2004. *Hello, Hello Brazil: Popular Music in the Making of Modern Brazil*. Durham, NC: Duke University Press.

Morse, Richard. 1958. *From Community to Metropolis*. Gainesville, FL: University of Florida Press.

Prefeitura de São Paulo. Available from http://ww1.prefeitura.sp.gov.br/portal/a_cidade/urbanismo/zona_leste/index.php?p = 372&more = 1&c = 1&tb = 1&pb = 1; INTERNET.

Rama, Angel. 1996. In *The Lettered City*, edited by John Chasteen. Durham, NC: Duke University Press.

Resina, Joan Ramon. 2003. The concept of after-image and the scopic apprehension of the city. In *After-Images of the City*, edited by Joan Ramon Resina, and Dieter Ingenschay. Ithaca, NY: Cornell University Press, 1–22.

Rheda, Regina. 1994. *Arca sem Noé: histórias do Edifício Copan*. São Paulo: Paulicéia. English, translation in the volume *First World/Third Class and Other Tales of the Global Mix*, ed Charles A. Perrone. Austin, TX: University of Texas Press, 2005.

Sassen, Saskia. 2001. *The Global City: New York, London, Tokyo*. 2nd edn. Princeton, NJ: Princeton University Press.

Sevcenko, Nicolau. 1992. *Orfeu extático na metrópole: São Paulo, sociedade e cultura nos frementes anos 20*. São Paulo: Compahnia de Letras.

United Nations Department for Economic and Social Information and Policy Analysis. 1993. *Population Growth and Policies in Mega = Cities: São Paulo*. New York: United Nations.

Veloso, Caetano. 1978. Sampa. *Muito*. Polygram Brasil.

Whitaker Ferreira, and João Sette. 2000. Globalização e urbanização subdesenvolvida. *SP Perspectiva, Revista da Fundação SEADE* 14 (4): 10–20.

Wigley, Mark. 2001. Network fever. *Grey Room* 4 (Summer): 82–122.

Beatriz Jaguaribe

FAVELAS AND THE AESTHETICS OF REALISM: REPRESENTATIONS IN FILM AND LITERATURE

Favelas and the crisis of the city

Perched on the mountains overlooking the beaches of Rio, sprawling horizontally at the edges of São Paulo, or facing the sewage-choked lagoons in Salvador, favelas are an overwhelming feature of city life in Brazil.[1] The contradictory relations between the favela and the city constitute a key issue of the Brazilian urban experience because they translate how the expectations of the modern metropolis have been both frustrated and partially fulfilled. They have been defeated because the material promise of modernity as access to goods and services has been undermined by the radical economic and social inequality between the rich and the poor. Yet, they have been enacted also because the modernizing urban scenario is a crucial site for the invention of new forms of social identity, democratic struggle and individual social mobility.

Cast as both the locus of the 'national imagined community' and as a 'fearful stain' on the landscape of modernity, the favelas were often metaphorized as an emblem of Brazil's uneven modernization. Celebratory versions of the favela as a samba community composing carnival lyrics coexist with images of armed adolescents shooting police forces during drug raids. Since the 1980s the increase in social violence produced by the globalized drug trade and the flow of media images, consumer goods, and new cultural identities produced a crisis of representation of the 'national imagined community'. Indeed, the overwhelming presence of the media centred foremost on television, and the circulation of globalized consumer goods, lifestyles and political agendas have transformed expectations and cultural identities. Such transformations are keenly felt in the invention of youth cultures, where the formerly national samba has lost much of its influence to funk and hip-hop in the favelas of Rio de Janeiro and São Paulo.

Images and narratives of a globalized favela emerge as the former national portraits of Brazil become increasingly fragmented. The fraying of previous narratives and images of national identity has also brought to the limelight new cultural icons shaped by the media and popular culture. In the wake of these changes, contemporary literary and cinematographic productions are attempting to come to terms with new portraits of Brazil that focus on marginalized characters, favelas, drug cultures and the imaginaries of consumption.

The main contention of this essay is that a crucial element of the fabrication of the new representations of the favelas is the usage of different forms of the 'aesthetics of realism'. Evidently, not all the cultural representations of the favela rely on a realist register, but those that have had a greater repercussion and press coverage have made use of the impact of verisimilitude associated with the realist encoding of the 'real'. Guided by Simmel's classic definition of the hyperstimulation of urban culture, I argue that these realist narratives and images produce the 'shock of the real' by means of artistic defamiliarization.[2] In Simmel's account, the rapid pace of the city, the anonymity of the metropolis and hyperstimulation produced by new forms of transport, commodities and entertainment induced urban inhabitants to adopt a blasé attitude and means–end rationalization in their daily lives. The blasé attitude cushioned the city dweller from a bombardment of sensorial stimuli. In contemporary terms, urbanites may continue to shield themselves from urban chaos but the blasé defensiveness is threaded through by the perplexity of uncertainty. Cities have become increasingly difficult to map. Furthermore, the very territorial boundaries of the city no longer persist. The shock of the new and the culture of hyperstimulation that were formerly perceived as part of the metropolitan experience have surpassed the boundaries of the urban environment. The city itself no longer has readily defined limits. Yet, in a world of globalized branding and intense cultural hybridity, cities continue to provide what Baudelaire termed to be the 'commotion of the modern'. If the shock of the new and hyperstimulation can be bought and experienced in computer games, theme parks, tourist sites and shopping malls, the 'commotion of the modern' still implies experiencing the tumultuous rush of the urban maze. It evokes the street scene, the unexpected encounter, the meeting with the stranger, the presence of the crowd, and the sensorial impact of the sights and sounds of the urban realm.

Experiencing the city also implies creating a range of representations that express the different vocabularies of modernity. These maps of urban living and 'stories of the street' are in continual dispute.[3] An overflow of media images and narratives coexist with personalized memories, historical events, architectural constructions and lived experiences. Contemporary urban dwellers are not only subject to the 'shock of the new' and the tumult of hyperstimulation analysed by Simmel, but they are also increasingly caught in a maze of representations where local knowledges are combined with globalized representations. Furthermore, as cities gain complexity and become deterritorialized, the experience of being in the city entails varying degrees of direct exposure to metropolitan living itself. Gated condominiums, communitarian neighbourhoods, isolated slum areas, all of these urban layouts emphasize, for better or worse, territorial limits. Yet, what distinguishes these urban configurations from their similar nineteenth- and early twentieth-century versions is precisely the flow of global communications and commodities. This not only implies the emergence of urban lifestyles and forms of identity that surpass local and national boundaries but also allows narratives and images to circulate.

Transmitted by film, television, radio, Internet and advertising such narratives and images also fabricate representations of the city itself, its enticement and allure, its danger and threat. The phantoms of fear that haunt cities have their specificities and historical avatars. They come in the shape of unexpected terrorist explosions in public places, they lurk as the menacing criminal in the dark corners of parking lots, they feature as the riotous mob or dangerous individuals, and they are centred in particular urban zones of manifest violence and poverty.

For inhabitants of large metropolitan areas in Brazil, the fear of urban spaces is tied to the usual threats of rape, robbery, kidnapping. But such forms of violence can occur in any section of the city and are viewed as part of the menacing experience of the streets. Yet within the urban maze, the favelas – as is evidenced by the dramatic drop of real estate prices of houses and apartments located near them – are seen as specific danger zones of violence and poverty. To experience the city entails facing these contradictions, ambiguous spaces and cultural contagions. Disparities between the rich and the poor are directly mirrored in the layout of urban scenarios where favelas face luxurious shopping malls, street children cluster around well-heeled pedestrians and public spaces such as the beach in Rio de Janeiro are both a congenial meeting ground of different classes and arenas of tension.[4] Indeed, inhabitants of cities such as Rio de Janeiro and São Paulo are constantly assaulted by uncertainty[5] – an uncertainty that feeds on the fear of violence, that mirrors the transformations of the urban design, that grows with the fluctuations of a volatile economy and that expresses the fast pace of cultural change.

In such an uneasy terrain, the aesthetic options that are chosen to represent the favela and the city become narrative ballasts that insert the weight of the 'real' in what appears to be a fraying tissue of a dissolving reality. The aesthetic forms of realism have a particular density because they establish codes of apprehension anchored on the verisimilitude of quotidian existence. Imagined communities in cities and the construction of daily existence are created by a multiplicity of discourses, where the languages of realism in the press, television coverage, personal narratives and social events have become a naturalized encoding of the 'real'. Yet, the disputes concerning the register of the 'real' reveal that the very fabric of social construction is being debated and that perspectives of the future are being called into question.

Ongoing disputes concerning the nature of the 'real', the combination of codes employed by fictional films that use the realism of documentary films and documentary films that fictionalize the 'real' provide a floating terrain of symbolic mappings. The close contact between 'fiction' and non-fiction does not necessarily erase the boundaries between the 'real' and the fictional, but it questions the status of representation and our access to experience largely tied to a media 'culture of the spectacle'.[6]

Yet, the frontiers between the 'real' and the imaginary are also constantly being blurred in advertising, the media and our own personal daydreams. Journalistic disputes over the narration of the real insist on offering distinctions between sensationalist coverage and objective news. Despite the legitimacy of these distinctions, the overall spectacularization of daily life and the very nature of representation make it practically impossible to experience facts without media mediation. The sense of the real becomes increasingly packaged and yet the shock of the real is insistently sought.

Since the 1990s, the Brazilian public has consumed an outpouring of realist literary and cinematic representations of the favela. Such fictional productions were matched by a rising interest in documentary films, biographies and journalistic accounts of first-hand experiences in places of extreme social hardship. The absorption of these new realist registers is far from being a Brazilian phenomenon. From the manifestos towards an authentic cinema to the debunking of magical realism by a new generation of Latin American writers, new forms of the 'return of the real' have emerged as globalized narratives.[7] Despite an immense variety of aesthetic codes and allegiances, such realist inventions are also a response to televised fabrications of the 'real' and to the mainstream productions of the culture industry. Nevertheless, in our daily existence we make constant use of the imaginaries of the media and we establish a complex negotiation with the realm of fact and fiction. Yet, rather than insisting on the return of a 'real' uncontaminated by spectacularization and media aesthetization, the demands of new realist fictions seek to revitalize experience producing a defamiliarized 'shock of the real'.

In the specific case of Brazil, the realist register has a deeply embedded cultural trajectory that began with the naturalist and realist novels of the nineteenth century and continued to prevail throughout the twentieth century. With the formidable expansion of television in the 1970s, the narratives of the 'real' gained greater visual impact and influence in journalistic programmes. If the *Jornal Nacional* was the reality principle shaping the nationwide televised imagined community, the soap operas of Rede Globo were the realms of fantasy that connected millions of viewers to the same fictional narrative. The entrance of cable network and the weakening of Globo's hegemonic position altered the centralization of the 'imagined televised community'.[8] Furthermore, social and economic upheaval, the disruptive violence of urban centres, conflicting agendas for the future, and the demise of hegemonic discourses all contribute to a sense of crisis and perplexity. Evidently, the rise of realist aesthetics is not automatically conditioned by social forces, just as the very notion of what realism is varies immensely. Nevertheless, new realist codes that focus on marginal characters, urban violence, poverty and extreme experiences are producing narratives and images that avoid avant-garde experimentation and cancel flights of fantasy that menace the pact of mimetic legitimacy with the spectator or reader. The predominance of such realist representations led me ultimately to question how fictional imagination shapes our existence and how the option for a realist aesthetics was often at odds with and a response to the enchantments of everyday life that we pursue in advertising, in dreams, beliefs and non-rationalized narratives. Moreover, I was struck by the discrepancy between 'realist' depictions of the poor and the marginalized in the favelas and the realms of fantasy that are often at the centre of so many Brazilian social fabrications ranging from carnival practices to religious beliefs.

A key element of the prevalence of the realist register is also related to the perception of realism as being closely tied to the construction of modernity. Whereas religious beliefs, inner realms of fantasy and collective carnivalesque practices may actually feature in realist productions, the controlling reality principle is given by the rationalist realist code. Realism brackets the realms of the imaginary, the transcendent and the irrational by means of a predominant codification of an objective reality. Often, the dramatic centre of realist fiction is precisely the conflict and discrepancy between internal subjective self-fashionings and the social perception of the self, or between the desires of achievement of an individual or social group and the thwarting circumstances that deflate such expectations. Individual and collective imagination are pitted against the reality principle informed by the realist register. As this code becomes a standard form of narration in media productions that provide news and information, it also serves as a generalized form of communication. This does not imply that contemporary realism cancels dialogical difference, nor that it censors subjective projections. Rather it suggests that different worldviews are translatable by means of a connecting communicative code.

Realist favelas

The importance of the realist code in artistic productions in Brazil was and still is largely tied to the necessity of cognitively mapping the contradictions of a nation on its path towards modernity. The favela with its flimsy, insanitary and densely packed constructions was always the very opposite of modernist urban planning. But even more problematic, the poverty and unruliness of the favela were located at the very centre of the modernizing project, inside the city itself. Modernist productions of the 1920s and 1930s altered previous early twentieth-century conceptions of the favela ruled by positivist paradigms and eurocentric values. In the 1930s, the urban popular culture of Rio de Janeiro gained nationwide projection with the broadcasting of samba by the national radio. As the site of popular culture, the favela was celebrated for withstanding the scarcity of services, goods and means through a cultural hybridity that adapts, transforms and upholds its ethos in the midst of adversity.

But if both experimental modernist and social realist depictions of the favela catered largely to middle- and upper-middle-class sectors, the cultural production of the favela itself was tied to samba and the mass media productions of the radio and television. The importance of Carolina de Jesus's book, *Quarto de Despejo*, published in 1960 was precisely her authorship, the fact that she wrote a book about her life in the favela using her daily existence as the source for a written documentary.

In the pages that follow I will discuss a selective group of representations ranging from *Quarto de Despejo* (1960) to *Cidade de Deus* the novel (1997), and the film (2002), in order to discuss how the differing usages of realism and the popularization of the realist canon occupy a central role in the construction of an image of social exclusion in the city and how such images provide the 'shock of the real'. I begin with Carolina de Jesus's famous book precisely because she anticipates the impact of testimonial literature but does so without the political agency that would later be developed in the writing and reception of such accounts in the 1970s. For different reasons, I bypass the well-known Cinema Novo films of the 1960s that depicted the favela, precisely because their production is related to a political agenda of the social transformation of Brazil, but their cinematic aesthetics had scant repercussion among popular cinema viewers. In contrast, both recent documentaries and fictional productions on the favela have not only catered to large audiences but more importantly have established an interpretive code of realism that allowed them to become focal points of discussion concerning the real events and experiences of Brazilian cities.

When Carolina de Jesus's diary was printed in book form with the title *Quarto de Despejo* it achieved astounding success. Seven editions were published and the book was translated into 13 languages. Carolina de Jesus had been 'discovered' by the newspaper correspondent Audálio Dantas who wrote for *Cruzeiro*, then the most widely read magazine in Brazil.[11] For Carolina de Jesus, the usage of the realist register was a form of testimonial evidence and access to memory in a metropolis where the poor were largely silenced. She is one of the first favela writers to emerge in the twentieth century. Her diary, however, did not spawn an outpouring of testimonial literature or induce a fabrication of literary favelas by favela dwellers. On the contrary, her book constitutes a singular event just as her disengagement from any political party or grassroots movement made her personal narrative an exemplary and yet isolated phenomenon.

In contrast with both the films of the Cinema Novo that depicted the favela and the literary writings of modernist writers that expressed the lives of the poor, Carolina's narration was not a product of the cultured intelligentsia. She was not even a writer who had overcome humble origins and entered into the domains of the artistic circles. Carolina was a *favelada* who barely made a living by gathering paper and reselling her scraps to local shop owners. The title of her diary, *Quarto de Despejo* (Scrap Room), is not metaphoric but literally the rendition of her material circumstances. Making a living out of scraps, rubbish and garbage, Carolina de Jesus and her children lived in utmost poverty in the shantytown of Canindé situated on the banks of the river Tietê in São Paulo. Carolina gained visibility where no poor black female slum dweller ordinarily would. She was not a samba star, a naïf painter, a seeker of the limelight in carnivalesque television shows, nor was she a protagonist of a sensationalist horror story told by the press. Carolina emerged as an author who uses the written word as her means of expression. Furthermore, she made use of her daily existence as a form of narration.

The transcription of the 'real' in the form of narrative realism is the key element that renders Carolina de Jesus's story so convincing and the reality of her biographical existence is given photographic visibility in the pictures of Carolina in her slum dwelling. Her grim narrative of gathering paper, making meals from very little, fetching water, listening to the ruckus of neighbours is as repetitive and exhausting as scraping a living from day to day can be. Yet, the bare bones of realism are often coated with lyrical musings and a cultured literary usage of words appears amid numerous grammatical errors. The entrance into the domain of the letter is also a form of extricating herself from the narrative of sheer survival that emerged from the daily activity of gathering waste paper. Despite negative references to politicians, a heightened perception of racial discrimination and a pointed critique of male abusiveness in the favela community, Carolina de Jesus's voice is not affiliated to pre-established codes of political usage or social demands. The basis of her reception is conditioned by a humanitarian notion of the rights of citizens upheld, in her specific case, by her personal dignity in the midst of degrading circumstances and by her appreciation of 'high culture'. A 'high culture' that is not, however, processed as mere emulation but is filtered through personal experience and seen as a source of redemption. Symptomatically, Carolina read the saccharine nineteenth-century abolitionist novel *A Escrava Isaura* [Isaura the Slave Girl] (1875) and wept for the plight of the chained slave.[12] In her published diary Carolina seldom mentions literary references, although she does specify that the opinions surrounding her writing activities and bookishness are incisively summed up in the commentary of a neighbour: 'I never saw a black woman like books as much as you do.'[13] Yet, if she regards the act of reading as an 'ideal', her written word becomes denunciatory evidence, a confessional document, a register of scarcity, a form of epiphany. In all these instances, the crucial point is the vital connection between the written word and the lived experience, between her narration and her biographical truth.

But if the narrative represents an anchoring of memory and a projection of visibility into the future, the future of the favela itself is suspended in the void of barren necessities. The favela is not exoticized. It is not the 'imagined community' of the nation, it is not the terrain of the proletarian revolution. Rather, Carolina's words reinforce the notion of the favela as a 'fearful stain'.[14] Despite her pronounced antipathy towards the politician Carlos Lacerda, Carolina actually endorses what Lacerda himself would espouse in the 1960s: the eradication of the favelas by state authorities. It is therefore symptomatic that the day she left the favela of Canindé she was pelted with stones by her neighbours. She did not project herself politically as the voice of the oppressed but, rather, she denounced her living conditions and expressed her adamant will to be free of the bondage of scarcity. The luxury of writing was the only means of breaking the cycle of mere subsistence. Media visibility through the domain of the written word became the way out of the favela. Yet, when Carolina left Canindé she also destroyed her access to the testimonial narration of life within the favela. The loss of that lived testimonial narration eventually closed off all her paths, left her without readers, and placed her once again in appalling conditions of poverty. By then, she was too far gone and broken to articulate her word again. The novelty of her authorship had worn off and Carolina Maria de Jesus died as she had lived most of her life: utterly destitute.

The same ingredients of the veracity of lived experience were also used to promote the narrative of a radically different book, Paulo Lins's bestseller *Cidade de Deus* [City of God]. First published in 1997, the novel was hailed by prominent literary critic Roberto Schwarz as an 'uncommon artistic adventure' as it articulated a new range of discursive strategies combining ethnographic research, literary naturalism and cinematic flashes in order to reveal an explosive scenario of social exclusion and violence.[15] Although Schwarz's laudatory review veers away from personalizing the figure of the author, the overall reception of the novel was influenced by the fact that the author, Paulo Lins, was a former resident of the Cidade de Deus favela. Yet, the true novelty here was that his authorship was radically different from the writing of previous favela writers such as Carolina de Jesus. Lins was research assistant to Alba Zaluar, one of Brazil's leading anthropologists on urban violence, favelas and the drug trade. Zaluar herself had published a full-length study on Cidade de Deus entitled *Machine and Revolt* (1985) and years later, when Paulo Lins was her research assistant, she published the collection of essays, *The Devil's Condominium* (1994).[16] As Zaluar's research assistant and as a resident of the favela, Lins acquired a dual role as anthropological researcher-informant and as community member. Both the legitimacy of his authorship and the subject matter of a new, radically violent drug culture within the favela offered middle-class readers an insider's view of an unknown terrain. Moreover, if the subject matter had evident cinematic qualities manifest in the usual display of murders, escapades and exchange of bullets, the social dimensions of such warfare and the protagonists of the bloody feud were distanced from the aesthetics of violence as seen in American films or narrations. The multitude of characters are given scant psychological depth, their ethical conflicts surface minimally, they are ruled by desires that are constantly thwarted by the very violence that constitutes and dissolves them. The literary 'shock of the real' is fabricated by a series of brutal crimes, violent disputes, tumultuous events where the possibilities of a banal quotidian, the maintenance of identities, are continuously destroyed. Children are not children in Cidade de Deus and lives are worthless in the constant drug disputes, police raids, inner wars. Lins stresses that he is narrating a neo-favela as he begins the novel in the 1960s and ends the narrative in the 1980s where the scale of violence wrought by the drug trade and by patterns of social exclusion in a society mesmerized by consumption surpasses previous parameters. However, the social existence of Lins himself suggests a complex scenario where the relation of the favela to the city reveals contact zones based on radically unequal exchanges.

Viewed by millions of spectators, reviewed by all the major newspapers in Brazil and granted critical acclaim in international film festivals, the film *Cidade de Deus* (2002), based on Lins's novel, galvanized public attention and was at the centre of polemical opinions. With fewer characters and fewer episodes of straightforward violence, the film's narrative swiftness is achieved by a mutative camera eye that alters its visual register from documentary to video-clip montage in an accumulative narration that tells the saga of several bandits and drug dealers. The film has caused far greater impact than the original novel. Such an impact is not only achieved because of the sensorial quality of the visual medium, nor is it based exclusively on the cathartic mobilization of a public cinema viewing that caters to far larger numbers of people than the reading of a novel that is both solitary and demands literacy.

Cidade de Deus became the focal point of a battle of representations concerning the nature of the 'real', the fabrication of society, the viability of cities and the nature of violence. It has been allegorically read as a synecdoche of the nation while being upheld as an example of realism. Conversely, it has been denounced as a spectacularized Americanized action film devoid of realism. Critics who have placed it in the category of an entertainment action film either extolled it as an example of competent cinematic narration or disparaged the film as a 'cosmetics of hunger', in contrast with the previous neorealist tenets of the Brazilian Cinema Novo in the 1960s that extolled 'an aesthetics of hunger'.[17] In a brief newspaper review, anthropologist Alba Zaluar criticized the lack of white characters in the film and undermined the supposed analogy between the 'similarity of the favela/American black ghetto, not withstanding the great racial and cultural differences between the American ghetto and the Brazilian favela'.[18] Zaluar further questioned the racial inversion in the film where the most violent and ruthless gangster is black when in real life he was an 'almost white' north-easterner. Others emphasized that viewing the film was a 'civic duty', or that aesthetic discussions concerning the qualities of the film were beside the point because the film brought forth the camouflaged fact that Brazilian cities are facing a war, a war wrought by social exclusion, poverty, injustice and the rampant abuse of the drug trade. A war that has had a greater death toll than the city of Sarajevo when it was at the epicentre of an ethnic strife.[19] By contrast, MV Bill, a famous rapper from Cidade de Deus, praised the aesthetic qualities of the film but announced that it would only benefit its makers, whereas the actual community of Cidade de Deus would be even further ostracized as a living hell, as the most violent favela in Brazil.[20]

Whether denouncing its lack of true realism or celebrating its realist impact, *Cidade de Deus* was judged largely in relation to its appraisal of a disruptive social situation. The demands of realism were sustained by the cast of unknown actors recruited from the favela communities of Rio de Janeiro. The acting talents of these unknown children and adolescents became a source of constant praise and generalized consensus but the dividing line between fact and fiction was further blurred by the social origins of these actors who escaped the fate of their fictional characters, yet lived in direct contact with the contradictions of the favelas. The film itself insists on the ambiguity between the 'real' and the fictional by pairing off at the end of the narration the pictures of the actors with the photographs of the real drug dealers that they had been embodying.

The question then arises of why so much was read into a film whose focus is actually very narrow as it essentially depicts the violent disputes between outlaw characters in different periods of the favela's history. The diverse critical reception given to *Cidade de Deus* indirectly evoked the spectres that expressed the quintessential Latin American dichotomy of the nineteenth century: civilization versus barbarism. In its nineteenth-century configuration, the 'barbarians' were cast as rustic rural remnants in the provinces or backlands, peoples that would inevitably be obliterated by the inexorable march of progress. In the cities, the 'barbarians', identified as non-Europeans, were to be subjected to educational reforms, sanitized and modernized. Even in their nineteenth-century configurations such polarizations collapsed and often revealed the contradictory montage of social relations and legacies. The destabilizing element in the dichotomy was the very real presence and existence of mestizo cultures and of the ongoing processes of cultural hybridization that ensured a porousness of cultural influences. Such cultural influences are depicted in the film by the presence of a youth culture centred on drugs, music, sexual exchanges, and relationships of affection that surpass class boundaries and territorial divisions. It is also mirrored in the trajectory of the protagonist, the young man from Cidade de Deus who enters into the world of journalism as an amateur photographer, has an amorous encounter with a white woman journalist and becomes a mediator between the city and the favela. Nevertheless, disruptive violence as featured in both the novel and the film *Cidade de Deus* produces a vision of otherness, of encapsulated worlds that revolve around an almost Darwinian survival of the fittest. In this process of social implosion subjectivity and imaginative construction are undermined by the hammering of corrosive violence. Critical dismissal of the film's usage of video-clip camera movements and aesthetization obliterates the attempt by the director, Fernando Miereles, to essay a new form of realism. A realism that does not rely on the direct unfiltered documentary camera but introduces the aesthetization of daily life with the symbolic and cultural components that constitute the imaginary of the characters in the plot. The drug dealers' competition for the limelight, the search for some kind of media notoriety, the choice of consumer goods and musical genres, in this case, the presence of James Brown in the late 1970s and early 1980s, a choice that would later include funk and hip-hop, all these elements are used in order to evoke the role of the imagination in the process of self-fashioning. What this 'new realism' cannot do is produce totalizing images of the national narrative even though the demands that are placed on it are centred on a vindication of a new portrait of Brazil.

The dispute over an apprehension of the 'real' and the invention of a new realism centred on the favela and the urban poor has also engendered different documentary films. A documentary film maker such as Eduardo Coutinho provides an anti-aesthetics of the real, an anti-spectacularization of daily life, by focusing on anonymous people in peripheral conditions who are struggling to survive and yet fabricate their lives in narrative tales told to the camera. Once again, the favela is a favoured documentary site but, in tune with anthropological arguments that stress the rights of self-representation, the participants in several of these films represent themselves, as they are registered with minimal intervention and the camera filters without special effects. Pauses in the conversation, redundancy, noises and the presence of the interviewer or the vision of the filming camera emphasize that the spectator is viewing a film in the making. Thus, the effect of reality is rendered by the exhibition of the conditions of the filmic fabrication. What engages the spectator is not the aesthetic resources of the camera, or the voyeuristic espionage of veiled intimacies, and even less the display of violent imagery, as Coutinho's films avoid the 'shock of the real'. What arrests the spectator is the real-life narrative that pours from the lips of the filmed participants who engage the spectator's attention, as they become personalities imbued with their own visions of the world. In films such as *Santo Forte* (1999), *Babilônia 2000* and others, the camera movement is minimal, the aesthetic effects are practically non-existent and the register is direct without making its plainness a source of self-conscious non-aesthetization. Centred on the speech of the favela dwellers, the striking components in many of these films are the inner worlds, the realms of belief, the mobilizing force of personal and collective imaginations of people attempting to make sense of their lives, to rise above their circumstances, and to obtain their freedom through religion, politics, consumption. Coutinho's films are dialogical in the ethnographic diversity of voices that emerge from the screen, but they adhere to realist representation as the imaginaries of the speakers are not projected as visual imagery. Coutinho's resistance to the lure of the image is also a form of sustaining documentary veracity against the spectacularization of the real undertaken by reality shows and sensationalist media coverage. It is a documentary grounding of authenticity imbued with a political agenda that seeks to potentialize characters, and humanizes anonymous people while holding at bay their attempts at fictional projection. This minimalist aesthetics controls carnivalization because the social inversion of roles or the fictional masks the interviewees might wish to fabricate are solely available through their speech, as wish images, as instances of self-fashioning. As part of the portrayal of the lives of the poor, Coutinho has a selective panel of what represents 'ordinary people'. His narratives bypass the reworking of clichés of violence by avoiding the presence of drug dealers, bandits, outlaws. Yet, by centring the focus on particular communities, they do not address the multiplicity of urban voices, mappings, commotions that make cities arenas of change. At the end of the film *Babilônia 2000*, a favela dweller invites people to come up to Babilônia hill and view the famous New Year's celebration on Copacabana beach from the favela overlooking the city. 'People make wrong judgements about us', he claims.

The invitation to enter the domains of the favela and join the party extended by the favela dweller in *Babilônia 2000* would constitute a veritable impossibility in João Moreira Salles's documentary *Notícias de uma guerra particular* [News from a private war] (1999). Filmed in the favela Santa Marta, in police headquarters and in institutions for juvenile delinquents, the film offers a corrosive view of the ongoing dispute over the drug trade in the midst of urban poverty and rampant violence and yet it also focuses on the speech of the favela dwellers and the working-class people of Santa Marta. Amid the violence of both the police and the drug dealers, a critique of social exclusion is undertaken even by specific sectors of the police. But the most grating image of the film is the depiction of the adolescent drug dealers who voice their passion for clothing, the acquisition of consumer goods and their rejection of normative work ethics. What is telling in these interviews is not so much the social view that is being displayed in a favela world of brutal options, but the dramatization of such a self-fashioning in front of the camera. Their heavy posturing and the drawling accent become an acting out of the gangster role-playing that is overtly theatricalized and self-conscious.

As the drug trade recruits more and more children and adolescents precisely because of their immaturity, the image of the revolutionary drug dealer that surfaced in the 1960s and 1970s with underground cinema and in the artistic installations of avant-garde artists increasingly loses credibility.[21] Counter-cultural movements of the 1960s and 1970s expressed their critique of authority during the military dictatorship and it was in the context of the oppression of the authoritarian regime that they assigned a role not only to the favela but also to the outlaw as a figure of resistance. Both the democratization of Brazil and the unleashed violence of the drug trade have undermined the exaltation of the favela bandit. The famous installation of the artist Helio Oiticica that carried the slogan 'Be an Outlaw, Be a Hero' has become dated and yet the imaginaries of the heroic guerrilla leader continue to surface in the figure of the communitarian drug dealer. The controversial figure of Marcinho VP, former drug leader of the favela Santa Marta, is an example of an alternative 'rebel' self-fashioning as he claims to wish to organize a revolution in the favelas.[22] Marcinho VP was catapulted to fame when pop star Michael Jackson's music video, 'They don't care about us' was shot in the favela Santa Marta. In order to film in the steep hills of Santa Marta, the film director, Spike Lee, had to ask the permission of Marcinho VP. Not only were the local authorities reduced to incompetent bystanders, but also the overwhelming attention of the media transformed the relatively unknown Marcinho VP into an instantaneous celebrity. Thus, the metaphoric and representational uncertainties surrounding the favelas, the uneasy negotiation between national popular culture and marginalized outcasts, the embracing of hybridity and the fear of social violence are further intensified with the emergence of a new kind of media visibility. This new media visibility largely connected to television offers a range of representations of the favelas, the poor and the outlaws. The new ingredient is given by the internalization of the media component by the drug dealers, the favela dwellers, the poor. Those who manage to appear on the screen are able to voice their condition in front of TV cameras, documentary films, music videos and feature films.

Realist defamiliarization

As I have argued throughout this essay, the realist register in recent representations of the favela in film and literary fiction has been variously used as a means of engendering artistic 'defamiliarization' and as a form of translating the new cultural experiences of the globalized favela. As the site of defamiliarization, art – according to the famous words of Victor Sklovskij – is what makes the 'stone, stony' and its aim 'is to convey the immediate experience of a thing as if it is seen instead of recognized; the device of art is the device of making things strange…'.[23] The strangeness of art as evoked by Sklovskij is related to a heightening of perception that peels away the wrappings of the customary and provides unfamiliar awareness. Avant-garde experimentation tended to provoke a dramatic rupture between the stone and its stoniness, whereas modernist experimentation often dismissed the aesthetics of verisimilitude in order to evoke another 'realness'. Realist representation in its many guises and epochs emphasizes the palpability of experience and lays particular claims to its capacity to make the 'stone, stony'. Yet, how to enforce the tangibility of the 'real' essential to the realist experience in media cultures saturated with images, hyper-stimulations, spectacularized events and technological reinventions of nature?

In the case of the realist narratives and images examined in this essay, the aesthetics of realism resurfaces as both a shock response and as a means of reworking the connections between representation and experience, in an attempt to engender interpretive frameworks that produce a vocabulary of recognition in the midst of the tumultuous uncertainty of Brazilian cities. As the focal site of urban unease, the favelas are once again thematized but now they are no longer buffered by modern narratives of future utopian redemption that prevailed in the agendas of the Cinema Novo and much of the previous modernist inventions. Contemporary depictions of the favela provide defamiliarization without radical aesthetic experimentation because this 'strangeness' may demolish the petrification of daily habits, but it channels perception to specific interpretive vocabularies and aesthetic codes. While the actual democratization of Brazil has failed to alter significantly economic and social disparities it has, nevertheless, dramatically changed the production of cultural codes. Media culture and new forms of consumption have created new elites, celebrities and role models. Yet the same media culture and the allure of consumption also foment increasing frustration within the youth cultures of the urban poor hampered by harsh economic options that curtail consumer expectations and social possibilities. As never before, these social frustrations, expectations and desires are being voiced by a number of artists that come directly from the favela communities or from the ranks of the urban poor. And distinct from the lyrical productions of the former samba composers that relied on both Afro-Brazilian traditions and yet were also influenced by the poetic forms of a culture of letters, these new expressions of favela culture are shaped by local/global visual and musical cultures that are not necessarily connected to previous national narratives or elite models of expression.

The prevalence of the realist code attests to a veritable anxiety for uncovering these pluralistic portraits of Brazil, while making both empathetic connections between the daily experiences of the urban centres and artistic representations. While televised soap opera productions still largely portray the romances and expectations of the urban middle classes, cinematic and literary realist productions have centred their attention on the poor, the excluded, the marginalized as an attempt to instil a critical perspective and ensure their access to a wide audience. The impact of such productions forms part of an ongoing dialogue concerning the feasibility of the nation, the possibilities of urban living and the agendas for the future. As a battle of representations unfolds around themes of urban violence, social exclusion, justice and the depiction of the popular, the aesthetics of realism both forms part of the culture of the spectacle and yet it politicizes representation. Perhaps a crucial danger of the realist aesthetics is its masking of its own mechanism of fiction making and its silencing of forms of imagination that subvert the codes of the realist real. Yet, in the most powerful realist productions, the reductive mechanism is countered by a convincing rendering of experience that brings to the surface the claims of authenticity that had been discarded by theoretical deconstruction and postmodern relativism. It is the debate surrounding social exclusion, urban violence and security measures, as exemplified by the conflicts of the drug trade in the favelas, that is encouraging a plurality of voices to emerge and discuss the future of Brazilian society. The favelas — as seen through the lens of the 'shock of the real' — are sites of contention in the cities of a nation that is now openly discussing the narratives and images that express its reality in the making. Yet, within its complex structure and given its extensive exchange with the city, the favela speaks of a cultural hybridity that bypasses polarities and provides the cities without maps of the twenty-first century.

Notes

1. The word favela designates the slum areas without basic sanitation and infrastructure that exist in almost all the cities of Brazil. The origins of the term favela began in the late nineteenth century when homeless soldiers returned from the backlands of Bahia after having exterminated the messianic rebel uprising of Canudos. While fighting in Canudos, the soldiers had camped on a hill covered by vegetation known as 'favela'. Upon returning to Rio de Janeiro, the soldiers never received the promised government housing and built makeshift shacks on a hill near the centre of Rio. They named their location Favela in a clear reference to Canudos. According to the 2000 census undertaken by the IBGE, favela populations have increased throughout Brazil. In a city such as Rio de Janeiro, the favela population increases in one year by what the urbanized city population increases in six.
2. In his excellent essay 'Modernity, hyperstimulation and the beginnings of popular sensationalism', published in *Cinema and the Invention of Modern Life* (Berkeley: University of California Press, 1995), Ben Singer makes use of Simmel's classic essay 'The Metropolis and Mental Life' and argues that the hyperstimulation of metropolitan living also fomented sensationalist press coverage and entertainment. My argument concerning the crisis of Brazilian cities and the aesthetics of 'the shock of the real' follows a similar reasoning by suggesting that realist aesthetics surface as a response to urban uncertainty as a form of competing with media fabrications of everyday life.
3. See: De Certeau, M. 1990. *L'invention du quotidian, arts de faire*. Paris: Gallimard.
4. In the early 1990s, funk gangs provoked panic on the beach of Ipanema. The debate surrounding their representation in the press and the role of funk culture in Rio de Janeiro has been studied by Micael Herschmann. See: Herschmann, M. 2000. 'As imagens da galera funk na imprensa'. In *Linguagens da Violência*,

organized by Carlos Alberto Messeder Pereira, Elizabeth Rondelli, Karl Erik Schollhammer and Micael Herschmann. Rio de Janeiro: Rocco: 163–97.

5   The promise of the modern city was precisely the possibility of envisioning alternative futures distinct from the tradition-bound premises of the past and diverse from the hierarchical constraints of rural existence. As either the scenario of the revolutionary masses or the conquering ground of the enterprising individual, the modern city was to fulfil the dreams and aspirations of a better future. The persistence of such acute social polarizations reflects the failures of modernizing projects as well as their triumph. Favelas have increased throughout Brazil. Yet, the term favela encompasses such an urban variety that it no longer has a singular vocabulary that can account for its diversity. If there are many aspects to the lives of the poor and a diversity of cultures of poverty, there are also many forms of social critique that have increasingly surfaced within the urban tissues of the great cities. The global impact of the media, neighbourhood associations, NGOs and new role models set by the several agendas of identity politics provide a wide range of social options. The struggle for representation is particularly relevant in the depiction of the marginalized. It is strategic in the emergence of the new visions of the favela and instrumental in decoding the validity of the notion of the 'divided city'. In the case of Rio de Janeiro, dramatic social violence such as the massacre in 1993 of favela dwellers in Vigário Geral by police forces seeking revenge on local drug dealers, and the murder of street children also in 1993 in front of Rio de Janeiro's cathedral, were among a host of events that spelt the carnage of unleashed violence. In the wake of these events, the term 'divided city' coined by journalist Zuenir Ventura in his book of the same title gained currency as an apt description of Rio de Janeiro. Yet, such polarizations and even a close reading of Ventura's own book reveal that, more than just being a 'divided city', Rio de Janeiro is a tumultuous urban maze of inequality and social juxtaposition. Between the favelas and the neighbourhoods of the rich and the middle class are numerous exchanges and, indeed, it is the ambiguity of these contact zones that allows both violence and cultural socialization to occur simultaneously. See: Ventura, Zuenir. 1994. *A cidade partida*. São Paulo: Companhia das Letras. For a discussion of the concept of the 'divided city' and the press coverage of the favela, see Mariana Cavalcanti's master's thesis, 2001: 'Demolição, Batalha e Paz: favelas em manchetes'. ECO/UFRJ.
6   See: Debord, Guy. 1967. *La Société du spectacle*. Paris: Gallimard.
7   See: Foster, Hal. 1994. *The return of the real*. Cambridge, MA: MIT Press.
8   For a discussion of the breakdown of TV Globo's media hegemony see Isabel Christina Esteves Guimarães's doctoral dissertation, 2002: 'Ratinho: A Crise da TV Brasileira e as Reinvenções do Popular'. ECO/UFRJ.
9   From the beginning of the twentieth century, literary descriptions of the favela were undertaken by a variety of Brazilian authors in a diversity of literary styles. The incursion into the favela was also a crucial feature of the journeys of foreign artists. Marinetti, Le Corbusier, Blaise Cendrars, Camus, Orson Welles and many others ventured into the favelas and produced narratives, photographs, images and architectural designs. Residing in Rio de Janeiro for many years, the American poet Elizabeth Bishop wrote several poems that metaphorized the favela and in one particular ballad, 'The Burglar of Babylon', Bishop narrated the saga of the outlaw Micuçú as he attempted to escape from the police in the favela of Babylon. Armed

10 For a discussion of the modernization policies of the Brazilian engineers at the beginning of the twentieth century see: de Carvalho, Maria Alice Rezende. 1994. 'Engenheiros na Belle Époque Carioca'. In *Quatro Vezes Cidade*. Rio de Janeiro: Sette Letras.

with powerful binoculars, Bishop watched the escape on Babylon hill, located above the building where she lived.

11 De Jesus, Carolina Maria. 1960. *Quarto de despejo: diário de uma favelada*. São Paulo: Livraria Francisco Alves. For a discussion of her diary see: Vogt, Carlos. 1986. 'Trabalho, pobreza e trabalho intellectual (*O Quarto de Despejo* de Carolina Maria de Jesus)'. In *Os pobres na literatura brasileira*, edited by Roberto Schwarz. São Paulo: Brasiliense.

12 Written by Bernardo Guimarães, the abolitionist novel *A Escrava Isaura* (1875) narrates in sentimental prose the plight of the lovely Isaura who was born a slave and was subjected to cruel torments by her lustful master. The crucial point about Isaura is her complexion, as Guimarães casts her as a white woman of African descent. Made into a soap opera by Globo Network in the 1970s, it was a tremendous public success in Brazil and also in Cuba and China where it was exported.

13 Ibid., p. 27. The translation from the Portuguese is mine.

14 See Janice Perlman's critique of the 'myth of marginality' cast upon the inhabitants of the favelas of Rio de Janeiro in her 1977 book, *O mito da marginalidade: favelas e política no Rio de Janeiro*. Rio de Janeiro: Paz e Terra. Carolina de Jesus's prose does not reinforce the 'myth of marginality' because she does not endorse the clichéd view of the poor as 'lazy', slothful', 'backward'. Yet, her portrait of the miserable conditions of the favela has practically no redeeming features, as the people she depicts tend to lack solidarity or cultural inventiveness.

15 Schwarz, Roberto. 1997. 'Uma aventura artística incomum'. *Folha de São Paulo*, Caderno *Mais* 7 September: 5–12.

16 The translations of the Portuguese titles are mine. See Zaluar, Alba. 1985. *A máquina e a revolta: as organizações populares e o significado da pobreza*. São Paulo: Brasiliense, and 1994. *Condomínio do diabo*. Rio de Janeiro: Editora UFRJ.

17 Film critic Ivana Bentes created the term 'cosmetics of hunger' and her expression has circulated in the written and televised debates on the film *Cidade de Deus*. See her critique of Cidade de Deus in a 2002 review: '*Cidade de Deus* promove turismo no inferno,' *Estado de São Paulo*.

18 See Zaluar, Alba. 2002. 'A tese do gueto norte-americano'. *Jornal do Brasil*, Caderno B 2 September. The English translation of Zaluar's quoted words is mine.

19 João Moreira Salles, the director of *Notícias de uma guerra particular*, wrote a review on *Cidade de Deus* entitled: 'Cidade de Deus: o que fazer?' In *no mínimo*, Internet newspaper, 8 September 2002. The title in English is 'Cidade de Deus: what to do?'. In the review he stresses, 'In Brazil and especially in Rio de Janeiro we are and we aren't at war. It is true that there aren't formal declarations or clear aims – requisites of any war. Yet, more people died in Rio during the four-year siege of Sarajevo than in the city of Sarajevo itself that was directly ambushed and in open and direct conflict.' The English translation of his words is mine.

20 See: interview with MV Bill, 'Rapper da Cidade de Deus diz que filme prejudica moradores', *Folha On Line* 28 August 2002.

21 See: Dowdney, Luke. 2002. *Child combatants in organised armed violence: a study of*

children and adolescents involved in territorial drug faction disputes in Rio de Janeiro. Iser/ViVa Rio.

22 For an overview of the newspaper coverage of Marcinho VP, see: Thiago Melamed Menezes's 2002 graduation project, 'Marginais Midiáticos'. ECO/UFRJ.
23 Quoted from Fokkema, D. W. and Elrud Kunne-Ibsch. 1977. *Theories of literature in the twentieth century*. London: C. Hurst & Company: 16.

Ignacio M. Sánchez-Prado

AMORES PERROS: EXOTIC VIOLENCE AND NEOLIBERAL FEAR[1]

Let us imagine for a moment that we find ourselves in an affluent neighbourhood in Mexico City. Suddenly, a vagrant whose appearance is not-too-subtly reminiscent of Karl Marx fires two shots through the front window of a five-star restaurant into the back of a prominent businessman, killing him. In another part of the city, around the same time, an automobile accident involving a pair of youngsters fleeing from a group of criminals and a Spanish supermodel going to the store is the point of departure of a series of events that will entwine the lives of a group of urban characters. These images, from Alejandro González Iñárritu's film *Amores perros*,[2] are symptomatic of the transgression performed by crime and violence in the urban, middle-class environment – an environment whose sense of security is dissolving in tandem with the Partido Revolucionario Institucional PRI state in Mexico. Neoliberal and violent, caught between a nationalist imaginary and the desire of transnational projection, Mexican culture at the end of the century was faced with the absence of a centre of gravity that could determine its political position. In recent years, this destabilized culture has produced new images of violence that allegorize the sense of uncertainty which is a product of the fall of the paternalistic state and of the ideas attached to revolutionary nationalism. The result is a cultural repositioning of violence, which has ceased to be a marginal manifestation and has become the very centre of a newly emerging identity. This identity begins to define forms of citizenship and imaginary in the context of Mexico's political transition.

Violence is a category that has become increasingly used in Latin American cultural analysis. It has permitted the construction of a new cultural cartography whose axes are urban experience and a sense of social instability, both of these instances of the shaping of a new sense of community[3]. Susana Rotker has noted that the sense of insecurity in Latin America's capitals 'has been gradually changing the way in which people relate to urban space, their fellow citizens, the State and with the very concept of citizenship'[4]. In Mexico's case, the emergence of these 'citizenships of fear' coincides with the decay of notions of citizenship stemming from PRI discourse and, in a certain sense, resolves an identity crisis created by the radical cultural and political transformations of the 1990s. At this point, as violence and criminality occupy an increasingly prominent place in both the national imaginary and the image that Mexico projects on a transnational scale, I would like to propose an analysis of *Amores perros* in terms of a paradoxical ideological articulation. On one hand, *Amores perros* is the ultimate product of the imaginary generated by the country's urban middle classes: social groups that see their class interests affected by the new urban configurations and invent myths about the marginalized sectors as a means of conveying their fears and insecurities. On the other hand, the film appeals to a transnational market that reinterprets violence as an allegory of the new possibilities of political expression after the fall of the Berlin Wall. In this sense, *Amores perros* is the most recent version of a new form of commodification of Mexico and Latin America: the configuration of an imaginary that simultaneously appeals to the worldview held by the privileged groups that benefit from the region's neoliberalism and to the voluntaristic politics of the progressive and pseudo-progressive sectors of Western intelligentsia, desperately searching for new ways to relate to the Third World.

The interpretation of violence in *Amores perros* emerges from an ideological matrix that is far more conservative than its sophisticated formal resources would suggest. Behind the formal mask, the stories that comprise the film share the common trope of the family. Paul Julian Smith has noted that the absence of the paternal figure is a constant motif throughout the film[5]. Furthermore, it is imperative to observe that the catalyst for the actions of all three of the film's plotlines is either infidelity or family abandonment. In the first storyline, Octavio, played by Gabriel García Bernal, falls in love with Susana, his brother's battered wife. In order to free Susana from her husband's violence (and of course with the ulterior motive of 'getting the girl' for himself), Octavio enters into the underground world of dog-fighting – an adventure that leads to the car chase mentioned at the beginning of the article. The second plotline centres on the story of Daniel and Valeria. Daniel is a one-time family man who leaves his wife and daughters to live with his mistress, Valeria. Valeria, however, is involved in the same car accident as Octavio, and thus begins a process of convalescence in which Daniel's life is converted into a living hell. In the third plotline, El Chivo is a hit man at the end of a personal odyssey that began in the 1960s, when he left his family to join a group of revolutionaries.

The plot of the movie, then, is constructed upon the consequences of these actions. The surface unity of the film might seem to be given by the intertwining of these stories attendant on the car crash, but in reality the structure of the movie is constructed upon allegories (not to say parables) that reflect the consequences of a series of moral decisions. Let us use El Chivo as an example. He decides to leave his family in the name of the revolution and this triggers a series of moral decisions that include complete alienation from his family (he does not contact them after his incarceration, letting his daughter, Maru, believe him to be dead), and his subsequently becoming an assassin. El Chivo's path to redemption also begins with a moral decision. In his final job, instead of completing the hit for a man who has paid him to kill the contractor's brother (who, incidentally, is an adulterer), El Chivo decides to confront both of them when he learns about their relation to one other. In short, this narrative development, like those of the other two plotlines, suggests that people are always judged in terms of a transcendental moralism that makes no allowance for circumstances. It is irrelevant here whether El Chivo's cause is just. What is relevant is simply his abandoning of his family, which makes him equivalent to Daniel, the adulterer of the second plotline (who also leaves his family). According to the movie's moral code, there is no difference between Daniel and El Chivo. That the former leaves his family for another woman whereas the latter does so for sociopolitical reasons has no bearing on the consideration of the fact that they both leave their families. Both characters share parallel fates: as a consequence of their actions, both go through purgatory of sorts (Valeria's accident and El Chivo's descent into crime), and both are finally given the opportunity to return to their respective families: Daniel calls his estranged wife over the phone, although does not dare to speak to her; El Chivo leaves a message on Maru's answering machine.

One might ask what would happen if, for a moment, this scale of values was inverted. For instance, an alternative reading of Octavio and Susana's story might be constructed from the point of view of a moral system without absolutisms. In terms of the film's values, Octavio's tragic error (i.e. his adulterous desire for his sister-in-law), drives him to a series of poor decisions: his involvement in the criminal network of dog-fighting, his attempt to confront one of the neighbourhood's most notorious criminals, his decision to stab this man after he shoots Octavio's dog, etc. The three characters from the first story, consequently, receive 'just' punishment: Ramiro – thief, abusive husband and adulterer – dies in a gunfight during a robbery; Octavio, who attempts to steal his brother's wife and finance their escape with his illegal activities, ends up alone at a bus station, physically battered and penniless. We know little about Susana's fate; perhaps her punishment is concealed because of her final fidelity to her spouse. However, because she did succumb to temptation, she is left on her own with her child, pregnant for a second time. If adultery were removed as the driving force of the justice meted out by the plot upon its characters, the interpretation of their acts might be very different. If Octavio and Susana fell in love, and we then followed this logic against the film's plot, then we might be able to think of a possible narrative that does not conclude with Octavio's punishment. It is possible to think of a storyline in which Octavio's decision results in a 'happy ending' with Susana, or even in a narrative in which Susana makes the same final choice, but Octavio's departure would still be presented in redemptive terms. These possibilities tell us much about the film's ideological wager: it does not attempt to place the characters into a set of circumstances from which they measure their decisions, but rather creates an absolute moral compass that evaluates everyone using the same criteria. The morality outlined here is, in the end, conservative: the vindication of unquestionable family values under three very different circumstances. Therefore, Octavio and Susana's relationship is always represented in an uncomfortable manner: its ethical possibility is cancelled a priori by the moralism through which the film interprets its characters.

This counterpoint between a conservative moralism grounded in the family and an ethics founded in specific circumstances is clear precisely in the film's representation of Octavio and Susana's first sexual encounter. Paul Julian Smith establishes that, even when this encounter is emphasized by the movie itself (upon being placed in a scene with background music, after half an hour without this resource), all of their sexual encounters are interrupted by some unfortunate background noise. The first time Susana's baby is present, next to them. The second sexual encounter includes not only Octavio looking at himself in a broken mirror but also a montage that shows Ramiro having sexual relations with one of his co-workers, Ramiro being assaulted by Octavio's friends and the heavily ironic use of the rock ballad *Lucha de gigantes*[6]. In other words, the act that could lead Susana and Octavio's love to be seen in another light and that would, consequently, lead to a more empathetic interpretation of their story is always interrupted by images that induce guilt: the baby reminds us of the illegality of the relationship; the montage of images links the couple to Ramiro's errors and also with a criminal act linked to Octavio's attempt to win Susana's love. Any possibility of transforming the characters' situation is annulled by the film's own narrative.

Precisely because this master narrative of adultery is at the film's core, all of the manifestations of violence in the film, fortuitous (like the car crash) or not, are direct consequences of moral actions and are never interpreted from a social point of view. As Laura Podalsky has observed, the movie uses an emotional register stemming from soap operas as a way to obscure or question the social and political register of the characters' actions. This, continues Podalsky, manifests 'an epistemological crisis that has destabilized the subject's understanding of contemporary society and, perhaps, more importantly, his/her ability to make substantive proposals for a better future'.[7] Carlos Monsiváis has emphasized this point in his analysis of the melodramatic structure of the *thriller*, and he makes an observation particularly pertinent to the reading of *Amores perros*: 'Cinema retains melodrama and brings it up to date, giving it an appropriate context: social decomposition.' In this dimension, the cinema of violence 'is constituted in the distorting fairground mirror where characters live out previously inconceivable roles with grotesque energy'.[8] This narrative structure has profound consequences in terms of the manner in which violence is understood by Mexico's conservative middle class, whose frames of reference are represented by this movie. Ultimately, in the history of the use of melodrama in Mexican culture, from the liberal novelists of the nineteenth century through the cinema of the 1930s up to Televisa, it has been consistently utilized by the dominant classes to generate imaginaries and political consensus eventually naturalized by viewers. The resort to melodrama in *Amores perros* is the latest instance of this process.

The conservative ideology of *Amores perros*, then, cannot be reduced to the story of three assaults on morality. El Chivo's story not only transmits the failure of the utopian and revolutionary discourse of the generation of the 1960s but also, in several ways, allegorizes the interpretations of this event that the 'citizenship of fear' constructed by Mexico City bourgeoisie has incorporated into its imaginary. The figure of the assassin embodies the culminating point of the process of moral decay responsible, according to this imaginary, for the emergence of urban violence. In the first place, all violence is unleashed, as I mentioned earlier, by a series of personal decisions: abandoning the family, participation in a clandestine movement, the decision to become a hit man on being released from prison, etc. Furthermore, in so far as one follows the trajectory of this character, it must be emphasized that, within the movie's code, the return to the family offers the only possibility of redemption. Hence, El Chivo's final assignment (which once more involves an adulterer and his treacherous brother) is not resolved by murder but rather by a sort of the angel-of-death ethics, in which El Chivo turns into an agent of Solomonic justice. Finally, when El Chivo decides to make amends to his daughter Maru, he cuts his hair and shaves off his beard, transforming his Marx-esque appearance into a somewhat grotesque image of a 'good citizen'. In this sense, the film's presentation of El Chivo's evolution is not surprising: his journey from revolutionary, to prisoner, to criminal natural and profoundly undermines the dissident quality of the narrative. El Chivo is imprisoned because of a bombing (note here how the revolutionary is reduced to a terrorist, and this in a country where leftist movements are not particularly characterized by revolutionary violence), imprisoned and later incorporated into the world of crime via a corrupt police agent. Is this not the way in which the conservative middle class characterizes the figure of the revolutionary? From their perspective, any threat to the status quo of Mexico City's affluent zones becomes a manifestation of criminality: the dissident who places a bomb in the middle of a shopping centre to further the cause of social justice and the hit man who kills for money in broad daylight are the same person, since both actions attack the protective bubble that surrounds the middle and upper classes. From the perspective of the movie, the ethical, political or ideological motivation that lies behind the act is rendered irrelevant.

This entire framework leads us to think that, far from being a progressive film, *Amores perros* simply deals with a catalogue of urban bourgeois fears. The film interprets these fears using precisely the same conservative moral measure that considers violence to be a product not of profound social and economic differences but of the decline of family values that accompanied the fall of the strong state after 1968. For this reason, in spite of the fact that González Iñárritu has expressed in various interviews the idea that crime is the poor people's way to make a living,[9] the movie makes no effort to problematize the ethical position of its characters and everything functions as some sort of divine justice in which each person reaps what he/she sows in terms of a black-and-white moral scale: the adulterers come to grief, the beautiful woman is left mutilated, and those who abandon their families live in the purgatory of nostalgia. This imaginary permits one to infer that this particular 'citizenship of fear' does not lead to, as Rotker suggests at the end of her famous text, the emergence of movements that recognize 'difference as the space in which to deepen democracy and self-management'[10] but rather to the rise of images that deepen the social, economic and cultural abyss in which violence is grounded.

In order to better understand this problem, we can set *Amores perros* against other representations of violence emerging from the era of neoliberalism: *Todo el poder*, a film by Fernando Sariñana that appeared shortly before the González Iñárritu work, and *Nostalgia de la sombra*, a novel by Eduardo Antonio Parra.[11] *Todo el poder* tells the story of an unemployed documentary director who, after several encounters with Mexico City crime, loses his ex-wife's SUV (sports utility vehicle) to a band of thieves and decides to take action. Along with a group of friends, he begins to track down the criminals in an investigation that brings in a police commander (a carnivalesque character named Elvis Quijano, after his conceit that he looks like the King of Rock) and Julián Luna, head of public security in Mexico City. The film has much in common with *Amores perros*: it is a commercial film, privately financed, distributed on the back of a publicity campaign that was unprecedented for its time (*Amores perros* became the high point of this strategy).[12] Likewise, it is ultimately a film made exclusively for the urban middle class. It speaks to the same fear and the same sense of insecurity. In addition, the film is more literally based in the idea of a 'citizenship of fear' since it actually portrays a network of social solidarity that allows the criminal group to be confronted. In spite of the fact that *Todo el poder* lacks the formal pretensions of *Amores perros* and that poverty is simply invisible in the film[13] it still offers a more political interpretation of crime. The most crucial point here is the fact that violence and crime in *Todo el poder* are intimately linked to the neoliberal state's institutional network of corruption. Instead of falling into the temptation of parodying the ineptitude of the authorities, the film is interested in a much more profound problem: the collusion between crime and political power. In this way, the political system presented to us in *Todo el poder* is a combination of a profoundly inept bureaucracy (in one scene we see a secretary who is ignoring people reporting crime because she is eating at her desk) and the presence of criminals throughout the police force (certain members of a criminal gang have offices in the police station, and we eventually find out that Elvis Quijano is the gang's leader). This system shows up during a scene of simulated justice, meant to create the appearance of a crime investigation (it represents a confrontation between a group of assault victims and a series of randomly selected criminals, organized by Quijano to investigate a robbery that he himself committed). Corruption reaches to the highest ranks of political power. The movie's critique is so harsh that Luna, in his television appearances, speaks with a tone and prosody that is an almost perfect imitation of the political rhetoric used by both Carlos Salinas and Ernesto Zedillo, the two most prominent presidents during the PRI's neoliberal phase. Luna, then, represents the two faces of a neoliberal institutionalism that, in real life, manifested itself in the fall of Carlos Salinas: a political system that seeks to maintain a front of efficiency and modernization (as shown in the scene where Luna commissions a publicity campaign that emphasizes the statistical reduction in crime), even as it continues to be a direct participant in the problems that it is supposed to resolve.

In spite of its virtues, *Todo el poder* is a film that ultimately trivializes crime by dissolving it into a comedy of errors. However, a comparison with *Amores perros* nevertheless raises a very significant point: in *Amores perros,* political institutions are completely invisible. The only representative of the law in the film, the federal agent who organizes El Chivo's contracts, appears completely isolated and void of any relationship to the rest of the police body. He is, simply, just another (im)moral character in the film. This void not only allows for the reduction of crime and violence to the moralism that I have previously described, but also results in a profound inability to articulate a truly political criticism of neoliberalism and its violence. Of course, the literal appearance of the institutions of the state is not an indispensable condition for a political critique. Rather, the point is that there is not a single manifestation of crime or violence in the film that cannot, ultimately, be reduced to a moral decision. Both the film's critical commentators and González Iñárritu himself have over-emphasized the historical context of *Amores perros*, pointing to its relationship to the Mexican transition. Claudia Schaefer, for example, has pointed out that 'the film places individual characters' despair within an undeniably political setting'.[14] It seems to me, however, that this 'undeniably political setting' exists more in the film's sociohistorical context than in the film itself. Ultimately, this interpretation follows a somewhat imprecise formula: Mexico City represents, in Carlos Bonfil's words, 'a modernity that only offers the proliferation of social injustice, political corruption and ... neo-liberal dogma'.[15] Consequently, situating a movie in this city and showing these contradictions represents in itself a political *mise-en-scène*. Regardless of how valid this reading might be in other contexts, when it comes to *Amores perros* it results in an imprecise interpretation given that neither injustice, nor corruption, nor neoliberalism has anything to do with the film's plot. In the film's narrative structure, there is no causal relationship of any kind between these factors and the narrated events. Actually, the 'political dimension' of *Amores perros* seems to be situated in the will of its audience, which, during one of the country's moments of political unrest, imposed upon the movie a critical intention that is simply not there.

To be fair to *Amores perros*, it is indeed possible to argue that the plotline of Valeria and Daniel offers a critique of the immorality of the emerging neoliberal classes.[16] In effect, Daniel and Valeria are part of the media industry (he is an editor of a prominent magazine and she is a successful model participating in a renowned publicity campaign), a sector that enjoyed a particular ascent during the neoliberal years. In other words, Daniel and Valeria are part of this new urban bourgeoisie whose wealth comes from the emerging economic sectors. The same can be said about the brothers involved in El Chivo's contract. They are two young businessmen, part of the same emerging business class. Immorality, then, is not only a sin of the poor who opt for crime: the bourgeoisie is also responsible for adulteries, abandonment and fratricide. This emerging class, in the eyes of the film, is also an active part of moral decline and social decomposition. This, however, does not change the fact that the critique of this social class is also moralistic and apolitical: they are simply additional performers of the same immoral symphony.[17]

Before addressing the question of why, in spite of everything I have said up until this point, the interpretation of the movie as a progressive and political film persists, I would like to make a detour in order to illustrate an alternative to these narrations of violence that avoids both the moralism of *Amores perros* and the literalism of *Todo el poder*. *Nostalgia de la sombra* is a text that profoundly problematizes the moralistic interpretations of violence by tracing the trajectory that transforms the everyday man into a murderer, by way of a journey through a series of distinct territorialities in the map of urban violence. In her article, '¿Guerreros o ciudadanos?', Rossana Reguillo classifies the way in which urban imaginaries represent violence in three fields of meaning: 'a territory inhabited by poverty; night as a time of exception; and an environment characterized by moral laxity and vice'.[18] If I had to describe the importance of Parra's novel for Mexican representations of violence, I would say that it is perhaps the text that best puts these three fields of meaning into question. The novel tells the story of Ramiro Mendoza Elizondo, a family man who is attacked in the streets of Monterrey. During the attack, he kills his aggressors and, instead of returning to his family, he embarks on an odyssey that takes him to the border, to the rubbish dumps, to prison, and ends ups with his transformation into a hit man. It is important to emphasize that, unlike El Chivo, Ramiro's turn to crime is a product of crime itself, and not the result of a moral (like Octavio's) or political (like El Chivo's) decision. The novel is structured by two intersecting time-lines: on the one hand, the process by which Ramiro is transformed from citizen to murderer and on the other Ramiro's reservations regarding his most recent contract, which targets a woman.

The world of Ramiro's journey is complex because violence is not a product of moral choices but rather something that happens, a consistent presence that becomes a constitutive part of the social tapestry in the distinct environments he navigates. In other words, violence does not function as a flat continuum that as in *Amores perros* equates political violence with crime or family violence. Actually, poverty, violence and other social factors become polyvalent indicators whose consequences manifest themselves in terms of their relationship with other components of the social tapestry.[19] Thus, on the border, violence is an instrument of control exercised by those holding the power to cross it; in the rubbish tips, it is a mechanism related to a particular code of honour and survival; in the territories of organized crime it always functions in relation to the political and economic interests of society's most privileged strata. Following this line of thought and returning to Reguillo's categories, in *Nostalgia de la sombra* we encounter not only a narrative of violence far removed from the idea of 'moral laxity' but also a portrayal that puts into question any deterministic relationship between poverty and violence. The novel's characters are not violent because they are poor. Violence is, rather, a social code that enters the urban environment as a strategy of social relationships and as a component of subjectivity. Far from the 'citizenship of fear' that presents violence as an otherness seeking to maintain itself outside of the boundaries of the individual, *Nostalgia de la sombra* is the narrative of a 'citizenship through violence', in which violence is not an enemy to conquer but rather a component that passes through subjectivities and communities, and is, irrevocably, part of both.

Through the dual structure of the novel it is possible to discern two functions of violence: first, as the instrument that allows Ramiro to both link to and separate himself from the two distinct territories that he passes through; second, as a constituent element of his personality, completely normalized within the narrative. The act of violence that leads to the emergence of Ramiro's self (when he kills three men who are trying to kill him) becomes a mark that radically transforms his subjectivity. Symptomatically, this transformation is described by the phrase 'the fear had gone for good'.[20] Here, then, it can be understood that a 'citizenship of fear' such as the one represented in *Amores perros* or *Todo el poder* dissipates when an act of violence displaces the urban, middle-class bourgeoisie to the margins. This new formation of the urban subject, in the novel, opens precisely in the moment in which fear stops being the element that grounds citizenship and violence integrates itself into the realm of daily life. For this reason, Parra's book does not narrate an anxiety drawn by the fears of the privileged groups, but rather a world with diverse social and ideological layers that cannot be approached from the point of view of a strict or fixed moral code. Thus, classic citizenship and family life in this text are not conceived as the origin of a moral scale or even a secure environment. Both function, rather, as shadows – ghosts that haunt the 'citizen through violence', who has always inhabited his complex social space, in the light of their loss. As Miguel Rodríguez Lozano has already pointed out, these shadows articulate in a single image the nostalgia for what is lost and the presence of the night as an allegory of violence.[21] In this way, the night is not conceived of as the time or space of violence but as an allegory for a state of mourning that in a certain sense reflects the fall of identitarian certainties in a violent and neoliberal Mexico.

The example of *Nostalgia de la sombra* indicates that a representation of violence can only be political when it is understood as part of the social network that transcends it. In other words, violence per se has no political valence and, because of this, to assume that a film or novel would be political simply because it shows urban violence or because it was made during a specific historical moment is extremely imprecise. Rather, violence is an element that is used strategically in cultural representations in order to validate specific political and social perspectives.[22] Therefore, in *Amores perros*, where violence is self-evident and problematized by its social dimension, it serves as an indicator of the consequences of the country's moral decline. Violence is the argument that the conservative discourse invokes in order to caution against the dangers of immorality. In this sense, *Amores perros* is not far from made-for-television melodrama or from nineteenth-century *costumbrismo*, which interprets crime as sickness and as the consequence of moral decadence.[23]

Everything that I have argued leads to the question of why *Amores perros* is such a successful film, in spite of its representation of violence and the profound ideological problems behind its narrative. The answer lies in its unusual ability, within the Mexican and Latin American film world, to convert violence and crime into commodities. The reason behind this is that *Amores perros* is the most expensive film in Mexico's history, filmed exclusively with private funding.[24] Therefore, the recovery of the funds invested became a particular problem, given that no prior film in Mexican history had ever grossed an amount even equivalent to the final cost of *Amores perros*. In consequence, appealing with an unprecedented intensity to both the international market and the national middle class that generally sees only Hollywood productions was crucial for the film's success. This need forced *Amores perros* to make a fundamental decision: to avoid the bureaucratic apparatus around Mexican film production, controlled by the Instituto Mexicano de Cinematografía.[25] By virtue of this, *Amores perros* eschewed the traditional distribution network for Mexican cinema, which generally includes a modest commercial run, a pair of international festivals and a stint in art-houses. Upon accepting private funds, *Amores perros* took a chance on not being seen as simply another art-house film made for a pre-selected minority and set its sights on a greater audience.

A second consequence to take into consideration is that *Amores perros* was conceived in a manner distinct from the *auteur cinema* that had flourished in Mexico under the aegis of Imcine. In contrast to Arturo Ripstein or Jorge Fons, Alejandro González Iñárritu is not a 'traditional' filmmaker. His roots are in the communications industry. On one hand, he was one of the best known radio hosts of WFM, a very successful commercial radio station. On the other, he was one of the key publicists behind campaigns that redefined the market during the neoliberal years, and the owner of a major advertising company. In fact, González Iñárritu defines himself as 'self-taught' when speaking of his entrance into the world of movie-making.[26] Taking this into account, it seems that *Amores perros* should not be considered as a cinematographic work on the same level as other independent films but a product packaged and advertised in order to sell. The *Amores perros* product, then, extends far beyond the movie and its production. Part of the *Amores perros* product includes a soundtrack consisting not only of songs that appear in the movie but also a number of songs 'inspired by' the film, from figures central to the Mexican music scene (Julieta Venegas, Control Machete, etc.). With this, inside the national market, *Amores perros* perfects a strategy first used by Antonio Serrano's *Sexo, pudor y lágrimas*:[27] appealing to a public already constituted by groups of alternative rock (a public that includes the young middle class that also sees Hollywood's films) in order to generate interest in the film. This comes along with a new strategy of filmmaking, stylistically closer to the music video than to the slower rhythm of traditional Mexican cinema (for example, Ripstein's films). Therefore, *Amores perros* brings us face to face with a dynamic, vertiginous, visual aesthetic that entails a profound renovation of Mexican cinema and at the same time brings about a renovation of its public: as films start speaking MTV's language, its audience is drawn by this type of cinema. In this sense, it is crucial to understand the role that Iñárritu's advertising experience plays in the movie's aesthetic. The visual language of commercials, on one hand, and his knowledge in terms of packaging products define the positioning of *Amores perros* within Mexican cinema: the inclusion of these external discourses in the cinematographic canon lead to a renovation that would have been impossible within the prevailing aesthetic. Therefore, if the film deserves some credit, it would be precisely for its break with certain stereotypes of the Mexican cinema industry at both the national and international levels: no longer did it have to do with the 'aestheticized vision of Latin American society' and the visual nihilism of Arturo

Ripstein[28] or the idea of a folkloric Mexico full of guitars and drug traffickers, such as the one seen in Robert Rodríguez's films.[29] González Iñárritu has tirelessly declared his intention to break free from these traditions and represent 'el mundo en el que vivo'.[30] Certainly, one cannot help but share this vocation. However, this proposition is suspended both by the moralism that I have presented and by its own narrative consequence: violence. In the end, González Iñárritu breaks with the exoticism inherited just as much from magic realism (Alfonso Arau's proverbial *Like Water for Chocolate*[31]) as from the 'dirty' Mexico of the North American western (Gore Verbinski's *The Mexican*), thus establishing a new exoticism: that of a fast-paced, violent, postmodern Mexico. With this, obviously, I do not intend to say that violence does not exist within the Mexican world. Rather, my point is that *Amores perros* operates within a new cinematographic world where violence is the new trademark of Latin America.

The representation of violence seen in *Amores perros* is based on a profound contradiction between meaning and form. On one hand, the film gives the Mexican middle class audience a testimonial and almost therapeutic discourse of violence in which one can identify a system of values similar to that of Mexican neo-conservatism, represented at the time by the presidential candidacy of Vicente Fox. On the other hand, we have an audiovisual system that transmits the image of an urban subculture consisting of avant-garde musical groups and vertiginous images of city life that, in a transnational context, has brought positive appraisals that establish the film as some sort of renovatory force for progressive Mexican cinema. However, as can be seen even in the positive reviews, the movie is founded on a subculture that puts the possibility of social transformation under erasure.[32] Ultimately, this contradiction is the same contradiction of Mexican neoliberalism: the image of a modern, avant-garde country, en route to becoming part of the First World, that uses this mask for the preservation of both the deep class divisions and the conservative ideology that throughout history have obstructed the promises of change.

This contradiction flourishes if we give some thought to the specific cinematographic genealogy of *Amores perros*. The critics have pointed out three films that share both the violent aesthetic of González Iñárritu and the international success that permitted the reception of this brand of movie: David Cronenberg's *Crash*, Tom Tykwer's *Lola Rennt* and, very specifically, Quentin Tarantino's *Pulp Fiction*.[33] Rather than addressing the formal and visual connections between these films and *Amores perros*, a topic that has already had its share of discussion, I would like to point out a difference crucial in comprehending one of the film's central problems. For Tarantino, Tykwer and Cronenberg, violence is never social: it is metacinematographic. Directly appealing to a postmodern discourse of simulacrum and pastiche, these directors' portrayal violence is always aesthetic and exists in their films to the extent that it exists in the genres they are revisiting. This is clear in Tarantino, who appeals to a graphic form of violence in films that belong to the *pulp* discourse (*Pulp Fiction* and *Reservoir Dogs*) or to minor genres such as Japanese samurai films or classic spaghetti westerns (*Kill Bill*). Meanwhile, when referring to a genre based more on plot and less on violence, such as the one revisited by *Jackie Brown*, the films are noticeably less violent. The point here is to observe that Tarantino's movies are essentially asocial: their violence has no base in social or political matters. They are based, simply, on an aesthetic simulacrum of classic movie genres.

Tarantino's filmmaking results in a stylistic revolution of contemporary cinema, with ramifications that extend far beyond the scope of the present work.[34] In the specific case of *Amores perros*, its appropriation of this discourse of violence is based on a problematic interpretation of *Pulp Fiction*: the use of an essentially metacinematographic discourse for the expression of a social problematic. In other words, Tarantino's simulacrum is put to use by González Iñárritu to produce a narrative that is, in the end, realistic. The motivation for this appropriation can be traced back to the emergence of the city as the centre of the visual discourse of Mexican cinema. Unlike the traditional nationalistic cinema or that of provincial and rural environments, both templates used by Ripstein and other directors, *Amores perros* aspired to capture Mexico City in the midst of a cinematic tradition that lacked the style for doing so. The stylistic problem faced by *Amores perros* may be defined by invoking the words of Jesús Martín-Barbero: 'seen from the heterogeneity of experience, the city challeneges our mental habits to the point of making it unthinkable'.[35] In this sense, González Iñárritu understood that the insertion of this environment into the cinematic imaginary required a new language. Finally, as Martín Barbero observes, after Benjamin there has always been a relation between emerging mediations of cinema and the transformation of the urban experience.[36] In this sense, the Tarantino discourse makes it possible for González Iñárritu to incorporate into cinema a new way to give account of this experience. Marvin D'Lugo moves in this direction when he observes that González Iñárritu's films use 'pulp fictions' in order to 'help sustain the lives of characters in the city' and that the 'decisive fiction is one of an easy modernity to which nearly all of the characters seem to subscribe'.[37]

However, this aesthetic choice brings with it the key problem of its own insufficiency. In the end, Tarantino's language is not constructed to speak of urban chaos but rather to represent cinema and its stereotypes. This generates a crucial blind spot that may also be articulated through Martín-Barbero's words: 'What is in play here is not so much the difficulty of integrally thinking the city as the possibility of perceiving it as a public matter and not just the sum of private interests.' This leads Martín-Barbero to warn of a danger: 'It is therefore indispensable to sketch out the possibility of a total view of the city, of its nostalgic complicity with the idea of unity or lost identity, leading to a culturalist pessimism that is preventing us from understanding what the fractures that are exploding are made of.'[38] If we connect this insight with the moralistic discourse that I have outlined in previous pages, *Amores perros* only creates the impression of a progressive discourse set in the urban context: underneath, its narrative is 'a culturalist pessimism' that is incapable of recognizing the profound social and political contradictions that transcend the very world that the film narrates. In this sense, what is left is the admission that, in spite of its fight to break with social stereotypes, *Amores perros*, in the end, succumbs to them. Jorge Ayala Blanco astutely names the only social classes present in the film ('the lumpen stratum or ruling class, with nothing in the middle'), a problematic ethical attitude ('Bestialism is the only idea or experience of humanity'), and a concept of the city that is, ultimately, unreal: ('An exasperated and hypothetical city which is grotesquely anti-human and is reduced to spaces without place and places without space').[39] Unconsciously, the cinematographic discourse found in *Amores perros* does not escape Tarantino's metageneric tendency. It is, partly, a simulacrum of *costumbrismo* and, partly, an aestheticization of soap-opera melodrama. It is in not coincidental that, when asked 'What do you think of violence?' the response given by González Iñárritu was 'It is part of our nature, unfortunately. It is painful for those who deliver it or receive it, and also confusing. This being against our nature forms part of us.'[40] Not social, not political, not economic. The violence in *Amores perros* is natural. And aesthetic. In this sense we should not forget that, in the same text referred to by Martín-Barbero, Benjamin cautions of the dangers of aestheticizing politics and violence. Benjamin also observes that the course to follow is not the aestheticization of politics but rather the politicization of art.[41] In consequence, the ultimate failure of *Amores perros* stems from its essentially moralistic base and its interpretation of violence. From such a position, it is not possible to articulate the public dimension so crucial for Martín-Barbero. In its incapacity to transcend the sphere of private life, the politicization of violence is, in the end, impossible.[42]

An interpretation of *Amores perros* such as the one that I have been elaborating up to this point cannot but conclude with an interrogation of the increasing status of violence as an indicator of the Latin American experience. The other result of the Tarantinesque aesthetic adopted in *Amores perros* is the legibility of the film in the international cinema market. It is enough to point out that *Pulp Fiction* was a film that was very well received in circuits such as Cannes, Sundance and the Academy Awards, where *Amores perros* acquired its international audience, especially since it was given the Critic's Week Prize at Cannes. *Amores perros* is part of a larger group of Latin American films that have ridden a wave of success in metropolitan markets: Fernando Meirelles and Kátia Lund's *Cidade de Deus* and Barbet Schroeder's *La Virgin de los sicarios*, for instance, enjoyed much more box office success and critical praise than the average Latin American film. This situation, along with other cultural manifestations such as the Colombian literature of the *sicarios*,[43] or the increasingly popular Latin American 'crime fiction',[44] has changed the form in which the metropolitan discourse conceives Latin America. To use Sylvia Molloy's term, the 'magic-realist imperative' is now accompanied by a 'violent imperative'.[45] In a sort of perverse *neomacondismo*, the discourse of civilization and barbarism is rearticulated as metropolitan spectators begin to think of an otherness founded on violence. The pleasures of the tropical come spiced with the spectacle of the Other's misery. Mabel Moraña has warned of the dangers of 'the construction of the new postmodern version of Latin America, elaborated in the centers, [which] in great measure makes of Latin America a construct that confirms the centrality and the globalizing, theoretical, avant-garde status of those who interpret it and aspire to represent it discursively'.[46] Moraña attacks the 'boom del subalterno' as an attempt to 'cover all those sectors subordinated to the discourses and praxis of power'. It is necessary to articulate a critique of the 'boom of violence' that could be characterized by the same terms used by Moraña: violence is promoted as 'part of an external agenda, connected to a market where that notion is affirmed as an ideological exchange and use value and as a brand that is incorporated through various strategies of promotion and ideological reproduction into globalized cultural consumption'.[47] *Amores perros*, in this sense, appeals to an emerging conceptualization of Latin America (and of much of the Third World) as the site of violence, as the place where a vertiginous life of misery and otherness fascinates the pseudo-progressive audiences of international film festivals. Precisely because *Amores perros* required this type of success to recover the capital invested, its cinematographic language and its publicity campaigns are adjusted to this 'violent imperative'. It is in no way coincidental that the movie's international success preceded its national success. Once the film's publicity campaign produced recognition at Cannes, Mexican audiences acquired a renewed sense of national pride and went to see the movie.[48] To put it even less euphemistically, once the metropolitan intelligentsia approved the film as an acceptable representative of 'Mexican cinema',[49] Mexicans were convinced that the film proudly represented them. It is hard to find a more convincing portrait of the neo-colonialism prevalent in the commercial success of many current Latin American films.

If one is consistent with an analysis critical not only of *Amores perros* but also of the semantic field of violence that begins to configure the Latin American imaginary, the only possible conclusion is to avoid falling for these representations at all costs. Carlos Monsiváis has demonstrated the role that cinema has played in the confirmation of identities in our region,[50] and, in so far as movies like *Amores perros* encounter unusual degrees of acceptance inside our countries, we begin to naturalize this vision of violence and accept it as constitutive of our identity. This, I believe, should be resisted. Since it would be absurd to postulate that violence is not a situation present in the daily life of the Latin American city, it must be stressed that this category is insufficient to describe the social sphere. Martín Hopenhayn has observed that drugs and violence are both ghosts, since there is a constitutive gap between their perception and their reality.[51] *Amores perros* is the product of these ghosts. The film conveys a profoundly erroneous cultural perception of violence in Latin American countries, constantly reproduced on both national and transnational circuits. *Amores perros* helps us see that violence as a category of analysis is a double-edged sword: in transnational terms, it contributes to the characterization of Latin America as a site of barbarism and a region incapable of articulating a truly political discourse. In national terms, it fortifies the privileged position of the neoliberal middle class as the centre of citizenship and the exclusion of marginal subjects from this realm. Rossana Reguillo describes this phenomenon as follows: 'With a relatively sedentary and enlightened middle class strengthened, the developmentalist model in place and the country being increasingly integrated into an international dynamic, the pincers are closed and an imaginary is produce that turns these actors into enemies of modernity and into potential carriers of the danger of return'.[52]

To accept violence as an identifying feature and as a representative sign of Latin American countries in the transatlantic market implies complicity with the neoliberal agenda embedded in these discourses. All references to violence should be a critique of violence, a comprehension of its profound economic, social and political roots. Above all, it is imperative to understand that what defines the Latin-American experience is a contradictory legacy of colonialism and resistance, of conflict and heterogeneity. Violence is only a by-product of these relationships: to place violence at the centre of analysis or cultural production leaves aside the central questions of our culture and leads the way to an imaginary where violence and social conflict are irrevocably naturalized. In so far as violence is converted into an increasingly popular indicator for the understanding of Latin American culture as a whole, it is also important to leave open the question of the profound depoliticization implied both within the academic context of cultural studies and in the way in which social and communitarian identities adapt themselves to the ultimate violence of the neoliberal system. To celebrate *Amores perros* as a revolution within Mexican or Latin American cinema, in spite of the film's undeniable accolades, results in complicity with a model of comprehension that dissolves our conflicts into a cheap morality disguised as avant-garde culture. The continent is in urgent need of a sophisticated critical spirit that is not swept along with the changing tides of a perception that, in this ulterior instance, is nothing more than the most recent manifestation of a long tradition of imperialism.

Translated by Kara N. Moranski, revised by Citlali Martínez

Notes

1. The final version of this paper was possible thanks to discussions and suggestions made by various people. I want to thank Mabel Moraña, Joshua K. Lund and Hermann Herlinghaus for the initial dialogue and debate on the ideas presented here. I also want to thank Juan Poblete and Emanuelle Oliveira for their comments during the presentation of an earlier, much shorter version of this paper in the LASA conference held at Las Vegas. Roberto Fernández Retamar, John Kraniauskas and Philip Derbyshire were of great help in the publication of this text, which first appeared in Spanish in *Casa de las Américas* 240 (2005). The present translation presents some additions and modifications with respect to the Spanish publication. Finally, I want to thank Kara N. Moranski for her translation and Citlali Martínez for the revisions to this version.
2. México: Altavista Films/Zeta Films, 2000.
3. See, more specifically, the collected volumes *Ciudadanías del miedo*, edited by Susana Rotker. Caracas: Nueva Sociedad, 2002 y *Espacio urbano, comunicación y violencia*, edited by Mabel Moraña. Pittsburgh: Instituto Internacional de Literatura Iberoamericana, 2002. These volumes compile an ample representative sample of this theoretical turn to violence.
4. *Ciudadanías del miedo*: 14.
5. *Amores perros*. London: British Film Institute, 2003: 14.
6. *Amores perros*: 44.
7. 'Affecting legacies. historical memory and contemporary structures of feeling in *Madagascar* and *Amores perros*'. *Screen* 44(3) 2003: 284.
8. 'El melodrama: "No te vayas, mi amor, que es inmoral llorar a solas"'. *Narraciones anacrónicas de la modernidad. Melodrama e intermedialidad en América Latina*, edited by Hermann Herlinghaus. Santiago de Chile: Cuarto Propio, 2002: 120. It should be pointed out that here Monsiváis exemplifies this process with Quentin Tarantino's *Pulp Fiction*, a film with an enormous resonance in *Amores Perros*.
9. See Claudia Schaefer. *Bored to distraction*. Albany: State University of New York Press, 2003: 87.
10. *Ciudadanías del miedo*: 18.
11. Eduardo Antonio Parra. *Nostalgia de la sombra*. México: Joaquín Mortiz, 2003.
12. I will address in greater detail the production of *Amores perros* and its publicity campaign below.
13. In fact, *Todo el poder* falls far short of being a movie that could be held up as a model for Mexican cinema. Jorge Ayala Blanco quite precisely points out the film's profound

ideological problems: '[*Todo el poder*] is a phoney thriller whose success is prefabricated, classist and completely leaving out the theme of poverty ... an ode to the trivial dilemmas of the autistic national middle class with a thievable this-year's-model Cherokee' (*La fugacidad del cine mexicano*. México: Océano, 2001: 471). In spite of the fact that I share Ayala Blanco's critique, it still seems worth mentioning that, being a film that is cynically (or honestly) commercial, it has a political dimension simply absent in a more pretentious film such as *Amores perros*

14 *Bored to distraction*: 87.
15 Cited in *Bored to distraction*: 87.
16 I owe this point to Juan Poblete, who brought it to my attention during my presentation of an earlier version of this work at the LASA conference in Las Vegas.
17 Daniel and Valeria's story has also been the object of feminist readings. Deborah Shaw's interpretation, for example, suggests that the characters represent the collapse of the discourse of 'machismo', therefore articulating a critique of patriarchy itself. Valeria is interpreted as a character that validates the social and racial structures of patriarchy (she is a European model that validates the racism of the media, oppressing people of colour). Her accident and ensuing mutilation can be seen as a sort of 'happy ending' that opens the door to the possibility of a 'post-model' life for her. (*Contemporary Cinema of Latin America: 10 Key Films*. New York: Continuum, 2003: 64–6). Even when Shaw recognizes the dimensions of *Amores perros*'s conservative discourse (such as the way El Chivo's life turns out by comparison with his revolutionary ideas), the interpretation based on a critique of patriarchy seems somewhat voluntaristic. I do not share her conclusion with respect to Valeria. While she is right in pointing out that Valeria plays a role that legitimizes patriarchy (in that she accepts that a man would leave his family for her) and racism (capitalizing on the fact that she is European in a television industry that excludes the country's racial majority), Shaw's 'happy ending' does not exist. There is, however, a moral justice that cannot be explained by the critique of patriarchy but rather demands it own logic: Valeria receives a fairly severe punishment in return for participating in an adulterous relationship, whereas Daniel simply returns to his family. There is, thus, a crucial gender difference in the punishment for the same deed.
18 ¿Guerreros o ciudadanos? Violencia(s). Una cartografía de las interacciones urbanas. *Espacio urbano, comunicación y violencia*: 56.
19 Here I do not wish that my discourse be reduced to the anachronistic argument of the novel being a genre 'superior to' or 'more complex than' cinema, nor am I interested in a nostalgic defence of the novel as the figuration of all things social. The point that I am illustrating is a conceptualization of violence as something more complex than a series of moral decisions, which is seen very clearly in *Nostalgia de la sombra*. This has much to do with the simple fact that Parra's novel has no need to meet the commercial expectations of *Amores perros* or *Todo el Poder* and, therefore, is not anchored in this middle-class vision of the world.
20 *Nostalgia de la sombre*: 55.
21 *Sin límites ficcionales. Nostalgia de la sombra de Eduardo Antonio Parra. Revista de Literatura Mexicana contemporánea* 2, 2003: 69.
22 This point is illustrated, for example, by the comparison that John Beverley established between Fernando Meirelles's and Kátia Lund's *Cidade de Deus* and Víctor Gaviria's films. Beverley observes that, even if both address analogous problematics (for example gangs, drugs, etc.), there is an important structural difference: the first is

the *Bildungsroman* of a youth who leaves the ghetto and enters the bourgeoisie (consequently supporting an ideology that is, ultimately, middle class), while Gaviria is more concerned with a project representing subalternity. 'Los últimos serán los primeros': Notas sobre el cine de Víctor Gaviria. *Osamayor* XV: 34.

23 One example is *La génesis del crimen en México* (1900) by Julio Guerrero (México: Conaculta, 1996), which condenses the positivist visions surrounding the theme. It would undoubtedly be instructive to make a comparison between the arguments of books such as this one and the stereotypes presented in many contemporary accounts of violence.

24 The overview of the production of *Amores perros* that I make here is amply based on the detailed assessment elaborated by Smith in his book about the movie.

25 A brief summary of the failure of Imcine and the emergence of commercial cinema can be found in Shaw, *Contemporary Cinema of Latin America*: 52–3.

26 Un puzzle canino. Entrevista con Iñárritu. Available at: http://www.clubcultura.com/clubcine/amoresperros/ perros02.htm; INTERNET.

27 *Sexo, pudor y lágrimas* is perhaps the first representative of the commercial Mexican cinema that emerged in the late 1990s. The movie is a comedy of errors that tells the story of two couples with their relationships in crisis, and of two external figures putting them in further danger. The film's logic is similar to that of a myriad of Mexican movies from the latter part of the last decade whose plotlines centre on infidelity, a logic that resounds in *Amores perros*. Fidel Moral has stated that the movies' logic is based on 'punishing the free and condemning the disfunctional to stay together' (cited in *La fugacidad del cine mexicano*: 443). This logic is not far off from that of González Iñárritu film. To address the soundtrack, its title track was recorded by pop artist Aleks Syntek; the song's success doubtlessly generated interest and contributed to the film's eventual success. Martin D'Lugo has also studied the soundtrack strategy in Quentin Tarantino's films. (Amores perros. In *The Cinema of Latin America*. London: Wallflower Press, 2003: 227.) It is fitting here to address the fact that there is something different at work in Tarantino's films: while his soundtracks are well articulated to the development and aesthetic of his films, a considerable portion of the *Amores perros* soundtrack is not even featured in the movie.

28 This point is made by Marvin D'Lugo. 'Amores perros': 229

29 *Once upon a time in Mexico* is the most obvious example. Robert Rodríguez takes his stereotyped vision of the border (developed since his first film, *El Mariachi*) and combines it with the visual language used in the Almada brothers' *narcocine* and also in the *fichera* cinema sponsored during the administration of President José López Portillo, in the late 1970s and early 1980s. The result is an accumulation of stereotypes that shatters any cinematographic problematization of the country. It is, simply, a metacinematographic approach that has more to do with Rodríguez's textual and cinematographic references than with Mexico itself. This aesthetic is also present in the recent North American films such as Gore Verbinski's *The Mexican* or Steven Soderbergh's *Traffic*.

30 Cited in Deborah Shaw. *Contemporary Cinema of Latin America*: 54.

31 For a contrast of this film and *Amores perros*, refer to *Contemporary cinema of Latin America*: 36 and ss.

32 See, for example, Serna, Juan Antonio. El discurso de la subcultura transgresora en el film mexicano *Amores perros*. Ciberletras 7. Available at: http://www.lehman.cuny.edu/ faculty/guinazu/ciberletras/v07/serna.html; INTERNET.

33 See D' Lugo 'Amores perros': 227, *Bored to* distraction: 86–8.

34 The most interesting study of the climax of Tarantinesque cinema and its implications can be found in Botting, Fred, and Scott Wilson. *The Tarantinian Ethics*. London: Sage, 2001.
35 *Al sur de la modernidad. Comunicación, globalización y multiculturalidad*. Pittsburgh: Instituto Internacional de Literatura Iberoamericana, 2001: 127.
36 *Las ciudades que median los miedos. Espacio urbano, comunicación y violencia*: 25. The Benjamin text referred to is 'The work of art in the age of mechanical reproduction'.
37 D'Lugo. 'Amores perros': 227.
38 *Al su de la modernidad*: 127–8.
39 *La fugacidad del arte mexicano*: 486.
40 Un puzzle canino.
41 *La obra de arte en la era de su reproductibilidad técnica*. México: Ítaca, 2003: 96–9.
42 An example of a possible counterpoint can be found in the work of Carlos Monsiváis, who seeks to explain the metropolis from the point of view of its public spaces, while articulating a profound critique of the bourgeoisie's moral discourses. See *Los rituales del caos*. México: Era, 1996. I have discussed this point in my article, De ironía, desubicación, cultura popular y sentimiento nacional: Carlos Monsiváis en el cambio de siglo. *Revista de literatura mexicana contemporánea* 20 (2003): 15–23.
43 This term refers to the recent Columbian narrative that depicts violence from the perspective of the *sicario*, the name for a young assassin working within the world of drug cartels. Notable authors in this genre include Fernando Vallejo, Jorge Franco Ramos and Mario Mendoza.
44 See Braham, Persephone. *Crimes against the state*.
45 Latin America in the US imaginary: postcolonialism, translation and the magic realist imperative. In *Ideologies of Hispanism*, edited by Mabel Moraña. Nashville: Vanderbilt University Press, 2005: 189–200.
46 El *boom* del subalterno. *Teorías sin disciplina. Latinoamericanismo, poscolonialidad y globalización en debate*, edited by Santiago Castro-Gómez y Eduardo Mendieta. México: Miguel Ángel Porrúa, 1998: 239.
47 'El *boom* del subalterno': 240.
48 This account can be found in Smith. *Amores perros*: 13–27.
49 Smith observes that this year's Oscar awards were characterized by the press as having a 'Hispanic accent', due to the presence of *Amores perros* along with two of the United States' most recent neo-exotic films: Julian Schnabel's *Before Night Falls* and Steven Soderbergh's *Traffic*.
50 *A través del espejo. El cine mexicano y su público*. México: El milagro, 1994. This book also includes a text by Carlos Bonfil.
51 'Droga y violencia: fantasmas de la nueva metrópoli latinoamericana'. In *Espacio urbano, comunicación y violencia*: 69–88. After a lengthy social analysis, Hopenhayn demonstrates that the reality of drugs and violence often operates counter to ideas generated by cultural manifestations.
52 ¿Guerreros o ciudadanos?: 60.

References

Ayala Blanco, Jorge. 2001. *La fugacidad del cine mexicano*. México: Océano.
Benjamin, Walter. 2003. *La obra de arte en la era de su reproductibilidad técnica*. México: Ítaca.

Beverley, John. 2004. Los últimos serán los primeros. Notas sobre el cine de Víctor Gaviria. *Osamayor*, no. 15: 34.

Botting, Fred, and Scott Wilson. 2001. *The Tarantinian ethics*. London: Sage.

Braham, Persephone. 2004. *Crimes against the state, crimes against persons: detective fictions in Cuba and Mexico*. Minneapolis: University of Minnesota Press.

D'Lugo, Marvin. 2003. Amores perros. In *The cinema of Latin America*, edited by Alberto Elena, and Marina Díaz López. London: Wallflower Press, 2004: 225–35.

Guerrero, Julio. 1996. *La génesis del crimen en México*. México: Consejo Nacional para la Cultura y las Artes.

Hopenhayn, Martín. Droga y violencia: fantasmas de la nueva metrópoli latinoamericana., In Moraña and Herlinghaus: 69–88.

Martín-Barbero, Jesús. 2001. *Al sur de la modernidad. Comunicación, globalidad y multiculturalidad*. Pittsburgh: Instituto Internacional de Literatura Iberoamericana.

Martín-Barbero, Jesús. Las ciudades que median los miedos., In Moraña y Herlinghaus: 19–36.

Molloy, Sylvia. 2005. Latin America in the US Imaginary: Postcolonialism, Translation and the Magic Realist Imperative. In *Ideologies of Hispanism*, edited by Mabel Moraña. Nashville: Vanderbilt University Press, 189–200.

Monsiváis, Carlos. 2002. El melodrama: 'No te vayas, mi amor, que es inmoral llorar a solas'. In *Narraciones anacrónicas de la modernidad. Melodrama e intermedialidad en América Latina*, edited by Hermann Herlinghaus. Santiago de Chile: Cuarto Propio, 105–23.

Monsiváis, Carlos y Carlos Bonfil. 1994. *A través del espejo. El cine mexicano y su público*. México: El milagro.

Moraña, Mabel. 1998. El boom del subalterno. In *Teorías sin disciplina. Latinoamericanismo, poscolonialidad y globalización*, edited by Santiago Castro Gómez, and Eduardo Mendieta. México: Miguel Ángel Porrúa, 233–44.

Mabel, Moraña, and Herlinghaus, Hermann, eds. 2002. *Espacio urbano, comunicación y violencia*. Pittsburgh: Instituto Internacional de Literatura Iberoamericana.

Parra, Eduardo Antonio. 2003. *Nostalgia de la sombra*. México: Joaquín Mortiz.

Podalsky, Laura. 2003. Affecting Legacies: Historical Memory and Contemporary Structures of Feeling in *Madagascar* and *Amores perros*. Screen 44 (3): 277–94.

Reguillo, Susana. 2003. ¿Guerreros o ciudadanos? Violencia(s). Una cartografía de las interacciones urbanas., In Moraña and Herlinghaus: 51–68.

Rodríguez Lozano, Miguel. Sin límites ficcionales. *Nostalgia de la sombra* de Eduardo Antonio Parra. Revista de Literatura Mexicana Contemporánea IX (21): 67–72.

Rotker, Susana, ed. 2002. *Ciudadanías del miedo*. Caracas: Nueva sociedad.

Sánchez-Prado, Ignacio M. 2003. De ironía, desubicación, cultura popular y sentimiento nacional. Carlos Monsiváis en el cambio de siglo. *Revista de literatura mexicana contemporánea* no. 20: 15–23.

Schaefer, Claudia. 2003. *Bored to Distraction: Cinema of Excess in End-of-the-century Mexico and Spain*. Albany: State University of New York Press.

Serna, JuanAntonio. 2002. El discurso de la subculture transgresora en el film mexicano *Amores perros*. Ciberletras no. 7. Available at: http://www.lehman.cuny.edu/faculty/guinazu/ciberletras/v07/serna.html; INTERNET (accessed 8 December 2005).

Shaw, Deborah. 2003. *Contemporary Cinema of Latin America: Ten Key Films*. New York: Continuum.

Smith, PaulJulian. 2003. *Amores perros*. London: British Film Institute.

Zayas, Manuel. 2001. Un puzzle canino. Entrevista con Iñárritu. Available at: http://www.clubcultura.com/clubcine/amoresperros/perros02.htm; INTERNET (accessed 8 December 2005).

Post/Colonial Toponymy: Writing Forward 'in Reverse'

QUETZIL CASTAÑEDA

Amerigo Vespucci the voyager arrives from the sea. A crusader standing erect, his body in armor, he bears the European weapons of meaning .... Before him is the Indian 'America,' a nude woman ... an unnamed presence of difference ... the conqueror will write the body of the other and trace there his own history .... She will be 'Latin' America ... initiated here is a colonization of the body by the discourse of power. This is writing that conquers. It will use the New World as if it were a blank, 'savage' page on which Western desire will be written. It will transform the space of the other into a field of expansion for a system of production. (Michel de Certeau, *The Writing of History*)

The past is very near the surface in Mérida. (Nelson Reed, *The Caste War of Yucatan*)

When the Spaniards discovered this land, their leader asked the Indians how it was called; as they did not understand him, they said uic athan, which means, 'what do you say' or 'what do you speak,' that 'we do not understand you.' And then the Spaniard ordered it set down that it be called Yucatan .... (Tzvetan Todorov, *Conquest of America*)

Listening in Place of Writing: *Mise-en-Scène*

The discourse on place names initiates the collision between Maya and European as it nonetheless repeats the founding acts of Maya societies. Let us consider the scene of initial encounter between Maya and Spaniard, a scene that had always already been a trope of cultural collision but since the 1980s has become a trope of colonial discourse analysis. It is said—said endlessly by tour guides, in guidebooks, by Yucatec intellectuals, in regional histories, by Mayas and Mayeros, in villages and cantinas—that when the Spaniards landed—landed on this 'tierra del faisán y venado' this 'land of the pheasant and deer'—the Indians called it 'u luum cutz, u luum ceh'; and, when they met the natives who approached, they asked, 'what is the name of this land?'. Not understanding the k'astrant'aan (i.e. Spanish), one Maya turned to the other and exclaimed, 'Uuy ku t'aan!' [Listen how they talk!]. Up to this point in the story this much is certainly known and known with certainty, albeit with some variations to be explored below. But what happens after this moment in the encounter and in the stories of the encounter is total speculation—despite what *some* may assert with finely polished claims of authority.

Having, as an anthropologist, an 'ethnographic sensibility' of village life among the Maya of what is now Yucatán, the spectacular story that I tell meets the approval of my colleague, Juan Cocom, who is not only an anthropologist and a Maya, but also a descendent of a noble lineage of these lands of the pheasant and deer. Listen: ... and the Spaniards asked the two Maya standing by their houses on the neck of land at the edge of the sea, 'what is the name of this land?' Not understanding what *it* was that had washed ashore, the one Maya said to the other not a little surprised, 'Uuy! Ku t'aan!' [Listen! It talks!]. The other, no doubt poking the first in the ribs with his elbow while expelling a very nasal and elongated aspiration, 'Háah ...' [Yes!] and sternly pointing with his nodding chin to the bearded, smelly, pink person in shiny clothing, responded, 'Uuy a watan!' [Listen to your wife (talk)!] Listening attentively (no doubt) to repeat the words—'uuy ku t'aan' 'uuh yu ku tan'—but without having a course in phonetics, the Spaniards figured—figured *somehow*—that these new lands must be called 'Yucatán'.

Commentators across five centuries have proliferated different words and possible sentences in their conjuring up of conjectural reconstructions of this mythic event that inaugurated the invasion and conquest of what has come to be known as 'Yucatán'. Consider another sixteenth-century version that has itself become a trope for twentieth-century critics. This discourse on the naming of Yucatán has become a topos not only of Yucatán but of Latin American colonial discourse criticism, since it economically marks the complex textual invention of alterity forged in the encounter between European and Indian. See for example Greenblatt (1992, p. 104), who recontextualizes a quote from Inga Clendinnen (1987, p. vi) which is itself a quote from Antonio de Ciudad Real (1588) which also happens to be the source of Todorov's (1984) recitation and reiteration:

> When the Spaniards discovered this land, their leader asked the Indians how it was called; as they did not understand him, they said uic athan [or: uuyik a t'aan], which means, 'what do you say' or 'what do you speak', that 'we do not understand you'. And then the Spaniard ordered it set down that it be called *Yucatan* ... .

Notice first that these translations 'of the Maya' are not literal. They are metaphoric in terms of the actual words that are speculated as having been spoken. 'What do you say' and 'what do you speak' in contemporary Yucatec Maya would be *ba'ax ka walik, ba'ax ka waal*, or *ba'an ka t'aan*. 'We do not understand you' is *ma t naatik a t'aani'* or *ma t naatike'exi'*. While these sentences are possible reconstructions for the speech event, phonetic corruptions of these twentieth-century sentences and their sixteenth-century equivalents do not too easily render Yucatán. Thus, the colonialist interpretation and writing of history is clearly revealed as a colonizing writing that operates not simply 'after the facts' but more importantly 'in reverse': An event of dialogue in the past is blatantly reconstructed as an origin based on visions, logics and assumptions from the present. From the historical given that the toponym 'Yucatán' is given to the Spaniards by Mayas, the task becomes simply a process of offering messages whose semantic values would correspond to what a Spanish chronicler (and later a structuralist theorist and new historicist historians) imagine those Maya to have *thought* and *expressed* in the face of Spanish Conquistadores. While Beverley (1999) has suggested that postcolonial and/or subaltern critique need be a kind of historiography that deconstructs the colonialist/colonizing texts through analytical 'reversals' of meaning and power, here a certain 'writing in reverse' seems to be part and parcel of colonial discourse.

Second, notice that there was no invasion and conquest of some pre-existing entity, Yucatán. Rather, 'Yucatán' was itself an artifact, an imaginary place, invented with and at the 'moment' of invasion and conquest as a strategic weapon deployed to those ends—notice, however, that this moment is quite complicated as it not only spans several decades but includes Maya Conquistadores (see Restall, 1998)! The interesting point here is that since these contemporary re-enactments of the naming event by various cultural critics do not more than cite this as an example of the imposition of the European weapons of meaning, they reproduce and repeat this colonization of space, history and people. In seeking to reverse a writing that conquers there is recourse again to a history that colonizes the agency, speech/'voice' and participation of the 'subaltern'. The topographic order is inscribed in the colonial historiography and then re-inscribed again in the postcolonial text, now, however, with a lamentation of the voracious power of the European weapons of meaning and their colonizing effects. What is missing is a more rigorous decipherment of this glyph that traces the active participation of the Maya in its construction as historical truth and invention as reality.

Third, the pursuit of such complicity and complexity is necessary to understand the invention of the Maya without falling into the dual trap of positing the Indian as a pure artefact of European conquest (by sword and by historiography) or the Indian as an authentic, atemporal essence continuously linked to a proper (subaltern/subordinate) identity via a primordial origin. The task cannot be to find a Maya subaltern and to 'see' their 'voice' cursing and talking back. In this dense reiteration of recitations of the writing of a speech event, the alternative, however, is just as speculative, but we can avoid ventriloquism by 'surfing' the textual/discursive surfaces for semantic and perlocutionary divergences and 'reversals'.

The Maya—or more accurately groups among the peoples that are in the twenty-first century anachronistically called Maya (Restall, n.d.; Gabbert, n.d.)—also participate/d in this economy of re/citation in the discursive battle for authorial propriety and political legitimacy. In later efforts to render intelligible the name that the Spaniards gave, they 'translated' 'Yucatán'—rather, transcribed this word written in the oral encounters of Spanish histories into the sixteenth-century Maya books of history[1]—as *U-kal-peten*, or the Neck-of-the-land, which nonetheless, in the centuries following, becomes identified *in popular understanding* as the authentic and original, i.e., native, Eurocentric name:

> This is the name of the year when the foreigners arrived, the year one thousand five hundred and nineteen. This was the year when the foreigners arrived, here at our town, (the town) of us Itzá, *here in the land of Yucalpeten, Yucatán, in the Mayan Language of the Itzas* … . This is the year which was current when *the foreigners prepared to seize Yucalpeten [Neck-of-the-Land] here*. It was known by the priest, the prophet Ah Xupan as he is called. Christianity was introduced to us in the year 1519 … . (Roys, 1933, p. 119; emphasis added; cf. Edmonson, 1986, pp. 221–223)

The text goes on to cite the year for the arrival of yellow fever, drought, famine and related calamities. The key phrases translated in italics above, *uay ti luum yucalpeten, yucatan, tu than Maya Ah Itzaob lae* and *ca hoppi u ch'aic uba dzulob utial u chucicob uay yucalpeten lae* (Roys, 1933, p. 40, p. 63c), are traditionally interpreted as indicating the Maya correction of the Spanish invention of a name of the country based on a corruption of a misheard Maya word. Might this, instead, be a Maya rendition of a nonsensical sound pronounced in sixteenth-century Spanish? This thesis is supported by Edmonson's reasonable speculation that the name Maya derives from the name of the cycle of thirteen katuns, *may*, that organizes the space and time of social, political, astronomical and cosmological events; the Maya are people of the *may* and the term Mayab, 'of the May', is another name for both the 'country' (or sociopolitical and cosmological territory) in which the *may* reigns and in which the people live that propitiate this cosmological cycle of space/time (see Restall [n.d.] for an alternative speculation on the etymology of Maya).

In other words, this suggests that the name Yucalpeten is a Maya invention of a complex pun that was anchored to a Maya logic of toponyms. Maya toponymy manifests throughout the sixteenth-century books of the Chilam Balams, but is especially evident in the migration stories. For example, in the book of Chuymayel, places are listed as being the site where the group arrives and then these places are described through a pun on the toponym: 'Then they arrived at Panabha, where they dug [*panab*] for water [*há*]' (Roys, 1933, p. 70). In this manner each place is narrated as part of the migratory conquest of the Itzá (a Maya lineage group of Gulf Coast origin/ethnicity) as they arrive and take over Chichén Itzá—or, to use the Maya expression, 'seat' themselves 'at the mouth' [*chi*] of the 'well' [*chén*] of the 'Magicians' [*Itz*] 'of Water' [*há*].

A more complicated rhetoric of punning, placing and cosmology is expressed in what has been called the 'sermon' or 'song' of the *uinal*, which is Maya calendrical 20-day period. This is often metaphorically called the Maya 'month' because there are 18 of these periods within the Maya 'years' of 360- and 365-day cycles, called *tun* and *hab* respectively, as well as 13 periods in the 260-day cycle, whose name anthropologist have given it is *tzolk'in* ['count of the days']. The 'song' tells of the birth of time itself since the *uinal* is not only the building block of all three encompassing 'yearly' cycles. But, it is also about the birth of 'man' (*uinic*) and perhaps the human body (*uinkilil*), since these words share the same roots, linguistically and cosmologically speaking:

> This is the sermon of the occurrence of the birth of the *uinal*, which was before the awakening of the world Eurocent, and it began to run by itself, alone. Then said his [the *uinal*/man's] mother's mother, then said his mother's sister, then said his father's mother, then said his sister-in-law, 'What is to be said when a man is seen on the road?' So they said, whilst they were going along. But no man occurred. And then they arrived there at the east. And they began to say, 'Who is it that passed by here now? Here are his tracks, right here. Measure them with your foot according to the word of the planter of the world.' Who is the holy God. This was the beginning of saying the count of the world by footsteps [*xoc lah cab oc*]. [This was] Twelve Foot [a day name, Lahca Oc].[2] This is the account of his birth. For Oxlahun Oc occurred [a day name meaning Thirteen Foot], and they matched each other's paces and

> arrived there at the east. They said his name, since the days had no name then, and he [the man/*uinal*] traveled on … . The month [*uinal*] was born and the day name was born, and the sky was born and [so was] the earth, the pyramid of water and land, stone and tree. There were born the things of sea and land.

The text continues by calling each of the days by name in a perlocutionary act of giving the name to the day and naming that which was 'created' during that day of the uinal.[3] This text makes evident the Maya ordering of space, time, places and place names into a unified, coherent cosmology, to use the concept anthropologists traditionally apply to this cultural form. But such a cosmological chronotrope can also be grasped as a topography in the sense defined in this essay. These examples demonstrate the extensiveness and seriousness with which the sixteenth-century Maya (of this place that came to be called Yucatán) make use of word play to communicate political, religious and social values/meanings.

Let us recite again an Itzá Maya version of the arrival of the Spaniards: 'This was the year when the foreigners arrived, here at our town, (the town) of us Itzá, *here in the land of Yucalpeten, Yucatan, in the Mayan Language of the Itzas* … . This is the year which was current when *the foreigners prepared to seize Yucalpeten [Neck-of-the-Land] here.*' Can we speculate, then, that according to the Maya scribes, the Spaniards were 'taking hold' of the land in their attempt to 'strangle' the legitimate (indigenous) authority of this (fictional) Yukalpeten? In the transcription of a misunderstanding the Maya underscore the military seizure of the 'country' (*peten*) by the Spanish. Here the 'lands' (*luum*) and 'country' (*peten*) that are being seized by 'the neck' (*u kal*) are not marked as the proper/property of a specific Maya lineage or polity; that is, 'lands' is not qualified with reference to any pre-established sociopolitical boundaries or 'ethnically' named or controlled territory. Already, the Maya polities (here the Itzá are mentioned by name), their traditional structures, and all contesting claims to cosmo-political legitimacy, are rendered subordinate to a new arrival (Christianity) whose import contests the status quo. Thus, the name, its event and its retelling are a collision of misreadings—multiple transcriptions of difference into other languages. Here is a discourse of a name that covers the absence of an authentic meaning and the loss of an original referent with the veil of an identity constructed as the simple translation across codes of an integral essence or proper meaning. Thus, this text or textual web that binds a double encounter of naming and erasure (the Spanish overwrite the previous Maya word with a name, the Maya overwrite the Spanish name with another name) marks, in the form of a *confusion of tongues*,[4] the zero point of a war of knowledge waged in and as the topography of a space henceforth called *Yucatán*.

This discourse on toponyms proceeds, from this moment, backward, forward and askew through the events that have marked the Yucatec landscape and the histories of this topography. What 'explains' the ubiquitous presence of this discourse not only in tourist and academic literatures, but everyday talk across all ethnic and class lines? Certainly a history of its performance can be traced across various texts; but such an inquiry relies on a juxtaposition of occurrences that creates a meaning, i.e. the meaning of an explanation. On the other hand, we can simply understand this concern for place names as a 'cultural predilection': This act of naming a topos is valued and recognized among all Yucatecs as a key to the social history of a locality, the identity of its inhabitants and the everyday life of the community. Thus, place name itself becomes a topos of discourse[5] through the generation of a ceaseless commentary that re-enacts the transcription of an 'essence' into a proper name and vice versa, via the recounting of a storied event that accounts for the toponym and that constitutes a topography (i.e. a proper positioning and hierarchy of value: order).

This discourse of toponyms is clearly a speculative discourse. It is not mere intuition, although this is necessary, nor is it simply 'explanation' according to a logic of semantics that binds the name, in its act of being given, to the topos. There is an essential element, the propriety of the place, that is factored into the giving of the name through speculation. Operating here are speculative moves that both invest in a profit or a return according to the debts of giving and a sighting, along the logic of the gift itself, that declares a vision in which everything has its proper place: An order, immanent in space, is unveiled in the place of the proper name, the toponym. This dual system of topoi, the topos that is named and the topos of its speculation or discursive repetition, is a scene of writing. A spectacular scene, indeed, whose operations, whose economy, comprise the questions of this essay, or excursion in the topography of topoi.

Let us return again, now with Bishop Landa, to that moment when a logo-centric (Spanish, Christian, European) topography overwrites the hieroglyphic (Maya) landscape. What Landa tells us, 'was learned from one of the early conquerors, Blas Hérnandez, who came here [Yucatán] ... on the first occasion' (Gates translation, p. 24). Here, then, is not simply an eye(I)-witness, but an attentive *ear*, the ear of an entire jury, that not only *sees* but *listens* to what the evidence has to say. Having established his audience and courtroom scene, Landa is certain to extract the truth.[6] Through Landa's ventriloquism, let us listen with Blas to the speech of the evidence:

> When Francisco Hérnandez de Córdoba came to this country and landed at the point called Cape Catoch, he met certain fisherfolk whom he asked what country this was, who answered 'Cotoch,' which means 'our houses, our homeland' ... . When he then by signs asked them how the land was theirs they replied 'Ki u than,' meaning 'they say it' [or more accurately, 'they speak nicely,' 'sweet words'].

Here, then, is a different conjecture on the lost moment of contact between Maya and Spaniard, a moment considered original, even though secondary, because it is from this moment that 'conquest' is deemed to have progressed (be sent) to its rightful destination.[7] Regardless of how the encounter is speculated, the punchline remains the same, repeats itself: The unintelligible, unrepeatable and apposite words 'elicited' (evoked?) as 'an answer' to the *second* question asked by the Conquistadores (*Ki u than*) becomes trans-formed/scribed into the toponym, 'Yucatán'. Or, at least that is yet another version of this *founding act* of an origin of a topography of war between Maya and Spaniard.

First, let us be certain that this *fabulous* account (as was the previous speculation that I recounted) which not merely 'passes as' but *is* a historical truth (a speculation of an oral event verified in writing and through the authorization of the names attached: 'de Ciudad Real', 'Bishop Landa', etc.)[8] *is* a pure fiction (see Haraway, 1989, pp. 3–5 on fact/fiction). The text of this writing incorporates the reality outside that the text is to re-present and transforms this outside; a new truth is manufactured. This event of naming, then, is perlocutionary, performative, in both its original writing/being written and in its derivative, speculative orality. This is a new account of reality that erases and conquers the alterity of the Indian other and their past. Can we be certain that these Conquistadores, anxiously awaiting their destiny that God (and Crown) has designed for them, would exchange such pleasant, or at least contemplative, intercourse? Would they not have immediately read the letter of the required Proclamation, i.e. the *Requerimiento*, that Pope, King and Queen entrusted them to execute mercilessly? Upon arrival, would they delay this letter at its destination? Would they defer their destiny that is written therein according to providential design, which as its carriers they could then embark upon with its proper delivery? From the first-hand, eye-witness account of Bernal Díaz we find no mention of this verbal ritual of Conquest, but instead an anxious encounter of gestures with handsigns, swords and muskets. Whereas the eye-witness accounts focus on the military dimensions of the exchange, Landa's account presents a tranquil dialogue on the edge of the sea. The violence of the actual exchange of signs and the details of their transmission are deleted, erased from history and, therefore *loses* and is *lost*. (It both loses its position as the original moment of contact and is lost in the dusty archives from the circuitry of the general historical recollection.)[9] In substitution as the original interaction in the moment of initial encounter, the other scene of naming (the question/answer exchange), which as already noted is constituted by its own, 'internal' *mise-en-scène* is written into the histories as the (f)actual and the real.

Second, in this substituted event(s) of mispronunciations can be recognized the invention of the Maya in and through an apparatus of writing that began to operate some '500 years ago'. This scene and its recounting inaugurates an economy of knowledge, of sociopolitical practices in which the Maya have been and are still written as particular kinds of objects. Following De Certeau (1984, pp. 134–135), three critical factors of writing can be identified: One, the constitution of a 'blank page,' i.e. a proper place wherein writing is to occur, in which a Cartesian subject–object relationship is established; two, the construction of a text through articulated operations (literally writing and other gestures) that trace on this 'page' 'words', 'sentences' and, thus, a textual system (of meaning); three, the incorporation and transformation of the world 'outside' the text through a ceaseless manufacture of the 'external' reality according to the text's (cosmo)vision and objectifications.[10] The double *mise-en-scène* of the naming of the toponym clears the space for the European writing of the Maya and incorporation of this other within the text of European writing (history/knowledge). In a repetition and reflection this blank page is formed as the topos of the transcription of place names. Through this transcription of (mis)pronunciations, a text is constructed, a discourse of toponyms, that simultaneously designates a universe of meaning and locates the Maya in this discursive topography of the political imagination.

Third, there is another displacement, that of the indigenous topography in the Spanish inscription of the landscape according to its logic of names. Such (European) inscription is necessary as the first step to complete the travel, that is to transform the *destination* of the colonizing travel into the *oikos* ('home') or *point of departure* from which the exploration of lands preceded. As narrative, conquest is not 'completed' in either sociomilitary terms or ideological legitimization, until the travel that initiates conquest (a reconnaissance) returns full circle to its proper home, the topos of travel (colonization); however, one does not return to the same *oikos* (place of origin) but makes a new home of the destination (clears a blank space to be named and occupied as the place of identity to Sameness). Here there is a return without return, that constitutes (re)invention of the same 'as always' and of alterity 'as other': The otherness of the destination is domesticated in the guise of the same upon (the textualized) return in narrative, while the alterity of the place of departure (Spain) is 'returned' (restored) to the destination (pagan lands) upon (re-)arrival. The outside and the beyond is brought into the 'known world' (an *oikumene*, that is, this world of imaginary places or topography whose textualization is contested and thus exists in the contestation of those texts), which incorporates these new lands, this new home, according to the logic of the *oikos*, an *oikonomia* of travel (see Van Den Abbeele, 1992). This is called here a scriptural economy (see de Certeau, 1984), where a domesticating travel and multiform writing operate the invention of self and other in their proper places.

Fourth, from the (*mise-en-scène* of the) scene of writing and its speculation in a discourse on toponyms, a scriptural economy is put into operation. The Spaniards, according to Landa's account, land at a point which they called 'Cotoch'. Why? Notice a duplicity in this moment of contact that immediately differentiates a whole series of terms and sets these in motion. The initial moment of contact is itself split into two instances of dialogue, that of mutual intelligibility and of concerted misunderstanding: When De Córdoba *asked*—but here in a universal and crystalline language that apparently eliminated all false detours of meaning since it *spoke* in a voice that bound the essence of word and thing—the question was 'understood' as a question since it was *answered* 'as such' in a single word spoken and written down (in eye-witness memory and written histories); this word, in turn, was received as an answer whose meaning and reference was already intelligible, without misunderstanding and without mispronunciation: 'K toch'. How could such clarity of language occur in the first instance and not in the second when the name Yucatán is invented? Could it be that the sign language used in the second case caused the misunderstanding and mispronunciation? If so, what happened to the transparent or apparently divine speech of the first instance of dialogue? Passing between the Spanish understanding of the answer to their first question and their asking the second question was the collapse, seemingly, of a tower of Babel that ruptured communication.

Rereading the account left by an eye-witness, Bernal Diaz, especially over the shoulder of Clendinnen (1987, pp. 4–10), we might wonder how the event could ever be described by Landa as such a diplomatic encounter on the beach. On the contrary, the encounter was conducted entirely through sign languages in which one party, according to its customs, ritually and explicitly enticed the other to a battle and in which the other party construed what was initially viewed as a safe, friendly and warm reception as a treacherous ambush. In these texts, the Maya, all dressed for war, 'beckoned them towards the town, saying something which sounded like "cones catoche, cones catoche", which the Spaniards guessed [How? When? No one explains; when did they understand that it] meant "come to our houses", and which was to lead them to name the headland

Cape Catoche' (Clendinnen, 1987, p. 7). Again, the details of the transmission of messages and meanings is erased, the gaps and delays in and between locutionary speech, listened understanding, perlocutionary hortatory ('write it down'), misheard text—listen to the words!—are whitewashed, all as if to make a blank page, a *mise-en-scène*, on which another history is written, a history of European desire to possess. Here, then, is a writing that conquers through its own legitimization.

But, listen again, to the written text: Was the pronounciation of the Maya words a 'k toch' meaning 'our house' or was it 'ka toch' meaning 'your house'? Certainly, the Spanish ear would have added a vocalic value after the consonant 'k' to render it repeatable and writeable. Was it 'come to our house' or 'come to your house'? Then again, 'ka' is two: 'come to [the?] two house' or 'come to [the] dual house.' Indeed, it is a dual or double house: ours/yours.

Listen: 'K(a) toch' (our house/your house) 'Ka toch'. And the Spaniards repeat the words (repeat there on the path to the blood-drenched temples in the centre of town, there in the historical remembrance of an originary moment of belonging) whose ambivalent meaning transforms from our (Maya) to your (Spanish) house, from your (Spanish) to our (Spanish) house: 'Catoch'—and we can here imagine their emphasis on *our* house, *our* home. Arriving at their destination, the Spaniards give the name of this point, Cape Catoch, 'our *oikos*', with its echoes in the Spanish ears as 'our world' and the destiny of possessing the/ir world. For notice that this toch, this oikos, this home, is not the home to which they will not return in Spain as rich hidalgos (in spite of being the goal of this travel), but the home that by design they have 'returned' to after their travails during their 'voyage of conquest'. They—and here speaking of the Spaniards as whole to which the crew of de Córdoba's ships are a synecdoche—have reached their destiny: They have reached their (new) home, even as de Córdoba's crew fled from the cruel 'ambush' of savage, even cannibal, hospitality even as Hernán Cortez, later, returns to this coastline and departs again to find *his* home in the Mexican capital, even later, as another three generations of Montejo *Eurocentric* each arrive at their imagined home of conquest only to depart and return again until finally a *fragile military domination is established, tentatively*.[11] On this foundation, the colonial regime is erected, or, as in the Maya trope of political possession, 'seated' in its *proper place*.[12]

But, listen here! This is not the final destination of these transcriptions. To add to this confusion of tongues seeking to speak the proper name and to thereby possess its property, consider that:

> ... possession in Roman Law was based largely upon the principle of bodily occupation: 'possession is so styled,' the Digest of Justinian explains, 'from the 'seat,' as it were 'position' (*a sedibus quasi positio*), because there is a natural holding, which the Greeks call *KATOCHE* by the person who stands on a thing.' By means of a striking inversion, this principle of positioning—that is, occupation by virtue of placing one's body upon a piece of property—is then made to apply to the placing of a piece of property upon one's body. (Greenblatt, 1991, p. 27, cf. p. 157 fn 6; original emphases)

'Konex k toche.' Listen to the words. *Listen* to how the Spaniards listened to these words as they were spoken. Imagine them listening: How they must have resonated in the Spanish historical memory, that is, in the collective recollection of reiterated encounters of interpretation. These words must surely have echoed, and echoed with distinct inflections of meaning with each reiteration, not simply in the ears of ambushed Conquistadores swearing their return to avenge Indian treachery, but in the legal minds of the *Scholastics* —those authentically Greek-Spaniard hybrids who developed their own transcultural philosophico-theologico *mestizaje*, scholasticism—obsessed with the lawful legitimization (of everything generally, but especially) of the 'Christian wars of conquest' (Pagden, 1982; Keen, 1971). Listen to how Landa, as he writes decades later a legal defence of his inquisitorial actions in Yucatán, listens to the words of a speculated Maya speaking and how he imagines—or repeats in advance what the anthropologists five centuries later are to imagine again—that the Maya sounds Greek, that is, like Greek-come-Spanish philosophy of law spoken by a Spaniard-come-Greek Scholastic lawyer: 'Koneex k toche, Koneex Katoche.' 'Come to our home. Let's go to your home.' 'Possess your home.' Uuyik u t'áan.

What an event! It is an event so speculative that it appears hallucinatory as we 'listen' to its destined arrival in the Yucatec landscape of this text. It is an event that is purely theoretical (visual, speculative, conceptual, imaginary, reconstructive, deductive, and grounded in a self-serving perspective that effaces its self, its positionality). An event whose value resides precisely in being theoretical and, as such, being a double theatre of memory and of drama through which a war is waged in its place, in its name.

Is this not precisely how Landa[13] rewrites the event in his account, which in turn is an apologia and justification of his own war of religious conversion, that is, the Inquisition that he began in 1562 with an Auto de Fé (see Clendinnen, 1987)? Whereas Columbus's meticulous ritual of possession is enacted as naming (Greenblatt, 1991, pp. 52–85), Landa's is a legitimization (and re-enactment) of violence performed as a simple writing of (the history of a transcription of) a spoken name. In his text, only a brief 'Description of Yucatán' precedes this founding act of epistemic violence, which is entitled 'Etymology of the Province: Its Situation'. Here, then, we can say with the certainty of Derrida that the letter never arrives at its destiny and always already arrives at its destination: In communication the message (a text, a letter) is destined to arrive at its place of the receiver with a difference in meaning than what was sent by the sender; and yet this detour through the (mis)interpretive frames of the receiver is its destination. But look: The Maya who understood perfectly the first spoken question are now impressed or amused by the *sign language* used to ask the second. And these spoken 'letters' *sent* by those attending Maya are not addressed to Spaniards, but reach their destination nonetheless, only to be sent again on another circuit, another travel and other toponymic destinations: uic a than. 'Yucatán.' 'Yukalpeten.' In the logic of this word(s) the Mayab 'land of the pheasant and the deer' is overwritten by a mishearing, mispronunciation, transcription, and a pun of political discourse. Here we may say that the letter is always already de/signed to arrive at its sender.

Assuming that there even was such a speculative theatre of diplomatic dialogue on the beach by 'our houses,' the travelogic of toponymy enacts a writing that conquers. From this transcription of mispronunciations a scriptural economy arrives at Cape Cotoch that is destined to invent a new topography. From this (mise-en-)scene of writing, Maya and Spaniard depart from Cape

Cotoch to travel, in an endless tour of marking boundaries and contours, a *Yucatec* landscape. Enfolded in the hieroglyphics of this toponym are the histories of multiple collisions of heterogenous 'cultures'. Listening to the topography, we might hear the creaking of these landscapes scraping against each other like pen against paper. And notice the illusion of the moment of origin as a tranquil act of speech by the sea. But, it is not merely the act, rendered in such soft tones, that is illusion. The figures enacting this encounter—'the' Maya and 'the' Spaniard—are themselves historiographic fictions that are actualized in part by fables such as these that name and define the spaces of colonial engagement.

Postcolonial Topography

A certain trajectory within postcolonial discourse/studies begins with a consideration of travel and travelogues in the Americas (e.g. De Certeau, Hulme, Todorov, Pratt, Greenblatt) and reaches an apogee with the multitude of studies questioning aspects of the 1492–1992 problematic (e.g. Jara and Spadaccini, 1989, 1992) and Latin American Eurocentricities/postcolonialism (Chanady, 1994; Dussel, 1995; Benitez-Rojo, 1996; de la Campa, 1998; Mignolo, 2000). Key moments in this discursive trajectory—Todorov, Greenblatt, Clendinnen—revisit the topos of the toponym of Yucatán. Might we listen with our eyes to these words again to hear what they write about this landscape of postcolonial theory/discourse in which the words are performed as a perlocutionary writing that carves up space and settles in it a strategic order?

The juxtaposition of quotes by De Certeau about the Amerigo–America encounter and by Todorov of the event of listening/writing the words of Yucatán as rewritten, which begin this essay, might initially strike one as redundant. They 'say' the same thing. The event of listening/writing the perlocution of *uy k a taan* becomes in the postcolonial studies that recite 'it' or De Certeau's recitation of it (e.g. McClintock, 1995, p. 25), a trope that functions to quintessentially define the power/knowledge relations of colonizing and colonizer–colonized dynamics. But, do they 'say' the same thing? Or, is it rather that the interpretations of both within this discourse of postcolonial studies come to the same analytical point: There is a pre-given binary of elements that come into contact that not only establishes a political hierarchy of domination but an erasure of the original dialogic and corporeal event of contact by a colonial historiography that instead stages its own *mise-en-scène* of purities colliding as the condition of the perpetuation of this writing that conquers. The postcolonial disclosure repeats again this *mise-en-scène* of essential identities in collision. This is clearly evident in the work of Todorov, who in his meticulous tracing out of the colonial logic of identity/difference in the 'conquest of México' reproduces an all the more insidious and, thereby, refortified Eurocentric racism (see Root, 1988; Clendinnen, 1990).

In the works of Greenblatt and Clendinnen, the trope of Yucatán does not work to this unfortunate effect. Although these analyses leave the story of listening to the words as emblematic, they seek to disclose the inventiveness of agents and how their actions hybridize the relations of identity and cultural logics that become engaged in colonial encounters. The hybridity of colonial cultures is mutual on both sides of the 'great divide' of power. Yet, this divide is only enlarged and fortified if we imagine it in our panoply of analytical machines and historiographic weapons as a separation that resolutely imposes itself such that the agency of its targets is erased. To listen to words and silences before that erasure is often a speculative enterprise, yet it may be among the few ways to 'reverse' the effects of particular modes of discursive-epistemological structures of domination and to avoid the self-deluding ventriloquisms that construct subaltern voices from the past. The analytical speculation would then be, as it were, a writing *forward* from here, but 'in reverse'.

Notes

1. Sixteenth-century Maya polities 'of Yucatán' also recorded visions of past and current events in books known as the Chilam Balam ('Jaguar Spokesman'). These are notoriously difficult for Western logics and hermeneutics to penetrate. An initial problem of course is that although these texts are written in the Roman alphabet, there is not a standardization of punctuation, spacing and capitalization. Thus, the initial act of reading these texts is a highly interpretive process that requires the reader to 'collate', as it were, the letters into words and sets of words into sentences. This aspect of the transcription and translation of the texts has given room for various translators to assert that the Maya scribe/author has made errors in writing the text. While perhaps such might be the case, these errors are noticeable in the first instance because an aspect of the text does not comply with the logic of interpretation that the translator has imposed on the text in his/her efforts to render it intelligible.
2. There is alliterative and poetic punning here in the Maya text. *Xoc lah cab oc*, 'count all [the] world [by] footsteps' and the day name called *Lahca Oc* ['Twelve Foot'] sound very similar except for the first word *xoc*, which also has the semantic value of 'read'. One would therefore read: 'Xoc lah cab oc, Lahca Oc'.
3. It can be noted that this is a story of creation that has interesting points of resonance with and difference from Christian cosmogenesis. As in the creation story of the Popol Vuh or Pop Wuh, there is room for different interpretions of syncretism, assimilation, transculturation, etc. To my mind, however, the text is not very Christian and no doubt written in theological opposition to Christian thought. Further, it manifests a logic that bears an uncanny resonance with Derridean logic of differánce, in which there is a double articulation of the spatialization of time and the temporalization of space such that that which structures is already structured by that which it structures. Leaving this comment as no more than a suggestive tease, we could call this logic of the *uinal* Maya differánce or a Maya theory of differánce.
4. This is an allusion to an organizing theme of analysis in Clendinnen's (1987) detailed reconsideration of the Spanish—Maya interface between 1517 and 1570. While she attunes her analysis to a hermeneutic recovery of meaning (what actions/words meant to Maya and Spaniard and how meaning was cross-culturally misconstrued), the inquiry here is oriented towards the mechanisms and operation of discursive practices and their conflictual intersection. A similar analysis, which has influenced my thinking, is Greenblatt's (1992) work on the encounter of 1492, specifically his discussion of Columbus's 'ritual of possession' (pp. 52–85) and the 'kidnapping of language' (pp. 86–118). See also Seed (1994) on the ceremonies of European possession-taking.
5. Among the non-Maya, this tradition may have been initiated by the questionnaire distributed among the first *encomenderos*; questions nine and thirteen concern toponyms and their etymologies (de la Garza et al., 1983, pp. xliv—lvi, lxix—lxx, 7–12). It is not clear to me what the relationship may have been between this widely deployed questionnaire of the Spanish Crown and the sixteenth-century humanist treatises prescribing the correct methods of travel. These methodologies, which are formalized along Ramist principles, give marked attention to place names in relation to the social, historical and political characteristics of the visited place (see Stagl, 1990, 1995). Much later, in his apologia, Landa is also concerned with place names (see Tozzer, 1941) and provides interpretations of these. But note that he is reporting what his Maya informants said to him, thus 'acculturating' himself to the Maya practice, which no doubt extends well beyond the Spanish invasion, or he is 'syncretizing' two parallel traditions. For example, the Chilam Balams (e.g. Roys, 1933) clearly illustrates that the Yucatec Maya developed a hermeneutics of place names with intricate punning that operated in political discourses

of domination, legitimacy and control. Derived from this initial colonial concern, it has become standard practice for Yucatec intellectuals to discuss and debate the meanings and correct interpretations of these names (e.g. Cirerol Sansores, 1951, pp. 17, 20–21; Pacheco Cruz, 1959; INAH, 1965, p. 2; Sansores, 1979; Díaz Bolio, 1972, pp. 15–26; Piña Chan, 1987, pp. 13–15; Roche Canto, 1987). Roys's (1935) contribution to this discourse is now reprinted in pamphlet form in order to circulate in the tourist market. Guidebooks on Yucatán, or the sections pertaining to Yucatán in books on Mexico, employ a standardized trope whereby etymological snippets are typically situated in the text after phonetic transcriptions of localities, so as to suggest a natural order between pronounciation of the name and the meaning of the place (e.g. Díaz Bolio, 1972; Arochi, 1974, pp. 21–25; Zapata Alonzo, 1984; Mallan, 1986; Brosnahan and Kretchman, 1983; Broshanan, 1989).

6. Landa directed the Spanish Inquisition in Yucatán. See Clendinnen (1987) for a psychosocial analysis of his persona and motivations in executing his plan for extracting the truth of Maya heresies. Clendinnen's drama-focused hermeneutic of meaning provides substantial secondary evidence for the present argument in that her analyses demonstrate the creative, transcultural, adaptive agency of Maya caught in the colonial structures of power that they did not choose.

7. Here and throughout the essay, analytics rely on and make use of the debate between Derrida (1990) and Lacan (1973) on the meaning and value of Poe's short story, 'The purloined letter', as an allegory of the problem of signification (see also Mehlman, 1973; Johnson, 1977). While Lacan reads this text as a psychoanalytical fable about the phallus, power, signification and 'truth', Derrida's reading converts the story into a deconstructionist fable about language, text, and mis/communication, and 'truth'. Without getting into the details that have stimulated wide-ranging discussions (e.g. Muller and Richardson, 1990) my use of these issues, debates, terms and concepts is limited to an articulation of the problematics of how communicative acts are addressed and received through an interpretive mode that necessarily revises the meaning of messages in ways that it (the message) becomes both different and the same as the message that was sent. This understanding follows Derrida's argument that interpretation always necessarily entails a shift in meaning or, to phrase it another way, interpretation is always a kind of misinterpretation because the meaning of messages cannot be controlled or determined in advance; when received, the message/meanings of the text are occasions for endless re-interpretation (see also Derrida, 1979, 1980, 1988) that alters, however slightly, the message if for no other reason that the context of its receipt creates different meanings. The interesting aspect of this theory of (textual/literary) signification and communication is that it is not simply phrased, but theorized and formulated within a terminology of travel: it is a theory of travel, a travelogic theory, and a travelogue of theory (see Van Den Abbeele, 1992). Messages are 'letters' and 'postcards' that are open to endless re-visioning by receivers at their point(s) of destination, where destination has a double valence of receiver and context, or 'place' of the receiver. The 'detouring' of mis/interpretation entails a proliferation of destinations (what in other texts Derrida calls dissemination) that are both intended and unintended and, therefore, that ultimately include the sender as among the destinations of communicative signification. That messages are often expressed with the pretext of being for another but are actually addressed to oneself–or what might be called the 'self-addressed return' quality of signification–is economically signalled by the concept of postcard, which is often written to another but for oneself. Intrinsic to the discussion of the purloined letter, and especially to Derrida's continued elaboration of the theme (e.g. Derrida 1980), is the problematic of the gift, in that 'sending' is a mode of signification that is related to giving. This thematic no doubt contributed to Derrida's even later turning to question of the gift and then to ethics in his returning engagement with Levinas. This elaborate elaboration is appropriate in a footnote as this indeed forms a subtext of this essay on toponymy, the propriety of names, and the topography of discourses.

8. Bernal Díaz, in his eye-witness account of the landing, does not detail this dialogical interaction, but instead focuses on the gestures of war that were exchanged (i.e. 'friendliness,' 'aggression', etc.). In the eyes and re-memorization of the participant Spaniards, the Maya tricked the Spaniards into an ambush. Here the trope is that of the good/bad Indian that Hulme (1986) shows to derive from the ethnological distinction Carib/Arawak which in turn is premised on the moral differentiation between cannibal/docile Indian (Pearce, 1988, ch. 7).

9. Without getting into polemics of historical truth, my comment refers to the historical memory of a generalized discourse of contemporary life; of course, the rarefied and esoteric memory of historians and anthropological scholarship does not forget these details of different accounts.

10. A less theoretically loaded phrasing can be found in Mary Pratt (1992), who has argued that (specifically) travel writing has produced the world. Although citing Foucault's discussion of the discursive production of the real, Pratt qualifies the scope (Eurocentrism) of this assertion/thesis with idea that she is analysing how the world is produced by (travel) writing *for a European readership*.
11. The crucial histories in English for the 'conquest' of Yucatán are Chamberlain (1948), and Scholes and Roys (1948). The idea that some Maya 'of Yucatán' were not conquered until the eighteenth century and others not until the twentieth and even others have yet to be conquered is a theme that resonates implicitly in the epigraph from Nelson Reed, which holds, to paraphrase in the inverse, that the (European/Spanish, Criollo) present is only a light or slight 'surface' on the (Maya) 'past'. Studies by Roys (1943, 1957), Tozzer (1941), and Farriss (1984) are important for their analyses of Maya society before and/or after Spanish colonization. Clendinnen's (1987) treatment of Landa's Inquisition and Jones's (1989, 1998) study of the 'conquest' of the southern Maya margins are important revisionist histories that demonstrate that the unqualified use of the term 'conquest' is itself a historiographic manifestation of colonizing desire and colonialist will to power. Restall (1997, 1998) has provided a different revisionist and even 'reversalist' history of 'the conquest' based in Maya sources and interpretations. This revision can be summarized in three points: one, Restall's work argues that the social basis of Maya society was other than what had been imagined, i.e. based in community and lineage not kingships; two, that different Maya groups participated, whether in 'actuality' or only in their after-the-fact historiography of the Spanish invasion, as conquistadores, thus the phrase 'Maya Conquistadors'; and, third, that some groups we know today as Maya did not call themselves Maya but rather sought to conquer other groups that they considered, in a pejorative sense, Maya (see Restall, n.d.). Restall contributes to a series of works (cf. Gabbert, n.d.) that deconstruct the ethnic-racial identity term 'Maya' as something that was invented at the end of the nineteenth century.
12. See Seed (1994) for a different kind of historical analysis of the rituals and logics of possession in the colonial encounters of the Americas than that which is elaborated here (cf. Greenblatt, 1992).
13. Perhaps it is here that we should note that there is now some questioning about the text that is authored by the name Landa. Landa's Relación may not be Landa's (Matthew Restall, personal communication, 2002). Landa, like the Maya, seem all to be artifices of historiographic imagining and desires for solid and stable entities.

References

Luis E. Arochi, *La Piramide De Kukulcan Y Su Simbolismo Solar* (México: Panorama Editorial, 1974).

Gloria Anzaldúa, *Borderlands/La Frontera* (San Francisco: Aunt Lute Press, 1987).

Michael Aronna, John Beverley and José Oviedo, eds. Postmodernism Debate In Latin America (Durham: Duke University Press, 1995).

Trevor J. Barnes and James S. Duncan, eds. *Writing Worlds* (London: Routledge, 1992).

Antonio Benitez-Rojo, *Repeating Island* (Durham: Duke University Press, 1996).

John Beverley, 'Writing in reverse: the subaltern and the limits of academic knowledge, in *Subalternity and Representation* (Durham: Duke University Press, 1999), pp. 25–40.

Tom Brosnahan, *Frommer's Mexico On $25 A Day, Plus Belize and Guatemala* (New York: Simon & Schuster, 1989).

Tom Brosnahan and June Kretchman, *Frommer's México* (New York: Simon & Schuster, 1983).

Quetzil E. Castañeda, *In The Museum of Maya Culture. Touring Chichén Itzá* (Minneapolis: University of Minnesota Press, 1996).

Robert S. Chamberlain, *Conquest and Colonization of Yucatán, 1517–1550* (Washington, DC: Carnegie Institution of Washington, 1948).

Amaryll Chanady, ed., *Latin American Identity and Constructions of Difference* (Minneapolis: University of Minnesota Press, 1994).

Manuel Cirerol Sansores, *Chi Cheen Itsa* (Mérida: Talleres Gráficos Del Sudeste, 1951).

Inga Clendinnen, *Ambivalent Conquests: Maya and Spaniard In Yucatán, 1517–1570* (Cambridge: Cambridge University Press, 1987).

Inga Clendinnen, 'Cortés, signs, & conquest of México', in *Transmission of Culture In Early Modern*

Europe, ed. by A. Grafton & A. Blair (Philadelphia: University of Pennsylvania Press, 1990), pp. 87–130.

Roman de la Campa, *Latin Americanism* (Minneapolis: University of Minnesota Press, 1998).

Mercedes De La Garza et al., [1579–1581] *Relaciones Historicos–Geograficas De La Gobernacion De Yucatan (Mérida, Valladolid Y Tabasco)*, 2 vols (México: UNAM, 1983).

Gilles Deleuze and Felix Guattari, *A Thousand Plateaus* (Minneapolis: University of Minnesota Press, 1987).

Jacques Derrida, 'Freud and the scene of writing', in *Writing and Difference* (Chicago: University of Chicago Press, 1978), pp. 196–231.

Jacques Derrida, 'Living on: border lines', in *Deconstruction and Criticism*, ed. by H. Bloom et al. (New York: Seabury, 1979), pp. 75–175.

Jacques Derrida, *The Post Card* (Chicago: University of Chicago Press, 1980).

Jacques Derrida, *Limited, Inc.* (Evanston: Northwestern University Press, 1988).

Jacques Derrida, 'The purveyor of truth', in *Purloined Poe: Lacan, Derrida, and Psychoanalytic Reading*, ed. by J.P. Muller and W.J. Richardson (Baltimore: Johns Hopkins University Press, 1990), pp. 173–212.

José Díaz Bolio, *La Serpiente Emplumada, Eje De Culturas* (Mérida: El Mayab, 1957).

José Díaz Bolio, *Instructive Guide To The Ruins of Chichén Itza* (Mérida: El Mayab, 1972).

José Díaz Bolio, *La Serpiente De Luz De Chichén Itza* (Mérida: El Mayab, 1982).

Michel De Certeau, *The Practice of Everyday Life* (Minneapolis: University of Minnesota Press, 1984).

Michel De Certeau, *The Writing of History* (New York: Columbia University Press, 1988).

James S. Duncan, *City As Text* (Cambridge: Cambridge University Press, 1990).

James S. Duncan and David Ley, *Place, Culture, Representation* (London: Routledge, 1993).

Enrique Dussel, *The Invention of The Americas* (New York: Continuum Publishing, 1995).

Munro Edmonson, *The Ancient Future of The Itza* (Austin: University of Texas Press, 1982).

Munro Edmonson, *Heaven Born Merida* (Austin: University of Texas Press, 1986).

Nancy Farriss, *Maya Society Under Colonial Rule* (Princeton: Princeton University Press, 1984).

Wolfgang Gabbert, 'Violence and ethnicity in the Caste War of Yucatán', *Journal of Latin American Anthropology*, in press.

Stephen J. Greenblatt, *Marvelous Possessions* (Chicago: University of Chicago Press, 1992).

Donna Haraway, *Primate Visions* (London: Routledge, 1989).

Peter Hulme, *Colonial Encounters* (London: Routledge, 1986).

INAH (Instituto Nacional De Antropología E Historia), *Chichén Itza: Official Guide of the INAH* (México: Departamento De Publicaciones, 1955).

INAH (Instituto Nacional De Antropología E Historia), *Ciudades Mayas: Guia oficial INAH* (México: Departamento De Publicaciones, 1965).

Rene Jara and Nicholas Spadacini, eds, *1492–1992: Re/Discovering Colonial Writing* (Minneapolis: Prisma Books, 1989).

Rene Jara and Nicholas Spadacini, eds, *Amerindian Images and The Legacy of Columbus* (Minneapolis: University of Minnesota Press, 1992).

Barbara Johnson, 'The frame of reference: Poe, Lacan, Derrida', *Yale French Studies*, 55–56 (1977), pp. 457–505.

Grant D. Jones, *Maya Resistance to Spanish Rule* (Albuquerque: University of New Mexico Press, 1989).

Grant D. Jones, *Conquest of the Last Maya Kingdom* (Stanford: Stanford University Press, 1998).

Benjamin Keen, *The Aztec Image in Western Thought* (New Brunswick, NJ: Rutgers University Press, 1971).

Jorge J. Klor De Alva, 'The postcolonization of the (Latin) American experience: a reconsideration of "Colonialism," "Postcolonialism," and "Mestizaje"', in *After Colonialism*, ed by Gyan Prakash (Princeton: Princeton University Press, 1995), pp. 241–278.

Jacques Lacan, 'Seminar on the purloined letter', *Yale French Studies*, 48 (1973), pp. 38–72.

Jacques Lafaye, *Quetzalcoatl and Guadalupe* (Chicago: University of Chicago Press, 1974).

Fray Diego De Landa, *Yucatán Before and After The Conquest*, trans. by William Gates (New York: Dover Publications, 1978 [1937]).

José Limón, *Mexican Ballads, Chicano Poems* (Berkeley: University of California Press, 1992).

José Limón, *Dancing with the Devil* (Madison: University of Wisconsin Press, 1994).

Octave Mannoni, *Prospero and Caliban* (Ann Arbor: University of Michigan Press, 1990).

Chiki Mallan, *Guide to Yucatan Peninsula* (Chico, CA: Moon Publications, 1986).

Anne McClintock, *Imperial Leather* (London: Routledge, 1995).

Jeffery Mehlman, 'The floating signifier', *Yale French Studies*, 48 (1973), pp. 10–37.

Walter Mignolo, *Local Histories/Global Designs: Coloniality, Subaltern Knowledges, and Border Thinking* (Princeton: Princeton University Press, 2000).
John P. Muller and William J. Richardson, eds,. *Purloined Poe: Lacan, Derrida, and Psychoanalytic Reading* (Baltimore: Johns Hopkins University Press, 1990).
Anthony R. Pagden, *The Fall of Natural Man* (Cambridge: Cambridge University Press, 1982).
Americo Paredes, *With his Pistol in his Hand* (Austin: University of Texas Press, 1958).
Roy Harvey Pearce, *Savagism and Civilization* (Berkeley: University of California Press, 1988).
Santiago Pacheco Cruz, *Diccionario de etimologías toponímicas mayas. Con sugestivo prólogo del Señor Don Francisco J. Santamaría* (Merida, published by the author, 1959).
Santiago Pacheco Cruz, *Diccionario de etimologías toponímicas mayas. Con sugestivo prólogo del Señor Don Francisco J. Santamaría* (Merida, published by the author, 1959).
Román Piña Chan, *Quetzalcoatl: Serpiente Emplumada* (México: Fondo De Cultura Economica, 1985).
Román Piña Chan, *Chichén Itza* (México: Fondo De Cultura Economica, 1987).
Mary L. Pratt, *Imperial Eyes* (New York: Routledge, 1992).
Nelson Reed, *The Caste War* (Stanford: Stanford University Press, 1964).
Matthew Restall, *The Maya World: Yucatec Culture and Society, 1550–1850* (Stanford: Stanford University Press, 1997).
Matthew Restall, *Maya Conquistador* (Boston: Beacon Press, 1998).
Matthew Restall, 'Maya ethnogenesis 1500–1850', *Journal of Latin American Anthropology*, in press.
Roberto Fernández Retamar, *Caliban and Other Essays* (Minneapolis: University of Minnesota Press, 1994).
Conrado Roche Canto, *Patronimicos Y Locativos en Toponimos Mayas* (Mérida: Talleres Gráficos Del Sudeste, 1987).
Renato Rosaldo, *Culture and Truth* (Boston: Beacon Press, 1989).
Deborah Root, 'Imperial signifier: Todorov and the conquest of America', *Cultural Critique*, 1988, pp. 197–219.
Ralph L. Roys, *The Chilam Balam of Chumayel* (Washington, DC: Carnegie Institution of Washington, 1933).
Ralph L. Roys, 'Place-names of Yucatán', *Maya Research*, 2 (1935), pp. 2–10.
Ralph L. Roys, *The Indian Background of Colonial Yucatan* (Washington, DC: Carnegie Institution of Washington, 1943).
Ralph L. Roys, *The Political Geography of the Yucatan Maya* (Washington, DC: Carnegie Institution of Washington, 1957).
José David Saldivar, *Dialectics of our America* (Durham: Duke University Press, 1994).
Brito Sansores, 'Toponomástica de la Península de Yucatán', in *Enciclopedia Yucatanense* (Mérida: Gobierno De Yucatán, 1979), Vol. 10, pp. 343–403..
Patricia Seed, *Ceremonies of Possession in Europe's Conquest of the New World, 1492–1640* (New York: Cambridge University Press, 1994).
France V. Scholes and R.L. Roys 1948. *The Maya Chontal Indians of Acalan-Tixchel*, Publication 506 (Washington, DC: CIW Publications, 1948).
Justin Stagl, 'The methodising of travel in the 16th century', *History and Anthropology*, 4 (1990), pp. 308–338.
Justin Stagl, *A History of Curiosity: The Theory of Travel, 1550–1800* (Chur, Switzerland: Harwood Academic Publishers, 1995).
Tzvetan Todorov, *The Conquest of America* (New York: Harper & Row, 1984).
Alfred M. Tozzer, 'Landa's Relacion de las Cosas de Yucatan', in *Peabody Museum of Archaeology and Ethnology, Papers*, 18 (1941).
Van Den Abbeele, *Travel As Metaphor* (Minneapolis: University of Minnesota Press, 1992).
Gualberto Zapata Alonzo, *An Overview of the Mayan World* (Mérida: G. Zapata Alonzo, 1984).
Sharon Zukin, *Landscapes of Power* (Berkeley: University of California Press, 1991).

Agnes Lugo-Ortiz

MATERIAL CULTURE, SLAVERY, AND GOVERNABILITY IN COLONIAL CUBA: THE HUMOROUS LESSONS OF THE CIGARETTE *MARQUILLAS*

This essay discusses how ephemeral artifacts of daily material culture, such as marquillas *– the colorful lithographed papers that were used to wrap bundles of cigarettes during the second half of the nineteenth century in Cuba – partook of the symbolization of emergent forms of racialized governability towards the end of slavery on the island. When the para-carcelary regime of the slaveholding plantation was near its final collapse, what sorts of imaginaries and sensibilities were deployed to formulate new fantasies of domination over bodies that once were, theoretically and juridically, the objects of constant surveillance, spatial coercion, and arbitrary punishment? This essay argues that through their humorous content and seductive appearance, these* marquillas *articulated complex and widespread discursivities by which people of color were reimagined not just as objects of derision but also as temporally immobilized (thus devoid of historical existence) in the cognitive and visual fields of a masterly gaze. In particular, it focuses on two series: the visual narratives of the lives of* mulatas, *who appear hilariously trapped by an unavoidable punitive destiny, and on an almanac where the lives of poor free blacks and slaves are ridiculously and inescapably bound to a monotonous and repetitive moral tempo.*

Preliminaries: a sketch on time and the political field of racialized humor

Paved with blood and sorrow, with state violence, censorship, and war, the path that led to the legal demise of slavery in colonial Cuba in 1886, and to subsequent attempts to redefine its racialized social contract, was also paved with laughter. It may be difficult to ascertain, though, to what extent slaves themselves actually laughed at the prospect of their manumission and at the price they had to pay for it, or if they expressed any sense of ironic humor at the bittersweet and equivocally promising disciplines offered by a regime of wage labor and unequal citizenship in the post-abolition era. Silent about that possible laughter, our current historical archive, on the contrary, is rich in the intensity of its pathos. It records the centuries-long slave experiences of torture and pain, the objects and technologies by which that suffering was inflicted, and the many tactical acts of rebellion that resisted such an order of things. The Cuban record, in particular, is eloquent in its account (both factual and fictional) of slaves' insubordinations and insurrections and of their decisive participation in the wars of independence – a process that lasted, interruptedly, for a long period of thirty years (1868 to 1898). Partly because of the overwhelming number of slaves and free people of color in the ranks of the revolutionary armies, both as foot soldiers and as prominent military officials, in their bloody course these wars were progressively and torturously, yet unambiguously, transformed from a strictly political project (i.e. achieving national independence) into a struggle for the abolition of slavery during the period from 1868 to 1878 and for a rearrangement of the racialized social compact around the post-abolition era, after 1886 (Cepero Bonilla, 1948; Carbonell, 1961; Moreno Fraginals, 1970; Scott, 1985; Ferrer, 1999).[1]

Thus, not comedy but the solemnity of *epos* seems to have been the privileged mode that emplotted the black experience towards emancipation in Cuba, and *thanatos* the ominous sign marking that road.

At least with regard to the articulation of public discourses (no claim could possibly be made here about the more subtle and informal practices of everyday life), for slaves and free people of color in Cuba, more generally, the belligerent path towards emancipation and citizenship was quite probably no laughing matter. However, the same cannot be said of their political opposition. As Ada Ferrer (1999) and Aline Helg (1995) have demonstrated, one of the most consistent concerns of many Cubans of color engaged in the struggle for equality throughout the period of the wars of independence and during the post-abolitionist years pertained to the battle of derisive images and skewed identifications waged against them by racist and pro-colonial forces on the island. From the institutions of civil society and the state, as well as the ranks of the revolutionary army itself, Cubans of color were represented either as anachronistic menacing savages or as not yet fully civilized creatures (i.e. as figures of categorical or cultural evolutionary in-betweeness and scorn) whose belonging to the national community and to an order of rights was at best unadvisable and problematic.

One of the main fronts for such attacks was the vigorous humoristic and satirical press entirely identified with the colonial regime that flourished in Cuba between the late 1850s and the 1890s. Through verbal and visual humor, publications such as *El Moro Muza* (1859–1875), *Don Junípero* (1862–1867), and *Juan Palomo* (1869–1874) aggressively, and even viciously, engaged with the current social and political issues, and were adamant in their racialized mockery of the revolutionary movement and their leaders – as exemplified in an 1870 caricature published in *El Moro Muza* by one the most remarkable artists working in Cuba at the time, the Basque painter Víctor Patricio Landaluze (figure 1).[2]

Landaluze's drawing, 'Céspedes, anti-republicano y farsante' ('Céspedes, anti-republican and charlatan'), is emblematic of the ideological tenor that characterized the political visual field of the revolutionary years. It satirically portrays the 'father' of Cuban independence, Carlos Manuel de Céspedes, as an inebriated and aloof monarch – his drunkenness in this and other caricatures is typically marked by the darkened color of his prominent nose. Céspedes, who later was to be iconically mythified in Cuban nationalist imaginary for beginning the war against Spanish colonialism by freeing his own slaves and burning his estate, La Demajagua, on October 10, 1868, appears here indulgently served by two infantilized black men. In order to comply with Céspedes's arrogant royal wish that they lift his mantle, these dwarf-like figures are servile enough not to require the action of the lash that is delicately held in the revolutionary king's

FIGURE 1   Víctor Patricio Landaluze, caricature published in *El Moro Muza*, 1870. Biblioteca Nacional José Martí, La Habana, Cuba. 'Céspedes pintado por los suyos. Céspedes anti-republicano y farsante. Gran retrato copiado exactamente del natural por los acreditados artistas Ignacio Agramonte y Manuel R. Silva' ("Céspedes" painted by his own people. Céspedes anti-republican and "Charlatan". Grand portrait copied directly from life by the renowned artists Ignacio Agramonte and Manuel R. "Silva").

right hand. Yet, their obedience is nonetheless carefreely surveyed by a backward-looking Céspedes, whose prominent scepter-whip seems to subtly mark the steps of his march forward.

This image is a visual elaboration of three major issues of political conflict during this period: first, the imminent, although short-lived, triumph of liberal republicanism in Spain, which will culminate in the brief establishment of the first Spanish Republic in 1873; second, the inner conflicts within the revolutionary leadership that pitted advocates of a centralized conduct of the war and a delay in the abolition of slavery (represented by Céspedes) against those who pressed for the immediate establishment of a liberal republican government to lead the war efforts and declared an immediate end to slavery in 1869; and, third, the fearful and ever-present image in the nineteenth-century Cuban political imaginary of 'Haiti' as a signifier of the ominous idea of a black republic (Fischer, 2004; Sklodowska, 2009). In this cartoon, however, the political future promised by the caricatured revolutionary leadership is not that of a republic but of a degraded kingdom, one led not by a delirious black king à la Henri Christophe but by a laughably debauched and autocratic Cuban white *Criollo*. The subjects of this kingdom are, in no uncertain terms, child-like blacks.[3] Rather than a progressive movement towards freedom, the Spanish liberal, republican, and pro-colonial historical perspective of the cartoon conceives of the war for Cuban independence as a march retrogressively moving forward, as an oxymoronic proleptical inversion of historical progress: not as a movement towards liberal republican freedoms, but towards autocratic monarchy; not towards adult citizenship, but towards infantilizing enslavement and serfdom; not towards individual actions that are obedient to the State on the purported basis of the rational deliberation of a free will, but on stultifying violence and coercion; a march not towards civilization, but towards black savagery. It is a derisive and racialized inversion of the teleological liberal creed of modern temporality, one in which the struggle for freedom is nothing more than a farce, as the title of the cartoon itself very well indicates: 'Céspedes anti-republicano y farsante' (Céspedes anti-republican and charlatan). In his delusional march sustained by barbarians, Céspedes obstinately persists in looking backwards.[4]

Thus, against the *thanatos* of the wars, the epic solemnity of national foundation (with its promises of a future palingenesis), and the social and imaginary reconfigurations produced by the abolition of slavery and the subsequent repositioning of Cubans of color within an order of rights, the pro-colonial response was made up not only of counter-military strategies and political repression, but also of laughter. This was laughter that, as a breaking point, appeared to be racially waged against the conception of historical mobility, against the historical narrative lines unleashed by revolutionary discourses and practices. Contrary to their modern proleptical sense, in the pro-colonial visual production of the period these discourses and practices were inversely construed as a suspension of the forward movement of historical time: as an obstacle to be overcome either through the infliction of death or through the fixation of their political impulses as a march towards retrogression (as in the royal and counter-progressive leadership of Landaluze's Céspedes). In both cases, temporality (acceleration, suspension, retrogression) is what lies at the core of the racialized politics of humorous visuality and its deadly inversions.

Laughter and the symbolic elaboration of material culture: the cigarette *marquillas*

While the world of satirical cartoons makes particularly evident this racialized war of humor against an emancipatory temporality, a less apparent, but nonetheless notable, site from which this war was also launched were *marquillas cigarreras* (cigarette labels), the lithographic and chromolithographic prints that appeared on the paper sheets used in Cuba to wrap packed cigarettes during the second half of the nineteenth century. Among the rich array of subjects represented on these artifacts, people of color and their aspirations for social mobility appear as some of the most remarkable comic objects of derision (figures 2 and 3). In this essay I will explore the mechanism of this laughter: the subtle forms of symbolic constraint that the *marquilla* image deployed through pleasurable mockery (partly enabled by their aesthetic qualities) and the manner in which these engage epistemological questions of narrative and temporality, so saliently indexed in the broader pro-colonial visual production sketched above.

Between the 1860s and 1890s, Cuban cigarettes, which, unlike cigars, were exclusively produced for the local market, were sold in small bundles instead of cardboard packages as is done today. One of the functions of the *marquillas* was to tightly wrap the cigarette bunch in the shape of a cylinder. In a self-referential gesture, one of the extant examples of these objects, *La cajetilla bocoy* (The pack-barrel, figure 4),

FIGURE 2 C. A[nillo], ¡ ¡ ¡ *Vengan a ver esto!!!* [Just look at this!!!], cigarette *marquilla*, Para Usted factory, Cuba, ca. 1860s–1880s.

provides an image of how such lithographed papers were used at the time. The term *marquilla* denotes the particular quality of the material used for its production: a thick, lustrous, deep white paper that was highly suitable for drawing, and which is known in Spanish as *papel de tina* or *papel de marcar* (marking paper). The term *marquilla* also refers to the act of marking or branding merchandise to distinguish it from other products (Núñez Jiménez, 1985: 64–5; 1989: 33–4; n.d.: 173–4).[5]

The *marquillas* themselves were relatively small pieces of paper measuring about 12 x 8.5 centimeters. By law, they had a highly standardized visual structure: (1) the invariable trademark that had to be placed on the right side of the label; (2) the *escena* or *estampa*, the rectangle at the center where different subjects and themes could be represented once approved by the censor; and (3) the *orlas*, the elaborate two-inch visual frames that partly surround the *estampa*. Although the law required that the name and address of the factory appear somewhere on the *marquilla*, the names of the graphic artists who designed these objects are mostly unknown since the majority of the images are unsigned.

The *marquillas* were usually issued in thematic series purposely designed to transform what was basically a utilitarian and marketing device into a collector's item. The subjects serialized in these prints were of encyclopedic proportions: from butterflies, rare animals, or exotic landscapes to portraits of cultural and political personalities; from entwined patterns of letters and numbers to mythological figures; from visual narratives of *Don Quijote* and other novels popular at that time to incessant and rather obsessive displays of colonial, Spanish, and international military fashions and armaments, images that appear similar to toy soldiers (Núñez Jiménez, 1985: 67–85;

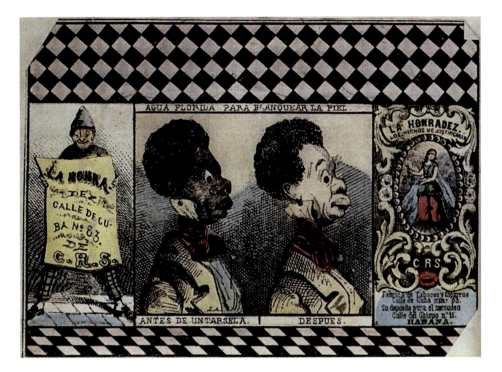

FIGURE 3 Anonymous, *Agua Florida para blanquear la piel. Antes de untársela. Después.* [Flower water for bleaching skin. Before and after], cigarette *marquilla*, La Honradez factory, Cuba, ca. 1860s–1880s.

n.d.: 177–248). The historical specificity of these rather complex objects is, thus, constituted in the intersection of multiple values: their functional/use value as a disposable wrap; their commodified symbolic exchange value as advertisements; and their aesthetic value as a collector's item destined for preservation. Aesthetics, use, and exchange values are all integrated in the very materiality of the *marquilla*.

The drive towards collecting is constitutive of both the *marquilla's* market and aesthetic value, of its impersonal/exchangeable condition as a commodity and its potentiality as an auratic object. Collecting here is, most decisively, not the afterthought of the object. The collector that these objects aimed to instantiate had, in no uncertain terms, an anonymous, homogeneous quality, in that he or she would achieve satisfaction through the restitution of the individual *marquillas* to their serialized (imaginary) pre-existent whole. The intended accumulation of these objects entailed an incitement towards possession and completion and also an epistemological dimension – the desire to restore the encyclopedia produced and promised by the individual images: the taxonomical organization of flora and fauna, the biographical serialization of world leaders, the knowledge of Greek mythology or of contemporary military might.[6]

A remarkable core within this epistemologically luscious production was devoted to the humorous and injurious depiction of Cuban blacks and mulattoes, or, to say it differently, to laughing at people of color. They were part of the items to be collected, of the grand visual encyclopedia of the *marquillas*, right next to images of rare animals, exotic flowers, or foreign armies, and, we must add, beautiful white women, deployed

FIGURE 4 Anonymous, *La cajetilla bocoy* [The pack-barrel], from the series *Alegorías infantiles cubanas del cigarro y del tabaco*, cigarette marquilla, La Honradez factory, Cuba, ca. 1860s–1880s.

for all sorts of allegorical and non-allegorical functions. Significantly, their injurious incorporation within that complex body of visual(ized) knowledge took place precisely at the moment when Cubans of color were attempting to constitute themselves as political subjects by embracing the promises of revolutionary agency and/or by demanding in the civic sphere a different position within an order of rights. In both cases, an anti-stasis of the social, a certain sense of motion, of shifting gears and historical acceleration were all intensely at work.

If, by engaging Judith Butler's reflections on 'injurious speech' (1997) and her assertion that our vulnerability to hateful utterances is a consequence of our being constituted by language, we were to further inquire into the power that, not verbal language, but visual humor may have to injure, we may very well conjecture (in a Lacanian complementary twist) that it is a consequence of our being constituted also by visuality. What is then the character of the political injury produced by the visual humor deployed in the *marquillas*? To what extent could their symbolic and affective technologies be seen as a means to contain the pace of emancipatory temporal dislocations and as part of the anxious imperatives for governability in the face of a post-slavery era?

On the (humorous) collecting of people of color

Saidiya Hartman, in her remarkable book *Scenes of Subjection*, has suggested that hypervisibility is the ruling visual logic of modern plantation slavery (1997: 36).[7]

The condition of the slave as the permanent object of a surveying gaze is the fantasy deployed very early on by plantation legal discourses in the Americas, starting with the nefarious 'Barbados Act' of 1661, up to the 1665 Louisiana *Code Noir*, the 'Virginia Slave Code' of 1705, and the 1842 'Hispano-Cuban Slave Code' (Engerman *et al.*, 2001: 43–142). Within this legislation, it was clearly stipulated that in the daily practices of plantation slavery, the slave was expected by law to be permanently visible (even when absent) to the eye of the master or to the eye of the master's figurative substitution, the overseer.

This drive towards the hypervisible that defines the legal/visual logic of the plantation system, with its cognitive and pornographic fantasy of total dominion, is one that strove to prevail during this period as a form of epistemological re-enslavement in the humorous visual depiction of people of color. At the transition from slavery to wage-labor, from coercion to discipline, the racialized humor deployed in the *marquillas* (with its pleasurable, rather banal, but nonetheless rich visual rhetoric) became a symbolic technology by which to create the illusion of 'fixing' or 'narratively immobilizing' people of color as a *déja*-known object. These series had to be reconstructed through the ambiguously commodifying practice of serialized collecting in its double axes of possessive accumulation and completion. Unless, of course, such operations were undermined by an indifferent consumer for whom the image was just a wrapper to be casually looked at, ephemerally enjoyed, used, and discarded.

Two series among the diverse production of *marquillas* were particularly intense in their attempt to reassert the hypervisibility, the procured *déja (mais non vraiment)*-known quality of people of color. Through a game of narrative redoublings and repetitions that at times read as baroque variations, these series freeze time or make a (collectible) frieze of time within a spatial/visual frame. Visualized space becomes the container for narration and temporality in a move parallel to that performed by the legal/visual logic of the plantation upon the existence of the slave. The first of these series is a satirical almanac entitled *Almanaque Profético para el Año 1866* (Prophetic Almanac for the Year 1866); the second is a complex core comprised by four series organized around the visual biography of 'the mulatta', constructed here as the subject of a satirical and punitive archetypical narrative.

In both series, humorous visuality is waged as a disciplinary device to fix the movement (the mobility) of people of color in a narrative analogous to the proverbial character, evoked by Bergson in his theorization of the meaning of the comic, who absentmindedly slips on a banana peel and falls while rushing down the street. For Bergson, in such a case the comic effect, the inducement to laugh, is the result of a lack of 'elasticity', of a 'physical obstinacy' that emanated from a 'rigidity or momentum' and which led 'the muscles [to continue] to perform the same movement when the circumstances called for something else' (thus the slipping on the banana peel). The narrations at work in these *marquillas* implicitly or explicitly construct the life of people of color either as inapt slowness and repetition or as an acceleration of movement. In any case, to say it with Bergson, what is at stake within this representational/humorous logic is the visualization of a lack of 'flexibility', an inadequacy with regard to the demands of a hegemonic social temporality; the fantasy that something unreflectively mechanical 'has been encrusted upon the living'. While the underpinnings of such a construction are in actuality the opposite – that is, the resistance and refusal of ideological racist imperatives to adapt to the transformations of the social – the scenarios visualized in the *marquillas* invert the loci of inelasticity and rigidity by projecting them onto people of color as the agents of an inappropriately mechanized tempo. Through this inversion laughter acquires a rather normative role, divergent from the socio-ethical concerns that Bergson attributed to it as a potential device for the enhancement of difference. In Bergson's reflection, laughter at *'mechanical inelasticity'* could be seen as a salutary *'social gesture'* that allows society to take on the 'rigidity of the body, mind and character' from which it needed to be 'rid [...] in order to obtain from its members the greatest possible degree of elasticity and sociability'. In its most unadulterated forms, rigidity is the comic and laughter its corrective (Bergson, [1911] 1999: 9–10; 20–1). In these *marquillas*, however, laughter is an attempt to symbolically instantiate an injurious immobility. This is indeed the temporal drive at work in the humorous mechanics of these *marquillas* in their derisive attitude towards the acceleration of time incited by revolution and abolition and the undoing of racialized normativity they mobilized.

Slowness and seasonal repetition: *Almanaque Profético para el Año 1866* (Prophetic Almanac for the Year 1866)

Comprised by twelve *marquillas*, one for each month of the calendar year, ten of the items in this series satirize or caricature people of color by representing their behavior as a compulsive and immoral lack of discipline. The 1866 almanac (issued two years before the beginning of the Ten Year War) proposes and prophesies, almost as an inevitability, a 'racialized tempo' marked by the four seasons of a cyclical 'colored morality'. These seasons are comprised by four satirical themes that recur throughout the series within its different *estampas*: (1) fiesta (figure 5, *Enero. Los diablos coronados castigarán tus pecados,* January. The crowned devils will punish your sins); (2) sex (figure 6, *Abril. Habrá esposición* [sic] *de cañas gordas,* April. There'll be a fine showing of fat canes); (3) alcoholism (figure 7, *Julio. Chicharrón te volverás,* July. You'll turn into cracklings); and (4) idleness (figure 8, *Diciembre. Pasarán trabajos comiendo guanajos,* December. They will sweat to eat turkey). In its chronological/temporal axis the series begins in January with 'fiesta' and ends in December with 'idleness'. Furthermore, each of the carefully crafted designs of the *orlas* comes to synthesize two of the remaining moral 'seasons' developed in the series (i.e. 'alcoholism' and 'sex'), thus elegantly reinforcing and completing the humorous ontological rigidity of the *marquilla*'s temporality within virtually the entire spatial totality of the sheet's design (*estampa* and *orla*). Such a satirical intensification runs parallel to the liturgical calendar that appears in each of the objects, indicating the many religious festivities of the month. Religion and profanity, the sacred and the mundane are placed in contiguity within the same field of vision, barely separated by a thin black borderline, on the verge of potential and mutual contamination.

The first *marquilla* in this series, corresponding to the month of January (*The crowned devils will punish your sins*, figure 5), is a caricature of the festivities celebrated in Cuba since the early colonial period on Epiphany, which for Catholics falls on January 6th. On that day throughout the slaveholding era, slaves were allowed to come from the rural areas into the cities and take over the streets, dancing and asking the neighbors for an *aguinaldo*, the monetary present given in exchange for their dances and performances (Ortiz, [1920] 1993: 64–75). Víctor Patricio Landaluze's *Día de Reyes en La Habana* (Epiphany in Havana, figure 9) give us a more complex representation of what those

FIGURE 5 Anonymous, *Enero. Los diablos coronados castigarán tus pecados* [January. The crowned devils will punish your sins], from the *Almanaque Profético para el Año 1866*, cigarette *marquilla*, La Honradez factory, Cuba.

celebrations may have entailed with regard to the performative dynamics of urban public space and the intersubjective social exchanges it may have generated, while still exploiting bodily poses to comic effect. One of the distinctive features of these fiestas was that each African *cabildo*, the institutions authorized during the colonial era to organize the sociability of the different African ethnicities (Ortiz, [1921] 1993: 54–63), would crown a king and a queen for that day – in Landaluze's painting, for example, the king is the figure on the left side of the canvas that is elegantly dressed in a Western tuxedo and distinguished by a sash and a scepter and who courteously and solicitously extends his hat to the white ladies that remain well-guarded in their gated interior. *The crowned devils will punish your sins* is an allusion to these festivities and the carnivalesque inversion of royal dignity that they stage.

By contrast to Landaluze's work, this *marquilla* greatly lessens the visual energy and complexity of the fiesta. The caricature virtually cancels the city as a historically identifiable environment (which in Landaluze is marked by the recognizable dome and tower of the church and convent of San Francisco) and the systems of cultural and monetary exchanges between heterogeneous social and racial sectors enabled in the streets of Havana by the fiesta. It also, and perhaps most saliently, diminishes the semiotic richness of the diverse costumes: the festive carnivalesque inversions meant to be enacted through the use of Western garb and the relation to a whole system of cultural transmissions and memories connected to Africa indexed in the traditional costumes and masks (so perceptively rendered by Landaluze), and which in the image appear just as simplified and rather ridiculous feather headdress, skirt, and crown.

FIGURE 6 Anonymous, *Abril. Habrá esposicisión* [sic] *de cañas gordas* [April. There'll be a fine showing of fat canes], from the *Almanaque Profético para el Año 1866*, cigarette *marquilla*, La Honradez factory, Cuba.

Showing the slaves practically naked and displaying exaggerated dance steps and facial expressions, this *marquilla* atemporally suspends them in pure affect, apparently disconnected from any system of social and cultural meaning in the present (e.g. via the appropriation of Western clothing) and from any ancestral tradition from the living past (e.g. via the display of identifiable African costumes). The disconnection staged by this *marquilla* would have certainly been complete if it were not for the ominous relational caption that warns the viewers, from a safe space of verbal exteriority with regard to the figurative frame of the image, that these crowned devils one day will punish their sins. What sins? Whose sins? What day? The year 1866 thus starts with an ominous fiesta, one in which the caricatured slaves in their temporal suspension could nonetheless, and humorously, become Satanic dancing ghosts.[8]

The endpoint of the chronological frame of this prophetic *Almanaque* is, of course, the month of December. The image that closes it, *They will sweat to eat turkey* (figure 8), is a reference to the turkey dinner to celebrate Christmas Eve or day, and it satirizes the supposed work that people of color may need to endure to enjoy the holidays, thus closing the chronological axis of the series with the theme of 'idleness'.

The chronological frame of this series is further enhanced by the framing designs of the *orlas*. The *orlas* satirically complete the four thematic seasons of the year by reference to alcoholism and sex. Here three ape-like and semi-naked figures (the men wearing loincloths, the woman exposing her breasts) compete for a bottle of alcohol (figures 5, 7, 8). In *July. You'll turn into cracklings* (figure 7), the competition is resolved in the *estampa*, where the woman of the *orla* is shown in possession of the bottle, getting

FIGURE 7 Anonymous, *Julio. Chicharrón te volverás* [July. You'll turn into cracklings], from the *Almanaque Profético para el Año 1866*, cigarette *marquilla*, La Honradez factory, Cuba.

drunk under a smoking, burning sun and the surveying, almost expectant, gaze of a sketchily drawn white man (who protects himself from the sun with an umbrella).

The second design of the *orlas* pertains more directly to the subject of sex and is more complex in composition and interplay of meanings (*April. There'll be a fine showing of fat canes*, figure 6). The image in this *orla* is divided into two different axes (one vertical, the other horizontal) that establish a visual distinction between present and past, history and myth, reality and fantasy. On the left side of the *orla*, on the vertical axis, are caricatures of two dark skinned ape-like men, one perched on top of the other, with Sambo-like grins on their faces. The one on top spies with lustful delight through a window (a window, one could say, that opens up the black men's unconscious to the viewer's gaze) onto a fantastical bucolic space, arrayed along the horizontal axis, where a group of white women are sensually resting. In this dream-like mythological scenario the four carefree women enjoy the delights of an intimate rustic moment in front of a pond where a white swan swims. The scene is, of course, an evocation of the mythological rape of Leda by Zeus in the shape of a swan (a rape that, we may recall, gave birth to beauty in the form of their daughter Helen and to a heroic belligerent contest between men for the possession of that beauty).

Thus, the threat of rape in this image is played out as an ironic inversion of the whiteness of the swan with the blackness of the slaves. However, the image assuages the fears (and pleasures?) that the visualization of such a fantasy could produce in a white male viewer by inscribing, with humor, the promise of a quick and imminent punishment of the transgressors. For in the left distance, the principle of repression

FIGURE 8 Anonymous, *Diciembre. Pasarán trabajos comiendo guanajos* [December. They will sweat to eat turkey], from the *Almanaque Profético para el Año 1866*, cigarette *marquilla*, La Honradez factory, Cuba.

appears, a spectral figure with a whip in his hand, (sketchily drawn much like the white surveying figure in *July. You'll turn into cracklings* figure 7): this is the overseer, rushing to punish the black man's fantasy. In this particular *marquilla*, the situation posed by the *orla* – its possible fears and pleasures – is re-elaborated as well by displacing and heightening the erotic charge of the *orla* into the rather vulgar but comic dynamics of the *estampa*. At the center of the *estampa* we see a black woman flanked by two black men (possibly the same ones from the *orla*) who hold '*cañas gordas*' (thick sugar cane stalks) in front of their crotches, to the black woman's immense delight. In so doing, the image restitutes black men's supposedly unbridled sexuality (no way to miss those large and erect phalluses) to its proper object – the black woman – who also appears here as a figure of potential sexual excess by having at her disposal not one but two well-endowed men. The image, then, moves from and in between the figuration of black men's sexuality in the realm of a fantasy (a mythical desire to possess a white woman in the *orla*) to its deployment in its 'proper' place (the scenario of the black woman's body and of desire in the *estampa*). This is a game in which the image actually duplicates white fantasies about black sexuality, offering the viewer, with the reassuring and amusing intercession of the overseer, its full visual spectrum.

From the racist narrative perspective of the artifact itself, the humorous pleasures deployed in the *Almanaque Profético para el Año 1866* enable the comforting fantasy of placing people of color light-heartedly in their 'proper place' by constructing them as quaintly caricatured humorous objects – be this because of the amusing fiction of an

FIGURE 9 Víctor Patricio Landaluze, *Día de Reyes en La Habana* [Epiphany in Havana], ca. early to mid–1870s, oil on canvas, 51 × 61 cm, Museo Nacional de Cuba, Havana.

ontological inevitability and repetition or due to the illusion of capturing their existence in a slow but steady temporal unfolding of a risible immoral sameness. Yet, it is even more in the figure of free mulattas that the plantation gaze strove to fully reassert itself and deploy its greatest epistemological visual lust and laughter – to the point of making humorous racialized conventions the implicit substance of tragedy.

Acceleration and punishment: the life of the mulatta

Few other subjects received the kind of obsessive and systematic treatment in the visual production of the *marquillas* as the mulatta. Besides the numerous free-floating images that show her as an object of both repulsion and desire, there were at least four different series that staged her as the subject of a highly codified moralistic visual narrative, one in which her life was construed as a sequence of incomplete or failed aspirations for social mobility: *Historia de la mulata* (History of the Mulatta, from the Para Usted factory, eight scenes); *Vida de la mulata* (Life of the Mulatta, from La Honradez factory, seven scenes), *La vida de la mulata* (The Life of the Mulatta, also from La Honradez, seven scenes); and *Vida y muerte de la mulata* (Life and Death of the Mulatta, from the Llaguro factory, fifteen scenes).[9]

The series entitled *Historia de la mulata* does not concentrate on the life of a single mulatta but on scenes of immoral behavior supposedly common to all mulattas, regardless of their age, complexion, or social class. These images insinuate that mulattas are ubiquitous beings and that their immorality pervades all aspects of the social sphere by targeting white men of all classes. They appear to move in a carefree fashion through public spaces, from the street to the market to sumptuous interiors, engaging with sailors and merchants as well as with old and pachydermic magnates (as in *El palomo y la gabilana* (sic), Male dove and female hawk, figure 10).

The *Vidas* (with the strong hagiographic connotations of the word), on the contrary, visualize and narrativize the life of the mulatta in a linear temporal fashion – with a beginning, a middle, and an end – thus producing the mulatta as a discernable and knowable diachronic entity. All of these *Vidas* start with a scene of literal or metaphorical 'birth' that corresponds to the first *marquilla* in the series. *La vida de la mulata. El nacimiento* (Birth, figure 11) depicts a biological birth (what makes the scene hilarious is the expression of domestic bliss on the faces of the new parents), while *Vida y muerte de la mulata. 1a. El que siembra coje* (1st. He who sows will reap, figure 12) narrates the beginning of her corrupt genealogy. This last image, which belongs to the longest and most complex of the three series, shows a black woman in the street engaging in a monetary exchange with a white man. Figuratively, it is a moment that conveys the act of conception, equating the origins of the mulatta with a corrupt sexual/monetary transaction. Even before birth, she is already marked by immorality.

In a sort of moral inversion of the hagiographic model – in which, as Michel de Certeau has observed, everything in the life of the saint has been given from the very beginning, with a 'vocation' and an 'election', thus producing the life of the saint as nothing but the unfolding epiphany of the god-given gift of sainthood – everything in

FIGURE 10 Anonymous, *El palomo y la gabilana* [sic]. [Male dove and female hawk], from the series *Historia de la mulata*, cigarette *marquilla*, Para Usted factory, Cuba, after 1862.

FIGURE 11 Anonymous, *El nacimiento* [Birth], from the series *La Vida de la mulata*, cigarette *marquilla*, La Honradez factory, Cuba, ca. 1860s–1880s.

the life of the mulatta has also been pre-ordained, with an 'initial ethos'.[10] The unfolding path of the mulattas' life throughout these series is unequivocally one of progressive, but narratively prefigured, moral degeneration that ends with the mulattas' final demise either by illness (*La vida de la mulata. La conducen al hospital* [They take her to the hospital]) or death (*Vida y muerte de la mulata. 15a. Fin de todo placer* [15th. End of all pleasure]). Like the 1866 *Almanac* — where the lives of people of color unfold between fiestas and idleness, alcohol and sex, marking the meaning of their existence through a predictable temporality — the lives of the mulattas show a similar drive to produce her as an immoral certitude. Her becoming in time is nothing but the confirmation of her essential truth, one that is offered to the viewer through the many (serialized and collectible) satirical repetitions performed in the *marquillas*. These repetitions draw a horizon of expectation where the viewer could see and know, without surprises, what is coming — a horizon of expectation not so different, to recall Bergson once again, from the banana peel in the street that elicits the viewer's anticipation of the laughable fall. Within the logic of these *marquillas*, the comic pathos of the mulatta is that we can predict the pitfalls of her accelerated movement through the social environment. What makes her risibly pathetic is that her acceleration negates any real movement (of change and difference) — it is just the repetitive actualization of a frieze.[11]

This drive to visually and narratively produce the mulatta as a knowable being is a response to and a re-enactment of the uncertainties and anxious ambivalences that her figure actually came to signify in the decades before the legal abolition of slavery in 1886 and in its aftermath. Far from a certainty, the mulatta was conceived as a

FIGURE 12 C. Anillo, *1a. El que siembra coje.* [1st. He who sows will reap], from the series *Vida y muerte de la mulata*, cigarette *marquilla*, Llaguno factory, Cuba, ca. 1860s–1880s.

dangerous enigma, like in Franciso Muñoz del Monte's 'La mulata,' published in Havana in 1845:

> De blanco y negro inexplicable engendro,
> sublime, cuando quiere se enamora,
> insaciable en sus iras como el tigre,
> apacible en su amor como paloma.
>
> Antítesis viviente de dos mundos,
> cambiante anfibio, esfinge misteriosa,
> que el enigma propone a los pasantes,
> y al que no lo descifra lo devora. (Muñoz [1845] 1981: 196–7)
>
> Inexplicably engendered by white and black,
> sublime, she falls in love as she likes,
> insatiable in her wrath like a tiger,
> peaceful in her love like a dove.
>
> Living antithesis of two worlds,
> ever-changing amphibian, mysterious sphinx,
> who poses a riddle to the passerby,
> and devours those who cannot solve it. (Trans. Kutzinsky, 1993: 27)

The poetic voice in these stanzas from Muñoz del Monte's poem appears puzzled at the existence of the mulatta, a being that was 'inexplicably engendered by white and black'. The bad faith about the sexual violence of slavery is barely disguised here. In the poem the mulatta (whose origins are a puzzle) is herself an enigma, an 'ever-changing amphibian' (that is, a protean being whose shape eludes clear recognition). She is a 'mysterious sphinx' – an epistemological challenge. The inability to elucidate that mystery, the poem tells us, could be a deadly predicament; it will 'devour' those who cannot solve it. What is the enigma at stake here? First, of course, that of racial identity itself since the mulatta could pass as white, thus deceiving her white lover. This was an anxiety that was repeatedly inscribed in the *marquillas* of this period, just as in one from the *Historia de la mulata. Café de escauriza, el ponche de leche* (The milk punch is nothing but watered-down coffee). This image shows a masked mulatta, solicitously surrounded by a group of elegant white men (but also under the inquiring gaze of a black boy who stares in knowing puzzlement at the scene) while the voice of the caption defines (and unmasks, so to speak), with a play on words, the truth of the situation for the viewer.

The enigma in Muñoz's poem seems to be resolved with self-assurance by the visual production of the *marquillas*. Insofar as the mulatta defies physiognomic categorization, solving the enigma requires exceptional visual skills. A visual lack, so to speak, could lead to an undesirable transaction, to an inappropriate recognition (as the image described above suggests), but, more seriously, to incest. The fear of incest associated with the mulatta as an epistemological enigma (an awareness of who she really 'is') was partly thematized in the most important novel published in Cuba during the nineteenth century, *Cecilia Valdés* by cirilo Villaverde. At the center of its plot is the romance between a beautiful mulatta (Cecilia Valdés) and an irresponsible young *Ccriollo*, Leonardo Gamboa, who, of course, happens to be her brother. At the end of the novel, Cecilia is pregnant with her brother's child and all sorts of tragedies ensue, including her confinement in a sanatorium (a fate not so different from the mulattas of the *marquillas*). At the beginning of the novel, though, the omniscient narrator, whose own desire for Cecilia is barely concealed throughout the text, describes her physical appearance with sensual gusto and then wonders:

> ¿A qué raza, pues, pertenecía esta muchacha? Difícil es decirlo. Sin embargo, a un ojo conocedor no podía esconderse que sus labios rojos tenían un borde o filete oscuro, y que la iluminación del rostro terminaba en una especie de penumbra hacia el nacimiento del cabello. Su sangre no era pura y bien podía asegurarse que allá en la tercera o cuarta generación estaba mezclada con la etíope. ([1882] 2001: 73)

> What was, thus, her race? It is difficult to say. Nevertheless, a connoisseur's eye would not miss that her red lips had a dark edge, and that the lightness of her face ended in a sort of shadow at the growth of the hair. Her blood was not pure, and it can be assured that in the third or fourth generation it was mixed with that of the Ethiopian. (Trans. Helen Lane [1882] 2005: 13)

The racial truth of the mulatta, or the production of the mulatta as a racial truth, requires the eye of a 'connoisseur'. This is the eye that is redeployed in the *marquillas* not so much as an act of physiognomic recognition (as we have in Villaverde's novel) but as a moral eye that can ascertain without ambiguities (and in a totalizing fashion) the shape of her moral destiny – a destiny that, as we have seen, has no other conclusion than punishment and demise. Or to say it differently: to recognize the physiognomics not of a body but of a moral countenance.

Punctuated by ironies and satirical observations, the *marquillas* devoted to the life of the mulatta nevertheless exhibit as well the signs of melodrama and perhaps tragedy, even if there is no nobility in her 'heroism'. However, in all of these series, and despite brief moments where moral judgment may give way to glimpses of potential compassion or identification, the process that led to pain and suffering most decisively becomes an object of uncontrollable hilarity. This hilarity does not necessarily emanate from the impersonal moralistic viewer that guides our perceptions and interpretations of the scenes through most of the captions (and whose laughter is rather wittily circumspect). Rather, it emerges through the systematic and overt visual insertion, in each scene, of a mocking spectatorial eye. Without exception, in all of these sequences, there is a moment of comic anagnorisis whose agent is the gaze of a black man, a figure who seems to believe that the melodramatic spectacle of the mulatta is a laughing matter.[12]

In the non-linear narrative of the *Historia de la mulata*, for instance, we find, among its fragmentary diversity, an image with the caption *Nuevo sistema de anuncios para buscar colocación* (New system to publicize job wanted ads, figure 13) in which, at right, a black lad is laughing very heartily. What is he laughing at, and what is so funny? It is the elegant mulatta in this image, who coquettishly reciprocates the gallant attentions and desirous gazes of the solicitous white men who approach her as she walks in the park. Is it possible that the concealed face that elicits such laughter from the boy may resemble, in humorous terms, something like the 'whiteface' portrayed in *Agua Florida para blanquear la piel. Antes de untársela. Después* (Flower water for bleaching skin. Before and after, figure 3) – that is, her face reveals an aspiration for social mobility conceived

FIGURE 13 Anonymous, *Nuevo sistema de anuncios para buscar colocación* [New system to publicize job wanted ads], from the series *Historia de la mulata*, cigarette *marquilla*, Para Usted factory, Cuba, after 1862.

here as a process of 'whitening', as an act of unwelcome acceleration that upsets the normative, naturalized order of things and which can only be perceived as a hilariously grotesque joke?

In the *Vidas* series, the judgmental mockery is no less subtle. The *Vida y muerte de la mulata*, for instance (figure 14), radicalized the mockery by showing a drunk mulatta ready to respond to the sexual propositions of the black carriage driver, who with derisive and aggressive vulgarity asks her if she wants him to 'light her up' ('¿quieres mecha?'). At this point, the series seems to be violently restituting the mulatta to her 'proper place' within a system of sexual exchanges defined by racial segregation, very much like the image of the 1866 *Almanac* discussed earlier, *Abril: Habrá esposición de cañas gordas* (figure 6). What is at stake in both of these images is a stark opposition to interracial relationships under threat of punishment.[13]

In all of the mulatta series the black man is a figure of displacement, one loaded with the laughter and the scorn of the white male racist gaze that organizes the tragic comic spectacle of the mulatta. What do these black men laugh about? They laugh about the aspiration for social mobility of women of color; that is, at the same kind of humor by which 'uppity blacks' were invented as performative incongruences (dancing the minuet, figure 2) and as ontological inevitabilities (staying physiognomically or, more accurately socially, black no matter what, figure 3). They laugh at the satirical capturing of the mulatta's existence as the temporal unfolding of an immoral sameness; again, at the same sort of humoristic presuppositions we saw deployed in the 1866

FIGURE 14 Anonymous, 12a. *"Caridad", Quieres Mecha? ¡¡Siaa!!* [12th, Caridad, do you want me to light you up? Suuuure!!!!], from the series *Vida y muerte de la mulata*, cigarette *marquilla*, Llaguno factory, Cuba, ca. 1860s–1880s.

Almanac in which the tempo of people of color's existence was immorality and vice. It could be said, then, that they certainly laugh at the mulatta, but also that their laughter is a projected complicity with the structures of racist humor through which all people of color (socially mobile blacks, the free poor, and the slaves as well) were rendered knowable as fixed entities that ought to be kept in the 'proper' social place.

As the totalitarian pretensions of dominion waged by the slaveholding plantation gaze had to progressively confront the new tasks of governability demanded by the slow and violent transition to a (nominally) exclusive regime of wage-labor — one in which subordination had to be (at least legally) procured no longer by coercion but through discipline, and where space (especially the space of the plantation) ceased to be the legally predetermined border to the movement of workers — the humorous temporal logic of the *marquillas* appears as a symbolic re-elaboration and reassertion of fantasies of control and immobility that the end of slavery would not be able to fully uphold. This fantastic elaboration is intensified by the illusion of cognitive completion incited by the accumulative and possessive structure of serialized collecting itself. The humor of this fantasy is certainly not exempt from pain, in fact rather the opposite. If anything, the laughing black men in the mulatta series could also be seen as the ultimate form of mimicry (of a non-musical minstrelsy, if you will), one that intensifies the white racist mockery at the tragicomic acceleration of the mulatta by visually canceling empathy and solidarity amongst expected kin, by intensifying the injury through radical dissociation. Only tragedy could ensue from such injurious laughter, as these series, even against themselves, and in the fault lines constitutive of their immobilizing teleological narrative, let us know.

Acknowledgements

I would like to thank Marianne Hirsch, Stephan Palmié, Leo Spitzer, and Ana María Reyes for their kind and encouraging reading of this essay, as well as Raida Mara Suárez Portal, Margarita Suárez, and Zoila Lapique Becalí for their support and our many conversations about the *marquillas* under the sun of Havana. I am also grateful to the anonymous readers at the *Journal of Latin American Cultural Studies* for their clear and thoughtful suggestions. Diane Miliotes, as always, gave me her "tough love" and helped me with the editing of its many versions. But my special gratitude ought to go to Angela Rosenthal, who read an earlier version of the essay with her usual intellectual passion and generosity and made many crucial and timely recommendations. Her mind and love live on in the best parts of this piece; its shortcomings are simply the result of my own limitations.

Notes

1. In this essay I will use the terms 'people of color' or mulattoes, which was the language used in the second half of the nineteenth century to refer to persons of African descent.
2. Landaluze is best known in Cuban art history for his extraordinary and complex *costumbrista* depictions of mulattoes and of urban scenes pertaining to Afro-Cuban life. For a basic introduction to Landaluze's biography, see Lázara Castellanos's *Víctor*

Patricio Landaluze. The most comprehensive study to date on this rather understudied artist is Evelyn Carmen Ramos, 'A Painter of Cuban Life: Víctor Patricio de Landaluze and Nineteenth-century Cuban Politics'.

3 On the broader humorous and caricaturesque iconographic field deployed in the battle between empires within the Spanish-speaking Caribbean at the end of the nineteenth century, and in which the infantilization of people of color and 'natives' had a prominent role, see John J. Johnson, *Latin America in Caricatures*; Manuel Méndez Saavedra, *1898. La Guerra Hispanoamericana en caricaturas/The Spanish American War in Cartoons*.

4 On the question of temporality and space with regard to colonial and post-colonial discursive formations, see Anne McClintock's *Imperial Leather. Race, Gender and Sexuality in the Colonial Contest* (1995: 36–42); and Johannes Fabian, *Time and the Other. How Anthropology Makes its Object*.

5 For a beautiful and well-documented history of nineteenth-century Cuban lithography, also see Zoila Lapique Becalí's *La memoria en las piedras*.

6 A few extant albums preserved in the archives of the Museo Colonial and at the Oficina del Historiador de la Ciudad, Palacio de los Capitanes Generales, in Havana give us some idea of the possible identities of collectors, among them children and upper-class women, and of the organizational logic applied to the collecting of *marquillas*. Judging from this small sample, these collectors carefully organized the images in scrapbooks, one of which displays the complete series in succession and features an elegant leather cover with the initials of the owner inscribed in gold letters. It is difficult, though, to say how widespread such practices were since the archival evidence is so scarce. However, the manufacturers' marketing choice to produce illustrated series in the first place is indicative of the allure that collecting as a practice was believed to have had at the time. Significantly, the decades under examination here for the production of *marquillas* (circa 1860–1890) also coincide with the beginning of fine art collecting and the proliferation of cartes-de-visite on the island. Thus, the *marquillas* may also be seen as part of a broader reorganization of visual economies and cultures in Cuba during the second half of the nineteenth century. The mapping of this complex visual field is a task that still remains to be done.

7 A development of the concept of hypervisibility vis-à-vis slave (de)subjectification is found in Angela Rosenthal and Agnes Lugo-Ortiz's 'Envisioning Slave Portraiture'.

8 Roberto González Echevarría has observed that the sins to be punished by these ghostly dancing slaves are those of slavery (observation made in a lecture delivered at the University of Chicago, October 2007). For his view of the relationships between art, literature and *fiesta* in Cuban culture see his *Cuban Fiestas*. Similarly, Diana Aramburu, in a suggestive reading of the *Almanaque Profético para el Año 1866*, states that in these *marquillas*, the figure of *la culona* (the 'big-ass woman', who is a conventional character of the *fiestas*) carries as well a charge of defiance: 'Ella simboliza el tiempo festivo donde se puede "tirar todo a relajo", donde reina la risa liberadora y el "'choteador"' ['She represents festive time, when everything can be "taken as a joke" and in which liberating laughter and the Cuban joker prevail']. See Diana Aramburu, 'Las fiestas afrocubanas en las marquillas cigarreras del siglo XIX: el *Almanaque profético para el año 1866*.'

9 Vera Kutzinsky puts forward an intelligent reading of the relationships between gender, race, and the masculinist gaze in the series *Vida y muerte de la mulata* is one of the rare *marquilla* series that in signed, by a 'C. Ancillo' about whom nothing in yet know. *Sugar Secrets. Race and the Erotics of Cuban Nationalism* (1993: 43–100). Feliza

Madrazo has also addressed these issues in her '*Ni chicha ni limonada*'. *Depictions of the Mulatto Woman in Cuban Tobacco Art*; and so does Alison Fraunhar in her '*Marquillas cigarreras cubanas*: Nation and Desire in the Nineteenth Century'. For a broader and insightful discussion of the mulatta as a hermeneutic device in post-abolitionist Cuba see Jill Lane's *Blackface Cuba* (2005:180–223).

Let known is one of the rare *marquilla* series that is signed, by a 'C. Anillo', about whom nothing is yet known.

10 Cf. Michel de Certeau, 'Una variante: La edificación hagiográfica' in his *La escritura de la historia*. Trans. Jorge López Monctezuma ([1978] 1985: 294). For the historical distinctions between hagiography and biography, see Daniel Madelénat, *La biographie*. On the issue of secularized sainthood in nineteenth-century revolutionary Cuba, see Agnes Lugo-Ortiz, *Identidades imaginadas: Biografía y nacionalidad en el horizonte de la guerra (Cuba 1860-1898)* (1999: 76–9).

11 The construction of the mulatta that we find in the Cuban *marquillas* seems to diverge profoundly from that found in the works of Agustino Brunias within the eighteenth-century British West Indian context. Kay Dian Kriz has convincingly argued that during that juncture, Brunias exploited the perceived racial/ontological ambiguity of socially mobile mulattas 'to represent civilized society under development in a place "in-between" civilized Europe and savage Africa' (2008: 45). The social aspirations of these British colonial mulattas were produced as indexical of the benefits of colonialism, of its refining cultural influences upon the primitiveness of black Africans (a construction that Kriz makes clear did not exclude a simultaneous elaboration of their bodies as sexually charged; the mulatta incorporated both rudeness and refinement). Bespeaking the particular tensions of late nineteenth-century abolitionist/revolutionary Cuba, in the *marquillas* the mulatta's aspiration to social mobility and cultural refinement is, on the contrary, thoroughly punished by the visual narrative, and it is in no way contemplated as a positive by-product of colonialism. Kay Dian Kriz, 'Marketing Mulâtresses in Agustino Brunias' West Indian Scenes', in *Slavery, Sugar and the Culture of Refinement. Picturing the British West Indies, 1700-1840* (2008: 37–69).

12 Both Fraunhar and Aramburu mobilize Jorge Mañach's discussion of the term *choteo* to describe the kind of humor deployed in the *marquillas*. Mañach's pivotal lectures of 1928 (published under the title *La crisis de la alta cultura en Cuba: indagación del choteo*) are concerned with what he deemed to be the crisis of 'high culture' in Cuba during the post-independence era. For him, *choteo* stands for a problematic and impertinent sort of Cuban (national specific) humor that indiscriminately denies gravitas to the serious facts of social and personal life, thus impoverishing it. Or to say it differently, it is humor geared towards melting all that is solid. Such humor, as he saw it, had started as a feature of the lower classes and has progressively contaminated all social stratas. In my view, Mañach's *choteo* is a figure that allows him to critically articulate his own anxieties about the social and cultural dynamics of early Republican Cuba and not necessarily an analytical category to project retrospectively (and with the risk of ahistoricity) into the dynamics of the nineteenth century. Thus I will refrain from naming the humor of the *marquillas* as *choteo* or from suggesting that their humor could be seen as a sort of an anti-colonial expression of *Cubanness* (as Fraunhar seems to suggest). Del choteo, *La crisis de la alta cultura en Cuba: indagación del choteo*.

13 On interracial marriages in colonial Cuba see Verena Martínez-Alier, *Marriage, Class, and Colour in Nineteenth-century Cuba: A Study of Racial Attitudes and Sexual Values in a Slave Society*.

References

Aramburu, Diana. 2010. Las fiestas afrocubanas en las marquillas cigarreras del siglo XIX: el. *Almanaque profético para el año 1866*. *Afro-Hispanic Review* 29 (1): 11–34.

Bergson, Henri. [1911] 1999. *Laughter*. Translated by Cloudesely Brereton and Fred Rothwell. London:Mac Millan.

Butler, Judith. 1997. On Linguistic Vulnerability. In *Excitable Speech. A Politics of the Performative*. New York/London: Routledge.

Carbonell, Walterio. 1961. *Cómo surgió la cultura nacional*. La Habana: Ediciones Yaka.

Castellanos, Lázara. 1991. *Víctor Patricio Landaluze*. La Habana: Editorial Letras Cubanas.

Cepero Bonilla, Raúl. 1948. *Azúcar y abolición. Apuntes para una historia crítica del abolicionismo*. La Habana: Editorial Cénit.

de Certeau, Michel. [1978] 1985. Una variante: La edificación hagiográfica. In *La escritura de la historia*. Translated by Jorge López Monctezuma. México: Universidad Iberoamericana.

Engerman, Stanley, Drescher, Seymour, and Paquette, Robert, eds. 2001. *Slavery*. Oxford/New York: Oxford University Press.

Fabian, Johannes. 2002. *Time and the Other. How Anthropology Makes its Object*. New York: Columbia University Press.

Ferrer, Ada. 1999. *Insurgent Cuba: Race, Nation, and Revolution, 1868-1898*. Chapel Hill/London: University of North Carolina Press.

Fischer, Sibylle. 2004. *Modernity Disavowed. Haiti and the Cultures of Slavery in the Age of Revolution*. Durham/London: Duke University Press.

Fraunhar, Alison. 2008. *Marquillas cigarreras cubanas*: Nation and Desire in the Nineteenth Century. *Hispanic Research Journal* 9 (5): 458–78.

González Echevarría, Roberto. 2010. *Cuban Fiestas*. New Haven: Yale University Press.

Hartman, Saidiya. 1997. *Scenes of Subjection. Terror, Slavery, and Self-Making in Nineteenth-century America*. New York/Oxford: Oxford University Press.

Helg, Aline. 1995. *Our Rightful Share. The Afro-Cuban Struggle for Equality, 1886-1912*. Chapel Hill/London: University of North Carolina Press.

Johnson, John. 1980. Marketing Mulâtresses in Agustino Brunias' west Indian scenes. In *Latin America in Caricatures*. Austin: University of Texas Press.

Kriz, Kay Dian. 2008. *Slavery, Sugar and the Culture of Refinement. Picturing the British West Indies, 1700-1840*. New Haven/London: Yale University Press.

Kutzinsky, Vera. 1993. *Sugar Secrets. Race and the Erotics of Cuban Nationalism*. Charlottesville/London: University of Virginia Press.

La Gráfica Política del 98. n.d. Extremadura, España: CEXCI, Junta de Extremadura, Consejo de Cultura y Patrimonio.

Lane, Jill. 2005. *Blackface Cuba*. Philadelphia: University of Pennsylvania Press.

Lapique Becalí, Zoila. 2002. *La memoria en las piedras*. La Habana: Ediciones Boloña.

Lugo-Ortiz, Agnes. 1999. *Identidades imaginadas: Biografía y nacionalidad en el horizonte de la guerra (Cuba 1860-1898)*. Río Piedras: Editorial de la Universidad de Puerto Rico.

Madelénat, Daniel. 1984. *La biographie*. Paris: PUF.

Madrazo, Feliza. 1999. *'Ni chicha ni limonada.' Depictions of the Mulatto Woman in Cuban Tobacco Art*. Albuquerque: The University of New Mexico Research Paper Series No. 34.

Mañach, Jorge. [1928] 1991. *La crisis de la alta cultura en Cuba: indagación del choteo*. Miami: Ediciones Universal.

Martínez-Alier, Verena. 1974. *Marriage, Class, and Colour in Nineteenth-century Cuba: A Study of Racial Attitudes and Sexual Values in a Slave Society*. Cambridge: Cambridge University Press.

McClintock, Anne. 1995. *Imperial Leather. Race, Gender and Sexuality in the Colonial Contest*. New York/London: Routledge.

Méndez Saavedra, Manuel. 1992. *1898. La Guerra Hispanoamericana en caricaturas/ The Spanish American War in Cartoons*. San Juan: Comisión Puertorriqueña para la Celebración del Quinto Centenario del Descubrimiento de América y Puerto Rico.

Moreno Fraginals, Manuel. 1970. Desgarramiento azucarero e integración nacional. *Casa de las Américas* XI (62): 6–22.

Muñoz del Monte, Francisco. [1845] 1981. La mulata. In *Poesía afroantillana y negrista (Puerto Rico, República Dominicana, Cuba)*, edited by Jorge Luis Morales. Río Piedras: Editorial de la Universidad de Puerto Rico.

Núñez Jiménez, Antonio. 1985. *Cuba en las marquillas cigarreras del siglo XIX /Cuba as Portrayed in 19th-Century Cigarettes Lithographs/Cuba dans les lithographies de cigarettes au XIXe Siécle*. La Habana: Ediciones Turísticas de Cuba.

Núñez Jiménez, Antonio. n.d. *El libro del tabaco*. Nuevo León, México: Pulsar Internacional.

Núñez Jiménez, Antonio. 1989. *Marquillas cigarreras cubanas*. España: Ediciones Tabapress.

Ortiz, Fernando. [1920] 1993. La fiesta afrocubana del Día de Reyes. In *Etnia y sociedad*. La Habana: Editorial de Ciencias Sociales.

Ortiz, Fernando. [1921] 1993. Los cabildos afrocubanos. In *Etnia y sociedad*. La Habana: Editorial de Ciencias Sociales.

Ramos, Evelyn Carmen. 2010. A Painter of Cuban Life: Víctor Patricio de Landaluze and Nineteenth-century Cuban Politics. PhD diss., University of Chicago.

Rosenthal, Angela, and Agnes Lugo-Ortiz. 2012. Envisioning Slave Portraiture. In *Slave Portraiture in the Atlantic World*, edited by Agnes Lugo-Ortiz, and Angela Rosenthal. Cambridge: Cambridge University Press.

Scott, Rebecca. 1985. *Slave Emancipation in Cuba*. Princeton: Princeton University Press.

Sklodowska, Elzbieta. 2009. *Espectrosy espejismps. Haití en el imaginario cubano*. Madrid/Frankfurt: Iberoamericana/Vervuert.

Villaverde, Cirilo. [1882] 2001. *Cecilia Valdés*. edited by jean Lamore. Madrid: Cátedra.

Villaverde, Cirilo. [1882] 2005. *Cecilia Valdés*, edited by Sibylle Fischer. Translated by Helen Lane. Oxford/New York: Oxford University Press.

Freya Schiwy

INDIGENOUS MEDIA AND THE END OF THE LETTERED CITY

What can indigenous media – the booming production of documentaries, docudramas, fictions, and community television by indigenous movement organizations – contribute to understanding the logic of power and representation in the age of multiculturalism? Do indigenous media contribute to the 'decline and fall of the lettered city' (Franco, 2002)? While the concept of the *lettered city* is well known to those working on Latin American literature and culture, perhaps, given the limited circulation of scholarship produced in Spanish, it has had less resonance in the wider subaltern studies debate. The late Uruguayan literary critic Angel Rama had coined the term in order to denote a continuity in the collusion of power, knowledge and technologies of representation from the colonial period to the present (Rama, 1996). For Rama literacy became an auratic practice sustaining a class of *letrados* (lettered men) who, at the service of the state, controlled the symbolic and discursive production of reality. Their writing incorporated indigenous topics, myths and even language structure into Latin American literature in the twentieth century, thus extending and intensifying those allegorical literary representations that relied on *costumbrista* (local folkloric) elements in the nineteenth century. These literary forms, together with the exercise of literacy, created a national imaginary that negotiated ethnic and class differences of colonial origin.[1] Rama traces the transformations of the lettered class from the conquest to modernity, showing, in particular, how in the nineteenth century the apparent democratization of literacy served the bureaucratic needs of the newly independent states. In this view the lettered city has continuously re-created intellectual elites whose practice seeks to discipline a mostly illiterate population, while at the same time coming to rely on an increasing public readership that allows for the profession of the writer.

As a critical concept the lettered city has primarily compelled literary and cultural studies scholars. Julio Ramos' *Divergent modernities* (2001), for instance, challenges Rama's thesis on the grounds that literature, particularly in the nineteenth century, served as much to challenge and subvert state power as it did to imagine and inscribe *mestizaje* – cultural and biological miscegenation – as its civilizing project.[2] Even for those more explicitly arguing from subaltern studies, such as John Beverley, the concept of the lettered city has remained bound to literature, becoming most productive when thinking about challenges to the literary institution through hybrid genres such as the *testimonio* (1999: 4–8). Ultimately, this link to the literary is one of the major reasons why, more recently and in light of the increasing importance of film and television, some argue that the term has begun to lose its critical relevance. As Jean Franco (2002) suggests, the persuasive logic of the lettered city has ceased to explain the present. The literary institutions have disintegrated and alphabetic literacy seems to be losing importance in the face of new technologies. More importantly, the notion of the lettered city cannot grapple with the dominance of global multicultural markets and the expansion of mass media. Jesús Martín-Barbero (1998: 257–333) argues for mass media's new democratic potential where the people's ideas and desires find expression. Néstor García Canclini, although adamantly defending the importance of the nation-state, places his hope for civil society in consumer choice, that is in the consumption of urban cultural expressions such as rock music, comics and videos (2001:151).

When placing Rama's study in dialogue with indigenous media, however, two key notions entailed in the lettered city open up, requiring closer attention. First, reading indigenous media against the lettered city suggests considering Rama's argument in terms of literacy (not merely literature) constituting a hegemonic technology through which both the exercise of power and its contestation are enacted. The lettered city thus retains a quality akin to Foucault's notion of capillary power, that is, as a technological site where power congeals as a result of dominance and contestation. Second, as I will show below, the opposition between literate and oral cultures that underlies Rama's own literary discourse and much of the critical engagement with Rama's thesis appears more unstable than at first sight. Ultimately, I suggest, current media practices by indigenous movement organizations push us toward refining our understanding of literary and audiovisual media as similarly constituted technologies of representation. They appear linked rather than opposed. This coherence, on the other hand, demands questioning the implicit teleology underlying the notion of a world-historical progression from oral to literate cultures to those shaped by the proliferation of audiovisual and digital technologies. Instead we continue to live a struggle over power and representation that still has colonial contradictions at its heart.

Decolonizing the soul

If Rama's thesis on power and technology has had limited circulation, indigenous media, despite their increasing proliferation, may be similarly unfamiliar to those outside Native American studies and visual anthropology. The production of indigenous film and video has been booming during the past 10 years with films such as the US production *Smoke Signals* (1998) and the Canadian feature *Atanarjuat, The Fast Runner* (2001) achieving box-office success. Aboriginal video and community television in Australia, documentaries by the Chiapas Media Project (a US-based solidarity organization that promotes video production in the Mexican state of Chiapas), the Brazilian Video in the Villages, CEFREC-CAIB's award-winning docudramas and fiction shorts[3] and other such initiatives are similarly reaching ever-wider audiences. The films are seen at indigenous film and video festivals in Latin America, Canada and the USA, and they are regionally distributed among rural communities. Members of rural indigenous communities – men and women such as Julia Mosúa, Lucila Lema, Carmen Vitonás, Marcelina Cárdenas, Alfredo Copa, Patricio Luna, Jesús Tapia, Marcelino Pinto, and urban migrants such as Reynaldo Yujra, Juan José García, and many others – have been training as audiovisual communicators and are now primarily in charge of the production of indigenous media. They create the scripts, wield the cameras, act, edit and post-produce the films in a collective process that also includes using non-indigenous advisers such as Iván Sanjinés, Guillermo Monteforte,

Vincent Carelli, and the cameraman César Pérez, among others. Most of these advisers are members of CLACPI, an organization of independent filmmakers (both indigenous and non-indigenous) who began organizing training workshops and international festivals in Latin America in 1985.[4] While there are many localized efforts – such as the production of video by the Colombian Regional Indigenous Council of the Cauca, CRIC (*Consejo Regional Indígena del Cauca/Regional indigenous council of the Cauca*) that has incorporated video into its bilingual education programme – many indigenous media are increasingly networked, communicating diverse indigenous populations.

Bolivia and the transnational Amazon region is one of the most dynamic sites for indigenous audiovisual communication in Latin America, due to the initiatives of indigenous communicators from different cultures and rural communities who formed CAIB in 1996. Together with CEFREC, a non-profit organization that was also the headquarters of CLACPI until 2005, this multiethnic group of indigenous communicators has created a vast, ongoing audiovisual production of documentaries, docudramas and a growing number of fiction shorts. Indigenous communicators in Bolivia are also broadcasting documentaries and news programmes on community television, and CEFREC-CAIB's 30-minute news programme *Entre Culturas/Between Cultures* has been airing on Bolivia's National Television station (Canal 7). The success of CEFREC-CAIB's films at festivals and in the rural communities is without doubt due to the continuous training and reflection process in which the communicators have been taking part. This process follows the parameters set up in the 1996 'Indigenous People's National Plan for Audiovisual Communication of the Indigenous Peoples of Bolivia'. The plan is based on an agreement between CEFREC, CAIB and the major indigenous and peasant union organizations in Bolivia. It is independent of the Bolivian state, but national, even supranational, in its reach and ambition. In a progressively expanding and diversifying effort CEFREC and CAIB have created communication networks among villages in five of Bolivia's seven departments as well as in the transnational Amazon basin. The network allows for a process of intercultural reflection as indigenous facilitators circulate multimedia packages containing fictions and documentaries on DVD and VHS tapes as well as radio shows on CD on a regular basis. So-called facilitators (members of CAIB) screen these productions in the villages and guide community discussions (Schiwy 2003; Himpele 2004; CEFREC 2005b).

International institutions – such as the Spanish Agency for International Cooperation (AECI), the Bask NGO Mugarik Gabe, and the Dutch foundation SEPHIS (South-South Exchange Programme for Research on the History of Development) – have supported this process financially in the name of fostering multiculturalism and human rights. They have handed out grants for specific elements of the Indigenous Peoples' National Plan, such as for the creation of a Latin American indigenous video archive, for the first five-year training plan, and for the community television pilot project in Bolivia's Alto Beni region. While international backers emphasize the notion of multiculturalism, the video makers embrace the term less wholeheartedly. While making use of the global currency of the term, indigenous communicators also agree with indigenous social movements that multiculturalism risks reducing the process of strengthening indigenous culture to a superficial commodification of diversity that is utterly compatible with neo-liberal capitalism. The critique of neoliberal reforms has recently brought down two presidents in Bolivia and contributed to the election of the Aymara Evo Morales as the region's first indigenous head of state. The communicators organized in CAIB favour the term 'intercultural' as they work to create the conditions for multi-ethnic inter-indigenous communication where alternative forms of development can be imagined. Crucial to this process is the revalorization of indigenous cultures and traditions of transmitting knowledge that have been subalternized throughout a long colonial history and continue to be considered markers of superstition, the premodern or, at best, as folkloric tourist attractions. Video makers, like the indigenous organizations they are associated with, work to create a new self-confidence from which to pressure national governments to think about and negotiate alternatives to the global neo-liberal market paradigm by thinking precisely from indigenous cultural traditions, ethics and ways of knowing.

In the intercultural discussion process that audiovisual communication enables, video makers, their communities and their indigenous audiences critically reassess the thinking that devalues indigenous traditions and ways of life as backward and prone to disappear.[5] Since the expanding reach of state education continues to disseminate such ideas through the canon of literary works and social studies, video responds to an urgent need, felt by many in the communities, to redress this influence. Indigenous media production hence challenges the ideological products of the lettered city, particularly the guidelines of nation building that literature helped to map out in the nineteenth and twentieth century. Through literary and other forms of alphabetic writing, Rama argued, elites have not only imagined communities but also performed the integration of illiterate masses into the projects of nation-building and colonial rule before that (1996: 66–73). Instead of mestizaje and transculturation toward a nation modelled on Europe and North America,[6] indigenous communicators like the social movement organizations they are allied with, in contrast, explore possibilities of 'indianizing the white man' (*indianizar al q'ara*), as the Aymara politician Felipe Quispe, el Mallku, once put it (Sanjinés 2004: 165).

Building on a longstanding tradition of community radio, indigenous communicators are, at the same time, reshaping the representation of indigenous people in mass media. Rather than address the reading and cinema-going upper and middle classes of the urban centres that literature and cinema have primarily engaged, CAIB's video distribution network (*RED*) has focused on communicating to rural audiences. These communities have lived diverse histories of contact with colonial and postcolonial state power as well as with television media. Some villages do not have electricity but may run one or more television sets on generators, others have full access to electricity and mass media. Many members of these communities travel to urban centres where they are also exposed to television, pirated and legal DVDs, and the ubiquitous VHS streaming on cross-country buses. Alexandra Halkin, founding director of the Chiapas Media Project, and Amalia Cordova from the National Museum of the American Indian in the USA put it succinctly:

> Indigenous communities are often on the frontline of corporate globalization and government efforts to privatize natural resources. Rarely does mainstream media address scenes of inequality so prevalent in these communities. When they do, they present the people as stuck in poverty and unable to draw on their own communities and cultures. Alternatively, media representations often include romantic portrayals and superficial analyses of culture. Through silence and misrepresentation, mainstream media contributes to economic injustice and lack of respect toward indigenous communities. (Halkin and Córdova 2004: 1) (1)

In other words, faced with a world that denigrates indigenous culture or commodifies diversity as folkloric tourist attractions without letting go of entrenched ethnic stereotyping and without seriously addressing the social and political injustice that has resulted from colonialism, indigenous communicators and their audiences critically examine the resources of indigenous cultural traditions.

Close-up

Some of CEFREC-CAIB's videos address racism and discrimination through intimate personalized stories. In the drama *Angeles de la Tierra/Angeles of the Earth* (2001), for example, a young Quechua goes to the city Cochabamba in search of his brother who had migrated there as a young boy only to find him having renounced his indigenous ethnicity and denying the youngster any help in time of need. *Yawar Mallku/Blood of the Condor* (1969) had compellingly addressed the problem of cultural alienation, concluding with the return of the prodigal son to his native community in order to lead an armed revolution. *Angeles de la tierra*, in contrast, ends with a question mark; the protagonist dies in deep regret but there is no militant solution. Most indigenous videos, however, eschew the realist exploration of the 'Indian problem' that dominated so-called *indigenista* literature and cinematography in the twentieth century. The films are both aesthetically and arguably a far cry from testimonial third cinema. Most of CEFREC-CAIB's fiction films produced in the late 1990s – such as *Qati Qati/Whispers of Death* (1999), *El Espíritu de la Selva/Forest Spirit* (1998) or *El Oro Maldito/Cursed Gold* (1999) – frame *cuentos* (traditional stories) that are set in daily village life and filmed in geographically and culturally very distinct indigenous communities. The films attest to a process of *decolonizing the soul*, that is, the need to counteract the self-denigrating reaction to colonial racism at the heart of the communities.[7] These low-budget videos

FIGURE 1 Pedro Gutiérrez and Ofelia Condori in *Qati Qati*. Production still. Image courtesy of **CEFREC**, Bolivia.

FIGURE 2 Pedro Gutiérrez and the Flying Head in *Qati Qati*. Video still. Image courtesy of **CEFREC**, Bolivia.

seek to redress the colonial subalternization of an order of knowledge that is based on a combination of storytelling, the embodied transmission of knowledge and the visual.

A closer look at the prized short *Qati Qati/Whispers of Death* may help to explain what I mean.[8] *Qati Qati* is a key example of the video makers' effort to 'recuperate'

FIGURE 3 Pedro Gutiérrez in *Qati Qati*. Video still. Image courtesy of **CEFREC**, Bolivia.

indigenous culture (CEFREC, 2005a, n.p.). It also challenges the conceptual division between orality and literacy. This 35-minute short narrates the story of Fulo (Pedro Cornello Gutiérrez), who no longer believes in the traditional myths, stories and ethical values of his community. His wife tries to convince him and their children of the relevance of these traditions. She dies at the end, converted into a rolling head, a *qati qati*. This plot is parallel to another apparently unconnected story about a robbery. Although the video makers exploit editing conventions that implicate the protagonist Fulo by cross-cutting from close-ups of his face to scenes where the robbery is discussed, he is innocent and not linked to the crime. In fact, Fulo's innocence is never overtly questioned and does not form part of either story, that of his wife Valentina's (Ofelia Condori) death or that of the robbery. Instead, the *chullpa* (ancestral mummy) consulted by the elders reveals a young man and minor character in the film as the culprit. The two narrative strands in this complexly layered short are, however, linked, though – at least for this viewer – in a surprising way.

The video's central scene depicts a dream where the protagonist approaches a mountain stream and prepares to take a bath. He laughs as a detached head dripping blood floats by and remains unconcerned when a black bird flies overhead. As he sees himself stepping into the ice-cold water, splashing his face and upper body, the water turns to blood. Before he awakens his puzzlement gives way to joy. He happily waves goodbye to his wife who is departing on the back of a truck, the blood-red liner of her bowler-hat mirroring the colour of the stream. This dream scene is key because it provides the missing link that connects the two story lines, which the spectators need to piece together. The dream constitutes a premonition of Valentina's death that should be responded to through a ritual, just as in the case of the robbery. Since Fulo no longer believes, he fails to enact the ritual that would save his wife.[9]

The dream in fact joins several narrative strands. Besides the story of the robbery, there is the main narrative of Fulo's awaking to the power of spirits, and by extension a greater social ethos carried by the *qati qati* myth. This greater ethos becomes apparent in Valentina's actions. One evening when the couple hear a noise outside their hut, Fulo looks around and claims it was nothing. Valentina, however, insists it was a flying head to whom she promises salt and chilli peppers. She then tells a variant of the *qati qati* story to her children, warning them to drink water before going to sleep so their heads do not fly off at night. Fulo, his children, and we as spectators laugh in disbelief. The next day, unfailingly, a neighbour stops by to ask for the condiments (though denying having come around as a *qati qati* the night before). An elder, 'Tata Anselmo' (the actor is not explicitly identified in the credits but is a member of the Comunidad de Ullajsantia where the video was filmed), tells another variant of the story according to which a woman's head can fly off at night, and her braids can get caught in thorny bushes, thus causing her demise. Fulo's second dream visualizes Valentina's death in precisely this manner before he finds her lying in bed lifeless, as the final version of the *qati qati* tale becomes 'real' in the diegetic space.

The structure of the film not only recuperates oral storytelling but corresponds to the braiding of plots called *k'anata* in Aymara storytelling and songs. These oral forms invoke a visual context of transmitting knowledge through weaving (Arnold *et al.*, 1998: 185). Weavings encode epistemic meaning and continue to survive in the Andean highlands as a material form of transmitting knowledge, where women are primarily in charge of producing and 'reading' these woven texts. The anthropologists

Denise Arnold and Juan de Dios Yapita have argued that the subalternization of weaving as a technology of knowledge is based not only on the dominance of written documents or the general pressure of alphabetic writing but also on their very association with the female body within the *ayllus* (indigenous communities) (Arnold and Juan de Dios Yapita, 1996: 376).

Gender and colonial legacies

In many of CEFREC-CAIB's fiction films women protagonists embody the guardians of traditional knowledge and indigenous ethics. Young, able-bodied men, in contrast, confront the dilemma of defining their masculinity in rational terms and within the framework of objective thinking that follows the legacies of rationalism and positivism laid out in the nineteenth century's lettered city. Representing indigenous knowledge as embodied by woman is an ambiguous strategy.[10] On the one hand, such a link inscribes a dual gender essentialism and denies the changing roles and participation of women in indigenous audiovisual communication itself. On the other, the transmission of indigenous culture through the female body attributes new value to the notion of illiterate otherness in the lettered city. Orality is not only racially inscribed but also conceptually associated with femininity. As is well known, in the discourses of colonialism science is associated with a civilized masculinity, and intuition is credited to a romantically constructed idea of femininity. Nature, rural space, oral and indigenous culture is symbolized as female — threatening and out of control, or benign, infantilized and calling for male guidance.

In *Qati Qati* the female-embodied order of knowledge is first ridiculed — as Fulo and his children laugh at Valentina's 'superstitions' — and then revalorized. The film ends with Fulo admitting 'it might be better to believe'. The symbolic and overarching relevance of the *qati qati* story — that is its reference to *ayni* and a reciprocal economy — as well as its means of transmission are put up for debate in the context of community screenings. The film uncovers remaining traces of colonial thinking and opposes an idealized epistemic framework grounded in storytelling, the sacred meanings of mountains and lakes (as Tata Anselmo insists), of textiles (including weaving and *kipus*), and of dreams.[11] Crucially, the representation of the dream — like Valentina's embodied storytelling and the woven structure of the film — also establishes a visual dimension in the transmission of knowledge. The dream's visibility on screen draws attention to the visual character of 'invisible' signs encoded in other forms such as spectres and the symbolic meanings of snakes and black birds that are framed in many other indigenous videos.

To briefly give another example, *El Oro*, an allegorical fiction short that criticizes the US-backed coca eradication in the Bolivian Chapare, features a gold prospector who seeks easy riches (and who symbolizes those who cultivate coca for cocaine production instead of traditional usage) and disregards the local knowledge and way of life that would prevent his death. As this film makes a case for the relevance of a Quechua order of knowledge where dreams, spectres and bad omens in animal form abound, it alludes to principles of a shared pan-indigenous cosmovision. The snake in *El Oro Maldito/Cursed Gold* parallels the black birds in *Qulqi Chaliku/Silver Vest* and in *Llanthupi Munakuy/Loving Each Other in the Shadows*. The devil, a syncretic figure rendered as a plain-clothed elderly man, who seems visible only to the audience and the protagonist, represents the military forces occupying the region. He also reflects the undead made visible in other films such as *Qulqi Chaliku/Silver Vest*. Together these fiction shorts insist on the visual quality of the apparently invisible, which contains an epistemic value, just like the stories, dances, rituals and other oral and embodied ways of transmitting knowledge that are enacted on screen.

By joining embodied storytelling with references to visual and tactile media indigenous media invoke a regime of knowledge transmission that explodes the reigning idea of an oral culture diametrically opposed to the lettered city. Indeed, as I propose in the next section, Rama's overarching study, at least regarding his analysis of the colonial period, itself contains references to the interrelation of literacy and other systems of signs.

The lettered city's visual economy

Instead of understanding literacy as a technology of the intellect (Goody, 1977; Ong, 1982) and as a natural expression of the progress of civilization, for Rama literacy becomes hegemonic through the exercise of power in a global colonial context. Literacy is in the hands of an elite that continuously changes its social make-up, but it is also a hegemonic form of enacting power. In other words, literacy is not only a form of exerting power where lettered elites act in the service of the state; it is also the privileged mode of contesting power where 'any attempt to ward off, defy, or defeat the imposition of writing passes necessarily through writing' (Rama, 2004: 82; my translation).

A key example of such contestations is literary *testimonio* where those marginalized from institutionalized literary, ethnographic and historiographical modes of representation seek to gain a voice, or are sought to be given a voice by sympathetic editors. Yet, as is well known, the *testimonio* has also encountered serious limitations. On the one hand, readers have expected the genre to conform to testimony (telling truth rather than constructing narratives). On the other, although *testimonio* was to destabilize the colonial foundations of literary institutions, it has been incorporated into existing power structures. As John Beverley phrased the problem:

> ... if literature ... was functionally implicated in the formation of both colonial and postcolonial elites in Latin America, then our claim that it was a place where popular voices could find greater and greater expression, that it was a vehicle for cultural democratization, was put into question. (Beverley 1999: 8)

In light of the literary institutions' colonial history and Rama's account of literacy, apparently oral cultures are condemned to working through the pitfalls of these hegemonic forms of representation. Yet Rama's account of the construction of the lettered city also opens up a view on a more varied semiotic arrangement. Rama emphasizes that in the sixteenth century the power of the lettered lies not only in their management of written documents and the law but also in their creation of symbols and graphic diagrams. The colonial powers constructed a sense of inalterable signs in opposition to an apparently ephemeral orality. In one sense, Rama's exploration highlights the colonial construction of modern power/knowledge through literacy. In another, he gives much consideration to the architectural inscription of colonial authority as a city of letters. In Rama's study we glimpse part of a plethora of complex visual representations and bodily performances of authority that accompanied lettered practice. Besides architectural design and urban planning, visual and performative transmissions and contestations of authority included, for example, the creation and display of religious paintings and iconography, the enactment of the *requerimiento* (the ritual of taking possession of the land during the conquest), the use of clothing, etc. (Gruzinsky 2001; Taylor, 2003).

Rama, however, does not elaborate on how orality, as an idea, abstracted from other varied forms of signifying. He disregards visual and performative means of creating and transmitting knowledge in different indigenous cultures. Before the conquest and in a more subdued manner afterwards, such representations were realized through codices, glyphs, knotted *kipus* and weavings, inscriptions of meaning into the landscape, dance and rituals, etc. Diana Taylor has argued that:

> ... the separation that Rama notes between written and spoken word, echoed in de Certeau, points to only one aspect of the repression of indigenous embodied practice as a form of knowing as well as a system for storing and transmitting knowledge. Nonverbal practices — such as dance, ritual, and cooking, to name a few — that long served to preserve a sense of communal identity and memory were not considered valid forms of knowledge. (Taylor, 2003: 18).

The colonial construction of power/knowledge worked through the subalternization of varied and multiple material and embodied forms of signifying. This process of subalternization forms part of the 'coloniality of power', that is the collusion of economic exploitation, Eurocentric discourse, and the oppression of indigenous forms of creating and transmitting knowledge.[12] Indeed, as Brian Street (1984) had already argued in the 1980s, orality has perhaps never existed in a pure form. The teleology that proposes literacy as evolving from orality is flawed, as is the idea that only literacy can enable analytic thought. Even within oral modes there are discourse types and mnemonic devices that impede arbitrary changes to oral 'messages' over time and space (Street, 1984: 48). Oral communication involves as much classificatory intellectual procedures as writing and is, in principal, equally at work in all languages and cultural contexts (1984: 38).

The Spanish colonizers and missionary zealots, to be sure, considered both mimetic and abstract visual and textile representations works of the devil, threatening the religious project of colonialism. Similarly, the roles of the *tlamatinime* and the *amauta*, those trained in reading and performing the knowledge encoded in visual, textile and/or tactile material, were suppressed (Mignolo, 1994; 1995: 69–122). These material forms of signifying, along with bodily enactments and storytelling, are far from ephemeral. They have been transformed in the process of colonialism but have not disappeared (Taylor, 2003: 43). As in *Qati Qati/Whispers of Death* — where the cinematographic horror genre is blended with Andean tales of the walking dead and integrated into oral-visual, tactile and performative Aymara traditions of transmitting knowledge — some of them find their way back into the process of present-day indigenous audiovisual communication. Indigenous social memory and identity continue to be transmitted through the repertoire of embodied performance in rituals and celebrations, in the parodies of colonial history enacted in Andean carnival, but also through the daily embodiment of dress, hairstyle and language use.[13] In the Andes the prevalence of visual and other material forms of transmitting knowledge remains overwhelming. Indigenous communicators and the communities participating in the creation of fiction and documentary films represent and enact these traditions on screen.

Alongside storytelling, song, dance, ritual, kipus, pottery design, etc., indigenous communities transmit knowledge, historical memory and belonging through the meanings they attribute to ruins, to mountains, lakes and *wak'as* (odd-shaped rocks and natural formations). In the case of *Qati Qati/Whispers of Death*, the *chullpa* that solves the robbery, for instance, is not shown as a mummy but as the badlands of an eroded hillside. The lakes, mountains and mother earth (whose power Fulo belittles) are a visual presence in the video that Tata Anselmo calls attention to. Material artefacts and the bodily transmission of knowledge are here intimately connected. In another fiction short, *Qulqi Chaliku/Silver Vest* (1998), postcard-like shots of ruins, the village church, of individuals, animals and of small groups of people in conversation are cross-cut as they create the transition between the action sequences. *Qulqi* constructs an imagery of the Aymara people that relies more heavily on the visual than on dialogue. The visual dimension even seeps into the audio space. The original soundtrack composed for this film creates sound-bites or audio-icons of a particular highland setting. As cultural and geographic markers they situate the video in the much wider inter-indigenous debate that encompasses extremely diverse regions, from the arid high plains of the Andes to the tropical Amazonian lowlands. Similarly, viewers in other regions will recognize the shots of tropical vegetation, bags of coca leaves and ominous tropical snakes in *El Oro Maldito/Cursed Gold* as cultural-geographic markers of the coca-growing Chapare. Like *Qati Qati/Whispers of Death* and *Qulqi Chaliku/Silver Vest*, *El Oro Maldito/Cursed Gold* claims the importance of indigenous traditions and forms of knowing that are transmitted through a combination of storytelling, performance, the visual, tactile and textile forms, etc. Indigenous media expand and vitalize storytelling, performance and visual means of transmitting knowledge by using film technology – an oral, visual and performative medium. Indigenous media hence point to visual and performative forms of signifying as part of what have been designated 'oral' cultures.

The audiovisual medium liberates its users to a large extent from the requirements of literacy and state education. Many fiction shorts privilege images and soundtrack over dialogue; subtitles can be read out loud and interpreted by the facilitators who form part of the distribution network. During production film scripts are often drawn or memorized. Indeed, not all of the video makers and viewers are fully literate. Video thus bypasses the basic social and ethnic heterogeneity that the Peruvian literary critic Antonio Cornejo Polar (1998) spoke of as separating the realms of literary production and consumption from its indigenous referent. At first sight the proliferating use of digital video technology and community television by indigenous organizations (in Australia, New Zealand, North America, and Latin America) might hence be seen as bypassing the paradigm of literacy/literature and contributing to the fall of the lettered city. Upon closer examination, however, indigenous media indicate shortcomings in the concept of the lettered city. In this light, the separation between orality and literacy that the lettered city emphasizes is insufficient for understanding the contestation of power, and not only since the age of mass media. Such a separation disregards the roots of indigenous video in the complex traditions of transmitting and enacting knowledge and social memory. Indigenous forms of transmitting knowledge have been subalternized, but the tale of intellectual progress, encoded in a transition from oral cultures to literacy and technology, is itself a colonial construct. The lettered city's fall appears similarly ambiguous. As indigenous communicators integrate digital technology into pan-indigenous forms of knowledge production, representation, property and exchange they reshape the lettered city's visual economy. They indicate that visual and embodied representations have always accompanied the inscription of literacy as power. At the same time, indigenous-made documentaries and fictions as well as the social practice and economy of video production and diffusion show that, like literacy and literature, visual and audiovisual technologies are not neutral.

Vision and coloniality

In the twentieth century cinema established its own codes of legibility, projecting racial imaginaries rehearsed in nineteenth- and early twentieth-century Andean paintings and photography. Such visual representations formed an important part of the lettered city. Paintings mirrored the imperial vision of early nineteenth-century English and German travellers, who reinvented the Latin American continent as a savage land, emptied of its population and waiting to be civilized by the new European Empires (Pratt, 1992). Photography imbued paintings and drawings, particularly the portable portraits (or *cartes de visite*) that also began to circulate early in the nineteenth century, with a new, seemingly objective and ontological value that supplied scientific racism with its apparent visual proof (Poole, 1997). In her study *Vision, race, and modernity* Deborah Poole deconstructs these images as she reads the *mise-en-scène* and the manipulations of light and shadow against the apparent objectivity of the camera:

> The carte de visite's flattening effect also proved perfect for caricaturing physiognomic traits. Just as artificial lighting could be used (...) to downplay clients' more undesirable facial features, so too could it be made to emphasize the 'deviant' or 'lower-class' features of criminals, peasants, beggars, prostitutes, and 'freaks' portrayed in the commercial cartes de visite. Harsh or direct lighting, for example, could be used to emphasize the high cheekbones and to broaden the noses of Andean Indians. Through such lighting effects, and by removing the subjects' hats and caps to reveal unkempt hair and phrenological contours, it was possible to suggest conformance with ruling physiongnomic defnitions of bandits and other 'criminal types' (Poole 1997: 117-118)

In the early twentieth century, photography also provided the means for visualizing the romanticized image of an Inca past as a blending of Andean and Greek imagery that served to construct a distinct sense of civilization in the Peruvian highlands. Photography helped to redress the discourse of the powerful elites in the coastal capital of Lima who relegated the highlands to the realm of barbarism, associated with the indigenous Quechua-speaking populations. As a powerful technology of representation photography was also coveted by middle-class Quechua families, who performed their class distinction in front of the camera, while seeking to fashion themselves as bourgeois subjects (1997: 168–97).

On a global scale cinema has similarly contributed to the construction of racial otherness by establishing a gaze that is both masculine and imperial. Film became an important means of documenting the colonial experience since the end of the nineteenth century. It has transported images captured by Western travellers in Asia and Africa and built on an imagery first developed centuries earlier in the Americas. It became part of the colonial enterprise, documenting and controlling 'the "primitive" cultures' that missionaries, administrators and the military encountered' (Kaplan, 1997: 61). At the same time, the movies became an important tool for visualizing the tropes and metaphors of conquest and colonization put forth by literary accounts and human exhibitions. Cinema thus helped to spread the enthusiasm for the imperial projects beyond the elites and into the popular strata (Shohat and Robert Stam, 1994: 100). Cinema proposed the centrality of a Eurocentric male gaze; pretending to see objectively, it projected images of colonial power relations, fraught with the anxiety of having the gaze returned, both on screen as well as by parts of the audience (Rony, 1996; Kaplan, 1997).[14]

Hollywood cinema has been a staple for urban audiences in the Andes. Together with home-grown literary and filmic representations Hollywood has shaped the thinking of the lettered elites. Its images also inform the consciousness of indigenous populations. Like literature and photography, film has also been a contested medium. In the 1960s, for instance, anti-colonial filmmakers in Latin America and Africa explored alternative aesthetics and practices of film production and distribution in order to turn cinema into a tool for the revolution. Similarly, indigenous media build on indigenous visual and performative traditions but these films also enter the lettered city's visual economy. Indigenous video makers assert a need to produce their own images in the face of cinema and TV's mainstream production and distribution practices that have inscribed the medium into the archive of the lettered city – whether as bourgeois art form or as a product of industrial cinema permeated by an easily digestible and marketable multicultural content. Production and distribution of audiovisual media, such as cinema and television, are dominated by few global corporations that curtail access and monitor content in terms of its profitability (Miller et al. 2005; Sinclair 1999; Sinclair and Turner, 2004). If the lettered city is indeed built upon not only literacy but also embodied and visual forms of transmitting knowledge, arguments about its demise in the face of mass media are weakened. If visual media have criss-crossed the lettered city, the creation of an audiovisual global marketplace does not render irrelevant the structures of power/knowledge/technology that came into being with the colonial experience. Rather, audiovisual representation demands critical inquiry, particularly in terms of a textual negotiation of the colonial gaze, but also with respect to market compatibility.[15]

Acknowledgements

This article would have been impossible to write without the kind support of members of CAIB (Audiovisual Indigenous Communicators of Bolivia). The author would like to thank particularly Jesús Tapia, Julia Mosúa, Alfredo Copa, Marcelino Pinto, Faustino Peña, and Marcelina Cárdenas; CEFREC (Center for Formation and Training in Cinematography, Bolivia), especially Iván Sanjinés and Reynaldo Yujra. She also appreciates the help of Mario Bustos and Lucila Lema at the CONAIE (Indigenous National Council of Ecuador) and of the staff at the consulate of the CRIC (Indigenous Council of the Cauca) in Bogota, Colombia. Versions of this article have been presented at several universities in the US and Canada. Many thanks are offered for the insightful comments received on each occasion as well as to Walter Mignolo, on the research project as a whole. Jacqueline Loss, Susan Antebi, and anonymous reviewers have offered detailed comments. Thank you. All shortcomings are the author's own.

Notes

1 *Narrative transculturation* generated a modern and progressive literature that incorporated and transformed the vestiges of indigenous oral traditions as well as the regional conservative narrative conventions by putting them into contact with the literature of Joyce and Faulkner, generating thereby a modern homogenous fusion (Rama, 1982). The task, certainly, remained in the hands of the lettered classes (Cornejo Polar, 1998).
2 Julio Ramos, in his recently translated and revised study *Divergent modernities*, details how, in Latin America, the nineteenth century brought about a significant split among the lettered classes that was related to the aesthetics of representation. Ramos shows that state thinkers, such as Faustino Sarmiento whose writings were influential beyond his native Argentina, sought to control orality by converting the voice of a largely illiterate people into literary representation and thereby symbolically enacting the subjection of oral social groups to the educated urban elites. Ramos, however, also indicates that the professionalization of the writer and the subversive strategies of modernist poetry allowed not only for a resistance to positivism in the figure of the *literato* (lettered man), but also for a lettered practice that resisted the state (Ramos, 2001: xliii; 60).
3 CAIB (Coordinadora Audiovisual Indígena de Bolivia) brings together a diverse group of Bolivian indigenous and aboriginal (*originarios*) communicators. They work with CEFREC (Centro de Formación y Realización Cinematográfica), a training centre in cinematography with headquarters in La Paz, Bolivia.
4 CLACPI, the Latin American Council of the Indigenous People's Film and Video (*Consejo latinoamericano del cine y video de los pueblos indígenas*). CLACPI recently renamed itself Coordinadora Latinoamericana del Cine y Video de los Pueblos Indígenas y Originarios.
5 Only after a five-year process of questioning the self-denigrating effects of colonialism are video makers now moving towards creating an intercultural debate with 'national society' (CEFREC, 2005b).
6 John Beverley discussed the difference between transculturation as a project designed by the state in contrast with reverse transculturation or '*transculturación al revés*' (1998: 271) designed by indigenous social movements in the brief essay 'Siete aproximaciones al problema indígena', a comparative study of the drama Ollantay, the Sandinistas, and Rigoberta Menchú's testimonio.
7 The concept of the colonization of the soul borrows from Frantz Fanon's analysis of colonialism in *Black skins, white masks*; it has acquired particular resonance in Bolivia (Rivera Cusicanqui, 1991).
8 *Qati Qati / Whispers of Death* was shot and produced by members of CAIB and CEFREC. Reynaldo Yujra, an Aymara actor and member of CEFREC directed or, as CAIB prefers to phrase it, "is responsible for" the short. The piece has won prizes at international indigenous film and video festivals in Guatemala, Ecuador, Montreal and it has screened at the Native American Film and Video Festival in New York.

9   Many thanks to Reynaldo Yujra for clarifying this aspect. In my conversation with him, Yujra also asserted that indigenous audiences are not at all surprised by this connection.
10 This gendering of tradition is a problem for postcolonial politics, as Partha Chatterjee (1993) and Ann McClintock (1995), among others, have argued for different contexts.
11 During the first years of the Indigenous Peoples' National Plan there were few explicit references to weavings. Male producers and protagonists were privileged and the films resisted more extensively exploring male violence as it appears, for example, in the opening sequence of *Qulqi Chaliku/The Silver Vest* (1998), where the protagonist Satuco (Reynaldo Yujra) physically threatens his wife. With the recently growing attention to gender and women's rights in the communities – as well as in the international arena – CAIB-CEFREC have begun to incorporate the topic of gender and weaving into the diegetic space. A recent documentary by Marcelina Cárdenas compares and investigates weaving and embroidering in highland and lowland cultures. (Thanks to Marcelina Cárdenas and Max Silva for letting me see an almost finalized cut of the documentary in August 2005 in CEFREC's office in La Paz, Bolivia.) At the same time, the film's structure is, like *Qati Qati/Whispers of Death*, modelled on the idea of weaving different threads together. *Llanthupi Munakuy/Loving Each Other in the Shadows* (2001) begins to question indigenous patriarchy itself. The fiction *Venciendo el miedo/Overcoming fear* (2004) directly addresses the issue of women's rights.
12 On the concept of the coloniality of power see Quijano (2000) and Mignolo (2000); as well as Escobar, forthcoming. Coloniality of power does not understand power/knowledge as a product inherent to Europe's modernity. Rather, modernity itself is understood as constituted fundamentally through the colonial experience, beginning with the conquest of the Americas. It involves the construction of racial categories along with epistemic hierarchies or Eurocentrism, as well as deeply unequal and exploitative economic relations.
13 There is much literature on embodied forms of transmitting social memory and indigenous identity (e.g. Dover *et al.*, 1992; Abercrombie, 1998; Harrison, 1989; Taylor, 2003).
14 See also Shohat and Stam (1994, especially chapter 3). Brian Winston (1996) argues that even the development and use of dyeing processes in colour film responded to racist ideas about skin colour and privileged the mimetic rendering of whiteness over blackness. Colour technologies that would have actually recorded the structure of colour and been able to realistically represent hues of white and black were neglected. As Winston summarizes, 'essentially, the research agenda for colour film (and more latterly colour television) was dominated by the need to reproduce Caucasian skin tones' (1996: 39).
15 For a brief exploration of indigenous media's relation to the film market see Schiwy (2005).

References

Abercrombie, Thomas A. 1998. *Pathways of Memory and Power. Ethnography and History Among an Andean People*. Madison: University of Wisconsin Press.
Angeles de la Tierra/Angels of the Earth. 2001. Collective Responsibility. Prod. CEFREC/CAIB. 50 minutes. Distr. CEFREC/CAIB, Bolivia.

Arnold, Denise, and Juan de Dios Yapita. 1996. Los caminos de Qaqachaka. In *Ser mujer indígena, chola o birlocha en la Bolivia postcolonial de los 90*, edited by Silvia Rivera Cusicanqui. La Paz: Ministerio de Desarrollo Humano, Secretaría de Asuntos Etnicos, de Género y Generacionales, Subsecretaría de Asuntos de Género: 303–91.

Arnold, Denise Y., Domingo Jiménez A., and Juan de Dios Yapita. 1998. *Hacia un orden andino de las cosas: Tres pistas de los Andes meridionales*. La Paz: Hisbol/ILCA.

Beverley, John. 1998. "Siete aproximaciones al 'problema indígena'". In *Indigenismo hacia el fin del milenio: Homenaje a Antonio Conejo-Polar*, edited and introduced by Mabel Moraña. Pittsburgh, PA: Instituto Internacional de Literatura Iberoamericana. 269–83.

Beverley, John. 1999. *Subalternity and representation: Arguments in cultural theory*. Durham: Duke University Press.

CEFREC 2001. Home page. Available from http://videoindigena.bolnet.bo; INTERNET (accessed 15 September 2001).

CEFREC 2005a. Componentes. Available from http://videoindigena.bolnet.bo/plan2.htm; INTERNET (accessed 13 January 2005).

CEFREC 2005b. Plan nacional. Available from http://videoindigena.bolnet.bo/plan1.htm; INTERNET (accessed 13 January 2005).

Chatterjee, Partha. 1993. *The nation and its fragments: Colonial and postcolonial histories*. Princeton, NJ: Princeton University Press.

Cornejo Polar, Antonio. 1998. 'Indigenismo' and heterogeneous literatures: their dual socio-cultural logic, introduction and translated by John Kraniauskas. *Journal of Latin American Cultural Studies* 7 (1): 13–27.

Dover, Robert V. H., Katharine E. Seibold, and John H. McDowell eds. 1992. *Andean cosmologies through time: Persistence and emergence*. Bloomington: Indiana University Press.

Escobar, Arturo. Forthcoming. *Hybrid nature: Cultural and biological diversity at the dawn of the twenty-first century*. Durham, NC: Duke University Press.

Espíritu de la Selva, el/The Forest Spirit. 1999. Responsible Faustino Peña. Prod. CEFREC-CAIB. 25 minutes. Distr. CEFREC, Bolivia.

Fanon, Frantz. 1967. *Black Skin, White Masks* [1952] Transl. Charles Lam Markmann. Grove Press.

Franco, Jean. 2002. *The decline and fall of the lettered city: Latin America in the Cold War*. Cambridge, MA and London: Harvard University Press.

García Canclini, Néstor. 2001. *Consumers and citizens: Globalization and multicultural conflicts*, introduction and translated by George Yúdice. Minneapolis and London: University of Minnesota Press.

Goody, J. 1977. *The domestication of the savage mind*. Cambridge: Cambridge University Press.

Gruzinsky, Serge. 2001. *Images at war: Mexico from Columbus to blade runner (1492–2019)*, translated by Heather Maclean. Durham, NC and London: Duke University Press.

Halkin, Alexandra and Amalia Córdova. 2004. "Red de Iniciativas Por el Video Indígena Latinoamericano (RIVIL)/Latin American Indigenous Video Initiative (LAIVI)." Typescript.

Harrison, Regina. 1989. *Signs, songs, and memory in the Andes: Translating Quechua language and culture*. Austin: University of Texas Press.

Himpele, Jeff. 2004. Packaging indigenous media: an interview with Ivan Sanjinés and Jesús Tapia. *American Anthropologist* 106 (2): 354–63.

Llanthupi Munakuy/Loving Each Other in the Shadows. 2001. Resp. Marcelina Cárdenas. Prod. CEFREC-CAIB. Distr. CEFREC/CAIB, Bolivia.

Kaplan, E. Ann. 1997. *Looking for the other: Feminism, film, and the imperial gaze*. New York: Routledge.

Martín-Barbero, Jesús. 1998. *De los medios a las mediaciones*. Bogotá: Convenio Andrés Bello.

McClintock, Ann. 1995. *Imperial leather: Race, gender, and sexuality in the colonial conquest*. New York: Routledge.

Mignolo, Walter D. 1994. Afterword: writing. In *Writing without words*, edited by Elizabeth Hill Boone and Walter Mignolo. Durham, NC: Duke University Press, 293–313.

Mignolo, Walter D. 1995. *The darker side of the renaissance. Literacy, territoriality and colonization*. Ann Arbor: Michigan University Press.

Mignolo, Walter D. 2000. *Local histories/global designs: Coloniality, subaltern knowledges and border thinking*. Princeton, NJ: Princeton University Press.

Miller, Toby et al. 2005. *Global Hollywood 2*. London: BFI.

Ong, Walter. 1982. *Orality and literacy: The technologizing of the word*. London: Methuen.

Oro Maldito, el/Cursed Gold. 1999. Resp. Marcelino Pinto. Prod. CEFREC-CAIB (Santa Cruz). 35 minutes. Distr. CEFREC, Bolivia.

Poole, Deborah. 1997. *Vision, race, and modernity: A visual economy of the Andean image world*. Princeton, NJ: Princeton University Press.

Pratt, Mary Louise. 1992. *Imperial eyes: Travel writing and transculturation*. London and New York: Routledge.

Qati Qati/Whispers of Death. 1999. Resp. Reynaldo Yujra. Prod. CEFREC-CAIB (La Paz). 35 minutes. Distr. CEFREC, Bolivia.

Quijano, Aníbal. 2000. Coloniality of power, eurocentrism, and Latin America. *Nepantla. Views from the South* 1 (3): 533–80.

Qulqi Chaliku/The Silver Vest. 1998. Resp. Patricio Luna. Prod. CEFREC-CAIB (La Paz). Fiction. 25 minutes. Distr. CEFREC, Bolivia.

Rama, Angel. 1996. *The lettered city*, edited and translated by John Charles Chasteen. Durham: NC Duke University Press.

Rama, Angel. 1982. *La transculturación narrativa en América Latina*. Mexico: Siglo XXI.

Rama, Angel. [1984] 2004. *La Ciudad Letrada*. Prologue by Carlos Monsiváis. Chile: Tajamar Editores.

Ramos, Julio. 2001. *Divergent modernities: Culture and politics in nineteenth-century Latin America*, translated by John D. Blanco. Durham, NC and London: Duke University Press.

Rivera Cusicanqui, Silvia. 1991. *Pachakuti: los aymara de Bolivia frente a medio milenio de colonialismo*. Chukiyawu: THOA.

Rodowick, D. N. 2001. Dr. Strange Media; or, how I learned to stop worrying and love film theory. *PMLA* 116 (5): 1396–404.

Rony, Fatimah Tobing. 1996. *The Third Eye. Race, Cinema, and Ethnographic Spectacle*. Durham: Duke UP.

Sanjinés, Javier. 2004. *Mestizaje upside-down: Aesthetic politics in modern Bolivia*. Pittsburgh, PA: University of Pittsburgh Press.

Schiwy, Freya. 2003. Decolonizing the frame. Indigenous video in the Andes. *Framework*, 44 (1): 116–32.

Schiwy, Freya. 2005. La Otra Mirada: Video Indígena y Descolonización. *Miradas. Revista del audiovisual 8*. [Online] Available from http://www.miradas.eictv.co.cu/index.php

Shohat, Ella, and Robert Stam. 1994. *Unthinking eurocentrism: Multiculturalism and the media.* London and New York: Routledge.

Sinclair, Jonathan. 1999. Latin American Television. A Global View. Oxford, New York: Oxford UP.

Sinclair, Jonathan and Graeme Turner, eds. 2004. *Contemporary World Television.* London: BFI.

Street, Brian V. 1984. *Literacy in theory and practice.* Cambridge, London, New York, New Rochelle, Melbourne and Sydney: Cambridge University Press.

Taylor, Diana. 2003. *The archive and the repertoire: Performing cultural memory in the Venciendo el miedo/Overcoming fear.* 2004. Resp. María Morales. Prod. and Distr. CEFREC-CAIB, Bolivia.

Taylor, Diana. 2003. *The Archive and the Repertoire. Performing Cultural Memory in the Americas.* Durham: Duke UP.

Winston, Brian. 1996. *Technologies of seeing: Photography, cinematography, and television.* London: BFI.

Ivana Bentes

SUBJECTIVE DISPLACEMENTS AND 'RESERVES OF LIFE'[1]

Morrinho, a 300m^2 maquette in the Favela do Pereirão, Rio de Janeiro, is an *al fresco* miniature duplicate of the favela itself forming an impressive construction of clay, painted bricks, recycled material and chicken wire. It is a chaos-construction of houses, streets, miniature cars, street lamps, and sundry objects: an impressive jumble. Moreover, this giant-miniature-model is inhabited by locals and visitors, little figurines made from blocks of LEGO and moved by the hands of their creators.

And in addition to this impressive architecture, life in the favela is re-created, re-signified through toys: miniature cars, a LEGO armoured police van, a LEGO motor-taxi, a LEGO storyteller (*mestre* Renato), LEGO street urchins, LEGO housewives, a complete LEGO samba school, a LEGO drug dealer, a LEGO cop, and even a LEGO artist, a LEGO Saci Pererê (a traditional Brazilian folk hero), and miniature versions of toy dinosaurs from the newspaper stand. In short, it is an entire life-world, but one that does not simply reproduce a state of things, but is itself full of virtualities. It grew out of an innocent and original children's game, started in 1998 by Nelcirlan Souza de Oliveira in his backyard when he was fourteen.

Seven more kids joined in the game and they were to give life to the micro-community coming into existence in Nelcirlan's backyard. The game was so intense that it took over the boys' lives, every one of them playing out different characters/LEGO puppets, giving them a voice, a unique style and attitude, making them up as they went along.

The maquette of Morrinho became a tourist attraction in Pereirão – it was featured on the popular television show *Domingão do Faustão*, toured in Germany, Austria, etc. – and perhaps it would have turned into yet another sightseeing curiosity (along with the sand sculptures on the beach and Favela Tourism in Rocinha) if the project had not evolved into TV Morrinho, a series of mini-films in which the boys themselves document the stories, games and dramas of their community of LEGO puppets. Afterwards, TV Morrinho expanded into NGO Morrinho, and within that there are projects such as Morrinho Exhibition, Morrinho Social Club, etc.

The fascination with the maquette/scenario, the art-game, the documentary of the lives/fictions of the LEGO puppets and their creators, led to the project's selection for the 52nd Venice Biennale, in 2006. The favela-maquette was transported and re-built in the gardens of the Biennale in Italy.

For those who know the project, this is all very impressive, but the specific question that concerns us here is the transmutation of life into language, of their fusion. How did a game played by favela boys transform something without value, that is, idle time, stolen moments before and after school, between one chore and the next, into value, beauty, work-in-action, mobilizing the entire lives of these boys?

This transmutation of life into language, this turning point in the trajectory, occurred when the stories that were being invented and played out in the backyard, where everyone played the part of a LEGO character, investing it with time, subjectivity, a voice and gestures, started to be documented/fictionalized by the boys themselves, resulting in remarkable micro-films: fictional documentaries or documentaries of their fabulations.

The videos in TV Morrinho (*Saci in Morrinho, Peri's Swimming Pool, Samba School of Morrinho I and II, The Revolt of the Puppets*) last only for a few minutes and are all shot in the maquette. They dissolve the border between documentary and fiction, effectively functioning as a form of auto-ethnography, inventing daily life, fictionalizing reality, an existential game.

The aesthetics of these micro-films interests me as a point of departure for an initial mapping and analysis of documentaries produced outside the corporate sphere (the 'professionals'): that is, documentaries emerging from the periphery produced by amateurs and non-professionals, by youngsters from vocational schools for cinema and audiovisual arts, by the urban 'precariat', in workshops that are springing up everywhere in the country.

These questions are not exactly new. It suffices to take a brief look at the history of cinema, at the fascination for the banality/singularity of the everyday in early cinema: scenes of street life showing passers-by and curious people, their reactions in front of the camera, crowds standing in front of shop windows or strolling by, or else absorbed in their work, as in the descriptions by Benjamin and Baudelaire. Or take Vertov's city as a 'factory of facts,' Eisenstein's mass-subject of History, *cinéma vérité* and Direct Cinema, Jean Rouch's disquiet in the face of otherness, Godard's anti-heroes, and so forth up to the contemporary context of modern Brazilian cinema.

These are distinct problems and moments in the history of cinema, which we shall not explore in any detail here: rather we will merely highlight some recurrent concerns: the conceptual fragility of the search for and affirmation of 'social identities,' and the insufficiency of theories of social representation in accounting for the uniqueness of life-languages (*vidas-linguagens*).

The question, then, is not to fetishize the production of those other subjects of discourse, related to the territories of poverty, niches and ghettos (which very often reproduce dominant clichés and aesthetics). Nor is it a matter of marking these productions with the stamp of 'authenticity' or authority, (as in the affirmative discourses of identity and group legitimation that fall into the trap of 'essentialism' in their quest for ready-made identities), which are more or less common currency in the marketplace of culture and often merely produce new 'clichés' and discourses of truth.

The surprising thing about TV Morrinho's micro-films is that they restore and transfigure the 'commonplace' – not merely the 'state of things' and the banality of daily life – in all its lyricism and/or brutality. They also act out the media discourse that has contaminated contemporary Brazilian cinema with films that are often merely replicas-maquettes of 'common sense', duplicating exhausted and de-potentialized social matrices.

Although the films of TV Morrinho also make use of ready-made discourse (and a certain disconcerting infantilism), they are nonetheless crisscrossed with life-languages. Here we can see the emergence of new qualities and singularities that are capable of potentializing the poverty of discourse and that of the settings and scenery, which become exuberant in their imaginative miniaturization, bringing out richness in poverty. Here is a *bios* turned into aesthetics and language, breaking through and mortally wounding the very clichés that might occasionally find their way into the stories.

The question is of interest if we want to tackle and think about those 'out-of-place' audio-visual productions that come to us from alternative territories and subjects, and that carry with them a political-aesthetic potential. They are, we might say, capable of constituting a *bio-aesthetics* that we can attempt to define by a question: *What are the aesthetic possibilities that these lives enclose?* Or simply: *What are the possible becomings, the potential transformations they can undergo?*

The surprising thing, then, about these videos and films from the 'outside' – not only from the favela and its characters, but from the maquette of the favela where life is documented and fictionalized – is their capacity to produce aesthetic values, style, and subjective modulations, as well as sensibilities and spaces where relations unfold along with the struggle for and production of power (bio-politics).

The force of those micro-films lies in the tension between the colourful, vital and rough setting/maquette and the lives of the LEGO puppets (which are visibly being moved by the boys' hands, while their voices originate off-screen). What is surprising is the life-aesthetic, the language that is born from the confrontation between, on the one hand, the different elements of the maquette and the LEGO characters, and, on the other hand, the voices, hands and gestures of the boys who narrate their own lives.

The first time I saw these doc-fables, I was moved by their uniqueness and ambiguity. There was a certain lack of measure, an incommensurable quality apparent in the explicit life-language of these fictitious mini-documentaries. In 'Saci in Morrinho' (made for the Nickelodeon channel in 2007), the LEGO character *Mestre* Renato tells the tale of a disturbing incarnation of the one-legged folk urchin Saci Pererê who moves into the favela of Morrinho. Here Saci is a sinister, hollow-voiced figure, full of slang and gangster-talk, who frightens and punishes a favela thief given to stealing sweets from children. The tales merge childhood and childishness with the day-to-day characters of Morrinho.

The video starts with a child in the favela humming a song when an older boy accosts him ('Yo, shrimp! Gimme your sweets, they're mine now! Gimme your sweets unless you wanna feel my knuckles on your head') and ends with a righteous Saci thrashing him, forcing him to behave. Brazilian and urban folklore are cross-contaminated and merge into amoral narratives and tales that are shot through with images from the wider world – the cinema, the media – as in the story about the invasion of the favela by dinosaurs, with its soundtrack of shrill voices, roars, shouts and confusion.

That mixture of infantile games and 'naïve' pranks – punctuated by cruelty and violence in the gestures and voices that animate the settings, the characters and objects – creates a life that transcends the 'state of things' and the clichés about favelas, violence and drugs.

We are not being given information here. Instead, the fairy-tale register of the narrators (who are responsible for the voices of the puppets) and the footage shot by the kids of TV Morrinho, which is incorporated in the game (the camera plays an 'active' part), stage a series of tensions.

In 'The Revolt of the Puppets' (2008), made by TV Morrinho and NGO Morrinho, the tensions between the real and the fictional reach a sophisticated meta-linguistic level when the LEGO puppets discover that the boys, who give them their voices, are going to travel to the Venice Biennale without taking them along. They start a rebellion in Morrinho (the maquette) demanding to be allowed to accompany their creators to Italy.

In the middle of a shoot-out scene in the maquette, complete with an armoured police van, BOPE special forces units, gun shots, confusion and threats, the puppets rebel and stop the scene when they find out that the boys are going to go abroad without them. They stop the scene to question their own status as 'toys/workers' as opposed to the world of the artists/creators, the active work of the stories' authors versus the passive work of the puppets who stay behind 'dossing around' while the boys are travelling. The puppets act in threatening fashion, with protests and strikes. They clear the stage, thus creating a space devoid of life: an exodus, a desertion (fleeing as a bio-political strategy that empties the places of power). 'If I don't go to Venice, we'll quit, the Morrinho will go bust, it will be a right mess! We'll stick it on the Internet and on YouTube! All hell will break loose if we don't come along!'

The boys appear on camera, enter the story of the LEGO puppets and decide to reconsider. The 'original' LEGO puppets will go to Venice, not just the new replicas that have no 'history'. The final scene: joyful puppets with bags and suitcases in their hands and on their backs, crossing one of the alleyways of the maquette. In the midst of all the artifice and play, the LEGO puppets cross paths with a column of real *saúva* ants, a sign of these strange or estranged lives: the lives of objects and images, which begin to throb and pulsate, turning into genuine documentaries, only of a different kind, just as they experience intervention by the fictional.

The production of TV Morrinho (raw, direct) revolves around the same questions that we find in many documentaries and productions made outside the professional sphere. They consist of language games, passions, affects; forms of conceiving and experimenting with collective fabulations; alternative organizations of the sensorial and of space-time. Many of these productions lack explanations and references, which puts us before another way of thinking the political. What matters more than knowing the reasons behind this or that life is 'the direct confrontation between a life and its potential,' as Jacques Rancière has put it with regard to the films of Pedro Costa, in particular to *In Vanda's Room* (*O Quarto da Vanda*) (Rancière 2005).

The point is that these 'backyard' films can be made both in the factual world (literally in the backyard) or in those other spaces, those 'reserves of life' (*reservas de mundo*) that the territories of poverty, niches and ghettos have become. These are places that, for a wide variety of reasons, cannot be thought of merely as the most visible signs of social collapse, the crisis of State and the crisis of 'rational' urban planning.

Even less can they be reduced to the contemporary *doxa* of 'fractured spaces,' with 'islands' of affluence and functionality on one hand and closed-off territories on the other, as if it were possible to separate elements of the urban fabric into isolated ghettos. These enclosures or reserves of life, these heterogeneous territories, are places for the production of the sensorial, of times and spaces, forms that go well beyond debates about the 'topics' (the 'information' and 'characters') of the documentaries.

In the midst of various crises, these territories represent laboratories of subjectivation, laboratories for an alternative experience of the city that functions alongside, in partnership with or even in opposition to the State. They operate within the tension between new cultural productions, self-organized 'substitute economies,' and the state of exception they are subjected to (like the favelas and the global ghettos).

The 'backyard' can be taken literally, but it can also refer to personal computers, lan houses, the bedroom, or to data clouds on the Internet, when these are turned into laboratories, 'living' rooms and workshops. It is therefore necessary to create/count on these enclosures of life, more so, perhaps, than on a 'second life.'

I insist on these questions of place, inhabiting and being, because many documentaries made in the non-professional sphere base their aesthetics on these kinds of relations between art, work and the arrangement/disposition of social space. To once more quote Rancière at length on this configuration of the sensorial:

> Art is not political because of the messages it transmits or the way in which it represents social structures, political conflicts, or social, ethnic or sexual identities. It is political above all for the way in which it configures a spatio-temporal sensorium that determines our modes of being together or separate, outside or inside, in front or in the midst of. It is political to the extent that it demarcates a determinate space or time, to the extent that the objects it uses to populate this space or the rhythm it confers on this time determine a specific form of experience, conforming or breaking with other forms: a particular form of visibility, a modification of the relations between sensible forms and regimes of signification; particular velocities; but also and above all forms of coming-together and of solitude. Because a politics, even before it becomes the exercise of or the struggle for power, is the demarcation of a particular space of 'common occupations'; it is the conflict over the determination of the objects that are or are not part of these occupations, the subjects that do or do not participate in them, etc. If art is political, it is so to the extent in which the spaces and times it demarcates, and the forms of occupying these spaces and times, interfere with the very demarcation of spaces and times, of subjects and objects, of private and public, of competence and incompetence, which defines a political community. (Rancière 2005)

Subjective inclusion

The question posed by Rancière can be applied to documentaries and fictions produced by new subjects of discourse, in particular when he insists that 'what the proletariat lack is not the conscience of the condition they are in, but the possibility of changing the sensible being [Em português está 'o ser sensível', enquanto o tradutor usou 'o estado de percepção.' Ele pode ter se baseado numa tradução inglesa do Rancière. Você sabe como está no original?] that is tied to that condition.'

At the moment when the city is thought of as a 'new factory,' as Antonio Negri proposes, or even as an experimental laboratory of cognitive capitalism, we can say that urban culture is at the base of this very idea of productive 'multitude' made up of singularities that can no longer be represented in a traditional way and that start to act collectively and in shared projects and collaborative actions.

Nowadays urban culture is being understood as the production of wealth, and the city, the metropolis, is to the masses what the factory was to the workers, an open-air laboratory of bio-aesthetics. The spread of productivity and creation of value have been displaced to the field of social relations, of flows and exchanges. The city itself is becoming digitalized and informatized, as are production and labour. Urban culture is becoming one of the bases of capital that seeks to extract value from the networks that are spread out over the city: cultural networks, knowledge networks, affective and social networks.

But what are the conditions of possibility for the networks of urban culture to appropriate and dynamize the urban territory? 'There is no inclusion without subjective inclusion' – this statement from the *Reperiferia* project of Nova Iguaçu (Rio de Janeiro) may be articulated with the question we have been developing up to this point, concerning the transformation of the sensorial and the reserves of life, charged with aesthetic potential and life languages.

In effect, there can be no 'inclusion' or sharing without taking ownership of languages, which is the last wall or barrier that obstructs the sharing-out of sensibilities. Systems of information and communication that permit cheap, autonomous and collaborative communication are as important as mere access to a technological infrastructure and networks, since these systems – with the use of computers, software, digital cameras, free internet and collective spaces where one can 'get together' – generate an increase in social productivity.

These, more than the technologies of communication, are the conditions that will allow the functioning of new social processes and the creation of social capital, thus augmenting the 'intelligentsia of the masses' and social productivity at all levels. But what would that sustainability and subjective inclusion be, an issue as important as the existence of a technological infrastructure (low-tech or high-tech)? Many aspects of this 'immaterial' and symbolic sustainability are equally or more important than more material and concrete questions such as the need for free and public technology to be installed in the body of the city.

Taking possession of language

In the context of urban networks and culture, we must highlight the diversity of languages and their incorporation as the determining element of the new forms of politics and action. Among these urban languages, music and audio-visual forms are the prevalent manifestations across the contemporary field of cultural, educational and aesthetic production.

The majority of urban cultural groups in Brazil do not work with a single, exclusive language. Instead, diverse languages are mobilized in their production, but all groups recognize the current transition from a lettered to an audio-visual culture as a decisive dimension, resulting in the need to 'take possession' of these languages and of their potential, which becomes as important as the ownership and deconstruction of the idioms of power.

In fact, there is a vague, undefined desire to experience all the languages, to share the emotions, the intelligence, wrestling them away from mass culture, in order to empower the discourses, to take possession of processes, and to create languages, style and value.

It is interesting, then, to think of urban cultures as radical experiences of a non-formal education in which audio-visual experience (amongst others) appears as ludic knowledge, and where possession of language is the privileged entry to subjective inclusion and living labour. [seu original era 'trabalho vivo'. Será que 'trabalho não-alienado' funciona aqui?]

In undoing the opposition between the written and the oral, the popular and the erudite, technology and artisanship, urban culture incorporates the most diverse aesthetics, making use of anything from the most experimental forms to languages already circulating in mass culture. The strategies for this appropriation of languages are multiple.

It is a recurrent dynamic in the constitution of groups, collectives and urban cultural projects to start from the already existing references of youth culture, whatever these may be. This is a very different idea from that of classical forms of training, which work with a repertory of pre-constituted references.

A young girl from the Open Cinema Academy of Nova Iguaçu, for instance, wants to produce video clips for the evangelical songs of her church; a boy wants to learn how to make action films in the manner of James Bond. Their teacher is not going to dissuade them from their projects and motivations, but will present them with new references. Meanwhile, in the 'Image Collectors' project, the class is engaged in an analysis of the recordings of everyday events made by each participant. Daily life is the starting point for thinking about an aesthetics or a language that can be expanded towards other fields, repertories and references.

At the TV Lata project in Bahia, a boy shows video images of his younger sisters bathing in their innocent nudity. The mediator/teacher, Joselito Crispim, has to ask if the boy himself thinks he can show his sisters to everyone. The boy hesitates, and concludes that it is perhaps better not to expose his sisters to the curiosity of strangers. An ethics of the image thus emerges from the process of making images, and reflecting on them. Images we will often re-encounter in a state of drift, fragmentation, disconnection: they are discarded, abandoned to be picked up at random from the open sewer of images. Found footage, sampling and remix are the basis of a culture of excess, of leftovers, of a surplus of references and their potentials.

In many of these projects, it is a matter of starting from the concrete in order to arrive at the concept and the ethics (never conceived as abstraction, norm or transcendence). It is to arrive at their own history of cinema and video-art. To work from the codes of melodramas and *telenovelas*, so as to reconfigure sensibilities. To start from the already familiar, from consumption, in order to access other fields of reference: as in the script about a boy who wants to incorporate the brand name Nike into his own nickname and has it tattooed on his skin, which was given as an example by Luciana Bezerra from the Rio de Janeiro-based film and audio-visual association *Nós do Morro* ('*Us from Up There*', with the implied sense of 'from the favelas').

The *Nós do Morro* audio-visual group precisely sets out from the state of affairs, only then leaving behind the subjective ghetto, to go beyond the demands and discourses that create a consumption 'niche' for films and videos produced in or coming from, the periphery. They are not always successful, but leaving the ghetto also has another meaning: abandoning the place that was given to them, and moving beyond this conceptual space constructed by problematic concepts such as subalternity, marginality, exclusion, periphery, which are fast becoming new theoretical clichés.

Initially known for their theatrical work, the group *Nós do Morro* has been involved in audio-visual experimentation since 1996, with some impressive results, such as 'Picolé, Pintinho and Pipa' by Gustavo Melo with a script by André Santinho (2006). Their films are fictional works punctuated by documentary elements that have a freshness to them stemming from the bodies, gestures, speech and locations which are filmed. The favela, in this case the *Morro* of Vidigal, with its slopes and corners that look out over the sea, introduces a different spatio-temporality, harking back to the times when a minivan would appear in the alleyways, offering to trade in scrap metal, empty bottles, wash basins, old cloths, and wine jugs for popsicles, chickens and kites. The announcement made over a loudspeaker causes a stir; children are spurred into action and hurtle down the streets, rubbish tips and stalls of knick-knacks.

Time speeds up and gives an urgency to the small dramas and dilemmas played out when the inhabitants are confronted with the promise of trading rubbish/scraps for desired objects. In many of these short films the reinvention of childhood and the child, or of the idea of youth, conjures up ideas of a different sociability, different temporalities: the time that is spent playing games on the sofa in front of the television, eating junk food or sleeping, but also the expanded time of made-up games invented in the streets, the time of 'idleness' to which children are entitled when they have not yet been subjected to standards of productivity.

'Time': is that not the greatest luxury that the poor and those who have not definitively entered the discipline of production have left today? This experience of the sensorial is also what is being explored, to a greater or lesser degree, in the short films, starring, for the most part, members of *Nós do Morro*. Gustavo Melo and André Santinho's script was awarded a prize in a competition organized by the Ministry of Culture, which financed the production of the film in 2006. This shows, not least, how these groups can enter, and challenge, the cultural marketplace.

In other short films by *Nós do Morro* – 'Mina de Fé' (Faithful Chick, 2004) by Luciana Bezerra and 'Neguinho and Kika' by Luciano Vidigal – we also see fiction being traversed by documentary flotsam. There is an attempt to excavate the real; these films start from an idea of objectivity and its stereotypes (the 'bandit's wife' from 'Mina de Fé', the 'boy wanting to get out of the drug trade' in 'Neguinho and Kika') and move towards questions of subjectivity, the affective fold that forges an alternative relation with what we see and hear. These are prosaic questions that emerge from the gaze of an adolescent girl, the local drug gangster's sweetheart expecting his child. That in itself exposes problematic issues of teenage pregnancy, the instability of relationships between adolescents, and girls vying for the alpha male of their small plot of land, which are intensified by the experience of having to live it all in accelerated time, the space of a few months or years, before the next shoot-out, the next death, widowhood, flight, abandonment.

It is all about temporality – no longer extended, but accelerated, precipitated. Time is accelerated, life is short, and decisions are made prematurely. These issues are also addressed in the short film 'Neguinho and Kika' by Luciano Vidigal, which also limits itself to the world of children/adolescents who are growing up and are being displaced by decisions and dramas that beset their adolescence.

What is new in these films is the emergence of a different space-time, alternative ways of living together: amity, temporary alliances, improvised communities in which violence and affection are experienced in diverse ways.

'O Campim' (The Pitch, 2006) is a documentary by *ClanDestino Filmes*, with the support of *Nós do Morro*. It was made in the complex of favelas of Alemão (Rio de Janeiro) by Jéferson de Oliveira (Don) and Eduardo Dornelles, two favela-dwellers from Morro da Grotta. It offers a unique sensory experience of space-time, 'which determines our modes of being together or separate, outside or inside, in front or in the midst of' (Rancière 2005). Something as prosaic as the creation of a football field in the neighbourhood on a piece of land used as a rubbish tip and pet cemetery brings into existence 'a common cause,' the powerful experience of self-organization – of 'leisure,' social relations and life.

A community springs up around the field and faces difficult questions of organization, problems and conflicts with neighbours, issues of leadership, all centred on a space of 28 by 9 metres, and this disrupts the neighbourhood's social life. It is affected by links of friendship that surround the project and that derive from organizing and sharing: we see the creation of a space of collaboration, but also the little rivalries and grievances. The football that breaks the water tap of the neighbouring woman, the difficulty of fencing off the field, the need for leadership, the complaints surrounding the magical plot – among all this, the 'campim' of the favela emerges as a little universe full of potential, the wealth of poverty.

The documentary follows the daily life of the inhabitants who use the plot or are affected by it for a year and a half. The director incorporates the language of DJs and VJs, editing and manipulating his images in order to flesh out his characters, but he also gets to the heart of the favela with uncut sequences in which time just elapses.

The recurrent use of long takes of favela streets and alleys is a constant factor in these films ('Picolé, Pintinho and Pipa,' 'Neguinho and Kika,' 'Mina de Fé,' '7 minutos,' de Cavi Borges, and many more).

Penetrating the 'real', tinkering with the sensory experience of space-time, describing, monitoring, scanning data: these are the manifold functions of this camera that enters the favelas and makes us feel that we are witnessing an event that is unfolding right in front of our eyes. The camera 'takes aim' in a singular, unrepeatable act, violently monitoring and scrutinizing the area traversed in those long takes where the viewfinder acts like the sights of a rifle scanning the terrain.

There is, in my view, a fundamental ambiguity to many of the projects, workshops and audio-visual training programmes at vocational academies and film schools. With the inclusion of audio-visual education in the primary school curriculum the danger was that these experiences would conform to an 'education for the poor,' in which languages and experiences would remain restricted to certain repertoires. Yet, some projects have started to question this form of educating the poor and have begun to incorporate other languages and aesthetics that come from video games, fashion, advertising, experimental cinema, video art. They do not restrict themselves to producing 'documentaries' in the classical sense of the term. For them, it is the possession of these languages (even if then to withdraw from and abandon them) that enables these groups to challenge contemporary discourses.

For many groups that work with marginal youths, the task of educating/occupying/training youngsters begins with a certain confinement to a politics of fixed identities and subjective ghettos that affirm the new 'essentiality' or exceptionality of these groups. In spite of the political legitimacy of such propositions, we need to ask how a sense of social 'belonging' (an enclosure of life, or of 'recognition') can be created. How can we create a subjective 'community,' a commons, an insertion through the sharing-out of languages, aesthetics, modes of being-in-the-world, without negating their uniqueness?

These strategies are still ambiguous, but they point towards a transition from being objects to being subjects of discourse, a social mobility that means more than just moving through codes, languages and aesthetics of power, but which produces alternative languages, aesthetics and values, affirming their place in contemporary urban culture. That is the radical change inherent in the productions from the margins and from the open film and video workshops and academies. It is a struggle for the sensorial, which in its 'sharing out' can produce clichés but also real events.

In that sense, we have to recognize the shortcomings of the theoretical discourse which analyses those productions and tends to legitimize them solely as sociological fact, social representation, 'augmentation of self-esteem,' 'belonging,' appropriation of discourse, and so forth. Such a view celebrates the 'slum celebrity,' that new figure on the cultural stage that has created a whole new 'genre' or audio-visual niche.

Today, new kinds of propositions are booming in Brazil, promoting modes of informal audio-visual education with very different methodologies, durations and objectives. Apart from the aforementioned groups, there are innumerable film festivals that follow these principles. A prime example is the workshops of *Kinoforum*, held since 2001 at the International Short Film Festival at São Paulo, the output and archives of which have been posted online. Since 2001, 751 students have produced, directed and shot 174 short digital films, always using their own scripts. Other festivals specifically aimed at that type of production have sprung up, such as the *Visões Periféricas*, the film festival of the CUFA (Central Única das Favelas, a cultural and political NGO of slum-dwellers) in Rio, the *Fórum de Experiências Populares em Audiovisual* (FEPA) which reunites various programmes on a national level, but also favela-based cinema clubs like the *Cineclube da Maré*, and so forth. Then there are partnerships between these groups and universities (for instance, between the communications course of the CUFA and the School for Communication of Rio de Janeiro Federal University), partnerships with private companies, with the State, etc. All this is still unmapped territory and a form of production that has not been 'legitimized' as part of a body of work appropriate for aesthetic and critical analysis.

At the same time, with the proliferation of urban culture originating from the margins, it is necessary to problematize the 'assistentialist' and patronizing discourse that presents itself as the 'saviour,' 'Messiah' or 'guardian' of these emerging movements, which are breaking with old discourses of poverty. Groups like *Nós do Morro* are eager to leave behind the patronizing discourse of projects that declare their mission to be 'getting youngsters out of drugs and off the streets.' Their discourse is a different one, namely, putting these youngsters in charge, giving them back their autonomy and creating new conditions for subjective inclusion or indeed 'social intrusion.' Their challenge is one of technological and symbolic appropriation: everything that produces an increase in potentiality/autonomy/self-determination. 'Don't put us in a ghetto.' Don't reduce us to the production of a 'peripheral aesthetics.' Even more importantly, don't reduce us to a picturesque poverty. This is one of the recurring issues of peripheral urban culture, the second stage, breaking away from the discourse of 'identity' and 'ghetto.'

Other circuits

At TV Ovo in Rio Grande do Sul, the audio-visual education of youngsters aims at teaching and multiplying instructors, moving beyond instruction and towards production and exhibition, and so creating alternative circuits.

An example: TV Ovo on the bus, a scheme which produces short films to be shown on public transport buses that are fitted with a television. The bus becomes an exhibition space. Passengers miss their stop because they want to finish watching the video on *Bus TV*. Another example of the creation of circuits is *TV Minuto*. Lightning debates on the road are organized when the traffic lights are on red, with a small plastic stool and a topic for the debate – a parody of television debates during which nothing is really being debated. The rush and the worry that the traffic light will go red or green is enough to 'entertain.'

In another example of new forms of circulation, *Filmagens Periféricas*, which also organizes video workshops in Tiradentes (São Paulo), exhibits material that has been produced for the MIS (Museum for Image and Sound) and the CCBB (Cultural Centre of Brazil's National Bank), places to which many of the residents of Tiradentes, on the outskirts of São Paulo, have no access. They may not even know what they are. So the 'Peripheral Cinema' was launched with the idea of copying all the videos produced for the *Filmagem Periférica* on VHS or DVD and to distribute these among the video rental stores of Tiradentes.

In 2003 with the aid of the Programme for the Support of Cultural Initiatives from the São Paulo City Council, *Filmagem Periférica* managed to produce 120 copies containing 13 short films that were distributed to seven video stores and could be taken out free when clients rented an ordinary film.

What do these projects have in common? The horizontality of the networks, the tendency to abolish the rigidity of hierarchy and bureaucracy. What suburban and favela culture (music, theatre, dance, mass media, video, fashion, education) offers is a political discourse that is 'out of place' – it does not come from the university, nor from the State, nor from the mass media, nor from political parties. This discourse puts the spotlight on those other facilitators and producers of culture, the emerging 'precariat' of rappers, *funkeiros*, b-boys, young actors, performers, slum-dwellers, the unemployed, the under-employed, the participants of the so-called informal economy, urban artists, groups and discourses that have been revitalizing the territories of poverty and reconfiguring the urban cultural scene. They crisscross the city and reach the mass media in a way that is often ambiguous, enabling them to assume an urgent, innovative political discourse within informational capitalism itself.

Those local cultural networks are being constituted in contrast to the public politics that are directed from the centre, ultra-hierarchical and centralistic in their design and thus incapable of solving social inequalities or of managing to reduce them to an acceptable level. Today, we have a historical opportunity for experimenting with alternative models of public politics that are still embryonic, and with socio-cultural networks that function horizontally, in a de-centralized, rhizomatic way, organizing their own production.

Translated by Sander Berg

Note

1 'Reserves of life' is a translation of 'reservas do mundo', which carries the connotations of spaces of the life-world which are outside the political order and perhaps can act as sources of renewal of the world.

References

Bentes, Ivana. 2007. Redes Colaborativas e Precariado Produtivo. In *Caminhos para uma Comunicação Democrática*. São Paulo: *Le Monde Diplomatique* e Instituto Paulo Freire.

Brasil, André. 2008. *Modulação/Montagem: ensaio sobre biopolítica e experiência estética*, PhD Thesis (Tese de Doutorado), Programa de Pós-Graduação da Escola de Comunicação da UFRJ, Rio de Janeiro.

Deleuze, Gilles. 1988. *Foucault*. São Paulo: Brasiliense.

Foucault, Michel. 1988. *História da sexualidade: a vontade de saber*. Rio de Janeiro: Edições Graal.

Hardt, Michael, and Antonio Negri. 2001. *Império*. Rio de Janeiro: Record.

Hardt, Michael, and Antonio Negri. 2005. *Multidão: guerra e democracia na era do Império*. Rio de Janeiro: Record.

Lazzrato, Maurizio. 2006. *As revoluções do capitalismo*. Rio de Janeiro: Record.

Migliorin, Cezar. 2008. *Eu sou aquele que está de saída: dispositivo, experiência e biopolítica no documentário contemporâneo*, Post-graduate thesis of the Escola de Comunicação of the UFRJ, Rio de Janeiro.

Rancière, Jacques. 2005. 'Política da Arte.' presentation at the seminar *São Paulo S.A, práticas estéticas, sociais e políticas em debate*, São Paulo, Sesc Belenzinho, April 17–19, 2005.

Rancière, Jacques. 2008. *Le spectateur emancipé*. Paris: La Fabrique Éditions.

Index

Entries in *italics* refer to illustrations.

abjection 12, 14, 198, 227, 292–3
abolitionism, elite 206
abra 124–33, 136.n29, 137.n40
ACACPCD (Cooperative Association of Residents of Campaña) 250, 257–8, 260, 263.n11
academic field, limits of 30–1, 33
acarajé 208–9
accentuation, clashes of 32
Acción Democrática 235
Adorno, Theodor 123, 176
advertising, visual aesthetic of 341
advertising images 268, 270, 272
aestheticization of politics 87, 344
aesthetic radicalism 3
aesthetics: of frustration 147; of hunger 192, 324; of realism 15, 318–20, 328–9; of violence 323
affective turn 11
African-Americans 219–21
African diaspora 16, 220
Afro-Brazilian culture 208, 215–16, 328
Afro-Brazilian music 11, 189, 193–7
Afro-Brazilians: Brazil's debt to 213; in popular culture 211, 217–19; representations of 204–6, 221–2; urban populations of 223.n10; words used for 224–5.n33
Afro-Brazilian women 206, 208–10, 214, 218
Afro-Cubans *see* Cubans of color
Afro-Venezuelans 235–6, 244.n10
after-image 302, 304–5, 307, 309, 312–13, 314.n20
aftershock 7
Against 189
agency, non-elite 2, 208, 232
Águila, Guz 172
air-writing 134.n13
La alameda de la memoria (Boulevard of Memory) 39–41

Alborta, Freddy 7, 55–8, 73.n3; photograph of Guevara 56, 74.n17
alcoholism 376, 378, 383
Alemão 418
Alianza 13, 249–50, 262
allegory, in post-dictatorship 28
Almanaque Profético para el Año 1866 375–6, *377–80*, 383, 387, 389.n8
Almodóvar, Pedro 181
Alonso, Carlos 63–7, 74.nn19,23
Alsina, Adolfo 95, 97
alterity: hybrid 155; and seriality 33–4
Álvarez, Ana Gabriela 9, 11–13
Alvarez, Chacho 249, 262.n1
Alvarez, Santiago 70
ambiguity: and censorship 154; of Coatlicue 117; and sexuality 253, 255
Americanization 86, 170
Amerindians: Andean 404; colonialist construction of 354, 358; of Mexico 108, 111–12, 167; of Patagonia 94–6, 103.n3; of Peru 120–1, 123–7, 129–32; in Spanish Empire 294.n3; *see also* Aymara people; Aztecs; indigenous cultures; Maya; Quechua culture
Amores perros 10, 15; awards for 349.n49; cinematographic genealogy of 342–5; feminist reading of 347.n17; marketing of 340–1; and middle-class imaginary 333–4, 337; morality of 334–6, 338–9, 342, 346
ananké 178, 182
Andean culture 22, 25, 120, 125–6, 131–2
Andean landscapes 99, 125
Andean magical beliefs 25
Angeles de la Tierra 397
Anhangabaú Valley 307–8, 311
animality 150
anomalous happenings 255
anthropological discourse 267–9
anticipation 283

INDEX

anti-production 124, 135.n21
APRODEH 39, 46
Aramburu, Diana 389.n8, 390.n12
Árbenz, Jacobo 1
archival technology 270
Argentina: annexing Patagonia 93–7; battle for memory in 40; Catholic revolutionaries in 62; cultural criticism in 23–4; debt crisis in 8; military coup of 1966 63; military government of 1976-83 6, 18–19, 162–3; national parks 98–100; police powers in *see* Police Ordinances (Argentina); secret poetry boom in 9, 162–5; sexualities in 255; working classes of 72, 251; xenophobia in 264.n13
Argentinian art: in late 1960s 62–3; post-crisis 9
Arguedas, José María 6, 8, 22, 120, 122–3, 125–33
art: political 63, 415; primitive and Western 144
assassins 285, 334, 336, 349.n43
audiovisual communication 3, 12, 394–6, 403, 405, 413, 416
audiovisual education 419–20
auratic art 122, 144, 150, 393
auratic space 143, 151, 158.n9
authenticity: and *boleros* 179, 182; documentary 326, 329; in global art market 9, 153; in Latin-Americanism 81, 176; in rock music 201.n15; and Sepultura 10, 189, 198–9; and theory 177
authoritarianism 22, 47–8
avant-garde: in Cuba 143, 152; in Mexico 342
avant-garde film 320, 328
Avelar, Idelbar 7, 10–11, 28, 34.n2
Avenida Paulista 300, 308, 311
Ayala Blanco, Jorge 343, 346–7.n13
ayllus 123–4, 126–33, 134.n12, 136.nn29,36, 400
Aymara people 395–6, 399, 402–3
Azevedo, Artur 211–12
Aztecs 106–8, 111–18

Babilônia 2000 326
backyard films 411–12, 414–15
bad taste 265, 274, 278
Bahia: black originality of 218; food of 215; music of 201.n16; urban culture and film 417
baiana 208–10, 212–16, 218
Baiano (singer) 212
baião 188, 198
Baker, Josephine 219–20
Bariloche 98, 100
Barthes, Roland 32, 176–8, 238, 272
Baudelaire, Charles 318, 412

Baudrillard, Jean 92
Bello, Andrés 22, 82
Belo Horizonte 189–90, 198–9
Beneath the Remains 192
Benjamin, Walter 3, 60, 129, 132–3, 158.n9, 182, 343–4, 412
Bentes, Ivana 16–17
Berger, John 55, 58, 60–1
Berni, Antonio 66
Bestial Devastation 189–92
Beverley, John 87, 347.n22, 393, 401, 406.n6
Bezerra, Luciana 417–18
Bhabha, Homi 294, 311
bio-aesthetics 413, 415
biopolitics 2, 7–8, 11, 413–14
Bishop, Elizabeth 330–1.n9
Black Mother *see Mãe Preta*
blackness: in popular culture 204–5, 208, 210, 217–22; and whiteness 407.n14
Black Sabbath 200
Black women 208, 216, 223–4.n18, 237, 322; *see also* Afro-Brazilian women; Cubans of color; *mulata*
blasé attitude 318
bodies: and cities 284, 286–7, 289–90; deviant 11; in Guevara images 59; mutual affectations between 12; and technology 89.n5
body without organs 121, 134.n11
boleros 10, 166, 174, 176–83
Bolivia, indigenous media in 16, 395
borders, Latin-Americanists defending 79, 81–3
Borges, Jorge Luis 23, 164, 177, 295.n6
Bourdieu, Pierre 198, 242, 244.n9
bourgeois respectability 251
Bourricaud, François 136.n34, 137.n40
Brazil: anti-World Cup protests in 5; artistic representations of 328–9; created through broadcasting 307, 315.n26, 320; First Republic in 203–4, 208–11, 221, 284; informal audiovisual education in 420–4; languages of urban culture in 416; poetry in 163; popular music in 10–11, 185–6, 188–91, 193–4, 198, 211–12, 307 (*see also* MPB); Portuguese language of 195–6; 'racial democracy' of 12, 206, 210, 220–2, 235; space in 14–15
Brazilian art, realism in 320–1
Brazilian cities 295.n4, 317, 321, 324, 328, 329.n2; *see also* favelas
Brazilian film: banality in 412; *see also Cidade de Deus*; Cinema Novo; documentary film
Brazilian rock 198
Brooksbank Jones, Anny 277–8, 279.n2
Brown, Carlinhos 194–7
Brunias, Agustino 390.n11
Buena Vista Social Club 159.n20

INDEX

Buenos Aires: culture of 24; local politics of 13, 248–9, 261; prostitution in 249–51, 253, 255–9, 262.n3; texts about 14; *travesti* activism in 9, 250
bullfighting 125–7, 130, 136.n34
bureaucracy, cultural 153–4
Burri, René 71, 73.n1
Bustillo, Exequiel 100–1
Bus TV 421
Butler, Judith 201.n14, 254, 270–1, 374

cabecitas negras 253, 263.n8
cabildos 377
Cabrera, Sergio 183.n1
Cabrera Infante, Guillermo 14, 177–8, 284, 287–90, 292–3, 295.n11
Cacciari, Massimo 293
CAIB (Coordinadora Audiovisual Indígena Originaria de Bolivia) 16, 395–6, 406.nn3,8, 407.n11
Calendar Stone 108
California, Mexican-Americans in 168
Calloway, Cab 171
camp 10, 176, 179–82
O Campim 418–19
Campo de Marte, Lima 37, 50
candomblé 197, 208
Canindé 322–3
canja 212, 225.n40
cannibalism 120, 311, 360
Cantinflas 10, 166–7, 170–1, 173
Canudos 284–7, 294, 295.nn4-6, 329.n1
capitalism, cultural turn of 7
Caracas uprising of 1989 234, 237–9
carioca 208–9, 211, 213, 215
Carmona, Pedro 242
carnal pleasure 289–90
'Carne Argentina' 64, *67*
carnival: Andean 402; in Brazil 208, 210–11, 213–15, 317, 320
carnivalesque 204, 211, 214, 322, 337, 377
carnivalization 326
Carrera, Arturo 9, 164
Carter-Torrijos Treaty 77
cartes de visite 270, 404
Cartesian dualism 282, 286, 289, 358
cartoons: from colonial Cuba *370*, *371*; from contemporary Venezuela 228–33, *229*, *231*, 236, *240*
Castañeda, Quetzil 16
Castells, Manuel 302–4, 311, 313, 314.n13
Castillo Zapata, Rafael 176–8
Castro Castro prison massacre 42–5, 49
Castro-Gómez, Santiago 241
catastrophic torsion 30
Catholic Church, revolutionary tendencies in 62
Cavalera, Igor 189, 192–9, 202
Cavalera, Max 189, 192–7, 200.n7, 201.n11

"caviar left" 38, 44
Caymmi, Dorival 201.n16
CEFREC (Centro de Formación y Realización Cinematográfica) 16, 394–5, 397, 400, 406. nn3, 8, 407.n11
censorship: in Argentina 63, 68; in Cuba 153–4
Centro Novo, São Paulo 307, *308*, 311
CEP (City Executive Power) 258, 261
Céspedes, Carlos Manuel de 369–71, *370*
chachachá 175, 180
champagne 274
Chaos AD 189, 192–4, 198
charanga 192–3, 201.n11
Chaskel, Pedro 56
Chávez, Hugo 4, 12, 227–8, 242–3, 244.n10
Chávez, Marcelo 168
Chavism 227, 230–1, 233–7, 241; internet text satirizing 245–7
Chiapas 266–7, 394, 396
Chicana feminism 106, 117, 279.n10
Chilam Balam 355, 363.nn1, 5
children, and regulation of sexuality 257–8, 262
Chile: battle for memory in 40–1; and Patagonia 94–5, 103.n3; post-dictatorship transition in 5, 27–30, 33
choteo 390.n12
Christian iconography 61–2, 69
Chubut 97, 103.n2
chullpa 399, 403
'cidade/city/cité' 309–11, *310*, 313
Cidade de Deus / City of God 321, 323–5, 331. nn17,19, 344, 347–8.n22
Cidade Nova, Rio de Janeiro 214
CIDH (Inter-American Court of Human Rights) 42–6
cinema: banality of the everyday in 412; color 407.n14; in *La Habana para un infante difunto* 288; and imperialism 404–5; indigenous 396–7; Mexican nationalistic 341, 343, 345, 348.n29; micro- 412–13; parody in 175, 196; political 68; of violence 336; *see also* documentary film; Mexican cinema
Cinema Novo 192, 321–2, 324, 328
cinematography 69, 341–2, 348.n29, 397
cinéma vérité 412
cities: becoming lost in 295.n17; clandestine 285; divided 330.n5; as essay and as tragedy 293–4; inverted 284–6, 295.n6; maps of 14, 291–2, 318; networks in 303; as new factories 415–16; representations of 318–19; and time 311; utopian visions of 282–3; wealth gap in 301, 304; *see also* global city; improper cities; Latin American city; urban spaces
citizens: and the mob 241; ordinary and perverse 13, 286; and residents 257; and the State 94, 99; subjects becoming 88, 90, 284, 298

429

INDEX

citizenship: academic construction of 82, 86; as enlightenment 124, 299; of fear 333, 336–7, 340; liberal ideal of 249, 256; struggle for 2; through violence 340
city-scapes *see* landscape, urban
Ciudad del Saber 80
ciudad letrada: end of 16, 393–4; and improper city 293–4; Rama on 2, 14, 282–3, 287, 295. n18, 299, 401–2; visual economy of 403–5
ciudad real 295.n18, 299
Civic Alliance 241
civilization and barbarism, dichotomy of 282, 284, 287, 294, 304, 325, 344
civil society: and the mob 228, *230*, 234, 243; in Peru 38
CLACPI 395, 406.n4
class: and Gramsci's hegemony 244.n15; and humor 390.n12; in Laclau's populism 243. n7; *letrado* 299, 307, 393, 406.n2; in Mexican cinema 166, 343; in MPB 198; neoliberal 338–9; performance of 272; racialization of 120; in Rossell's photography 268, 274, 278
class conflict 125, 166, 216, 393
classificatory logic 269–70
Clendinnen, Inga 353, 359–62, 363.n4, 364.n6, 365.n11
Coatlicue 8; in contemporary Mexico 117–18; and Mexican nationalism 111–17; statue of 106–11, *107*; story of 109
coca 400, 403
Cocom, Juan 353
Co-existence Code (Código de Conviviencia) 249–51, 255, 258, 262.n2
coffee, in Brazil 304–6
Coffin Joe 196
Cogumelo Records 189–90, 192
collecting 373–4, 389.n6
collective memory 39, 42, 50
Colombia: peace accords in 1, 7; *sicarios* of 344, 349.n43 (*see also* assassins)
colonialism: and film 404–5; obverse 14, 298, 314; and science 400
coloniality: of power 402, 407.n12; textual configurations of 16
Columbus, Christopher 159.n20, 361, 363.n4
comic effect 375, 377
commercialization of memory 40
commotion of the modern 318
communal lands 127–8
communication, suppression of 18
Communist Party of Argentina 63
Communist Party of Peru *see* Sendero Luminoso
Companhia Mulata Brasileira 218–19
Companhia Negra de Revistas 217–20, 226.n68
Condori, Ofelia *397*, 399
Conquest of the Desert 23

Conquistadores 354, 357–8, 361, 365.n11
consensus: imaginary of 240–1; neoliberal 7; post-dictatorial 31–3
consolation 295.n15
Constituent Assembly (Buenos Aires) 248
consumer culture 13, 265–6, 271–2, 275, 279
consumer goods, in the *favela* 317, 325, 327
consumption, and identity 265, 271–2, 274
continuities, reinvention of 20
convulsion, time of 22
Cooder, Ry 159.n20
Cooke, John William 72–3, 75.n40
cordiality 12, 206, 211
Cornejo Polar, Antonio 4; and Latin Americanism 8, 81–5, 88; on literature 403; and *Yawar fiesta* 124, 126, 131–2
Coronil, Fernando 94
corruption: in Argentina 262.n1; crusade against 2; in Mexico 15, 265, 337–8; in Peru 37
Cortez, Hernán 360
cosmopolitanism 15, 85–7, 299
costumbrismo 269, 340, 343, 393
counter-insurgent imaginary 13, 242–3
Coutinho, Eduardo 326
Coyolxauhqui 109
creole imaginary 125
Creole State 24–5
CRIC (Consejo Regional Indígena del Cauca) 395
crime: and art 151; commodification of 340–1; in Mexican film 333–9; and Police Ordinances 251–2; and poverty 266; prostitution as 258–9
critical incidence 30
critical irrecoverability 31
critical labor 5, 34
Cronenberg, David 342
cross-dressing 215; *see also* drag queens; *travestis*
crowds, violent containment of 12
Cuba: crisis of high culture in 390.n12; end of colonial era in 368–71; reactions to *La hora de los hornos* in 69–71; Special Period 9, 141–2; US rapprochement with 1; US seizure of 78, 85
Cuban art: hyperrealist 156–7; international market for 152–6; new 140–4, 147, 150–8; new 158.n8; online dissemination of 158–9. n17; V Biennial 143–4, 155
Cuban cigarettes 371; *see also marquillas*
cubanidad 9
Cuban Revolution 1, 62–3, 70–1, 75.n40, 147, 154
Cuban Revolutionary Party (PRC) 87
Cubans of color: Landaluze's depictions of 388. n2; temporal immobilization of 368, 375, 380–1, 387–8; in visual humor 369–71, *370* (*see also marquillas*)

430

INDEX

CUFA (Central Única das Favelas) 420
cultural assimilation 31, 235
cultural capital 61, 167
cultural criticism 3–4, 22–3, 25, 32, 35.n12, 187
cultural critique: decentering and transversality in 31; and the imaginary 302; and urban landscape 14
cultural exchange 85, 159.n20
cultural fields 2, 19–20, 22, 24, 26
cultural identities 12, 35.n12, 267, 317
cultural nationalism 113
cultural performance 270–1
cultural self-knowledge 177
cultural signs, destruction of 19–21
cultural studies: decentering and transversality in 31; disciplinary boundaries in 22; in neoliberal era 5; and politics 2; *see also* Latin American cultural studies
cultural studies questionnaires 2, 4
cultural symbols, national and imported 275
cultural world 18–19, 141
culture: authentic 20, 208, 216; as battlefield 32; curated 140, 143, 152; dis-location of 311; globalization of 83, 88; territorialization of 6
culture industry 10, 55, 240, 320
curators 9, 144, 150–4, 156
Curet Alonso, Tite 178, 180
CVR (Truth and Reconciliation Commission, Peru) 37–9, 41–6, 49

da Cunha, Euclides 14, 284–7, 292, 294
dangerousness 11, 251
Dantas, Audálio 322
Danzón 179
Darío, Rubén 106
Darwin, Charles 92–3, 96, 254
Davidson, Robert 297–8
Dawson Island 103.n3
de Andrade, Mário 307
death metal 11, 185, 188–9, 193
de Campos, Augusto 309–11, 313
de Campos, Haroldo 14
decenterings 31
de Certeau, Michel 302, 358, 362, 382
De Chocolat 217, 220
de Ciudad Real, Antonio 353, 357
decollection 21
de Córdoba, Francisco Hérnandez 357, 359–60
defamiliarization 7, 318, 327–8
de Ferrari, Guillermina 9
degeneracy 210, 219
Degregori, Carlos Iván 41–2
dehumanization 69, 306
de-ideologizing 19
de-Indianization 123, 131
de Jesus, Carolina 321–3, 331.n14

De La Rúa, Fernando 13, 248–50, 252, 255–6, 262
del Barco, Oscar 4
Deleuze, Gilles and Guattari: Félix 121, 124, 134.nn11-12, 135.n28, 163
Delgado, Angel 150–1, 158.n15
del Sarto, Ana 4–5
del Vega, Florencio 253
de Melo Gomes, Tiago 12
democracy, and culture 16
democratic transition 1
de Nieve, Bola 178, 181
Derrida, Jacques 32, 361, 364.n7
descastamiento 170–1
desencuentros 14
desert, Patagonian 93, 96–7, 99, 101, 104. nn7,12
despojo 127–8, 130, 132
deterritorialization 6, 21–4, 135.n28
deviance 12–13, 270, 275, 404
Día de Reyes en La Habana 376–7, *381*
Diario de Poesía 9, 162, 165
Díaz, Bernal 358–9, 364.n8
Díaz Pimienta, Alexis 140–1, 151
Díaz Rodríguez, Manuel 239
differánce 363.n3
difference, incompleteness and uncertainty of 34
diglossia 83
Direct Cinema 412
dirty war 18
disappearances, in Peru 18
disciplinary lighthouses 39
disease, and the city 292
disenchantment, aesthetics of 157.n5
dismembering 8, 25, 110, 118
D'Lugo, Marvin 343, 348.n27
document, memory as 29
documentary film: about *favelas* 321, 326; Brazilian 326–7; Che Guevara in 56, 68, 73. n3; indigenous 393–5, 404, 407.n11; from the periphery 412, 414–15, 418–19
dominant systems, intellectual criticism of 32
Doña Herlinda y su hijo 178–9
Dorsal Atlântica 190–1
Douglas, Mary 255, 295.n14
drag queens 176, 183, 250, 253, 271; *see also travestis*
Drinot, Paulo 7, 37
drugs: in Brazilian Portuguese 195–6; in *favelas* 323–7, 329, 330.n5; as a ghost 345; police control of 252–3; and violence 317
drum solos 193–4
dual city 301
Duchamp, Marcel 158.n15
Duno Gottberg, Luis 12, 16

Eco, Umberto 57
efficient discourses 28

INDEX

Eloy Blanco, Andrés 235
embodied performance 270, 402
embranquecimento see whitening
emergencia 1
Emergency Zones 18
English language, in heavy metal 191, 196
Engracia das Frutas 216–17
Enlightenment 109, 112, 269
enunciation 13, 23, 29, 123, 136.n28
epistemological re-enslavement 375
erotic mapping 287
escena avanzada 3
A Escrava Isaura 322, 331.n12
Espina, Eduardo 9, 164
essentialism 181–2, 400, 412
estampa 372, 376, 378, 380
Estévez, Abilio 145, 147, 156
Estrada, Martínez 98
ethnography 267–8, 278, 401
ethno-populist discourse 237, 243–4.n7
Eurocentrism 311, 354, 360, 362, 365.n10, 402, 405, 407.n12
European imaginary 81
everyday life: in Cuban art 150; in early cinema 412; enchantments of 320; in urban utopias 284
evolution, theory of 93
experience 295.n16
EZLN (Ejército Zapatista de Liberación Nacional) 117, 266

Fanon, Frantz 16, 69, 406.n7
'la farándula' 181
FARC 1
Favela do Pereirão 411
favelas: chroniclers of 217; community media in 17, 411, 413, 417–20, 424; cultural representation of 15, 319–25, 328–9, 330.n9; documentary films of 326–7; as emblem of Brazil 317–18; new visions of 330.n5; as reserves of life 414; word 195, 329.n1
feijoada 215
femininity: performed 215; sexualized 265, 288–9
feminism, and Coatlicue 117
Fenianos 214–15
FEPA (Fórum de Experiências Populares em Audiovisual) 420
Fernández, Justino 110, 112–14, 116
Fernández Meijide, Graciela 248–9, 262.n1
Fernández Retamar, Roberto 88
Ferrari, Léon 63, 74.n13
fetishisms 8, 122, 125, 263.n9
fiction: and non-fiction 319, 325; realist 320
figuras contravencionales 252
film *see* cinema; documentary film
Filmagem Periférica 422–4
First World: Brazil as part of 313; cultural paradigms of 143; images of Latin America in 155; Mexican wealthy as part of 274, 342; and Third World 298, 302
First World cities 298, 301, 313
FLC (Fundación Ludwig de Cuba) 155–6
flexibility, lack of 375–6
FLH (Homosexual Liberation Front) 9
Flores Galindo, Alberto 6, 11, 22, 24, 128–9, 133.n5
forests 78, 98, 100, 286, 295.n7
forró music 14, 306–7, 309
Fort Clayton 77–80
Foucault, Michel: on the actual 32; on capillary power 394; on discourse 152; sexuality and power 251, 254
Fourth World 14, 303–4, 313
Fox, Vicente 342
Francis, Pope 5
Franck, Henry 78–9
Franco, Jean 2, 8, 11, 393
Frankfurt School 4, 241
FREPASO 248–9, 255–6, 262.n1
Frey, Emilio 104.n5
Frith, Simon 187
Frivolous Theatre 166, 172–4
Frondizi, Arturo 1, 252
Frosh, Paul 269–70
Fuentes, Carlos 106, 113, 115
Fujimori, Alberto 19, 37–8, 41–2, 46, 49
Fujimoristas 7, 46, 50
funk 190, 196, 317, 325, 329.n4
futures, alternative 7–8, 330.n5

Gailard Avenue 77, 79
Gallegos, Rómulo 230, 235
Gamio, Manuel 111
gamonalismo 22, 120–1, 123, 128, 133.nn2,5, 136.n36
Gandhi, Mahatma 197
Garaicoa, Carlos 144, 147, 152, 156
García, Alan 5, 38, 43, 46, 50
García, Juan 172, 174
García Canclini, Néstor 6, 20–1, 136.n36, 157.n1, 275, 394
gauchesque genre 23–4
Gaviria, Víctor 347–8.n22
gay people 9–10, 164, 176–81, 250, 255–6, 263.n9
Gelderman, Carol 158.n14
gender binary 254–5
gender performativity 265, 271
gender roles 179–80, 275, 279.n10
La génesis del crimen en Mexico 348.n23
genocides 23, 40
gentrification 301
Geralda 207, 210–11, 217
Gerzso, Gunther 112
Getino, Octavio 68, 70
global city 297, 299–301, 304, 312–14

INDEX

globalization: and cities 14, 299, 304 (*see also* global city); and Latin-Americanism 80–3, 88; and measurement 297–8; in Mexico 267, 277; and poverty 301–2, 313; and the Third World 298
Globovisión 237
golpe 7, 29, 35.nn7-9
Gómez Landeros, Humberto 172
Gonzaga, Luiz 306–8
González, Abigail 147, *148*, 156
González Echevarría, Roberto 295.n5, 389.n8
González Iñárritu, Alejandro 333, 337–8, 341–4, 348.n27
Gorgas, W. C. 78
Goulart, João 1
governmentality 1–2
Gramsci, Antonio 239
Granma 151
Green, Derrick 201.n10
Greenblatt, Stephen J. 353, 360–2, 363.n4
gringification 170
Grosz, Elizabeth 286, 289, 295.n8
Groussac, Paul 104.n13
Grzegorczyk, Marzena 13–14
'La guagua' 140–4, 151
Guevara, Alfredo 68
Guevara, Ernesto 'Che': in Argentinian art 63–7, *65–6*, 74.n18; in Argentinian cinema 68–71; death of 57–8, 73.n4; disappearance of body 76.n43; photographs of 6–8, 55–6, 58–62, *60*, 71; reactions to death of 71–3
Guha, Ranajit 227, 242
Guillot, Olga 177–8, 181
guitar solos 187, 194
Gutiérrez, Pedro Cornelio *397–8*, 399
Gutiérrez, Pedro Juan 147, 150–1, 156, 157.n5
Guzmán, Abimael 47

hagiography 382, 390.n10
Haiti 370
Hartman, Saidiya 374
Harvey, David 93, 314.n11
Havana: and Che Guevara 56, 75.n32; and Cuban art 144, 147, 151, 153; depicted on *marquillas* 377; as improper city 284, 287–90
heavy metal: in Brazil 10–11, 185–6, 190–1, 193, 197–9, 200.n8; and classical music 200.n5; genre boundaries of 187–8; origins of 200.n6; production of power in 186–7; *see also* death metal; thrash metal
hegemony, and symbolic production 239–41
hermeneutics of culture 3
Hérnandez, Blas 357
Hernández, Helmo 155
Hernández, Orlando 150

Herschmann, Micael 11, 329–30.n4
heterosexuality 179, 215, 251, 254–6, 263.n9
La Higuera 55, 58, 72–3
hip-hop 189–90, 306, 317, 325
Hispanism 90.n19
hispanoamericanismo 82–3
history: official 41–2; ruptured 27–8
Hobsbawm, Eric 227, 239
Hollywood 167, 341, 405
Holocaust 40–1, 67, 291
homogeneity 7, 13, 24, 32–3, 81, 267, 373
homosexuality *see* gay people
Hopenhayn, Martín 345, 349.n51
La hora de los hornos 68–71, *69*
Hudson, William 92
Huitzilopochti 106, 108–10, 116, 118.n4
humanism, inhumane 306
humanities 2, 11, 82, 297–8, 343
human rights organizations 38, 41
human trafficking 8
humor, racialized visual 368–9, 371, 374–5, 388, 390.n12
hunger: aesthetics of 192, 324; cosmetics of 324, 331.n17
Huyssen, Andreas 40–2
hybridity: cultural 20, 25, 318, 321, 325, 329; in genre 201.n12
hyperliteracy 309, 311
hyperrealism 143, 156–7, 158.n14
hyperstimulation 318, 328–9
hypervisibility 374–5, 389.n7
Hypodermic City 290, 292–3

ICAIC 68, 70–1
identity: cinema confirming 345; feminine 265, 271, 279.n9; fragmentation of 278; political 19, 261; proof of 252, 263.n6; of the rich 271–2; social 204, 317, 412; visual 268
identity categories, naturalization of 270
identity crisis 268, 333
identity discourses 84, 268–9, 271, 279
identity politics 3, 330.n5
ideology: exhaustion of 150; reproduction of 241
idleness 376, 378, 383, 418
illiteracy, in Brazil 304, 307, 309, 311, 314.n13
images: ethics of 417; non-institutional 270; process of production 206, 269–70, 302; staged 271; *see also* photography
image-scape 304
image world 269–70, 279
imagined communities 182, 307, 317, 319–20, 323, 396
Imcine (Instituto Mexicano de Cinematográfia) 341
immigrants 87, 264, 301, 306

INDEX

imperial imagination 8
imported goods 274
improper, use of term 294.n1
improper cities 14, 282–4, 286–7, 290, 292–4, 294.n3, 295.nn6,13
impurity 293, 295.n14
Indians *see* Amerindians
indigenism 120, 122, 124–6, 132–3, 135.n24
indigenous cultures 111, 267–8, 395–7, 399–400, 402
indigenous media 9, 16, 393–7, 401, 403–5
indigenous objects, consumption of 275
Indigenous People's National Plan for Audiovisual Communication 395, 407.n11
injurious speech 374
Inkarrí 25
intellectual practice, and academic culture 31, 35.n10
interculturalism 396, 406.n5
interdisciplinarity 297–8
Internet, in Cuba 158–9.n17
interpellation 8, 82, 88, 99, 228, 240, 243.n7, 257
Iron Maiden 190, 192
Istúriz, Aristóbulo 244.n10

Jackson, Michael 327
Jacoby, Roberto 63
Jaguaribe, Beatriz 14–16
Jauretche, Arturo 4
Jesus Christ: as guerilla 74.n16; Guevara compared to 58, 61–2, 69, 75.n30
Jesus María, Lima 39, 45
Jiménez, Reynaldo 164
Jobim, Antônio Carlos 193
Joelho de Porco 200.n8
Journal of Latin American Cultural Studies, history of 3–5
Just War 21–2

Kaliman, Ricardo 4
Kamenszain, Tamara 9, 164
k'anata 399
Katz, Leandro 56–7, 73.n3
K'awarasu 129, 132
K'ayua 123, 129–30, 137.n40
Kinoforum 420
kipus 400, 402–3
Kirchner, Néstor 4
Kisser, Andreas 189, 193–4, 196–7
knowledge: indigenous transmission of 399–403; Latin American theory of 22; political economy of 5; production of Latin American 82–4
knowledge of loss, and loss of knowledge 27
Korda, Alberto 7, 55–6, 63, 71
Kraniauskas, John 4, 6, 8
Kristeva, Julia 28, 35.n4, 292–3

Kubitschek, Juscelino 1
Kuitca, Guillermo 14, 282, 290–4

Lacan, Jacques 163, 364.n7
Lacerda, Carlos 323
Laclau, Ernesto 2, 12, 122, 135.n23, 243.n7
Lamborghini, Leonidas 164
Lamborghini, Osvaldo 164
Lampião 196
land: accursed 93–4, 96–7; 'savage' 121–2, 127–30, 132, 134.n12, 404
Landa, Bishop 357–9, 361, 363.n5, 364.n6, 365.n13
Landaluze, Víctor Patricio 369, 371, 376–7, 388–9.n2
landscape: as cultural medium 99–101; embodying the nation-state 94; urban 289–90, 299, 304; virtual 14
la Negra, Toña 178–9
language: mixing of 135–6.n28; taking ownership of 416–17; and values 293–4
language games 414
Lara, Agustín 10, 168, 178–81
As Laranjas da Sabina 211–12, 225.n41
Latin America: cities of 13–14; commodification of 334; geographical configuration of 8; as global brand 15; incorporation into the world 85; as intelligible primitive space 155; knowledges of 80, 82–4; knowledge transmission in 16; violence as representing 342, 344
Latin American city 282–5, 298–9, 301–6, 313, 345
Latin American cultural studies: and post-dictatorship moment 1–3; and race 14; vernacular tradition of 4
Latin-Americanism 5, 8, 80–8, 313
Latin American literature, and Spanish literature 90.n19
Lauer, Mirko 120, 125
laughter, normative role of 376
Lee, Spike 327
legitimacy: and culture 2, 141, 240; mimetic 320; political 227, 354
LEGO 411–14
Leguía, Augusto 120–1, 133.n5, 136.n38
Lerner, Salomon 37–8, 41, 44
letrados 14, 299, 307, 393
lettered city *see ciudad letrada*
Lévi-Strauss, Claude 144, 156
Lewis, Gabriel 80
Leyva, Alexis (Kcho) 144–5
Liberation Theology 44, 62
lieux de mémoire 51.n15
life-languages 412–13, 416
Lima: as colonial city 294.n2; as head of Peru 25; and indigenous communities 120–1, 125, 130–1, 404; monuments in 7, 39

INDEX

Lino, Maria 213, 216
Lins, Paulo 323–4
literacy: and citizenship 82, 299, 393; liberation from requirements of 403; and orality 16, 394, 399, 401–2, 417
literary criticism 22–3, 163
literary institutions 86, 124, 393, 401
literature: and citizenship 86; testimonial 75.n37, 321–2
Llanes, Lllilan 155
Llanthupi Munakuy 400, 407.n11
Llesterdei 182
local knowledges 84–5, 87–8, 318, 400
looting, in Venezuela 234, 237–9, *240*
Los Angeles, and *pachuco* culture 168
loss of the word 27, 30, 34.n1
Lubiano, Wahneema 223–4.n18
Luck, Elaine 10, 12–13
Ludmer, Josefina 6, 23
Lugo-Ortiz, Agnes 16
lumpen 230, 233, 243, 343
La Lupe 178, 180–3
luxury objects 274, 278

McClary, Susan 187
McKinley, William 79
macrismo 5
Made in Brazil 200.n8
madness 285
Mãe Preta 209, 211, 218, 220–2, *221*, 225.n46, 226.n70
Magellan, Ferdinand 93
magic, reconsideration of 25–6
magic realism 320, 342, 344
La Malinche 275, 279.n10
mambos 175, 180
Mañach, Jorge 390.n12
Mansilla, Lucio 294
Mantegna, Andrea, *Lamentation over the Dead Christ* 58, 61, *64*, 70, 74.n11
maps: of Americas 79, 85; Kuitca's paintings of 290–2; of Patagonia 95
maracatu 194–5, 198, 201.n12
Marchant, Patricio 27, 34.n1, 35.n7
Marcinho VP 327, 332.n22
marginality, myth of 331.n14
Marginal Pinheiros 300, 311
Mariátegui, José Carlos 120–1, 123, 125–6, 131–2, 133.nn2,5
market rationality 19–20
marquillas 16, 368, *372–3*; collectors of 389.n6; Cubans of color on 16, 371, 373–4, *376–80*; designs of 371–3; mulattas on 381–8, *382–4*, *386–7*, 388, 389–90.n9; name of 372; racialized humor of 375–6; *see also Almanaque Profético para el Año 1866*
Martí, José 84–7

Martín-Barbero, Jesús: on the city 343; communication theory 2; culture as mediation 15–16, 227, 240; and mass media 394
Martínez Solares, Gilberto 172, 174
Marx, Karl 127–8, 134.n11, 135.n26, 314.n11, 333, 336
Marx Brothers 167, 171–2
Marxism 62, 120
mass media *see* media
material culture 13, 265, 278, 368, 371
Mato Grosso 197
May, Lyn 266
Maya: and Aztecs 111; encounter with Spanish 352–7, 359–62, 363.n4, 364.n8; European writing of 358, 361; pre-conquest society of 365.n11; toponymy and cosmology of 355–6; written records of 363.n1
Mayan iconography 110
media: counter-insurgent imaginary of 242–3; and cultural mediation 20; democratic potential of 394; hiding by revealing 244.n9; producing the mob 12–13, 227, 233, 240–1; violence in 239; *see also* Venezuelan media
media arbitration 242
media scandal 278
mediation: culture as 15; mediatic and social 12–13, 240–1; as space of struggle 227
media visibility 323, 327
mega-cities 14, 303
Megadeth 190–1
megaprojects 300
Mejía, Ramos 98
melancholy 7, 10, 27–8, 30, 34.n2, 35.n9, 137.n40, 165
Melo, Gustavo 417–18
melodrama: in *Amores perros* 336, 343; in *marquillas* 386; and outsider film making 417; and Tin Tan 167, 175
memorization 29
memory: battles for 37, 41–2; culture of 18, 40–1, 51.n12; popular 20, 212, 240; *see also* collective memory; social memory
memory-work 6
Menarezzi, Ana 211
Menem, Carlos 19, 248, 262.n1
messianism 295.n8
mestizaje: ideology of 108, 111, 275; Venezuelan 234–5, 237
mestizos 24, 108, 124, 234–6, 269, 325; *see also mistis*
Mestman, Mariano 7
Metallica 187, 190–1, 193
Mexican-Americans, Mexican attitudes to 170
Mexican-American War 84
Mexican cinema: comedians in 166–7; commercial success of 345; crime and violence in 337–8, 343; funding of 341; golden age of 10, 174; *pachucos* in 168–70

435

INDEX

Mexican nationalism 106
Mexican photography 265, 267–9, 278–9
Mexican Revolution 111
Mexico: 1985 earthquake in 232; incorporating indigenous culture 111–16; as *mestizo* homeland 108; student movement of 1968 5, 114, 267; violence and class in 333–4, 336–7; wealth gap in 265–6, 272–5, 278
Mexico, Splendors of Thirty Centuries 115–16
Mexico City: films about 15, 343; *pachucos* in 171; wealth and poverty in 277, 333, 336–8
el México Feo 266
Mictlantecutli 110–11
Miereles, Fernando 325
migrations, mass 89, 305
military dictatorships 1–2, 6, 27, 327
Miller, Paco 168
'Mina de Fé' 418–19
Miranda, Carmen 209
Miro, Cris 253
mise-en-scène 338, 358–60, 362, 404
misinterpretations 16, 364.n7
El Misitu 127, 129–32, 136.n36
mispronunciations 358–9, 361
mistis 121–2, 124, 127, 129–33
the mob 11, 227–32, 229, 234, 236–9, 241–3, 243.n1, 244.n14, 319
modernity: imperial 93; in Latin America 14, 85, 87; and literacy 393; in Peru 24–6; and realism 320
Monsiváis, Carlos 10–11; on Agustín Lara 180–1; on cinema 336, 345, 346.n8; on cities 349.n42; on Coatlicue 117; and Mexican earthquake 232
Montesinos, Vladimiro 49–50
Montoya, Rodrigo 6, 24–5
monumentality 41
monuments: cultural and political use of 41; destroying 37–8; memory as 29
Morales, Evo 395
Moraña, Mabel 344
Morbid Visions 189, 192
Moreiras, Alberto 3, 30
Moreno, Francisco P. 95–6, 98–9, 101
El Moro Muza 369
Mosquera, Gerardo 143–4, 151, 153–5, 158.n7, 159.n18
motorbikes, and the mob 237, 238, 242
Motörhead 190, 192–3
Mouffe, Chantal 2
mourning, in post-dictatorship 7, 11, 27–30, 34.n2, 35.n9
MPB (Brazilian Popular Music) 11, 185–6, 198, 200.n2
Mraz, John 268
mulata: in Brazil 210–11, 214–19; in British West Indies 390.n11; in Cuban visual humor 375, 381–3, 386–7; as uncertain figure 383–5

multiculturalism 154, 267, 279.n8, 393, 395
munguzá 214–15
Muñoz del Monte, Francisco 384–5
musical theatre revue 211, 213, 217
Mutal, Lika 39, 42–5, 49
MV Bill 324

El Nacional (Venezuela) 228, 233, 236, 238, 243
NAFTA (North American Free Trade Agreement) 10, 115, 117, 179, 265–7
Namuncurá, Ceferino 103.n4
narrative images 208–12, 216–17, 223–4.n18
Nation 189, 192
national culture: and class struggle 88; fragmentation of 278; and global markets 9; imposing on Indians 23; and the media 20; and the visual 267
national identity: in Brazil 14; in Mexico 111, 265, 268; in music 10, 196–9, 201.n10
national ideologies 108, 298
national integration 82
national liberation 1
nation-states: critique of 2; and globalization 277, 297; Idea of 104.n14; and race 12; territoriality of 20–1, 94–5, 99, 103, 104.n10; weak 47–8
nature: icon of 99; struggle against 94, 96–7, 103.n3
negation/radicalization dialectic 188
Negri, Antonio 136.n35, 415
negro, North American use of term 218–20
'Neguinho and Kika' 418–19
neighborhoods: in Buenos Aires 249–50, 252–3, 258–62; urban 174
neobaroque 9, 147, 162, 164–5
neobarroso 164
neo-indigenismo 267
neoliberal idiom 3
neoliberalism: closure of 34; and identities 13; and intellectual labor 5; in Mexico 267, 277–8, 337–8, 342, 345–6; and Pinochet dictatorship 6; and rationalization 20
neomacondismo 344
Neruda, Pablo 86
network society 302–4
network theory 303
nihilism 10–11, 186, 191, 200.n3, 341
non-violent actors 38, 47–8
Nora, Pierre 40, 51.n15
Nós do Morro 417–18, 420
nostalgia: as camp 181; and deterritorialization 21; and homosexuality 176–7, 179, 183.n1; and slavery 209
Nostalgia de la sombra 337, 339–40, 347.n19
Notícias de uma guerra particular 326–7
Nouzeilles, Gabriela 4, 8
Nova Iguaçu 416–17

436

INDEX

Novaro, María 179
Novo, Salvador 170

objectivism 165
Ocampo, Victoria 100
O'Gorman, Edmundo 111–12
Oiticica, Helio 327
El Ojo que Llora (The Eye that Cries) monument: and battle of memory 7, 38, 41; creation of 39–40; names of terrorists on 42–6, 49; vandalism of 37, 50
Olinda 295.n4
Once Upon a Time in Mexico 348.n29
orality: indigenous 16, 398–400, 402–3; speculative 358; in urban culture 417
Orientalism 80–1, 90.n13
orlas 372, 376, 378–80
El Oro Maldito/Cursed Gold 397, 400, 403
Osbourne, Ozzy 190, 193
otherness, pulsion of 33
'Our America' (Nuestra América) 79, 81, 84
outrage 250, 252, 255–7
Overdose 190–1

pachucos 10, 168, 170–2, 174–5
paintings: Andean 404; and photography of Che 57–9, 61
El País newspaper 144, 151
Palermo, Buenos Aires 256, 258–9, 262.n3, 263.n11
Palestine 192–3
pampas 101, 104.n10, 286
PAN (Partido Acción Nacional) 266, 277
Panama Canal 8, 77–80, 82–3, 85
Panama City 283
pan-Americanism 79–80, 84–5, 176
Pará 190
parda / pardo 207, 210–11, 217
Pardavé, Joaquín 174–5
parody: in Andean carnival 402; and camp 179; in Cuba 141; in heavy metal 186, 200.n8; in Peruvian literature 20, 23; Rossell's use of 266, 271; Tin Tan and 10, 174–5
Parra, Eduardo Antonio 339–40, 347.n19
Parra, Victor 168
the past, mythic and real 40
Patagonia 8; in colonial imagination 92–3; establishing sovereignty over 93–7; landscape of 93, 95, 98–102; natural resources of 96–8; prisons in 103.n3; territorialization of 103
Paulo Jr 189, 193, 196
Payró, Roberto 97
Paz, Octavio 10, 108, 113–18
PDVSA 230, 243.n4
Pedrosa, Mário 4
Peña, René *149*, 158.n13
Péret, Benjamin 112

Pérez, Fernando 142, 156
Pérez Balladares, Ernesto 79
performativity 211, 255, 270–1
periphery: of art world 143, 153, 155–6; and globalization 88
Perlman, Janice 331.n14
Perlongher, Néstor 9–10, 295.n17
Perón, Eva 76.n43
Perón, Juan 1
Perónism 19, 68, 71–2, 262.n1
Peru: battles for memory in 37–41, 45; causes of violence in 47–9; cultural criticism in 24–6; ethno-racial division of 124–5; human rights violations in 43–4, 49–50; landowner power in 120; post-conflict 7
Peruvian civil war 19, 21–2
petit bourgeoisie 253, 261
Philippines 78, 85
photography: captions in 60; in Cuba 144–7; and identity 267–71, 279; naturalism of 156, 158.n14, 238, 272, 404; and the performative 270–1; portrait *see* portraiture; *see also* Guevara, Ernesto 'Che'
picaresque 173
pink tide 1, 13
Pinochet, Augusto 3, 6, 20, 33, 103.n3
pishtaku 25
place: and experience 292; propriety of 289
place names *see* toponymy
plantation slavery 368, 374–5
pluralism, conformist 32
pocho 170–1
poetics: critical 28–9; radical 3; urban 283
Poleiro 214–15
Police Ordinances (Argentina) 11, 248–53, 255, 257, 261–2, 263.nn7,10, 263–4.n12
pollution: and ambiguity 255–6; industrial 93
polyrhythms 192–3, 199
Ponte, Antonio José 141, 156
Poole, Deborah 125, 269–70, 279.n11, 404
popular culture: blackness in 204, 208; *carioca* 211; Che Guevara in 72; and culture industry 10; and *favelas* 321, 327; gay men in 176, 178, 180, 321; in Mexico 170
popular music 185–8, 191, 198–9, 201.n15, 211–12
populism 243.n7
portraiture 268, 271, 273
Portuguese language: in heavy metal 191, 195–7; in poetry 309, 313
positivism 96, 133.n6, 321, 400, 406
postcolonial theory 362
post-dictatorship: critical thought in 29–31, 33–4; Latin America in 1; memory and mourning in 5, 7, 11, 27–9, 40; and music 185
postmodernism, in Latin America 157
Potosí 294.n3

INDEX

poverty: blaming poor for 216; images of 278; in realist art 320; in São Paulo 300, 311; territories of 414, 424; urban 287, 301–2, 319; and violence 339
Power, Kevin 152–3
power chords 11, 186, 200.n4
power/knowledge 127, 362, 401–2, 405, 407.n12
power structures 294, 401
Pratt, Mary 365.n10
precariat 412, 424
pre-Columbian civilizations 106, 108, 111–17
PRI (Partido Revolucionario Institucional) 265–7, 276–7, 333, 338
Primer sembrado de hongos alucinógenos en La Habana 144–7, *146*
primitive accumulation 127–8
Proceso de Reorganización Nacional 6
prostitution: in Argentina 250, 252–3, 256, 259–62, 263.n10; Cuban art about 141, 144; in Panama 77; as work and as perversion 258
Psychopathia Sexualis 263.n9
public intellectuals 83
public space, democratic character of 99
Puerto Rico: debt crisis in 8; US seizure of 78, 85; workers' movement in 87
Puig, Manuel 10, 177–8
Pulp Fiction 342–4, 346.n8
punarunas 127–9
punning 256, 355–6, 363.n2, 363–4.n5
Puquio, Peru 120–8, 130–1

Qati Qati/Whispers of Death 397–8, 399–400, 402–3, 406.n8
Quarto de Despejo 321–2
Quechua culture 18–19, 22, 24, 397, 400, 404
Queenshrÿche 191
queer 12, 176, 179–83; *see also* gay people
Quetzalcoatl 115–16
Quijano, Anibal 14
quintadeiras 12, 207–9
Quipus of memory 39, 45; *see also* kipus
Quiroga, José 10
quitandeira 208–9, 211, 218, 225.n41
Qulqi Chaliku/Silver Vest 400–1, 403, 407.n11

rabble 227, 230, 243
race: and madness 285; and space 14–15
racial hierarchy 14
racialization 234, 237, 376
racial taxonomy 269
racism: and color film 407.n14; indigenous media confronting 397; and the mob 235–7; *pachuco* confronting 168; scientific 210, 217, 404
Radio Caracas Televisión 242
Rais, Hilda 163

Rama, Ángel 2, 4, 13–14; on cities 282–6, 295–6.n18, 299, 304; on literacy 393–4, 396, 401–2; as public intellectual 82; on real/imaginary 302
Ramos, Julio 8, 16, 393, 406.n2
Rancière, Jacques 17, 125, 135.n24, 414–15
rape 319, 379
'Ratamahatta' 194–7
rationalization, politics of 19–20
rationalism, and masculinity 400
rationality: political 232, 243; urban 284–7, 296.n18
Ratos de Porão 192
reactionary mass movements 1
Read, Justin 9, 14
the real: artifactuality of 32; return of 320; shock of 318–21, 324, 326, 329.n2
Real Academia Española 158.n16
real estate, speculative investment in 300
realism: in Cuban art 142–3, 147, 150–1; and defamiliarization 327–8; depicting *favelas* 322, 324; new 15, 156, 158.n15, 325–6; reality and imagination in 320–1
reality, becoming-other of 32
reality effects 7–8, 34, 57, 238
reality/virtuality dichotomy 302
re-articulations 2, 15, 176, 206, 265, 298
reason *see* rationality
recognition, spaces of 240
Rede Globo 320
referentiality 144, 150, 152, 156, 257
La regata 144, *145*
regional identity 80, 209
regional knowledge 82, 84
Reguillo, Rossana 339, 345
re-Indianization 123, 131–2
relajo 167, 172, 175, 389.n8
remainder, post-symbolic 7, 27–8, 33, 34.n3
Rembrandt van Rijn, *The Anatomy Lesson of Doctor Nicolaes Tulp* 58, *59*, 61, 64–6, 74.n11
Reperiferia project 416
representation: coup against 27–8; demand for 242; local and globalized 318; of rebellious subjects 227–8, 233, 238–9, 243; social 412, 420; technologies of 394; of violence 337, 340, 342
representational visibility 268
representativity, violence of 257
A República 211–12
Requerimento 22, 358, 402
resentment 1, 13, 166, 239–40
reserves of life 17, 414, 424.n1
residents, in civic democracy 249–50, 261, 298
resignification 29, 62
Resina, Joan Ramon 302, 304, 365.n11
reterritorialization 21, 249
'Revolt of the Puppets' 413–14

INDEX

revolutionary heroism 147
revolutionary nationalism 267–8, 276, 333
revolutionary Perónism 68, 72
El rey del barrio 173–4
Reyes, Alfonso 82, 85
rhetoric of the overlooked 270
Ricas y famosas 265–6, 268, *273–4, 276–7*, 278
Richard, Nelly 3, 6–7, 11, 87
Rio de Janeiro: *favelas* in 317, 325, 329.n1, 330.n5, 331.n14, 411, 418; popular culture of 211 (*see also* carnival); School of Medicine protest in 203–6; street vending in 208–9, 216; *see also* Rock in Rio
Rio Grande do Sul 420
Ríos, Alicia 5
Ripstein, Arturo 341–3
Rivera, Diego 112
rock, national 197–8
Rock in Rio 190, 193, 200–1.n9
rock pauleira 190, 200.n8
Rodó, José Enrique 86–7, 90.n28
Rodríguez, Robert 342, 348.n29
Rodríguez, Tito 178, 180
Roorback 189
Roosevelt, Theodore 77–80
Roots 189, 192, 194, 199
Rossell, Daniela 13, 265–6; and identity 267–70; and nationalism 276–7; and performativity 271–2, 276; use of objects 273–5; wealth and poverty 278
Rowe, William 2–3, 6, 9, 16

SAAP (Sociedad Argentina de Artistas Plásticos) 63
Sabina 12; appropriation of image of 207–8; carnival groups portraying 214–15; as character in popular culture 211–14; in elite narratives 216–17; embodying narrative images 208–11, 218; as former slave 223.n7; personal opinions of 207; and School of Medicine protests 203–6
saca-ojos 25
'Saci in Morrinho' 412–13
sacrifice: Guevara as 58–9, 72, 75.n30; in Mexican civilization 107–12, 116–17
sacrificial ethic 75.n30
Said, Edward 80, 90.n13
Salesians 103.n4
Salinas, Carlos 266, 338
Salinas, Raul 266
Salles, João Moreira 326, 331.n18
salvation, memory of 41–2, 50
samba: as national genre 201; and Sepultura 196–8.n16
Sánchez, Luis Rafael 177–8
Sánchez Prado, Ignacio 10, 15–16
Santa Fé, Argentina 165
Santinho, André 417–18

São Paulo: Afro-Brazilians in 219–21; after-images of *305, 312,* 314.n20; de-centered urbanization of 308–9, 311–13; *favelas* in 300, 306, 317; as global city 298, 300; historical genealogy of 304–6, 314–15.n21; music of 306–7; rich and poor in 14
Sapene, Eduardo 242
Sarduy, Severo 164
Sarlo, Beatriz 19, 24, 74.n16, 82, 87–8
Sarmiento, Faustino 96, 104.n12, 230, 282, 287, 406.n2
Sassen, Saskia 299–302, 304, 313
Schiwy, Freya 9, 16
Schizophrenia 189, 192
Schwabsky, Barry 265
Schwarz, Roberto 1, 323
scriptural economy 359, 361
Seigel, Micol 12
Seixas, Raul 188
self-exoticization 143, 155
self-fashioning 272, 325–7
self-musealization 40
self-reflexivity 127
self-representation 32, 79, 217, 271, 326
self-surveillance 19
semantic polyvalency 28
Sendero Luminoso 6, 18; and national identity 24–5; official narratives of 7, 37, 43–4, 46; violence of 21–2, 47–8, 50
sense of loss, and loss of sense 29
sentimentalism 166, 172–3
sentimentality, Latin American 177, 180–1
Sepultura 10–11, 185; in Brazilian context 190, 194–9; cover art of 192; language used by 191–2, 195–7; musical evolution of 188–9, 192–4
seriality 13, 33, 273
Serrano, Antonio 341
sertão 14, 284–5, 287, 292, 295.n5, 306–7
servants, images of 278
Sexo, pudor y lágrimas 341, 348.n27
sexual dimorphism *see* gender binary
sexuality, normal and abnormal 251, 254–6, 262, 263.n9
Shaw, Deborah 347.n17
Shining Path *see* Sendero Luminoso
significant relations 28
signification: break in 28; irrecoverability of 30
sign language 357, 359, 361
signs: industrial order of 307; invisible 400
Singer, Ben 329.n2
Sinhô 214
slavery: and American history 14; in Brazil 205, 209–11, 213, 223.n10, 305; in Cuba 368–71, 376–8; sexual violence of 385; in Venezuela 235; visual logic of 374–5
Slayer 190–1, 193

INDEX

soap operas 320, 331.n12, 336; *see also telenovelas*
social amnesia 18
social capital 416
social categories 204, 215, 223.n18, 271
social contracts 82, 293, 368
social control 239, 261
social exclusion: and *favelas* 321, 323–4, 327, 329; as Fourth World 303–4; and heavy metal 11; and representation 240; in São Paulo 304
social fabric, emptying-out of 6
social hierarchy 204, 269–70
social intrusion 420
social invisibility 7
social memory 18–19, 29, 402–3
social movements, new 3
social spaces: and globalization 302; and memory 18
Sociedade Dançante Carnavalesca Familiar Kananga do Japão 214
Soderbergh, Steven 348.n29, 349.n49
Sodré, Azevedo 223.n13
Solanas, Fernando Pino 68–70, 75
Sontag, Susan 59–60, 271
soundtracks 68, 341, 348.n27, 403, 413
Souza de Oliveira, Nelcirlan 411
sovereignty 8, 77, 93–4, 102, 249
space: annihilated by time 314.n11; fractured 414; and globalization 298; mathematization of 104; in photography 272; racialized/ethnicized 14–15; and sovereignty 93–5, 98, 103; and time 55, 92–4, 133, 302, 355, 402; virgin 100, 177; visualized 375
space of flows 302–3, 309, 313
space/time 355, 414, 418–19
Spain, First Republic in 370
Spanish-American War 8, 78–81, 84, 87, 90. n19
Spanish imperialism: crisis of 1898 90.n19; and logocentrism 402; racial narratives of 389. n3; and toponymy 358–61, 363.n5; urban aspirations of 283, 285, 294.n2, 299
Spanish Inquisition 361, 364.n6
Spanish language: 'curator' in 151–2, 158.n16; teaching in North America 83; Tin Tan's use of 170–1, 175
spectacularization 319–20, 326, 328
squatting 259–61
states of emergency 19
statist investments 286
stereotypes: of blackness 204; and image production 270; of indigenous peoples 125; of the poor 217
Stewart, Susan 13, 272–3
stock images 218, 270
street vendors *see quintadeiras*
subalternization 120–1, 124–5, 131, 400, 402

subalterno, boom del 344
subaltern voices 86, 88, 363
subjectivation 8, 414
subjectivity: imaginary 34; improper 286; media-created 228–30, 233; and objects 272–3
sublime, and Patagonian landscape 99, 104.n9
substitution, and mourning 28
surdo 194–5
symbolic, emptying of the 18–20, 26
symbolic production 2, 18, 239
synthesis, in the city as essay 293

Tanaka, Martin 44
Tarantino, Quentin 342–3, 348.n27
Taylor, Diana 270, 402
Teatro Experimental do Negro 226.n68
techne 78
telenovelas 20, 266, 417
Televén 242
Temple complex, Mexico City 106, 109–10
temporal dislocations 122, 374
temporality 16, 130, 136.n36, 371, 375–6, 383, 389.n4, 418
'Territory' (music video) 192–4
terrorism: Peruvian narrative of 7, 38–9, 42–7, 51.n8; revolution and 336
testimonio 11, 393, 401
testing zones 32
Texas, Mexican-Americans in 168
Thayer, Willy 5, 34.n1, 295.n16
Third World: studies of 298; 'transfecting' First World 313; and violence 344
Third World art 144
Third World cities 14
Third World music 192, 199
Third World politics 62
Thomson, E. P. 227, 239, 244.n15
thrash metal 190, 195, 198, 200.n7
time: acceleration of 376, 418; and space 55, 92–4, 133, 302, 355, 402 (*see also* space/time)
timelessness 60, 285, 295.n5, 303, 311
timelessness
Tinhorão, José Ramos 206, 212, 223.n7
Tin Tan *see* Valdés, Germán
Tiradentes 422
Tlatelolco 113–15
Todo el poder 337–40, 346–7.n13
Todorov, Tzvetan 352–3, 362
toponymy: of Patagonia 96, 104.n5; of Yucatán 16, 352–3, 355–7, 361–2, 363–4.n5
Torres, Camilo 62
Torrijos, Omar 77
Toscano, Salvador 112
tourism, in Patagonia 93, 98–102, 104.n13
traditions, vernacular 4, 86
tragedy 55, 61, 179, 293, 386

440

INDEX

transculturalism 126
transcultural torsion 123–4, 127, 133
transculturation 123, 128, 363.n3, 396, 406.nn1,6
transdisciplinarity 31
transfection 14, 313–14
translation: in heavy metal 191; politics of 4
transposition 28
transversalities 31
transvestites 10, 176, 179, 181, 183.n1, 252, 262–3.n4; *see also* drag queens; *travestis*
trauma 6–7, 27, 35.n9, 37, 87
travel writing 365.n10
travestis 9, 13, 250, 253–60, 262.n2, 262–3.n4, 263.nn10–11
Trigo, Abril 2–3, 5
tropical medicine 78
tropics, in Latin American culture 176
Tudo Preto 217–22
turba 227, 234, 237
turupukllay 125, 127, 129–32; *see also* bullfighting
Tutti Frutti 200.n8
TV Lata project 417
TV Minuto 421
TV Morrinho 411–14
TV Ovo 420–1
Tykwer, Tom 342

UCR (Radical Civic Union) 249–50, 262.n1
uinal 355–6, 363.n3
Último Reino 9, 162, 164
uncertainty: in cities 319; zones of 34
UNEAC (Unión Nacional de Escritores y Artistas Cubanos) 154
'unicity' 298–9, 309, 311, 313
United States: ghettos of 324; hegemony over Latin America 77–9, 84–5; Latin-Americanism in 83; and Mexico 267; migration to 89; *see also* African-Americans
urban configurations 318, 333
urban culture 318, 415–17, 420, 424
urbanization: in Brazil 211, 217; globalized 301–2; in Latin America 299, 304; and natural space 93; sociocultural interpretations of 297
urban networks 311, 416
urban planning 282, 321, 402, 414
urban spaces: disruptive 249, 284, 299; fear of 319, 333; in Kuitca's art 290, 292; production of 13; reterritorialization of 249, 261; virtualization of 304
Urdaneta, Orlando 237
utopia: anti-American 154; Patagonia as 94–5, 97; urban 282, 286

vagina dentata 287
Valdés, Germán 10, 166, 168, 170–5

Valdés, Zoé 156
Vallegrande, Bolivia 7, 55–8, 63–6, 68, 73.n3
vampirism 25, 128
Van Halen 187
Varga, Chavela 178
Vargas Llosa, Mario 19, 44–6
Veloso, Caetano 200.n2, 307
Venevisión 242
Venezuela: 2002 attempted coup in 12, 227–8, 230–2, 238, 242–3; the mob in literature of 239; racism in 234–6
Venezuelan media 227, 230–4, 236–42
Venice Biennale 411, 414
Venom 190, 193
Verbinski, Gore 342, 348.n29
vernacular culture and traditions 81–2, 85–6
Vespucci, Amerigo 352, 362
Viaduto do Chá 307–8
Vianna, Hermano 199
victims, in Peruvian civil war 7, 21–2, 37, 39–46, 48–9
Vida y muerte de la mulata 381–3, *384*, *387*, 389.n9
Vidigal, Luciano 418
Vietnam War 62–3, 67, 70
Villaverde, Cirilo 385
Viñas, David 6, 23
violence: against dissidents 103.n3; in *Amores perros* 334, 336–7; commodification of 340; culpability for 47–9; in cultural analysis 333–4; decontextualization of 237–9; delegitimization as precursor of 243; destroying memory and communication 18–19, 26.n1, 27; and the *favela* 319–20, 323–7, 413; film depictions of 342–4; generalized 25; as a ghost 345; legitimacy of 7, 22; mapping effects of 6; memorialization of 38, 40–1, 46–7, 50; sacred 132; social 22, 239, 317, 327, 330.n5; and sovereignty 94; urban 15, 320, 323, 329, 336, 339–40
violent imperative 344–5
Virgin of Guadalupe 116, 275, 279.n10
virtual cityscapes 14
Visôes Periféricas 420
visual codes 271
visual culture 267
visual economy 279.n11, 389.n6, 404

Walser, Robert 186–7, 193, 200.n5
Walsh, Rodolfo 71–2, 134.n15
war: against mosquitos 78; and national memory 42; and Patagonia 94, 96, 103.n3; and state of emergency 19; *see also* Just War; Peruvian civil war; Spanish-American War; Vietnam War
weavings 16, 399–400, 402, 407.n11
Whitaker Ferreira, João Sette 300
whitening 210–11, 217, 220, 235, 386–7

INDEX

Wigley, Mark 289
Williams, Raymond 2–3, 15
Willis, Bailey 98–9
Witchhammer 191
women: and indigenous knowledge 399–400; social control of 261; *see also* Black women; *mulata*
working-class movement 87
worlding 8, 77–8, 81, 84–5, 88
'world music' 11, 197, 199, 201.n15
wrestling 5
writing in reverse 354, 363

Yawar fiesta 8, 120–8, 130–3
Yawar Mallku 397
youth cultures 317, 325, 328, 417

Yucalpeten 354–6, 361
Yucatán 16, 352–7, 359, 361–2, 363.n1, 365.n11
Yucatec Maya 352, 356–7, 361–2, 363–4.n5
Yuyanapaq photographic exhibition 38–9, 41

Zaluar, Alba 323–4, 331.n18
zambo 237, 244.n10
Zapatistas *see* EZLN
Zeballos, Estanislao 96
Zedillo, Ernesto 338
Žižek, Slavoj 38
Zona Leste 300, 306
Zona Oeste 300, 306, 308
zoot suits 10, 168
Zumbi 196